Contents

The Consolidation of the Roman Catholic Church in Ireland, 1860–1870

PAUL CARDINAL CULLEN, ARCHBISHOP OF DUBLIN
(courtesy of the President of St. Patrick's College, Dublin)

The Consolidation of
the Roman Catholic Church
in Ireland, 1860–1870

Emmet Larkin

The University of North Carolina Press

Chapel Hill and London

To My Mother

Both the initial research and the publication of this work
were made possible in part through grants from
the National Endowment for the Humanities,
a federal agency whose mission is to
award grants to support education, scholarship,
media programming, libraries, and museums,
in order to bring the results of
cultural activities to a broad, general public.

Library of Congress Cataloging-in-Publication Data

Larkin, Emmet J., 1927–
The consolidation of the Roman Catholic Church
in Ireland, 1860–1870.

Bibliography: p.
Includes index.
1. Catholic Church—Ireland—History—19th century.
2. Ireland—Church history—19th century. I. Title.
BX1505.L36   1987   282'.415   86-25059
ISBN 0-8078-1725-2

Preface

In the first published volume of this work I explained how and why I embarked on writing a history of the Roman Catholic Church in Ireland in the nineteenth century;[1] I will not, therefore, burden the reader again on that score. I have once again adopted techniques of style and scholarly apparatus that are not quite orthodox, and I think it would be helpful to repeat to some extent what I said in my earlier volumes about technique. The richness in the quality and quantity of both the general archival materials and the personal papers of the principal characters in this study is still very impressive. In presenting the evidence, therefore, I have again used a technique that I call "mosaic." The many varied and colored bits and pieces of evidence have been selected and arranged to create a portrait of the Church between 1860 and 1870. There are, I believe, a number of advantages in using the mosaic technique when the materials are appropriate. Because the writing of history can never result in more than a representation of what was "true," a historical portrait in mosaic is perhaps more "realistic" than might at first be supposed. The technique of mosaic allows for the inclusion of a great deal more of the evidence in its original form and contributes, therefore, not only to the immediacy of the actual experience but to the authority of the representation, thereby

1. *The Roman Catholic Church and the Creation of the Modern Irish State, 1878–1886* (Philadelphia, 1975).

enhancing the reality of the portrait. In all representations, and perhaps even more so in a mosaic, appreciation has a great deal to do
with the proper relationship of the elements to the mind's eye—in a
word, the achievement of perspective. If I have been successful, then,
in constructing my mosaic, the numerous details should integrate and
the various parts should harmonize when the volume is read as a
whole.

Because the system of footnoting in this volume is also somewhat
unorthodox, I think an explanation to the reader is again in order.
Most of the ecclesiastical as well as the lay correspondence quoted
here has not been catalogued in any more systematic way than by
date. The correspondence, therefore, has been noted in the text simply
as K (Kirby), C (Cullen), D (Dillon), and so forth, with the dates and
correspondents also indicated in the text. The problem of showing a
break or omission in any particular letter quoted has been resolved by
using the word "then" in parenthetical interpolation: for example,
"The Fenian Brotherhood," Cullen explained to Kirby on November
18, "is a very dangerous secret society" (K). "We shall undoubtedly,"
he then added, "have to ask Rome for a formal condemnation," indicates that between the last quotation and the previous one there has
been a break in the original text. Sometimes the letter used for quotation was a copy rather than the original, as is revealed in the designation. For example, if Cullen wrote Kirby and the designation is C
rather than K, the letter quoted is obviously a copy. If there has been
any variation from this procedure, it has been noted. The various ab-
breviations used for the correspondence are listed on page xiii.

Given the fact that this volume is the fifth published in my projected ten-volume history of the Roman Catholic Church in Ireland in
the nineteenth century (1780–1918), it may not be out of place here to
explain that the volumes so far published are III (1850–60), VI (1878–
86), VII (1886–88), and VIII (1888–91). I am presently writing the sequel, V (1870–78), to this present volume IV (1860–70), and when it is
done I shall have completed the 1850–91 portion of my history in six
volumes. There are then two volumes projected for the period 1780–
1850, I (1780–1829) and II (1829–50); and two for the period 1891–
1918, IX (1891–1905) and X (1906–18). Because these projected ten
volumes are primarily concerned with the high politics of the Church
in Ireland in the nineteenth century, and though they are certainly
the necessary preliminary to grasping the basic frame of what was
fundamentally a hierarchical institution, they are not sufficient in
themselves to understanding the social and pastoral role of the Irish

Church in that century. If vouchsafed the necessary longevity, therefore, I also propose to write a companion volume, "The Devotional Revolution in Ireland, 1780–1918," in order to explain how the Irish people became that uniquely pious and practicing religious phenomenon they have essentially remained down to the present day, and thus provide, in some measure at least, a social dimension to my history of the Irish Church.

In turning to the many obligations I have incurred in the research and writing of this volume, I must again explain that there is no one to whom I am more indebted than the late Dr. Donal Herlihy, Bishop of Ferns and formerly Rector of the Irish College in Rome. I also sincerely thank the Most Reverend Dr. Dominic Conway, present Bishop of Elphin and formerly Spiritual Director and then Rector of the Irish College in Rome, for all his help and kindness. I am also under considerable obligation to the late Most Reverend Dr. Dermot Ryan, Pro-Prefect of Propaganda and former Archbishop of Dublin, and the Most Reverend Dr. Kevin McNamara, present Archbishop of Dublin, for their permission to research in the Dublin Diocesan Archives, as well as to Professor James Dillon, of Trinity College, Dublin, for his permission to research in the John Blake Dillon papers. I must once again thank the Most Reverend Dr. Thomas Morris, Archbishop of Cashel, for his permission to read the Leahy correspondence on microfilm in the National Library of Ireland, and I am also under obligation to the late Bishop of Elphin, the Most Reverend Dr. Vincent J. Hanly, for his permission to read the Gillooly correspondence on microfilm. Both Dom Mark Tierney, O.S.B., who has arranged and catalogued the Leahy papers in the Cashel archives, and Father Kevin Kennedy, former archivist of the Dublin Diocesan Archives, were once again most helpful. My debt to the late Mina Carney for all her help in the researching of this volume is very considerable. To the staffs of the Dublin Diocesan Archives and the National Library of Ireland, I offer my sincere thanks for their unvarying kindness, patience, and help. I must particularly thank, however, Miss Mary Purcell and the present archivist, Mr. David Sheehy, of the Dublin Diocesan Archives, and the former and present Directors and the Assistant Keeper of the National Library, Mr. Ailfred MacLochlainn, Mr. Michael Hewson, and Mr. Gerald Lyne, respectively, for their generous help. I should also like to thank the staff of the Newberry Library, where a considerable amount of the research for this volume was done, and especially its President and Librarian, Dr. Lawrence W. Towner, and its Academic Vice-President, Dr. Richard H. Brown, for all their help and encouragement.

Finally, I should like to thank my good friend and former colleague
Karl F. Morrison, for having read portions of this book and for his wise
advice and counsel in regard to them.

For all the various opportunities to continue my research through
numerous grants-in-aid, I thank the American Irish Foundation, the
American Philosophical Society, the Social Science Research Council,
the American Council for Learned Societies, and the National Endowment for the Humanities. I must also especially thank the division of
Social Sciences at the University of Chicago, without whose generous
aid the research, writing, and publication of this volume would have
been impossible. In conclusion, I should like to take this opportunity,
inadequate as it is, to express my thanks to all those who had a hand
or part in the making of this book, and indeed of my history of the
Church in Ireland over the years, and especially my more recent
graduate students Mr. John J. Thompson, Mr. Frederick Bruner, Mr.
Daniel Lipsher, and Miss Julie Rogers, as well as our hardworking and
hard-pressed secretarial staff, Mrs. Marnie Veghte, Mrs. Augustine
Lehman, and Mrs. Elizabeth Bitoy. No one but myself, of course, is
responsible for any of the errors that may yet be found in this volume.

The Roman Catholic Archbishops and Bishops in Ireland, 1860–1870

Archbishops of Ireland
Armagh:
  Joseph Dixon, 1852–66
  Michael Kieran, 1866–69
  Daniel McGettigan, 1870–87
Dublin:
  Paul Cullen, 1852–78
Cashel:
  Patrick Leahy, 1857–75
Tuam:
  John MacHale, 1834–81

Bishops of the Province of Armagh
Ardagh and Clonmacnois:
  John Kilduff, 1853–67
  Neal MacCabe, C.M., 1867–70
Clogher:
  Charles McNally, 1843–64
  James Donnelly, 1864–93

Derry:
  John McLaughlin, 1840–64
  Francis Kelly
  (administrator), 1849–89
Down and Connor:
  Cornelius Denvir, 1835–65
  Patrick Dorrian (coadjutor),
  1860–85
Dromore:
  Michael Blake, 1833–60
  John Pius Leahy, O.P.,
  1854–90
Kilmore:
  James Browne, 1827–65
  Nicholas Conaty
  (coadjutor), 1863–86
Meath:
  John Cantwell, 1830–66
  Thomas Nulty (coadjutor),
  1864–98
Raphoe:
  Patrick McGettigan, 1820–61

Daniel McGettigan
(coadjutor), 1856–70

Bishops of the Province of
Dublin
Ferns:
Thomas Furlong, 1857–75
Kildare and Leighlin:
James Walshe, 1856–88
James Lynch, C.M.
(coadjutor), 1869–96
Ossory:
Edward Walsh, 1846–72

Bishops of the Province of
Cashel
Cork:
William Delany, 1847–86
Cloyne:
William Keane, 1857–74
Kerry:
David Moriarty, 1854–77
Killaloe:
Michael Flannery, 1858–91
Nicholas Power (coadjutor),
1865–72

Limerick:
John Ryan, 1828–64
George Butler (coadjutor),
1861–86
Ross:
Michael O'Hea, 1858–76
Waterford:
Dominic O'Brien, 1855–73

Bishops of the Province of
Tuam
Achonry:
Patrick Durcan, 1852–75
Clonfert:
John Derry, 1847–70
Elphin:
Laurence Gillooly, C.M.,
1856–95
Galway:
John MacEvilly, 1856–78
Killala:
Thomas Feeny, 1847–73
Kilmacduagh and Kilfenora:
Patrick Fallon, 1847–66
John MacEvilly
(administrator), 1866–83

Abbreviations

A	*Acta Sacrae Congregationis*, Propaganda
C	Cullen Papers
D	Dillon Papers
F.O.	Foreign Office Papers
G	Gillooly Papers
Gl	Gladstone Papers
I.C.D.	*Irish Catholic Directory*
K	Kirby Papers
L	Leahy Papers
M	Monsell Papers
Ma	Manning Papers
S.R.C.	*Scritture riferite nei congressi*, Propaganda
W	Woodlock Papers

Prologue

This is an attempt to tell the story of the political dimension of the consolidation of the modern Irish Church during the 1860s. The key to that consolidation was to be found in the institutionalization of the Irish bishops as a body. That institutionalization, in turn, was the result of the Irish bishops' being able to maintain their unity as a body in response to all the various challenges—pastoral, educational, political, and constitutional—to their corporate wholeness during this period. What gave this process of consolidation its dynamic were the ways in which the bishops responded to the various challenges. Those challenges, in fact, were not entirely new. They might even be described as a projection of those issues that had divided the bishops as a body over the previous twenty years, and that, by 1860, they had managed either to contain or partially to resolve. How they would continue to respond to those challenges in a corporately effective way, and institutionalize themselves as a body, was therefore the question of the decade as far as the consolidation of the modern Irish Church was concerned.

The decade certainly began auspiciously enough for the effecting of the harmony and unity in the episcopal body on which the eventual consolidation of the modern Irish Church would depend. The crisis precipitated by the Kingdom of Sardinia's aggressive designs on the Papal States in late 1859, and the consequent deprivation of Pius IX by Victor Emmanuel of the largest part of his temporal power during

1860, resulted in the Irish bishops' mounting a very formidable agitation on behalf of the pope in Ireland. In late 1859 and early 1860 the bishops not only launched a series of monster meetings in every diocese in Ireland to protest the spoliation of the Papal States by Sardinia but also inaugurated a collection for the pope that realized the incredible sum of £80,000, and they then proceeded to raise an Irish brigade of more than a thousand volunteers to defend what was left of the pope's patrimony. This impressive demonstration of loyalty and affection among the Irish people for the pope was really a formidable religious revival that contributed significantly to the focusing of an Irish-Catholic consciousness on a national scale. Ireland had seen nothing like it since the heady days of Catholic Emancipation in the 1820s and the movement for the Repeal of the Act of Union in the 1840s. The focusing of this Irish-Catholic consciousness, moreover, was intensified by the fact that none were more forward in support of Sardinian designs on the temporal power of the pope than the English government headed by Lord Palmerston, and Irish Catholics were forcibly reminded once again that their hereditary enemy was still the deadly foe of their race, their creed, and their nationality.

The momentum and general euphoria induced by this national agitation on behalf of the pope during 1860 did not survive the new year. This was the result less of the dreadful defeat of the papal army at Castelfidardo in late September, and the consequent reduction of the pope's temporal power to the city of Rome and its environs, than of the disastrous harvest of 1860. When this harvest, which was the worst since the catastrophic year of the Great Famine in 1847, was then followed by successive equal disasters in 1861 and 1862, with the crop most affected being the people's staple, the potato, the plight of those at the base of the social pyramid became really desperate. The government, in this deepening social crisis, refused to provide any relief for the distress beyond what could be obtained by resorting to private charity or the hated poor law, and the people once again began to emigrate at the rate of more than one hundred thousand a year. At this point the indignation, not to say the bitterness, of those who felt they had a real social responsibility to their people may be easily imagined. In this awful testing time the Irish people not only learned once more as a people how Catholic they were but also learned again in their bitterness how Irish they were, and it is not too much to claim that it was in these years that the Irish-Catholic identity focused by Daniel O'Connell before the famine, and reinforced by the Devotional Revolution in the years immediately after, was finally crystallized.

In this psychologically very complex and rapidly deteriorating socioeconomic situation in the early 1860s, the Irish bishops attempted to respond to the various challenges posed to their harmony and unity as a body. Their most taxing challenge was certainly the political. The three successive bad harvests of 1860–62 and the refusal of the government to help alleviate the consequent distress created a social situation that proved to be most conducive to the rise of the revolutionary politics of the Fenian, or Irish Republican, Brotherhood, whose purpose as an oath-bound secret society was to establish an Irish Republic by force of arms. The Irish bishops, moreover, by denouncing the government for its callous disregard of the needs of the suffering poor, while at the same time refusing to sanction the launching of a constitutional political agitation to bring the government to a sense of its duty, created a dangerous political vacuum that the Fenian Brotherhood rapidly began to fill. Between 1862 and 1865, in fact, the Brotherhood was most successful in recruiting large numbers of members in Ireland and among the Irish emigrants in both Britain and the United States. Becoming alarmed at the growth of the Brotherhood, and appalled at the increasing exodus of their people, the bishops finally decided to meet the revolutionary challenge by approving the launching of a constitutional political movement in the National Association.

In spite of its inclusive three-point program of reform—disestablishment of the Irish Protestant Church, compensation by landlords for tenant improvements, and episcopal control over a system of denominational education on all levels—the association failed to capture the political imagination of the country and did little, in the last analysis, to impede either the growth of Fenianism or the increase in emigration. By the time it became evident that the National Association had failed in late 1865, however, the Fenian Brotherhood was already in the early stages of disintegration as a viable revolutionary conspiracy because of a series of crucial arrests and convictions at the leadership level by the government. Throughout this long crisis posed by Fenianism, which finally wound down with an abortive rising in March 1867 and a number of outrages in England at the end of the year, the Irish bishops as a body refrained from formally condemning the Brotherhood. Though a few of the bishops, including the leader of the Irish Church and archbishop of Dublin, Paul Cullen, did indeed condemn the Fenians by name, the body of the bishops in the aftermath of all the arrests, convictions, and long sentences, given the very divisive nature of the issue among the laity, obviously concluded that the more prudent course in the long run would be to continue attempting to ride out the storm. The important point to be made, however, was that the bishops remained essentially united on the issue.

In the meantime, the bishops had to face two challenges besides that posed by their efforts to contain the revolutionary politics of Fenianism. The first of these had to do with the question the bishops as a body virtually had come to view as their own—education. The second had to do with the constitution of the Irish Church, and particularly with Cullen's role in the governing of that Church. In the area of education, the bishops by 1860 were all agreed that neither control by the state nor mixed education between Catholics and Protestants was desirable. The real question in the 1860s, therefore, was how the bishops were to gain and maintain control over the Irish educational system on all its levels, while at the same time making it purely denominational. On the primary level, the problem of mixed education was less serious than that of state control because by 1860 the educational system, outside Ulster, was virtually denominational. The real difficulty for the bishops was that the primary system was supported by the state, and the bishops did not have the resources to finance an alternate system. They therefore decided to tolerate the system for the good that was in it, while agitating at the same time for greater control and more denominationalism. In adopting these tactics, they assumed, and as it turned out, correctly, that as long as they remained united in presenting their demands, time was on their side.

On the other hand, the secondary, or intermediate, system, which had emerged slowly after the relaxation of the penal laws in the late eighteenth century, and which had never received any state aid, had been greatly expanded by the bishops after 1850 to meet the increasing needs of the Catholic community. Indeed, by 1870 the bishops succeeded in setting up a secondary system that was not only adequate to Catholic needs but completely under their control and strictly denominational. As regards university education, the very aggressive line pursued by the bishops during the 1860s, though unsuccessful, proved to be perhaps even more significant, at least from the point of view of policy, than their considerable achievements on the elementary and secondary levels. Though the bishops had founded a Catholic University in the 1850s, that institution had not flourished in either students or funds because it had failed to secure a charter from the state that would allow it to incorporate and grant degrees. The reason why Parliament refused to grant a charter was that the bishops refused to allow Catholic laymen any real voice in the governing or control of the University. In adopting this very hard line against lay participation, which was entirely approved of by the Roman authorities, the bishops gave a clear and early warning that they were determined to secure an absolute control in the long run over the whole of the Irish educational system.

The final challenge to the unity, not to say the harmony, of the bishops as a body was precipitated when Cullen was raised to the rank of cardinal in the spring of 1866. Since his appointment as archbishop of Armagh and apostolic delegate by Pius IX in 1849, and then his translation to Dublin in 1852, Cullen had acquired considerable power and influence in the Irish Church. Though his role as leader had been regularized in the governing of the Irish Church by 1860, and further modified between 1860 and 1866, he continued to remain the acknowledged leader of the Irish bishops and the favorite of both the pope and the Roman authorities. After his appointment as a cardinal, however, Cullen was no longer merely the first among equals; he was now superior in rank to his brother bishops, and the formal head of the national hierarchy. As a member, moreover, of the congregation of Propaganda, which was administratively responsible for the affairs of the Irish Church, Cullen would now be consulted by virtue of his office on all Irish business, and most especially in the crucial matter of Irish episcopal appointments. In a word, in the future his voice was likely to prove even more determinant in shaping the Irish bishops as a body than it had been in the past. The critical moment came finally for the bishops as a body, and for their constitutional role in the governing of the Irish church, in late 1869, when Cullen attempted to have his thirty-six-year-old protégé and secretary, George Conroy, appointed archbishop of Armagh and primate of all Ireland. In the end the bishops of the province of Armagh, with the tacit approval of the cardinals of Propaganda and the pope, were successful in resisting Cullen's efforts on behalf of Conroy and finally secured the translation of one of their own body to the see of Armagh. In thus containing Cullen, the bishops were ultimately able to demonstrate their own independence and integrity as a body in the governing of the Irish Church.

As the bishops were successfully making their corporate will effective in regard to both the education question and their constitutional role in the Irish Church, the Fenian challenge, which they had been prudently attempting to contain for nearly a decade, also finally climaxed in late 1869. This crisis was brought about by the celebrated Patrick Lavelle, the parish priest of Cong in the diocese of Tuam, who had the unique distinction in the Irish Church of having been suspended three times on the direct orders of the pope between September 1863 and April 1864 for his scandalous conduct in denouncing

Cullen and defending Fenianism in the public press. Even after his
rehabilitation in the summer of 1865, Lavelle continued to be a painful thorn in the sides of both Cullen and the bishops as a body because
of his public support of the Fenian cause. Finally, in November 1869,
he capped all his previous audacity by addressing an open letter to the
Irish bishops maintaining that the Fenian Brotherhood had not, in
fact, been condemned by Rome and that the members of the Brotherhood were not subject to excommunication, as Cullen had declared in
a recent pastoral letter on the subject. When, some two weeks later,
the dean of Limerick, Richard B. O'Brien, issued a circular letter to the
Irish clergy asking them to sign a declaration in favor of amnesty for
the Fenian prisoners then in custody, and when within several weeks
nearly half of the Irish clergy signed the declaration, the Irish bishops,
the great majority of whom were in Rome attending the first Vatican
Council, decided to petition the pope for a formal and authoritative
condemnation of Fenianism. The pope, through the Holy Office of the
Inquisition, responded to their petition almost immediately, on January 12, 1870, with a decree condemning the Brotherhood, which was
formally promulgated by the bishops in Ireland the following month.
By their firm and united action, the Irish bishops gave the Brotherhood a blow from which it never really recovered, for in each succeeding year after 1870, it became a smaller and more ineffectual revolutionary sect in the Irish political spectrum until it was finally
eclipsed in the constitutional politics of the Parnellite period.

   In the meantime, however, and before they finally persuaded the
pope to condemn Fenianism, the Irish bishops had to deal with yet
another kind of political challenge. This challenge was made real for
them when William Gladstone, the leader of the Liberal party, declared in early 1868 that justice must be finally done to Ireland and
proceeded to adopt, in effect, the program of the then-moribund National Association. Gladstone promised to disestablish and disendow
the Protestant Church in Ireland, pass a Land Act that would protect
the Irish tenant from capricious eviction, and settle the University
question to the satisfaction of Catholics. The Irish bishops took up
this proffered Irish-Liberal alliance with great enthusiasm both as a
constitutional answer to the revolutionary politics of Fenianism and
as a solution to those outstanding grievances that would perhaps finally give Ireland peace in the British connection. In the ensuing general election of 1868, therefore, the Irish bishops and their clergy supported Gladstone and the Liberal party in Ireland with great effect,
helping him to achieve an overall majority of some 130 in the new
House of Commons.

True to his election pledges, Gladstone disestablished the Protestant Church in Ireland in 1869 and then proceeded to attempt to provide a solution to the land question. By the time he was able to introduce his bill in early 1870, however, Irish opinion on what would be an acceptable solution to the land question had radically changed, and the Irish bishops as a body had also moved with the times. Five years before, in endorsing the program of the National Association, the Irish bishops had been willing to settle for a measure involving tenant compensation for improvements. By 1870 they were unwilling to approve anything less than fixity of tenure at a fair rent as an acceptable solution. Caught between his majority in the House of Commons, which was basically committed to the rights of private property, especially in land, and the radical exigencies of the Irish-Liberal alliance, Gladstone opted for the more conservative course, and the alliance, of which the bishops and their clergy had been the mainstay in Ireland, was severely shaken. Still, in hammering out their own consensus on the Land Bill, the bishops not only had managed to retain the confidence of the Irish portion of the alliance but also had succeeded in remaining united.

Though the lesson of the Irish-Liberal alliance was the same as that of the education question and Fenianism, what must not be forgotten was that all of the various challenges not only resulted in the bishops' finally crystallizing their policy concerning each but also had a cumulative effect in institutionalizing the corporate character of the bishops as a body. When all was said and done, however, it was the constitutional challenge that proved to be the crucial one to their institutionalization as a body. If that problem had not been satisfactorily resolved, the consolidation of the modern Irish Church would not have been possible. It was, therefore, the success of the bishops in gradually resolving the problems of the distribution of power in the Irish Church that finally gave them the determinant voice in the governing of that Church. Indeed, without that developing confidence in their corporate will in the 1860s, the Irish bishops would hardly have been able to meet the challenges cumulatively presented by the various aspects of the educational and political questions. In the last analysis, then, it was their success in regularizing their relationship with Rome and their ability to contain Cullen in his role as leader of the Irish Church that allowed the bishops to institutionalize themselves as a body and effectively consolidate the modern Irish Church.

Part I

The Bishops as a Body

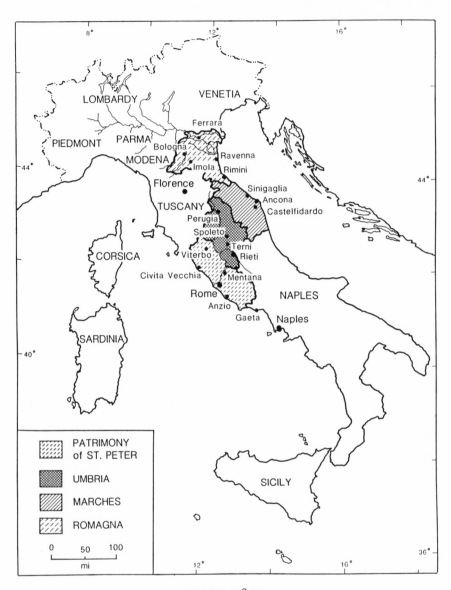

ITALY, 1859

I

The Temporal Power

August 1859–March 1861

During the winter of 1859–60, the Irish people became involved in Italian affairs to an extent that had never prevailed before and never would again. That involvement, moreover, was to have a profound influence in the shaping of modern Irish nationalism. This curious and unanticipated course of events had been initiated when France, in alliance with Sardinia, had become involved in a war with Austria in northern Italy in April 1859. By July the French and Sardinians had driven the Austrians out of Lombardy and annexed that province. In the meantime the duchies of Tuscany, Parma, and Modena, which had in effect been Austrian satellites, were taken over by pro-Sardinian governments. There were also pro-Sardinian uprisings in the Papal States to the south and west, particularly in the Romagna, where the papal authorities were unable to maintain themselves because the Austrian garrisons, which had provided the effective police power in the province, had all been withdrawn. Though the papal authorities were quickly able to reestablish their control in the Marches and Umbria, a Sardinian-inspired provisional government was successfully set up in the Romagna in spite of the vigorous protests of the pope.

In Ireland, meanwhile, the Irish bishops at their general meeting in early August 1859 had called the attention of their flocks, in concluding the usual pastoral address issued on such occasions, to "the machinations of wicked men, at once enemies of the Holy See, and the disturbers of all order, who, in casting off allegiance to their lawful sovereigns, as they had already cast off the restraints of religion, are seeking to disturb the peace of the pontifical states."[1] "Nor, as it would seem, have these lawless men wanted the sympathy," the bishops added, alluding to the English prime minister, Lord Palmerston, and his cabinet colleagues,

> if even the direct encouragement, of those who from their position should be the friends of order. Catholic Europe, the Catholic world, has been shocked to see that unscrupulous Statesmen, contrary to the principles of justice and international law, which they themselves are the loudest to invoke at other times, and from no assignable motive save that of a deadly animosity to the Holy See, would fain despoil the Roman Pontiff of those dominions which he has held and holds by a title the oldest as well as the most sacred of any in Europe.

Indeed, indignation in Ireland at the treatment of the pope was beginning to rise to a boil during August as Palmerston, and particularly his foreign secretary, Lord John Russell, became more openly pro-Sardinian and antipapal. "The attacks on His Holiness," the archbishop of Armagh, Joseph Dixon, reported to Tobias Kirby, the rector of the Irish College in Rome, on August 31, "by Russell, Palmerston, and Gladstone have pierced the very breasts of the Irish clergy and people. The indignation of the Irish people will hurl these men from power shortly after the next meeting of Parliament, and I trust that we shall never see them in power again."[2] The antipapal fury in England, however, continued to increase during the late summer and early fall, as the Protestant evangelicals thought they saw in the imminent collapse of the temporal power of the pope the prelude to the final demise of his spiritual power as well. In early October, therefore, the pope's apostolic delegate in Ireland and the leader among the Irish bishops, Paul Cullen, the archbishop of Dublin, attempted to stem the rising antipapal tide. On October 9 he issued to the clergy and laity of his archdiocese a long pastoral letter entitled "Some Recent Instances of Bigotry and Intolerance."[3]

The greater part of Cullen's very able letter was taken up with a defense and justification of the pope's temporal power. "It would be

1. Patrick Francis Moran, ed., *The Pastoral Letters and Other Writings of Cardinal Cullen* (Dublin, 1882), 1:695–96.

2. Kirby Papers (K), Archives of the Irish College, Rome, quoted also in E. R. Norman, *The Catholic Church and Ireland in the Age of Rebellion, 1859–1873* (London, 1965), p. 38.

3. Moran, 1:652–81.

impossible," Cullen explained, "to notice all the attacks that are directed by the press against the Pope's authority, and perhaps it would be almost useless to answer them; for they are made by persons blinded by passion, and inaccessible to reason, who appear to have nothing in view but to inflict a wound on the Head of the Church. It is not hatred of oppression or love of freedom that animates them, but a virulent hatred of Catholicity, and of that rock on which it stands, and will stand forever." "But without entering into lengthy discussions," he added,

> it may not be useless to notice one or two of the arguments generally alleged on this question.
>
> The first and principal ground of complaint against the Pope appears to be that he is not willing to extend to his dominions that liberal form of government, which under English influence, and with the applause of the British Press, has been introduced into the kingdom of Sardinia by its ministers Cavour and Ratazzi [*sic*]. But is there anything in the fruits obtained in that kingdom by the liberalized form of government to induce the Pope to adopt it? What has been the effect of the reforms of those applauded ministers? Under their auspices the property of convents and monasteries has been confiscated, nuns and friars dispersed, priests and bishops exiled or persecuted, the rights of the church invaded, heresy and error patronised, and the fountains of knowledge poisoned by anti-Catholic and infidel teaching. All this had been done under the name of progress and liberality; but to show how hypocritical is such a pretense, we may add that the boasted liberty of the press has been assailed, every Catholic newspaper suppressed, and intolerable and most oppressive burdens placed upon the people, so that under the care of the friends of progress, and those who are put forward as models of good statesmen, a country, which twelve years ago was happy and flourishing is now almost reduced to a state of utter destitution and bankruptcy, and groaning under a fearful despotism.[4]

"Another ground of complaint which is continually repeated," Cullen then pointed out, "is that the people of the Pope's states are dissatisfied, that foreign troops are employed to keep them in obedience, and that misery, poverty, and crime abound in them." He went on:

> In answering this objection it is necessary to recollect that no human institution is free from defects, and that no government

4. Ibid., p. 668.

can render all its subjects rich, happy, and contented. Political economists and enthusiastic statesmen sometimes promise to bring back the golden age, and to banish misery from this world. But their schemes are mere delusions. The earth is only a place of exile and banishment, where man's lot is to suffer and to earn his bread with the sweat of his brow. There will be always poverty in this world, and we are to recollect that it is not a crime to be poor, for our Redeemer himself, and the blessed Virgin, and the Apostles were poor; and our Lord has said "blessed are the poor." Crimes will always disgrace this earth; for the children of Adam, tainted by original sin, are prone to evil and disobedience. Hence, even in the greatest and best governed States, there are restless spirits seeking for changes, which frequently only aggravate their miseries; and mutinies, and seditions, and rebellions spring up from time to time.

"Even the British Empire," Cullen added, cleverly twisting his knife by referring to the bloody Sepoy mutiny in India, "is not exempt from such evils, and very lately it has been considered expedient to repress them in India by fire and sword, by destroying and pillaging great cities, and even by blowing unfortunate soldiers to pieces from the mouth of the cannon."

"But if great and powerful states," he then continued in the same vein, "cannot always satisfy all their subjects, is it just to pretend that the sovereign of a small territory, and comparatively weak, should succeed in so arduous an undertaking?" "Undoubtedly there are poor in the Pope's states," Cullen admitted,

but there is none of that squalid and degrading poverty which you see in London and the great cities of England; and we never heard of millions of his subjects dying of famine, or having been turned out by exterminating agents to perish of want on the high roads. There are crimes, of course, in the Pope's states; but yet you do not hear of continual child-murdering, nor of systematic poisoning, nor do you witness that degrading and scandalous exhibition of immorality which renders it impossible for a stranger to pass through many British cities without being shocked and horrified. Unhappily, too, there is some discontent in a part of the Papal territory; but it is not general, and does not extend to any considerable portion of the inhabitants; and what is more, it owes its origin to foreign influence, and to the intrigues and emissaries of Secret and Bible Societies, and frequently to English money.[5]

In finally concluding his long pastoral Cullen exhorted his clergy and laity, as had the bishops in August, to pray for the pope that he might be safely delivered from his enemies.

When the antipapal agitation in England showed little sign of abating, Cullen obviously decided that the boldest course was best and launched a very formidable counterattack in early November. He opened his campaign by calling a meeting of the Dublin clergy on November 10, in the procathedral, at which he presided. An address and a series of resolutions sympathizing with the pope in his difficulties were presented and adopted.[6] The following day, November 11, Cullen's secretary, C. B. Lyons, forwarded the address and resolutions to Kirby in Rome, informing him that the archbishop wanted them put into *"nice* Italian" for presentation to the pope, and expressing the hope that the Dublin meeting would set the example for the clergy in other dioceses (K). Lyons also explained that the meeting of the clergy would be shortly followed up by a meeting of the Catholic Young Men's Society of Dublin. The meeting of the society was duly held in the Rotundo in Dublin on November 15, and though Cullen did not attend because he was unwell, he wrote the spiritual guardian of the society, Father J. C. Spratt, a Carmelite, a long letter to be read to the young men. On November 28 Spratt also wrote Kirby explaining that Cullen had asked him to forward the address adopted at the meeting, which had been "attended by about *10,000* young men!!!" (K). It would be a great encouragement, Spratt added, if Kirby could secure *"a few lines* from the Holy Father *in his own handwriting* imparting to them the Apostolic Benediction."

The agitation launched by Cullen quickly caught fire, and from late November until late June of the following year, the developing enthusiasm in Ireland for the pope's cause was simply incredible. In every diocese in Ireland, the bishops began to organize meetings of the clergy and laity to present addresses to the pope. For example, the bishop of Elphin, Laurence Gillooly, informed Kirby from Roscommon on December 4, "I am now engaged in organising a Meeting of the Catholic Gentry etc. of this diocese. It will be held in Elphin on the 28th Inst.—and will, P.G., be largely & respectably attended. A requi-

---

5. Ibid., pp. 669–70.
6. *Irish Catholic Directory* (I.C.D.), 1860, pp. 247–62. The date given there, September 3, 1859, is incorrect.

sition is being signed by the leading gentlemen of the County, requesting me to convene the meeting. I will send you an account of our proceedings in early Jan^y" (K). "Those meetings," he further assured Kirby in conclusion, "will arouse the Catholic feeling of the Country—and exercise a salutary influence on our government." That same day, December 4, Gillooly's neighbor, the bishop of Ardagh and Clonmacnoise, John Kilduff, wrote Kirby from Longford, also complaining about the antipapal policy of Lord Palmerston's government (K). Kilduff reported that he and his clergy were going to hold meetings in every parish in his diocese before the opening of Parliament in January to protest any ministry that supported rebellion in the Roman states. From the southwest the bishop of Kerry, David Moriarty, assured Kirby on December 14 that the propapal agitation was going on gloriously in the diocese (K). The speeches in English at their recent meeting in Killarney, Moriarty informed Kirby, were as nothing compared to those in Irish. One priest had asked those present, in Irish, what they would do if they had arms in their hands. From the crowd, Moriarty explained, came the reply, " 'Into the guts of the enemies of the Holy Father.' " "I never," he concluded heartily, "enjoyed such a day of real fun."

The agitation on behalf of the pope in Ireland continued to pick up momentum throughout December and into the new year. "I am happy to tell your Eminence," Cullen reported to the cardinal prefect of Propaganda, Alessandro Barnabò, on December 20, "that throughout all Ireland there is an extraordinary attachment being shown for the cause of the Holy Father. Vast meetings have already been held in Cork, Waterford, and other cities to protest against the insults that have been offered to the Holy See, and not only bishops and priests but many laymen have made eloquent and learned speeches. I believe that there was never seen in any country such a manifestation in favor of the rights of the Holy Father, and it may be hoped that it will result in great good."[7] "What is most amazing in this whole movement," he noted, "is that everything has been conducted with the greatest order, and even though in some instances fifteen or twenty thousand persons gathered there was never the slightest disturbance."

Several days later, the cardinal prefect received independent corroboration and more of all that Cullen had reported about the progress of the agitation in Ireland in favor of the pope. Daniel O'Connor, who was serving as a curate in the parish of Parteen in the diocese of Lim-

---

7. *Scritture riferite nei congressi, Irlanda* (S.R.C.), vol. 33, fol. 1061, Archives of the Society for the Propagation of the Faith, Rome.

erick, wrote Barnabò his annual letter on December 22, thus fulfilling his obligation as an alumnus of the College of Propaganda in Rome.[8] "Your Eminence will, I am certain," O'Connor reported, "be pleased with the news that we have offered public prayers this year for peace, and especially for his Holiness, which the good people responded to with real zeal and fervor." "A great public meeting," he further assured the cardinal, "will be also held on the 26th of this month in Limerick to protest the meddling of the English ministers in the affairs of the Papal States and to sympathize with the Holy Father in his misfortunes. There will also be manifestations on the part of the Catholic nobility of Limerick, the members of Parliament, the magistrates, the municipal councillors, and all the civil dignitaries together with the general public and the clergy in support of the temporal power of the pope." "In conclusion," O'Connor added finally, "your Eminence will allow me to sympathize with you and to reveal the regret that not only I but all [my] parishioners feel because of the wicked attempts that are now being plotted against the rights of the Holy See, and the peace and well being of the people who are subject to her."

The agitation in Ireland to sustain the temporal power of the pope finally climaxed on January 9, 1860, in Dublin at a large meeting convened by Cullen on the requisition of more than twenty-three thousand signatures. The lord mayor and all the Catholic municipal dignitaries were in attendance; the procathedral was filled to overflowing and a huge concourse of people congregated in the streets outside. Cullen, who presided, spoke for more than an hour and a half on the rights of the Holy See. His discourse when published totaled some fourteen thousand words in nearly forty printed pages.[9] In forwarding a copy of his effort to Kirby on January 12, Cullen explained that he had stuffed as much as he could into it not only because he hoped the Protestant papers would take offense and publish all of it but also "with a view of not leaving too much time to the lay speakers who sometimes go astray on religious matters" (K). The meetings finally began to wind down during the latter part of January, until they were in effect concluded on February 7 with two large meetings in Castlebar and Clones, which were chaired respectively by the archbishop of Tuam, John MacHale, and the bishop of Clogher, Charles McNally.

The course of events in Italy, however, was about to give the agitation in Ireland not only a fresh impetus but a new direction. In early January the recently established provisional government in the Roma-

8. Ibid., fol. 1062.
9. Moran, 1:710–49.

gna had proceeded to expel the Jesuits and to decree the confiscation of the property of the regular orders. When Pius IX was then informed by the emperor of the French, Napoleon III, his erstwhile protector, that he thought the pope should surrender his claim to sovereignty over the Romagna, Pius IX was at last persuaded by his advisers that he could rely only on his own efforts to sustain what was left of the temporal power. Accordingly, he issued an appeal to the faithful of the world to aid him materially with money and men in order to reorganize the papal army. The effective desertion of the papal cause by Napoleon III was taken very hard in Ireland. The archbishop of Armagh, Joseph Dixon, was incensed, and on January 14 he wrote a scorching open letter to the people of Drogheda on the subject of the emperor of the French, which concluded with the apostrophe " 'ROBBER TAKE YOUR HAND FROM THE THROAT OF THE VICAR OF CHRIST.' "[10] Cullen was no less appalled at the news from Rome, but in writing Kirby on January 17, he explained that though the news was terrible, he thought Dixon's letter too strong (K). Cullen was convinced, however, that the Church would come out of the struggle purer and stronger. He also expressed the hope that Kirby had been able to give an account of the recent meeting in Dublin to both the pope and his secretary of state, Giacomo Cardinal Antonelli. "You will say," Cullen noted, referring to the pope's recent request for aid, "that it is all smoke up to the present, true, but probably we shall soon be able to send some roast. I expect to originate a collection in a few days, and undoubtedly the people will give a hearty response."

Cullen was not able to launch his collection for the pope for some two weeks, however, apparently because he was unwell. In any case, he finally announced on February 2 that he would make his collection on February 26, the first Sunday of Lent. Most of the Irish bishops immediately followed suit and scheduled their collections either for the first or for one of the other Sundays during Lent. Only the archbishop of Tuam, John MacHale, Cullen's implacable enemy among the Irish bishops, refused to follow his archepiscopal colleague's lead. In a letter to the editor of the *Freeman's Journal* dated February 3, and published on February 6, MacHale complained:

In the morning *Freeman* of yesterday you state that collections will be made in every parish church in Ireland on the first

10. *Freeman's Journal* (Dublin), January 16, 1860.

Sunday of Lent, and on the preceding Sunday, the officiating clergy will afford the necessary explanations &c. I am not aware as far as this diocese is concerned, you had authority from me for any such communication. The topics of his Pastoral Letters for Lent or for any other season, are selected by the judgement of the Ordinary, and the collections, if such there be, are regulated by his instructions. It may not be known to you, that for several years the parochial collections on the first Sunday of Lent, have been uniformly devoted, in this diocese, to the support of schools and missions, and other diocesan objects. You may not be aware that according to our provincial statutes, no officiating clergyman is permitted to make extraordinary collections in his church on any account without asking and obtaining the sanction of the Ordinary.

"Of the claims of the Holy Father," MacHale added, "especially in his present afflictions, on the Catholics of Ireland, as well as on the Catholics of the entire world, there can be no question. But all things must be done according to order, nor would it be respectful to his Holiness, even in the matter of these contributions to violate the laws which have his own sanction. Whenever the faithful are appealed to in behalf of his Holiness, in a legitimate manner, there is no doubt but the appeal will be generously responded to."

"Such a clergy and people," MacHale then assured the editor of the *Freeman*, "do not require the unauthorized interference of anyone to instruct them in their duty to the Pope, or to specify the time and mode of its performance. That shall be done by the Ordinary, and the clergy and people of Tuam will, as usual, do their duty." "In the article alluded to," MacHale continued,

you introduce, you say, a Pontifical Legate [i.e., Cullen], to sanction, I suppose, what must appear as extraordinary proceeding.

However, as you have on more occasions than one introduced him, it is high time to inform you that we know of no such personage in Ireland; nor do I find any address from a venerable prelate, purporting from the name of his diocese and particular regulations not applicable to any other, to be intended exclusively for his own. To this address you append a commentary, giving it a far wider application than it bore on the face of it, connecting the plea of the Pope's claims on which the clergy of Ireland require no new information, with strange pretensions, which, if you were not seasonably set right on, would soon upset in Ireland the ancient boundaries of which the church is so jealous, and gradually subvert all due subordination.[11]

Cullen was naturally very annoyed at MacHale's demurrer, and in writing Kirby on February 7 he pointedly observed, while enclosing MacHale's letter, that one would think that the archbishop of Tuam did not want the collection to be a success (K). Earlier in his letter, however, Cullen had noted that he had already received £500–£600 in the last four or five days and that he would send £1,000 before the end of the week because the pope might be in need. Several days later he forwarded the promised £1,000 to Kirby, cautioning him to tell the pope "not to be too generous with his money. He may want a little for bad times."[12] In the next two weeks the enthusiasm for the pope's collection began to build, and Cullen was able to forward another £1,000 to Kirby on February 17, and yet another on February 24, two days before the general collection was to be made in Dublin. On the Sunday of the collection Cullen was obviously elated, for he dated the letter he wrote to Kirby that morning, February 26, "Pope's tribute day" (K). He anticipated that the collection would amount to between £10,000 and £12,000 and asked Kirby to have a good address in Latin drawn up by one of the professors of rhetoric in Rome for presentation to the pope with the collection. Before closing his letter, however, he noted with some obvious satisfaction in the margin, "12 o'clock. Up to this hour £600 collected at the door of Marlboro St. Church—£150 at the door where the poor enter. This makes nearly £2,000 from my parish alone! Cosi va la Madonna evviva il Papa!" A short time later he reported in yet another marginal note, "The total amt. from St. Mary's parish (mine) is £2,150. The collection at the door of S. Andrews—Westland row exceeds £1,000. I think we shall have £12,000 altogether."

The following day, February 27, Cullen wrote Kirby a carefully penned letter in Italian for Roman consumption about the results of the collection (K). Seven of the largest city parishes, he explained, had contributed some £6,800, and seven of the country parishes had collected another £2,350, for a total of some £9,150. He added, "I imagine that the collections in the other 40 parishes will be at least £3,000 more. In all it will be £13,000 or 325,000 francs. Let us hope that the

---

11. What the editor's loose use of the term "Pontifical Legate" to describe Cullen referred to was, of course, Cullen's rank as apostolic delegate of the Holy See in Ireland. As delegate, Cullen's authority extended only to those matters connected with the observing of the statutes and decrees enacted at the Synod of Thurles in 1850, and not to any right to interfere in provinces or dioceses not his own.

12. K, n.d. [ca. February 10, 1860].

other dioceses will contribute respectable amounts. From all Ireland it will perhaps amount to a million and a half francs [£60,000]." "This is a very convincing reply," he observed further, "to Protestants who boast of having extinguished the Catholic religion in Ireland. A good example is also given to English Catholics who have so many pretensions and seek to make it appear that the Catholics of Ireland are worthless, and never lose the opportunity to outdo them. Now let them go and imitate the good example."

Whatever may be said of the example set by Cullen for English Catholics by his collection, he certainly gave his brother bishops in Ireland a good example. Indeed, his own early estimates of what Dublin would contribute had been too low. In the end Dublin contributed nearly £16,000.[13] This was a prodigious sum, and the collections in the other dioceses between March and July were in scale equal to it. By early July, therefore, when all the collections had finally been made, the Irish people had raised some £80,000 for the pope.[14] No such sum had ever been raised before in Ireland in the nineteenth century. In 1851, for example, when the Irish bishops called for a general collection to launch the Catholic University, the total amount collected was only £18,000, of which Dublin contributed some £3,600.[15] When the bishops then authorized another collection for the University in 1854, the total amount collected came to only about £10,000, of which Dublin again contributed some 20 percent, or £2,000.[16] Not even O'Connell's celebrated Catholic or Repeal rent at the height of the agitations for Emancipation or Repeal had come to more than £1,000 per week in any given year. In the long run, however, the real significance of the pope's collection was less the initial response, perhaps, than the successful institutionalizing of that enthusiasm in the annual Peter's pence collection, which became a permanent feature of Irish life. In the next fifty years, in fact, the Irish people would contribute more than £500,000 in Peter's pence to Rome.[17]

In the short run, the staggered nature of collections between March and early July helped to sustain and increase the enthusiasm that had been initiated between December and February by the mass meetings

13. K, Cullen to Kirby [April 10, 1860].
14. K, Cullen to Kirby [July 28, 1860].
15. Emmet Larkin, *The Making of the Roman Catholic Church in Ireland, 1850–1860* (Chapel Hill, N.C., 1980), p. 432.
16. Ibid.
17. Emmet Larkin, "Economic Growth, Capital Investment and the Roman Catholic Church in Nineteenth Century Ireland," *American Historical Review* 72 (1966–67): 866.

in favor of the pope. Then in the midst of the enthusiasm created by the ongoing collections, the general excitement was further increased when the news of the project to raise a brigade in Ireland for the pope gradually became general knowledge. The project of an Irish brigade had apparently been inaugurated in early February when Kirby wrote Cullen and a number of other Irish bishops reminding them that the pope had called for men as well as money in his appeal in January. Initially Cullen proved to be something less than enthusiastic about this idea. "It is nonsense," he told Kirby rather plainly, "to talk about getting men in Ireland—it w^d require two years to train them—the people do not know how to fire a gun, and without training they c^d do nothing."[18] In his letter Kirby had also obviously explained very confidentially to Cullen that the papal government had commissioned an Austrian nobleman of Irish extraction, Count Charles McDonnell, to recruit volunteers in Ireland. Cullen was not surprised by the news, for he dryly informed Kirby that the fact that the count was preparing to come to Ireland to recruit had already been reported in the public press.

McDonnell finally arrived in Ireland during the last week of February, armed with a letter of introduction to Cullen from the secretary of Propaganda, Gaetano Bedini. In writing to Cardinal Barnabò on February 24, Cullen cautiously explained that he would certainly do what he could to help the count, but the project had already been somewhat compromised by discussion of the count's visit and its purpose in some detail in the daily papers.[19] In writing to Kirby two days later, on February 26, Cullen was even more pessimistic about the count's mission (K). One of the reasons, of course, why Cullen was so guarded and cautious about discussing the proposed brigade was that he was only too well aware that it was against the law in Ireland to recruit subjects of the queen for service in foreign armies. It seems that Count McDonnell, however, was little daunted by either the complexities or the illegalities. He shrewdly began his campaign by enlisting the aid of A. M. Sullivan, the editor of the Nation, and then in his company embarked on a tour of Ireland to find recruits.[20]

One of those whom McDonnell found to be most enthusiastic in

18. K, Cullen to Kirby, n.d. [ca. February 10, 1860]. See also K, Cullen to Kirby, August 19, 1859: when Kirby apparently mentioned the possibility of raising troops in Ireland, Cullen replied there was not much chance because "the wages are too high, and it costs too much to pay soldiers at such a rate. Besides men are really very scarce."

19. S.R.C., vol. 33, fol. 1121.

20. A. M. Sullivan, New Ireland (London, 1882), pp. 211–13, quoted in G. F. H. Berkeley, The Irish Battalion in the Papal Army of 1860 (Dublin, 1929), pp. 19–20.

the cause was the bishop of Kerry, David Moriarty. Moriarty had, in fact, already written Kirby on February 15, declaring that since money "is the sinew of War," it "must be procured before men" (K). "I expect," he added, "we shall have a noble offering from the Irish people. I advise *all* to give a little each so that there may not be [any] down to the child sucking at the breast who will not reach a hand to the Holy Father. We were chary about talking of *men*, lest a failure should subject us to the taunt of vain boasting. We had to consider how they were to be officered, how equipped, how sent to their destination etc. etc. etc. If all these preliminaries were arranged on some well digested plan—I doubt not we should have volunteers in plenty." "A practical way," he explained, "is suggested to me. You are making railroads in the R[oman]. states. Charter a vessel to take out labourers direct from Ireland—if they have not to fight let them be sure of work. So that as need may be, they may take up the pick or the pike." When Count McDonnell left Rome, Kirby had apparently provided him with a letter of introduction to Moriarty, for after the count's visit Moriarty proved even more enthusiastic. "*Men*, & big men too," he reported to Kirby from Killarney on March 28, "are coming in every day to offer themselves for the service of the Holy Father. We cannot without sanction from Rome use the offerings made for the Holy Father for the purpose of sending them out. We want then either a special fund for the purpose or leave to apply this the money subscribed. We want also agencies along the line of route. All this should be looked to."[21] "The friend you introduced to me," he assured Kirby finally, referring to the count, "is I believe now in France. He has found everywhere the same readiness to fly Romewards."

Moriarty had undoubtedly suggested to McDonnell that the best way to avoid the penalties of the Foreign Enlistment Act was to provide the volunteers with the means to emigrate to the Papal States, where they ostensibly could find work; when they arrived they could then formally be enlisted in the pope's service. Moriarty's further suggestion about using a portion of the money collected for the pope in Ireland to support the "emigration" was also eventually adopted. Some of the bishops apparently enjoyed the subterfuge. "We are thinking of sending a portion of it," the archbishop of Armagh informed Kirby on April 4, referring to his collection for the pope, "by some Irish *navvies*, who are going out to work at railways and other things" (K). Cullen, however, continued to be most guarded and cautious.

21. See also Kieran O'Shea, "David Moriarty (1814–77): III, Politics," *Journal of the Kerry Archaeological and Historical Society*, no. 5, 1972, pp. 89–91.

While admitting to Kirby on April 10, for example, that many in Ireland were ready to fight for the pope, he also reminded him that he had not as yet received any authority from Rome to proceed, and that such activity, moreover, was against the law in Ireland (K).

Kirby obviously took the hint, for in the time required to receive a reply from Rome to his letter, Cullen had moved into action. He set up an "Emigration Committee," which was managed by two of his most able and trusted priests, Laurence Canon Forde and James Murray, both of whom had been educated in the Irish College in Rome in the 1840s when Cullen had been rector. Cullen still continued, however, to be very cautious in promoting the brigade. In his correspondence, for example, he always referred to those officers and enlisted men who volunteered in Ireland as "students" and "emigrants," respectively. "Dr. Forde," he alerted Kirby on April 27, "is gone to pay you a visit. You can regulate with him all matters about future students" (K). "You and Don Giacomo," Cullen added, referring to the papal secretary of state, Cardinal Antonelli, by their adopted code name for him, "can see what is best to be done and tell him everything." "I wrote to you before," he then reminded Kirby, "about the emigrants who are going out or wishing to go. I c^d say nothing to them. Those who have some employment at home ask will they be sure of something abroad. You have the opportunity of letting us know." "Pay as much attention," he then advised Kirby in a postscript, "as you can to any students that go out. Beg of D. Giac° to assist them." Kirby obviously replied by return of post, for Cullen was able to inform the bishop of Elphin, Laurence Gillooly, on May 9, "I received some days ago a letter from Rome in which it was stated that the authorities there would be happy to give employment there to any emigrants who might go out from Ireland, and that it would be fully satisfactory that any money destined for Rome should be employed in defraying their traveling expenses."[22] "I do not like to write much about these matters," he added, "lest a false interpretation should be put on my words by our enemies, but I suppose it is quite free for anyone that wishes to emigrate, and for us to assist them if we can."

By this time, however, the British government had become concerned and had instructed its unofficial representative in Rome, Odo Russell, to ask Cardinal Antonelli if the rumors that an Irish contingent was on its way to Italy to join the papal army were true. "I inquired of the Cardinal Secretary of State," Russell reported to his uncle and foreign secretary, Lord John Russell, on May 10,

22. Gillooly Papers (G), Elphin Diocesan Archives, Sligo.

what truth there was in the report that the Papal Government expected one thousand Irish recruits at Ancona by way of Belgium and Trieste.

His Eminence replied that since the War Department was no longer under his control, the formation of the Papal Army was entirely in the hands of General de Lamoricière and he was not thoroughly acquainted with all the measures taken by His Excellency but he believed the general reckoned on obtaining one thousand Irishmen for the Papal Army. They came of their own free will to Italy and enlisted here, nothing will induce the Papal Government to attempt enlistments in Ireland. They had too much respect for the laws of other countries, and since it was prohibited to enlist in the Papal States for foreign armies, the Pope respected in other states the laws he wished to see respected in his own dominions. His Holiness was constantly receiving letters from Irish gentlemen offering to bring him from three to five thousand men at any time, but the Sovereign Pontiff had always declined to entertain such offers.[23]

"His Eminence did not," Russell added,

for many reasons think it desirable to have a large number of Irish soldiers in the Papal Army. But the question at present was to form an army sufficiently strong for all police purposes in the Papal States, so as to make the French occupation cease altogether and free the Papacy from all foreign intervention and he most sincerely hoped and believed that for the sake of this long desired and much discussed object, Her Majesty's Government would generously throw no impediments in the way of such of Her Roman Catholic subjects, who, of their own free will, proceeded to Rome to offer their services to the Pope.

By the time Lord John Russell received this dispatch from Rome, Cullen was writing to Kirby that a group of prospective officers were on their way. "I have heard," he reported, "that several very respectable students have left or are about to leave for Rome. I have not seen any of them but I have heard that they will make a very good Camerata [class] in yr. college. You know it w^d not be well that any of them c^d send home bad accts of the College."[24] "You know," he further cautioned Kirby, "what going into a *gabbia* [cage, jail] is. Well I do not want to make such an experiment." "Some of the people in Rome

---

23. Foreign Office Papers (F.O.), 43/77, Great Britain, Public Record Office, London.
24. K, n.d. [ca. May 13, 1860, because it covers enclosed letter dated May 12, 1860].

write as if they wish D^n Placido there," he explained, referring to himself by his code name. "He w^d be sent if he c^d be caught. Mr Talbot and others write as if he c^d give Commissions etc. Were he to do so he w^d soon be locked up. It is a felony to do certain things." Cullen was so concerned, in fact, about the possibility of breaking the letter of the law that he asked William Monsell, the senior member of Parliament for county Limerick and a prominent Catholic convert, to solicit a legal opinion. "A distinguished member of Parliament," he explained to Kirby on May 16, "has just written a letter to ——— in which he writes as follows:—

> 'I have looked carefully at the Foreign Enlistment Act and have taken a good opinion on the subject. No one may accept a military Commission in any foreign Service or enlist as a soldier or sailor therein or go abroad with the intent or to enlist or to endeavour to procure any person to enlist—but anyone may go into a foreign service as a policeman. In other words a police force that exists in Ireland might be formed by Irishmen at Rome without offending the law.'[25]

It will be well for you," Cullen advised Kirby, "to have the above. The statement of the M.P. is to [be] relied on. . . . There was some talk in Parliament. The government are determined to prevent anything from being done."

Cullen's surmise was correct, for the government had taken action that very day. "I send you," Cullen alerted Kirby in Italian two days later, on May 18, "a copy of a proclamation that was posted in all the streets of this city yesterday against those that want to enlist in foreign armies. I fancied that such a document would be published. The Cork newspapers announce that 150 young men arrived in that city led by two priests appointed to take them to Rome, and that they were full of enthusiasm for the cause. Other newspapers have made similar announcements, so that the government was obliged to take notice."[26] "Anyhow," he added, "many still want to go to Italy, and they can go as emigrants if they want to. The difficulty is in regard to their success in that country. Will they be well received, will they be able to obtain the means to live[?] For myself, I fear that many will go out warm friends and return enemies." The government's effort to dampen support for the pope in Ireland does not appear to have met with much success. The Dublin proclamation of May 16, warning

25. K; this letter is not signed, but it is in Cullen's handwriting.
26. K; this letter is also unsigned and in Cullen's handwriting. The enclosed proclamation was apparently dated May 16 and posted in Dublin on May 17.

against foreign enlistments, in fact resulted only in greater publicity for the efforts to raise a papal brigade in Ireland. The Irish Catholic members in the House of Commons, for example, took advantage of the issuing of the proclamation to criticize the government's pro-Sardinian policy in general and Lord John Russell in particular.[27] In any case the enthusiasm for the pope's cause in Ireland continued unabated. "Very many here," Cullen assured Kirby again on May 26, "are anxious to go to Italy. They are going away in any case to Australia or America. If they got any hope of success they w^d stay nearer home. About 400 have gone—they are going thro' Germany. I fear that the C^t McD is taking them that way to show he is a g^t man" (K). "Poor fellow," he shrewdly advised Kirby, "has not I fear much judgement. Be cautious with him."

A week later, on June 1, Cullen was finally able to report with some obvious relief to Kirby that all the "emigrants" had now been sent off (K). Those from his part of the country, he noted, were respectable-enough Catholics, but those from Kerry, though very robust, had scarcely any shoes or clothes. The enthusiasm for the pope's cause in Ireland apparently continued to be very great during the next few months. That enthusiasm, however, was not reflected in Cullen's correspondence with Kirby. "Great complaints," Cullen warned Kirby on June 8, "have been published here. It is stated in Ancona that they [the recruits] were put in *un fienile* [a hayloft] and that on the road they had to suffer *assai* [a great deal]. There is no knowing the truth—but of course *la cosa non puo andare bene* [the affair cannot go well] as no one here can have anything to do with it on acct of the law. Everyone does as he wishes" (K). "I fear the Count," Cullen added for good measure, "was no good to organise matters in Germany. I think it is a *pazzia* [folly] for people to go round the world through all Germany when they could get to Rome in four days by Marseilles." Some two weeks later, Cullen was still in a very pessimistic mood when he wrote Kirby, on June 21, that he thought there would be a good deal more trouble about the brigade before it was all over (K). "Probably," he prophesied, "the whole affair will end up a fiasco—like some of the Crusades."

———◆———

Indeed, the situation with regard to the brigade was a good deal more serious than even Cullen realized. In early June the recruits, who had

27. *Hansard Parliamentary Debates*, 3d ser., 158:1767.

recently arrived and were assigned to garrison the town of Macerata near Ancona, mutinied. The Roman authorities immediately dispatched a number of Irish priests to calm the recruits and to act as chaplains. As one of those chaplains, Father Bonaventure McLaughlin, an Irish Franciscan, explained to Kirby from Macerata on June 7, "I was very anxious to have some leisure to write you a long letter about the arrival of the Irish—the state of mutiny in which I found them, and the exertions (successful thank God) that I had to make in order to get them safely lodged in their excellent and comfortable barracks at Macerata" (K). He elaborated:

> The arrangements for their transfer from Ireland are very much complained of, and persons taking an active part in the movement are condemned *nominatim*: but much allowance must be made for everything new; and first arrangements are naturally defective. As regards individuals no one of experience will hastily condemn them on the evidence of disappointment or irritation. Nevertheless it appears to me that the arrangements are capable of much improvement: and the agents might get such instructions as would prevent the recruits from having it in their power to say, on arriving, that they were deceived. A certificate of good conduct should be a *sine qua non*: we have got some shoking [*sic*] fellows amongst us, but they are few as yet.
>
> I am entirely too occupied—dizzy from want of sleep, and weak from over-exertion to attempt entering, at all, on details: but you cannot attach too much importance to the remarks I have made, for they are the result of a painful and evident experience.

"I think," McLaughlin added, "they are most appropriately made to you, who are in Rome the representative of our nation and our church; and your long experience in business matters, will enable you to represent them to the authorities in proper form." McLaughlin then prudently concluded by introducing the bearer of his letter, a young Irish sublieutenant stationed at Macerata, who would provide those details necessary to help Kirby read between the lines.

"This moment," Patrick Moran, vice-rector of the Irish College, reported to Cullen that same day, June 7, "a young officer, Lieutenant Doyle, has arrived from Macerata. His accounts are very bad. There are, he says, about 150 Irishmen in Macerata. About 40 of them are from Kerry; these latter have given a deal of annoyance; nothing but discontent and fighting, & wishing for this and for that."[28] "Sullivan

28. Cullen Papers (C), Dublin Diocesan Archives, Dublin.

who had been in the *Phoenix* society," Moran explained, referring to a recruit who had been a member of a celebrated secret society in West Cork and Kerry, "had the model of a Cap: and a number of them insisted on getting this. They threw off the Roman cap & jumped on it. They also insist on getting green coats." "Father Bonaventura is altogether killed from them," he added. "Captain Russell who has got the charge of drilling them is beginning to get them into some order. He sends them without any mercy to the black-hole. God grant that they may behave themselves." "One of them," Moran noted interestingly, "gave a characteristic answer to Father Bonaventura when he asked him to keep quiet. Oh, he said, we came out to fight, and 'till we meet Garibaldi we must have a spree amongst ourselves." "They were kicking up such rows in Macerata," he reported finally, "that we have been told, the people there are getting up a petition to the Government to have them removed. You see we are Paddies ever more: all the way from the Kingdom of Kerry."

The news of the disturbances at Macerata was not long in becoming general knowledge. "I learn," Odo Russell reported to Lord John Russell on June 12, "through some officers lately returned from Macerata that the greatest dissatisfaction prevails among the Irish recruits of the Pope. They vow that they have been enlisted under false pretenses and that the authorities have not kept faith with them. Irish priests have been sent from Rome to pacify them. I have as yet no further details to give your Lordship on the subject."[29] Some ten days later, on June 23, Russell was finally able to supply the details. He reported that the Irish priests sent to Macerata had "instead of preaching submission" taken "the part of their countrymen and declare they have been unfairly treated by the Papal military authorities. In consequence they have all been ordered to Rome to be placed under the immediate orders of General de Lamoricière."[30]

As far as I can learn they are treated exactly in the same manner as all the other foreigners who enlist in the Pope's army, —no difference is made, I believe, but these poor deluded men, relying on the golden promises of their priests at home, have found their own hopes and expectations deceived.

In the first instance they say they were promised two shillings a day instead of which they receive five *bajocchi* (about fourpence).

2nd they expected to be commanded by Irish officers.

29. F.O., 43/77.
30. Ibid.

3rd they expected to form a Legion and wear a special uniform and

4th they complain of their bed, food, barracks, —everything in short, and the men who were enlisted as officers have been reduced to the ranks on arriving at Macerata.

As they have become very riotous at one time and set fire to their barracks, gendarmes were sent to keep them in order, but they declared they would murder any foreign officers who attempted to command them.

Wherever they have been, the subjects of the Pope have had to complain of their behaviour and at Macerata the authorities declared they preferred even a Spanish garrison to an Irish one.

"I must repeat again," he noted finally in conclusion, "that General de Lamoricière, who is most kind to his soldiers, seems very well disposed towards them, and in all probability the true cause of their present disappointment must be attributed in great measure to the exaggerated promises and expectations held out to them by their priests in Ireland, and it must also in truth be said that the Irish priests in Rome who surround them are most zealous in their behalf and minister both to their spiritual and bodily comforts."

Several days later the British consul in Rome, C. T. Newton, also reported the behavior of the Irish recruits to Lord John Russell. "I have the honour," he explained on June 25, "to enclose herewith translations of a pamphlet anonymously printed, containing suggestions in reference to the mode of raising and training Irish Volunteers for military service in the Roman States. These remarks are, I should imagine, drawn up by some Irish Ecclesiastic, and seem to contain some useful practical suggestions."[31] I have further," Newton added, "the honour to report that Irish volunteers to the number of about three hundred have arrived here in successive small detachments from Macerata within the past week. It is said that discontent prevails among them and that they committed disorders on their march from Macerata. The Irish Catholic clergy here seems, as far as I can judge, to think that these volunteers have not been as yet fairly dealt with and that the

---

31. F.O., 43/80a, "Suggestions on the Addition to the Pontifical Army of Irish Volunteers, Who Offer Their Services to the Holy See." The pamphlet pointed out, in part, that until matters were properly arranged it was necessary "to govern the Irish soldiers by religious motives principally, for this end, making use as far as possible of the priestly influence of the Chaplain. Or, at any rate, permitting this wholesome influence to aid in a great measure, in the support of military discipline." The anonymous author of this pamphlet was apparently Laurence Canon Forde. See K, Forde to Kirby, January 15, 1861.

promises held out to them in Ireland have not been fulfilled in Italy." Five days later, on June 30, Newton reported again that the behaviour of the Irish recruits in Rome was deplorable.[32] "Two or three days ago," he noted, "the conduct of several of them was so mutinous that one of the officers who had been called to quell the disturbance cut down one of the most refractory with his sabre, wounding him severely on the head. Much drunkenness and quarreling prevails among them, as they are generally recruited from among the lowest class of Irish. . . ." Earlier in this letter, however, Newton had explained that about twenty of the recruits were from the Dublin Metropolitan Police and that there were at least four men who had come out on the understanding that they would receive commissions, which there was no hope that they would get.

Finally, on July 10, Odo Russell summed up the whole situation in a long dispatch from Rome.[33] "The Irish recruits of the Pope," he reported to Lord John, "amount now to about thirteen hundred and the enlistment in Ireland has been stopped. They continue to be very riotous and disorderly, and are a source of trouble to the Papal authorities. At Macerata, Spoleto and lately at Ancona they have committed various excesses. They have exasperated the inhabitants and terrified the authorities and their officers do not appear to have much control over them. They are a wild set of fellows who seem to enjoy a rare amount of exuberant spirits." "Here at Rome," Russell further explained, "a good many of them have called at the British Consulate complaining that they had been deceived in Ireland by every kind of promise, that they had never enlisted but had simply come to look for work and were compelled to enter the Papal Army against their will, and they claimed to be sent home to Ireland at the expense of Her Majesty's Government." "They had been advised," he added, "to address their complaints to the priests and officers under whose care they had placed themselves."

"I next called on Cardinal Antonelli," he then continued,

and told him that although I had no instructions to do so, I wished privately and on my own account to call his attention to the complaints made by Her Majesty's subjects in the Pope's service and to inquire of him whether anything can be done to render them more satisfied with their present condition.

His Eminence replied that he was glad I mentioned the subject to him since he wished to tell me that he had given orders to

32. F.O., 43/80a.
33. F.O., 43/77.

send home all those who since their arrival in the Papal States objected to serve in the Pope's army, —that the Pope only sought volunteers and wished no one to serve him against his own free will. All those, therefore, who asked to go home would be sent back to Ireland at the expense of the Papal government, and those who wished to remain were treated with great kindness by General de Lamoricière who had taken a fancy to their fine military appearance. He begged I should give him the names of any of the men I thought were in trouble and he would see at once what could be done for them.

"His Eminence," Russell added, "related many anecdotes about the excesses they had committed, and said he now understood why I had eight months ago so strongly urged him not to form an Irish Legion,— that the Pope as well as himself had not known the Irish character to be so energetic, —and that he could also now appreciate the difficulties experienced by the British government in dealing with Ireland."

The stories about the misplaced energy and exuberance of the Irish recruits were also an embarrassment at the Irish college, but the embarrassment was tempered with a difference. "We must only hope," Moran explained to Cullen on June 13, "that the Irish who come here will not bring down any disgrace on our country. Up to the present some fine young men have come, but as the Cappelano F. Bonaventura wrote to us some time ago, there are *some shocking fellows* amongst the soldiers. They get drunk and beat one another and some of the Italians into the bargain" (C). "There was quite a scene in Vienna," he reported, by way of example, "when one of the batches was passing through. An Irishman got drunk, the Austrian police seven in number went to arrest him: he made opposition, they drew their swords, but with the shillelah that never missed fire he knocked down three of them, and the others ran for their lives." Indeed, nearly all of Moran's letters during this period are good examples of this curious mixture of embarrassment and pride: an embarrassment at the lack of discipline in his fellow countrymen and yet, at the same time, a real pride in their raw physical courage and apparent fearlessness, which he then proceeded to sublimate in a tolerant amusement in his correspondence.

Meanwhile, Kirby had early reported both to Canon Forde, who had since returned to Dublin after his visit to Rome in early May, and to Cullen that all was not well within the brigade. Forde, who had a tendency toward irascibility, at least on paper, was very annoyed. "When," he complained to Kirby on June 16, "just as everything has been got into a most prosperous and well working order here we find things in such utter confusion, as reported, beyond, and so many English intermeddlers here as well as in Rome anxious to make confusion worse confounded for the sake of discrediting the Irish, that I have just received new marching orders and to my excessive annoyance, am obliged to leave tomorrow for *Macerata*, via Brussels—Vienna and Trieste—so that the next letter you receive will be from some or other of these places" (K). "Meantime," he added,

not to excite any *antagonism*, I will go merely as a *tourist*—without assuming any official character etc.

I hope McLaughlin will allow me to *cooperate* with him—he must have been *davvero qui incapace* [truly incapable] not to have managed our poor Irish better—McDonnell too has acted very injudiciously to say the least—he has kept all our young men capable of being of any use, acting in Vienna and elsewhere as clerks—writing orders[,] telegraphic dispatches etc, while meanwhile he left the task he assumed to himself of organising the route from *Bodenbach* south completely neglected—took no care of our men and hence *illae lachrymae* [those tears]. I will not however upbraid *him* when I see *him* as I think I can get round him—He has been beset from the outset with an idea that unless the affair was *Austriaed* it could not succeed—and while he carefully avoided corresponding with us to let us know what he was doing by the Vienna route, as soon as by the instructions I got in Rome, we attempted to get up a second route through France without in the least abandoning the first, instead of minding his business he kept on sending offensive telegrams—the tone of which you may understand when he was not ashamed in one sent to the *Primate* to accuse the Irish working party of *Gallican thimble rigging*. I will not however get angry with the Count—indeed I am quite satisfied that if I had only him to deal with him [*sic*] I should get things to right very soon with God's assistance—but the count is made a tool of by an English or Anglo-Roman conspiracy—Bowyer—Talbot—Wallis of the *Tablet* —somebody who calls himself *Petre* (is he anything to the vagabond that was in Rome about 16 years ago[?]) Blake, M.P. etc. being the conspirators.[34]

34. All the names mentioned by Forde were closely connected in a political way to the archbishop of Westminster (and the primate of the English Church), Nicholas Cardinal Wiseman. In the general election of 1859 Wiseman had attempted to throw English Catholic political influence to the side of Lord Derby's Conservative party and against

"I am not I say afraid of these," Forde then confided, "but there is a wild priest called *Shanahan* from Limerick, gone out with his men who will *leave* after him as he goes a *legacy* of insubordination. He openly tells the men or says it before them that they are not to obey anyone but an officer from their own part of the country of his own apptment. Is there no way of flattering him and getting him off *quietly*—I say *quietly* because if he goes by force he will surely turn the minds of the men before he goes." "I will give you," he finally promised in conclusion, "full details, and particulars as to the conspiracy when I next write, as far as may be necessary to protect Irish influence at Rome and Dr. Cullen for these are the two great objects of attack. Meanwhile tell them at Rome to exercise a little of that virtue which they exact so much from others[,] *holy patience*[,] and all will be yet *so well*, that I am free to wager that before six months they will make an unlimited demand on our resources for men."

Kirby, who had also written Cullen on June 15, had obviously also complained that some of the recruits were most undesirable types. "I was sorry to hear," Cullen replied promptly in Italian on June 22, "that there are some rascals [*birboni*] among the emigrants that have gone to Italy. The thing however was inevitable—and it would not amaze me to hear that with the usual machiavellianism which now prevails that some were sent to spoil the effort and discredit everything" (K). "Meanwhile every effort," he then complained, taking up Forde's line of English conspiracy, "is made in London to discredit what has been done in Ireland—*The Tablet* writes furiously against us. Lord Petre has written a letter to an Irish member of Parliament inveighing against Irish swindlers [*imbroglioni*] and maintaining that the emigrants are dying of hunger in Trieste etc. without being able to go on or return home. This letter has been shown to everyone in Dublin and has upset everything, the result is that an end has been put to the emigration for the present. Canon Forde however has gone to Vi-

---

Lord Palmerston. Sir George Bowyer, an English Catholic and M.P. for the Irish borough of Dundalk, had been most forward in support of the Conservative ministry previous to its fall in 1859 and in the general election that followed. John Wallis, the editor of the English Catholic weekly, the *Tablet*, had no small share in this effort to bring about a Catholic-Tory political alliance. Monsignor Talbot, private chamberlain to the pope and Wiseman's strongest and most influential supporter in Rome, was also very partial to English Catholics' allying themselves with the Conservative rather than the Liberal party, especially in view of the latter's obvious preference for the politics of Cavour and Garibaldi in Italy. Lord Petre was a prominent English Catholic who had also moved considerably to the right in the English political spectrum in recent years. John A. Blake, M.P. for Waterford city, who had been supported by Wiseman in his reelection in 1859, had also been, like Bowyer, most forward in his support of the Conservative party in Parliament and in Ireland.

enna and Trieste to see how things are." "Perhaps the Count," he concluded more hopefully, "has made a mess of it."

When Cullen learned in early July that there was still considerable dissatisfaction among the recruits in Italy, and that some were returning home, he became very concerned that their complaints would become public knowledge. Still, though he again sourly complained to Kirby on July 10 that he had always told him so, he supposed that they must make the best of it, as nothing could now be done (K). The adverse rumors and reports, however, do not appear to have dampened either the interest in or the enthusiasm for the brigade in Ireland. Bernard Durcan, the dean of the diocese of Achonry, for example, had written Kirby on July 9, while enclosing some £670 for the pope, "I hope the Irish Brigade will prove themselves worthy sons of Erin. That they will do honour to the cause that they are gone to defend and to the country that sent them" (K). A short time later Daniel Murphy, the vicar apostolic of Hyderabad, who had just returned to his native land after a brief visit to Rome, also wrote Kirby about the brigade. "We are looking forward," he assured him on July 21, "with the greatest possible interest in the success of the brigade. The irregularities of some of them instead of discouraging has only amused their friends, and increased their hopes, for they are convinced that when organised, they will form the best soldiers in the world" (K).

The difficulties with regard to the morale of the recruits, however, continued to be a good deal more serious than their friends in Ireland were aware. "I have heard today with great pain from Major O'Reilly," the archbishop of Armagh, Joseph Dixon, informed Kirby on July 23, referring to the commander of the brigade, "who writes to me—that our workmen in Italy will not *engage* for want of higher pay. Between ourselves I thought that those who went out were prepared to make greater sacrifices and exhibit greater chivalry than this *dead lock* in the affair shows. At the same time the matter appears to be now urgent; and I beg of you if you can to prevail on the Roman Government to add at least 2^d per day to the pay of the men—even if their time of service should be shortened on this account" (K). "The whole affair," he warned Kirby, "will bring great dishonour on Ireland and injury to the sacred cause, which we have at heart, if it is allowed to end in the catastrophe which appears to be apprehended." "I have great hopes," Dixon explained in conclusion, "that the Archbishop of Dublin will be able to have things put right: but I thought that this expression of my views might also help to strengthen your hands in the application which I trust you will now make to the government as the matter is very urgent."

By the time Dixon had written to Kirby, however, the situation had become more than urgent; it was critical. In fact, only two days before, Father Bonaventure McLaughlin, the Franciscan chaplain who had helped quiet the recruits after the mutiny at Macerata in June, wrote Cardinal Barnabò a frantic letter from Spoleto, explaining that his men were now again on the verge of mutiny and begging him to take the measures necessary to prevent such a calamity. "The Irish Battalion still exists" McLaughlin reported somewhat melodramatically on July 21, "notwithstanding the vigorous attempts made to destroy it: But the latest blow threatens to be decisive. This is nothing less than to reject the nomination (still provisional) of the officers who have the merit of having formed the Battalion, who enjoy the respect of the troops and to whom the provisional appointments have been promised!"[35] "If Monsignor Mérode," McLaughlin warned, naming the papal minister for war,

> persists in this madness the Pontifical Government will be more discredited by his Excellency than by all the articles that have ever been written in the "Times." I well realize that this is a bold letter, but I also know well that your Eminence will excuse me when I foresee an imminent calamity.
>
> The Irish troops are now so numerous, so unfairly harassed, and so ill humored that I am with difficulty able to restrain them from great rashness. Among the officers who are being made light of are three especially very deserving of the Holy Father, namely Messrs. Darcy, Cronin and Stafford. To give these a provisional appointment is a very small recompense for what they have suffered and worked for in the cause: but to deny it to them, while it is given to unworthy persons would be a scandal without comparison. As I believe that Canon Forde is animated by the sentiments of Monsignor Cullen in this particular, I wish to write to him by this post so that he may have an interview with your Eminence when he could give you more detailed information; since your Eminence for us fills the role of a Cardinal Protector, you will be able to inform the Holy Father whose sovereign voice alone will be able to arrest the torrent of evils that are inundating us.

"I know," he confessed again in conclusion, "that this is not the kind of a letter that should be written to a Cardinal but your Eminence will

35. S.R.C., vol. 33, fols. 1203–4.

pardon my rashness in consideration of the rectitude of my intentions, and of my desire to prevent an imminent scandal."

The crisis at Spoleto had apparently been building for some time, because several days after McLaughlin had written Barnabò, the acting British consul in Rome, Thomas McKenna Hughes, wrote Lord John Russell to apprise him of the recent developments. "I have been informed," Hughes reported of the Irish on July 24, "that at Spoleto and especially on the march of the last detachment from Macerata they were guilty of great excesses, plundering shops, drinking and refusing payment, and committing violence even on the persons of those with whom they came into contact."[36] "There is a party among them," Hughes added, "who have been guilty of very violent conduct both towards some of those who wished to return and towards those who have been suspected of being spies of the English Government." Earlier in this dispatch Hughes had also reported that he had received a visit the day before from Count Ferdinando Giraud, adjutant to Monsignor de Mérode. "He said," Hughes had noted, "that the Irish were quite savage and uncivilized and added that it was not much to the credit of the English Government to have left any part of the Kingdom in such an uncivilized state." The difficulties with the Irish at Spoleto apparently continued well on into August, because C. T. Newton, the British Consul in Rome, reported to Russell on August 7 that many of the Irish were returning home in disgust, and on August 21 that those Irish who were still in prison in Spoleto were there for insubordination and rioting.[37]

The real cause for the continuing ferment among the Irish, however, had less to do with a lack of discipline than with an aggrieved sense of nationality. They deeply resented the various attempts that had been made to subvert their character as an Irish brigade by incorporating them into other papal units. When Newton reported to Russell on August 7, for example, he noted that General Lamoricière, the commander of the papal army, wanted to break the Irish up and that their priests were very annoyed about the way their countrymen were being treated by the papal military authorities.[38] The Irish also, moreover, violently objected to serving under any officers other than those of their own nationality. When the archbishop of Cashel, Patrick Leahy, heard that perhaps the worst was about to happen—English

---

36. F.O., 43/80a. See also Berkeley, pp. 54–57, for the march from Macerata and for some of the mitigating circumstances governing the ill discipline of the Irish.

37. F.O., 43/80a.

38. Ibid.

officers were to command Irishmen—he asked Kirby on August 6 "to make known from me to the authorities that, if Englishmen are placed over the Irishmen now in Italy on the Pope's service, it will be a most unhappy thing, —will tend utterly to demoralize our country- men, and is moreover in direct violation of the understanding had here in Ireland with those who helped forward the Emigration move- ment" (K). A compromise was apparently reached in early August that did a great deal to restore order and discipline among the Irish. The brigade, which now consisted of about eleven hundred officers and men in eight companies, was assigned to Ancona and Spoleto in two main bodies, which were placed under the immediate supervision of their own officers and chaplains.[39]

The architect of this settlement was apparently Canon Forde, who had arrived in Rome via Vienna, Trieste, and Ancona in June. When the disorders broke out in Spoleto he was obviously immediately dis- patched there by the authorities to deal with that difficult situation. He was still in Spoleto on August 24 when he wrote Kirby explaining why he had been delayed (K). He had been engaged in both necessary and good work. The necessary work, he reported, had to do with straightening out the men's accounts and seeing that they received what they had coming to them. The good work consisted of taking up not only the letters and messages of the men to deliver to their friends in Ireland "but principally as much of their bounty as I can get, this being the best means of keeping them from *drink*[,] our *only remain- ing difficulty*." "I am thus too," he explained, "brought into personal contact with the mean [*sic*]—give them a little advice etc. and am enabled to ascertain their dispositions which are of *the best possible*. In fact all *guasto* [damage] is being rapidly restored—the military as- pect of the affairs too is *most satisfactory*. We are the only soldiers and do all the garrison duty of the town." He went on, referring to Monsignor Pericoli, the papal delegate in Spoleto, "Monsignore Dele- gato is most kind to us, thinks highly of us and is most considerate for our defects and failings. Indeed, I believe, the same might have been said from the commencement of all the prelates placed in similar po- sitions who came into contact with our men. I know it was the case in *Ancona* and I have heard equally so at *Macerata*. As for the excellent Archbishop [Spoleto] his really personal solicitude for our men and cause is *beyond all praise*." Forde then turned to the way in which the terms of the recently effected compromise were being observed. "You

39. Berkeley, p. 50. Companies one to four were based at Spoleto; five to eight were based at Ancona.

will be sorry to hear," he informed Kirby, "that despite of de Mérode's promise to you Piotti has been maintained in relations with our men. *Anzi* has been promoted to a more enlarged sphere of mischief, where he is in contact not only with *ours* but with all the troops of the garrison when they are present in town. This is *qui vero tradimento del povero Santo Padre* [real treachery here to the poor Holy Father]." Forde finally concluded his long report to Kirby by promising that he would return to Rome in a few days to visit him at the Irish College's summer retreat at Tivoli before setting out for Ireland the following week.

———————◆———————

Meanwhile, Cardinal Antonelli had written to Cullen both to ask him not to send any more recruits and to ask him to do his best to promote subscriptions in Ireland to the papal loan that had just been floated by the Roman government. "Card. Antonelli has written to me," Cullen reported to Kirby on July 20, "to prevent any further emigration. I suppose it cannot be completely stopped, but many more will not go. You recollect what I wrote so often that I feared many w^d return enemies who went out friends. *Pare che si verifichi la cosa* [It appears that the thing has come to pass]. Many have returned *e sono malcontenti* [and are unhappy]. *Ebbene* [Well] it is like the end of the Crusades."

Regarding the *imprestito* [loan] I think they do not understand the condition of Ireland. In the 1st place about £70 or 80,000 have been collected—that is more than any country has given in the same circumstances. *Poi* [Then] the people have not the sums to dispose of worth putting at interest. A man that has £20, or £30, or £50, or £100 will not put such sums at interest. In France it appears they put £3 or £5 at interest and receive some few shillings yearly. No one here is accustomed to do such a thing. I suppose there are scarcely any Catholics who put small sums in the funds and those who have large sums are not the most generous. I think it would be easier to get a second collection here than to raise the loan. [K]

"I suppose," Cullen continued, returning to his original theme, "you are pretty well tired of the emigration—it c^d not go on well as there was no authority to control anything. However in the end things may get right—of course a little disgrace is incurred by bad conduct in Belgium, Austria, France and Italy—what was destined *a fare onore fa vergogna* [to do honor does shame]. *L'uomo propone, Dio dispone* [Man proposes, God disposes]." "I told Dr. Forde over and over," he then added, "that mere verbal instructions were altogether unsatisfactory. *Mutatis circumstantibus* [In altered circumstances] such instructions are forgotten or modified. I wrote to you several times that it was hard for us to act here *senza ricevere una riga in carta* [without receiving a line on paper]. However you must tell Dr. Forde to be very patient, and to let others have their own way of thinking. You know he is very right in his way of thinking—but all cannot be made to agree." "Take the world quietly," he then finally advised Kirby. "Do not be alarmed. Things will go on as God wishes or as He allows them. I think you will have bad work thro' Italy—probably *il clero soffrirà assai* [the clergy will suffer much]. I think the Pope's States too will be disturbed. Lamoricière has not men enough nor money to defend them. What can he do against Naples, Piedmont, France & England[?]"

When he wrote Kirby a week later on July 28, however, Cullen was in a more somber and less philosophical frame of mind (K). By that time he had learned from Major O'Reilly that the recruits had demanded an increase in their pay, and he was afraid that it would prove contagious among the other units in the pope's service. He was also very upset that those who had returned from Italy were complaining very loudly and that some of them were supplying information to the Orange press. "I am fearing everyday," he confessed to Kirby disconsolately, "to hear of an explosion in the Pope's states. The crisis is certainly approaching. The prayers of the world may avert it, but humanely speaking there is no hope." The reason Cullen was so despairing at the end of July, of course, was that Garibaldi and his redshirts, who had landed in Sicily in May, had occupied the whole of the island by the middle of July and were now poised for an attack on the mainland to put the finishing touches to the Kingdom of Naples. Indeed, Garibaldi crossed the straits of Messina on August 18, and by September 7 he had taken the city of Naples. As the climax approached, Cullen's anxieties about the deteriorating situation in Italy increased. In a letter that he began on August 31 and did not close until September 5, he explained to Kirby that "all the accounts from Italy are unfavourable. The English appear to know all the secrets of the [word illegible]. If they are well informed the Pope's states will be in a blaze" (K). In a postscript he then added, "The news today from Italy 5th September very bad. I suppose you will have war immediately. The Neopolitans *si sono sporcaficati* [have disgraced themselves]."

"It is useless," Cullen wrote Kirby again on September 11,

to tell you that the affairs of Italy are to us all the occasion of alarm and grief. Naples is fallen, and what is worse the Army, the Navy, generals, ministers and princes have covered themselves with disgrace.

What can you say now to Protestants when they point out the conduct of pious practical Catholics, and tell you that the Romish system produces such fruits. If at least anyone had acted a noble part—but the whole lot were fit only to eat macaroni. *Ebbene, jacta est alea* [Well, the die has been cast] for Naples, and I fear the turn of Rome will come on next. God grant that at least in Rome and the Roman states the people may show more Catholic spirit than has appeared at Naples. According to the English papers who enjoy the confidence of Garibaldi there is no doubt that the Pope's states will be seized on immediately. What will become of all the emigrants[?] I fear they will not be able to make much resistance. [K]

"The powers of darkness," Cullen then added, "now appear to triumph. God grant that their triumph may be short. All the Protestants are shouting with delight that Babylon is fallen, is fallen."

As Cullen had feared, Garibaldi's lightning success in conquering the Kingdom of Naples boded ill for the pope's dominions. In order to forestall Garibaldi, who was expected to attack the Papal States as soon as he had consolidated his position at Naples, Count Cavour, the Piedmontese prime minister, decided that his government had to take immediate action itself to conquer the pope's dominions. On September 11, therefore, three Piedmontese armies, some 36,000 men strong, crossed into the Papal States. General Fanti, with an army of 12,000 men, invaded Umbria and advanced quickly on Perugia, while General Cardona, with 7,000 men, struck directly south into the Marches with the town of Gubbio as his goal. General Cialdini, with the remaining 17,000 men, attacked along the Adriatic coast road and quickly took Pesaro, Fano, and Sinigaglia in rapid advance on Ancona. Cavour, meanwhile, had also apparently had the foresight to secure Napoleon III's guarantee that the French army stationed in and around Rome would not interfere on the pope's behalf as long as the Piedmontese armies confined their activities to Umbria and the Marches. General de Lamoricière, the papal commander, however, had apparently been informed by the Roman authorities that he could count on French help in defending the pope's dominions in the event of an attack. He very sensibly, therefore, decided to make an effort to concentrate his small army of some 12,000 men at Ancona. He thus hoped to place the Piedmontese in the precarious strategic position of having to deal with a French army on their right and a papal force on their left the further south they advanced into the Papal States.

Of the four Irish companies at Spoleto, the first had been sent some ten days before the Piedmontese invasion to strengthen the garrison at Perugia. The second and third Irish companies remained at Spoleto under the command of Major O'Reilly. The fourth, however, was assigned to accompany Lamoricière when he began collecting his force in Umbria for his dash to Ancona. Perugia was taken on September 13, and though most of the garrison of 1,200 men proved to be of little use in its defense, the Irish were reported to have shown conspicuous courage in the fighting that did take place. Spoleto fell four days later, on September 17, after a spirited defense by O'Reilly and his garrison of some 750, about half of whom were Irish. Lamoricière, meanwhile, had collected his troops and set out from Foligno for Ancona on September 12, with some 6,000 men. In a series of forced marches he reached Loreto on the Adriatic coast, a distance of some seventy-five miles over the back of the Apennines, in four days. He was not, however, quick enough, for he was intercepted by Cialdini on Monday, September 17, ten miles south of Ancona.

That evening John McDevitt, the chaplain of the some 500 Irish stationed at Ancona, wrote Kirby asking him to pray for them all, for the day of battle was apparently at hand (K). "I am really fatigued," McDevitt explained, "hearing their Confessions, and preparing them to die happily, but the fatigue of last night, and a little freedom today with *hated liquor* has (I fear) made them forget themselves." The approaching ordeal, McDevitt then pointed out most revealingly, "will be dreadful, as I fear the citizens[,] especially the *basso popolo* [lower classes][,] are against us." The following day, September 18, the papal and Piedmontese armies joined in battle at Castelfidardo, about ten miles south of the now-besieged Ancona. The papal army was overwhelmed by the numerically superior Piedmontese, though Lamoricière and a few of his staff officers were able to make their way through the enemy's line to Ancona. The Irish appeared from all reports to have fought as well at Castelfidardo as they had at Perugia and Spoleto. When the roll was called after the battle by Martin Kirwan, the captain of company number four, nearly one-third of the company was reported as killed, wounded, or missing.[40] When Lamoricière reached Ancona he decided to continue the struggle. In fact, he held out for ten more days until he was obliged to surrender the fortress on

40. K, Kirwan to Kirby, October 25, 1860.

September 28, when the Piedmontese naval forces under the command of Admiral Persano finally penetrated his harbor defenses and had the fortress at their mercy.[41]

The story of the final days at Ancona was told some two weeks later to Kirby by McDevitt in a letter from Genoa, where he had been taken as a prisoner of war. "We responded to the enemy's fire," he informed Kirby on October 12,

by sea and land perhaps for nearly a fortnight or ten days. And you may depend we peppered them pretty well, when they came within *shell range* [?] or *gun reach* of us.

Remember we had only about four thousand men altogether between the town and the fortress, while the enemy had about seven vessels of war bombarding us by sea and about forty-five thousand men by land. By land the enemy stormed one of our outer batteries[,] "Monte Pelago[,]" but were gallantly repulsed by only one battalion of Austro-Papal Bersaglieri. Again they returned with two regiments and the Austrians having spiked the guns, retired to the next battery of San Stefano, where great numbers of the enemy coming to the assault three different times were severely repulsed by only one regiment of our Bersaglieri, and were obliged to retire leaving the ground strewn with dead bodies. However we could not stand by sea, so that on the last day of the siege three or four steamers of war attacked the battery of the "Lanterna" which commanded the entrance of the harbour, and after a fierce struggle of about three hours, silenced it. I was looking on and General Lamoricière was running about— directed himself one of our guns but when he saw the battery silenced, he came into the magazine where I was standing wiping his eyes with his handkerchief and ordered the white flag of truce to wave from our battlements, retaining the honour of not giving in to the land force, but to the naval—against which we had no means of combating. [K]

"Oh!" McDevitt then noted of the Irish, "how indignant the greater number of them felt at capitulating at all without having the satisfaction of strewing the ground around them with the dead bodies of their enemies. I saw a Tipperary fellow come up, when the flag of truce was hoisted, before Lamoricière take off his cap and fling it on the ground

41. Berkeley, pp. 213–15. See also, for an account of the Irish Brigade at Ancona, the four letters from "W.C." in the *Freeman's Journal*, November 16, 21, and 29 and December 6, 1860.

with an exclamation of grief and disgust. Poor Lamoricière looked at him with a piteous look and a look of compassion."

Several days after the news of the disaster at Castelfidardo and reports of the Irish garrison's surrender at Spoleto had reached Ireland, Cullen reported to Kirby that it was all very sad. "Nothing," he maintained on September 21, "can be more afflicting. God appears to have abandoned His people to a spirit of vertigo, and the devils in hell seem to have been let loose" (K). "*The Times*," he then added even more sadly, "says the Irish have disgraced themselves. I hope it is a calumny." Indeed, the day before, the *Times* had in its editorial columns leveled some incredible charges against the Irish in the pope's service. "We never had any Irish in our service," the *Times* maintained on September 20,

> who behaved with the cowardice these men have shown, or who have so softened under the tuition of their priests. But indeed we never sought out the class of Irishmen fit for the work to which these were destined.
>
> So ends the Pope's Irish Brigade. It is a disgrace. The country must feel rather as a family feels when a *mauvais sujet* whom they know to be a ruffian turns out also to be a sneak. Six hundred men ought to have made a fight for the Pope after taking his money. Much as we hate their cause we have a natural interest in their pluck. We all expected at least some rough good fighting from them. Perhaps however we ought to have known better. . . . If there is no market in Europe for such services as they can render, the best thing they can now do is to steal back to their homes and hide themselves; they will serve as a warning to their neighbours against temptations by recruiting priests.

A very worried Cullen reported to Kirby a week later, on September 27, "We have received no letter from you for the last 15 days. You may imagine how anxious we are to hear something about Rome and accurate accounts about Perugia and Castelfidardo" (K). "*The Times*," he explained again, "published a most atrocious attack on the Irish brigade, stating that they had acted as cowards[,] that they were a disgrace to the British Empire etc. The accounts since received shows [*sic*] that *The Times* was at its old work telling lies." Still, Cullen remained in a very chastened mood some days later. "I believe," he confessed to Kirby on October 5, "this is the *tempus tacendi* [time for silence]. Like Joab the greatest of the calamities must make us silent. However God is good and just and I trust, He will bring down the enemies of religion—but speculations are useless. *Fiat Voluntas Dei*

[Let God's will be done]" (K). "On next Friday," he reported, "we shall [have] an office and mass for the men who were killed at Ancona, Spoleto, Perugia etc. I shall sing it—after mass I think we shall hold a meeting and denounce to the world the assaults made on the Pope." "I hope," Cullen then added more pugnaciously, "he will not yield an inch. *Vestigia nulla retrorsum* [Not a footstep backward]—tell Card. Barnabò to be courageous and not to yield. Albion will now cease to have the exclusive right to be called *perfida* [perfidious]. France has usurped the title."

Meanwhile, the five hundred Irish taken prisoner at Spoleto and Perugia had been removed to Genoa. Those taken later at Castelfidardo and Ancona were also sent to Genoa. Lamoricière, his staff, and the other officers were transported by boat from Ancona via the straits of Messina, while the enlisted men were marched overland. McDevitt, who was shipped with the officers, arrived in Genoa on Monday, October 8, after the week's sea voyage, where he found the officers and men taken at Spoleto and Perugia, though his own men had not yet arrived from Ancona. McDevitt then learned that the officers had been told that they were free to go home whenever they wished, and that they could take their men with them, but that they would have to make their own arrangements. In the meantime the prisoners were placed at liberty on their word of honor. In reporting all this to Kirby on October 12, McDevitt also explained that they had just received that same day a telegram from Dublin and a letter from Canon Forde assuring them of help (K). Kirby wrote Cullen the next day, October 13, assuring him that all was now quiet in Rome and telling him what he knew about the situation of the prisoners in Genoa. "How things are," Cullen replied on October 19, "I know not, but we are trying to get some money to bring home the prisoners. I suppose 7 or 8,000 pounds will be required. Having had so many collections this year it is not easy to get that sum. Dublin subscribes very generously but the provinces are very slow, and if you observe you will find that Connaught gives little or nothing except talk. However I hope the poor fellows will get on to Ireland or to Rome—if the Pope wants them notice ought to be sent to Genoa or Marseilles. It is a pity I think to let them return as they are now pretty well trained" (K).

"I am glad," Cullen continued, "that the Romans are thinking of the Peter's Pence. They are much richer than the people of Dublin, and they ought to make up 20 or 30 thousand pounds as we have made up in our poverty 15 or 16 thousand." "If France and Austria and Spain," he further conjectured, "were to give as much in proportion as Ireland the Pope would not be in want of men or money. There are five millions of Cath. in Ireland and every [correctly, they] gave about 63 or 64 thousand pounds. There are thirty-six millions in France[,] as many in Austria, and as many more in Spain, Belgium, Bavaria, Prussia[,] say one hundred millions. At the rate given by Ireland they could give 1 million, 300 thousand pounds. Say same of men. Five millions gave one thousand and one hundred millions ought to give 20,000." "We had ere yesterday," Cullen added, "a meeting of the clergy. I sent you the report. The speeches were very good, but I do not know whether they are well reported. I thought it well to have a meeting to stir up the spirit of the country."

The Roman authorities had meanwhile decided to take action with regard to the Irish prisoners of war at Genoa. "On yesterday (20th October)," McDevitt reported to Kirby, "we embarked near 600 of our prisoners on board the steamer 'Byzantine' a French steamer in the employment of His Holiness. She was sent with Captain Russell from Civita Vecchia by order of Merode for transmission of Irish prisoners to Marseilles" (K). Since the *Byzantine* could take only six hundred men, McDevitt explained, he thought it better to charter another ship to transport the remaining five hundred to Marseilles, rather than wait for the return of the first ship. He had telegraphed Forde, who was arranging the receiving of the first group of prisoners in Marseilles, and Forde replied that he should do what he thought best in the circumstances. McDevitt then explained that he would charter a vessel the next day. From Marseilles the eleven hundred men of the Irish Brigade proceeded to Le Havre via Paris. "McDevitt," Cullen informed Kirby's vice-rector, Patrick Moran, on November 2, "has written to me from Havre. He will be in Cork tomorrow or rather this evening. They will get a g^t reception there and money will be thrown away. Here we are trying to collect as much as will help them home— but it is very hard to get £8,000 or £10,000 and every farthing of that sum will be necessary" (K). "Many," he added dryly, "are for giving g^t dinners, swords etc. A good frieze coat and a pound note w^d be much better."[42]

"The reception of the Brigade," Cullen reported again on November 8, writing to Kirby from Dublin, "is enthusiastic to madness here and in Cork. You will see acct. in papers" (K). "Here," he then added, "all the Protestants are Garibaldians. They have got Gar. hats & cloaks. Even the ladies (Protestant) have *red* Garibaldi cloaks and a sort of Garibaldi hat with red feathers. The Tory and Orange papers are more

42. Cullen had announced the collection to his clergy on October 24, 1860, for the following Sunday.

revolutionary than the Whigs themselves. I believe Lord Derby w^d be as bad as Lord Palmerston." A week later, when the festivities attendant on the arrival of the brigade had calmed down, McDevitt wrote Kirby from the College at All Hallows in Dublin, where he was staying. "We had a very favourable passage from Havre to Queenstown of about forty hours sail," he reported on November 16; "no accident occurred notwithstanding the crowd on board except a fire that broke out for some hours in the engine room. You already know by the papers how the men, on their arrival, were cared [sic], and feasted, not only in Cork but in every city of the United Kingdom, where they went; nothing but dinners, soirées, and 'fetes' of every description, for the heroes of the Irish Brigade, in their several districts" (K). "This reception," McDevitt further explained, "has done invaluable good to the cause, because such kindness and sympathy shown the poor men on their arrival brought consolation to their troubled hearts, and calmed down every feeling of murmur and dissatisfaction therein engendered by the many trials they underwent, especially during the late campaign." "So much have they been pleased and contented," he finally assured Kirby, "by this reception, and kind treatment, that they are now proud of being the Pope's soldiers, donned their old campaigning caps, and are ready to a man again to flock to the standard of His Holiness, if required." Cullen too had been very concerned about the evident unhappiness of the brigade, the great majority of whom had apparently elected in Genoa to return to Ireland rather than to Rome to continue in the pope's service.[43] He was very pleased therefore that the reception in Ireland had improved the disposition of the brigade. "I was afraid in the beginning," he confessed to Kirby on November 22, "that g^t mischief w^d be done by the men returning to Ireland. They appear to be all satisfied—so we shall not have to complain that religion has been injured" (K). "All however," he added by way of qualification, "speak with the greatest contempt of the Italians."

———————◆———————

Over the next few months and well into the new year, however, the affairs of the brigade continued to place a considerable strain on Irish-Roman relations in a number of significant ways. In late October Cullen had received a letter from Cardinal Antonelli, the papal secretary of state, explaining that given the sad state of the pope's finances, the Roman government was making every effort to establish the Pe-

43. K, McDevitt to Kirby, November 16, 1860.

ter's pence on a worldwide basis. "We will immediately," Cullen had assured Kirby on October 26, in Italian, "set up a Committee to organize the matter, and I hope that we will be able to do something substantial. Unfortunately, the harvest has been very bad, and the people will be able to do little this winter. There will be many poor" (K). "It will not be easy," he then added, "to induce all the Bishops to help in the work of the Peter's pence—there is so much jealousy. Dublin however will do as much as possible." On October 26 Cullen, as good as his word, forwarded some £200 of Peter's pence as a first installment. (K). "We are organizing the Peter's pence," he reported some three weeks later to Kirby in a letter that can be dated November 17 from internal evidence; "the plan w^d have been out ere now only Dr. Furlong is sick—and the other bishops of the province are anxious we s^d all come out together" (K). On November 29, however, Cullen managed to send another £300 of Peter's pence to Kirby for presentation to the pope (K). He explained that he was very sorry that it was so little, but the harvest had been very bad and the people were in very great misery.

When Kirby answered on December 12, he must have told Cullen that the Roman authorities were disappointed that the Peter's pence had not been taken up in a more systematic way in Ireland. In his reply to Kirby on December 21, Cullen was obviously annoyed (K). "You will see," he pointed out, "what expense the Brigade entails on us. The expenses are beyond £7,000. Only very few dioceses have done anything in the case. The whole West gives zero. Still the money must be collected." "In Rome," he added, "they sh^d understand that all this money goes for the Papal Government. They were obliged to send home the Brigade—indeed I believe they are obliged to keep them for four years. But of course no one w^d think of asking such a thing. However it is well that they sh^d understand that we are expending £7,000 for them." "Why do not the English contribute to this expense?" he asked more petulantly. "They w^d like to command but they leave others to pay." "Explain to Dr. Dixon this case," Cullen then instructed Kirby, referring to the archbishop of Armagh, who was in Rome fulfilling his required *ad limina* visit, "and it will show why we are slow about the Peter's pence. We can not make too many demands at once. If the Brigade were once paid for, we c^d set the Peter's pence on foot all at once."

By this time, however, Irish-Roman relations had been further complicated by a letter Canon Forde had received from his old friend in Rome, Bernard Smith, who had served for a number of years as Kirby's vice-rector in the Irish College. Cullen informed Kirby on December

24, "I have seen a letter from F. Smith in which he speaks of a conversation with Mr Mérode [the pope's minister for war]. Monsignor [Mérode] stated that he c^d have no Irish brigade and no communication with the Dublin committee, because we are all favourable here to Buonaparte, and looking out for a French invasion" (K). "Do not mention F. Smith's name," Cullen advised Kirby, "but if you see Monsignor Mérode be so good as to tell him in my name that he is doing a great deal of mischief to the Pope's cause by indulging in such foolish observations. Tell him also that probably I will write a letter to His Holiness complaining of him." "At all events," Cullen observed, "his absurd charges will prevent us from doing anything more in the case. He treated the Irish very badly when he had them. He is now spreading false charges against them. Of course he is inspired by the good Inglesi—it is very provoking to have such a man at the head of affairs."

In writing to Kirby again several days after Christmas, Cullen was still obviously very much annoyed with Mérode. After explaining that the affairs and expenses of the brigade were nearly all settled, Cullen complained again that the brigade had undoubtedly been treated very badly both in the passage to and in Italy. "Some of the persons who have come home," he reported on December 27, "state that shoes were sent to them big enough only for children, and coats and shirts that w^d scarcely go on a good boy. There must have been either *gran perfidia, o gran trascuranza negli impiegati* [great wickedness or great negligence among the clerks]. Monsig^r Mérode ought to have looked to such things, but he appears to have more talent for blustering than for acting" (K). "It appears," Cullen further charged, "that he was not fortunate in his selections, and the few foreign officers he selected to command the Irish were a *razza cattiva* [bad breed]. Count Guttenberg who came to Ireland passed himself off here as nephew of Card. Reisach. In Rome Myles O'Reilly assures me he told General Lamoricière that he was my nephew. Who is he or what? I suppose a clever adventurer. he asked me for money here—of course I did not give any." "The conclusion I draw from all this statement," Cullen summed up, "is that I will have nothing more to do with Brigades, and I think no one ought to go out unless the conditions be plainly understood."

In Rome, meanwhile, Pius IX had unfortunately precipitated yet another crisis in Irish-Roman relations by deciding to have a silver medal struck to reward all those who had defended him in the late campaign. Those few soldiers of the Irish Brigade who still remained in the pope's service, some thirty in number, were presented with their medals on November 18 in Rome by the archbishop of Armagh, Joseph Dixon, on behalf of the pope. When it came time for the distribution of the medals to those who had returned to Ireland, however, Monsignor de Mérode did not choose to use the good offices of Dixon, who was planning to return to Ireland about the middle of January. Instead, he entrusted the task to an Irish Catholic layman and M.P. for King's county, John Pope Hennessy. Cullen, who found Hennessy's politics of independent opposition in Ireland most obnoxious, had written Kirby twice on December 21 and 24, warning him about Hennessy and advising him to leave that slippery and artful man to their English brethren in Rome. Cullen had also taken the precaution of writing to William Monsell, M.P. for county Limerick and a prominent Catholic convert, who was also visiting Rome. "I have heard," he warned Monsell on December 24, "that Pope Hennessy M.P. is in Rome acting as the representative of English and Irish Catholics. His conduct with regard to the Cork election was so strange that I would not wish to be represented by him."[44] "I trust you may be able," Cullen suggested, "to explain the real position of that gentleman. He seems to be rather a representative of the Irish orangism rather than anything else—and I do not understand how we can form a league with that wicked faction so hostile to all our interests."

Early in the new year, however, Mérode finally capped his folly with the Irish by proposing to Dixon that the brigade be reconstituted in part at least and returned to Rome. When Forde heard of the proposal he obviously felt that his cup had been filled to the brim and wrote Cardinal Barnabò explaining why he thought the project was not feasible. In effect, Forde told the cardinal that in the first place Mérode could not be relied on to honor his agreements, and in the second place the monsignor had fallen under English influence in Rome in the management of Irish affairs. "With reference to these two causes," Forde reported to Kirby on January 15, 1861, enclosing his letter to Barnabò, "as compared with each other you may say to his Emce that the latter operates on us much more powerfully than the former" (K). Forde then explained,

> With reference to the two distinct heads of difficulty considered in themselves—it may be useful to observe 1st as regards the *conditions* which we have thought well to make—that we never

44. Monsell Papers (M), National Library of Ireland, 8317 (3). The Monsell correspondence contains a portion of the correspondence of David Moriarty, the bishop of Kerry. These are a number of letters to Moriarty therefore designated by the letter M in the text. See also Peadar MacSuibhne, *Paul Cullen and His Contemporaries*, vol. 3 (Naas, 1965), p. 313.

here in Ireland thought of assuming the arrogant and odious position of dictating terms to the Gõvt of His Holiness. The Bishops who interested themselves actively in this matter, simply sent *suggestions* in reply to the request that was made of them by the *Agent* of the Holy See. Having been asked their advice they were certainly entitled to give it. They stated certain arrangements as best calculated to guard against very great dangers that were inseparable from a first effort at an Irish force for the Pope.

"This motive of necessary prudence," Forde insisted, "and not any extravagant *National* pride, however just and laudable, was the real source of what are called the *conditions* imposed by the Dublin committee."

"A few words now," he then continued, turning to the second and more important of his complaints about Mérode,

> on the point of *British* interference. Writing to a Cardinal of acts attributable to a Minister of His Holiness I could not qualify things as they deserved. I simply said that results followed from viewing things through such a medium as, *per dire il meno* [to say the least], were *sommamente inopportuno—disgustosi, scandalosi, o disastrosi* [highly inopportune—disgusting, scandalous, or disastrous] would have been better words or rather the *only* fitting terms to employ. And after all, what is it, but disgusting, scandalous, and disastrous, to insult in the most reckless manner, Irish Bishops, priests and distinguished laymen—and those especially who were distinguished in leading the Irish people in the noble example of devotedness to the See of Peter, which they have given to the entire world[?]

Forde went on, referring to a young English priest who would eventually make his career in the Roman Curia, "The conduct of the War Office in selecting Mre Howard, while I was still in Rome, to do the work which I was formally commissioned by Doctors Cullen[,] Dixon and others to do should not be easily forgotten. Of course the offense is not against me but those who sent me."

Forde further charged, making reference to the influential Anglo-Irish convert and private chamberlain to Pius IX, "While in Rome expressly for the purpose of being of what assistance I could on a matter purely regarding *Ireland* and the Holy See, it was openly avowed to me that Mre Talbot's advice was that which was followed. I was myself even referred to him on the subject of an Irish chaplain." He continued:

I say nothing of how Dr. Dixon was treated in person by the same parties—but all is eclipsed by the late arrangement about the medals.

Whereby the Primate is passed over in favour of an Anglo-Irish adventurer and Major O'Reilly treated, as though instead of exposing life and family in the service of His Holiness he had cowardly betrayed his trust—a bad encouragement surely for men of honour and position to give signal evidence of their attachment to religion and its August Head. I cannot speak much just now for the country districts, but I assure you without exaggeration there are few things could have shocked and scandalized the clergy of this diocese so much as this proceeding has done—showing as it does on the part of persons whom the public ordinarily associates with the Sovereign Pontiff such a recklessness of insult or such incapacity. Dr. Cullen is very much annoyed by it.

"Letters too," Forde then continued, "are commencing to pour in from country priests jealous of their political opponents whom Mr. Hennessy has selected as distributors of the Papal honours—and last not least the men themselves are writing complaining that they are grossly injured—that men who did not serve, never were out or came home before the campaign are getting the distinctions due to them." "Indeed," Forde maintained, "how it can be otherwise I do not know for it is perfectly impossible that Mr. J. P. Hennessy can discharge the duty he has assumed. You see therefore what a nice kettle of fish Mre de Mérode has made of the *whole* business from *beginning* to *end*— while he gave his confidence to Parliamentary adventurers they were using him for their own purposes." "They have however," he assured Kirby in conclusion, "overshot the mark—and have roused an opposition to English interference in Rome in our affairs . . . but what is of more importance, in Irish ecclesiastical affairs in general." Kirby was obviously impressed with Forde's indictment, because he was convinced from his own experience that the facts as related by Forde were essentially true; at the same time he was undoubtedly shaken, for the crisis it precipitated required very careful handling in Rome. The governing factor as far as Kirby was concerned, of course, was Forde's assertion that Cullen was very annoyed. Indeed, Kirby had ample evidence in his own recent correspondence with Cullen that he was very annoyed, and particularly with Monsignor Mérode. To add salt to the soup, moreover, Dixon was also very much upset and surely did not leave Rome in a positive frame of mind with regard to either the future of the brigade or Mérode.

On February 18 Cullen wrote Barnabò his final word about both the brigade and Mérode: "When the Irish soldiers who were taken at Spoleto and Ancona, were sent to Genoa, a collection was made in Dublin, Cashel, Armagh and some other dioceses to help pay the expense of their return to Ireland. The collection has produced about five thousand pounds sterling."[45] "It seems that Monsignor de Mérode," Cullen then pointed out, "desires that some of these men return to Rome. He acts however in a way to hinder the success of such a project, even if it be expedient, of which there is doubt enough." Cullen continued:

I have seen a *memorial* sent by that Prelate to the archbishop of Armagh that is well calculated to provoke the Irish, who however, and especially Mr. O'Reilly, do not appear to have merited the many insinuations spread about them by Monsignor de Mérode. I hope that this *memorial* will not be published. The things that are written to Monsignor Dixon or to me do not make a great impression, but if Monsignor de Mérode writes similar things to our laity, or if there are intercepted in the post (as happens) letters similar to that *memorial*, great damage will be done to religion in this country.

Monsignor [Mérode] is not even very fortunate in his choice of persons. Recently he has sent medals to be distributed to the soldiers but the persons entrusted are so little respected, that in their hands the medals lose their value—they ought to have been sent to Mr. O'Reilly who knew his companions in arms. Moreover the men who returned to Ireland complain that two Germans were placed over them, Guttenberg and Schmidlein, both thieves and a certain Bruder, who sought to establish houses of ill fame in Spoleto to corrupt the men, and that he was only prevented from this wickedness by being well thrashed as he deserved. I tell these things to your Eminence not to complain, but to indicate the reasons why it is not believed expedient that men should be sent to Italy solely at the request of Monsignor de Mérode. If however the Holy Father or the Secretary of State or your Eminence wished it, I am convinced that a great many would be ready to respond to the call.

"I am very sorry," Cullen added in concluding, "to write unpleasant things because I well know that your Eminence has enough to suffer in the actual circumstances in Rome without having to put up with the tribulations from abroad. I beg you however to take what I have written about Monsignor de Mérode as past history." Kirby meanwhile

45. S.R.C., vol. 34, fols. 39–40.

had obviously done his best to revive some interest in the brigade and Rome's need by writing Dixon about the middle of February. In his reply, however, Dixon, in a definitive and dignified way, simply brushed aside Kirby's latest efforts. "I have given up," he informed Kirby tersely on February 26, "all interest in the Irish brigade; because until Monsg. de Mérode will understand a little more of the Irish view in this matter it seems to me that it would be a mere waste of words to write or speak about it" (K). Kirby had apparently in the meantime been attempting to persuade the authorities that something must be done to reassure the Irish that Forde's charges of the paramountcy of English influence in Rome with regard to Irish affairs had no real foundation in fact. He was partially successful, for when he finally answered Forde's long letter of January 15 some seven weeks later, on March 5, he was at least able to inform him that the pope had appointed Forde a monsignor as a *Cameriere d'Honore*.[46]

Forde's long letter of January 15, complaining of Mérode and English Catholic intrigue at Rome, was only another manifestation of the developing resentment, which was deep and general among the Irish clergy, of English influence in their affairs at Rome and at home. English Catholic influence in Irish affairs had not, in fact, counted for very much since Cullen had been appointed archbishop of Armagh and apostolic delegate by Pius IX in 1849. When in the spring of 1859, however, the English primate and archbishop of Westminster, Nicholas Cardinal Wiseman, took the unprecedented step of interfering in Ireland at the general election in the interests of Lord Derby and his minority Conservative government, the differences between Cullen and him regarding the correct policy to be pursued in British and Irish politics, which had been up to this time successfully muted, became public knowledge. Though Derby with Wiseman's help gained some nine seats in Ireland, he was still unable to form a government, and the Liberals led by Lord Palmerston again returned to power. Because Palmerston and his colleagues were deeply and publicly committed to the Italian cause as espoused by Cavour and Garibaldi, the pope and his advisors were persuaded that a Conservative government led by Derby would be more sympathetic to their cause. As the pope became more intransigent about Piedmontese aggression and the English government's open support of it, a number of prominent English Catholics began to disavow their traditional Liberal allegiance and adopt a more Conservative posture in English politics. Moreover, Monsignor

46. K, Forde to Kirby, January 5, 1861. This was a note made by Kirby at the conclusion of Forde's letter.

George Talbot, Wiseman's Roman alter ego and the pope's private chamberlain, began to gain rapidly in influence with Pius IX because of his firm support of the intransigent position. At this point English Catholic influence began to appear more formidable at Rome, especially to the Irish.

Forde's complaints in his correspondence with Kirby about the malign effects of English influence were, of course, seconded not only by Cullen but also by Kirby, who was, if anything, even more resentful and suspicious than his friend and mentor, the archbishop of Dublin. When, for example, Wiseman, who was visiting Rome in early 1860 on English ecclesiastical business, organized a deputation of the British Catholics in Rome to present an address of sympathy to the pope, and invited Kirby to join the deputation, Kirby refused. Monsignor Talbot wrote Kirby on February 16, the evening before the audience, to explain that he had heard that Kirby had some objection to attending (K). "Now," Talbot added, "I write to say that I think your absence will be observed, and commented on and perhaps unworthy motives will be given as reasons for your not coming, such as a spirit of nationality, an anti-English feeling, or even jealousy of Cardinal Wiseman." "I therefore write to you," he further explained, "as a friend, and as an Irishman myself, although I am a citizen of the world in feeling, to say that I should be much gratified by your coming." In his reply the next morning, February 17, Kirby, in effect, politely snubbed Talbot's invitation (K). "I am prevented from attending personally," he explained, "through several motives, (different from those you mention); but the absence of so insignificant a person from a meeting of British Catholics can in no wise detract from either its respectability or importance."

Kirby immediately reported to Cullen what he had done, for Cullen replied on February 24, reassuring him that he had been right "not to go with the English address" (K). Indeed, Kirby had apparently decided to organize a deputation of his own, for on Sunday, March 11, he presented an address of sympathy to the pope at the Vatican, accompanied by more than three hundred Irish Catholic gentlemen, clerical and lay, as well as the entire student body of the Irish College.[47] Among those present was that "citizen of the world" Monsignor Talbot. In a gesture obviously designed to reassure the Irish about their good standing at Rome, the pope had *proprio motu*, the evening before his audience with the Irish deputation, appointed Kirby one of his own *Camerieri Segreti*, or private chamberlains. A week later the new

47. I.C.D., 1861, p. 135.

monsignor led another large delegation of Irish Catholic gentlemen and students to the Vatican to pay their customary homage to the pope on St. Patrick's Day, and the pope returned the compliment by visiting the Irish College, attended by Cardinals Antonelli and Barnabò. "It must be very gratifying to you," Dixon wrote, in congratulating Kirby on April 4, "to find that the Roman authorities were so much pleased with the firm stand that you made for old Ireland in the affair of the deputation to the Vatican" (K).

In the meantime, Kirby had also written his old friend, Dominic O'Brien, the bishop of Waterford, informing him of his refusal to be part of the British deputation. In his reply O'Brien, who had unsuccessfully pitted his political influence against Cardinal Wiseman's candidates at the late general election in Waterford and who was obviously still very sore about it, gave full vent to his anti-English feeling. "I do not know what other prelates may think of your conduct on the occasion," he assured Kirby on March 5, "but for my part I highly approve of it. It has been my opinion for many years that Cardinal Wiseman would like to have the Irish Church at his feet. He would be glad to see our ancient and independent hierarchy absorbed by England of which he himself is the head. May God forbid that such a consummation should ever take place" (K). "We have," he declared, "a regularly constituted hierarchy unbroken since the days of St. Patrick, and we wish to maintain it in immediate connection with the Holy See." He added in conclusion, "I think you deserve the thanks of the Bishops and clergy of Ireland for the manner in which you acted upon this late occasion. We should always keep ourselves separated from the English in those public demonstrations; or otherwise they would extinguish us as a distinct national hierarchy."[48]

The anti-English Catholic sentiment expressed by Kirby and Cullen and their friends became more acute, of course, as their difficulties over the brigade began to mount. For example, by June of 1860 Forde had come to see Count McDonnell as the unwitting accomplice in an Anglo-Catholic conspiracy bent on discrediting the Irish. By the new year he had come to the even more unsettling conclusion that Mérode was actually a willing instrument of that conspiracy. Cullen too had come to view Anglo-Catholic interference in Irish affairs with a very jaundiced eye, and both he and Dixon had apparently begun to agree with Forde regarding Mérode and the Anglo-Catholic conspiracy. That

48. See also K, George Butler to Kirby, April 25, 1860, explaining that John Ryan, the bishop of Limerick, approved of what Kirby had done regarding the deputation. "It would never do," Butler added, "to have the representatives of our Country at Rome come before the Holy Father at the tail of the English."

Wiseman and his friends were something less than loyal both at home and at Rome to their Irish co-religionists, and took advantage of their various embarrassments with the brigade, was certainly true, but whether their actions amounted to a systematic conspiracy directed against the Irish is quite another matter.

When it is realized that the English Catholics, those who, like Wiseman and Talbot, held the ultramontane position, were in serious difficulties of their own, which had little or nothing to do with the Irish, their very aggressive behavior at home and at Rome becomes more understandable. Not only were the English ultramontane Catholics a miniscule minority in a nation that had come to view the temporal power of the pope as an anachronism in terms of liberty and progress, but they were also perhaps a minority in their own church with regard to both the temporal power of the pope and their ultramontane principles. Indeed, Wiseman visited Rome in 1860 to put down a cisalpine revolt in the English Church led by no less a person than his coadjutor with the right to succession, George Errington, the archbishop of Trebizond. Though Wiseman would, with the aid of Talbot, eventually persuade the pope and the authorities to remove Errington, the effort expended was very considerable, and it resulted in binding the English ultramontanes even more closely to Rome, especially if they hoped to continue to survive in a nation that was inveterately hostile to, and in a church that had become deeply resentful of, ultramontane influence. The English ultramontane party's aggressiveness, and the advantage it tended to take of Irish difficulties, therefore had perhaps less to do with any concerted conspiracy against the Irish than with the English ultramontane Catholics' need to consolidate their position at Rome if they were to continue to control the English Church.

Still, the Irish had become convinced that there was an English conspiracy. What was even more important, however, was that it was the ultramontane portion of the Irish Church led by Cullen, which was presumably less susceptible to ultra-nationalist prejudices, that had come to hold this belief. The Roman reaction to the Irish jealousy of the English may be easily imagined. The Romans could hardly be blamed for finding the nationalist propensities of the Irish tiresome, if not indeed irksome, especially because most of their own recent difficulties were rooted in the Italian brand of that same phenomenon. Still, when dealing with the Irish vis-à-vis the English, the Roman authorities had learned by long experience to tread warily. When Kirby decided to make his stand for national honor and identity in the affair of the British Catholic deputation to the pope, the pope responded reassuringly by making Kirby a domestic prelate. The following year the Roman authorities again attempted to reassure their obviously disgruntled Irish brethren by promoting Forde. By this time, however, the anxiety of the Irish about their standing at Rome was so great that they apparently needed a larger gesture of reassurance than the creation of another monsignor. The archbishop of Armagh, for example, in writing Kirby on April 3, 1861, explained that he was very pleased that Forde had been promoted but then went on to refer to a promotion that would give even greater satisfaction in Ireland (K). "I trust," Dixon noted very pointedly, "that the rumour of the coming promotion of the archbishop of Dublin is well founded. That would be indeed the cause of joy to the people." Cullen was not, in fact, promoted to the rank of cardinal at that time; indeed, he would have to wait another five years for his red hat.

The real significance of the various efforts made by the Irish people and their Church on behalf of the temporal power of the pope during 1860 was of course not to be found simply in the perceptible cooling that took place in Irish-Roman relations. What was really significant about those efforts was the way in which they cumulatively resulted in the deepening of an Irish national consciousness. The launching of a national agitation, the inaugurating of the Peter's pence, and the raising of a papal brigade by the bishops and clergy all resulted in the Irish people's thinking and acting more in national, and less in regional, terms. This energetic focusing on the needs of the pope, moreover, not only deepened that consciousness but intensified it in a way that made the Irish people even more aware of how very Catholic they were. What was thus being focused and strengthened, therefore, was not simply an Irish, but an Irish-Catholic consciousness, which was to have profound consequences for their future as a people. This developing Irish-Catholic consciousness was further hardened, meanwhile, by the English reaction to it. The undisguised delight of the English at the imminent demise of the temporal power of the pope, and their unconcealed contempt for everything Irish and Catholic, caused the Irish not only to become more aware of themselves as a people but also to perceive more clearly how profoundly different they still were as a people from the hereditary enemy of their nation and religion.

II

The Economics of Politics

September 1860–September 1863

In the course of the next three years the Irish were going to become even more aware of how Irish they were, and how very different they were as a people from the English. This further deepening of their awareness was the result of yet another of those harrowing experiences that appear to have been their lot as a people in the nineteenth century. The Irish harvest failed in 1860, 1861, and 1862. Not only was each of the harvest failures a particular calamity, because the crop most affected was the people's staple, the potato, but they were also a cumulative disaster, because the existing social and economic structure was unable to provide the means necessary to relieve the inevitable increase in misery and destitution. When the government was asked to help mitigate the distress and suffering, and it, in effect, refused to do so by denying that the Irish appeal for relief had any real basis in fact, the reaction of the Irish—the bitterness about and even hatred of the English connection—may be easily imagined. The depth of that Irish antipathy was made amply clear in these years in the increased power and influence of those who advocated the overthrow of the English connection by force of arms and the establishment of an Irish Republic. The result was that those politicians who were still prepared to argue for a constitutional solution to the question of Irish self-government and who were attempting to hold their political ground against the extremists were obliged, in the face of the appalling social and economic condition of their people and the government's apparent indifference to it, to indulge in an even fiercer political rhetoric, thus increasing the chances of an explosion in an already dangerously overcharged political atmosphere. As the Irish political spectrum shifted more radically to the left, none were perhaps more severely tested in the crisis than the Church and its clergy, who found themselves cruelly caught between their duty to the established order and their loyalty to their people.

When Cullen wrote Barnabò on February 18, 1861, complaining about Monsignor de Mérode, he also attempted to explain at the end of his letter why he had not yet established the Peter's pence collection in his diocese on the more formal basis recommended by the Roman authorities: "Here," he admitted, "we are late in helping the Holy Father. There are however circumstances that explain the delay. Last year we made three collections—the first for the Holy Father, which produced about £16,000, that is 400,000 francs, the second for the Syrians, which amounted to almost £3,000, and the third for the Irish soldiers which in this diocese amounted to about £1,200, while all the other dioceses have not given a quarter of that sum."[1] "Moreover," he added, "we have collections every Sunday for the maintenance of an infinite number of orphans, widows, and sick in this city; and besides, the harvest of last year has been ruined to such an extent by rain that the labourers all find themselves much afflicted." "These reasons explain our delay," Cullen noted in conclusion, "but I hope that we shall be able to do something fitting on next St. Patrick's day."

Indeed, the harvest had been a disaster, especially for the poor and the small-farming class, because the crop that had been hardest hit was their staple, the potato. At the end of August the bishop of Cloyne, William Keane, wrote Kirby from Fermoy in county Cork that the rain had delayed the harvest and that the hay crop was seriously damaged.[2] He added that the potatoes were damaged by blight but that because the crop promised to be a good one, the overall loss would be mitigated. The rain, however, continued unabated for the next two weeks, and Cullen reported somberly to Kirby on September 21 that "the harvest has not come in as yet, and it is feared we shall have very great misery next year. Potatoes rotting" (K). In the next few weeks the rain finally abated, and the reports were somewhat more encouraging, if still grim. Though the harvest had been severely damaged, Cullen informed Kirby on October 6, the weather had lately been so dry that a considerable part of the corn crop at least would be saved

1. S.R.C., vol. 34, fol. 40. The figure cited for the Syrian collection by Cullen was the amount collected in all Ireland; the other figures were for Dublin alone.
2. K, August 31, 1860.

Provinces and Dioceses of IRELAND

Raphoe

Derry

Down & Connor

ARMAGH

Clogher

Dromore

Armagh

Killala

Kilmore

Achonry

Ardagh & Clonmacnois

Elphin

Tuam

TUAM

Meath

Galway & Kilmacduagh

Clonfert

Kildare & Leighlin

Dublin

Tuam

Kilfenora

DUBLIN

Killaloe

Ossory

Ferns

Cashel & Emly

Limerick

Waterford & Lismore

CASHEL

Kerry

Cloyne

Cork

Ross

—— Ecclesiastical Provinces

—— Dioceses Boundary

0   60   120

miles

N

PROVINCES AND DIOCESES OF IRELAND

(K). The oats were good, though the wheat would probably yield only about half as much as usual. What was left of the potatoes, most of which had rotted because of the continuing rain, Cullen added, had at least been saved, so that there would be no immediate want of provisions.

Two days before, on October 4, the bishop of Cloyne had also written Kirby in the same vein (K). Though the harvest had been very late, Keane reported, "it was saved in better condition than expected & on the whole it is said it is fair enough. The loss of the potatoes was not so great as '46 or '47." "This, of course," he admitted, "is a serious drawback; but it will not be so much felt as it was at that time, when the whole Social System rested principally on a Sound potato Crop. Now the People are more accustomed to bread diet; they are fewer in number; they are better employed; and they get better wages." These reports, however, were too optimistic, at least as far as the poor and the small-farming class were concerned. The potato crop was, in fact, down some 40 percent from what it had been, if the average yields of the years 1856–58 are taken as the norm.[3] The turnip crop, moreover, on which the poor and small farmers greatly depended for not only food for themselves but feed for their pigs and supplementary wages for labor, was down 35 percent. The hay and corn crops, which were the mainstay of the larger farmers, were up to the average in their yields, except for wheat, which was down some 12 percent. Indeed, when the picture became clearer, the last word was had by Cullen, who understood better than most of his colleagues both the import of a bad harvest in Ireland and how to take his comfort in his best sorrow. "I fear we are in for gt. distress next season," he confessed to Kirby on October 19. "The wheat is of no value—the potatoes are bad, and at least half rotten. *Fiat voluntas Dei*" (K). "It is better," he added in conclusion, "to have famine than revolution."

Though Cullen was obviously alluding to Italy in referring to "revolution," he was also very much aware of the recent efforts toward a new political agitation in Ireland. A movement had been launched in September by A. M. Sullivan of the *Nation* to petition the queen to authorize a public referendum in Ireland on whether the Act of Union between Great Britain and Ireland should be repealed.[4] On November 14 the National Petition Committee of Dublin wrote Cullen asking for his permission "to have the Petition forms placed for signature

3. James S. Donnelly, Jr., "The Irish Agricultural Depression of 1859–64," *Irish Economic and Social History* 3 (1976): 36–37.
4. A. M. Sullivan, *New Ireland* (London, 1882), pp. 242–43.

within the enclosed space surrounding Marlborough Street Cathedral on next, or the following Sunday" (C). Some two weeks later, on November 30, the committee addressed a circular letter to all the Irish bishops, calling their attention to an aggregate meeting to be held in Dublin on December 4 at the Rotundo to endorse the petition and asking the bishops to support the movement (C). "The National Petition[,] my Lord," the committee explained,

> is designed to test the sincerity of the English government in their declaration of the right of every people to choose their own rulers and form of government. By their assertion of that principle English ministers have encouraged revolt in the Papal States and sought to justify rebellion against an ancient legitimate, and rightful Sovereignty. But in their haste to overthrow the Holy Father they seem to have forgotten that Ireland might demand the application of that principle to her affairs, and might truly say that grievances such as she is compelled to endure have had no parallel in the Roman States.

In concluding their circular, the committee then asked the prelates, if they approved of the views expressed, to let them know. The committee was to be severely disappointed, for by the time of the aggregate meeting the only bishop who had replied positively was the archbishop of Tuam.

At the meeting on December 4 the chair was taken by The O'Donoghue, member of Parliament for Tipperary and a strong advocate of the Irish policy of independent opposition in Parliament.[5] Among the principal speakers on the occasion, besides O'Donoghue, were John Francis Maguire, member of Parliament for Dungarvan, who was also a forward advocate of independent opposition, and John Martin, who had been transported to Tasmania for his Young Ireland activities in 1848. What was very significant, however, was how few clergy were in attendance, and that, of those who did attend, only two addressed the meeting—Robert Mullen, curate of the parish of Sonna in the diocese of Meath, and Patrick Lavelle, administrator of the parish of Partry in the archdiocese of Tuam.[6] Two of the high points of the meeting were the reading of letters of encouragement from William Smith O'Brien, leader of the Young Ireland uprising in 1848, and

5. *Freeman's Journal*, December 5, 1860.
6. Ibid. In addressing the meeting both Mullen and Lavelle were careful to point out that they had their respective bishops' blessing for their appearance on the occasion. In all there were only eight priests present. Mullen, moreover, was misidentified as "Richard" and "administrator" of Ballinacargy.

from "the ever national patriotic Lion of the Fold of Juda," John Mac-Hale, the archbishop of Tuam. "When the heart of the country went earnestly with the measure," MacHale explained, referring to the Repeal movement of Daniel O'Connell in the 1840s, "it was a gratifying duty to labour in a cause fraught with such national blessings. Though crushed for a time by the combined influences of famine and desertion, its justice will always animate with such a vitality that it can never be entirely abandoned."[7]

"At the same time," MacHale pointed out, "I trust that its sanguine advocates at this juncture can rest on more solid and more hopeful arguments than those supplied by the inconsistency of Her Majesty's ministers, denying us the same right of choosing our rulers which they glory in preaching up to all the nations of this earth." "The Repeal of the Union," MacHale then assured his listeners,

> rests on a far firmer basis, and a thriving and vigorous Irish project would give the measure a vigor and efficiency which all the decrepit and heartless political fallacies, borrowed by English statesmen from foreign infidel schools, could not bestow. To make the youth of Ireland able and willing to achieve, with legal and constitutional might, the Repeal of Union, you must inure them to the preparatory and interminable campaign of working out their freedom, and the fall of that most enormous of all despotisms, the Protestant Establishment. These are the ends. The means of obtaining them must be as distinctly understood and defined. The most explicit independence of all political parties, the most entire freedom of education, distinctly meaning a perpetual opposition to the National Board and the infidel colleges; the utter confinement of its little political sect of all the benefits of the Established Church; and above all, the steady uncompromising oppositions of the Catholics of Ireland to every one—candidates, members of parliament, of the cabinet, and finally to the cabinet itself—that shall attempt to continue longer the humiliation of the Pope or the persecution of the people, or to the sustaining of an Establishment, of which the wailing mothers and children on the bleak mountains of Partry should at least teach it that its days are numbered.[8]

A few days after the meeting, George Henry Moore, former M.P. for county Mayo and a devoted political ally of MacHale, indicated that

7. Ibid. See also I.C.D., 1861, pp. 260–61.
8. *Freeman's Journal*, December 5, 1860.

he was prepared to recommend even more drastic action and wrote a public letter in which he explained that it was not by petitioning the English government that the Irish would realize their heart's desire.[9] "Freedom is not," he maintained, "to be had for the asking. It is a fair lady that faint heart never won, and in the parallel sought to be instituted between Ireland and Italy the essential was omitted. Neither Lord John Russell nor Lord Palmerston had said that every people had a right to change their government by presenting a petition. They must not only utter their disaffection but prove it; they must not only wish for the right to choose their own government but win it." "I tell the people of Ireland," Moore then added, "that if they seek for national independence and separate rule, they must struggle for it as the Italians struggled. They must suffer for it as they suffered, and, if necessary, die for it as they died; and then out of that union, out of that struggle, suffering, and death, they have a right to hope for a national resurrection." "But if, on the other hand," he concluded eloquently, "we have no heart for such a struggle, let us at least draw a decent cloak over our infirmities; let us not hawk about our wounds, as mendicants their sores for alms, or stand in the highway of nations reciting to deaf ears a beggar's petition."

Cullen, who had a sharp eye for developing political agitations, immediately took notice of the rumblings. "I fear," he wrote Kirby on December 7, "we are at the eve of a bad agitation here. Some who abused the bishops in 1854 are now coming out. G. H. Moore, etc. and they are preaching the doings of 1848" (K). Some two weeks later Cullen was still very concerned about an imminent agitation, and especially about the direction it was likely to take. "I think," he explained to Kirby on December 21, "we shall have trouble with the Young Irelanders again. G. H. Moore, Dr. McHale's[10] great friend has published a most revolutionary letter. In all the towns there is a set of radicals ready for mischief. Probably the government spies pay some of them" (K). Cullen's premonitions proved to be only too justified, for the proponents of an agitation on behalf of Repeal apparently concerted their efforts with a series of letters published on New Year's Day, 1861, to rouse the national political consciousness.[11] George Henry Moore, in emulation of the great Daniel O'Connell, published

9. Maurice G. Moore, *An Irish Gentleman, George Henry Moore* (London, n.d.), pp. 275–80.

10. It should be noted that in all his correspondences Cullen consistently misspelled Archbishop MacHale's name as "McHale." I have not corrected the misspelling.

11. I.C.D., 1862, p. 211. See also *Freeman's Journal*, January 2, 1861, for MacHale's letter to Palmerston.

an open letter on the state of Ireland and the present condition of her people, which, needless to say, he found to be deplorable. Archbishop MacHale that same day addressed yet another of his famous letters to the English prime minister, Lord Palmerston, complaining about the misgovernment of Ireland in general and the evictions in Father Lavelle's parish of Partry by the Protestant bishop of Tuam, Lord Thomas Plunket, in particular. John Martin and William Smith O'Brien then added salt to the soup in an exchange of letters discussing whether in the event of a French invasion Irishmen should support the French or the British. Several days later, on January 7, The O'Donoghue published an address to the people of Ireland, discussing their demand for a national government in terms of the Repeal of the Act of Union.[12] His further plea for greater activity in securing signatures to the Repeal petition was in itself, however, a sign of the public's languishing interest.

In a last desperate effort to enlist the aid of the bishops in the petition movement, O'Donoghue finally decided to write directly to Cullen. "Will you," he asked him plainly on January 27, "allow me to affix your name to the National Petition?" (C). "Believe me my Lord," he then assured Cullen, "the aim of English legislation, is to make Englishmen of us all. So long as there is a large population who remain faithful to the Church, and who love Ireland, the work is one of great difficulty. Consequently every facility is afforded for the destruction of the population." "In 1851," he then reminded Cullen, "the Bishops endeavoured to create an independent Irish Parliamentary party. The Bishops were unable to create such a party, both they and the country were betrayed, and the result has been great loss of influence to the Bishops, and the diffusion through Ireland of the belief that there is no such thing as public virtue—amongst public men. Every voter now believes in his heart, that it is a matter of indifference for whom he records his vote. . . ." "To rouse the spirit of the Nation," O'Donoghue assured Cullen, "without the cooperation of the Bishops is next to impossible, therefore it is my Lord that I implore you to sign the National Petition. The Declaration of five hundred thousand Irishmen, *headed by the Bishops of Ireland*, that they have no confidence in the English Government, can not fail to produce *most beneficial results*." What O'Donoghue meant by "*most beneficial results*," of course, was that the National Petition, when duly rejected, was to be but the prelude to a national agitation, the end of which would be the creation of an independent Irish Parliamentary

12. *Freeman's Journal*, January 7, 1861.

party in the House of Commons backed by a solid phalanx of the bishops, priests, and people of Ireland. What O'Donoghue certainly failed to appreciate, however, was that Cullen was of no mind to help launch a political agitation that would once again embroil the priests in politics and sow dissensions among the bishops. Needless to say, he did not sign the petition, though a few of the Irish bishops, including William Keane of Cloyne and John Cantwell of Meath, did support the movement in company with MacHale.

All the various efforts to launch a successful agitation on behalf of Repeal therefore proved to be abortive. Even when MacHale and the bishop of Cloyne, William Keane, attempted to blow some life into the agitation in their Lenten pastorals in February, they failed. "Here," Cullen reported to Kirby on February 15, with some satisfaction, "all is quiet—you will see however that the pastorals of Dr. Keane and Dr. McH. call for agitation" (K). "At Dr. O'Connell's consecration, Dr. Cantwell," he added, referring respectively to the former director of the missionary college of All Hallows in Dublin, who had just been appointed vicar apostolic of Marysville, California, and the bishop of Meath, "made a post-prandial speech to the students on the necessity of wholesome agitation. Unfortunately the priests and the other agitators who join will not agitate against any but Catholics, and especially other priests and Bishops—they have no intention of agitating against the abuses of Government, or the Prot. Church or bad education."

Some further insight into Cullen's political views at this time is provided by some remarks he made earlier in this letter about a by-election then pending in county Cork. The election had been occasioned by the appointment of Rickard Deasy as the Irish attorney general in Lord Palmerston's ministry, which made it necessary for him to stand for reelection. Because the more nationalist and Catholic portion of the Cork electorate was not pleased with the attitude of either Palmerston or his foreign secretary, Lord John Russell, they were casting about for a viable candidate to run against Deasy. "Myles O'Reilly," Cullen informed Kirby, naming the late commander of the papal brigade, "was invited to stand for Cork. The expenses wd be about £3000—*et incerta victoria* [and victory doubtful]. He wisely refused to go in debt." Cullen prophesied bitterly, referring to the likelihood that a contest between two Liberals would allow a Tory to sneak in, "An Orangeman will be returned—I think that in the course of 4 or 5 years all Ireland will be represented by Orangemen. The Catholics are losing influence every year. The exorbitant pretensions of the Young Irelanders and independents have done gt mischief, but the great cause is that the voters have no leases, and everyone that votes against a Landlord is turned out." "Lord Derby," Cullen then pointed out, naming the Conservative leader, "goes with the Orangemen. Lord J. Russell is just as bad against Catholics. Between them *stiamo male* [we are badly off]." "Some of yr good people in Rome," he finally added ironically, "think we ought to put ought [*sic*] J. Russell. We have as much chance of doing that as they have of putting out Cialdini or Cavour."

Though O'Reilly had wisely declined the invitation to contest county Cork, those who had invited him persisted in their quest for a candidate and finally persuaded Viscount Campden, an Englishman of Catholic and Conservative antecedents, to run against Deasy as a Liberal. The bishops and clergy of county Cork, which included all the dioceses of Cork, Cloyne, and Ross and part of Kerry, could not agree, and Deasy defeated Campden handily by some twenty-three hundred votes in a poll of more than nine thousand. Cullen was simply appalled at the result. "Dr. O'Hea and Dr. Keane," he reported sadly on March 4, referring respectively to the bishops of Ross and Cloyne, "urged on by my friend Pope Hennessy put forward a Tory candidate[,] Lord Campden, and inscribed the *Pope* and *Catholic Education* on their banners" (C). "They acted," he added, "most imprudently and got a frightful beating. *In primis* Pope Hennessy was no man to guide them. 2° Lord Campden[,] an Englishman and as deaf as a poker, and a Tory was not a fit candidate. In 3° *loco* Deasy was very popular and not likely to be defeated." "As for me," he then concluded even more sadly, "I am very sorry that the Catholic party was defeated in Cork but I think they did wrong to engage in the contest. The clergy was fairly divided—two bishops against two bishops—and the clergy of Cork versus the clergy of Cloyne & Ross—it is in this way that we lose all power."

At this point the question naturally arises why the bishops and clergy did not respond with the same enthusiasm as they had in the past to an agitation for Repeal. The question is especially pertinent not only because they had just proved their mettle in raising a formidable agitation on behalf of the temporal power of the pope but also because they must have understood how much a political agitation could do to take the sting of despair out of the recent failure of the harvest and therefore to help mute social discontent. The answer is very complicated, but any answer must involve the need to distinguish between a religious and a political question in the Irish social context. Both Cullen and MacHale, for example, agreed that the agitation on behalf of the pope was incumbent upon them as a religious duty. When it came to an agitation on behalf of Repeal, however,

Cullen refused to involve himself or to allow his clergy to become involved, not simply because he regarded it as a political issue, or even because the leaders involved were tainted with the principles of Young Ireland, but rather because it was an issue on which the Catholic laity were divided, both on the feasibility of Repeal and on the means to be used in realizing it. MacHale, on the other hand, tended to equate religious and political issues. He understood the cause of Irish nationality and independence to be a sacred cause because it was essentially a Catholic cause. To MacHale, the survival of the Irish people as a Catholic people was the real issue, and he was prepared to commit himself, his clergy, and inasmuch as he was able, the Irish Church to that sacred cause.

The problem faced by Cullen in this context, therefore, was how to keep the Church united in the face of a political issue that would divide the laity and result in the clergy's also taking sides. His solution to the problem was simple. In politically contentious situations the clergy should assume a very low political profile and quietly do their utmost as peacemakers to produce that harmony and unity so necessary to any effective Catholic action, political or otherwise, in Ireland. In this way, Cullen argued, the clergy not only would preserve their clerical character but would greatly enhance their very real power and influence with their people. MacHale saw Cullen's position as tantamount to forsaking the cause of Catholic nationality and deserting their people.[13] He believed that the clergy should be in the front rank of any agitation on behalf of the people, and if the laity were divided about ends or means, those who were on the wrong side, as defined by him and his clergy, should submit in the interests of their common nationality. While Cullen and MacHale were both able, in their respective archdioceses, to enforce their views with their clergy, the real difficulty was that there were also some twenty-six other bishops in Ireland, who also exercised that same jurisdiction in political matters over their priests.

13. Ibid., February 9, 1860. At a banquet on Tuesday evening, February 7, 1860, after a mass meeting that afternoon in Castlebar in support of the temporal power of the pope, MacHale had said: "Thanks, then, to the Sovereign Pontiff, whose cause had awakened the country to a knowledge of its sufferings, and reanimated them with the desire to have their grievances redressed (hear). But why was it that in Ireland demonstrations of the magnitude and importance of that which had passed off a few hours before were inoperative and without effect? It was owing to the spirit of division that prevailed, marshalling the forces of the people in opposite directions, or plunging them into what was still worse—a general apathy (hear, hear). If that apathy had not existed for some years in Ireland, they would not have been obliged to assemble to defend the cause of the Holy Father, or to reorganize another vigorous agitation for its delivery, and the delivery of the Catholic Church (hear, hear)."

For more than ten years, in fact, the bishops as a body had been attempting to regulate and control the political conduct of their clergy. By enacting more stringent decrees at their national and provincial synods, with the express encouragement and approval of Rome, in the 1850s, the Irish bishops had finally established the canonical framework within which they could regulate the political conduct of their priests. The great difficulty was that if an individual bishop, of whom MacHale was the outstanding example, did not choose to enforce the national or provincial regulations governing the political conduct of his clergy, there was actually little or nothing the bishops as a body could do. They might, of course, appeal to Rome against the offending bishop or bishops, but that course of action in the long run was only subversive of their own authority as a body. Still, by 1860, the problem of individual bishops taking their own line, or allowing their priests to take their own line, in political matters had been considerably reduced by Cullen's very great influence at Rome in the making of Irish episcopal appointments. By 1860, in fact, Cullen had reduced the episcopal dissidents in political matters to the redoubtable MacHale and perhaps three or four supporters in a body that numbered twenty-eight.[14] While MacHale and his supporters might continue to commit themselves and their clergy to an active participation in politics, they were no longer numerous enough to turn that commitment into an effective national agitation. The key, then, to any successful agitation on any issue, religious or political, was whether the bishops as a body were prepared to commit themselves and their clergy to it, and as long as Cullen was able to persuade the great majority of the bishops that his view rather than MacHale's was the correct one, the possibility of focusing the national political consciousness in a constitutional agitation was not very promising.

The price paid by Cullen and the majority of the bishops, however, for the political curbing of their priests proved in the end to be incredibly high. They created, in effect, a political power vacuum, which would soon be rapidly filled by the secret, oath-bound, and revolutionary Irish Republican, or Fenian, Brotherhood. The Brotherhood had been founded in the United States in early 1858 and had made very rapid progress among the many emigrants embittered by having been forced to leave their homeland. The organization made slower progress in Ireland. The enthusiasm generated on behalf of the pope during 1860 and the implacable hostility of the Church to all forms of

14. The MacHale supporters, on many issues, were the bishops of Meath, Clogher, Clonfert, and Killala.

secret societies certainly contributed to inhibiting its growth. The failure of the harvest in 1860 and the consequent severe distress during the winter, however,[15] combined with the abortive efforts to launch a constitutional agitation for Repeal early in the new year, created a more congenial atmosphere for the advocacy of extreme measures. "At present," Cullen informed his cousin, Patrick Moran, vice-rector of the Irish College, on April 5, "I fear we are likely to be beset by secret societies. I hear they are springing up. Their object is to promote a French invasion. They are as mad as possible" (K). "It is a sad thing," he noted, "to think that they can place their hopes in a man who is doing so much to destroy the authority of the Pope [i.e., Napoleon III]. Here in Dublin and Leinster the people are not at all inclined to side with the Sphynx, but in the South they are quite enthusiastic for him." Cullen added:

> We are altogether in a most extraordinary state—between Orangemen our deadly enemies here and held up in Rome as our loving friends, and Whigs the open enemies of the Pope, pretending here to give fair play to Catholics. It is hard to see what course ought to be adopted, but what appears certain is that schemers under the pretence of opposing the enemies of religion, are getting up secret societies and plotting to get in that great friend of Catholics who resides in Paris. There is an arch-Presbyterian or infidel by name Mitchell who is promoting this work of course thro' love of the Pope. You see what troubled waters we have to navigate in.

"The secret soc. I mentioned," he then finally explained, "are called the Brotherhood of S. Patrick. I learned from a sacerdote that some members are bound by oath—others, the inferiors not. Their object is to protect the cause of Ireland—*quod fieri debet per arma aliena* [which ought to be brought about by foreign arms]."

15. K. In February 1861 an old friend of Kirby and his brother, William, James Clampett, wrote explaining that Limerick city was not what it was when William lived there, "for Limerick is now a scene of great distress in provisions being very dear almost a total want of business and tradesmen and labourers idle for want of an imployment [sic] and our workhouses ful [sic] of poor and distressed peopple [sic], rates threefold more than former years. I regret to say I [am] suffering my part as my tennants [sic] who live as weekly in some houses I hold in the old town are not able to pay any rent and most of them [are] in the poor house." In explaining to Kirby on February 20, 1861, that there had been nothing but rain lately, T. Benson, writing from Springfield, Clonard, near Limerick, reported, "The poor of Ireland are at present very destitute even in Limerick—indigence is very prevalent—as yet no deaths on that account have occurred—It is hoped that the Government will shortly give means of relief."

Cullen's information, however, was only partially accurate. The Brotherhood of St. Patrick, the bulk of whose members did not take an oath, was really only a front organization for the secret and oath-bound Fenian Brotherhood. Both organizations apparently continued to recruit members throughout 1861, but just how successful they were still remains something of a mystery. At their general meeting in April the bishops thought the matter serious enough to take occasion in their joint pastoral to denounce secret societies. They declared on April 25, referring to the cause of the pope's present difficulties in Italy,

> Moreover, from the misfortunes now afflicting the fairest regions of Europe, let us learn the great evils of secret societies, which undoubtedly, are the scourge of humanity and the bane of religion. On account of such evils all who are sworn in as Freemasons or Ribbonmen, or join in any other similar illegal combination, have been excommunicated by the Pope, and cut off as rotten branches from the Church. If any designing man endeavour to promote such societies among you, continue as for the past to be on your guard against them, and preserve yourselves and your country from the dangers to which any participation in those designs of darkness would involve you.[16]

While there is no further mention of secret societies in any of the clerical correspondences for the next six months, the surprise and excitement they created, especially in clerical circles, when they did appear again in late October indicate that they had gained considerable ground, at least as far as Irish public opinion was concerned. The occasion for the increased clerical concern was the proposed funeral of Terence Bellew McManus, a Young Irelander who had been transported to Tasmania for his part in the 1848 rising and who had died in comparative obscurity and poverty in California in January 1861. The Fenian organization in California decided that he should be given a hero's funeral in Ireland and shipped his remains from San Francisco to New York, where the archbishop of New York, John Hughes, eulogized him as a patriot in the funeral sermon he preached for him in St. Patrick's Cathedral.

As McManus's remains were en route to Ireland from New York, the organizers of the funeral arrangements requested the bishop of Cork, William Delany, to allow the remains to lie in state in his proca-

---

16. Patrick Francis Moran, ed., *The Pastoral Letters and Other Writings of Cardinal Cullen* (Dublin, 1882), 1:839.

thedral. Delany refused and when the remains arrived in Queenstown (Cobh) on October 31, 1861, they were removed to a church there, Queenstown being within the spiritual jurisdiction of the bishop of Cloyne, William Keane, who was more sympathetic than Delany to the aspirations of the Young Irelanders and Fenians. The funeral processions that took place in Queenstown and Cork, before the remains were moved on to Dublin, were very impressive. "The most favorable account," the head of the Fenian Brotherhood in Ireland, James Stephens, informed his counterpart in the United States, John O'Mahony, on November 16, "is far below the reality. The funeral procession in Cork numbered from 80,000 to 100,000, about 8,000 walking in regular order. Such men as Denny Lane, John Francis Maguire, John O'Donnell of Limerick, etc. were thunderstruck. They could not have believed such a demonstration possible without the cooperation of the clergy, at least, if not the leaders."[17]

The organizers of the funeral had also early asked Cullen to accord McManus a public funeral in his procathedral in Dublin. Cullen, of course, like Delany, refused. "A committee," he reported to Kirby on October 31, "wrote to me requesting of me to order a public funeral service for him in Marlboro' St. I answered that such things were not ordered unless for persons who had rendered gt services to religion or to the country, and I asked them to tell me what public services had been performed by McM." (K). "They have referred me," Cullen explained, "to the example of Dr. Hughes & Dr. Alemany in America [archbishop of New York and bishop of San Francisco, respectively] who gave public funerals. I have replied that I wish to know the precise services etc. I suspect that informers & spies are engaged in this work to divert public attention from real grievances & to get up odium against me if I refused a funeral, or to discredit me as a friend of rebellion if I grant it." "I will not," he declared adamantly, "do anything to approve of the folly of S. O'Brien and forty eight whatever odium I may incur." Indeed, in the next several years he incurred a great deal of odium.

Not only did Cullen refuse McManus a public funeral, but he refused to allow funeral masses to be said for him in any of the Dublin churches. This action resulted in a public letter from Patrick Lavelle, the administrator of the parish of Partry in the diocese of Tuam, to E. J. Ryan, secretary to the McManus Obsequies Committee, complaining about the treatment afforded McManus's remains in Dublin. Lavelle's letter, which was addressed from Tuam, was then printed up

17. Desmond Ryan, *The Fenian Chief* (Dublin, 1967), p. 176.

on a "broadsheet" and posted throughout Dublin on November 5. The letter read:

> Dear Sir—Enclosed I beg to forward to you 1£, the united mite of the Rev. U. J. Bourke, St. Jarlath's, Tuam, the Rev. Peter Geraghty. C.C., and myself, as our contribution towards the M'Manus Obsequies Fund.
>
> Alas! and alas! that in Ireland there should be a second sentiment on his claims to a national mourning and to national gratitude! He abandoned all for Ireland—wealth, friendship, peace and human happiness. He who, to obtain for his oppressed fellow-countrymen, groaning under the yoke of the tyrant stranger, some measure of fair play and rational liberty, flung every worldly consideration to the winds—who trampled under foot all those allurements that were so potent "to keep his proud soul under"—he, the Catholic and the patriot, the disinterested, the devoted, and the brave—he is denied the honours accorded to every Castle-slave, time-serving hypocrite, and whigling sycophant, whose creed is to sell his creed and his country together to the first buyer for prompt payment!
>
> Good God! M'Manus denied a momentary resting-place in any church of Ireland, though those whose fathers built those churches would shed the last drop of their blood to honour his memory!
>
> Oh! why not have brought those sacred remains to the Fane of Jarlath, that there the accents of tens of thousands of voices might mingle with the noble pronouncements of patriotic Cloyne, in honouring the man who died a martyr to his country's love[?]
>
> The Whig traitor who sells his country for his daily pound of flesh, the crawling place-hunter who worships only one God of the Dublin Castle, the *roue*, the debauchee, who may die rich without the blessings of Mother Church, they are honoured with voice prayers and fragrant incenses; the sanctuary is draped in deepest mourning to symbolise sorrow for their sins, though to the world it is the greatest gain—the sacred dirge is chaunted in solemn sadness around their unhallowed remains—the water is sprinkled over them, and the minister, unwilling though he may be, intones the mournful "From the depths I have cried to Thee, O Lord," yet the portals of the temple are closed against the bones of Terence Bellew M'Manus, the pure, the noble, the chivalrous, and the brave, in the bosom of the Land that gave him birth, and for which he laboured, exiled, sighed, and died.

Oh! Ireland! Ireland! is this your act? If not, in the name of creed, country, and people speak out your sentiment.

Did M'Manus die the banned of the Church? Then, my lord bishops of New York and Cloyne, explain your ecclesiastical homage to his memory. The laws of the church are the same in the City of the Hurdles as in Cove or the capital of Columbia. But, no, no. The Patriot died as he lived, true to his faith as to his country, annointed and annealed, in peace with the world and with God—with all except the enemy of all, cruel oppressor of his dear native land. Yet is he denied in that dear land the honours heaped upon the coward, the traitor, and the slave; the honours which, to-morrow, would be granted to those men who, for gain and interest, swore his precious life away, and would swear, to-morrow, mine and that of any bishop in Ireland.

St. Malachy, whom we this day commemorate—St. Laurence O'Toole—patriotic Oliver Plunkett, martyr to thy patriotism! Were you today alive would you deny Terence Bellew M'Manus a night's rest before the lamp of your sanctuaries? Oh! Ireland! Ireland! how art thou fallen! when shalt thou rise? Is this thy act? If not, speak out! Dare to speak it, Ireland!

Is patriotism a crime? Then let the patriot Primate of Hungary do penance in sackcloth and ashes. Let Ireland read his grand manifesto to the dominant alien foe of his country, and profit by the lesson. Are there Whig Prelates in Hungary? The brave Primate of Hungary is no Whig. He would never ostracise the honest Magyar who sacrificed all for the Fatherland.

And in Poland, there the strong hand of the Czar closes the Church against patriotic priest and people alive; here the Church closes herself against the Patriot Dead.

Dear M'Manus! honoured be thy memory in every land where freedom still dares to breathe. Thou art today ostracised in the heart of thy native land; but thy living countrymen have no part in the deed. Nay, thou art still dearer to them, far and far, from the attempt to dishonour thy name and thy grave, and the principles for which thou hast died, than thou ever would have been had the dim lamp of the sanctuary been permitted to cast its faint and melancholy light on thy precious remains. But thou art enshrined in our hearts a thousand times more than ever; and I, for one, vow never to enter the city in which thou art thus proclaimed on thy bier almost as I am in my parish, without pouring out my soul at thy grave, and vowing a new vow each time of hate and hostility to thy enemy and mine, the enemy of our Creed, our Country, and our Holy Father.

With my humble mite and that of my friends, I beg to convey these my sentiments, which, permit me to add, are those of every Catholic, lay and clerical, that I have met in this part of the country. If you allow matters to go much farther, prepare for a Veto.—I remain, &c.,[18]

"I hope you have received the Freeman's Journal," James Murray, Cullen's secretary, wrote Kirby on November 8, "which contained the wonderful letter of the far found father Lavelle. Did you ever read such a wicked and mischievous production during the whole course of your life? Wonders are never to cease" (K). "According to him," Murray complained, "we the clergy of Dublin are a sad lot because we do not side with rebellion and pay due honor to the principles represented by the Young Irelanders of 1848. At all events they might allow us to manage our own affairs, and let us live in peace with our people without exciting their worst feelings and follies against ecclesiastical authority." He went on:

> We are told they are making great preparations for the funeral on Sunday and the poor people[,] at least many of them[,] appear to be quite deceived by the representations of these men who have the management of the whole business in their hands. I was informed yesterday that they had not even a cross on the coffin, but were burning incense around it, so that you see even in Ireland the few rebels we have can make a display of what we may call their *Paganism*. When all shall have been over, I have no doubt but that the people will see the folly and the malice of those who were the leaders in the concern.

"I need scarcely say," he asserted further, "that the whole thing was got up for the purpose of sowing a political demonstration, and making us their servants in upholding their wicked principles. It is an attempt which if repeated would have a most terrible effect on our poor people by entirely separating them from the clergy and bringing on a state of things which is so prevalent at present on the continent." "May God," he concluded piously, "avert such evils from our poor country."

The next day, November 9, Cullen wrote to MacHale, who was Lavelle's bishop, complaining about his subject's letter in the *Freeman* and asking the archbishop to take appropriate action in the matter (K). MacHale did not give Cullen much satisfaction in his reply of November 11; he simply wrote that he would send Lavelle a copy of Cullen's

---

18. *Freeman's Journal*, November 6, 1861.

letter in order that Lavelle might answer for himself.[19] Meanwhile, the organizers of the funeral continued with their plans for a solemn procession on Sunday, November 10, to accompany McManus's remains from the hall of the Mechanic's Institute in Dublin, where he had been lying in state, to Glasnevin Cemetery. The crowds in attendance were reported to be in the hundreds of thousands, while some fifty thousand marched in the funeral procession. McManus was finally buried by torchlight as Father Lavelle said a few words by the graveside. His short oration deserves to be quoted in full because it is a prime example of that clerical-Nationalist rhetoric which resonated with such real effect during these years:

> Men of Ireland and men of Dublin, you behold in the grave today what was yesterday the symbol of your country, and is at this moment the symbol of resurrection. The demonstration of this day in the streets of Dublin will not be lost upon the oppressor. It was not my intention to speak on this occasion. It is not my privilege to preach the panegyric of the glorious and enviable dead; but I am here to pronounce that in Terence Bellew M'Manus, there died one of the bravest and best of Ireland's sons (cheers). It will be impossible for me to proceed if you make these manifestations. I am sure you must yourselves observe the awkwardness of this untimely response in this place. Perhaps it is better to bury the dead in solemn silence, and have his memory honoured by the eloquent, though silent, demonstration that has this day taken place in the streets of your city. That demonstration speaks more for the cause in which M'Manus died and for Ireland than all the tongues of all the priests and laymen in this country could utter. I am proud to see that the people of Ireland and of Dublin are not dead—that they have hope—that though the prophet be dead the spirit he evoked will outlive him, and even in the present generation raise his country from degradation to the glory of a nation (cheers). I regret exceedingly that I cannot proceed—I will say only that in M'Manus died a true Christian, a true patriot—that for your interests he sacrificed all his interests, and at length his life, and I hope the lesson will not be lost on you. As I fear to evoke any other response such as you have made, I will merely implore of you, for the great cause of suffering Ireland, that you will return to your homes peaceably, quietly, and constitutionally as you came here,

19. See S.R.C., vol. 34, fol. 201, for copies of Cullen's letter to MacHale and MacHale's reply, which Cullen forwarded to Propaganda.

and that by your silence and demeanour, you will show your enemies that though you are able to demonstrate your power, you are, at the same time, able to control it. I beg of you—I implore you of such in this vast assemblage that hear me, and not one tithe of a tithe of those around me can hear me—I implore of you, in the name of decency, in the name of Ireland, to disperse quietly and decorously, and thereby worthily terminate a demonstration which is one of the greatest Ireland has seen for the last century. We can pray wherever we like. We have said today the *De Profundis* for the dead. And when we have asked the guardianship of angels and the mercy of Heavens for the dead whom we honour, we shall all disperse.[20]

"The *De Profundis*," the *Freeman* further reported, "was then said by the Rev. Mr. Lavelle and the Rev. Mr. Courtney; and prayers being offered for the repose of the soul of Terence Bellew M'Manus, all present responded with a deep and solemn 'Amen.'"

Two days later, on November 12, Cullen wrote Kirby a long letter reporting on the whole affair to date (K). "I sent you some days ago," he explained, "Father Lavelle's proclamation in the Mazzini style about the McManus funeral. I now send you a copy of correspondence between Dr. McHale and me on the subject. I am expecting another letter from Lavelle who I suppose will write as directed by Dr. McHale. The whole business is most disgraceful—and all the priests and people here are greatly displeased with the lion." He continued:

I was thinking of suspending Lavelle ob delicta *hic* patrata, [for the offence of officiating as a priest *here*] his letter having been posted up here, but I thought it better to throw the onus on Dr. McH. He is now in a very awkward position. Lavelle dated his letter at Tuam—but he has been in Dublin for the last week, and he was here when the letter appeared—probably it was written here—but the publication is the offence.

The funeral was very large, and it was a pity to see a great many tradesmen making fools of themselves.

No Dublin priest attended except an old Capuchin F. Ashe. A priest from Bermingham [*sic*] by name Courtenay, and Father Kenyon were the only priests who accompanied Father Lavelle.

The whole business from California to Dublin was intended to be a declaration of adhesion to the foolish rebellion of Smith O'Brien in 1848, and a pronunciamento in favour of revolu-

20. *Freeman's Journal*, November 11, 1861.

tionary principles. I could not enter into such a matter without condemning all our doings in favour of the Pope, and in support of established authority.

Though there were crowds at the funeral there was little or no manifestation of feeling[;] it was rather pleasant amusement. Behind the hearse in a great cart there was an old fellow dressed in a white shirt and a big wig playing a harp, or rather drawing his fingers over the strings for he did not play. Some of the people cried out that he was Guy Fawkes.

The Americans who brought over the remains are sad fellows.

The government is delighted at the whole business, because it throws ridicule on us all, and weakens and divides the Catholics. They wd not allow such an exhibition, only they knew it wd end in ridicule.

"I wish you to ask them at Prop." Cullen charged Kirby, "whether Dr. McH. has a right to send out a priest of his diocese to insult the Bishops and priests and disturb the country. Is Dr. McH. free to send such answers as he has sent to me when I called attention to Lavelle's conduct? If so, I believe we may as well leave the Church to its fate."

What Cullen did not know, however, was that the apparent unanimity of the various political groupings participating in the McManus funeral had actually masked a very sharp struggle for power between those who still advocated constitutional methods (such as A. M. Sullivan of the *Nation*; The O'Donoghue, M.P. for Tipperary; and Father John Kenyon, the former Young Ireland priest cited by Cullen in his letter to Kirby), and the Fenian leadership (represented by James Stephens and Thomas Clarke Luby). The occasion for their confrontation was the question who should have control over the stage-managing of the McManus funeral. The struggle had begun in earnest when the Fenian leaders had early secured control of the various politically mixed committees that had been set up to welcome the dead patriot. They hoped thereby to exclude the constitutionalists, whom they derisively dubbed "Aspirationists," from any effective share in the arrangements. In an effort to work out a more acceptable accommodation, Father Kenyon met with Stephens and Luby, who agreed that Kenyon would be allowed to deliver the funeral oration. When they realized that Kenyon was determined on an Aspirationist oration, however, Stephens not only decided to select an American Fenian, Colonel M. D. Smith, to deliver the oration but also decided in the interests of Fenian orthodoxy to write it himself. During the week before the funeral, Kenyon and his Aspirationist supporters attempted at the various meetings of the Obsequies Committee to prevent any funeral oration from being delivered and failing in that, to have Kenyon substituted for Smith.[21]

The final confrontation took place on the evening before the funeral. "An infamous (I write deliberately) attempt," Stephens reported to O'Mahony in America, a week later on November 16, "was made on Saturday night to make the burial next day a failure. This attempt was the work of Father Kenyon, (the leader) John Martin, and such carrion as Cantwell etc., even The O'Donoghue allowed himself to be wheedled into the affair, though he had since disconnected himself from the miserable clique, who were all utterly crushed by the wise and manful action of the committee."[22] "Kenyon," Stephens then explained, "lost his wits all out—he insulted every member of the committee, and when leaving in a rage threatened to prevent the funeral the next day, declaring, 'You shall have no funeral,' etc. He and others then went to Miss McManus and by calumny, etc. endeavored to prevail on her to interfere and have the body taken from the American delegation, Dublin committee, etc. They were miserably disappointed, having succeeded in nothing but making themselves odious in Miss McManus's eyes as well as in the eyes of every true heart in Ireland." Though the Fenians were obviously able to contain Father Kenyon and his friends and retain control of the funeral arrangements, they were apparently taken by surprise by the ubiquitous Father Lavelle, whose graveside oration was unexpected and who managed to succeed in stealing some of the thunder of the Fenian-designated orator, Colonel Smith, who followed him.[23] In this context, it would be most interesting to know whether Lavelle had acted in concert with the Aspirationists or whether his effort was strictly impromptu. The ultimate irony, of course, was that Cullen, by prohibiting his clergy from taking any part in the McManus funeral, had unwittingly helped the Fenians turn the whole affair into a most successful revolutionary demonstration.

In any case, several days after his initial letter reporting the events of the funeral, Cullen again wrote Kirby attempting to have Propa-

21. Ryan, pp. 171–73.

22. Ibid., p. 173.

23. Ibid., p. 177. In an account quoted by Ryan, Thomas Clark Luby had noted at the time of the funeral, "The regular chaplain of the cemetery, pursuant to archepiscopal orders, I suppose, is conspicuous by his absence. Next Lavelle takes it upon him to deliver what he deems a patriotic harangue, which perhaps it may have been more or less." It must also be noted that Lavelle, by intimating in his impromptu oration that "solemn silence" was perhaps the better course on the occasion, and by then advising the mourners to disperse after the sacred words were said, was, whether intentionally or not, actually subverting the scheduled Fenian panegyric by Colonel Smith.

ganda take some action against Lavelle through MacHale. "All the respectable Catholics in Dublin," he assured Kirby on November 17,

> have been since asking, is there no law to punish such a man as Lavelle, who has given so much scandal? Is he to be allowed to trample on everyone with impunity[?] In order to have matters set right I have written an exposé of the whole business to the Cardinal, and sent him the three same documents I sent you. Try to get Lavelle's address translated. I could add his speech over McManus's grave, but it wd be useless to add anything to his address which was posted up in every corner of Dublin and in the neighboring towns and villages.
>
> The attempt to excite rebellion against the clergy was very wicked. However I trust that in a short time things will be right again. It was expected that meetings of the people wd be held all through Ireland to sympathize with the McManus obsequies committee—but this has not been done and the whole country has remained quiet. The men who came from America are probably dangerous fellows—one of them before he left Ireland attempted to burn a police barrack in Cappoquin. [K]

"Explain the affair to Cardinal Barnabò," Cullen suggested, "and make him send a philippic to the Leon of the West."

Indeed, the day before, November 16, Cullen had written a long and masterful letter to Barnabò in which he summed up the situation in Ireland for the cardinal prefect. Because the letter is useful, both as a summary and as an excellent example of the way Cullen told the truth he had to tell in dealing with Rome, it deserves to be quoted in full:

> Writing to your Eminence this month last year I was obliged to speak of the bad harvest that we had, and of the distress which consequently threatened the poor, but at the same time I added that our situation was to be much preferred to that of other countries which were subject to [in pieda] revolution, while we were exempted from the terrible calamity, although we had to see the people suffer the shortage of the means to live. This year unfortunately the harvest has been again destroyed by the continual rain, and the poor will have, without doubt, to suffer terribly in the coming winter and spring. I regret however that I am not able again to add that we are as immune from the effect of the revolutionary spirit, as we were able to boast ourselves to be twelve months ago. It is a strange thing to learn how that spirit has manifested itself among us in the last few weeks.
>
> Last January an Irishman named McManus died in California.

He had nothing to distinguish him or raise him above the level [*la torba*] of other men, if he had not been engaged in the year 1848 in a foolish revolutionary attempt here in Ireland, which was suppressed by a score of policemen without the intervention of regular troops. I said that the revolutionary attempt in which McManus was engaged was foolish, because in that year Ireland suffered a terrible famine, the typhoid fever claimed thousands of victims, and the people were without provisions, without money, and without arms. It was a real folly to excite such a people to resist the whole power of the English government, and they that have done it instead of being worshiped as heroes would deserve to be registered as lunatics. It is necessary to add that if perhaps the revolution went ahead, it is probable that religion in this country would have been destroyed, since the head of the revolution was a Protestant named Smith O'Brien, who in a work published afterwards showed himself infected by the principle of unbelief, and others of his companions fostered the maxims of Mazzini.

However that may be, McManus, of whom it is a question, without having done anything daring or worthy of admiration in any way, was arrested and condemned to death. Having been then pardoned, and sent into exile he was able to take refuge in America. He died there having first it is said received the sacraments of the church, and was buried in San Francisco.

Six or seven months after his death some crazy Americans and Irish determined to disinter him, and to transport the remains to Ireland, publicly declaring that they wanted recognition [*onore*] for the part taken by him in 1848, to manifest their adhesion to the revolutionary principle held by him, and to excite a revolutionary spirit in Ireland. To this object they engraved a figure of the Goddess of Liberty on the coffin that contained the remains of McManus, which Goddess held a liberty cap in one hand and with the other, signaled to the independence of Ireland, and those that brought the coffin to Ireland promised not to return without raising the standard of revolt. In this way matters were conducted in San Francisco and New York, and this is how they go on here in Dublin. The statements made in each place were openly revolutionary.

Before the remains of McManus arrived in Dublin a committee was constituted to receive them with honor. There were Protestants and Catholics on this committee, and some of them were known as persons who did not profess any religion. One of their first acts was to write to me asking me *to order* a solemn office and a requiem mass for McManus. They hoped to show the people in this way that they had the approval of the Catholic clergy and of the Church for the mad statements that they had made and for the maxims professed by McManus.

I found myself on this occasion in great embarrassment since I was certain to be insulted by the committee I have already described if I did not submit to their demands, and on the other hand I was afraid to give cause to the said committee to pretend to the people that the clergy favored revolution, if I placed myself in connection with men who did not take the trouble to give up their Mazzinian designs. Placed in these circumstances I asked the committee what marked services had McManus rendered to the church or to the country, and what were his merits, which would justify me in ordering a public funeral for a stranger, who had never lived in Dublin, and who had not any relation with our diocese, and not even with our province. This inquiry displeased the committee very much, but as there was no one able to give any other answer than the funeral was desired to honor the revolution, I was able to refuse every cooperation in the display that took place, and to save the clergy from doing anything that smacked of approval of the revolution. The committee and some newspapers threw themselves on me fiercely for the position I had taken, but all the regular and secular clergy of Dublin stood firm on the decision that I had mentioned, and no religious ceremony was held that could be connected with the revolutionary madness. There was however a great funeral procession held last Sunday at which were present perhaps twenty or twenty five thousand persons, almost all artisans or mechanics, but not one Catholic of any name or esteem took part.

Here perhaps it will be asked why the government did not prohibit this display? The reason is clear. In the first place as the people are without arms and without organization, the Government which has a powerful army, and a more powerful fleet, knows that the people can not make any serious move, and therefore permits them to amuse themselves. In the second place, it knows that these things divide the Catholics, and set them fighting among themselves. It also knows that by occupying the people with impractical madness, they no longer think about education and the condition of the poor and about other useful and necessary things, and so it allows a full field to do as it likes.

But to return to the funeral, it is necessary to mention a very great scandal that originated in connection with the same. While I and all the clergy of Dublin had taken up the role of not doing anything, a priest from the diocese of Tuam came to our city, who published a furious letter against me and my clergy and did all that he could to rouse the people to rebel against ecclesiastical authority. This priest is called Patrick Lavelle, and he is the same that raised the turbulence three years ago in the college in Paris, and gave so much scandal there. The letter of the priest was posted up in large letters in every corner of Dublin, and even in the surrounding villages. I am sending a copy of the letter to your Eminence in order that you may understand the cunning.

After Lavelle had published his proclamation, I wrote to Monsignor McHale sending a copy of it to him, and asking him to take some steps against Lavelle that he should judge suitable in the case. I enclose a copy of my letter, which was written with all due respect, as one might write to an archbishop.

Monsignor McHale however takes matters otherwise, and replies to me in a most discourteous way, and I may even say insolent. I am also sending an exact copy of his letter to confirm what I say. I will only add that Lavelle left thus to his own judgement by his ordinary, remained in Dublin for ten or fifteen days, and not only published the scandalous letter already mentioned, but even made patriotic speeches there almost every evening over the coffin of McManus, and harangued in a revolutionary sense at the grave when they were burying the remains of that pretended hero.

I believe that it is well that your Eminence knows these things so that you may be able to apply some remedy. The conduct of Lavelle has been the cause of affliction to good Catholics, and of exultation to all the enemies of the clergy. The good Catholics ask if a priest has the right to trample on the laws and all the proprieties with the consent, or at least with the connivance, of his ordinary? The scandal originated in this way is very great.

As for me I fear by the conduct of Monsignor McHale serious evils will arise if he does not receive orders from the Sacred Congregation to punish severely the misdeeds of Lavelle, and to force him to make some public reparation for the insults given to the clergy of Dublin, and for the scandal to all Ireland.

I leave the matter however in the hands of Your Eminence, but I hope that something will be done to prevent the evils that may arise from the conduct of priests like Lavelle when they are encouraged, or at least not curbed, by their superiors.

Before concluding it will not be out of place to mention the names of the priests who took part in the business of the McManus funeral—and who marched in the procession that took place on that occasion—the first is Patrick Lavelle already described from the diocese of Tuam, the second is a certain Kenyon of the diocese of Killaloe, who was involved in the rebellion of 1848, and who in general does not wish to obey his bishop—the third is a certain Courtenay [*sic*], priest of the diocese of Birmingham—the fourth an old Capuchin named Ashe. These among all the priests of Ireland wanted to take part in the demonstration that was made. Thus, thanks be to God, the clergy conducted themselves very well. I believe also that this abstention of the clergy will have the effect of preventing what the promoters of the McManus funeral wanted, I mean the propagation of revolutionary ideas and maxims.[24]

Perhaps the most interesting thing about this letter is what it reveals about Cullen's attitude toward revolution. He condemns the rising of the Young Irelanders in 1848, for example, not because it is inherently wicked to resist established authority but rather because the people were without money or arms and were laid low by famine and fever. The rising was also to be deplored because its leadership was Protestant or infidel, and the principles involved were Mazzinian. The day before he had written to Barnabò, Cullen had made his position with regard to revolution even clearer in a letter to Laurence Gillooly, the bishop of Elphin. "The whole McManus affair," he assured Gillooly on November 15, "wd seem to have been got up to turn away people's minds from everything useful, and to fill them with a wild revolutionary spirit. Some engaged in asking for religious ceremonies, were protestants, some infidels, who wd delight in setting us all by the ears. The great bulk of the poor people are now convinced that the exhibition was foolish and wicked" (G). "What a time," he added, "to promote revolutionary scheme[s], when the people are starving, and not a gun or an ounce of powder in their hands."[25] What would Cullen have said, it might well be asked, if the people were well armed and prepared, the leadership was impeccably Catholic, and the

24. S.R.C., vol. 34, fols. 190–92.
25. See ibid., fols. 207–8, Cullen to Barnabò, November 29, 1861, for more in the same vein.

end to be achieved was a Catholic confessional state rather than a secular Mazzinian republic? Cullen would have replied, of course, that in the context of the 1860s no answer was required because the propositions were all in the realm of fantasy. Still, it must be noted, Cullen's condemnation did not foreclose on a revolution in a just cause with a reasonable chance of success endorsed by a whole people. This was, in effect, the line that would be taken by the Irish Church for the next sixty years.

In his letter to Barnabò, moreover, Cullen had also decided to try to persuade the Roman authorities to take action against Lavelle through MacHale rather than to attempt to punish the offending priest himself. He had also carefully refrained from either overtly criticizing those members of the American hierarchy, especially Archbishop Hughes of New York, who had given their official blessing to the McManus demonstrations or noticing the action of the bishop of Cloyne in giving sanctuary to McManus's remains in a Queenstown church. Cullen did, however, cite the three priests who with Lavelle participated in the funeral ceremonies in his diocese. In all this it was obvious that Cullen was determined to pursue a consistent line by not saying or doing anything that was not covered by his own spiritual jurisdiction unless he received a clear mandate to do so from the Roman authorities. This decision was to prove a very significant one for the constitutional development of the Irish Church in the next decade. Finally, in his letter to Barnabò, Cullen cleverly set up an implicit cause-and-effect relationship between the two recent successive harvest failures and the rise of the Fenian and St. Patrick's Brotherhoods, a step that tended to lay the blame for their development on economic circumstances rather than on any lapse in Irish clerical zeal.

———◆———

Indeed, the harvest of 1861 had been even worse than the harvest of 1860, which had been the worst since that of the dreadful famine year of 1847 (see table).[26] How serious the harvest failure of 1861 was, and what the consequences were likely to be for the poor, especially in the west of Ireland, were well illustrated in a letter from Laurence Gillooly, the bishop of Elphin, to Kirby in early November. Gillooly, who had been one of the few Irish bishops to inaugurate a monthly collec-

26. If the average yields of 1856–58 are taken as the norm, oats, wheat, and barley were respectively down 12 percent, 31 percent, and 17 percent in 1861. The decrease in potatoes was an incredible 58 percent in 1861. See Donnelly, p. 37.

Crop Yields in Ireland, 1859–1863
(Percentage Deviation from Average Yields of 1856–1858)

Year	Oats	Wheat	Barley	Flax	Potatoes	Turnips	Hay
1859	91	102	94	92	95	84	84
1860	99	88	101	107	61	65	105
1861	88	69	83	88	42	80	95
1862	81	62	83	94	55	79	95
1863	101	104	107	116	89	93	95

SOURCE: Donnelly, p. 37

tion for the pope on a regular basis in his diocese, was finally forced to write to Kirby explaining why he was obliged to suspend them. "Our Peter's Pence collections," he reported on November 7 from Sligo,

would be far more successful were it not for the failure of the crops, especially of the potato crop—which is I regret to say very great and general throughout this diocese. We have no more than one third of an average potato crop—and the quality of what is saved is generally bad. They are by themselves unfit for human food. The price of Indian meal and oat meal is still moderate and I hope likely to continue so—but the people have not the money to buy—and unless they get extensive employment from the Landlords and the Government, there will be a great amount of destitution, which the Poor Law system will not or cannot relieve. I am at this moment providing information and preparing for public meetings in the hope of stimulating the Landlords and the Government to timely interference. I believe they set more value on our lives now than they did in forty-seven. [K]

He assured Kirby in concluding, "The people are, T. G.—everywhere industrious and peaceable. Our poor dear country presents in these respects and in all that appertains to religion and charity, the most consoling contrast with the other countries of the world. True religion and piety are becoming more widely diffused with education—the habits of our clergy are improved—they labour with untiring zeal—and never perhaps were they more loved and esteemed by their flocks."

The bishops and clergy in the west of Ireland soon took up Gillooly's example, and the reports of their activities received a good deal of attention in the nationalist press. Typical perhaps was the meeting of the clergy of the deanery of Castlebar on November 26, with the archdeacon of the archdiocese of Tuam presiding, at which the following resolutions were unanimously adopted:

Resolved—that the disastrous effects of the present inclement
season in the destruction of the potato crop, have created among
the people of this district the most alarming anticipations of an
impending famine vitally affecting the interests of all classes in
the community.

That we have carefully investigated the grounds of the general
alarm, and we feel it our bounden duty to the people, as well as
to the country, to state that scarcely one-fourth of the potato
crop of this year is safe from the ravages of the blight, and that
even this small remnant is so inferior in quality as to be unfit for
human food.

That no human foresight could have provided against a calamity so unforeseen as the destruction of the food of an entire people, and, therefore, that the salvation of the lives of the people
demands that the most prompt and comprehensive measures be
adopted by the government, to avert the horrors of famine with
which we are threatened.

That the unprecedented scarcity of fuel this year cannot fail to
add considerably to the privations which the poor are doomed to
suffer during the ensuing five months, and unless remedial measures be speedily procured, fever and dysentery, created by damp
and cold, will spread to an alarming extent amongst them.[27]

Some ten days before the western clergy had begun to move into
action, Cullen had also written Kirby in some alarm. "The winter," he
reported on November 17, "threatens to be very severe for the poor.
The potatoes are nearly all gone. The oats are bad—there is scarcely
any turf. What will become of the poor creatures?" (K). "Sir Robert
Peel," he explained, referring to the new Liberal chief secretary, who
had replaced Edward Cardwell in July, "has gone to visit the West to
be able to say that he examined things himself. His report probably
will be that the Government ought to leave the people to their own
resources and [not] to interfere with the corn merchants who expect
to enrich themselves on the miseries of the poor." "Some Scotch merchants in Sligo," he further charged, "proclaimed this maxim. Let the
poor starve, but do not interfere with our prospects of making money.
The same Scotchmen amassed large fortunes in the famine of 1847–8.
We may say to them *Pecunia tua est tecu in perditionem* [Your money
has been your damnation]." "Dr. Gillooly," Cullen noted in conclusion, "asked for an interview with Sir Robt. Peel in Sligo to explain

27. I.C.D., 1862, p. 268.

the state of the poor but the Baronet wd not receive him. It requires patience to hear such things but *est Deus in Israel* [there is a God in Israel]."

At the end of November the bishop of Cloyne, William Keane, took occasion to advise Kirby that given the very severe distress then prevailing not much could be done to establish the Peter's pence collection on a more regular basis in his diocese. Writing from Fermoy in county Cork, Keane explained on November 29, "A potato crop about as bad as in '47, and the worst corn crops ever remembered, and almost incessant rain, make fuel, food, work, and money unusually scarce" (K). A month later Cullen reported to Kirby that though the distress was very severe in the west, and was likely to become in time worse everywhere, the poor had been mercifully granted some respite in that at least the winter had turned very mild. "The distress is pretty grave in the west," he explained on December 27, "but it is not easy to get accurate information. Here as usual many poor, but the misery is not as yet greater than last year. However in the spring & summer things will be worse, as [i.e., when] the potatoes are all gone" (K). "God grant," he then added, "the fine weather may continue. There is a great dearth of fuel, as the turf could not be dried. The fine weather is a great blessing for the poor."

One of the important reasons why the distress was less serious in Dublin and in the north, east, and south of Ireland generally than in the west, as the winter deepened, was that the price of grain and particularly Indian meal was relatively cheap. Indeed, the crisis in the west was the result less of a shortage of food, as the bishop of Elphin had earlier pointed out to Kirby, than of the lack of ready money to purchase that food. The situation affecting the cost of food, however, had been seriously complicated by the ultimatum lately delivered by the British government to the American Federal government because one of the latter's naval vessels had intercepted a British ship on the high seas and removed two representatives of the Confederate States of America. The incident had very nearly brought the two nations to war, and the Irish, most of whose Indian meal was imported from America, were naturally much alarmed. "There are many conjectures," Bartholomew Moore, a curate in Multyfarnham in the diocese of Meath, reported to Kirby on January 2, 1862, "as to how a war with America would affect the markets. I am very much afraid provisions would rise and increase the miseries of the poor" (K). "There is no extreme want in this parish," he then explained, "but then there are a great many families almost on the verge of extreme want. They by great exertions make out sufficient for each day, but then they cannot say whether they will have anything for their dinner the next day. I see in the papers that there are parts of Ireland[,] particularly the West[,] where whole families are reduced to extreme want and in many cases actual starvation, so that the people are suffering an immensity."

Though the crisis with the American Federal government was satisfactorily resolved early in the new year, the British government's apparent lack of concern over the increasing distress in Ireland brought forth a steady stream of complaints in the press from the Irish clergy. Cullen took advantage of the government's bad press to call a meeting of a number of prominent clergy and laity at his residence in Dublin on January 23, at which a series of resolutions was unanimously adopted demanding the complete reform of the Irish poor-law system in reference to Catholics.[28] Several days later, when Cullen wrote Kirby about his recent efforts on behalf of the poor, he was still not only very upset at the government's continued lack of concern but also very annoyed by the attitude of its chief municipal representative, the lord mayor of Dublin. "The distress here," he reported on January 29, "is very great. The Government cd afford to give £500,000 to the Queen's Colleges, but it cannot afford a bajocco [twopence] for the poor. In summer I fear we shall have a famine or almost a famine. I sent a paper containing an acct. of resolutions adopted at a meeting I held here. I hope we shall get up a little agitation" (K). "There was a dinner ere yesterday," he then noted, referring to his latest effort on behalf of the poor, "of the Society of S. Vincent of Paul. I attended and we had a gt Catholic display of about 200 of the most respectable gentlemen of Dublin." "I was consulted," he explained, "about the *toasts* and made them put the *Pope* in 1° loco. The Lord Mayor, a Catholic, refused to attend because the Queen was not given the place of honour—at a religious society's meeting." "What a Catholic!" Cullen concluded, adding for good measure, "He has his son at Trinity College."

In the next few weeks, however, Cullen and the lord mayor apparently made their peace, at least to the extent that they joined in forming the Mansion House Relief Committee for the aid of the distressed poor. The committee, which was launched on February 17, soon became as much a vehicle for publicizing the plight of the poor as a modest source for their relief.[29] The western clergy, in particular, took

28. Ibid., 1863, p. 212.
29. Ibid., p. 224, June 12, 1862. "The Mansion-house Relief Committee publish a report from its formation on 17th February, to 31st May, 1862, in which from most authentic sources, and letters from the clergy and laity of about 50 parishes, mostly in

pains to accompany their requests for aid from the committee with doleful accounts of the sufferings of their poor. In explaining to Kirby on February 21 that the distress was deepening, and that the monthly Peter's pence collections he had recently inaugurated in Dublin were getting on slowly, Cullen suggested that perhaps the pope might be able to give the new relief committee some stimulation (K). "It would be well," he advised Kirby, "if the Pope were to send us £50 or £100 and authorise me to hand it into the hands of our relief committee out of the sums I may have for Peter's pence." "Such a thing," he assured Kirby, "wd produce a great effect on the Protestants and wd shame them to contribute. Sir Rob. Peel declares there is no distress. The Protestants all take up the same note because the poor are [not] Protestants—one way or other the poor are to be exterminated." "I have," Cullen reported to Kirby a month later, on March 21, "rec^d £100 from the Pope for the poor. I send a paper from which it will appear that the donation was well rec^d" (K). "The committee for relieving the poor," he then further explained, "is going on slowly—the Government has prevented by its declarations all Protestants and its own adherents from subscribing. *Intanto* [Meanwhile] the poor are suffering severely. Even here in Dublin we have gt distress. Provisions are low [i.e., in price] except meat, which is extravagantly dear. Indian corn is £7 10 s. a ton—in '48 I believe it was over £30. I hope the poor law bill be amended."

Given the various *ex parte* statements by the government on the one side and the western clergy on the other, it is difficult to gauge exactly what the actual level of distress was in Ireland. Some corrective is certainly provided in a letter to Kirby from Dominick Murphy, the very able dean and vicar-general of the diocese of Cork, who had just spent the winter in Rome on ecclesiastical business. "The cry of famine," Murphy maintained in writing Kirby on his return to Cork city on March 14, "that has been raised here and elsewhere has not been warranted by any very urgent necessity, at least in the South of Ireland" (K). "Though there is some increase," Murphy admitted, "in the distress of the larger towns, beyond other years; and the smaller occupiers and poor class of farmers are very much pressed and pinched by the succession of two wet and deficient harvests, there is abundance of food and it is cheaper than it has been in the beginning of the year." "The very lowest class," he further explained,

---

the West of Ireland, and in utter contradiction of the stupid or worse assertion of the English Protestant Secretary for Ireland [Sir Robert Peel], is set forth a mass of misery never known under the most despotic rulers."

such as labourers etc. are not the worst off, as there is very excellent remuneration for them and food is cheap; the small farmers and poor shopkeepers are those whose condition is the worst. I hope in the beginning of summer that all the poor will be in the enjoyment of work who are able to do it, and the conclusion to which I have come is, that though there is much said in the newspapers and elsewhere of great distress throughout the country, especially in the remoter districts, and therefore that probably there is some beyond the usual amount, that as far as I can see and hear from others with whom I have personal intercourse, there is scarcely anything beyond the usual condition of the poor and the people in winter.

Murphy's letter, of course, raises at least three important questions: how serious the distress was, where it was most prevalent, and what portion of the population was most affected. Without more detailed work in Irish social and economic history for this period, any answer to those questions must be tentative and largely impressionistic. Indeed, the general impression one gains from the clerical correspondence was that the distress was serious, that it became more serious as one moved west, and that the people most affected were those at the base of the social and economic pyramid. The clerical correspondence, however, also suggests that a number of important qualifications must be immediately applied to those rather simple propositions. First, there was no real danger of famine or starvation because food, and particularly Indian meal, remained plentiful and relatively cheap. Second, the sufferings reported in the press must be taken with a large grain of salt because they were mainly articulated by those western clergy under either the jurisdiction or the influence of that inveterate enemy of the British connection, John MacHale, the archbishop of Tuam. Finally, the brunt of the distress fell mainly on the destitute poor, the small-farming class, and the marginal shopkeepers, rather than on those laborers and cottagers who were able to earn a money wage.

Whatever the truth may have really been, there is little doubt that the intense campaign waged in the press by an indignant clergy and laity complaining of the suffering of the Irish poor and the British government's apparent indifference to it was certainly creating a climate of opinion that was becoming more and more congenial to political extremism. What Cullen in particular, and his clerical and lay supporters in general, did not apparently realize was that encouraging the denunciations of the government without committing themselves to an effective constitutional alternative was to play into the hands of the Fenian recruiters and the advocates of physical force. Priests such as Lavelle and Kenyon, therefore, could at least in this context be credited with attempting to prevent the initiative in Irish politics from falling entirely to the extremists by committing themselves to the side of the militant left in constitutional politics. Indeed, in the next few years Lavelle would make a veritable one-man stand among the clergy to preserve the image of the "patriot priest" in the national political spectrum. He was able, however, to sustain himself for as long as he did only because he had in effect the covert blessing of his diocesan, the archbishop of Tuam.

MacHale's long and arduous campaign on behalf of Lavelle had actually begun in early November, when MacHale replied to the letter Cullen wrote complaining about Lavelle's conduct immediately previous to the McManus funeral. In his reply on November 11, MacHale had informed Cullen briefly and insolently that he would forward his letter to Lavelle, who could answer for himself.[30] When Lavelle did finally reply on November 21, he explained to Cullen that he was sorry his letter had not pleased him and that he had not wished to give offense to any one, except the enemies of their holy religion, dear country, and Holy Father.[31] He thought, moreover, that his letter had done a great deal of good and regained a great many for religion. Because of English rule, Lavelle further maintained, religion had suffered, the country and the farmers were in misery, and their people were being evicted because they would not send their children to heretical schools. He then concluded by replying to Cullen's complaint that his letter had been posted up all over Dublin and that he had done nothing about it; it was no fault of his, he said, it had happened before he had ever arrived in Dublin. Needless to say, Cullen was not much appeased by Lavelle's apologia, and he forwarded the letter to Kirby for submission to Propaganda. "I send you a letter of F. Lavelle," he explained on November 26. "You will see how he tried to gloss over all his scandals. Dr. McHale is greatly to be blamed for letting such a man loose on the country" (K). Kirby replied on December 6 that he had submitted the letter and requested the authorities at Propaganda to take appropriate action.[32]

Meanwhile, Cullen had taken occasion in a pastoral to be read in

30. S.R.C., vol. 34, fol. 209.
31. Ibid., fols. 198–200.
32. Patrick J. Corish, "Political Problems, 1860–1878," in *A History of Irish Catholicism*, gen. ed. Patrick J. Corish (Dublin, 1967), 5:7, n. 15.

all the churches of his diocese on the first Sunday of Advent, December 1, to denounce secret societies, while at the same time pleading for greater efforts to be made on behalf of the suffering poor.[33] "Any one," he asserted, "who reads the history of secret societies for the last seventy years, and observes the effects of the revolutions which they have produced, will look on them with horror, and make every exertion to preserve himself and his country from so terrible a scourge. It cannot be denied that wherever secret societies and a revolutionary spirit prevail, religion is soon destroyed, and the worst principles of error and indifferentism introduced." "For these and other reasons," he then informed his clergy, "you will caution your flocks against all illegal combinations and secret societies, it matters not by what name they may be designated, and you will point out to them the censures and excommunications to which all Catholics are subjected who bind themselves by oath in such secret societies." "All Catholics," Cullen maintained, "enrolling themselves in Freemasons or Ribbonmen, or entering into any society or brotherhood established for purposes detrimental to civil society or religion, and bound by secrecy to oath, fall under the severest penalties, and are, *ipso facto*, excommunicated; their lot is miserable, indeed, for they are cut off like rotten branches from the Church."

The reason why Cullen refrained in his pastoral from denouncing the Brotherhood of St. Patrick by name was that the Brotherhood maintained that it was not an oath-bound society, and Cullen was aware that he could be sued for libel for saying it was. On December 10, several days after his pastoral was read, Cullen reported to Kirby that he had learned that the head of the Brotherhood was a Calvinist by the name of Underwood, who was assisted by two Catholics whose names were yet unknown (K). It also appears that those who supported the Brotherhood had recommended that instead of contributing to the Peter's pence, which Cullen had just inaugurated on a regular basis in Dublin in October, Irishmen would be better served if they contributed to a "Patrick's pence" and forwarded their contributions to Archbishop MacHale. In the next few weeks Cullen became increasingly upset by the turn events were taking, and when he had not heard by the end of December of any action being taken or contemplated by Rome with regard to Lavelle and MacHale, he became more uneasy. "I have never," he complained to Kirby on December 27, "heard a word from Propg. about the Lavelle business. He however exceeded bounds so much that I suppose he will scarcely leave home again. He has

33. Moran, 1:869, November 27, 1861.

never been in Dublin since—a word to Dr. McH. wd do him good, *ma si sa alla Prop. temono i Leoni* [but it is known they fear Lions at Propaganda]" (K). "The 'Patrick's Pence,'" Cullen further explained, "of which I sent you the *avviso* [notice] appears to have been a failure. There is no further mention of it in the papers—but it showed a bad disposition in those who set it a foot. The McManus affair is now about forgotten. The only thing I now fear is the establishment of secret societies. They are most ruinous, and it so happens, that they are managed by Protestants. The head of the Brothers of St. Patrick is a Protestant, and the managers not Catholics—but no one can denounce them[,] otherwise you would be exposed to legal prosecutions."

In early January 1862, however, Kirby was able to inform Cullen that Rome had finally taken some action. "It was a great pleasure," Cullen replied in Italian on January 17, "to hear that Propaganda had written to Monsignor McHale concerning Father Lavelle. Up to now however no result is seen. That priest has been in Dublin for *15* days, and I believe that his occupation is to promote the interests of the so-called Brotherhood of St. Patrick, which is really a secret society in the Mazzinian style" (K). "Their cry is," he argued, "long live Father Lavelle, down with the Dublin clergy. I remember having heard the Mazzinians shout in the time of the Republic, long live Padre Gavazzi, death to the Cardinals and the Pope. Father Lavelle goes about collecting, it appears, what he still calls Patrick's pence. He has contracted many debts and seeks to find the means to pay them with this collection that he makes here in Dublin." About a week later Cullen had apparently had enough of Lavelle's soliciting funds in his diocese without his permission and again wrote MacHale to complain. He explained to Kirby on January 29, "I wrote four or five days ago to Dr. McH. complaining of his subject, but he has not answered" (K). "Monsig^r Rinaldini's advice," Cullen added, referring to one of the officials at Propaganda, "is very good, but I do not wish to *imbrogliarmi con un prete matto* [involve myself with a crazy priest]. I wish to leave the imbroglio to his own Bishop who lets him go ahead. It wd be a strange business for me to take on myself the management of Dr. McH.'s priests and to let him then come out as the gt. defender of ecclesiastical liberty, and show me up as invading his rights." "The Propaganda," he finally pointed out, "if it is not determined to renounce its power ought to make Dr. McH. do his duty, or write to me to act under their authority."

By the time Cullen had written Kirby this letter, however, he had already learned that Lavelle had just raised the stakes in their ongoing political game. "Lavelle," he explained to his cousin and Kirby's vice-rector, Patrick Moran, in another letter that same day, "is about to give a lecture 'On the Catholic doctrine of the right to revolt' " (K). "I fear," Cullen concluded grimly, "he will do great mischief." In reporting Lavelle's lecture, the *Guardian* of London noted on February 12 that he "read from Thomas Aquinas to prove the right of the people to revolt against tyranny. Government is established for the good of the people; and when it loses sight of that end the people have a right to overthrow it; nay it is their duty if they are able." Lavelle "went on to prove that the Government of Ireland was far from being a good one" and then admitted " 'with shame, with a blush on his cheek, and with a down-looking brow, that he was born a slave.' But he had a light in his soul which pointed the way in which he would not die a slave." "The drift of the lecture," the *Guardian* concluded, "appears from the report to be that Ireland is so misgoverned that she has a right to revolt against the Queen, and in so doing she would have the sanction of the Church."

Meanwhile, MacHale had replied to Cardinal Barnabò's letter complaining about Lavelle's peregrinations by explaining that the priest in question had been absent from his parish for only a few days. Barnabò reported this letter to Cullen, and Cullen wrote Kirby on February 16, explaining that the cardinal should be advised not to write to Mac-Hale any more because Lavelle had, in fact, been absent from his parish for at least three months since the McManus funeral in early November (K). Several days later Cullen reported to Kirby that Lavelle was still in Dublin. "I send you a copy of the *News*," he explained on February 21, "in which you will see a letter from him dated in this city. He is here since last October more or less, except when he runs to other towns to lecture" (K). "Every day," Cullen added, "there are new proofs that the Brothers of S. Patrick are nothing more or less than Irish Mazzinians. I don't mean all, but the principal among them, and little by little the leaven will spread. It is a sad thing that there is no power to control a priest who favors and encourages such a sect." "I had a letter," he noted further, "from a Rev^d Mr. McDonald priest in Dundee Scotland. He says the Brothers are worse than Protestants there in their attacks on the priests. I am thinking seriously of suspending Lavelle. I have plenty of ground to go on. When his own Bishop lets him loose on the world, someone else must control him. He is getting some money, not much—and it is this that keeps him here. The Patrick's pence is a failure. It is to be sent to Dr. McHale to be disposed of by him." "I have just seen F. Timothy Mahony of Cork," he then finally reported, referring to a former student of the Irish College in Rome, "quondam of S. Agatha's. He says the Brothers of S.

Patrick are widely spread in the south, and doing mischief. He says they are mere *carbonari*. Unfortunately there are several priests, he says, mixed up with them. But what is that to Milan were according to the Armonia of today the ecclesiastical club counts about 150 *preti—"*

Even as Cullen's difficulties and perplexities with regard to Lavelle and the Brotherhood of St. Patrick increased, he was also involved with an ongoing verbal duel with the chief secretary for Ireland, Sir Robert Peel, who not only had denied that there was any serious cause for alarm about the distress among the Irish poor but also had earlier stirred up an educational hornet's nest by attempting to solicit the aid of a considerable number of the Catholic gentry in support of the Queen's Colleges. When the chief secretary then had the temerity to propose that perhaps religious property in Ireland should be taxed, Cullen denounced him and his proposal in a letter to the press.[34] This contretemps, moreover, took place in the midst of a by-election for county Longford, where Major Myles O'Reilly, the late commander of the pope's Irish Brigade and the hero of the siege of Spoleto, had offered himself as a candidate. The election soon became a test of strength between the government and the Catholic clergy, high and low. "An election," Cullen informed Kirby on February 25, "is to take place in Longford next Monday, just when you receive this. Myles O'Reilly is put forward by Dr. Kilduff and clergy. A Col. White is put forward to represent Lord Palm. and Sir Rob. Peel. There will be a severe struggle—if O'Reilly be returned, it will be a triumph, if he be beaten, we shall all be trampled underfoot" (K). "Dr. Kilduff," he assured Kirby, naming the bishop of Ardagh, "will fight to the last—but all the Tories and Whigs coalesce against the Catholic." The landlord combination, however, was unable to prevent the bishop of Ardagh and his clergy from winning a very considerable victory: O'Reilly was elected by 1,468 votes to 892 votes for White.[35] The lesson, of course, was that when the clergy and laity were united on their choice of candidate, their combined political will was still irresistible.

Father Lavelle and his friends did not allow Cullen to enjoy his brief moment of political respite for very long. Shortly before St. Patrick's Day, it was announced in the press that the Brotherhood of St. Patrick would hold a large dinner in Dublin on its name day and that Lavelle would attend. He was, in fact, unable to be present because he was previously engaged to speak at another gathering of the brothers that

34. *Freeman's Journal*, March 6, 1862. See also Chapter III, pp. 142–43.
35. Brian M. Walker, ed., *Parliamentary Election Results in Ireland, 1801–1922* (Dublin, 1978), p. 100.

same evening in Glasgow. Two priests, however, did attend and speak at the Dublin banquet. In rising to reply to the first toast of the evening—"The Irish People, the only legitimate source of power"—Father Jeremiah Vaughan, a priest of the Killaloe diocese, explained amid loud applause that he "had intended to be a silent spectator of the proceedings of the evening, but he would be dead to every feeling of his heart if he was indifferent to the call made upon him by any portion of his warm-hearted fellow-countrymen (applause)."[36] After noting that he was "one of the people," Vaughan then pointed out that he was "above all, one of the priesthood of the people." He believed, moreover, that their great strength in Ireland was that their Church was a voluntary and not an established one and that if they remained self-reliant and kept careful watch on their leaders and the press, "Ireland would be godlike in her march (applause)." Vaughan added that he was delighted with the progress nationality had made among them, and as far as the clergy were concerned, he would advise the people to "obey them when they taught the sound doctrines of faith and morals; but suppose a portion of the clergy in their civil capacity, enunciated a doctrine redolent of wrotten [sic] Whiggery, and subversive of nationality, it was their duty to follow their own course, and he had no hesitation in saying that until the Irish people understood that they would not proceed in the career of nationality. He could not understand how any enlightened Catholic could not follow that course and at the same time have a true respect for the clergy of his church (hear, hear)."

In rising to speak to the second toast of the evening—"The patriotic priesthood of Ireland"—Father John Kenyon began by admitting that though he did not have a "precise programme or advice to give them with respect to the future," he did think they were assembled there for a useful purpose that evening.[37] "What were they there for that night?" he asked. "They were there," he then replied,

> to protest that they were not free (cheers). Then being slaves how could they become free? Could they do it by parliamentary agitation? (no, no). Did they mean to say that they could do it by moral force? (no, no). Certainly never (cheers). It was a strange thing that enslaved men never yet won their freedom except by the strength of their arms (cheers). They could not explain it, perhaps, but so it was; they could not get into the position of

36. *Freeman's Journal*, March 18, 1862.
37. Ibid.

freemen unless they could win it by fair fight. The third question was, could they win it by fair fight? (cries of yes).

"No, no," Kenyon replied, "they were in the wrong there. It was a mistake and a delusion to suppose that." "What were they to do?" he then asked. "They were," he advised, "whenever they could—whenever the way was opened to them—to be free; but they should not indulge in fantastic and false notions (cheers). Three points were then established—first that they were slaves; second, that they could not be freemen unless they were able to win it by a fair fight; thirdly, that they were not able to win it at present (cries of 'we are,' and 'no, no'). But they were disposed and determined." "Two things were most important," Kenyon emphasized:

> first, they should be most tolerant to all classes of their country-men (cheers). At present they had bigots and fanatics preaching from high pulpits base and bad doctrines (hear, hear). People were at work for the English government, with very leading names too, setting Irishman against Irishman, Catholic against his honest Protestant and Presbyterian countrymen. He would tell that the soul of a Presbyterian Irishman was as valuable in the sight of God who made it, in the sight of Christ who redeemed it, in the sight of the Holy Ghost who watched over it, as the soul of any Catholic priest or bishop or hierarch (loud cheers). They were there that night to establish the principle of free toleration. No matter how high the pulpit from which the doctrine of bigotry was preached they denounced and despised it (cheers).

The second thing that was important besides tolerance, Kenyon then explained, was patience: "if they were patient, and always preserved in their hearts the true principles of nationality, which twenty generations of their countrymen fought and suffered for, died on the scaffold and in exile—if they kept that principle alive, and were patient, and were not led away into improbable speculations, but put their trust in God, and were tolerant to each other, although nothing definite was to be expected from that evening, yet the very gathering he saw around him would be an act of triumph in itself, and a stage toward their ultimate liberation (loud cheers)."

The most interesting thing about Vaughan's and Kenyon's speeches, perhaps, was really how moderate they were. Except for their respective allusions to Cullen in denouncing "Whiggery" and "bigotry," their speeches were, in fact, politically very tame. Vaughan had little to offer in the way of a practical program, and Kenyon actually rejected physical force as providing any immediate solution to making Ireland free. Cullen, however, affected to be scandalized by their action and immediately wrote Kirby citing them both. "At the meeting of the Brothers of St. Patrick here in Dublin yesterday," he explained in Italian on March 18, "two priests from the diocese of Killaloe were present. Both are already well known for their strange past conduct. I believe they do not consider themselves bound to obey their Bishop, Monsignor Flannery, who is entirely opposed to their madness. The scene that they made will be, without doubt, cause of grave damage to the clergy and to religion" (K). What Cullen still did not realize was that this was yet another attempt by Kenyon and his friends on the constitutional left to prevent the Fenians from having it all their own way, especially with regard to control of the Brotherhood of St. Patrick.

This position was made evident by the fact that both Vaughan and Kenyon spoke and also by the choice of John Martin as principal speaker of the evening. Martin, it will be recalled, had been Kenyon's chief supporter in his effort to prevent the Fenians from completely dominating the McManus funeral. If The O'Donoghue, moreover, had not been prevented from attending the banquet by the serious illness of his wife, the dominance of the constitutional left would have been even greater than it was. In the course of his long speech, Martin actually said that he had "no objection to anyone opposing secret societies—he saw no use for them, no occasion for them in Ireland under present circumstances, and was quite sure they might be perverted to very mischievous purposes. What, however, he would respectfully urge upon the consideration of the clergy was, that secret societies were a small matter when considered along with foreign rule, and that the first thing to be done in Ireland, for the cause of morality and religion, was to drive out the foreign rule (cheers)."[38] Martin was then followed by T. N. Underwood, whom Cullen had denounced to Kirby as the head of the Brotherhood of St. Patrick and a Calvinist. Underwood proceeded to deny flatly that he was

> in any way connected with secret associations, or that he approved of secret political organizations in the present conditions of Ireland. He also read a letter which he addressed to his Grace the Archbishop of Dublin on this subject, in which he assured his Grace that the National Brotherhood was a legal association, and not a secret body and that the doctrines or teachings were

38. Ibid.

not opposed to the Catholic Church no more than were those of the Catholic Association; also that he (Mr. Underwood) had always inculcated that a good patriot should be a good man, and that attachment to religion was the first sign of virtue.[39]

Cullen, however, was not impressed by all the various disclaimers, and he continued to keep up his barrage of complaints (reinforced by newspaper clippings) to both Kirby and the authorities at Propaganda about the brothers in general and Lavelle in particular. The main burden of Cullen's effort, of course, was to persuade Propaganda of the increasing seriousness of the situation created by Lavelle and his supporters and the consequent necessity of compelling MacHale to discipline his refractory subject.[40] "I have sent you," he informed Kirby on April 1, "several papers regarding the Brotherhood of S. Patrick. Read the *Irishman* of Saturday 29th March and you will remain convinced that the spirit is the same as that of the Young Irelanders in '48 and of the U. Irishmen in 1798. Their heroes are Emmett, the Shearses, Wolfe Tone, protestants or infidels and the whole tendency of the movement is to excite the people against the clergy" (K). "You will see," Cullen added, "they have put Dr. Machale's [sic] likeness between those of Emmet and Sheares, his grace will not like that, but why let his subject declare himself a brother & president of a lodge[?]"

In spite of Cullen's efforts, the Propaganda authorities continued to drag their feet. Their reason undoubtedly had to do with Cullen's having requested permission in mid-February to convene a general meeting of the Irish bishops to examine the state of the education question.[41] Barnabò, who had approved of the meeting, hoped that the bishops would at the same time settle the vexatious question of Father Lavelle and the Brotherhood of St. Patrick. When Cullen informed the Irish bishops on April 5 that a meeting had been ordered on the education question, he also noted in outlining the agenda that it seemed "desirable to examine the nature and tendency of some societies or brotherhoods now spreading through the country" (G). Whatever Cullen thought would be the result of the bishops' meeting, which was scheduled for May 6 in Dublin, he continued to hammer away about Lavelle in his usual stubborn fashion. He advised Kirby on April 15, "I sent you the *Irishman* of last Saturday. You will see in it that F. Lavelle has been elected Vic. Pres. of the Brotherhood of S.

39. Ibid.
40. S.R.C., vol. 34, fol. 353, Cullen to Barnabò, March 21, 1862; Peadar MacSuibhne, *Paul Cullen and His Contemporaries*, vol. 4 (Naas, 1974), pp. 113–14.
41. K, Cullen to Kirby, February 14, 1862.

Patrick, and that he is to lecture on S. Laurence in Dublin soon after Easter. *Pare che le parole di Roma non producono molto effetto* [It seems that the words of Rome do not produce much effect]" (K). "The brothers are," he explained, "I think beginning to fall away. They are getting no money—besides some of them fear to be excommunicated. Several have come to my house to give up. They swear to fight *pro Republ. Hibern* [for an Irish Republic]—they do not know who their head is, and who to command. . . . I guess that the head is some honest detective who will entrap them all." "Dr. Flannery," Cullen then reported, referring to the bishop of Killaloe, "is greatly displeased with Fathers Kennyon [*sic*] & Vaughan but I believe he can scarcely manage them. I will put in a paragr. on the Brotherhood in the pastoral for May. There is no doubt that it comes under the Bull of Leo XIIth." "Many are calling on me," he finally noted in a postscript, "to suspend Lavelle—he deserves it—but it is almost better not to make too much of him. I am often tempted to suspend him—but then if he break down himself, it will be better."

A week later Cullen wrote Kirby again. "The Brothers of S. Patrick," he reported on April 22, "are beginning to decline. A knock from the Bishops wd kill them out—but I fear some of them are afraid—to take any public step, and some say they have no existence in their dioceses. Dr. McHale if he come, will say that anything against them, is a measure against his clergy, or a member of it[,] F. Lavelle" (K). "I got the letter about the Brothers," he then assured Kirby. "I was going to denounce them in the pastoral for May—but I will now say little." But even the little that Cullen had to say was not allowed to pass by Lavelle. "In the pastoral letter of his Grace the Archbishop of Dublin," Lavelle declared in an open letter on April 29 to the members of the National Brotherhood of St. Patrick, "as published in the Dublin papers of yesterday, I find the following passage: —'Caution your flocks against Secret Societies and dangerous Brotherhoods; such institutions, being most baneful to religion and society, are severely condemned by the Church. Her censures have been fulminated not only against persons enrolled in them, but also against those who encourage, foster, or promote them in any way, directly or indirectly. Members of such societies, or persons connected with them cannot be admitted to Sacraments,' & c." (C). "Clearly," Lavelle maintained, "the 'Dangerous Brotherhood' here referred to is the National Brotherhood of St. Patrick. There is no other Brotherhood known in Ireland to-day, and Dr. Cullen has now gone the length of stating that every member of that Brotherhood is under the ban of the Church." "And I now, in the presence of God, who reads my soul," he then added, "solemnly declare that the assertions of Dr. Cullen are not true, in fact, as regards the Brotherhood of St. Patrick; that they are *in no sense of the word* a secret society; that they have no oaths, secret or otherwise; and that, therefore, they no more come under the censures of the Church than any pious guild in the city of Dublin." "So much for the fact," Lavelle further declared:

> Now as to the law. Dr. Cullen states that the censures of the Church are fulminated against SUCH societies as that of the Brotherhood of St. Patrick—in other words, against open and public Associations bound by no oath or by no sacred bond whatsoever. I say this is not the law—this is not the theology. To come under the censures of the Church in those matters, not only must the society be what is called a *secret society*, but it must be held together by the forbidden bond of a secret oath. It is high time this should be explained, and that there should be no further mystification on the subject—and if these words of mine contribute to enlighten the public mind on the matter, I shall have no reason to regret my pains.

"At a future day," he promised in conclusion, "I shall write more at length on this important subject."

In the letter from Rome that Cullen received before the publishing of his pastoral, Cardinal Barnabò apparently advised him that the bishops at their approaching general meeting on May 6 should take some effective action regarding Lavelle's connection with the brothers, but that this action was not to involve a public denunciation of the Brotherhood. At their meeting, therefore, the bishops as a body, over the strenuous protests of MacHale and the bishop of Clonfert, John Derry, decided that Lavelle not only should be obliged to resign from the Brotherhood of St. Patrick but should also make a public apology for his actions.[42] When it came to public condemnation, however, the bishops trod very warily. In a series of three resolutions condemning secret societies, they carefully avoided mentioning the brothers by name:

> That we have heard with deep regret that in some parts of the country persons have been known to administer unlawful oaths, and to entice foolish men to enter secret associations dangerous to religion and society.
> That we earnestly, and with all paternal affection, warn Catholics against all such combinations, whether bound by oath

42. Corish, pp. 9–10.

or otherwise, and especially against those that have for object to spread a spirit of revolution which, in other lands, is now producing such disastrous results.

That while we warn our people against those unlawful associations we cannot be blind to the many injustices they suffer, and the manifest inequality before the law which inspires some individuals with a spirit of alienation from authority and of resistance to public order leading in some cases to crimes which we and all good men deplore.[43]

On May 9, the day the bishops' meeting concluded, Cullen wrote Kirby a long report in Italian, which he conveniently summed up with a postscript in English: "I am half killed with the week's work. Only for Cardinal Barnabò's letter, I would have let things pass too quietly and Lavelle would have had a triumph. He must now humble himself. I fear however that he will do it most ungraciously—or perhaps offensively—Dr. McHale made a desperate fight—but everyone of the others if you except Dr. Derry; came out strongly and decidedly—so that the lion had to surrender" (K). At the end of this letter Cullen then explained that some nine bishops would set out for Rome the next day and that he and two others would follow on May 20. The occasion for the bishops' visit was the pope's invitation to all the bishops of the Church to assist in Rome at the canonization of the Japanese martyrs on June 8. The pope had also signified that he expected as many of the bishops to attend as possible in order to bear personal witness to him and his temporal power. In all, thirteen Irish bishops in a regular hierarchy of some thirty eventually assisted at the canonization.

Before leaving for Rome, Cullen issued still another pastoral for the month of May in which he denounced secret societies and associations lately established by those who were "mere enthusiasts" or worse. Cullen then advised his clergy:

> Caution young men against connecting themselves with such leaders, and point out the danger of the associations and brotherhoods which are fostering wild and hopeless projects or propagating maxims dangerous to religion and society. If any of your flocks join them, let them know that their connexion with them is a reserved case in this diocese, and that in all instances where anyone is bound by oath as a member, or encourages in any way the condemned associations, he incurs excommunication.
>
> However, as some good and virtuous young men may have been misled by a false spirit of patriotism, and a zeal, not accord-

43. I.C.D., 1863, pp. 268–69.

ing to knowledge, to redress civil and religious grievances, allowance must be made for their inexperience and their good intentions. If, therefore, they renounce their connexion with secret societies, dangerous brotherhoods, and make reparation for any scandal given, you may admit them to the sacraments. This privilege is to continue for all until the 15th August, the Feast of the Assumption of the Blessed Virgin, after which the reservation will be enforced.[44]

After quoting the three resolutions of the bishops at their late general meeting and recommending that the government could do much "to restore peace and happiness" in Ireland by relieving a Catholic people of the burden of supporting an established Protestant Church, Cullen then posed the crucial political question:

> Before we conclude, it will be well, perhaps, to answer a question sometimes proposed by those who think favorably of secret organizations. Are we, they say, to be indifferent to the sufferings of the people, or the wrongs of our country? Are we to forget Ireland, and give up every vestige of patriotism?
>
> My answer is, that the law of charity prohibits us to be callous to the sufferings of our brethren, and that we are obliged to sympathize with them, and assist them as far as we can. It is our duty also to call on the public authorities to relieve public distress, and to petition for such measures as may prevent its periodical recurrence. On the other hand our rulers are bound to examine into alleged grievances, and endeavour to remove them so as to leave no pretexts for complaint or for crime. When disturbances occurred some years ago in England this course was adopted; the disturbances in Canada were put an end to in the same way. If the same rule were applied to Ireland and her grievances redressed, undoubtedly all classes of society would be united, as in Canada, and peace and happiness would prevail.
>
> But in endeavouring to obtain redress, unlawful or unjust means should never be employed. It would be wicked and foolish to have recourse to force or violence; they would be only the cause of greater misery and ruin: nothing good can be expected from secret and dangerous combinations, which delight in deeds of darkness, and hating the light, cannot be blessed by Heaven. It is only through the protection of God that we can obtain anything good.[45]

44. Moran, 2:145–6.
45. Ibid., p. 147.

Cullen's pastoral was read in all the Dublin churches on Sunday, May 25, while he was on his way to Rome. Meanwhile, Lavelle had written Cullen, undoubtedly at the behest of MacHale, in response to the decision of the bishops as a body at their meeting. Lavelle explained to Cullen that although he had no wish to give offense, he could go no further with regard to the Brotherhood of St. Patrick than express his regret that he had joined this political association without the permission of his archbishop (C). This letter, which was undated but marked "received" on May 24, was apparently forwarded to Cullen in Rome. Shortly after Cullen's pastoral was read in Dublin, moreover, Lavelle published another letter in the press in which he asserted that Cullen's condemnation had no force as far as the Brotherhood of St. Patrick was concerned because the Brotherhood was in no way secret.[46] This letter was also surely forwarded to Cullen, who, before he left Rome at the end of June, raised the question what was to be done about Lavelle with no less a personage than the pope. The pope decided that MacHale should be ordered to discipline Lavelle in accordance with the decision come to by the bishops at their late meeting, and Kirby informed Cullen of this conclusion on July 21.[47]

For the next few months Lavelle maintained a very low public profile. He does not seem to have been in any hurry to make the submission required by the pope, and even MacHale was apparently having difficulties in dealing with him. When Lavelle again visited Dublin and Glasgow in October, Cullen wrote MacHale, as he explained to Kirby on October 26, complaining "that the resolution of the Bishops was trampled on" (K). "Dr. McH. gave me no satisfaction, but Dr. McEvilly," Cullen added, referring to the bishop of Galway, "says he [MacHale] wrote to Father Lavelle to be in his parish[,] Partry[,] before the next Sunday *sub poena suspensionis ipso facto incurrenda* [under the penalty of incurring suspension by the fact]. Father Lavelle the moment he rec[d] the order returned to Partry, stopped some hours[,] dined with the curate, and called on him to bear witness that he had obeyed Dr. McH's mandate[,] returning to the Parish before Sunday, and then left the place again and returned to Dublin or Glasgow to spend some longer time there." Still, for the rest of the year, though Lavelle did not make his required submission, he continued to keep out of the public eye. What Cullen and the Roman authorities did not realize, of course, was that this period of comparative peace during the last half of 1862 was merely the calm before the storm. The short

46. Corish, p. 10.
47. Ibid.

respite, however, was a welcome one to a Church and clergy that were about to endure the severe trials and privations of a third harvest failure in as many years.

———————◆———————

As usual, Cullen was the first to sound the alarm. "The weather here," he reported to Kirby from Liverpool on his way home from Rome, on July 17, "is wet—it is raining at present. The crops are quite green, and fears are entertained for the harvest" (K). "In Ireland," he added more ominously, "the weather is also very bad. God help the poor. Parliament is about providing for the manufactures in Lancashire where the distress is not very great—but they will do nothing for the poor in Ireland who are in such great misery—no fair play for a poor Catholic." A week later Cullen wrote Kirby somewhat more hopefully from Dublin. "The weather," he reported on July 23, "was cold and wet up to Sunday last. Since then it is fine and sunny—if it continue fine, the harvest will be good and the distress will cease—but if God does not give us fine weather we shall have a sad state of things" (K). The weather again turned wet and cold, however, and did not improve until the end of September; the archbishop of Armagh, Joseph Dixon, reported on the twenty-ninth that after a cold and dreary summer, "the people are now, in the most beautiful weather, gathering in a rich and abundant harvest" (K).

Dixon proved too optimistic. The weather again took a turn for the worse, and the bishop of Cloyne, William Keane, reported to Kirby from Fermoy on October 14 that they had nothing recently but rain, rain, rain (K). Three weeks later, when Dixon wrote Kirby again, he was in a more sober and somber mood. "Now that the harvest is nearly gathered in," he explained on November 4, "the produce is not found to be abundant, although much better than could have been expected after the wet summer we had. The prospects of this country in a temporal point of view are not encouraging" (K). "The poor people, however," he added more hopefully, "have potatoes and turf. Hence there is no danger of famine for the next season, nor much prospect of success for the soupers." Within a week the news became even more grim as the cold and wet autumn turned into an early winter. "We have had," Cullen reported to Kirby on November 11, "a heavy fall of snow these days—and what is worse even the corn is out in the fields in many places. It is the latest harvest on record. A good deal of corn not cut yet and what is in the fields must be wet and bad. God help the poor. Get the good people in Rome to pray for us" (K). He added bitterly, "A collection has been commenced here for the poor in Lancashire. The Protestants who gave nothing to the Irish poor are giving them large sums, though the distress is not so great as here." "The wheat," Cullen then noted, in concluding his tale of woe, "is bad here—the oats if they can be saved will be middling. The potatoes are better than usual. The poor very numerous. The small farmers and shopkeepers will suffer very much."

Cullen's assessment of the harvest of 1862 was all too accurate. Wheat and oats were down respectively some 7 and 8 percent from the previous year, while the barley crop was no better than that of 1861. The critical potato crop had improved some 3 percent over the previous year, but it was still down an incredible 45 percent from the average yields of 1856–58, whereas the turnip and hay crop yields were about the same as in 1861 (see table, p. 79). In absolute terms, therefore, the harvest of 1862 was at least as bad as that of 1861, and in relative terms it was worse because it was the third such harvest in succession. When the bishop of Cloyne wrote Kirby again on November 16, he explained that though he had finally managed to sell the twenty thousand lottery tickets that had been sent to him by the organizer of the papal lottery in Rome, the "great drawback just now, is the general depression among all Classes" (K). "In some instances," Keane explained further, "the harvest of this year is the worst since the famine. It is found to be even worse than I thought it to be, when I wrote to Duke Salviati. And it is the third bad harvest in succession." The compass of the disaster was finally boxed for Kirby by a letter sent to him on November 20 by the bishop of Raphoe, who wrote from Ballyshannon in southern Donegal (K). "A succession of unfortunate Seasons," Daniel McGettigan summed up, "is now ending with the worst of them all. We have had no summer. There is no harvest. An early Winter boisterous and pitiless is just on us, and the greater part of a very poor crop is lost in the storm. In travelling over a large district in this Diocese during the last fortnight, I found two thirds of the miserable corn crop still out in the fields. The straw is totally useless and the grain will not be fit for human food. Such is the lowering prospect before us. But we must look it manfully in the face."

The effect of a third bad harvest in succession was not only to prolong the sufferings of the poor for yet another year but also to increase the complaints of the clergy about the callousness of the government in refusing to do anything to relieve the misery. All the marks of the harvest failure of the previous year—the real misery, its increase as one moved west, and its affecting most seriously those at the base of the social pyramid—as well as all the qualifications of those respective marks—the cheapness of food, especially Indian meal, the articulation of the suffering in the press by mainly the western clergy, and the falling of the worst burden on those who did not or were unable to earn a money wage, such as the small farmers and marginal shopkeepers or the destitute poor—were also the main characteristics of the aftermath of the harvest failure of 1862. Still, given the obviously deteriorating situation, the condition of the poor in Ireland during the winter and spring of 1863 was probably no worse than it had been during the previous year. The reasons for this curious and apparent paradox were in the main two. Firstly, the charitable machinery set up for the relief of the poor during 1862 was greatly augmented by the very generous contributions from the Irish abroad, especially from America and Australasia. Secondly, the Irish began once again in 1863 to leave their native land in great numbers.

The main vehicle for relieving the distress of the poor in Ireland during 1862 had been the Mansion House Relief Committee, which was transformed in early November 1862 into the Central Relief Committee.[48] The resources at the disposal of the committee, however, would appear to have been always relatively modest. Up to the end of 1862, the committee had apparently collected only some £4,000, and in the first four months of 1863 it reported that it had collected another £3,500.[49] In the middle of May 1863 the committee reported that since its foundation some fifteen months before, in February 1862, it had expended nearly £11,500 in relieving the poor.[50] This expenditure had been made possible only by the sums it had received from America and Australia, given the amount that it had collected in Ireland. Indeed, the amount of money received in Ireland in late 1862 and in 1863 from the Irish abroad, over and above what had been received by the committee, was very considerable, though there are no precise total figures. In late October 1862, for example, MacHale reported that he had been sent £600 from America, and in November he acknowledged that he had received a total of £3,000 from the archbishops of Sidney and San Francisco and the bishop of Melbourne.[51] In early April 1863, at a meeting in New York at which Archbishop Hughes was one of the main speakers, £4,400 was collected for the relief of the poor in Ireland.[52] Later that month Cullen reported that he had received over £900 from the bishop of Newark in

48. I.C.D., 1863, p. 247, November 11, 1862.
49. I.C.D., 1864, p. 246, April 29, 1863.
50. Ibid., p. 253, May 14, 1863.
51. I.C.D., 1863, p. 238, October 29, 1862; p. 249, November 26, 1862.
52. I.C.D., 1864, p. 238, April 7, 1863.

the United States, and in the middle of May he acknowledged receiving £400 from the bishop of New Brunswick in Canada.[53] On May 27, moreover, Cullen wrote Kirby asking him to secure an audience with the pope for Father Leyden from Boston, who had just recently visited Ireland, bringing with him between £3000 and £4000 for the relief of the Irish poor (K). "I do not know," Cullen confessed on another occasion, "what our poor wd do, were we not so well supported by America."[54]

The crucial factor in the relief of distress during this period, however, was less the impact of the charitable contributions of the Irish at home and abroad than the large increase in emigration that took place in 1863 and the ensuing years. In order to appreciate the magnitude of this increase it is necessary to review briefly the trends in Irish emigration since the Great Famine year of 1847. In the six years after 1846, emigration from Ireland averaged about 220,000 per year, or nearly 1,300,000 persons between 1847 and 1852 of the estimated population of 8,500,000 in 1845. By the end of the 1850s emigration had fallen off considerably, but it was still averaging something more than 50,000 per annum in the years 1858–60. The tendency, especially after the very early years of the exodus, was for the vast majority of the emigrants (80 percent) to go to the United States. When the Civil War broke out there in 1861, not only did the total number of Irish emigrants fall sharply, to some 36,000, but the tendency to emigrate to the United States declined by about 5 percent. With the second successive harvest failure in 1861, however, emigration again increased to nearly 50,000 during 1862, and the tendency to avoid America became even more marked, as even fewer (67 percent) elected

53. Ibid., p. 245, April 23, 1863; p. 252, May 14, 1865. See also *Freeman's Journal*, June 19, 1863, for a report of a contribution of £7,150 from New York in April and May 1863 to the Central Relief Committee.

54. K, Cullen to Kirby, July 3, 1863. "America or rather the Irish there are sending in large sums of money. I got about £3000 last week, but it is only a *gocha nel Oceana* [drop in the Ocean]." As Cullen's remarks suggest, there are considerable difficulties in assessing the impact of relief on distress. Even if we did have firm figures regarding what was collected, which we do not, the largely subjective question whether it was enough to meet the need would remain to be answered. Donnelly (p. 48) points out that the Central Relief Committee and the Society of Friends Relief Committee spent between them only some £41,000 relieving distress over the two-year period 1862–63. He also points out that the lord mayor of Dublin guessed in August 1863 that since the previous winter £100,000 had been raised locally, and he rightly remarks that given the intensity of the crisis, the sum was not very impressive. Donnelly does not include, however, either the sums collected abroad or the very considerable sum, which averaged about £362,000 per year, remitted from North America by emigrants to their friends and relatives in Ireland. The most that can be said at this stage perhaps is that the money raised for relief helped prevent the worst effects of the distress, especially by making possible the purchase of food—in particular, maize.

to go to the United States. After the third harvest failure in 1862, the number who emigrated increased to 116,000 in 1863; 115,000 left in 1864, and another 101,000 in 1865. Over 80 percent of those 332,000 emigrants, moreover, chose to go to the United States in spite of the increasingly bloody conflict continuing to rage there.[55]

"We are again," the bishop of Elphin dolefully wrote Kirby from Sligo on January 10, "as you are aware, in the midst of great distress both here and in the southwest of Ireland. Our poor landholders are in far worse condition than they were last year. Numbers of them are being evicted and dispossessed for non-payment of rent. Those who have the means are flying from the country, even to the dis-United States, where our venerated friend, the Archbishop of New York is using his influence, like Magher [sic], for their destruction."[56] "We are in a sad puzzling condition indeed," Gillooly confessed, "—and it is a very hard thing not to become a declared rebel amidst the scenes that are rending our hearts." "When you come to see me next summer," he promised, "we'll give you the Shan Van Vaught with a patriotic chorus such as you never heard in Rome or Waterford." During January the campaign in the press was intensified by the clergy, and it was climaxed by a series of meetings in February for the relief of the destitute and suffering poor. Simultaneous meetings were held on February 1 in Galway, Kilkenny, Drogheda, Kingstown, Dublin, Cork, Kerry, and other parts of the country. Meetings were also held in Mullingar and Sligo later in the month. The agitation during the winter, however, was of no avail.

"Our poor people," the bishop of Galway reported to Kirby from Galway city on March 6, "are in a very bad way. I really believe if the American war were to cease tomorrow, and facilities for emigration afforded, half the numerical population of this province would leave before six months" (K). He added bitterly, "The cruelties practiced on the poor people by the landlords, agents and bailiffs are really incredible. The poor people cannot possibly pay the rents and then evictions [are] unmercifully resorted to." With the coming of spring and the terrors of the Atlantic winter passage over, the mass exodus finally began. "It would make your eyes run down tears," John Crotty, a recent alumnus of the Irish College then serving as a chaplain in Clonmel, wrote Kirby from Waterford city on March 12, "to see the

55. Emmet Larkin, "Economic Growth, Capital Investment and the Roman Catholic Church in Nineteenth Century Ireland," *American Historical Review* 72 (1966–67): 876, Appendix A.

56. K; the reference is to Thomas Francis Meagher, who became a brigadier general in the Union Army and used his influence to enlist his countrymen in the same cause.

wretched state of the people and the numbers who are steadily week after week going to America from their own poor but beloved home" (K). "The Catholic gentlemen," he added, "do not support the cause of the poor man as they ought. I fancy they think it vulgar to do so. The word of that bad young man, Sir R. Peel has more weight with them than the testimony or appeals of even Bishops."

Several weeks later one of the more important of those bishops also wrote Kirby in a very desponding tone. "All the small farmers," Patrick Leahy, the archbishop of Cashel, reported on March 27, "are utterly gone. So denuded are they of everything that even if left their land for nothing many of them could not hold on. All the fine young men and women of the country are flying away in thousands [to] any part of the world where they can find a livelihood" (K). Leahy added:

> If God in his mercy does not preserve to us a remnant of our people, in a short time the Protestants will outnumber us. For, mark you!—it is only the poor Celts, the poor Catholics, the beloved members of our flocks that are going—not one Protestant, I may say. The Landlord and Tenant laws are rooting the Celtic population out of the land, as surely as any physical cause produces its effect, —and this wicked Anti-Catholic, Anti-Roman, Anti-Irish, Anti-everything-dear-to-us-Government is looking on, laughing with delight, seeing that the direct, the certain effect of these laws is to root out our Catholic people, that in fact they are as effectual *penal laws* against our people as any ever enforced, and *therefore they will not raise a little finger so as to change these Laws as at once to do justice to both Landlord & Tenant.*

"God help us," Leahy summed up; "If He does not, I fear we are lost as a Nation, as a Catholic nation."

"Here in Ireland," the archbishop of Armagh informed Kirby a month later, on April 24, from Drogheda, "Emigration is the order of the day. At the same time the Spring is most favourable to the Country[,] unsurpassed in that respect by any Spring within our memory" (K). But nothing, it appears, could now stem the tide, for the bishop of Cloyne reported to Kirby on May 2, from Fermoy that "the young & strong" were off to America in the thousands (K). "What," he asked, "is to become of the country with this drain constantly going on? The war in America has no terrors for them. They are running from a worse war at home—the war of misery and hunger." Though the spring continued promising, the exodus persisted. "The prospects of the coming harvest," a curate in Waterford city, George Commins, assured Kirby on June 19, "are thank God most cheering. The weather is most propitious and the crops, so far, so good. But the continual emigration of the people is most alarming and melancholy" (K). "Every day," he explained, "the peasant class are leaving our Quay and no longer with that wild expression of sorrow with which they were accustomed to leave poor Ireland some years ago, but with the stolid coolness of men who have grown weary of the striving and poverty of home." "Providence," he concluded more piously, "no doubt has His own wise ends in this and has chosen them as instruments for a great work[,] viz. of carrying the faith into all parts of [the] world."

Whatever role Providence had in mind for the Irish people, there is little doubt that by 1863 emigration was well on its way to being institutionalized as a way of life among them. "One hundred and twenty-six emigrants," the correspondent of the *Tralee Journal* had reported from county Kerry on Friday, May 19, "arrived in Tralee on Tuesday evening from Tarbart and Listowel districts, and proceeded to Queenstown by the eight a.m. train on Thursday morning. They were of a better class than those usually seen emigrating to America. They appeared to be the sons and daughters of the farmers of the districts from whence they come."[57] "After arriving in Tralee," the correspondent further observed, "they attended evening service in the church of St. John the Baptist, where the Vincentian Fathers are now conducting a mission. Many of the intending emigrants availed themselves of the spiritual ministrations of the holy fathers, and prepared themselves for their perilous journey across the Atlantic by a visit to the confessional." "It was a pleasing sight," he concluded, "to see so many of Ireland's fair daughters and stalworth [*sic*] sons so engaged on one of the last evenings they were ever to spend in their native land."

A relatively bountiful harvest in 1863 and, indeed, good harvests for nearly a decade did little to stem the tide of emigration, which continued to average about 80,000 per annum in the next ten years.[58] The political consequences of this searing experience, whatever may be said of the economic, were very serious. The alleged indifference of the government to the consequences of three successive bad harvests and the subsequent mass exodus were taken together by a good many of the clergy, and especially by the Fenians and many of their sympathizers, as prima facie evidence that there was a conspiracy afoot to exterminate the Irish as a people. Because of the widespread distress and discontent, the Fenians had obviously continued since the Mc-

57. I.C.D., 1864, p. 254.
58. It should be noted, however, that 1863 and 1864 were not good years for graziers (Donnelly, pp. 35–36).

Manus funeral to make considerable gains in recruiting members for their counterconspiracy. "You will be glad to hear," the chaplain to the Presentation convent in Clonmel, John Crotty, had informed Kirby on March 12, "that the good Redemptionist Fathers are giving a very successful mission in Waterford. They concluded ours here about a month since, after having effected incredible good. It turned up during the mission that most of the young men about this place were sworn members of one of our secret societies lately so common in Ireland. Very cheerfully the poor fellows yielded to the good advice of the priests. They said they saw no harm in the world in the oath as they had no remedy in their distress."

The following day Cullen wrote to Barnabò in much the same vein as Crotty, but with something less than the Clonmel chaplain's compassion. After explaining to the cardinal once again, on March 13, that the government was doing nothing and that there was general discontent, "which the false liberals and revolutionaries make use of to propagate their ideas," Cullen added, "I fear that in this way great damage will be done to religion, introducing into their country the Mazzinian spirit, which is taught publicly by our Ministers, and which is then embraced by others to employ it against the government."[59] "I do not cease to tell Catholics," he assured Barnabò, "that it is pure madness to speak of revolution, as the people who are without arms, without money, and without any means of resistance in the manner of any popular movement, could not do other than give our enemies the opportunity to ruin us completely." "Unfortunately," Cullen concluded, "there are some madmen who do not wish to listen to such reasonable advice."

Another politically conservative Irish bishop, William Delany, reported to Kirby from Cork on March 28, "We are suffering a good deal of distress among some classes in Ireland. In certain localities the pressure is severely felt. Small farmers and all the classes of mechanics who lived by them and small shopkeepers who profited by them are reduced to a very low ebb" (K). "I suppose," Delany then conjectured, referring to the recent anti-English demonstrations on St. Patrick's Day in Dublin and Cork, "you have learned through the Irish newspapers, the shameful and violent proceedings of some of our poor misguided countrymen. They arrogate to themselves a monopoly of patriotism and bring discredit on the name by their unreflecting violence. I hope however the worst is over and that the erring are return-

59. S.R.C., vol. 34, fol. 909.

ing to their sober senses."[60] "We recovered," he added more brightly, "numbers from the secret societies by means of a late most successful mission in Cork." Though the violence did eventually die down, it resulted in a decidedly more aggressive tone among those who advocated a more active policy in Irish politics. And, once again, it was the ubiquitous Father Lavelle who was to be found in the vanguard.

In early February 1863 Lavelle had apparently given the undertaking required by Propaganda that he have nothing further to do with alleged secret societies and cease his campaign in the press.[61] He continued, however, to appear at public meetings and to publish letters in the press after his submission.[62] He was also certainly encouraged at this time by MacHale's example. In the middle of May the archbishop announced publicly that he was a subscriber to the *Irishman*, which had become notorious as the mouthpiece of the Brotherhood of St. Patrick. "I send Dr. Moran," Cullen informed Kirby soberly on May 22, "a letter of Dr. McHale declaring himself a subscriber to the *Irishman*[,] a newspaper very wicked for the past. He will say he does so in hope of amendment, but he ought to have waited to see some signs of penitence" (K). Finally, on June 13, Lavelle published in the *Glasgow Free Press* a letter dated the feast of Corpus Christi, in which he denounced Cullen for having made membership in the Brotherhood of St. Patrick a reserved sin, and maintained that the reservation should not deter any layman from joining the Brotherhood:

> I hope the Brotherhoods wherever they are will never mind any such denunciations. I have already shown scores of times that they are as untouched by any censures of the Church as Dr. Cullen himself. I have shown that papal constitutions have been misunderstood—or affected to be misunderstood—and misapplied. I have shown even that the form of reservation, used in a certain diocese in Ireland regarding it, is ludicrously invalid. And I now declare that no layman ought to be deterred from membership by any kind of intimidation from any quarter whatever. But, while I say this, I also say, and I say it with deep regret, that in certain places which I need not now particularise the conduct of individual members has brought discredit on the entire association. It has prevented sterling men from joining the ranks, and

---

60. See also *Freeman's Journal*, March 19, 1863, denying that the demonstrations represented Catholic feeling in Ireland.
61. Corish, p. 10.
62. Ibid., p. 11, n. 25.

even driven honest men away after their enrollment. It therefore behooves the Brotherhood to be careful and almost select in the admission of members. Let none but a *good man*, a *moral and sober man*, a *temperate liver*, and, as a Catholic, an attendant at his religious duties be admitted as a member. The man who is not faithful to God will hardly be faithful to his country. . . . [63]

Cullen forwarded Lavelle's "scandalous" letter to Kirby on June 21, noting that it not only encouraged people to join the Brotherhood but also urged "priests to despise the diocesan reservations" (K). He explained that he had written strongly to Barnabò that same day. After reviewing for the cardinal the history of Father Lavelle from the uproar he caused at the Irish College in Paris in 1859 to the present, Cullen went on:

> Matters being so, you will allow me to ask if things ought to be allowed to go on in this way forever—is there not some means of punishing Lavelle, or inducing his ordinary to prevent the scandal that the priest gives? I have mentioned several times, and I repeat it now, that the brotherhood of St. Patrick is a very dangerous society, and that it tends very much to the Mazzinian system.
>
> I hope that Your Eminence will take some measure that will put an end to the insolence of Lavelle. Otherwise there will arise some serious intervention for both him and his ordinary on the part of the clergy of Dublin who do not wish any longer to bear so many insults.[64]

Cullen was not the only one scandalized by Lavelle's letter, or the only one who thought Rome should take some action. "Between ourselves," the archbishop of Armagh wrote Kirby, somewhat ingenuously, on June 26, "it just now occurs to me to say that it is a very great pity that nothing is done for the purpose of stopping the Rev. Father Lavelle. His career for the last eighteen months is a source of great evil to this country" (K). "If His Eminence, Cardinal Barnabò," Dixon suggested, "would just ask the archbishop of Dublin for a brief statement of Lavelle's history for the last eighteen months, such a step on the part of His Eminence, would lead, I have no doubt to the applying of a remedy to this evil." "I make the observation," he as-

---

63. Ibid., p. 12, quoting the *Catholic Telegraph*, June 20, 1863, which quoted the *Glasgow Free Press*, June 13, 1863.
64. S.R.C., vol. 35, fols. 134–35.

sured Kirby in conclusion, "without having consulted any person about the matter."

What Dixon really intended in writing Kirby, of course, was to have Barnabò authorize Cullen once again to place the subject of Lavelle and the Brotherhood on the agenda of the upcoming general meeting of the Irish bishops. The meeting had been made necessary by various problems that had arisen in connection with the governing and financing of the Catholic University as well as the nagging nondenominational or "mixed" nature of the national system of education. Barnabò had written Cullen on June 1 authorizing him to convene a meeting of the bishops for the consideration of those problems (L). Cullen forwarded copies of Barnabò's letter to the bishops in early July, informing them that the meeting would be held on August 4 and subsequent days in Dublin.[65] When Barnabò learned of Lavelle's latest outburst, he wrote Cullen and again authorized him to submit the conduct of that priest and the Brotherhood of St. Patrick to the consideration of the bishops.[66] In late July, however, shortly before the bishops met, another letter from Lavelle was published in the Irish papers, a letter that he had written the previous April to the head of an Irish political club in San Francisco. In that letter he had been provocatively insulting to Cullen and had denounced him, in fact, for tyrannizing over the Irish episcopate.

"For a time," Lavelle confessed in the course of his letter to Thomas Mooney on April 18, "I was of the opinion that with the needful elements of success, the Irish priest would be found in the camp and by the ambulance with his struggling people. I now, to be candid with you, must admit that I fear I have greatly erred. He has not been taught, but *driven* into loyal *constitutional agitation*. There is an incubus over him, my friend." "The prophecy of Columbkille," Lavelle further explained, with a reference to Cullen, "seems to be coming out true to the letter—'A red-haired man shall be Bishop of Leinster, and he shall be the cause of great woe to the Gael.' I cannot, of course, vouch for the authenticity of the prediction: but . . ." He continued:

> The majority of our holy and respected prelates seem to be led blindly by this one man. They, of course, lead their priests; thus is the youth of Ireland fettered and log-chained, unless it rise up in apparent rebellion, against an authority which it has ever re-

65. K, George Butler to Kirby, July 13, 1863.
66. K, Butler to Kirby, July 27, 1863.

vered. I pray you understand me right. So far from pretending myself to a greater love of Ireland, or grief for the sorrows of her people than any other brother-priest in the Land, I do really believe that they all feel as much for their country as I do—many would be ready to sacrifice as much, which seems ALL, but the majority are rendered timourous by the emasculating policy at the assumed headquarters of ecclesiastical authority.[67]

More provocative than all, however, were the principles Lavelle enunciated several weeks later about the right of the Irish people to set aside their tyrannical rulers, which actually appeared in the press while the bishops were meeting. His categorical assertions have to be read in full in order to be properly appreciated.

1. According to all Catholic Divines (Bossuet alone, perhaps excepted), oppressive rulers may be deposed by their subjects.
2. No subjects in the world are more refinedly oppressed than the Irish people of the present day.
3. Therefore, we have the general and undisputable right to set aside our tyrannical rulers.
4. However, at this moment it would be madness or wickedness to make the attempt, because resistance would be useless.
5. Still, we have not alone the right, but we are bound by the duty, of making all preparations in our power against the day when our oppressor will herself be battling for her existence, and when our efforts will be morally certain of success. Is this treason? I am then a traitor. Is this disloyal. So am I.[68]

The bishops were not apparently much impressed with Lavelle's syllogisms on the right to revolution, for in the joint resolutions issued after their five-day meeting they finally condemned the Brotherhood of St. Patrick by name. "Several bishops," they declared, "having represented to the meeting that a society exists called the Brotherhood of St. Patrick, having for its object the support and defence by arms of what is called in the oath of membership the Irish Republic, or proposing to itself other such illegal ends, and that societies of the same character, though sometimes not bound by oaths, exist in some dioceses, it was resolved to condemn all such associations; and the assembled bishops do hereby condemn them, and the publication of

67. Corish, p. 12, quoting the *Catholic Telegraph*, July 25, 1863, which quoted Lavelle's letter of April 18, 1863, from the *San Francisco Irish News*, June 6, 1863.
68. E. R. Norman, *The Catholic Church and Ireland in the Age of Rebellion, 1859–1873* (London, 1965), p. 112, quoting the *Tablet* (London), August 8, 1863.

any defense of them under any pretext.[69] The bishops then entered their usual caveat about failure of the government to act responsibly in the present deplorable crisis:

> The bishops, whilst thus warning their flocks against those criminal combinations, cannot separate without declaring their profound regret that neither the government nor the legislature has taken any step to ameliorate the condition of the people of Ireland. The extreme destitution from which a vast proportion of the people suffered during this and past years was disregarded by both. A feeling of discontent naturally results from such indifference to their wrongs and privations, and leads to the forming of illegal societies. The bishops, therefore, in the interest of public order, as a duty to their flocks, and especially to the poor, respectfully call for such legal and administrative measures as will afford employment to the labouring classes in works of public utility, and in the development of the agricultural resources of the country, which would undoubtedly follow the enactment of a law that would secure to tenant farmers the rightful ownership of the products of their own industry and capital employed in the improvement of their holdings, and protect them from capricious evictions.

The day after the meeting closed, August 9, Cullen reported to Kirby in Italian that the bishops had unanimously condemned the Brotherhood and that all but MacHale and John Derry, the bishop of Clonfert, had condemned Lavelle's *Glasgow Free Press* letter of June 13 as being subversive of all government, civil and ecclesiastical (K). MacHale had put up a great battle for Lavelle, Cullen added, but the bishops decided over his protests and Derry's that Lavelle must make a public submission to the condemnation.[70] Several days later Cullen wrote Kirby again, expanding in English on the recent meeting. "Our meeting went on well," he explained gratefully on August 11, "thanks be to God—all the Bishops agreed in condemning the Brotherhood of S. Patrick. All except Dr. McHale and Dr. Derry passed a severe censure on Father Lavelle's writings and himself. Though Dr. McHale could not defend Lavelle, yet he was so unfortunate as to oppose all the other Bishops, and to refuse to say a word against him. Several

---

69. I.C.D., 1864, pp. 286–87. The pastoral is not dated.

70. *Acta Sacrae Congregationis* (A), vol. 228 (1864), fol. 99, "Ristretto con Sommario sull' adunanza tenuta dai Vescovi Irlandesi a Dublino nel mese di Agosto del 1863, Marzo, 1864" (fols. 96–110), Archives of the Society for the Propagation of the Faith, Rome. See ibid., Cullen to Barnabò, August 30, 1863, fol. 104.

Bishops lectured his Grace and told him that he was answerable to God and the Church for all the evils done by Lavelle and his Brotherhood" (K). Cullen, the bishops, the Roman authorities, and even the pope were soon to learn, however, that it was one thing to condemn Lavelle and quite another to enforce their condemnation.

One measure of the growth of secret societies, and particularly the Fenian, or Irish Republican, Brotherhood, was the bishop's condemnation of the Brotherhood of St. Patrick by name. Apparently, enough of the bishops had become convinced by the time of their general meeting that the danger from secret societies was real and something must be done about it. In their joint resolutions, however, the bishops had maintained that the responsibility for the growth of secret societies in Ireland lay with the English government. They pointed out that by refusing to relieve the misery and destitution of a vast proportion of their people both the government and the legislature had done nothing to allay that discontent which drove the people into joining illegal societies. By their open and public criticism of the government, however, the Irish bishops were also reminding their people that there was really little effective remedy for their grievances in a political system of which they were only nominally a part. By refusing to take an active part, or to allow their clergy to engage in mounting a constitutional movement to redress their people's grievances, the Irish bishops, in effect, contributed to the creation of a political power vacuum that the Fenian Brotherhood quickly filled. The bishops, therefore, must be asked to bear a very significant share of the responsibility for the rapid growth and success of the Brotherhood in the early 1860s.

III

The One Thing
Essential—Education

December 1859–June 1864

Even as the political situation was becoming more alarming and
threatening from their point of view, the Irish bishops as a body were
having considerably more success in dealing with a problem that had
sorely plagued them for almost as long a time. For more than twenty
years the education question had proved to be the most divisive in the
Irish Church. The issues at stake were in the main two. The first
involved the extent of the state's control over a system of education
attended by Catholics, and the second involved the concept of mixed
Catholic and Protestant education. But by 1859 these issues had been
largely resolved, at least as far as the Irish bishops were concerned; for
at successive general meetings in August and October of that year, the
bishops as a body finally determined those priorities and demands that
would govern their conduct on the education question for more than a
century. They declared, in effect, that the educational system on all
levels—primary, intermediate, and university—must be duly subordi-
nated to episcopal control. They also declared against the concept of
mixed education and demanded a denominational system on all levels. These priorities and the particular demands, or reforms, necessary
to their implementation were embodied in a series of resolutions in a
memorial to the Irish viceroy, which they forwarded through the chief
secretary for Ireland, Edward Cardwell, for the consideration of the
government.[1]

1. Emmet Larkin, *The Making of the Roman Catholic Church in Ireland, 1850–1860*
(Chapel Hill, N.C., 1980), pp. 467–68.

The bishops' memorial was largely concerned with the system of education at the primary and intermediate levels, because they had to adjourn their discussion of university education in August until the October meeting. When Cardwell finally replied on behalf of the government on November 28, therefore, he too confined his discussion to those levels. He immediately pointed out that the government desired "to express in the plainest terms their steadfast adherence to the principles in which the National System had been erected" (K). The government regretted to observe, Cardwell added, that some of the demands in the bishops' memorial were "wholly incompatible with the maintenance of these principles." "If those demands were conceded," he argued, "the National System would be overthrown, and a system of sectarian education substituted for it, calculated to revive social divisions in Ireland, —and to stimulate feeling which it is the object of every just and liberal government to allay." Though the government thus refused to have anything to do with any change that would undermine the principle of mixed education, Cardwell then softened his refusal by suggesting that the government ministers were ready to meet the objections raised by the bishops in that other fundamental principle of the national system—the providing of separate religious teaching, as distinguished from mixed secular teaching, for the different denominations that made up the system. "Consistently with these principles," Cardwell assured the bishops in concluding, "they are perfectly ready to examine, and if need be, to remove the ground of any complaint which the Heads of any of the Churches may prefer against the operation of the present rules, or of any of the present practice."

Cullen's reaction to Cardwell's reply was curious. His first response was that it was promising, and his second was that perhaps it was intended to sow discord among the bishops. His initial positive response was the result of his having been assured by the Irish attorney general, Rickard Deasy, that the government really intended to make concessions to meet the bishops' objections about the infringements on the principle of separate religious teaching that had taken place in the national system over the years. Cullen's negative response was the result of his reaction to what the reply actually said rather than what it was purported to promise, most particularly to its refusal to compromise on the principle of mixed education. When William Monsell, M.P. for county Limerick, who was influential in Liberal circles, also assured him of the government's good intentions, Cullen again became more positive.[2] Still, it must be admitted that with regard to

2. Ibid., pp. 477–78.

the two main priorities laid down by the bishops in their memorial, Cardwell's reply held little promise. Not only would the government not concede anything in denominational education, but it had not a word to say about the first of the bishops' priorities—the right of the bishops to control the whole of any system of education for Catholics.

When Cullen forwarded Cardwell's reply to the bishops in early December 1859, they were not very pleased. Apparently the only prelate who took any real comfort in Cardwell's reply was David Moriarty, the bishop of Kerry. Moriarty's position was that though the national system required improvements, it was dangerous to exchange it for a separate and denominational one at present. In writing to Cullen on December 8, Moriarty pointed out that the advantage would be with the Protestants if a separate system for Catholics were set up, because the Protestants would then be able to found schools with an even greater tendency to proselytize (C). "While the united system of secular education," he pointed out with inexorable logic, "gives us the great advantage of getting all the money—we can never be exposed to the dangers of a mixed system in a country where they have nothing to mix—where all are Catholic." "Suppose, as of course you do," Moriarty then noted shrewdly in conclusion, "that my opinions are not sound—yet is it not better to take advantage of Mr. Cardwell's offer to improve the rules, and then if your grace and the large majority of the Bishops—who are for an entirely separate system—wish to go further, the way is now open and a vantage ground is gained." At this point a number of Irish Catholic members of Parliament, prompted by two of their more prominent colleagues, The O'Donoghue and John Francis Maguire, representing county Tipperary and the borough of Dungarvan respectively, finally convened a long-deferred meeting in Dublin for December 15, to endorse the demands made by the bishops in their joint pastoral the previous August.[3]

Cullen had done nothing to encourage this lay initiative, which had been launched shortly after the pastoral had been published. Indeed, as he wrote Monsell on December 7, he thought that such a meeting would do no good.[4] After explaining that he had sent Cardwell's letter to the bishops and that he expected to learn their opinion very soon, Cullen added, "I think the meeting of the M.P.'s will do no good, but I have no influence with those who are promoting it. I believe O'Donoghue is amenable to reason if anyone were to speak or write to him and probably he cd act on Maguire and J. Ennis." Cullen further

3. E. R. Norman, *The Catholic Church and Ireland in the Age of Rebellion, 1859–1873* (London, 1965), p. 69.

4. M, 8317. See also Peadar MacSuibhne, *Paul Cullen and His Contemporaries*, vol. 3 (Naas, 1965), p. 273.

suggested, "P.S.—If the meeting of the M.P.'s be held, perhaps if you and Mr. O'Ferrall were present, you cd prevent any mischief." Though neither Monsell nor Richard More O'Ferrall, member for county Kildare, attended the meeting in Dublin on December 15, some eleven Irish members of Parliament did, and four more allowed their names to be appended to the seven resolutions adopted supporting the points made in the bishops' pastoral.[5] All those who put their names to the resolutions were apparently Catholics except Col. Luke White, the member for county Longford, who also fatally distinguished himself on this occasion by refusing to endorse the seventh resolution, upholding the temporal power of the pope. The bishops, however, had become increasingly uneasy of late about lay initiatives in educational matters. When Maguire, for example, had attempted to raise the question of securing a charter for the Catholic University directly in the House of Commons the previous July, he was told in no uncertain terms by the archbishop of Cashel that he had "no right to proceed in the matter without consulting the Catholic Bishops."[6] In the matter of a charter, the bishops preferred to approach the new Liberal government quietly by means of a deputation, as indeed they had done the previous March with the late Conservative ministry. At Leahy's request, moreover, Cullen had also apparently written Maguire instructing him to cease and desist in the matter of a charter.[7] Though Maguire had complied in July, when he and O'Donoghue again involved themselves in educational matters in December, their efforts were not much appreciated by the bishops.

All of Cullen's problems, however, were not simply the result of aggressive lay politicians' seizing the initiative in educational matters. He was also seriously concerned about the attitude of a number of his episcopal colleagues. Cullen was not eager, therefore, to have another general meeting of the bishops convened just then to discuss what course of action should be taken in regard to Cardwell's reply, lest a serious disagreement take place among the bishops and impair that harmony and unity so necessary to effective action on this important question. Hence, when Cullen wrote Cardinal Barnabò on December 20, he recommended that Rome not take any immediate action about the national system but that the Sacred Congregation charge some of the bishops or archbishops to demand of the government that it remedy all aspects of the system that the bishops found dangerous.[8]

5. Norman, p. 70, n. 6.
6. C, Leahy to Maguire, July 2, 1859 (copy).
7. C, Leahy to Cullen, July 2, 1859.
8. Larkin, p. 478.

The advantage of proceeding in this way, Cullen argued, was that the positive aspects would not be condemned along with the negative, and all Catholics would remain united on this important question. He then assured the cardinal that they could obtain all that was necessary from the government, though perhaps not all at once, if they would only be persistent. A week later Cullen wrote Kirby and put a most revealing gloss on his letter to the cardinal. "We have made no move as yet about the education question," he reported on December 27. "As there are seven or eight bishops at least *infermi in fede* (and especially Dr. Moriarty) on that question, it is well to move with caution. It is better for the Prop. to write that it will give no judgement at present, but that we ought to put forward our claims" (K). "It is impossible," he then explained, "to call the Bishops all together every week or month *e poi* [and then] even if they assemble, they are so numerous that they can do no business. I think Dr. McHale will refuse to act with the other three Archbishops. *Tanto meglio* [So much the better]. We have the finest case that can be imagined. We can show that the Government has violated for the past all its pledges, and that we can have no confidence in a mixed system any longer." "The Pastoral of last August," he admitted, "was not well drawn up. It did not give our reasons. As for our Memorial to the Lord Lieutenant it was a poor miserable concern. Dr. McHale drew it up, and all he seemed to think of was the insertion of long obscure Gibbonian sentences with a few hard words against the Government. No reason whatever was assigned to our petition. Why, you will ask, did we adopt the Memorial? Merely to keep Dr. McHale quiet, and to give the appearance of great unanimity to our proceedings."

There were, in fact, three main points of view represented among the bishops on the education question. Those who thought like Mac-Hale were adamant in their refusal to come to terms with anything less than a separate system supported by the state and under the control of the bishops. Those who agreed with Moriarty argued that the securing of a separate system was not only utopian but practically dangerous as far as proselytizing was concerned, and that the best course to pursue was to work for the restoration of the neutral system that had originally been set up in 1831 but had been subverted in the interim by Protestant, and particularly Presbyterian, pressure. A third group, including Cullen, Leahy, and Dixon—and they were in the great majority—agreed that in principle a mixed system was indefensible from a Catholic point of view but argued that the present system must be tolerated until they could persuade the government to grant a separate system, because they simply could not financially support a separate system. The proper course for the bishops, therefore, was to declare formally for a separate system, and in the meantime attempt to prevent the national board, which administered the system, from further encroaching on Catholic interests, while attempting to recover some of the ground lost in recent years by agitating for the reform of the board.

In early February Moriarty took occasion in a reply to a conciliatory letter from his metropolitan on the vexed educational question to explain his position at some length. "If you follow up the plan indicated in your Grace's letter," he assured Leahy encouragingly on February 6,

> you will be likely to have more unity & unanimity than if an extreme course is pursued. It is easy to be silent and inactive, but it is hard to talk & act contrary to strong convictions.
>
> I consulted every P.P. in this Diocese for our great meeting last summer. They were unanimously & decidedly of opinion that while the Nat. System required improvements, it would be dangerous to exchange it for a separate system. To get men with such opinions, in which I entirely concur, to hold meetings & pass resolutions to the contrary would be too great a farce. I think this is the opinion of the laity & that they will not be driven to the active advocacy of extreme views. We are all convinced that with a separate system the number of Catholic children in Protestant schools will be considerably increased in this part of the country, & we believe not diminished in the North.
>
> Assure us that under the separate system—or with separate grants, no Catholic children will attend heretical schools, in which they would have then no protection, & your Grace will find us the strongest advocates of the separation.[9]

"Dr. MacHale," Moriarty added, "will not give. I am sure he will not. This is a difficulty. Hence I would be inclined rather to let a few Catholic [?] members of Parliament work the thing out with Mr. Cardwell & the Government. The Bishops would not seem to change their position in the least, and the interference of our Members allowed but not officially recognized by us, might remove many grounds of complaint & justify our tacit acquiescence."

"The following list of amendments," Moriarty further explained,

> has been submitted to me by a member of the Government [probably the Irish attorney general, Rickard Deasy].[10] Although

9. Leahy Papers (L), Archives of the Archdiocese of Cashel, Thurles.
10. The model school system mentioned in item 4 in Moriarty's list of proposed amendments had been inaugurated in 1848. The commissioners of the Board of Na-

the letter was marked confidential I dare say it was submitted also to your Grace, but lest it should not I will transcribe it.

1.⁰ The appointment of a Catholic resident commissioner having coequal authority with Mr. McDonnell.

2.⁰ The alteration of the rule of 1855 as to allowing children to be present at religious instruction by making it more efficacious securing parental authority.

3.⁰ Separation of the pupils at the Training School by having separate domiciles for the different religions under the management of persons of their own religion.

4.⁰ Extension of the same separation to existing Model Schools.

5.⁰ Non-extension of the Model School System & gradual withdrawal from it.

6.⁰ Substitution of Non-vested or Training Schools.

7.⁰ Alteration of the rule as to vesting ordinary schools in the commissioners.

8.⁰ Revision of the school books.

"My answer to this proposal, which was not of course official," Moriarty noted, "was to request another call to your Grace. I do not know whether that has been done."

"I have told every member of Parliament with whom I have had conversation," he further reported, "that we can not stop where we

---

tional Education had earlier resolved on a system of thirty-two model schools, that is, one for each educational district in Ireland, but later reduced the number to twenty-six. "The ground rent and all building expenses the commissioners proposed to assume themselves. In return, the schools would be vested in them, not in local trustees. Each model school was to have an infant, a female, and a male school among its components, each division having a capacity of 100 students. Dormitory space was to be provided for three candidate teachers in the male school, and a residence was to be found for a female candidate in the neighbourhood. Candidate teachers were to be lodged and boarded at the commissioners' expense. Training was to take six months, thus allowing each model school to produce six trained male teachers and two trained female teachers each year. Following their work at the district model school, candidates were to teach for two years and after passing an examination on material that they were to study during their two years of teaching, then were to proceed to the central model school in Dublin. In order to fill the model schools with apt pupils on whom the candidates could practice the most promising students in local national schools were to be admitted free to the district model schools where they would act as monitors and receive a small weekly wage" (Donald H. Akenson, *The Irish Education Experiment* [London, 1970], pp. 147–48). The "Training School" referred to by Moriarty in amendment 3 was undoubtedly the central model school in Dublin, where, the Irish bishops complained, the students of various religious denominations (while segregated on the basis of sex) were permitted to live together without any special provision being made for religious supervision, instruction, or practice (Patrick Francis Moran, ed., *The Pastoral Letters and Other Writings of Cardinal Cullen* [Dublin, 1882], 2:74–119, letter of Irish bishops to Edward Cardwell).

are—that we must go forward to an entire separation or go back to the pure neutrality of the original System. The latter [is] I think the only practicable step." "I am going," he concluded, "to spend this evening with O'Donoghue. I never met a man so thoroughly devoted to the cause of the Church as he is. His fixed rule of action in these matters is to do as Your Grace will direct him as long as he is M.P. for Tipperary. He stands up for the Pastoral—the whole Pastoral & nothing but the Pastoral. I will not spoil him on you—as we say in Kerry." "P.S.," Moriarty added, "I fear very much the appointment of a resident Cath. commissioner. It would naturally entail the appointment of a Presbyterian with the Protestant, then the dismissal of the unpaid commissioner & then we would be one to two—or perhaps all three would be against us. Not unlikely that M.P. [John Pope] Hennessey would be the Catholic Commissioner. I much prefer the increase—to majority or at least equality—of our unpaid Cath. comm^{rs} who will not be mere tools in the hands of Government."

When Cullen made no move in the early new year to consult with the bishops as a body in reference to the reply to be made to Cardwell, rumors apparently began to circulate that whatever was to be done would be done without consulting the whole body. "A few days ago," the bishop of Cloyne wrote Leahy in some alarm on February 24, "I heard that there was a question of a meeting between at least *three* of the Archbishops and some of the Suffragan Prelates, having for an object to introduce certain modification in the 'Pastoral' so as to prepare the way for some united plan of action to be agreed to between them and the Government regarding national education" (L). "This was the first and the only intimation," he further explained, "I had of the subject and it was given so briefly and without explanation, that, not knowing what may be intended, I take the liberty of asking your Grace, whether such a project is entertained, and, if so, to what extent the Bishops' demands are to be modified." "In the present state of the question," Keane declared firmly,

> it is clear that the *mixed* system, in any of its departments, national, intermediate, or Collegiate, cannot be accepted.
>
> The principle is defective and dangerous. "Pur et simple," it cannot have the approbation of the Catholic Church.
>
> If the Government will not, or cannot, immediately grant the denominational system, there is nothing in the law to prevent them from returning of their own account to the spirit and letter of the rules of the Board as first laid down and acted on. Such a step would remove some of the dangers that give so much alarm to Catholics. . . .

No doubt the Government see and admit the injustice of the changes made by the Board; and clear as may be the necessity for a return to the original plan, they will not do so till they have exhausted all means of tiring out the patience of the Catholics, and of inducing the Bishops to become, as it were, one of the contracting parties, whose seal of approbation should be affixed to an education "mixed" plan, sanctioned by both.

"The language of the Memorial and Pastoral," Keane insisted in conclusion, "makes it impossible for the Bishops to accept with approbation anything short of separate grants. With a firm and earnest perseverance they cannot fail ultimately to succeed. Meanwhile, they will, as they have been doing for the last thirty years try and make the best of what they have unless a total break with the Board be forced on them."

Cullen, meanwhile, who had been working away at a comprehensive reply to Cardwell, had written Kirby that same day. "I send you," he explained on February 24, "a reply to Mr. Cardwell. Get in [*sic*] translated. I expect it will go in the name of all the bishops. If not I will publish it in my own. Examine it closely and suggest what you wish" (K). Some two weeks later Cullen reported to Kirby again. "I send you," he wrote on March 8, "a corrected copy of the reply to Mr. Cardwell. Try and get it translated. I think it hits the N. system very severely and temperately. I suppose Dr. McHale will not have anything to do with it. I have sent it to him today. Nearly all the other bishops will agree to it or have done so" (K). Cullen was right that MacHale would refuse to sign. "The gentleman secretary," MacHale explained to Cullen on March 13, referring to Cardwell, "having, in his answer to your memorial, expressed in the plainest terms the steadfast adherence of her Majesty's Government to the principles of the National System, I do not think that a second application would be more successful than the first in securing for Catholics the blessings of a separate education. I cannot, therefore, concur in having my signature put to any such rejoinder, from which no good result is to be anticipated." He advised Cullen ironically in conclusion, "The votes of ten or even five members of Parliament, strenuously resolved to see our application carried out, would, in my opinion, grounded on long experience, have more weight with the Government than twenty memorials and their rejoinders with the signature of all the episcopacy."

"I sent the letter to Cardwell," Cullen reported to Kirby on March

16, "in its corrected shape to Dr. McHale, who refuses positively to sign it. *Quid agendum* [What must be done?]. I suppose we must do without him. It is a real scourge to have to deal with him. If we act without him, we appear divided. If we do nothing our fetters will be bound tighter every day" (K). On March 23 Cullen wrote Kirby again:

> The Reply to Mr. Cardwell is now ready, but not sent as yet. Dr. Moriarty and Dr. Delany hold out against it as too strong. Dr. Moriarty appears to be much influenced by Protestant authorities. I had a long conference with him the other day, and argued over the Reply to Cardwell with him. He really had nothing to oppose to it—but I believe he went straight from me to the Resident Commissioner[,] Mr. McDonnell[,] to hear his teaching. Dr. Delany is I suppose afraid of the Cork spirit. I have written to him today. Dr. McH. probably will not sign—but that wd rather be an advantage, as it would indicate that the Reply was too moderate for him." [K]

"The Reply," he assured Kirby in conclusion, "tho' not long, cost a terrible deal of labour. I had to watch every word lest there cd be any contradiction given. I think it is now so guarded that Cardwell will find it difficult to answer it."

In reporting his discussion with Cullen to Leahy on March 21, from Killarney, Moriarty explained, "I think the best practical conclusion I can come to is this. If all sign—so will I. If there is to be a division I prefer to vote in the Minority, or in other words to be among the nonsigning. The latter I think the most truthful course, but I can bring myself to follow the former as there is nothing in the document wrong or bad *in principle*, and as to inexpediency, I may feel safe in the firm conviction that we will never get what we ask. God loves us too much" (L). "I believe," he added unrepentently, "that if the Devil got into his own uncontrolled management the affairs of the Irish Church he could do nothing better calculated to promote his interests than to give us a separate system of education." Cullen, who was nothing if not perservering, wrote Moriarty again on March 23: "I hope your Lordship has made up your mind to sign the Reply to Mr Cardwell. If the Government wish to make any concessions the reply does not prevent them from doing so, and there is nothing to impede us from accepting them though at the same time we ask for what is just and desirable[—]a separate System."[11] "There is nothing in the Reply," he further assured Moriarty, "to compromise anyone. If some

11. M, 8319 (4).

few bishops refuse their names it will give the Government reason to conclude that we are divided, and they will urge on their most dangerous plan of taking education altogether into their own hands as they are doing most effectually by their training and Model schools. I will keep over the letter until next Monday when I expect to send it. It is important that Cardwell shd have it before he bring[s] on the estimates for education. All the bishops of Ulster and Leinster have given their names and altogether we have 23 or 24 signatures." "The result I foresee in case of disagreement among the bishops," he warned Moriarty in conclusion, "is a total condemnation of the system by Rome in accordance with our desires of last August. If we could go on asking and getting something without divisions, we would be left to ourselves. Not being able to agree Rome must step in."

Though both Moriarty and Delany agreed in the end to sign the reply, MacHale remained adamant. In one last effort to make the reply unanimous Cullen decided to write him again. MacHale's reply was as insolent as it was devastating in adding insult to injury. "Having already stated," MacHale explained to Cullen on March 31, "why I declined affixing my signature to the rejoinder to Mr. Cardwell, I do not find in your Grace's recent letter any reason to make me come to a different determination."[12] "I have had occasion," he reminded Cullen, alluding cleverly to the fact that the apostolic delegate had once again avoided consulting with the bishops as a body, "to remark to your Grace more than once, that the mode of sending round letters to bishops soliciting their signatures for various objects without the opportunity of mutual consultation, was, in general, liable to grave exceptions. I scarcely ever knew it to be productive of good. It is certain that it has been productive of evils." He added, commenting on Cullen's complaint in his reply to Cardwell that Catholics had received hardly any share in the government's educational appointments in Ireland, "There is, in several quarters, more anxiety to get situations as commissioners and inspectors with large salaries under the present Board, than for separate grants for Catholics. And if those who look for such places could be gratified, but little solicitude would be left by them or their friends for the rights and duties of Catholic bishops regarding the education of their flocks." In a final note he alluded to the libel in ultra-nationalist circles that Cullen was a government bishop: "Your Grace acknowledges how unfairly we have been dealt with by the English Government, but you will not be much surprised

12. Bernard O'Reilly, *John MacHale, Archbishop of Tuam* (New York, 1890), 2:524–25.

when you reflect that the Government which has treated us so unfairly regarding such solemn interests is so vigorously and zealously sustained by several among those who complain of its unfairness, nay, encouraged by such earnest and extensive support to continue and aggravate the same unjust and insulting treatment."

Cullen's reply to Cardwell, which was dated from Dublin on March 18, though not sent off until early April, was a very able and temperate polemic on behalf of a separate system of education for Irish Catholics.[13] The reply, which came to nearly fifty printed pages, was divided into three unequal parts. The first and longest, which took up about half the reply, was a discussion of the three principles regarding education on which the government and the Irish bishops had concurred. They were the paramount importance of religious education, the necessity of granting separate religious training to the children of each religious denomination, and the right of the heads of the churches to oversee the religious education of those of their communion. Cullen then proceeded to argue that the system as then administered by the national board did not recognize any of those principles. The board did not admit the paramount importance of religious education and indeed secularized the teaching of history, philosophy, and even morality in those vested schools under its own control. It also denigrated Catholic religious practice by prohibiting any external religious manifestations, such as the sign of the cross, while even forbidding silent prayers and refusing to allow the crucifix itself to be set on any part of a school building. Cullen then pointed out that the second principle concurred in by the government and the bishops—the necessity of granting a separate religious training—was also not practically adhered to by the board. Combined religious instruction was, in fact, effected through use of national schoolbooks provided by board, which were compiled by Protestants, with the readings in them extracted from Protestant writers and divines. Finally, the third principle—the right of the heads of each Church to oversee the religious education of its flocks—was also violated in practice by the board. Catholic pastors were required to treat with the board through their flocks, and there was not a single case to date in which the board had recognized Catholic episcopal authority.

The second and third parts of Cullen's effort took up the remaining half of the reply in about equal portions. The second was primarily concerned with demonstrating how the national board had deviated from the principles first laid down by the earl of Derby, then Lord

13. Moran, 2:74–119.

Stanley, in 1831, when he was the chief secretary for Ireland, for the management of the national system of education. In fact, Cullen argued, the board had the ability to change the essential principles of the system because it needed only to secure the approval of the lord lieutenant of Ireland to alter any of the fundamental rules of the system. Over the last thirty years the board had accordingly modified the original system to the great disadvantage of Catholics. In setting up the training schools for teachers, as well as the agricultural and model schools, which were not managed with a due regard for Catholic interests, the board aggravated the anti-Catholic tendencies of the system. In the third and final part of his reply, Cullen addressed himself to an examination of the arguments urged in Cardwell's letter against separate education and in favor of the mixed system. Cullen pointed out that the three main arguments raised by Cardwell against a separate system—that it encouraged dissensions among the various classes of society, that it checked the progress of knowledge, and that it interfered with the proper distribution of public funds for educational purposes—would not stand scrutiny. What dissensions existed among the various classes in Ireland, Cullen noted, cleverly standing the argument on its head, were really the product of the mixed system of education; further, there was ample and disinterested testimony available about the efficacy of purely Catholic schools in the teaching and dissemination of knowledge, and Catholics not only had no designs on the public funds set aside for education but rather supported the view that the state should have, through inspection, the necessary control to secure the proper expenditure of public money.

Cullen then turned from the arguments raised by Cardwell against a separate system to those he adduced in favor of a mixed system. Cardwell had pointed out that it was the Catholics in fact who benefited most from the mixed system. Some 3,700 of the 5,500 schools in the national system were managed by Catholic patrons; 481,000 of the 573,000 children, a proportion of 84 to 16, were Catholics; and the proportion of Catholic to Protestant teachers was 80 to 20. What Cardwell was really saying, of course, was that because Catholics made up the poorer portion of the population they received far more from the public treasury for education than they contributed. Cullen rejoined by freely admitting that some good effects had been produced by the national system and that without forgetting their rights as citizens to participate in the public grant for education, the bishops were sincerely grateful for the benefits conferred on their flocks. Still, if the Catholics did receive a larger proportion of the public grant, and particularly the Catholic teachers, it was only because Catholics constituted the bulk of those who needed to be educated at public expense, having been in the past reduced to poverty by persecution, confiscation, and penal laws. Cardwell's statistics, Cullen then noted, also laid bare the anomaly of having a system that was more than 80 percent Catholic administered by an essentially Protestant bureaucracy. The resident commissioner and a large majority of the other commissioners were Protestants. Moreover, the majority of the other officials of the board were Protestants, and the proportion of Catholic to Protestant school inspectors had no relation to the number of Catholic schools and children in the system. The statistics also suggested, Cullen added cleverly, that because the system was for all practical purposes essentially Catholic, in fact it would require only very slight modification to make it completely denominational. This step would also resolve the further curious anomaly of having a separate system in England and a mixed one in Ireland.

"We speak," Cullen then reminded Cardwell in concluding, "for a population reduced to poverty by confiscation and penal laws. We speak in the name of a Church that has been persecuted and despoiled of all its property, and that has made great sacrifices in promoting public education. Though past injustices ought to be repaired, we ask for neither favours nor privileges; we seek for no monopoly, but for freedom of Catholic education—a freedom which implies a fair participation in the benefits of the State." "In the name of the same Church," Cullen then summed up,

we complain that solemn promises have not been maintained, and that our rights, which you, in the name of Government, profess to recognize, have been ignored. We complain that the administration of a system principally designed for a Catholic population is placed in the hands of a body in great part Protestant, and that in the appointment of inspectors and other officers, due regard has not been had to the number of Catholic schools and pupils. We complain that the rules of the Board of National Education have gradually undergone changes adverse to Catholics and favourable to Protestants. We complain of the dangers to which our children are exposed in schools where they are *induced* to receive Protestant religious instruction, or can receive no religious instruction at all. We complain that the books such as we have described them, are unfit for the education of Catholics. We complain that the whole National System has been developed in a narrow-minded, illiberal, and anti-Catholic spirit, and that the Catholics of Ireland, as if to remind them of the degradation of past times, are deprived of many advantages freely granted to all classes in England. In fine, we complain of grievances affecting ourselves and the children of our flocks. But far from seeking to usurp the education of Protestants, we restrict our care to those of our own household, leaving all who differ from us in religion to provide for the instruction of their own children in whatever way they consider most beneficial.

Cullen then concluded by expressing the hope that the government would recognize the justice and necessity of granting a separate system of Catholic education for Catholic children.

In writing to Kirby on April 10, shortly after he had sent off the reply to Cardwell, Cullen showed that he had few illusions about what its impact on the government would be (K). After complaining again about MacHale's refusal to sign, he explained that he feared "that we shall get nothing by the letter. The Government finds that education is placed very much under their control by the present system and they are anxious to keep it up on that account. However up to the present no great harm has been done. The sacraments are better frequented than ever and the collection for the Pope shows how strong the faith is of the people." Two months later he was somewhat more hopeful. "The National education question," he informed Kirby on June 8, "will be soon before Parliament. Concessions will be made to us—but probably only with a view of dividing. Dr. Moriarty says the system at present works so well in Kerry that he cannot wish for anything better" (K). Some six weeks later, on July 17, Isaac Butt, Liberal M.P. for the borough of Youghal, introduced a motion in the House of Commons for an address to the queen on the question of national education in Ireland. The defeat of Butt's motion, and an especially warm endorsement of the national system by Cardwell, apparently persuaded Cullen that the bishops needed to take some more decisive step. "I believe it will be necessary," he alerted Kirby on July 20, "to hold another meeting of the Bishops about the Nat. system. The Government will give us nothing. However we are advancing in public opinion. The letter to Cardwell of last March has done some good, and many are now with us, who were quite opposed to the first Memorial. Altogether we are getting stronger in regard [to] education. Speak to Cardinal Barnabò" (K).

A month later, on August 16, when the vote was taken in the

House of Commons on the Irish educational estimates for the year, Cardwell finally took occasion to announce what modifications the government was prepared to make in the national system:

There were one or two points in which the Government thought some change would be right, and advantageous to the system itself. They believed, in the first place, that the constitution of the Board was a matter of great and just objection to Roman Catholics. They thought that, the Roman Catholics having so large a proportion of pupils, and having so great an interest in the well-being of the system, it would be reasonable that their number at the Board should be raised to an equality. The principle of equality had already been admitted by former Governments in regard to the inspectors and administration of the system, and he did not understand why there should be any difficulty in carrying into effect the same principle of equality in that which was, after all, the great and important governing body of the whole. No member of any Church could say it was unreasonable to provide that the number of Roman Catholic members of the Board should be equal to that of their Protestant brethren. A question had also been raised with regard to the vesting of the schools. Originally the schools were vested, as in England, in trustees, and there appeared no reason why, instead of being vested in the Board as a corporation, the schools assisted by the State should not be vested in trustees, the terms of the trust-deeds being such as to secure the observance of the two cardinal principles of the system in a manner satisfactory to the Board and their legal advisers. Again, a great desire had been expressed for the revision of the books. . . . There was, for example, an almost entire absence of all reference to subjects of Irish interest, and he thought it would be easy to introduce much in connection with Irish topics without imparting at the same time anything either of a polemical or a political character. It was the intention of the Commissioners to appoint a Committee of their own body for the purpose of revising the books in the spirit he had indicated.[14]

Cullen, who had been making his customary visitation of his diocese during August, was obviously not much impressed with Cardwell's proposals. "I am just after returning from County Wicklow," he reported lackadaisically to Kirby on August 31 from Dublin, "where I

14. *Hansard Parliamentary Debates*, 3d ser., 160:1388–90.

spent some weeks visiting the several parishes. Thanks be to God the people are well instructed and devotedly attached to the faith. I thanked the various congregations for what they did for the Pope, and exhorted them to continue to pray for him. They are all most attached to His Holiness" (K). "I have confirmed since I began the visitation about 10,000 children," he explained. "They know the catechism very well in the country. They learn it in the National schools which are not mixed in this diocese except where there are model schools and training schools—which however only exist in Dublin and Athy. They are a great scourge, because frequented by prot. and catholic small children and teachers." "The debate in Parliament," he finally observed, "will do good, as it shows the movement for separate education is progressing."

By the end of August, however, Cullen had long decided what was the correct policy to be pursued regarding the national system. First of all, he understood that time was on the bishops' side. The system obviously posed no immediate danger either to the faith or to the practice of Catholics, and indeed in most areas where the system was essentially Catholic, faith and practice were actually enhanced by it. The policy to be pursued, therefore, was to agitate in the long run for a separate system while attempting to secure in the short run significant modifications in the present system. Cullen also understood, however, that the successful issue of this policy depended on two things. The first was that Irish public opinion had to continue to maintain that the present system was unsatisfactory, and the second was that the episcopal body must not allow itself to be divided on the issue. Cullen's understanding of these requirements does much to explain his various moves with regard to the education question over the previous six months. His efforts to keep Irish public opinion up to the mark, for example, explain why he wrote his reply to Cardwell in the first place and why he spent so much time on it when he obviously expected as little practical result from it as did MacHale. They also explain why he was pleased with the debates in the House of Commons during July and August, even though they too had little practical result.

Cullen's main concern over the previous six months, however, had been how to keep the episcopal body united on the education question. This was why he was so very annoyed at those bishops (especially Moriarty) who he suspected were not at one with the great majority of their brethren on the question. This was the reason why Cullen did not encourage the calling of a meeting of the bishops to discuss his proposed reply to Cardwell but chose instead to circularize them. The tactic was very clever, not simply because it was obviously impossible to have an open split if the bishops did not meet, but because it would minimize and contain what dissent there was on the question among the bishops. By isolating the dissenters, and giving each the impression that he was likely to be the only one not to sign the reply, Cullen very effectively coerced the minority. How well the tactic worked was made amply evident in the isolation and then the submission of even so very able and clever a prelate as Moriarty. Even MacHale's refusal to sign did not prove detrimental, for it was well known that he was an intransigent supporter of separate education and that Cullen's reply to Cardwell was, if anything, too moderate in its tone and content to please him. Indeed, he made his views known in two flaming open letters to the prime minister, Lord Palmerston, before and after the debate on the Irish educational estimates in August, in which he once again denounced the national system as yet another of those various schemes adopted and enforced by the British government to destroy the Catholic religion in Ireland.[15] The real reason why MacHale refused to sign the reply, of course, was that he viewed Cullen's bypassing of the bishops as a body as yet another attempt by the apostolic delegate to subvert the constitution of the Irish church.

But why, it may well be asked, did Cullen then request Kirby in July to speak to Barnabò about authorizing a meeting of the bishops to discuss the national system? The answer is that having just secured the bishops' virtual unanimity on his reply, he knew that they could hardly deviate as a body from what they had only recently and individually subscribed to. He also realized that Cardwell would soon introduce the government's proposals to modify the system, and a meeting of the bishops to discuss the government's proposals was something quite different from a meeting of the bishops called to frame their own proposals, which he had just successfully obviated by his tactic on the reply. Still, the danger was that even the government's rather tame proposals might divide the bishops, and this danger explained why Cullen became increasingly annoyed at and suspicious of Moriarty. When Moriarty wrote him, for example, in early October, apparently complaining that it was not wise to discourage Catholics from serving as commissioners on the Board of National Education, Cullen took occasion to read him a lecture on what he thought was the correct policy. He informed Moriarty on October 7,

15. Norman, pp. 72–73.

I beg to acknowledge receipt of your Lordship's letter regarding the important question of the National Schools. In reply I beg to assure you in the 1st place that I have not used any influence to prevent good Catholics from joining the board. I leave them altogether to their own discretion. However I see a great objection to accepting office, which I cannot remove. Those who become commissioners are I suppose, pledged to maintain the system as it is. They must uphold the model schools, and in doing so they throw the formation of all masters into the hands of a protestant government, and they contribute as far as in them lies, to undermine Catholicity in the country.

Your Lordship says that all the gentry of the country are against the Bishops. Fortunately the gentry do not represent the country—they are few, and I believe they were as much for the Veto as they are for mixed or infidel education.

Your Lordship is afraid that the Irish Cavour Party may get hold of the system. I entertain the same fear, and I think we ought all to fear such a result as long as we are at the mercy of a Palmerston or any other English minister. Such ministers may appoint Cavourites any day they wish according to the present system.

As the system is working actually it is in Protestant and Presbyterian hands, and the Catholics who were on the board and who were quite as zealous as those now spoken of, did not, perhaps could not, prevent the system from being made much more dangerous than it was in the beginning.

Hopes of changes are now held out but if they are really intended, why are they not officially announced[?]

As long as the model schools and training schools are maintained, I will oppose the system. I trust too to be able very soon to assail openly the model schools in this city. I will do it by ecclesiastical censures as soon as matters will be ripe for such a step.[16]

Cullen concluded firmly, referring to two prospective Catholic commissioners, "I have told Mr. O'Hagan this and I will tell Judge O'Brien and any others that speak to me on the subject. Of course this will not be pleasing to Commissioners—but I am convinced the only object the Government has in view is to fasten such institutions on the country, and it is necessary to oppose them while we can do so."

16. M, 8319 (4).

What had prompted Moriarty's complaint and Cullen's rejoinder was that the government had finally decided to increase the number of Catholic commissioners on the Board of National Education, as had been proposed by Cardwell in the House of Commons the previous August, and it was having considerable difficulty in finding acceptable candidates because of Cullen's attitude. To break the impasse the government had apparently requested William Monsell, the Liberal member for county Limerick, to intercede with Cullen and ask him to find out what the bishops' position might be about Catholics serving on the board. Cullen obviously said that he would informally ask those bishops who would be in Dublin at the end of October to attend the Maynooth and Paris college boards about their opinions on Catholics serving as commissioners. "I proposed the question," Cullen reported to Monsell on October 28, in a letter marked "Private & Confidential,"

> regarding the Commissioners of Nat. Education to about fourteen bishops on last Friday. Dr. Moriarty declared himself favourable to the opinion that good Catholics should accept the office. Dr. Leahy[,] archbishop of Cashel[,] said he could not see why it would not be *lawful* for Catholics to accept the office, but at the same time he said it might be inexpedient for them to do so. The other twelve bishops who were present expressed their opinion that Catholics ought not to give any sanction to a mixed system which of its nature is detrimental to Catholic interests, or contribute in any way to render it permanent in the country as good Catholics would do by accepting office. They all seemed to consider it dangerous to prop up the power of government in regard to education. They might give office now to good men, but they could bring dangerous elements into the body at any time. The general opinion of the bishops was to keep aloof—if the government in the meantime do any good, the bishops will be free to examine what may be done and act accordingly—if things be left as they are or made worse they seemed determined to break with the Board, and to hold out for a separate system.[17]

"I have spoken separately to others," Cullen then further reported, "and I think not more than three are satisfied with Mr. Cardwell's proposals, and they only wish to give them a trial. Dr. Moriarty is the only bishop who appears to be decidedly favourable to the present system, or satisfied with the proposed change."

17. M, 8317 (3).

Naturally the government did not want to announce its proposed increase in Catholic commissioners before it was certain, at least informally, that those places could be filled. The response of the bishops in late October, therefore, did not make the government's way any easier over the next few weeks. "More O'Ferrall," Cullen informed Kirby about November 17, naming the former governor of Malta and member of Parliament for county Kildare, "writes to say that the government is greatly upset about Nat. education. They do not know how to get on" (K). "If the Bishops c^d be kept in opposition," Cullen added, "the system wd soon be altered—but Dr. Moriarty is quite active supporting it. He is a sad man—a Young Irelander at one time, then upholding the government. However More O'F. thinks that if the bishops in general keep away, the system must fail or be changed." On November 22 Cullen again wrote Kirby, this time asking him to give a message to the archbishop of Armagh, who was then in Rome making his required *ad limina* visit (K). "Tell him," Cullen added, "that there has been nothing done about the education question as yet. The Government is promising to make some improvements—as yet they have done nothing." "I suppose," he then suggested, "we must hold a general meeting of the Bishops in January on the education question. Let Dr. Dixon speak about it to the Cardinal—as yet we do not know what government will do."

In December the government finally announced its proposed reconstruction of the Board of National Education.[18] It increased the fourteen-member board to twenty by raising the number of Catholic members from four to ten to give them parity with the Protestants. The six new Catholic members were the earl of Dunraven, a convert and important landlord in county Limerick; David R. Pigot, chief baron of the Exchequer; James H. Monahan, chief justice of the common pleas; Laurence Waldron, M.P. for county Tipperary; John Lentaigne, inspector general of prisons; and John O'Hagan, a prominent Dublin barrister. Cullen's first reaction to the new commissioners was ambivalent. "You will see in the papers," he informed Kirby on December 12, "the changes made in the Nat. Board. Whether any good will come of it I know not" (K). On Christmas Eve he wrote Kirby that Monsell was on his way to Rome and would tell him all about the education question (K). "He is favourable," Cullen reported of Monsell, "to Catholic separate education but wishes to give a trial to the new Commissioners. I fear they will do us no good." By early January 1861 Cullen had decided to bide his time with regard to the new

18. *Freeman's Journal*, December 19, 1860.

board, for he reported to Kirby on January 11 that it would be most unwise to say a word against it (K). "I shall however," he promised, "continue to scold."

Cullen had obviously decided that the question of the new board would be better left to the forthcoming episcopal meeting. "Dr. Dixon," he informed Kirby on February 2, "has arrived. Probably we shall have a general Meeting Ep[iscopor]um the 4 week of Lent to see about Education and anything else that may arise" (K). "Unfortunately," he added interestingly, "our gen. meetings do little good. Not one of the resolutions is observed. We may [sic] resolutions at least 3 or 4 times to have a collection for the University each year. Well in Connaught[,] except Dr. Gillooly and Dr. McAvily [correctly, Mac-Evilly], no one collects and I think the other dioceses have scarcely done anything. Meetings are little use unless what is agreed on be carried out." Two weeks later Cullen was in an even worse humor concerning the forthcoming episcopal meeting. "Regarding Nat. education there is nothing new," he reported to Kirby on February 15;

> I will call a meeting of the Bishops for the 16th April—to see *quid agendum*. These meetings however are of little use. No one goes to the least trouble in executing what is agreed on. We agreed at our last meeting to make a collection for the University. We did so in this province—but 15 or 16 dioceses did nothing. I will follow that example for the future. It is useless to attempt to do anything in common. Dr. McH. opposes everything, and when a resolution is adopted, he won't carry it out, and he gets a gt. no. of others to plead his example. No common action can be adopted in his adjunctis—to avoid disputes it wd be better to let everyone do as he wishes. I think Dr. Moriarty will go fully with the Government in the Nat. ed. question. Dr. Delany and others will accompany him. There is a great majority against them—but they say if it is lawful for others to disregard the resolutions of our meetings, why not allow us to do the same[?]
>
> It is great nonsense for me to preside at such meetings. I get a great deal of trouble and expense *e poi non si fa niente* [and then nothing is done].

"I do not like to bother Rome," he finally added most revealingly, "I know they wd not like to get into any row here with anyone—and they will rather abandon those from whom *non hanno niente da temere* [they have nothing to fear]."

With the approach of the episcopal meeting, Cullen's pessimistic mood continued to deepen. He disliked these meetings because they invariably involved him in a confrontation with MacHale that left him in a state of nervous exhaustion for days afterward. His anxieties were increased by the worsening situation in Rome for the pope's temporal power, and they were not helped by the recent harvest failure at home, which had also prevented him from effectively organizing the Peter's pence collection in his diocese. Though all these problems were serious, and certainly preyed on Cullen's mind, they were not what was really troubling him. What he was most concerned about was that the Catholic University was fast approaching another moral and financial crisis. Since Newman's effective resignation some three years before, the University had lacked any kind of consistent leadership. What was even worse, perhaps, was that the University was in serious financial difficulties. Expenditure was running at the rate of about £8,000 per year, whereas income from investments, tuition, and collections amounted only to something over £6,000 per year. What really rankled Cullen was that at their last general meeting in October 1859, the bishops had as a body undertaken to collect for the University, but as of March 1861, of the twenty-eight Irish dioceses, fifteen had collected nothing and several others very little. Of the £4,900 collected over that year and a half, moreover, the ecclesiastical province of Dublin contributed some £2,200, or nearly half of the total. If something were not done, and soon, the University must inevitably collapse, and its demise would be a most serious blow to Cullen's prestige at home and at Rome.

Given also the perceptible cooling in Irish-Roman cordiality over the brigade and Monsignor de Mérode, and the deterioration of Irish and English Catholic relations at the same time, it is little wonder that Cullen continued to be very irritable in his correspondence with Kirby. He reported somewhat crossly on March 29:

> We have not had any meeting of the Bishops—it is fixed for the 23$^\text{d}$ April. I suppose it will do no gt good—I wrote to Dr. McHale inviting him and he never answered my letter—this does not show much inclination to be civil—at our last meeting we adopted some resolutions—one was to have a collection for the University—but only about one half had it. Dr. MacHale never minded it—what use of meetings and wrangling when nothing is done that is agreed on[?] After this meeting I think, I will have nothing more to do with them. I find that everything that is undertaken by a Bishop in his own diocese flourishes. Almost every institution belonging to Dublin is most successful." [K]

"Well," he then added, "there seems to be a curse on our common undertakings—if the University had been taken up by Dublin alone, I am sure it wd have prospered. Now it is withering—the protection given by the meetings of the Bishops only helps to pull it down. No one wishes to do anything when he is assailed for everything he does by those who do nothing. I believe the organisation adopted by the church[—]that of provinces with a metropolitan over his own suffragans[—]is the best. Matters can go on then—but where you have 4 Archb[s] and 24 Bishops, you cannot get them to work harmoniously. However it is hard to know what is best."

"Will you tell Card. Barnabò," he requested of Kirby two days later on Easter Sunday, March 31, "that I have invited all the Bishops to meet on 23^{d} April. We are to treat of Nat. educat. 2. University. 3. Way of appointment of chaplains. 4th The poor laws. 5. The new laws about marriages" (K). "The question of the poor," he then explained, "is a vital one—all we can do is to send a petition. The nomination of the chaplains is now so arranged the Government names and removes. It is a very bad precedent. The education question is the same as usual." "I fear," he added more irritably, "we shall do no good as probably Dr. McH. will oppose everything. At the last meeting he put down all the other Bishops tho' he was alone. *E una vera miseria* [It is a sad situation]. As to me, I will not fight with anyone. I see my powers of Delegate are very uncertain—they are merely to carry out the Synod of Thurles whatever that means."

When the bishops did finally meet in Dublin, from April 23 to 25, all of Cullen's apprehensions proved to be unwarranted. MacHale did not attend, the bishops did a very considerable amount of useful work efficiently, and all was peace and harmony in the body. "I write one line," Cullen reported to Kirby on April 26, obviously greatly relieved, "to say that our meeting has gone on beautifully. We wrote a letter to the Pope which I send to Card. Barnabò. We adopted a remonstrance against the principles of the Nat. board to be sent to Government. We petition Parliament on the poor law—we examined what was to be done on the marriage question. We appointed Dr. Woodlock rector of the University—and we wrote a very long pastoral of which I will send you a copy tomorrow. The pastoral treats at length of the Pope. I think you will like this part of it; it also denounces secret societies—mixed education, the ill treatment of the poor etc. I drew it up as well as I could—but having so many affairs it is hard to write." "Dr. McHale," he then added in conclusion, "did not come to the meeting *nescio qua de causa* [I don't know for what reason]."

When the archbishop of Armagh wrote Kirby the following day,

April 27, he also drew an implicit cause-and-effect relationship between the fruitfulness of the meeting and MacHale's absence (K). "I trust," Dixon noted, "that we have done a great deal of useful business at our late general meeting. Dr. MacHale remained at home." It was left to the bishop of Cloyne, however, to appreciate what was really achieved at the meeting. "Without any doubt," Keane assured Kirby on May 1, "the difference[s] of opinion on education questions, that may have existed, are disappearing every day; and thus union of thought and action may with greater certainly be expected in the future" (K). Needless to say, the unanimity achieved among the bishops on the educational question at their meeting was, in the main, the result not only of Cullen's foresight and persistence but also of his masterfulness, not to say his cunning, in handling the bishops as a body in the course of the previous year.

Cullen was unable to forward to Barnabò his usual extended report of the general meeting for more than six weeks because he was obliged to visit Paris and London in the interim. The trip to Paris in early May was occasioned by the bishops' having commissioned Cullen and Keane to make the required annual visitation to the Irish College there; the visit to London was the result of Cullen's having agreed to give testimony before a select committee of the House of Commons appointed to investigate the poor-law system in Ireland. In any case, Cullen's report to Barnabò on June 12 was a full and able account of the recent meeting:

On April 23 last, a meeting of the Irish Bishops was held in a side chapel of the metropolitan church of Dublin. The Bishops were invited by me to attend there in compliance with a letter from the Sacred Congregation that was written me last autumn. All the Bishops took part except only three, namely the bishop of Raphoe, who was dying, and died several days after, the Bishop of Limerick, who is almost eighty years old and confined to his house, and the Archbishop of Tuam, who did not explain his absence, and who did not even reply to the invitation that I sent him to take part in our deliberations. The meeting lasted for three consecutive days, and everything was conducted with the greatest order and in synodical form. The matters proposed for the discussion were 1. national education, 2. The Catholic University, 3. the condition of the poor houses, 4. some matrimonial laws that have been proposed in these months in the English Parliament.

As for national education the bishops were of the opinion that nothing can be added to what they had written to the Sacred Congregation in the month of August, 1859. Matters remain approximately in the same state as then, only that the Catholic people begin to understand better than before the dangers of mixed education, and that the hope is growing, therefore, of being able to resist more effectively the designs of those who seek to poison the fonts of knowledge. The government itself has already begun to yield something—it has recently increased the number of Catholic commissioners who preside over education from five [correctly, four] to ten, and promises to change the books, and to reconstruct the model schools that form the greatest danger of the system. In these circumstances the Bishops decided to wait a little longer and to be satisfied with petitioning members of Parliament and the government to give us a Catholic system of education, exhorting the Catholic people at the same time to insist on their rights, and to be on guard against the dangers of mixed education. Probably in the end it will be necessary on this point to come to a break with the government, but it is always better that conciliatory means be exhausted before taking other steps, and that Catholics well understand what is necessary for Catholic education before we ask them to reject the education proposed by the government.

As for the Catholic University, the only thing to be done was to choose a rector. The Archbishop of Armagh proposed that Monsignor Woodlock, rector of All Hallows, be chosen, and almost all the Bishops approved the proposal so that Monsignor Woodlock was elected at once. The only opposition was on the part of Monsignor Moriarty, Bishop of Kerry, who proposed for rector Thomas MacHale, professor in the Irish College in Paris, and nephew of the Archbishop of Tuam. What motive Monsignor Moriarty had in putting forward Father MacHale, I have not been able to understand, but it is certain that if his candidate had been elected the University would be undoubtedly crushed. Everyone knows that Monsignor MacHale has always opposed the progress of that institution, and they would not attribute any other motive to the promotion of his nephew than the determination to effect its total destruction. It is necessary to say in regard to the Bishop of Kerry that in educational matters he sides with the government and is in opposition to the other Bishops. This is a very regrettable matter, for being a man endowed with eloquence and other excellent qualities, and being also very active he can do much damage to the good cause. As for the treatment of the poor, which I shall speak about later, he also sides with the government, although the poor are treated in a truly shameful way. Here, I do not have to say more than the college of All Hallows will not suffer any injury by the promotion of Monsignor Woodlock. Father Bennett, provincial of the Calced Carmelites, an excellent ecclesiastic, has served for the past six or seven years as vice rector in the missionary college and helps govern it. In this way things remain as they approximately were.

In the third place the Bishops have dealt with the condition of our poor Catholics in certain poor houses that were established about twenty years ago in this Kingdom. Of these institutes there are 163 scattered through all Ireland, and they are maintained by local taxes that actually amount to almost £500,000, and which in some years past amounted to almost £2,000,000. When these institutions were first introduced, it was hoped they might be a great blessing to the poor, and some Bishops declared strongly in their favor. O'Connell was the only one to raise his voice against them, but he was not listened to, and the experience of twenty years shows how much foresight he had. It is now recognised by all that the tax for the poor is a great burden on the people, that the poor do not receive any comfort from it. The poor houses are very badly administered, and the tax goes in great part to maintain a crowd of clerks, who are generally Protestants. The poor are half starved there, and the most corrupt persons are mixed there with boys and with girls in a way that anyone entering these houses comes out of them generally spoiled and ruined. Having examined the state of things the Bishops decided to present a petition to the House of Commons begging that the system be changed, and that the poor be treated with charity. The petition has already been presented, and we hope that some good will result from it. As I have already said the Bishop of Kerry has declared himself in favor of the present system regarding the poor—and he does not hide his feelings, for the other day after I had talked myself hoarse saying everything ill about the poor houses for almost four hours, one of the committee that examined [me on] that question, a Protestant member of Parliament, said coldly to me, ["]Yet one of your colleagues, the Bishop of Kerry, has told me things totally different from what you assert.["] Anyhow, the abuses are so atrocious that I believe it will be difficult to defend them or put up with them.

I come now to the last subject which was dealt with, namely

to the measures proposed with regard to marriage. Parliament was much occupied with this matter in these last months. One can see a great anxiety to take from us the freedom we enjoy concerning the celebration of marriages, which was the only freedom left, I do not know how, to Catholics in the times of persecution. Indeed although penal laws were made on everything possible, marriages contracted between two Catholics before a Catholic priest were always recognised as valid and the government never interested itself in the way in which they were celebrated. Now it seems that it is desired to replace this former tolerance, and a committee of members of Parliament has constituted itself, with the object of investigating the state of legislation on Catholic marriages in Ireland, and to propose to Parliament a plan of legislation about them. Nothing has yet been done, but it is to be feared, and there is reason to fear, that the committee will recommend that Parliament subject Catholic marriages to many restrictions, which will be the cause of serious inconveniences and injustices. In the actual circumstances, the Bishops were not able to do other than recommend that the Catholic members of Parliament oppose every innovation, and leave matters as they are, adhering to the rule, *quieta non movere* [let sleeping dogs lie].[19]

In the year that had elapsed between his reply to Cardwell and the general meeting of the bishops in April 1861, Cullen had maintained his course on the education question with a remarkable consistency. He had kept public opinion up to the mark in regard to the unsatisfactory nature of the national system of education. In doing so, however, he had done more than simply sow a sense of grievance in the public's mind about the system. By persuading Cardwell to a reform of the system he had also created the impression in the public mind that the government thought that there were legitimate grievances to be remedied. He had achieved all this, moreover, without giving any sanction to the legitimacy of lay interference in educational matters, and his cool reception of the increase in the number of Catholic commissioners on the national board was yet another reflection of his real conviction that only bishops ultimately could be trusted in such matters. By the time of the general meeting in April, Cullen had also brought those seven or eight bishops whom he labeled as being "infirm in the faith" in educational matters, if Moriarty be excepted, around to the views that he shared with the great majority of the body about the

19. S.R.C., vol. 34, fols. 130–32.

correct policy on the education question. Indeed, in the next ten years the attitude of the bishops would so harden on the education question that Cullen ironically would come to be regarded as a moderating influence on the body.

―――――――――◆―――――――――

On his visit to London in late May to testify before the select committee of the House of Commons on the poor law, Cullen found that the Whig ministry was very shaky. "The Irish M.P.'s," he explained to Kirby on June 7 from Liverpool, "are anxious to weaken the Whigs as much as possible without putting them out—they say that if there were a dissolution, and if it were brought on by the Irish Catholics, Palmerston & Russell wd raise the no Popery cry and they wd gain an immense majority—things wd [then] be worse than they are" (K). Cullen apparently also contributed his share to the ministry's instability while he was in London. "I got the Irish M.P.'s together when I was in London," he reported to Kirby on August 3, with reference to the government's proposed legislation on marriage, "and they agreed to object to everything. The result was that the Government has withdrawn all its bills, and we shall remain as we are for the present" (K). "The education question," he added, "is gaining ground. They have determined to change the books and to make some other concessions—but nothing serious will be done. We shall have to fight in the end."

The end, however, was to come much sooner than Cullen realized. Palmerston had apparently had more than enough of the recalcitrance of the Irish Liberal members, especially of the Catholics among them, and decided that they needed to be taught a salutary political lesson. At the end of July, therefore, Edward Cardwell was replaced as chief secretary for Ireland by Sir Robert Peel, and though Cardwell remained in the cabinet as chancellor of the duchy of Lancaster, Peel was not invited to join the cabinet. Not only was the Irish government thereby downgraded by being excluded from direct representation in the cabinet, but Palmerston, in choosing Peel, was also serving notice that the interests of the Irish Catholic Liberal members and their friends would receive very little attention in the future.[20] Cullen apparently did not immediately understand the significance of the change. "Sir Robert Peel," he reported good-humoredly to Kirby on August 3, "is now secretary of state for Ireland. *Pare che sia mezzo matto* [It seems

---

20. D. D. Olien, *Morpeth: A Victorian Public Career* (Washington, D.C., 1983), pp. 470–74.

that he is half mad]. He assailed everything Catholic from time to time, but they say he is clever, and perhaps in *una follia* [a fit] he may happen to do some good" (K). On his arrival in Dublin, Peel paid Cullen a courtesy call and invited him to dinner. Cullen declined the invitation, however, and these were apparently the last polite words exchanged between them for the more than four years Peel was to be chief secretary of Ireland.

In fact, from an Irish Catholic point of view, there could not perhaps have been a worse choice than Peel. He was at one and the same time an evangelical Protestant and an enthusiastic supporter of the policies of Garibaldi and the late Count Cavour in Italy—a most volatile mixture in Catholic Ireland. Indeed, the explosion was not long in coming. In early November Peel wrote to a large number of the Catholic gentry and nobility inviting them to subscribe to scholarships and prizes for the Queen's Colleges, and apparently he even mooted the possibility of establishing another Queen's College in Dublin. Cullen, who had been confined to his bed with an attack of bronchitis, did not hesitate; he denounced the new chief secretary on November 8 in an open letter to his clergy. "Whilst laid up," he reported to Kirby on November 12, "I heard from Mr. Monsell that Sir Robt Peel was writing to Catholic gentlemen urging them to make foundations in the Queen's Colleges. Sir Robt wrote to Lord Fingall and Sir Thos Esmonde among others. I thought this a good opportunity to let fly at him and I dictated the letter which I have sent you on Saturday. I think it was proper to expose his past delinquencies" (K).

In his open letter to his clergy, which had been published in the *Freeman's Journal* on November 9, Cullen had taken Peel to task particularly for his project "to establish and endow a Queen's College in this city; thus extending to the metropolis of Ireland that system which was branded by a member of Parliament for Oxford as a *gigantic scheme of Godless education*; and which must be reprobated from the bottom of his heart by every Catholic, since it has been condemned by the successor of St. Peter as intrinsically dangerous to faith and morals." Cullen then further charged:

> Our Secretary of State in his zeal to promote the condemned system has, it is said, given several endowments to the Queen's College; and as if anxious to increase the number of the few unhappy Catholics who set at defiance the teachings of the Church, he has been writing letters to Catholic gentlemen, or otherwise communicating with them, for the purpose of inducing them to imitate his own example by endowing Scholarships or Exhibitions. I make this statement on the best authority; it is

open to Sir Robert Peel to contradict it, if it be not correct. We are told it is through love for the Catholics of Ireland that the zeal of the Secretary of State is so active in this matter. I cannot adopt this view. I do not pretend to judge Sir Robert's merely political opinions; but in a religious point of view, I do believe that he is a most determined enemy of everything Catholic. He began his career by destroying the influence of the Catholics of Switzerland; he has lately vented his anger on the Catholics of Spain, where he formerly laboured with the zeal of an Exeter hall enthusiast. His eulogies of the arch-revolutionist and enemy of the church, Count Cavour, still echo through the halls of Westminster; and I need scarcely add, on every occasion, he has displayed the bitterest hostility to the venerable Pontiff who fills the chair of Peter, and to the institutions of the Holy Catholic Church.

"As Sir Robert Peel," Cullen then concluded, "has so openly and so emphatically declared his hostility to our holy religion, I need scarcely ask—Will the Catholics of Ireland be guided by his counsel in affairs connected with religion and conscience? Will they allow him to take into his hands the education of their children?"

Five days later, on November 13, Cullen reported to Kirby with even greater satisfaction that Peel had "felt the attack sorely and he stated at Derry that he *cried* (the good crocodile) when he saw that I was thwarting his good designs" (K). "Explain this matter also," he instructed Kirby, "lest they [the Propaganda authorities] sd think that I had assailed that gentleman without reason. *Provocatus in certamen descendi* [Provoked, I have descended into conflict]. Sir Robert Peel wrote to Mr. Bianconi, Sir Thos. Esmonde, Lord Fingall and other Catholics. He invites all to make foundations in the Queen's Colleges and to become members of a committee which he intends instituting to carry out his own views. He is a dangerous man, and I fear, he will divide the Catholics and set them to fight."

In writing Richard More O'Ferrall, M.P. for county Kildare and lay trustee for Maynooth College, several weeks later, Cullen obviously mentioned Peel and his efforts on behalf of the Queen's Colleges. "Sir R. Peel," O'Ferrall replied on December 8, "has not honoured me with an application and I fear he will not" (C). "I think," he added, "there is now an opportunity of doing something for the Catholic University. We may take a lesson from our opponents. I do not see why the 4 Archbishops should not address the Catholic laity asking them to found Burses and immitate [*sic*] the example of the protestants." "Before that can be done with success," he pointed out most interestingly, "it will be necessary to alter the constitution of the University and admit the laity who found Burses to a participation in the Govt of the University." "I believe," O'Ferrall then explained, "that many are dissatisfied that there is no lay element in the Govt of the University, such is my own feeling, and that it ought to be remedied. I admit there may be difficulties and dangers, but they can be met." "You need not," he assured Cullen, "be afraid of any layman who pays his money for a Burse, and you can always provide against traitors by keeping a majority of Bishops, and by giving the filling up of vacancies to the Board. My conviction is that if the university was well supported by lay opinion a few years would give us a Charter and all the privileges we require." "If anything is to be done," he advised prudently in conclusion, "we should proceed cautiously and ascertain beforehand that the application of the Bishops would be responded to. It would not do to fail."

Cullen apparently replied that though O'Ferrall's suggestion was certainly opportune, he was not sanguine about his proposed means to the desired end because the archbishop of Tuam, as one of the four to be approached, was not amicable to any lay representation on the board. "Your letter of this morning," O'Ferrall assured Cullen on December 18, "gave me great pleasure. I have remained these 10 years under the impression that Your Grace['s] influence alone excluded the laity from all participation in the Govt of the University" (C). "Now there is the opportunity," he then explained, "of rallying the upper classes of the Laity in aid of the University thereby giving us ground to meet the Queen['s] Colleges and demand a Charter, without leaving the ready excuse to the Govt that it was exclusively under clerical management." He added, referring undoubtedly to Cullen's having suggested that a division among the bishops or the Catholic body was just then to be avoided at all costs, "I am fully alive to the difficulty you suggest, and how much prudence and self denial is required to avoid greater evils than those I seek to remedy." "Do you see any difficulty or impropriety," he asked, "in my addressing his Grace of Tuam on the subject in a letter marked (private) framing it so, as not to be inconvenient if he committed the indiscretion of publishing it[?]" O'Ferrall and MacHale were fellow trustees on the Maynooth Board, and O'Ferrall went on accordingly: "We are such good friends on the Board, that I think he would send me a civil answer even if he rejected my appeal." "Even if he became angry," O'Ferrall assured Cullen in conclusion, "and hit me hard I am sufficiently insensible even to abuse as not to mind it, or enter into an angry contest with him." O'Ferrall's initiative apparently failed, because there is no further mention of it in the various correspondences, but the importance of this exchange between Cullen and O'Ferrall had less to do with its failure than with what it reveals about Cullen's attitude toward lay representation on the governing board of the Catholic University, and his perception that it was a potentially divisive issue. At this time Cullen was obviously anxious to give the impression that it was Mac-Hale rather than he who was responsible for the intransigence of the bishops as a body in regard to lay representation.

In any case, owing to Cullen's continued and serious preoccupation over the next several months with the difficulties raised by both the second harvest failure and the aftermath of the McManus funeral, his quarrel with Peel about the Queen's Colleges was reduced from a boil to a simmer. On February 14, however, shortly after the opening of Parliament, the chief secretary took occasion on introducing his proposals to put into effect the recommendations made in the report of the select committee on the poor law the previous June, to include a clause that would suppress the exemption from paying the poor rate enjoyed by religious, educational, and charitable buildings. In response, Cullen once again brought matters quickly to a boil by attacking him publicly in the press. "Lord Palmerston," Cullen complained to Kirby on February 25, "appears to have his bully in Sir Robt Peel" (K). "His last act," he then explained, "is to propose to tax our churches, poor schools, hospitals, and cemetaries. I wrote a letter against him about the matter yesterday." Cullen asked all the Catholic members of Parliament to oppose the obnoxious clause, and he especially exhorted Monsell to use all his influence against it. "I hope," he explained on March 7, "you will get all our M.P.'s to oppose the XIth clause of the poor relief Bill. It is monstrous to tax our churches in Ireland, and to leave the churches in England."[21] Cullen's efforts were successful, and some ten days later, on March 16, he was able to report to Kirby that Peel had withdrawn his tax proposal. "Sir Robt Peel," Cullen noted ironically, "has done us much good—if he remain he will make all of us good Catholics" (K).

By this time, however, Cullen had already decided to take advantage of Peel's political ineptness by calling another general meeting of the bishops in order to consolidate their position in the public's mind on the education question. He had, in fact, written Barnabò on February 14, requesting permission to hold a meeting; and that same day, in asking Kirby to speak to the cardinal, Cullen explained in Italian that the meeting was especially timely, "since Peel's letters have produced a good effect throughout the kingdom" (K). Barnabò quickly gave the

21. M, 8317 (3).

required permission "to examine the present state of the education question," and Cullen circularized the bishops on April 5, calling the meeting for May 6, in Dublin (G). He also explained that, besides the education question, it was "desirable that we should treat of the marriage registration bill and of a charity bill for Ireland, both at present under consideration in the house of Commons and also of any changes in the poor law that may attend to alleviate the miseries of the poor." At their meeting, which lasted for three days, the bishops rose to the occasion provided by Cullen and adopted a long series of resolutions on the privations of the poor, the poor laws, the charitable bequests before Parliament, the education question, the established church, and secret societies. Cullen summed up for Kirby on May 9: "We treated of the education [question] and adopted some very strong resolutions. We sent a petition against the marriage registration bill, a new charitable bequests bill—and the poor laws—we sent one also asking for a Catholic system of education—all I fear is that we were too Catholic" (K).

There was one subject, however, that had caused the bishops considerable concern in recent years that they did not treat at their meeting—the Catholic University. They left it alone because it had apparently been given a new lease on life by its recently appointed rector, Bartholomew Woodlock. Woodlock, who had been president of the missionary college of All Hallows in Dublin and who had been Cullen's choice to succeed Newman as rector from the start, had begun his tenure in April 1861 by addressing himself to the main problems faced by the University—leadership and finances. By working incredibly hard, increasing the number of students, and persuading the great majority of the bishops to hold collections in their dioceses, Woodlock had, in some six months after he had been appointed, succeeded in restoring the confidence of those most interested in sustaining the enterprise, and most especially Cullen. "Dr. Woodlock is working hard for the University," Cullen assured Kirby on November 17 (K). "He has done more in a few months than Dr. Newman did in years. He has got twice as many students as were ever in the University and I think he will get the money." "Dr. Newman thought," he then added in a more sour vein, "to act as an oracle—he was to sit in state to do nothing and others were to work. This would do very well in Oxford with £200,000 per an. or in Trinity College with £150,000—in a rising institution without funds people must strip off, and put their shoulder to the wheel." "The collection for the University," he reported further, "goes on over almost all Ireland today. Dr. McHale wrote to Dr. Woodlock not to attempt to collect in his diocese. He will not give, or allow others in his diocese to give."

Several weeks later, in writing to Barnabò on December 5 to report his recent disagreement with Sir Robert Peel over the latter's proposal to establish another Queen's College in Dublin, Cullen also explained that his exchange with the chief secretary had done the collection for the University a great deal of good. "We have at least obtained one good result," he assured Barnabò,

> that almost all the Catholics have declared themselves in favor of the University, and have contributed generously to the maintaining of the same. A collection being made for it in the churches of Dublin on the third Sunday in November, the sum received amounted to £1400–1600, and in almost all the parishes of Ireland something was contributed on that same day. The new rector, Monsignor Woodlock, has given a little life to the institution, and there are at the present moment in the Catholic University 110 medical students, about 80 students in letters and in science and there are about 150 matriculated youths, who must take the examinations, although they do not attend lectures. It may be hoped therefore that in spite of all the difficulties of the enterprise, the Catholic University will turn out successfully in the end. If Monsignor Woodlock had been said rector in the beginning in every probability at the present moment our University would be able to compete with the Protestant University, which has 1000 students and income sufficient for a good principality.[22]

Though there are apparently no figures available for the amount collected for the University for all Ireland in 1861, the sum must have been more than sufficient to meet its current needs. Cullen's obvious pleasure was certainly one indication, and the fact that Dublin generally accounted for about one-fifth of any national collection was yet another. The University's annual expenditure, it will be recalled, was about £8,000. Its only income, besides the annual collection and what it earned in tuition, was about £1,000 in interest earned on the £30,000 invested in government funds. In order for the University to remain financially solvent, then, the annual collection had to amount to at least £5,000 per year. Given Cullen's enthusiasm, the collection for 1861 must have come to between £7,000 and £8,000. Woodlock was so heartened by the general response, in fact, that he began not only to consider plans for acquiring a charter from the government for the University but also to make plans for a system of secondary schools that would serve as "feeders" for the University. In writing to

22. S.R.C., vol. 34, fols. 209–10.

his old friend the bishop of Kerry on December 12, 1861, to thank him for a recent speech on the subject of the Catholic University, Woodlock assured him that "Mr. Monsell & you have, indeed, given the ball a good blow. With God's blessing, we'll score a good many at these innings!"[23]

"I have written to Mr. Monsell," Woodlock further explained, "to thank him for his address. A-propos did he tell you of any correspondence I have had with him as to a mode of getting a charter[?] I mean by getting the Charter of the Board of Maynooth extended. I do not know whether I mentioned this plan to you in any of my letters. If not, I shall tell it to you, when next I write. I should not wish to have myself cited the author of the project; but, if it come to us from gov^t I think we might very well accept it." He continued, turning to a consideration of the secondary system,

And now to fulfill my promise to give you some of my thoughts regarding University-schools:

I.   It would seem to me the object of these University-schools should be to prepare students for the University. Ecclesiastical students should not be excluded: but aspirants to the Univ., and through it to the learned professions & to the numberless respectable positions open to educated men, and now unfortunately very generally occupied by Protestants, should form the greatest part of their students.

II.   I would propose to give in them a first-rate classical, scientific and commercial education, taking for model in this respect (of course mutatis mutandis), the High Schools of England, which have come down from Catholic times, Winchester, Westminster &c. I send you a pamphlet from the pen of Professor Haughton of Trinity College; at pp. 27–30 you will find my idea developed. The whole pamphlet will amply repay perusal.

III.   The school should be under the patronage of the Bishop & of the parochial Clergy, frequently visited by the latter &c.—; but its government should be vested in the University. The local managers would be: a Head-master, a first-rate man, with a salary of £250 or £300 a year; and an allowance of £200 a year more for three Ushers at £70 a year. Of course, these teachers should should not be appointed without the concurrence of the Bishop of the place; and should be removed when ever he required it.

IV.   These schools would not be boarding schools or Colleges:

23. M, 8319 (2).

at least for the present; as the outlay & liabilities in them could not now be prudently undertaken. For the convenience of boys not living in the town with their parents or guardians, certain respectable lodging houses might be procured, in which they might be placed by their friends, and frequently visited by the parochial clergy & by the authorities of the School & of the Univ. The Head-master, and even the under-masters might be allowed to take a limited number of boarders, if they wished to do so.

V. The cost to the University and through it to the country would, I think, be only about £300 or £350-a-year, for each of these schools; viz. £500, or thereabouts for salaries, as above; and £150—for rent and other expenses. Out of this sum (£650—), it might safely be calculated, the students' pensions would re-pay annually one-half or more: say 100 Students at £1-a-quarter, allowing one-fourth written off for bad debts &c.

VI. I would suggest that one of these schools be established in each Province, except Leinster; the place to be selected by the University-Board on the recommendation of the Bishops of the Province. Newry, or Belfast, Clonmel or Thurles, and Sligo might be deemed suitable locations.

May I beg you, my dear Lord, to give this plan your best consideration, and to help me with your advice; as I should wish very much to lay a Report as soon as possible before the Board, & get its sanction for making a beginning in Spring.

"If we do not bestir ourselves," Woodlock warned Moriarty in conclusion, "gov^t will, I fear, anticipate us, and it will be a sad thing for Religion & our country's liberty, if they once seize on middle-class education, as they are seeking to do in the model-schools. Indeed, I do not think the system I have just sketched, will ever be fully developed, till we have a school in every town, where there is a Model-School, or rather in every large town."

Woodlock apparently continued to work very hard at promoting the cause of the University and his ancillary system of "feeder" schools among the bishops, and he also persuaded a number of the Catholic magistrates in the country to declare in favor of the University and against the Queen's Colleges.[24] In March, moreover, the town council of Kilkenny and the Corporation of Limerick memorialized the government on behalf of a charter for the University.[25] In early April the

24. *Freeman's Journal*, March 10, 1862. See also ibid., March 11, 1862, for Moriarty's Lenten pastoral on the same theme.
25. Ibid., March 10 and 18, 1862. See also Norman, pp. 79–80.

subject of a charter was introduced and debated in the Dublin Corporation, and a resolution was passed in its favor. Other corporations soon took up Dublin's example, as public opinion began to mount in favor of a charter. Cullen was very pleased with the progress being made and on April 11 forwarded Kirby the newspaper reports of the debate in the Dublin Corporation for Roman consumption (K). "As to the education question," he reported to Kirby again some ten days later, on April 22, "things are coming around well. You have seen what a stir has been made in the corporations for the University" (K). "Dr. Woodlock," he further pointed out, "got one of the Jesuits to give a retreat to the students and professors before Easter. A vast no. attended and nearly all made their Paschal communion on Holy Thursday at the mass in the University Church." At their general meeting in early May, therefore, as has already been noted, the bishops decided to leave well enough alone; they said nothing about the University in the resolutions published after their meeting. They apparently preferred to continue their policy of petitioning the government for a charter for the University rather than have their representatives raise the question in Parliament, and on July 5 a deputation called on Palmerston to make the request. Monsell had attempted to smooth the way for the deputation by writing to Gladstone, the chancellor of the Exchequer, to assure him that no compromise of principle would be involved for Parliament if the charter were granted to the University.[26] Palmerston was obviously not much impressed, if indeed Gladstone interceded with him at all, for he informed the deputation that "Her Majesty's Ministers have made up their minds as to the nature of the education suitable for Ireland; they are firmly convinced that the best system for that country is a mixed system."[27]

The occasion for the Catholic answer to Palmerston's insolent dismissal of their deputation took place some two weeks later in Dublin at the long-awaited laying of the foundation stone of the University. On Sunday, July 20, in Drumcondra, at the largest religious demonstration ever seen in Ireland, 200,000 people assisted at the ceremony. "The manifestation in Dublin on last Sunday," Cullen reported to Kirby on June 23, "was the greatest and grandest ever witnessed in Ireland. I send you the description. Not fewer than 200,000 men women & children were present. The order was perfect[,] not the smallest accident or disturbance" (K). Cullen, unfortunately, had not been able to preside at the ceremonies because he had returned from

26. Norman, p. 81, quoting Monsell to Gladstone, July 2, 1862.
27. Norman, p. 81, quoting the *Freeman's Journal*, July 7, 1862.

Rome with a very severe cold and fever that confined him to his bed. His place, however, was amply supplied by the archbishop of Armagh, who was assisted by 35 Irish, American, English, and colonial bishops. Some 250 priests were also present. The attendance of such a large number of bishops was accounted for by the fact that they had all been recently in Rome for the canonization of the Japanese martyrs and had been invited by the Irish bishops to participate in the festivities. The ceremonies began with all the trades of Dublin assembling shortly before noon in Stephen's Green and then proceeding to the procathedral in Marlboro' Street to assist at a grand pontifical mass celebrated by the bishop of Elphin.

The sermon was preached by the archbishop of New York, John Hughes, and the procession from the cathedral to the foundation site occupied four hours. The solemn rite of laying the foundation stone was conducted according to the Roman pontifical, and appropriate speeches were made by representative bishops, priests, and laity, a process that took about another two hours. That evening the rector of the University invited the prelates and selected clergy and laity to a splendid dinner at which the archbishops of Armagh and New York, the bishops of Albany (USA) and Southwark (England), the rector, and The O'Donoghue and James Francis Maguire, among others, responded to the various toasts made.[28] The following day, July 21, a national conference of the mayors, chairmen, and other members of the various corporations in Ireland, who had come up to Dublin for the laying of the foundation stone, assembled at the Rotundo in the city to join in the national demand for a charter for the University. The *locum tenens* of the mayor of Limerick presided at the meeting; about five hundred men from all parts of Ireland and some two thousand others attended. Speeches were made by a large number of the local dignitaries, and a series of resolutions concerning the University were unanimously adopted.[29] That same day the *Freeman's Journal* declared that by their massive demonstration the day before, "the Catholics of Ireland—four million five hundred thousand people— made their election—took their side—declared their determination. . . ."

In the late summer and fall of 1862 Woodlock continued to work hard to take advantage of the enthusiasm generated by the agitation for a University charter. He took yet another step to strengthen the University when he finally set up a number of secondary schools de-

28. I.C.D., 1863, pp. 228–29.
29. *Freeman's Journal,* July 21, 1862.

signed to serve as much-needed "feeders" and to provide the University with a steady supply of students in the future. "Dr. Woodlock," Cullen informed Kirby on October 6, "has opened a University school in Waterford, and another in Ennis. This will prevent Government from opening mixed model or classical schools" (K). By the fall of 1862 the University had apparently reached its peak in enrollment, with about 300 students. Of this number 116 were in the medical faculty; some 80 were matriculated in the arts and sciences faculties; and about 100 attended evening classes. Woodlock had increased the paper enrollment of the University to 750 by the device of including some 450 students enrolled in the various schools and colleges throughout Ireland. In explaining all this at his first commencement address on November 25, at the University Church in Stephen's Green, Woodlock noted that the students

> residing outside of Dublin, although not receiving instruction from our professors, are in a position with respect to us similar to that in which the great majority of the students in Trinity College are placed; for it is well known that a large number of students of the Protestant University do not attend lectures therein, but merely come up for the examinations. This privilege we propose to allow to our students outside of Dublin. We recommend a course of studies, books, &c; we send an examiner to the schools, and thus we shall bring students, especially clever young men, from every part of Ireland, to compete for the same exhibitions, basics, and prizes, &c.[30]

Cullen, who was present in his capacity as chancellor of the University, reported the proceedings to Barnabò several days later. "In discussing education," Cullen explained on November 28, "Your Eminence will permit me to mention that the Catholic University begins to give hope that its happy success is by now well assured. The solemn commencement the other day was well done: there were 300 students present and a sufficient number of Professors."[31] "The rector, Monsignor Woodlock," he then added, ". . . made a speech that was received with great applause from twelve or thirteen of our Bishops, and from a throng of priests and laity, who were present. The said speech has been published in the newspapers, and I have sent a copy to Your Eminence. It appears that now the rector has united all the clergy and the people in the determination to have a Catholic Univer-

30. I.C.D., 1863, p. 271.
31. S.R.C., vol. 34, fol. 569.

sity." "Among the bishops," Cullen concluded, "there is only one [MacHale] who opposes the progress of affairs, happy to find himself in opposition to others." Cullen's letter to Barnabò, however, was perhaps more interesting for what it did not say than for what it did. The general University collection for 1862 had been held, as it had been in 1861, on the third Sunday in November, and Cullen did not mention it in his letter. The collection in Dublin had amounted to only some £1,100, and the total collection in Ireland eventually came to £6,400. The most disturbing feature was that neither Tuam nor Cork had held a collection, and if the past served as a precedent, their example would soon prove contagious. The inescapable fact was that the bishops had to collect at least £5,000 per year if the University was to survive, and the hard truth was that if they did not increase the University's capital sum of £30,000 at a rate greater than some £1,500 a year, the foundation stone they had laid with so much éclat the previous July would eventually serve as its tombstone as well.

Even as the bishops, and especially Cullen, were attempting to breathe new life into the University, they were also trying to bury that aspect of the national system of education which they thought to be most dangerous to the faith of their flocks—the model and training schools. Indeed, at their general meeting the previous May, the bishops had determined to declare war on that aspect of the system. The model or training schools had been set up throughout Ireland, with a central school in Dublin, to serve as models where teachers could be trained for the national system. The two features of the model schools that disturbed the bishops the most were that they were religiously mixed in both students and teachers and that they were under the absolute control of the national board. At their meeting, therefore, the bishops had decided to petition the government to demand that the Catholic teachers for national schools be trained in Catholic training schools, under Catholic professors, and that the training schools receive aid from the state as in England. In order to put some teeth into their demands the bishops further resolved:

> That convinced of the importance of Catholic teachers being trained in Catholic model schools only, we direct that no priest shall, after the first day of next term, send any person to be trained as a teacher, either in the central model school, or in any other model school, or in any way co-operate with other patrons

of National Schools, in sending after that date, teachers to be so trained, and that no teachers who shall be sent to be trained after that date in any model school, shall be employed as such by any priest, or with his consent.

That in consequence of the gradual development of the evil tendencies of the model schools, and to mark still further our disapproval of the dangerous principles, similar to those of the Queen's Colleges, on which they are constituted, we direct that our priests or religious shall not hereafter visit such schools even for the purposes of religious instruction or examination, nor otherwise countenance in any way, the attendance at them of Catholic children.[32]

Long before the bishops had decided as a body to move against the model schools, Cullen had determined to reduce their power and influence in his own diocese. Though there were, in fact, only two such schools in his vast archdiocese, one in the city of Dublin and the other in Athy, county Kildare, the school in Dublin was the largest and most important one in Ireland. Because the Dublin school was the showcase of the system, and the national board could be expected to make every effort to sustain it, Cullen initially concentrated his efforts on the school at Athy. By early September 1861 he had persuaded most of the Catholic parents to withdraw their children from that school. "In Athy," he reported with great satisfaction to Kirby on September 3, "the model school had last week only 9 Cath. childr. The Christian Brothers 160—is not that a good battle[?]" (K). "When things are prepared in Dublin," he assured Kirby further, "*si farà lo stesso* [the same will be done]." Several days later Cullen spelled out his policy even more clearly to Kirby: "As to the model schools, the country ones and the small ones can be put down readily. The big ones cannot be put down until there will be other schools to receive the children. They can be discredited and checked and when there will be other schools for the children, they may be prohibited but it is not safe to do anything unless where success is certain. Everything can be done gradually, but if we fail in any attempt, we lose immensely."[33]

Meanwhile, Cullen had been using his very considerable influence to have those bishops in whose dioceses the various model schools had been established take action similar to his own. When the national board had decided several years before to establish a model school at Enniscorthy in county Wexford, without consulting the

32. I.C.D., 1863, p. 267.
33. K, n.d. [ca. September 7, 1862].

bishop of Ferns, and in spite of his vigorous protests, Cullen was incensed.[34] To add insult to injury, moreover, Enniscorthy was not only the mensal parish of the bishop but his cathedral town as well. By early October 1862, however, the bishop of Ferns had apparently been as effective in Enniscorthy in preventing Catholic children from attending the local model school as Cullen had been earlier in Athy. "Mr. Cavanagh [*sic*] of the University,"Cullen informed Kirby on October 6, referring to a prominent Catholic apologist on educational matters and a professor of mathematics in the Catholic University, "has published a terrible letter about the new model school in Enniscorthy—no Catholic has gone to it—the parson has kept away the Protestants. There are only about 22 little Quakers and Presbyterians. The school however cost about £10,000 and it will take about £600 per annum to keep it up. That is a rather profligate expenditure for 22 children" (K).

Early in the new year, 1863, the movement against the model-school system was greatly accelerated when the bishop of Galway and the coadjutor to the bishop of Limerick make their moves against the large and long-established model schools in their respective dioceses. "You will be glad to learn," the bishop of Galway, John MacEvilly, informed Kirby on March 6 in a long and interesting letter,

> that I at the beginning of this year opened new schools for boys and girls under the care of monks and nuns to make provision for the reputable class of Catholic children who had been frequenting the Model School of this town. This class of children would not frequent the ordinary schools, and hence I opened schools for this class altogether apart from the poor schools. I never said a word til the schools were ready and then I sent round a short circular to be read on Sunday the fourth of January, denouncing the Model School, calling on the parents and guardians to withdraw the children and have them sent to the new Catholic schools, which at great expense and trouble were provided expressly for them. This short circular was read at every altar in Galway at all the masses. It thank God, had the desired effect. Nearly all the Catholic children left the Model School. There are upwards of 140 boys attending St. Joseph's school opened by the monks, not to speak of many more who went from the Model School to other schools and the new schools opened by the Sisters of Mercy are equally successful. [K]

34. Moran, 2:92–93, Irish Bishops to Cardwell, March 18, 1860.

"The Queen's College people," MacEvilly reported, "are furious at the unexpected success that attended the Catholic movement, and if I had no other proof of the evil tendencies of the Model School System, the rage and fury the movement against them here has caused the bigots of every class would be sufficient to condemn them in my eyes."

> I need not [tell] you, my dear Monsignor, that unless the extension of the Model School System receive a timely check, they will in the course of thirty years hence—and what is thirty years in the life of a System?—be spread over the country and the whole education of our people thrown into the hands of a hostile government. The System is not more than thirty-two years in existence, and in that period more than 100 [sic] Model Schools are either in operation or in the course of being so, and in fact the extension of the Model School System began within the last fifteen years. What then would be [sic] it be in 32 years more[?] These Model Schools are so many Queen's Colleges in miniature. They are regulated by the same principles. They [are] altogether in the hands of the government without any dependence on the pastors of the Church. No expense is spared in fitting them up and bestowing bribes and largesses in the shape of premiums to the children frequenting them. Hence, it seems to me there is no other way in which the faith of [this] poor afflicted country, for which our fathers "resisted even unto blood" is so seriously menaced. It is from this conviction that I have worked as hard as possible for the last four months to counteract [the model schools] by getting up Catholic schools equally good.

He then finally added, referring to the coadjutor to the bishop of Limerick, "It is a curious coincidence that on the same day without any previous concert Dr. Butler had been denouncing the Limerick Model School with equal success."

By the time Kirby received this letter, Cullen had also apparently decided to increase the pressure on the model-school system. In a short reply on March 19 to a letter from Major O'Reilly, recently elected to Parliament for county Longford, Cullen explained that he could not write at greater length because he was just then engaged in a visitation of one of his city parishes. "All I shall say at present," he added, "is that undoubtedly the Model schools ought to be assailed. They cannot be well defended. As to the M.P.s we will do everything possible to influence them."[35] O'Reilly, who proposed to offer a mo-

35. MacSuibhne, 5 (1977):9.

tion of censure in the House of Commons on the model schools, obviously wanted the bishops to use their influence with their M.P.'s to support his motion, and had written Cullen to enlist his aid. Matters became more complicated, however, when Daniel O'Connell, the son of the Liberator, decided to retire as the member for Tralee, and Thomas O'Hagan, the Irish attorney general, resolved to contest the seat. Though he was a Catholic and a commissioner of the Board of National Education, O'Hagan was a supporter of the principle of mixed education. When the bishop of Kerry, in whose diocese Tralee was situated, was reported to have endorsed O'Hagan's candidature, O'Reilly had some second thoughts about putting his motion of censure: he feared embarrassing the bishop of Kerry, because if O'Hagan were elected, one of his first acts as member of the ministry would be to vote against any such motion.

O'Reilly wrote Cullen explaining the dilemma he found himself in, but the archbishop advised him to persevere. "In fine," Cullen summed up on May 12, "if O'Hagan be returned and vote against your motion, he will only do what everyone knows his office compels him to do. Your motion I think stands on truth and justice, and it is well to bring it forward; it matters not what opposition you meet; *magna est veritas et prevalibit* [the truth is great and it will prevail]. I think the great mass of the people will be disappointed unless you persevere. I think nothing ought to prevent you from going on."[36] "I shall now merely add," he noted, referring to the model schools, "that in the returns you asked for it be necessary to have the religious denominations of the pupils specified. In Omagh, Derry, Enniscorthy there may be a number of Protestants but there are no Catholics. In Limerick it is the same, and the want of Catholics will show that the schools do not provide for mixed education or for the majority of the people." In the event, O'Hagan was elected in Tralee, and on May 17 Cullen wrote O'Reilly again.[37] "Mr. O'Hagan," he reported,

> will support the National system, but probably not on every point. I daresay he would give up the Training and Model Schools, or have them put on the same footing as in England. If this were done the common National Schools could be kept in order except in the North where Presbyterians are patrons of schools attended by Catholic children.
>
> I dare say it would be well to have some communication with Mr. O'H. on this subject, and try to gain him over. But if he undertakes to defend Training and Model Schools and the

36. Ibid., p. 10.
37. Ibid., p. 12.

schools under Presbyterian patrons, I think he will not damage us very much. On the contrary, it is probable that the people will be roused to greater exertions. O'Hagan's name and the hopes held out that greater changes would be made in the books etc. kept both bishops and priests from doing much during the last two years. It would be an immense advantage that he would declare himself openly either for or against us. If he resist your motion I think I will immediately assail the Model schools in Dublin. Every step for the past was prevented by saying all abuses would be corrected. When that hope will be abandoned it will be easier to do something decisive.

"However," he concluded characteristically, "I do not like to undertake anything until success is certain."

By this time, however, O'Hagan had already declared himself by eulogizing the national system of education in his election address thanking the electors of Tralee for returning him as their member. When Cullen read O'Hagan's address he decided to allow it to pass because he was apparently not yet ready to extend his quarrel with the government. But when O'Hagan's friends then published his address in pamphlet form as an appeal to the Catholics of Ireland in favor of his opinions on education, Cullen took up the challenge and replied with a scathing denunciation of the national system as then constituted. In an open letter to O'Hagan published on June 17, Cullen took issue with him on three points or assertions made in his pamphlet:

1. That the recent increase in the number of Catholic Commissioners has been the "noblest assertion of the principle of social equality, between Irishmen," which has been made since the time of the Emancipation;
2. That "the mischief of proselytism, on the one side or the other, is, at present, an impossibility" and
3. That, the National System is now on such a basis that it may be proclaimed "admirable in its conception, and in its working as admirable."[38]

The heart of Cullen's reply was really concerned with the first of these three points, and his discussion of the other two was obviously designed to add salt to the soup.

Cullen cleverly began his refutation by tacitly assuming that what O'Hagan really meant by "social equality" was "religious equality." On this matter, Cullen confessed, he was simply amazed at O'Hagan's

38. Moran, 2:185.

enthusiasm for what was merely "the addition of *four* [correctly, six] Catholic Commissioners to the six [four] already having places on the National Board, without giving them any additional power, without making any attempt whatever to correct the evils of the system, or to redress the grievances of which Catholics complain."[39] Parity, Cullen further maintained, was not be be confused with equality. The national board now consisted of one Unitarian, two Presbyterian, seven Anglican, and ten Catholic members. According to the Commissioners' Report of 1861, there were 663,145 Catholic and 140,219 Protestant children being educated in the national system, a proportion of nearly 83 to 17, and if equality had any relation to numbers of pupils the Catholic commissioners should number five to one to the Protestants on the board. Worse still, however, the so-called parity that did exist was only an illusion. All of the Catholic commissioners were busy men, and their record of attendance at the board meetings left a great deal to be desired if compared to that of the Protestant members. In fine, Cullen charged, Catholic interests were regularly managed by a Protestant majority. Moreover, the sole resident commissioner, who had a residence and a salary of £1,000 per year, was a Protestant and not only dispensed much of the official patronage of the board but also had the main administration of affairs in his hands.

Cullen then turned from the national board to the bureaucracy through which it administered the national system to apply the test of equality. The Inspection Department, Cullen pointed out, was more than half Protestant, and a large number of the Catholic inspectors had been selected from among the students of the Queen's Colleges, where "they could scarcely have imbibed much love for our holy religion. . . ."[40] The Central Office in Dublin, he further charged, "from the Resident Commissioner to the Head Porter, through every one of its Departments, exhibits Protestant ascendancy. For instance, after more than thirty years' working of the system, there is apart from several Protestant Heads of Departments, only one Catholic *First-Class* Clerk, whilst there are *five* Protestants, two of whom are reported to have renounced the Catholic faith."[41] Finally, the professors and teaching staff in the central training schools and the central and district model schools were all generally Protestants. Still, even if the commissioners, inspectors, and teachers were all nominally Catholic, that would be no satisfactory guarantee, because the bishops had a right to know "who those Catholics are, what are their merits, and

39. Ibid., p. 186.
40. Ibid., p. 193.
41. Ibid., pp. 193–94.

whether they are acting with the sanction of the Church and in conformity with its teaching and doctrines." In concluding his refutation of O'Hagan's claim for the "religious equality" of the system, Cullen then noted not only that the rightful authority of the bishops and pastors had been long ignored in the rules of the board, but that this authority was still being subverted by the practical action of the reconstructed board. Model schools had been opened in the past few years in Enniscorthy, Sligo, Londonderry, Omagh, and Parsonstown in spite of the protests of the properly constituted Catholic ecclesiastical authorities in those places. What was perhaps even more to be regretted, Cullen added, was that it was reported that one of O'Hagan's first acts in the House of Commons was to vote for the erection of a model school in the city of Cork in spite of the emphatic protest of the local bishop.

Cullen then took up the second of O'Hagan's assertions—that the national system was free from the danger of proselytism. Cullen pointed out that in the national schools in the north of Ireland, and particularly those taught by Presbyterian teachers where there was mixed attendance, the teachers gave a common religious instruction to all the pupils, regardless of religious denomination. "There is another effectual means of promoting proselytism," he continued, "a means which is very general throughout most of the Departments of the Public Service, and the existence of which under the Education Board ought not to be concealed from you and your Catholic Colleagues on the re-constructed Commission, I mean the bad example arising from placing Catholic youths in charge of persons who had abandoned the Catholic Church." "It is in Educational Institutions, however," Cullen then added, "that such an evil example is most pernicious; and it is to be regretted that at the head quarters of the National System, under the very eyes of the Board, which you glory in having reconstructed, we find some of the saddest cases of this deplorable scandal." "These scandals," he argued after having enumerated various examples of Catholic apostasy, "as well as similar ones in the District Model Schools, and the conduct of many of the Inspectors and other officers, some said to be Orangemen, or Freemasons, or to profess no particular creed, must exercise a most baneful influence on Catholic youth."

In treating of O'Hagan's third and final assertion—that the national system in its present form was admirable in its conception and working—Cullen, whose letter had now run to more than twenty printed pages, decided in the interests of brevity to make only one point. When the national system had been first set up more than thirty years before, the intention of its authors, he maintained, was that the children of each denomination in mixed schools would receive their religious instruction *in the schoolrooms from their own pastors.* That estimable intention had now been subverted by the rule of the board which provided that in those schools vested in patrons or managers, as distinguished from those vested in the board—and these were in the proportion of nearly 75 to 25—it was for the patron or manager "to determine whether *any* and if any, *what* Religious Instruction shall be given *in the schoolroom.*"[42] It was left to Protestant or Presbyterian patrons, in effect, to determine whether a Catholic child should ever be permitted to learn his catechism while in school, or receive any other than Protestant religious instruction in a Protestant national school. "Can you," he asked O'Hagan in conclusion, "consider this right of depriving poor children of all religious instruction, a feature in the Board worthy of admiration?"[43] Cullen then summarily ended his long letter by quoting that epitome of the evils of the national system with which he had concluded his letter to Edward Cardwell more than two years before, and which he had persuaded all the bishops except MacHale to sign.

While Cullen's letter to O'Hagan was not one of his best polemical efforts, because of its hurried and truncated form, it was certainly sufficient for its purposes. In the first place, Cullen had finally decided that nothing more was to be gained from the government in the way of concessions on the education question, and an open break was desirable. Given the ministry's demonstrated hostility in the attitude of Sir Robert Peel and, even more important, in that of Lord Palmerston, Cullen was undoubtedly correct in declaring war when he did. In the second place, by taking a more aggressive stand on the education question, Cullen would at least prevent the Catholic public opinion he had done so much to shape and mobilize on that subject in recent years from being debilitated and eroded by false hopes and promises. But why did Cullen make the publication of O'Hagan's address as a pamphlet the occasion for his break with the government? He did so because, by publishing his pamphlet, O'Hagan was no longer simply thanking his constituents for having placed their confidence in him but publicly endorsing a system of mixed education to which the bishops had individually and collectively voiced their most solemn objections in their pastorals to their flocks, in the decrees of their synods, and in their addresses to the government.[44] In a word, O'Hagan was juxtaposing his authority, as a prominent Catholic layman and a member of the government, to that of the bishops in a matter that

42. Ibid., p. 202.
43. Ibid., p. 203.
44. Ibid., p. 181.

they had come to look upon as peculiarly their own, and it was a challenge that Cullen could not allow to pass.

But why then, it may well be asked, did Cullen feel obliged to rush into print on June 17 to denounce O'Hagan? He certainly had no intention of doing so on May 17, when he was advising O'Reilly to speak to O'Hagan and try to win him over. He apparently was not even inclined to take action when he read O'Hagan's provocative address to the electors of Tralee several days later in the newspapers. Cullen's attitude apparently began to harden against O'Hagan when he learned that the attorney general was not going to remain passive in the debate that was scheduled to take place on June 18 on O'Reilly's motion of censure of the model-school system.[45] In other words, O'Hagan was preparing to defend the mixed system publicly and not simply to give the silent vote required of him as a member of the government. What probably finally pushed Cullen into denouncing O'Hagan's views, however, was that he undoubtedly had heard from O'Reilly or More O'Farrell that O'Hagan was attempting to persuade a number of the Irish Catholic members not to support O'Reilly's scheduled motion. In order to lessen the chances of a serious public split among the Irish Catholic members on the question of mixed education, not only was Cullen obliged to denounce O'Hagan's views, but he had to do it before June 18, when the expected vote on O'Reilly's motion was to be taken.[46]

In any case, in introducing his motion on June 18, O'Reilly made a very able speech criticizing the model schools.[47] He pointed out that the model schools "were foreign to the original system; they give an education to those who could afford to pay for it; they were extravagantly costly; they were unnecessary; they competed unfairly with other schools; they were fatal to free education; and above all, they were a step towards the system of centralized State schools which had been repudiated in England." Because it would be impracticable to move the rejection of the whole vote of £306,016 for public education in Ireland, O'Reilly proposed instead to reduce the item of £19,180 for the model schools by £268, "the cost of the Enniscorthy schools, which were attended by thirty-one pupils in order to afford the Com-

45. MacSuibhne, 5:13, Cullen to O'Reilly, June 3, 1863. Cullen reported to O'Reilly that one of the more able of the Catholic inspectors in the national system, Patrick Keenan, had gone over to London to assist O'Hagan in the making of his case in the House of Commons.

46. See K, Cullen to Kirby, June 21, 1863, in which Cullen explained that he had to hit O'Hagan hard because he seemed determined to force mixed education on the country and because, as a prominent Catholic, O'Hagan could do more harm than others.

47. *Hansard*, 171:1088–1111.

mittee [of the whole House] an opportunity of expressing an opinion that steps ought to be taken for the gradual abolition of these schools." After a spirited debate of several hours, in which O'Hagan vigorously defended the model schools, the committee finally divided, and O'Reilly's motion was defeated by a vote of 122 to 38.

Cullen was not in the least disappointed with the result of the vote. "I congratulate you most warmly," he wrote O'Reilly on June 22, "on the success which has attended your motion and your speech. Nothing could be more cheering. It is an excellent beginning. I regret, however, that the Attorney General has thrown himself heart and soul into the ranks of our enemies. I think he has taken a great responsibility on himself, and I am sure he has damaged his good name in Ireland. It will be necessary to fight our battles without any hope of assistance from those who sit on the treasury benches, and we must only trust to the justice of our cause. On our side is Erin and truth. On theirs is the Saxon and guilt."[48] "I shall see several bishops at Maynooth tomorrow," he assured O'Reilly in conclusion, "and speak to them about their M.P.s. We cannot complain in general when we reflect that there was never a division on the education question before, and no serious attack on Model schools." Not only was Cullen pleased with what he had done, but he characteristically had no regrets about it. "I am glad," he informed Kirby on July 3, "you like the letter to O'Hagan. The great mass of the people here were also well pleased—but old H. himself and the Government Catholics condemn it very much. They think they have a right to do what is wrong, and then they complain if anyone sets them right" (K). Whatever may be said about Cullen's views on education, there is little doubt that he was consistent about them. He had worked hard and long to establish two interrelated principles with regard to the education question in Ireland. The first was that the Catholic body must remain united on the education question if anything was to be achieved, and the other was that the only way of effectively guaranteeing that unity was to keep the initiative in all educational matters entirely in the hands of the bishops. When O'Hagan threatened those two principles, therefore, it was inevitable that he, and all those other lay politicians who thought like him, must be made aware that in Ireland the way on the education question was as strait as the gate was narrow, and that the only safe guides were the Irish bishops as a body.

---

48. MacSuibhne, 5:15–16.

Although this determination of the bishops as a body to brook no interference from the laity in educational matters would prove in the long run to be the cornerstone of their power and influence in the state, in the short run it had a disastrous effect on their efforts to provide for the higher education of Irish Catholics. By early 1863, in fact, it had become apparent to both Woodlock and Cullen that the Catholic University was once again in serious trouble. After the initial burst of enthusiasm occasioned by Woodlock's appointment as rector in May 1861 and the laying of the foundation stone and the agitation for a charter in the summer of 1862, the recent very considerable increase in the number of students began to level off and then decline, and the bishops' enthusiasm in collecting for the University began to wane. Like his good friend Richard More O'Ferrall, Woodlock had realized from the very beginning of his tenure as rector that the key to the eventual success of the University was to be found in the admittance of laymen to its governing body, for without that step there was no hope of the University's ever securing legal recognition from the state in a charter. In early February 1862, for example, Woodlock asked the bishops at a meeting of the governing board of the University "to consider the expediency of admitting lay-members to the Board," but the bishops apparently chose to ignore his request.[49] Woodlock, who was nothing if not persevering, returned to the subject at the next meeting of the board in October. His approach on this occasion, however, was a good deal more oblique. "What is the body," he inquired of the bishops on October 21, "for which we are asking a charter? How is it constituted? How is it to be kept up? (This question has been proposed to me by several influential public men. I deem it necessary to know the Board's views on this important point, in order not to commit their Lordships or myself; and in order to be able to publish them, if necessary)" (W). The bishops then resolved that Cullen and Woodlock should be asked to draw up a report on the subject for the next meeting of the board.

When the board met a month later, on November 25, however, the bishops deferred a consideration of the report until their next meeting (W). At that meeting, which took place on January 27, 1863, they duly received and considered the report (W). The document, which was entitled, "Report from the Archbishop of Dublin and the Rector on the admission of the laity to a share in the government of the University," had apparently been drawn up entirely by Woodlock. "The ques-

49. Woodlock Papers (W), Dublin Diocesan Archives, Dublin, "Minute Book of Board of Catholic University, 1861–1879."

tion," Woodlock pointed out, "of the modification of the University Board by the introduction of the lay element may be considered under a two-fold aspect: 1st—as to the advantage, or even necessity of such a change in itself; 2dly—as to its expediency at the present moment." Under the first heading Woodlock formally addressed five reasons in support of the change: it would strengthen the union of clergy and laity; it would shut the mouths of their enemies, who asserted that the clergy wanted to arrogate to themselves the control of all education; it would broaden the base of support for the University; it would, as an expression of confidence by the bishops, foster good feeling between them and the laity; and it would relieve the bishops from many arduous duties because the laity, owing to their experience, tended to be more proficient in practical affairs. "In time," he then noted, coming finally to his real point, "it must not be forgotten that we are looking for a charter from a Protestant Gov^t, which in the present state of public feeling in England could never think of chartering a body, composed exclusively of Bishops. . . ." In turning to his second heading, concerning the expediency of including the laity, Woodlock adduced four reasons: it would result in the acquiring of the advantages listed above; it would give a practical contradiction to the absurd rumor that the bishops wanted to make a big ecclesiastical seminary of the University; it would allow the University greater access to the capital necessary to the building of its facilities; and it would reward the laity who were now sound on the question of denominational education as well as enlist the aid of those who now held back.

In concluding his report Woodlock then made six practical recommendations by which he hoped to see his proposal implemented. The first four were largely technical, whereas the final two were more material in that they defined where real power in the proposed new governing body was actually going to rest. The first four recommendations were that the subsequent recommendations be approved by the bishops of Ireland at their next general meeting; that twelve laymen be added to the present board of twelve bishops and the rector; that the membership of the board be rotated each year, with three laymen going out; and that the resulting vacancies be filled by the board. The fifth, and most important, of the recommendations was "That the Episcopal Members of the Board alone be the judges in all cases regarding faith or morals, have a right to veto any appointment before it is made & to exclude any book without giving any reason for doing so; that they have a right to represent to the Board the teaching of any professor or other teacher as contrary to the doctrine or discipline of the Church, and the Board be thereupon obliged to suspend or dismiss

such professor." The sixth recommendation was that the body of the
bishops reserve to itself the appointment and removal of the rector.
After considering the report the bishops resolved that "the principle of
the admission of the laity is approved by the Board, & will be submitted to the Bishops of Ireland at their first meeting."

When the bishops of the University board met again some two
months later, on March 24, they further directed Woodlock "to prepare a long list of laymen, to which each of the Bishops of Ireland will
be requested to make any additions he deems desirable: twelve of the
laymen thus named to be elected by ballot by the Prelates at their
general meeting next June" (W). The bishops did not meet, however,
until the following August. In the meantime, shortly after the meeting of the board on March 24, Woodlock decided, with Cullen's approval, to go to Rome. Cullen provided Woodlock with a letter of introduction to Barnabò, and when he wrote the cardinal prefect himself
on April 14, he explained that Woodlock would soon be in Rome to
give him all the necessary details about the problems faced by the
University.[50] In Cullen's mind, the chief difficulty was to be found in
the attitude of the archbishop of Tuam, who was frustrating Woodlock
at every turn. "In order to please him," Cullen reminded Barnabò,
referring to MacHale, "a committee of Bishops was nominated four
years ago to govern the University, and he was one of those chosen. He
was present at the first meeting and then he did not want to know any
more about it, and I believe that he makes every effort to ruin the
whole business. It seems certain to me that he will not change his
manner of acting, and it is useless to deal with him about it." "Perhaps a general meeting of the bishops will be proposed," Cullen suggested obliquely, "and perhaps it will be useful to hold it. But in that
case, if I have to preside at it, it will be necessary to give me the most
precise instructions, otherwise the archbishop will continue to im-
pugn everything that I do or propose, and thus nothing can be done."

In writing to Kirby several days later asking him to take good care
of Woodlock, Cullen again adverted to the holding of a general meeting. "If the Propaganda," he alerted Kirby on April 17, "wish that I
should hold a meeting of Bishops, let them give me all the necessary
instructions" (K). "The last time I saw Dr. McNally," he explained,
naming the bishop of Clogher, who was a close friend and supporter of
MacHale, "he made a great attack on the interference of Rome in
regard to our meetings. He thinks we ought to assemble and act without any reference to Rome. When that course was adopted, there was

50. S.R.C., vol. 34, fols. 675–76.

nothing but fighting, and after the meeting no one cared about what was done. Some of the other Bishops think just like Dr. McNally." "It is not pleasant for me," he added, giving another exhibition of that bad temper he had shown before when the affairs of the University were in a precarious state, "to be acting under such circumstances—fighting and doing little good. *Poi* [Then] every meeting puts me to a considerable expense. I have always to entertain their Lordships and to get a good deal of printing done. Indeed all the trouble and expense in these matters has fallen on me for the last several years." "However," he then concluded more dutifully, "whilst the Head is so poor and in such difficulties, the members have no right to complain."

Shortly after Woodlock arrived in Rome, he was asked to submit a memorandum that would serve as a basis for a letter from Propaganda to the Irish bishops on the subject of the Catholic University. The memorandum, which was in Italian and dated from the Irish College on May 4, was headed—"Some reasons which show the utility or the necessity of the Catholic University in Ireland."[51] The memorandum was actually a series of notes or arguments not only about why a University was necessary, but also about why the lack of one was dangerous. His more positive points included the arguments that the pope and the Holy See had taken the project very much to their hearts, that a Catholic University was the necessary capstone to an Irish educational system, that the University was crucial to Catholic learning, that the increasing demand of the Catholic laity for Irish education had to be anticipated, that the prestige and honor of the Church both at home and at Rome were at stake, and that the great sacrifices already made by the Irish clergy and people must be sustained. On the negative side, Woodlock pointed out that Trinity College was a well-endowed, aggressive, and proselytizing institution, that the Queen's Colleges had been founded with the intention of taking higher education out of the hands of the clergy and secularizing it, and that the result was either the perversion of Catholics or the encouraging of a cold indifference to the faith of their fathers.

Woodlock had also been asked by the authorities at Propaganda to submit a memorandum on the role of the archbishop of Tuam in regard to the University. This memorandum, which was dated May 1, was a very severe indictment of MacHale's conduct and was also probably designed to serve as the basis for a letter to the recalcitrant

51. Ibid., fols. 697–700. See also ibid., fols. 695–96, for "Memorie per una lettera a Mgr Arcivescovo di Tuam in Irlanda." This memorandum is also unsigned, but it is in Woodlock's hand and dated May 1, 1863, from the Irish College, Rome. This was a very stiff indictment of MacHale's conduct with regard to the Catholic University.

archbishop.[52] Cullen had obviously persuaded Woodlock that if the survival of the University was threatened, the person most responsible was MacHale. In thus making MacHale the scapegoat (and given the archbishop's bad standing at Rome this was not very hard to do), Cullen was adroitly preparing for the worst with regard to the affairs of the University. In any case, Woodlock apparently made a favorable impression in Rome, for Barnabò wrote Cullen on June 1, not only authorizing him to convoke a general meeting of the bishops to consider the state of the University, but also exhorting the bishops in the name of the pope to give all the aid they could to an institution that served so useful a purpose. Barnabò also advised the bishops to determine what measures were necessary to safeguard the faith of Catholics in mixed schools.

Woodlock set out for home in early June and while en route received a letter from Cullen asking him to stop over in London to render O'Reilly what help he could on the motion he was to make in the House on the model-school system. While he was in London, Woodlock also learned that the English Catholics were mooting the foundation of a Catholic College at Oxford or Cambridge Universities, or both, and he was naturally very disturbed. "I fear such a scheme," he confided to Kirby from London on June 12, "if carried out, as is not (I think) unlikely, would be very injurious to the Cath. University & what is much worse, would produce all the evil results to Catholic & national spirit, which follow Trinity or the Queen's Colleges" (K). Meanwhile, Cullen had written Barnabò asking that the instructions about the meeting be sent in Latin in order that he might send copies to the bishops when he convened them. The meeting had initially been scheduled for some time in July, but when MacHale objected that it would be inconvenient for him to attend then, it was postponed to August 4. Meanwhile, the activities of the politically ubiquitous Father Lavelle had resulted, it will be recalled, in Barnabò's adding his case to the bishop's agenda, along with the University and mixed schools.

The bishops met on August 4, and it took them some five days to exhaust their agenda. Besides condemning the Brotherhood of St. Patrick and the conduct of Father Lavelle, Cullen explained to Kirby in Italian on August 9, the bishops had also dealt satisfactorily with the problems posed by the national schools and the University, and Woodlock had obtained all that he could desire (K). Several days later, when he wrote Kirby again, Cullen went into some greater detail about what

52. Ibid., fol. 695.

Woodlock wanted, and for the first time in all his various correspondences, he made known his real opinion on the subject of laymen being admitted to a share in the governing of the University. "Dr. Woodlock," he explained on August 11, "wants to get some laymen on the Board. Dr. McHale protested against it. The affair is now to be left to the Propaganda" (K). "I think," he added, "it is not of any great importance to have the laymen in question. They do without laymen in Belgium. We have scarcely any great laymen, who could help to keep up the University and it is in the body of the people that we must rely." On the same subject, nearly a month later, Kirby reported an interesting conversation to Cullen. "C. Barnabò," he confided on September 5, "told me this morning that Dr. McH. has written a fierce letter to the Pope contra tutti, and especially against himself the Card^l" (C). "He denounces the appointment of the seculars on the Univ^ty board," Kirby explained; "but the Card^l showed the Pope at once that you were quite opposed to that measure. The Card^l also disapproved others of his assertions." "Let your report," he finally advised Cullen, "when it comes to be pretty full as to the sentiments of the Bishops on these proceedings of his (Dr. McHale's)."

Cullen, who was both tired and unwell after the meeting, and who usually had to make a visitation of his country parishes during August, was not able to write his customary report for Propaganda until the end of the month. "I have written a long report," he informed Kirby on September 11,

> of our proceedings of the last meeting and sent it 10 or 12 days ago. I hope it will explain all things fully. In the report I stated that Dr. Woodlock proposed the admission of laymen to the Board and gave his reasons. I added that all the Bishops[,] except Dr. McH.[,] Dr. Derry and the coadjutor of Kilmore[,] voted for Dr. Woodlock's proposal as a matter of expediency. I gave the reasons *hinc inde* [on both sides], but stated that the reasons against the proposal were strongest. The laymen, I added, would be satisfied with things as they are were it not for Dr. McH. himself. He opposes everything. He prevents things from going on. The laity are naturally dissatisfied and think they could manage better than we have managed them. *Hanno molto ragione. Ma di cui è il torto* [They are very right. But whose is the fault?]. [K]

"If we could go on smoothly," he maintained, "and examine things quietly all would go well. But when *il Leone ruggisce e mostra i denti a ogni cose, che volete fare* [the Lion roars and snarls at everything, what can be done?]." In once again making MacHale the scapegoat in the affairs of the University, Cullen gave yet another example of his great skill in the subtle art of the dialectic. The actual reason why the laymen wanted a share in the government of the University, he maintained, was not that they really wanted it as a good in itself but rather that the affairs of the University were in such a deplorable state that they felt something must be done to remedy them. The reason why they were in such a sorry state, of course, was the continued obstruction and wrecking tactics of MacHale at every turn. This was a very clever performance by Cullen, for not only did it allow him to blame both the failure of the University and the demand for power sharing by the laity on MacHale, but even more important, it allowed him to continue to mask from Woodlock his own more crucial opposition to laymen on the board of the University.

Cullen also forwarded to Propaganda a formal account of the decisions the bishops reached at their meeting about the Catholic University. After reading Woodlock's report on the advisability of admitting laymen to a part in the governing of the University, Cullen explained in the third person that he had

asked the archbishops and bishops in succession, one after the other, their opinion as to the expediency of adopting the proposed change. When all had given their opinion, the Archbishop of Dublin gave his own, and announced that it was the general impression that some lay gentlemen should be associated with the Bishops in the government of the University.

His Grace then put the question—How many lay gentlemen should be so associated?

The decision was that the number should be eight.

It was then further decided that, as hitherto, there be, as Episcopal Members of the University Board, twelve bishops, viz: — Four archbishops, and eight suffragan bishops. The eight suffragan bishops to be as hitherto; two from each ecclesiastical province, elected by their respective comprovincial archbishops and bishops.

It was also decided that the eight lay gentlemen be also elected, two from each of the ecclesiastical provinces, Armagh, Dublin, Tuam, and Cashel, by the archbishops and bishops of those provinces respectively.

In answer to the further question, put by the Archbishop of Dublin, whether the Members of the University Board be elected for life or for a determined period, it was decided that they should be elected for life.

The Rector of the University is to be, ex-officio, a Member of the Board.

The Board is not empowered to elect the Rector of University. The bishops of Ireland are alone competent to elect a Rector.

It was also decided that the bishop members of the Board, shall have a veto in regard to the appointment of professors: that they shall be at liberty to exclude books, which they may deem objectionable; and that for the exercise of those powers they shall not be obliged to assign reasons. The bishops of the Board shall also be entitled to require of the Board to dismiss, or otherwise punish, professors to whom they may object on religious or disciplinary grounds.[53]

Though the bishops had modified a number of the recommendations made by Woodlock in his report of the previous January, such as the number, mode of election, and tenure of the lay members of the board, they fully endorsed the principle of absolute episcopal control of that board. In effect, in all important matters the bishops of the board voted by order rather than by head. In a body of twenty-one (twelve bishops, eight laymen, and the rector), seven bishops, or a simple majority of their lordships, would be sufficient to implement all the measures reserved in the last paragraph above. Even in the ordinary and less important matters, the authority of the body was not to be imposed upon, and that is why the number of laymen proposed was reduced from twelve to eight, for with twelve laymen and the rector, the bishops on the board would be in the minority. How the Bishops ever hoped, under these conditions, to persuade any self-respecting layman to join the board is one question, but how they expected that these proposals would ever pass muster in the House of Commons was an even more serious one.

Perhaps this was the reason why Woodlock's usual buoyant and infectious enthusiasm seemed to be somewhat diminished after this apparent vote of confidence by the bishops as a body on his recommendations. "I think," he reported ambivalently to Kirby on November 2, "things are progressing with us. As yet I cannot see much increase in our numbers; but the students we have are working harder, and it seems to me that greater interest in the work is getting up in many quarters. The Archbishop of Tuam has yielded to some extent: but he is still a great obstacle" (K). "I wrote last night to Dr. MacHale," Woodlock then confided, "expressing my hope, that he would direct the Collection to be made this year: that I hope the reasons are re-

53. Ibid., vol. 35, fol. 108.

moved which made him decline to do so last year, & that in any case, the Holy Father's wishes, which His Holiness told me He would communicate to him, will more than counter-balance his objections. We shall see what he says." MacHale apparently refused once again to collect for the University. "I send on the other side," Cullen explained to Kirby on November 17, the Tuesday after the third Sunday in November, when the bishops usually ordered their collections for the University, "the list of the collections for [the] University made last year [1862]. Some dioceses gave very little. Cork and Tuam nothing— this year it will be the same as far as Tuam is concerned" (K). The 1862 collection, it will be recalled, amounted to some £6,400.

The collection for 1863 was also not very successful, amounting to about £6,200. The problem was not so much that the bishops, Mac-Hale always excepted, refused to collect—for the pope's exhortation, in effect, made the collection mandatory—as that a considerable number of the collections did not amount to very much because all the bishops did not press their priests in the matter with equal energy. Woodlock still had to meet the current expenses at the University, and he was also committed to raising the necessary capital for an entire educational plant on the new site at Drumcondra. With income barely meeting expenses, therefore, the course decided on was to attempt to collect the necessary building funds in America and Australia, while trying to economize further on operating expenses. The problem with this plan was that in recent years the American and Australian bishops had become progressively more reluctant about allowing Irish priests to collect in their dioceses because of their own pressing financial needs, and some had even refused to allow the Irish to collect at all. Woodlock decided that the best way to overcome the American and Australian reluctance was to secure the recommendation of Rome for his project. In writing to Kirby in early February 1864, to ask him to help expedite Roman approval on this matter as well as on the proposal to include laymen in the governing of the University, Woodlock laid out his brief.

"This business is," he explained on February 10,

> 1st to get letters from the S.C. [Sacred Congregation] or from the Holy Father formally recommending the collection for the University (a) to the Australian Bishops, who otherwise will not admit our collectors; (b) to the prelates of America, to which country we are sending out two priests in the beginning of March—it is most important that this authorisation should be given as soon as possible, since our enemies are beginning to scoff at our long delay in building the University, of which we laid the foun-

dation stone with so much Pomp nearly two years ago; and we cannot proceed for want of sufficient means—2^{ndly} a matter, of still greater urgency is the question of the introduction of some lay members to the Board of the Univ^y. [K]

"The Bishops of Ireland," he added most interestingly, "at their meeting last August almost unanimously agreed to the expediency of doing so; but out of deference to Dr. MacHale, it was arranged to refer the matter to the Holy See. However, it is now all-important that the answer, which I have no doubt will accord with the views of our good Archbishop and the majority of the prelates, should come *without further delay.*" "Parliament," Woodlock continued, "as you know, has met; and all our efforts to promote the Univ^y with Gov^t are paralysed because this point is not settled. Meantime most precious time is now slipping by; for the present Parliament must be dissolved before very long, and it is all-important for us to show our strength before its dissolution. If The O'Conor Don or Mr. Monsell be still in Rome, they will explain all this to you much better than I can within the limits of a letter." "But I beg of you, my dear Dr. Kirby," he added in conclusion, "as you value the advancement of the Univ^y, in which you take so kind an interest, to try and hurry on this business."

Meanwhile, Cullen had written Barnabò some two weeks before, also asking for a decision concerning lay representation in governing the University. "Happening to be here in Dublin the other evening," Cullen reported on January 28, "a few Bishops begged me to write to Your Eminence to ask what decision had been adopted by the Sacred Congregation concerning the question whether the laity ought to be allowed to take part in the governing of the University. Some laymen are very desirous that they be admitted as members of the council that up to now consists of Bishops."[54] "Monsignor McHale," he reminded Barnabò, "opposed such a project at the last meeting of the Bishops, and I submitted the various reasons on one side and on the other of this argument. The Bishops I have recently seen, although they do not believe the question of great concern would wish to see a decision to foreclose further discussions." However, when the cardinals of Propaganda finally did meet to consider the matter on March 30, they decided because of the pressure of other business to postpone the decision until the next meeting.[55] Woodlock, who was obviously disappointed about the delay, took occasion on April 22, in the course of a letter to Barnabò requesting permission for an Irish priest, Robert

54. Ibid., fols. 1062–63.
55. A, vol. 228 (1864), fol. 99, "Ristretto con Sommario sull'adunanza tenuta dai Vescovi Irlandesi a Dublino nel mese di Agosto del 1863, Marzo, 1864" (fols. 96–110).

Dunne, to collect for the Catholic University in Australia, to explain why a decision was just then most expedient.[56] "We are, your Eminence," he reported, "every day expecting news of the supreme decision of the Sacred Congregation about the questions pertaining to the University referred to their Eminences last August." "The present," he assured the cardinal, "still appears to be the most opportune moment to promote our most just demands with the government and Parliament with regard to Catholic education, and especially this University." In then concluding, Woodlock added politely that regardless of how matters were decided, he was confident in his hope that an institution so dear to the heart of the Holy Father, and so useful and necessary in maintaining the faith in Ireland and the empire, would continue to grow.

Some three weeks later Woodlock again took occasion of a visit to London to write Kirby asking him to hurry things on. "I have come over here with the advice of our good Archbishop," he reported on May 10, referring to Cullen,

> to try and work forward the cause of Catholic University education. Thank God, I think our prospects are gradually improving, although I doubt if anything satisfactory will be done, as long as Lord Palmerston lives—however, we must be "agitating" the question, keeping our grievances before persons who may have the power to help us, and shaming, as far as possible, those who deny us the privileges granted to unbelievers and free-thinkers. But I am met here by one obstacle, which is putting an almost insurmountable barrier to all our programs: I mean, the unsettled state of the question regarding the admission of the laity to a share in the management of the secular part of the University. [K]

"His Grace, (as you know)," he explained further, "and nearly all the Bishops approve of my opinion that such a step is most desirable, if not necessary; but as in accordance with the wishes of Dr. MacHale and a very small number of the prelates the question was referred to the Holy See last August, we are anxiously awaiting its supreme decision." He went on:

> May I beg you, my dear Mğr, to hasten, if possible, the expediting of the decrees, and to let me know its purport *at the earliest possible moment*, and even by telegram. Every day is now of the greatest importance to us, for we are thinking (by the advice of

56. S.R.C., vol. 34, fol. 1151.

even a Protestant M.P.) of bringing the question before Parliament next month, when the education estimates for Ireland will be before the House. We are told, that by doing so although we might not get a favorable decision this year, we would prepare Parliament for a proper consideration of the matter next summer; and even at present, many things could in a debate on our business be said most appropriately respecting the monstrous grievance of the "Established Church" and "Protestant ascendency" in Ireland.

"Still," he advised Kirby in conclusion, "our friends cannot (or what is the same thing practically, will not) move till the question to which I have referred is decided. Hence my great anxiety to have the answer of the S.C. as soon as possible."

By the time he had returned to Dublin, Woodlock had received word from Barnabò that the cardinals of Propaganda would consider the question of lay participation in the University at their next congregation. Woodlock then decided that perhaps the boldest course was best and wrote Barnabò again. "A few days ago," he reported on May 19,

I returned from London were I was trying to promote the cause of the Catholic University in Parliament and with the government.

As there presently exists a great battle of parties, in which everyone is coveting for himself the highest offices of state, it seems that the moment is opportune to have our demands accepted for this University, which is still placed in a position of inferiority to the other Universities, the Protestant and mixed, because the government won't acknowledge our academic degrees. Still, among the enemies of our Holy Religion and of our country, who are to debate the question, are some who either for party interests or for reasons of natural uprightness would presently pay attention to the warnings of our friends. So even some heads of the opposed parties have given us to believe. But the Catholic members of Parliament won't move until the supreme decision of the Sacred Congregation is known. It will be asked in the House, they say, why the Catholic laity have not any part in the direction of the University, that is in a school in a great part secular, while this lay intervention is permitted in the ecclesiastical College of Maynooth; and was also permitted in the beginning of the same [Catholic] University.[57]

57. Ibid., fol. 1175.

"Being obliged to act," Woodlock explained, referring to the Catholic members, "in a few weeks (or in a few days) in the House of Commons on the mixed University, called the 'Queen's,' that will be the opportune moment to discuss and promote our cause. Hence the great utility, or the necessity, to have as soon as possible, the decision of the Sacred Congregation for our guidance and that of our member friends." "And therefore I beg Your Eminence," Woodlock concluded, "to be so kind as to communicate it to the Archbishop of Dublin or to me in the quickest way that is possible."

The cardinals of Propaganda finally decided on May 30 that laymen should not be included on the governing board of the University.[58] "I have received your letter of the 21st," Cullen wrote Kirby on June 28, "regarding the decision of the Propag. in reference to the C. University. I think the Cardinals were quite right" (C). He shrewdly explained: "The lay element that is anxious to take up the management of the University is not numerous nor important. Catholics of the highest class are only few in Ireland, they are not rich and they do not contribute much to the support of the University, nor will they send their children to it, as they are anxious to send them to England to form acquaintances there. The people who support all our charities are very glad to have them managed by ecclesiastical authority. The Cardinals have come to a wise conclusion." He added, referring to the recent Maynooth and Paris board meetings in Dublin, "I communicated it to the Bishops at the last meeting." "Dr. Woodlock," he reported finally, "is greatly annoyed about it—but of course he will abide by it." Two days later Cullen wrote Kirby again about Propaganda's decision. "All will be pleased," he assured him on June 30, "and Monsignor Woodlock although rather fanatical about the laity will be content. It seems to me the decision was very wise."[59]

A consideration of all the various stratagems, not to say machinations, that Cullen employed to frustrate the proposal of including laymen on the governing board of the Catholic University allows another interesting insight into the complex character of this very gifted man and also makes for a fresh appreciation of why the University eventually failed. Cullen's treatment of Woodlock in this affair certainly explains why he was so much distrusted and feared in the Irish Church. The more astute among the clergy and the laity undoubtedly recognized his fine Italian hand in the decision of the Propaganda. To ask

58. A, vol. 238, fol. 115, "Appendice alla Ponenza di Marzo 1864 sull'adunanza tenuta dai Vescovi Irlandesi a Dublino nel mese di Agosto 1863, 30 Maggio 1864" (fols. 111–16).

59. S.R.C., vol. 34, fol. 1222.

why Cullen was not more candid in his dealings with Woodlock is not to understand either his nature or his character. He simply was not candid by nature. If Kirby be excepted, he confided in no one, and he had the unusual gift of being able to keep virtually his whole mind to himself. His long Roman training, moreover, had enhanced these natural gifts, and it is not perhaps too much to say that few in the Irish Church were as adept as he in the art of dissimulation. Still, there are other reasons why he treated Woodlock as he did, and these reasons make some very good sense in both the lower and the higher worlds of Irish ecclesiastical politics.

In the lower world, Cullen could not afford to allow the University to collapse because both his own and the Holy See's prestige were at stake in the matter. The project had been undertaken some thirteen years before by Cullen at the behest and exhortation of Pius IX, and the survival of the University, at least, if not its success, was now a matter of Catholic honor in Ireland. Indeed, if Cullen had been more candid with Woodlock, who was determined on lay participation and who had recommended it to both the Irish bishops as a body and the Roman authorities, it is hard to see how Woodlock could have accepted Cullen's vote of no confidence in his judgment and continued as rector of the University. Woodlock's resignation would have certainly precipitated another crisis, and if the University did not collapse immediately, its days would have been even more obviously numbered. Cullen's problem, therefore, was how to block Woodlock's proposal for lay representation and at the same time secure his continuance as rector. This is why he threw the entire blame for the appeal to Rome on MacHale, a step that he also found most congenial, while privately recommending a Roman veto to Barnabò.

In the higher world of ecclesiastical politics, Cullen's efforts also made some real sense. He was determined to maintain a clerical monopoly in education on all levels in Ireland, and on this matter he had brought the great majority of the bishops around to his way of thinking in recent years. The most interesting assertion he made in explaining to Barnabò his reasons against lay participation in the University was that the bishops had voted for Woodlock's proposal as a matter of expediency. In other words, they had done so because they too realized that a vote of no confidence in the rector would be fatal to the University, and they had voted for lay participation as being the lesser of two evils. Cullen had probably also privately assured his reliable friends among the bishops, who were inclined to vote against the proposal, that it would not pass muster at Rome. That is why Cullen was able to report to Kirby that he had shown his letter regarding Propaganda's decision on lay participation to a number of the bishops and that they were well pleased. Though it is hard to say whether Woodlock realized that he had been undermined at Rome by Cullen rather than Mac-Hale, it is difficult to believe that he did not suspect something when the decision from Propaganda finally came.[60] If he did, he must have realized as well that in frustrating him Cullen had also saved his face in the Irish Church. In any case, Woodlock's continued compliance was yet another mark of Cullen's judgment and shrewdness in choosing him to succeed Newman as rector.

In the last analysis, then, the reason why the University failed was not simply the lack of leadership, or the shortage of funds, or even, as Cullen would have had everyone believe, the obstruction of MacHale at every turn, but rather the bishops' insistence on absolute episcopal control of higher education. In the political context of the day, such a monopoly made it a patent impossibility to secure a charter for the University from an English Parliament. Without a charter the University could not grant those degrees which its graduates needed to qualify for the fields and professions that required them. This is why that very small Catholic upper middle class in Ireland, who might have been expected to patronize the University and who willingly submitted to a clerical monopoly in education on the primary and intermediate levels, refused to send their sons to the University in any great numbers. Indeed, the medical school of the University was the exception that proved the rule.[61] From its inception the medical school had been the most successful branch of the University, and it had always accounted for more than half of the matriculated students.

60. See, for example, W, Dixon to Woodlock, June 1864.

61. Though written some years earlier, a letter in which Laurence Forde, then professor of canon law at the University, complained to Kirby about Newman sheds considerable light on the vitality and importance of the medical school in the University. Forde was particularly upset that although Newman had offered his resignation, he might yet be allowed to continue as "Rector on his own terms." "That is," Forde explained, "to stay away in England and write letters from time to time ratifying whatever his advisors[,] a couple of Oxford Converts[,] choose to suggest—meanwhile the University both in money and scholars, *magrisce* [grows thin]—the medical school excepted, which as its object is, *Superior Professional* education under Catholic management, and being moreover altogether, in the hands of ignorant Irish unconverted, and all as they are; continues to flourish and increase in numbers and stability in happy ignorance or disregard of the fact that the rules and regulations drawn up for the University by the English Savants do *not* admit of the Medical Pupils being recognised as students of the Catholic University. I apprehend however that before three years have elapsed it will form the only remnant of that Institution" (K, n.d. [ca. early 1858], fragment). See also *Freeman's Journal*, November 1, 1865, for the numbers of students receiving medical training at the various Dublin medical schools between 1854 and 1864. The total number of students being trained at the Catholic University in 1854 was thirty-nine and in 1864, ninety-three.

The school boasted a distinguished faculty, and its graduates were highly regarded in the profession. The bishops, moreover, had little to say about either the appointments to the medical faculty, except to approve them, or the curriculum, which was advanced for its day. The real reason for the medical school's success, however, was that it had early acquired, on the payment of a fee of £1,000, the required public seal that permitted the medical faculty, as the certifying body, to present its students for the necessary licenses to practice medicine. A charter from the state, therefore, was superfluous as far as the graduates of the medical school were concerned, but such was not the case for those students enrolled in the arts and science faculties—hence Woodlock's willingness to include laymen on the governing body and the unwillingness of the Irish M.P.'s to move on the matter in the House of Commons until the question of including laymen had been decided. The decision to exclude the laity was therefore the virtual end of any real hope for a charter and, by extension, the effective end of the Catholic University as a viable institution of higher education.

In any case, between 1859 and 1864 the bishops as a body had consolidated their position on the education question on all its various levels—primary, intermediate, and university. Though it would be some years before they achieved all that they desired in regard to education on all its levels, it was in this period that they finally crystallized those demands that would govern their policy as a body on education for more than a century. The architect of this consolidation, of course, was Cullen. In his reply to Cardwell, Cullen emphasized that control of Irish education by an essentially Protestant state was not acceptable to the Irish bishops, and by extension to Irish Catholics, and he later made it clear to O'Hagan that control by Catholic laymen, and by projection an Irish state, was no more acceptable to the Irish bishops as a body. Though the bishops did not succeed in gaining their way in this period, they did finally turn the tide of state control over education that had been running hard against them since the inception of the national primary system in 1831. By persuading Irish-Catholic public opinion in this period that it had serious grievances to complain of concerning both the control and the nature of the national system, the bishops were finally able to place the commissioners of the Board of National Education on the defensive. In then boldly declaring war on the model schools and successfully setting up an effective intermediate system of their own, the bishops finally seized an initiative they were never to relinquish again on the education question. None of this could have been achieved, however, if the bishops had not finally settled the differences that had plagued them as a body for more than twenty years on education, and their real achievement in this period perhaps was to be found less in discovering what was essential in education than in acquiring that harmony and unity which would make their will as a body effective in achieving those things.

IV

The One Thing Necessary—Unity

May 1859–April 1865

The efforts of the bishops as a body between 1860 and 1864 to acquire an absolute control over Irish education on all levels also had important consequences for the consolidation of their own body. For longer than a quarter century, the issue that had divided the episcopal body more than any other had been the education question. To secure the harmony of the body in the fifties, Cullen had gone so far as to threaten even its independence and integrity by invoking his very considerable influence at Rome. The bishops, however, had successfully resisted his efforts to bring some order out of chaos in the governing of the Irish Church, if such order were to come at the expense of the integrity of their body. By 1860 Cullen had become more wary about employing his influence at Rome, and Rome had become more circumspect in invoking its power in the Irish Church. As a result, the bishops as a body had acquired a greater confidence and responsibility in the governing of the Irish Church. For more than a decade, the most obvious measure of both Cullen's effective influence at Rome and Rome's real intentions in Ireland had been Irish episcopal appointments, and they continued to be watched, therefore, with an inordinate intensity and interest.

In Ireland between 1850 and 1859, there had been twenty appointments made in a hierarchy that numbered some twenty-eight regular bishops. In a decade, therefore, the Irish hierarchy had been virtually renovated, and it is not too much to say that in the great majority of these appointments Cullen's influence was paramount. Cullen's sine qua non for the promotion of any candidate had been that he should not be a friend or supporter of MacHale. Given that basic require-ment, Cullen's other priorities in recommending appointments to Rome were basically three. First and foremost, the candidate must be orthodox on the education question, and that meant that he must be opposed to mixed education on any level. Second, he must be an ar-dent pastoral reformer and prepared to enforce the decrees of the Synod of Thurles on that subject. Third, he must be ready to exercise a firm control over those priests who were too much inclined to in-volve themselves in politics. In any case, by 1860 Cullen could count on a very large majority in the episcopal body in support of these policies. The problem, however, was not simply one of creating major-ities but one of turning those majorities into that virtual unanimity which was absolutely necessary if the corporate will of the episcopal body was to have any moral or practical effect. This meant that the majorities must be very large in order to create a consensus morally strong enough to persuade the minority to submit not only in the name of the collective authority but in virtue of the collective wis-dom. The key to maintaining those large majorities, and the consen-sus that was dependent on them, was to ensure that those who were to be appointed bishops were in harmony with the general views of the body.

In the six years between 1860 and 1865 there were only six episco-pal appointments made in Ireland, and though there was obviously little change in policy in so modest a turnover, the appointments were significant both in themselves and cumulatively in the developing corporate character of the episcopal body. The first of these appoint-ments had arisen out of the pressing need to provide the aging bishop of Down and Connor, Cornelius Denvir, with a coadjutor.[1] For nearly ten years there had been constant complaints about Denvir's inac-tivity and the resulting spiritual destitution in his diocese. In the city of Belfast, for example, where the influx of Catholics from the country areas looking for employment had been very great in recent years, Denvir was charged with having refused to assign more than four priests to minister to the spiritual needs of a Catholic population that numbered more than fifty thousand. That situation was somewhat relieved after Denvir made his required *ad limina* visit to Rome in 1858, when the Roman authorities had the opportunity to discuss with him the various charges and complaints made by the clergy and

1. A, vol. 224 (1860), fol. 159, "Ristretto con Sommario sulla del Coadjutore pel Vescovo di Down e Connor in Irlanda, 4 Giugno 1860" (fols. 158–68).

laity of Belfast. Less than a year later, however, the archbishop of Armagh, as Denvir's metropolitan, had to write to Cullen, who was then in Rome, that the situation in Belfast and the diocese of Down and Connor was worse than ever and something drastic needed to be done. "What I should desire," Dixon explained on May 25, 1859, "would be that your Grace endeavor to bring Monsignor Denvir the charge from Propaganda to call a meeting of the clergy and to recommend a coadjutor in the due form. The advanced age of this prelate, his nervous apprehensions of the Orange party, the vast Catholic population of Belfast, and the extent of the diocese render this measure most desirable. If your Grace will bring such a document to Ireland, it will be a great work."[2]

Cullen had already left Rome when this letter arrived, however, and Dixon was constrained to write Kirby a month later, on June 28, charging him in Dixon's name to go immediately Barnabò and ask him to order Denvir to take the necessary steps for the nomination of a coadjutor without delay. Kirby did so, and on July 10 Monsignor Bedini, secretary of Propaganda, in an audience with the pope secured the necessary authorization to have Dixon and Cullen inform Denvir that the pope had ordered him to call a meeting of his clergy to elect a coadjutor.[3] "Having taken counsel with the Archbishop of Dublin," Dixon finally wrote Kirby on August 31,

> I communicated to Dr. Denvir the wish of His Holiness, that he would proceed to the recommendation of a coadjutor in the usual way. His Eminence will be gratified to know that Dr. Denvir received the communication in the best spirit; and would have summoned his clergy immediately, if I had so wished it. But I thought that for the convenience of the Bishops of the province, and for my own convenience, as I was then in the middle of my visitation, the meeting of the clergy and Bishops on the matter in Belfast might be deferred til the end of October. Dr. Denvir would thus have a convenient opportunity of inviting the Bishops of the province at our general meeting in October. [K]

"I am anxious," he cautioned Kirby in conclusion, "that you would not mention except to His Eminence this matter about a coadjutor for Belfast [sic]; as the knowledge of it in Ireland might lead to inconvenient agitation, not only in the diocese of Down and Connor, but elsewhere."

2. Ibid., fol. 163.
3. Ibid., fol. 159.

The meeting was finally held on November 29 in Belfast, and the clergy of Down and Connor commended the required three names, or *terna*, to Rome.[4] The *dignissimus*, or most worthy, was Charles Russell, the president of Maynooth, with sixteen votes; the *dignior*, or more worthy, was Patrick Dorrian, the parish priest of Loughinisland, with nine votes; and the *dignus*, or worthy, was John Fitzsimons, the parish priest of Cushendall, with four votes. The bishops of the province of Armagh, who met in Dublin on December 1 to report to Propaganda on the clergy's commendation, were unanimous in their choice of the first on the list.[5] Cullen reported to Kirby on December 3, "The election for Belfast [*sic*] has taken place. Dr. Russell 1st. He wd be well suited, but he says nothing will induce him to accept. The other two[,] Mr. Dorrien [*sic*] and Mr. Fitzsimons[,] are said to be good P.P.'s but I fear they are not up to the mark" (K). "If Dr. Russell refuse to accept," Cullen suggested, "then perhaps Dr. Leahy [bishop of Dromore] might be put in his place."

Cullen was correct about Russell's being not willing to accept the miter, for Russell wrote Barnabò on December 5, asking him to explain to the pope that he begged to be excused. Not only did he feel incapable of fulfilling so great a responsibility, but he had also had in recent years to take on a very heavy financial burden in order to save his family from disgrace, a burden that would seriously impair that freedom and independence so necessary to the office of a bishop. It was not unlikely, furthermore, that he would in the end be involved in litigation before the public tribunals, which could only bring discredit on the sacred office if he were a bishop. Both Dixon and Cullen, Russell finally noted, had been apprised of his sad situation, and they would attest to its very serious nature. Indeed, Dixon and Cullen wrote Barnabò the next day, December 6, confirming all that Russell had said. Barnabò then wrote Cullen asking what he thought should be done and what the merits were of the other two names on the *terna*. "After having consulted many prudent persons," Cullen replied on January 17, 1860, "I remain convinced that it is much better not to remove Father Russell from the College of Maynooth, the office of rector of that college being very important for all Ireland especially since at the present moment there cannot be found another person to succeed him. Perhaps it would be well to write to him to such effect to free him from the anxiety in which he finds himself."[6] "As for the other two candidates for coadjutor," Cullen explained, "I have still not

4. Ibid., fols. 163–64.
5. Ibid., fol. 164.
6. Ibid., fol. 166.

been able to obtain any news, but I hope soon to be able to obtain the necessary information."

Cullen was not able, however, to write Barnabò concerning the candidates for some seven weeks. He finally explained on March 4,

The distance of Belfast from Dublin has prevented me from obtaining accurate news about the subjects proposed for the coadjutorship of Down and Connor. As to the first, Father Russell, I do not have to say anything, given his decision not to accept the episcopal dignity. I have written in confidence about the second, Father Dorrian, to the coadjutor bishop of Newry [correctly, Dromore] who knows the said Dorrian well, and he says that he is a man of edifying life, and learned, and that he governs his parish with great zeal. In the diocese of Down and Connor spiritual exercises have never been given to the clergy, but Father Dorrian goes regularly to make his retreat in other dioceses, where spiritual exercises are held. The coadjutor bishop says in conclusion that the only difficulty that he has in recommending Father Dorrian is that he may lack that energy, which would be necessary in the present circumstances of the diocese of Down and Connor. Perhaps in a few weeks time more precise news may be obtained.[7]

As it happened, Cullen was unable to write Barnabò again on the subject for yet another seven weeks. "In complying with your Eminence's instructions," he finally reported on April 24, "I have made various inquiries about the candidates proposed for the coadjutorship of Down and Connor. Connections between that diocese and Dublin are very uncommon, and the clergy of this city know nothing of the priests of that distant part of Ireland. From the little news that I have been able to gather however it appears that Father *Dorrian,* who was second on the *terna,* is deserving of being a bishop. I have already written to your Eminence what I have been able to learn of his qualities, and I believe that there is nothing that presents an obstacle to his promotion."[8] A week later Cullen finally reported to Kirby what he had done. "About Down & Connor," he explained on May 1, "I wrote twice. All the information I could get from Belfast is favourable to the 2ᵈ[,] Mr. Dorrian[,] but there is scarcely any communication at all of an ecclesiastical nature between Dublin & Belfast, *sicche io non ho potuto far molto* [so that I have not been able to do much]" (K).

7. Ibid., fol. 167.
8. Ibid.

Cullen was obviously the central figure in this effort to choose a coadjutor for the bishop of Down and Connor. Two aspects of his role in the matter provide some interesting food for thought: his very long delay in securing the required information and his extreme diffidence, which was very unusual with him in such matters. The reason why he not only procrastinated but seemed to be less confident than usual in making his various recommendations to Barnabò was that he did not know Dorrian and had been unable to find out very much more about him than that he was a good and holy man. What Dorrian's views were on the education question, for example, was extremely important for Cullen to know, because for more than ten years Denvir had proved to be a painful thorn in his side on that question. If the new coadjutor should prove partial to Denvir's educational views, it could be disastrous for Cullen's current efforts finally to secure the unity he desired on that question in the episcopal body. The fact that Dorrian had been warmly recommended by the coadjutor to the bishop of Dromore, John Pius Leahy, who was also a good and holy man, was at that particular moment something less than reassuring, for Cullen was of the opinion that Leahy's views concerning the mixed nature of the national system were not as sound as they might have been. Cullen delayed making his final recommendation to Barnabò in order to find out more about Dorrian's opinions on those matters of great moment then facing the Irish Church.

Still, when Cullen did make his final recommendation to Barnabò on April 24, he chose to be very cautious. He pointed out to the cardinal, for example, that he had already in a previous letter endorsed Dorrian's qualities, thereby implicitly distinguishing between the candidate's qualities and his opinions. Cullen then went on to couch his recommendation in negative rather than positive terms by explaining that he did not believe there was anything that would prevent Dorrian's promotion. What Cullen was really saying, of course, and Barnabò was too practiced an ecclesiastic to have missed it, was that he could not take the responsibility for his recommendation given the insufficient information available to him. By the time Cullen's letter of April 24 had reached him, however, Barnabò had already received the necessary reassurance about Dorrian's opinions from another source. The vicar apostolic of Hyderabad in India, Daniel Murphy, a former Cork priest and an acquaintance of both Kirby and Cullen, was then in Rome on ecclesiastical business. Murphy, by chance, was also an old friend of Dorrian, whom he had first met some twenty-five years before, when they had been students together at Maynooth. Kirby must have asked Murphy, who generally stayed at the Irish College when he was in Rome, to speak to Barnabò about Dorrian, for the cardinal prefect asked Murphy to put his recommendation in writing so that it might be included in the *ponenza* to be submitted to the cardinals of Propaganda when they considered the appointment of a coadjutor to the bishop of Down and Connor. Murphy, who was obviously pressed for time, finally sent the requested letter to Kirby from Civita Vecchia on April 28, just as he was leaving Rome for Ireland. He asked Kirby to translate it and submit it to Propaganda in his name.[9] In concluding his letter to Propaganda, Murphy addressed himself to those two points that must have concerned Barnabò most in his correspondence with Cullen about Dorrian. "He well knows," Murphy assured the Cardinal of Dorrian, "all the spiritual needs of the Diocese, and he possesses not only the will, but also the energy to remedy them. He has also been an ardent supporter of those measures recommended by the Holy See for the advancement of religion in Ireland." Therefore, when the cardinals of Propaganda met on June 4 to consider formally the commendation of the clergy and the report of the bishops, they unanimously recommended Dorrian to the pope as coadjutor, with the right of succession, to the bishop of Down and Connor, and on June 10 the pope authoritatively approved their recommendation.[10]

Meanwhile, the bishop of Limerick, John Ryan, had also called a meeting of his clergy to commend a *terna* to Rome for a coadjutor with the right to succeed him.[11] On March 14, while visiting Dublin, Ryan had asked Cullen to forward to Barnabò his request for a coadjutor. In a covering letter enclosing the request the next day, Cullen explained to Barnabò that Ryan was nearly eighty years of age and almost unable to walk.[12] He also added that Ryan would like his request to be acted on as soon as possible in order to prevent intrigues from being set on foot in the diocese. On March 25, therefore, the pope, in an audience with the secretary of Propaganda, approved Ryan's request. The meeting of the clergy to elect a *terna* took place on May 2 in Limerick.[13] The three names proposed by the Limerick clergy were George Butler, dean

9. Ibid., fols. 167–68.
10. Ibid., fol. 162.
11. Ibid., fol. 410, "Ristretto con Sommario sulla scelta di un Coadjutore pel Vescovo di Limerick Nella Provincia Ecclesiastica di Cashel in Irlanda, 18 Settembre 1860" (fols. 404–26).
12. Ibid., fol. 405.
13. Ibid., fols. 410–11.

of the diocese; Robert Cussen, parish priest of Bruff; and Edmund O'Reilly, professor of dogmatic theology at the Catholic University and a member of the Society of Jesus. Curiously enough, in forwarding the three names commended by the clergy to Rome, neither Ryan nor the bishops of the province, who had met that same day in Limerick, mentioned the number of votes each of the candidates received. Moreover, the bishops in their report, in unanimously recommending the *dignissimus*, Dean Butler, failed to say a word about the merits of either the *dignior* or the *dignus*, Cussen and O'Reilly, respectively.[14]

In forwarding the report of the bishops to Barnabò on May 8, the archbishop of Cashel, Patrick Leahy, attempted to explain why the bishops did not, as they were required by the procedures in appointing to Irish sees, report on all three candidates.[15] The bishops had recommended Butler, Leahy pointed out, because he was the only candidate on which they were unanimous, and unanimity and concord among the bishops was just then the virtue to be most cherished in Ireland because the British government was by every artifice attempting to wound the Catholic religion. Though all the bishops esteemed O'Reilly for his piety and learning, Leahy added, they were concerned that because he was a Jesuit, the pope would be reluctant to promote him, and he was not the preferred of either the clergy or the bishop of Limerick. The bishop of Waterford, Dominic O'Brien, Leahy then reported, had been unable to attend the meeting because he became ill, but he had given him his permission in writing to add his name to that of the other bishops of the province for any priest that they considered worthy, except Butler. Why O'Brien had excepted Butler was that he had heard on good authority that the dean was in favor of mixed education and a supporter of the model-school system, and hence O'Brien's name was not added to the unanimous report to Propaganda in favor of Butler. The bishop of Limerick, however, Leahy further explained, had maintained that the charge was false, and he was supported in this claim by the bishop of Kerry. Leahy then added that he had told the bishops that if indeed the rumors were true concerning Butler's support of mixed education, he would write Rome retracting his endorsement of him. In a postscript Leahy then finally noted that the bishops were unanimous in thinking that the second on the list, Robert Cussen, though a good, laborious priest, was not really episcopal material. Some ten days later, on May 17, Leahy wrote Barnabò again, explaining that in the interim he had spoken to Butler,

14. Ibid., fols. 411–12.
15. Ibid., fol. 412.

who explicitly denied that he either favored the mixed system or supported model schools.[16] Butler also declared that he supported the position taken by the bishops in their 1859 synod in Dublin on the education question and again in their recent letter to Cardwell on that same question.

Cullen, meanwhile, had written Kirby twice about the Limerick *terna*. "Dean Butler," he reported in early May, "is 1st. He is clever, and respectable, but is said to be *mondano*, and fond of mixed education. He is a great friend of the Bishop and talks like him" (K). "Dean Cussen," he then added, "is a very good man—and does a great deal of good for religion—he is old. Dr. O'Reilly you know. He is I believe the best of all. His only fault is that he is a little undecided and slow." "Do not mention," he warned Kirby in conclusion, "what I have written at Propag. I will write when I hear more. Dean Butler I suppose has been recommended, as he is from Cashel, and a friend of Dr. Leahy." "I send you a letter from Limerick," he wrote Kirby again several days later, "which will help to show how things are there. Read it" (K). The enclosed letter, which was addressed to Cullen, was dated May 12 and signed "*Sacerdos Limericensis*."[17] "I consider it a duty, I owe to religion," the anonymous Limerick priest informed Cullen,

to call your Grace's attention to a few remarks on this matter, and to assure you that the greatest reliance can be placed on every statement herein made.

I have no hesitation in stating that the appointment of V. Rev. George Butler would be most unwise, as well as injurious, to religion in this diocese, at the present time. Within the last two years the priests have been divided, and cut up into two hostile parties. At some of the late elections the collision between them was most scandalous and disedifying. Very Rev. George Butler conducted himself so boisterously, that he had to be escorted through his own parish to his dwelling house by seven or eight dragoons. To such a height had the popular feeling been excited against him, on account of his conduct that some of his parishioners were heard to say they would rather die without Sacraments than to receive them at his hands. Truly my Lord, it would I beg to say be unwise to give us such a priest for our Bishop. We require a Bishop who will know nothing of our dis-

16. Ibid., fol. 412[a].
17. Ibid., fols. 413–14. Kirby submitted a portion of this letter—the first part, down to where the sodality in Butler's parish collapsed during his administration—to Propaganda in Italian translation.

sensions, who will be independent of both parties, and consequently be able to heal the wounds already inflicted on religion,
and unite the priests into one compact body. Such I beg most
respectfully to state is in my humble opinion the Very Rev. Dr.
O'Reilly. If a diocese ever required such a Bishop, it is the diocese
of Limerick at present.

"With regard to the Rev. George Butler's character," Cullen's anonymous correspondent added, "I must say that he is an exemplary priest,
and has given no scandal during his missionary career." "At the same
time," the letter continued,

> it must be confessed that he has no zeal, no efficiency. In the last
> 22 yrs he has not erected so much as *an altar*, in any of the
> missions where he has been placed: and it is a well known fact,
> that the pious sodalities established in St. Michael's parish fell to
> the ground during his administration. His present church is a
> miserable building wholly unsuited to the times, and still he has
> not made the least effort to improve it, or erect a new one in its
> place. He is all for pomp, and vanity, has the greatest penchant
> for dinner parties, and remains out until 12 o'clock at night, and
> sometimes returns home at one o'clock in the morning. Our dio-
> cese requires a most active and zealous Bishop, as the chapels,
> for the most part, are in a wretched state and the church furni-
> ture a disgrace to a Christian country. Will your Grace believe
> me when I tell you that there is no other lock to some of the
> chapel doors, but a bit of twine to fasten them to a nail[,] no lock
> to the chapel gates to prevent pigs and cows from coming into
> the yard. Such is the state of things in the parish of Donough-
> more, within two miles of the city, and in the parish of Bally-
> brown, Mr. Monsell's parish Church. I mention these in particu-
> lar as being convenient to the city, and under the observation of
> all[;] the chapels of the city are not much better.

"I now beg," he continued, turning to Butler's place on the *terna* as
dignissimus, "to call your Grace's attention to the manner in which
his election has been effected." He elaborated:

> During the last two years the vacant parishes were given only to
> such clergymen as were known to be his friends and supporters
> and at his request. The Rev. Richard O'Brien[,] late of All Hal-
> lows, was brought back to the diocese at the request of the Dean,
> who is his most intimate friend, and who does nothing without
> consulting him. I can give your Grace the names of the other

priests, who got parishes through the Dean. The last appointment has been that of the Rev. Mr. Hickey[,] a priest from another diocese who has been on the mission only six yrs. No one would say a word against the Bishop's act, were there any brilliant qualities in his character to reflect credit on the priesthood. But how does the case stand? This Rev. gentleman is more a huntsman, than a priest, he kept three race-horses and hounds and frequently appeared in the streets of Limerick dressed in large hunting boots. He had been robbed of his watch by a common prostitute on his return from a dinner party at 12 o'clock at night. The case came before the magistrates and everything connected with this scandalous business was brought before the public. These are the men, who got parishes within the last two yrs in order to secure a large number of votes for the Dean. Weeks before the election six priests on the part of the Dean canvassed almost every P.P. of the diocese holding out every encouragement to them in case they sustained the Dean. Three administrators got canonical possession of their parishes on the eve of the election in order to secure the first place for the Dean. It is for your Grace to say, whether such proceedings are to be tolerated.

"You Grace is aware," he then further informed Cullen, "that nothing has ever been done in this diocese for the Catholic University, nor to support the universal recommendation of the Bishops for the amelioration of the Nat. System. I believe I may fairly state that the Dean takes his lead from our Bishop on these subjects, and the Rev. Richard O'Brien and Dr. Moriarty have been heard to say that they were wholly opposed to a separate grant of money for Catholics. The writer of these lines heard conversation to this effect from the Rev. Richard O'Brien, who is the bosom friend of Dr. Moriarty."

"I have endeavoured," this Limerick priest then finally confided, "to lay before your Grace a few remarks on this most important matter, as I must confess I am not indifferent, as to our future Bishop. We want a holy[,] pious and zealous one. In God's name send us Dr. O'Reilly or Dr. Kirby. He had one vote, and perhaps the Holy Ghost watched over us so far." "Very Rev. George Butler," he assured Cullen again, "and the Rev. Richard O'Brien who is his law and his Prophet are party men, most violent and given wholly to dinner parties. Our chapels[,] and priests who frequent races notwithstanding the national and provincial statutes[,] require great improvement. I believe in my heart that the Dean will leave them as they are." "Will your Grace," he then requested of Cullen in conclusion, "kindly read over these few pages. I can vouch for the truth of every statement herein made. There is the greatest bitterness, and jealousy prevailing among the priests, and it would be most unfortunate for the Dean to become Bishop and most detrimental to religion. It has been considered unfair on the part of our Bishop to have invited the Bishops of the province to the meeting held in Limerick on second of May. It is to be presumed they took his advice in recommending his man to the Holy See."

When, several days later, Cullen had still not heard from Barnabò, who always asked his opinion in the making of episcopal appointments, he boldly decided to write the cardinal prefect about the Limerick *terna*. "Your Eminence will have already heard," he explained on May 8, "of the choice made in the three priests to be presented to the Sacred Congregation for the coadjutorship of Limerick. It appears that all three are persons of great merit, [but] I do not know which of them has been recommended by the bishops of the province."[18] He outlined what he knew of the three:

> The first among them, Father Butler, made his studies at Maynooth, and then went to Trinidad for some time as a missionary, but returned from there for reasons of health. He has the reputation of being a good preacher, and of administering his parish well: but at the same time he is considered a fair weather man [*uomo di bel tempo*], who likes to be invited to dine by the rich, and who spends much time in such things. Besides I have been assured that he is favorable to the mixed system of education. Monsignor Ryan, the actual bishop, has always strongly declared himself in favor of the said system, and probably Father Butler has adopted his views. It must be said in any case that the old bishop has done much to promote convent schools and the schools of Christian Brothers, although he speaks very favorably of the government's schools.
>
> The second on the list is Father Cussen: he studied in France and was a professor in the seminary of Meaux before the revolution of 1830. He is considered very learned, and zealous, and has made great efforts in his parish to establish purely Catholic schools. His major defect is his rather advanced age.
>
> The last on the list is Father O'Reilly. He studied in the Irish College in Rome, made a public defense at the Roman College in 1836, with the happiest result, and then obtained the chair of theology by concursus in Maynooth in 1838. He remained profes-

18. Ibid., fols. 412[a]–13.

sor in that College for 14 years, and then entered the Society of Jesus, and resides with those same fathers here in Dublin. He is in any case a native of Limerick, and nephew of the earl of Kenmare, one of the first noblemen of Ireland, and is connected with many other distinguished families. Father O'Reilly is a good preacher, gives spiritual exercises with great result, and is considered one of the most learned theologians in this whole kingdom. The bishop of Killaloe, Monsignor Flannery has written me that he would find it very desirable that the said O'Reilly should be appointed bishop. The diocese of Limerick is much divided into parties. Father Butler who is a native of Cashel, is not well looked on by many natives of Limerick, while Father O'Reilly belongs to that diocese, and at the same time having spent his whole life in Rome or Dublin is entirely removed from the intrigues of every party. Moreover, as no impetus was ever given under the actual bishop to the practices of piety in that diocese, it would be well that now a bishop devoted himself to them, who by life and learning might be an example to that whole clergy.

"I have made these few observations," Cullen concluded politely, "in the hope that they will throw some light for the Sacred Congregation on the important choice to be made."

Before this letter reached Rome, however, Cullen finally received a letter from Barnabò asking him for his views in the Limerick *terna*. Cullen replied on May 29, explaining that he had already anticipated Barnabò's request about the *terna* and that he had nothing really to add beyond what he had written.[19] "All three candidates," he noted again, "are worthy priests, but Father O'Reilly is undoubtedly superior to the others as a theologian and canonist. He is well known at the Irish College and at the Roman College, and if your Eminence asks Father Perrone, he will be able to give more accurate news of Father O'Reilly who has been his pupil. Besides being learned, Father O'Reilly is a man of great goodness, and singular piety. He certainly would be an ornament to the Irish episcopate." Several days later Cullen finally learned what had happened at the meeting of the bishops of the province on May 2 in Limerick, and he wrote Barnabò again. "After having then written," he explained on June 5,

I heard from the bishop of Kerry that the bishops of the province in their letter to the Sacred Congregation contented themselves with speaking of the merits of Father Butler, the first on the pro-

19. Ibid., fol. 416.

posed *terna*, without saying anything of the other two. The reason for this reticence was that the old bishop declared that he absolutely did not want to have another coadjutor than Butler, and that when the archbishop of Cashel, the bishop of Killaloe, and the bishop of Kerry said some words in favor of Father O'Reilly, the said old bishop became so excited that he appeared to be in danger of death. Then the bishops agreed to praise Father Butler, who has great merits, and to say nothing of the others, the merits of whom are still greater.[20]

"It seems to me," Cullen suggested, "that the Sacred Congregation ought to be informed of the merits of all three candidates, and therefore I would humbly suggest that the archbishop and each of the bishops of the province be written to inviting them to give their views about Fathers Cussen and O'Reilly who are the other two on the *terna*. The old bishop is in a worse state of health, and probably will not live many months. A little delay will do no harm in such a case, and if the diocese was vacant, the choice would be more free."

Barnabò decided to take Cullen's prudent advice and wrote the archbishop and bishops of the province of Cashel on June 21, asking them for their views on the *terna* commended by the Limerick clergy. In conveniently summarizing the opinions of the bishops in the *ristretto* later prepared for the consideration of the case by the cardinals of Propaganda, the secretary of Propaganda, Monsignor Bedini, explained:

> The archbishop of Cashel and the bishops of Kerry, Limerick, Ross, Cloyne and Cork persisted in believing Father Butler furnished all the talents necessary for the bishopric and [was] still preferable to the other two for the coadjutorship of Limerick. That of Kerry however said that if it was a question not of electing a coadjutor, but the bishop of Limerick, Father O'Reilly would be preferable to Butler, and if that was the object he would suggest a delay. The bishop of Waterford declared to have learned on irrefutable testimony, that Father Butler is too favorable to the system of mixed education, and that of Killaloe though he says he [Butler] is deserving of the bishopric he still believes that Father O'Reilly is still more deserving.[21]

In reviewing the bishops' opinions of Father Cussen, the second on the list, the secretary reported, "All the bishops are unanimous in

20. Ibid., fol. 418.
21. Ibid., fol. 407.

setting him behind the other two candidates. The archbishop however and the bishops of Limerick, Ross, Cloyne, and Killaloe do not believe him at all qualified for the episcopacy; those on the other hand of Waterford and Cork praise him, but agree that he ought not to be chosen." Finally, in summarizing the bishops' views on O'Reilly, Bedini added:

> The bishops are fully in accord in praising the eminent learning and piety of Father O'Reilly, but the metropolitan together with the prelates of Limerick, Ross, Cloyne, and Cork are not of the opinion that he ought to be elected to the coadjutorship of Limerick, since being a man of study, who has never had the care of souls, he lacks experience, and hence that practical prudence which is necessary to govern. On the other hand, the bishop of Kerry (as has already been noted) would be pleased that he was provided for the Church of Limerick, but only if it became vacant, and he would wish however that the choice of a coadjutor at present be not persisted in. The bishop of Waterford says that Father O'Reilly *est omni laude dignus* [is worthy of all praise], and while he seems to prefer him to the other two, he sees a difficulty in his appointment in his being a Jesuit, hence he defers to the wise judgement of the Sacred Congregation.

Indeed, the bishop of Waterford's premonition that difficulties would be raised because O'Reilly was a Jesuit was all too correct. In an interview in late June with the secretary of Propaganda, the father general of the Society of Jesus, Peter Beckx, declared himself averse to the proposed promotion. The secretary asked Beckx to put his objections in writing to the cardinal prefect for the consideration of the cardinals of Propaganda when they made their recommendation to the pope for a coadjutor to the bishop of Limerick. In writing to Barnabò on June 30, the father general adduced three main reasons for declining to approve O'Reilly's appointment—the general welfare of the Society, the particular needs of the Irish vice-province, and respect for O'Reilly himself.[22] As far as the general welfare of the Society was concerned, Beckx pointed out, their sainted founder had firmly established a tradition that its members were not to aspire to ecclesiastical dignities, and he had himself in recent years strongly advised the Sacred Congregation on similar occasions in writing that he was determined to uphold that tradition. As to the particular needs of the Irish vice-province, Beckx explained, the Society had established itself in

22. Ibid., fols. 417–18.

Ireland about forty years before but had remained in a languid state because the Society had been unable to establish a house in Ireland for the training of novices. The problem was not so much that the Society was unable to obtain vocations in Ireland as rather that it had lacked qualified men to supervise a novitiate in which the spirits and minds of its students could be properly formed. A house had now finally been built in Ireland for that purpose, which was to be opened in the fall, and Beckx had relied on having O'Reilly to form the novices. The Society, moreover, was in dire need of English-speaking missionaries to help provide for all those foreign missions where English was spoken. If O'Reilly were removed, Beckx argued, he did not see how he could be suitably replaced.

Beckx then turned to his third reason for declining to approve O'Reilly's appointment: he thought that little or no advantage would result from it either to the Church or to O'Reilly. "The said Father," Beckx explained, "is certainly a good religious, and also much esteemed for his learning, most highly in matters theological, but he is in the first place by character and natural disposition not at all fit to govern, I will not say a diocese, but not even a house. Besides being timid and scrupulous, and therefore always indecisive and irresolute in his deliberations, he has no experience in business, and much less of administration: and that is the judgement of all who know him. Now, how would he be able to regulate, principally in these times, a diocese, to win the trust and liking of the secular and regular clergy?" In the second place, Beckx then assured Barnabò, O'Reilly had a very great repugnance, which he had stated in writing to the father assistant in England, to being made a bishop, and he would have also written Propaganda to that effect except for a certain shyness about being thought presumptuous, especially as there were two other very worthy names before his on the *terna*. If indeed O'Reilly were appointed, Beckx continued, in the best Jesuit tradition he would of course obey, but he would be so afflicted and upset that he would be able to do little or no good. Moreover, all the great good that he could do in instructing the young and in giving spiritual exercises to the secular and regular clergy would be lost.

In winding up this very long and masterful letter, Beckx finally begged to be allowed to touch on two further points of some importance. First, he wanted to remind the Sacred Congregation that this would be the first case in which a member of the Society of Jesus was appointed for a regularly constituted see (*Sede propria*) and for a particular diocese in Europe—in effect, an awesome precedent. Secondly, the pope had had the goodness several years before to say in an audience that he was persuaded that members of the Society ought not to be appointed to *Sedi proprii* and that even in missionary areas, only in exceptional circumstances might they be obliged to be patient and yield either to necessity or to the greater good of the Church in the matter of accepting the episcopal dignity. Beckx then concluded by simply pointing out that he was sure, in the light of all these reasons, the Sacred Congregation would not recommend O'Reilly.

Because all of the bishops of the province of Cashel did not finally reply to Barnabò's circular letter of June 21 until early August, the consideration of the Limerick appointment had to be postponed until September. When the cardinals met on September 18, they decided to recommend that the whole matter be indefinitely postponed and that the cardinal prefect write the archbishop of Cashel "making some opportune reflections on his irregular proceedings, justifying the part taken by the Sacred Congregation in the postponement—the commendation and the formation of the *terna* not being really conducted with complete impartiality."[23] The pope approved this recommendation on September 23, and Barnabò wrote the required letter to the archbishop of Cashel on October 3. The cardinals had, in fact, little choice in making their recommendation, not so much because of the irregular proceedings of the archbishop of Cashel and his suffragans as because all three candidates on the *terna* had been eliminated in one way or another. Cussen had been vetoed by the unanimous voice of the bishops, and O'Reilly's unfitness had been made apparent in the devastating letter of the father general. Butler was undoubtedly deemed unacceptable because his reported opinions on the educational question were unorthodox. The cardinals had apparently chosen to accept Cullen's testimony about Butler's educational opinions rather than the explicit testimony of Butler as reported by the archbishop of Cashel. The cardinals had probably taken to heart the remark of the secretary of Propaganda in his *ristretto* that since Butler had spoken to Leahy *after* he knew that he had been recommended by the bishops, the "splendor of the miter might have perhaps influenced the aforesaid statement."[24] Still, the consideration that probably had the greatest weight with the cardinals was Cullen's assurance in early June that the bishop of Limerick was not likely to live very much longer. In the event of his death, it was obvious that the Propaganda could order a new *terna* to be commended by the Limerick clergy and could perhaps even require, given the circumstances, that none of the three names previously selected be presented again.

---

23. Ibid., fol. 409.
24. Ibid., fol. 406.

The bishop of Limerick, however, was to prove exceptionally resilient; he proceeded to defy all expectations of his early demise for nearly another four years. The problem presented by his recovery was compounded by the fact that in the process he had lost the use of his legs, so that the appointment of a coadjutor was more imperative than ever. The cardinal prefect was apprised of the new turn of events by the archbishop of Armagh soon after the latter arrived in Rome in early November to fulfill his required *ad limina* visit. Shortly after Christmas, Barnabò was given yet another account of the serious situation developing in Limerick because of the bishop's incapacity, this time by William Monsell, a distinguished Catholic convert and M.P. for county Limerick. Barnabò was obviously both impressed and concerned by Monsell's account, for he asked him to put his views and recommendations in writing. Monsell complied with a very able and interesting letter in French on December 30, 1860.[25] "I do not believe," Monsell explained, "that it will be necessary to respond at length to the questions your Eminence has posed on the present state of our diocese. There we Catholics are always faced with powerful enemies, who are incessantly on the watch, and who have on their side nearly all the aristocracy, and behind them a government ready to defend them."

Our bishop, who has done so much for our religious institutions, and for all the spiritual and material needs of our population, in his old age has become so weak that he is no longer able to govern. We have some excellent material—a generally zealous clergy, a faithful population—in the city of Limerick and in our small towns, the teaching is in great part in the hands of the nuns and the Christian brothers. But still the diocese is in a complete state of disorganization—when one asks the bishop to repress the scandals he says *liberavi animam meum* [I have cleared my conscience], I have asked for a coadjutor, I will not expose myself in my old age to disagreeable contentions—thus each priest is almost a bishop to himself. Those who are unruly know that they can act with impunity and one dreads each day the occurrence of new scandals. More, unfortunate appointments have been made and others will probably be made, which are and will be harmful to religion. I reply therefore to the first of your Eminence's questions by a solemn declaration of my deepest con-

25. A, vol. 225 (1861), fols. 461–62 (misnumbered 451–52), "Ristretto con Sommario sulla scelta di un Coadjutore del Vescovo di Limerick, e sopra un miglioramento proposto dal Vescovo di Kerry nei sistema d'elezione del Prelati Irlandese, 3 Giugno 1861" (fols. 458–67, misnumbered 448–57).

viction that the interests of religion will be gravely compromised if a coadjutor is not appointed at once.

It appears, according to what your Eminence has told me, there were some irregularities in the way in which the recommendation of the three names by the parish priests has been forwarded by the bishops of the province to Rome. I can not believe that this irregularity has been committed with any ill intention. Your Eminence knows too well the devotion of many of our bishops to the Holy See and their desire to maintain her dignity and her prerogatives to believe for an instant that they would have wished to encroach on her rights; but they probably felt the need to make a prompt choice and on this subject I could add that as some of the bishops either do not know Father Butler, or only very little or by reputation, that others differ in opinion with the actual bishop of Limerick, it is not likely to suppose that in these circumstances they would seek either to favor Father Butler or to please the bishop. In any case I am persuaded that your Eminence would not allow our diocese to suffer for a mistake in which it has no responsibility. A head is required to govern and to manage it. It contains one of the cities which most influences public opinion in Ireland. Its head ought to be a man endowed with uncommon and lofty qualities, great courage and great firmness as well as great style. I sincerely believe that Father Butler possesses these qualities to an uncommon degree. I know him well and I have great regard for him.

I am convinced that your Eminence will find that after having made some inquiries, that, as well as piety, zeal, detachment, and lofty sentiments on the rights and prerogatives of the Holy See, he has been since he studied at Maynooth, noted for his learning and for his capacity. Though very gentle and very prudent he comes to his conclusions with ease. He is one of the most courageous and most determined men I have ever known. He does not draw back before any duty his conscience demands. I believe that this is so well known that there would be an absolute submission to him on the part of even those who have acted most without regard for their bishop.

"I therefore sum up my response to your Eminence's question," Monsell continued, "saying that Father Butler is the only man in the part of Ireland where I live for whom I should take the responsibility of saying that I am certain that all those who will have to do with his appointment will in two years be proud of their work."

"Your Eminence has asked me," Monsell added, turning to the debit side of the ledger concerning Butler, "to reply to some allegations which have been made against him. These allegations are absolutely false." He elaborated:

1. He is not a relative of the bishop and there is no connection of any kind direct or indirect between his family and that of the bishop.
2. Though he was appointed dean by the intervention of the bishop who believed [him] the priest most worthy of that honor in the diocese, he never consulted him in the affairs of the diocese and did not even appoint him vicar general before the month of October last. The opinions of the bishop were formed before Catholic Emancipation and on the different questions that have been raised lately, such as the law of charitable bequests, public education, the Queen's Colleges, the Catholic University, his lordship and Father Butler were always opposed to each other. When Father Butler felt obliged to resist the bishop, as he has done for example on the question of the model schools, he has done it in so proper and respectful a way, he has not lost the respect of the bishop or of the other persons who thought differently.
3. I can absolutely affirm that before the month of October he has never directly or indirectly been responsible for any share of the administration of the diocese or for any appointment made by the bishop.

"I believe that I have now replied," Monsell concluded, "to all the questions that your Eminence has been pleased to put to me. If by chance there is anything that I may have forgotten, I beg your Eminence to remind me of it." "P.S.," he then added, "I beg his [sic] Eminence to keep this letter completely secret."

Before Monsell had left for Rome, he had apparently spoken to Cullen about the Limerick situation. He had also apparently made as much of an impression on the archbishop as he was to make on the cardinal prefect, for in writing Kirby on January 11, 1861, Cullen explained that Monsell was "most anxious for Dr. Butler's appointment" (K). "Perhaps," he added more surprisingly about Butler, "he wd do as well as any other. He has acted very well in regard to the Pope's collection, brigade etc." Barnabò then wrote both Cullen and Dixon asking them for their views on the proposed *terna* for Limerick in the light of Monsell's observations and also noting that it did not seem prudent to delay any longer in the appointment of a coadjutor. Dixon, who replied on February 13, agreed that it was unwise to delay any longer and strongly recommended that O'Reilly be appointed.[26] Cullen, who certainly realized from the cardinal's letter which way the wind was now blowing in Rome, was obviously perplexed about how to reply. "About Limerick," he confided to Kirby on February 15, "it is hard to say *quid agendum* [what must be done]—if Dr. O'R[eilly] go there *vivente episcopo* [the bishop being alive] he will have the hardest life. The Bishop is very infirm—perhaps this spring God may call him—it would be then easy to settle matters. I believe Dr. Butler acted very well for the Pope etc.—but he wd scarcely be able to reform the diocese" [K].

Cullen delayed as long as was reasonably possible, but the bishop of Limerick continued to defy all expectations. Indeed, when Ryan wrote Cullen on March 22, explaining that he could not attend the general meeting of the bishops scheduled for the following month, he also cleverly took occasion to dilate at very great length on why he needed a coadjutor and why it ought to be Butler.[27] At this point Cullen apparently realized that any further delay was impossible and grudgingly proceeded to do the necessary. In writing Barnabò on March 29, enclosing a translation of Ryan's letter, Cullen explained, "In reading this letter your Eminence will see how anxious he is for the choice of Father Butler. As for me, it seems that he has taken the matter so much to heart, that if another be appointed coadjutor he will make it impossible for him to do any good in the diocese."[28] "Though I have tried," he then added, explaining his long delay, "I have not been able to obtain other news about the candidates other than that I have already sent, and that which was passed on recently by the archbishop of Armagh. The only thing that I can add is that during the last year Father Butler has demonstrated great zeal towards the Holy Father, and I believe that the very considerable tribute collected in the diocese of Limerick is due principally to him. In the present times, it seems to me that this is a thing to be valued, and thus I believe a duty to mention it especially." "Besides," Cullen concluded, "I am convinced that the Sacred Congregation will make that choice most useful to the interests of religion, and for the good of the diocese of Limerick, which now without doubt, has great need of an active and zealous pastor." Therefore, when the cardinals of Propaganda met on June 3, they unanimously recommended Butler to the pope as coadju-

26. Ibid., fols. 462–63 (misnumbered 452–53).
27. Ibid., fols. 463–64 (misnumbered 453–54).
28. Ibid., fol. 463 (misnumbered 453).

tor to the bishop of Limerick, a choice that the pope confirmed on June 9, 1861.[29]

Though the circumstances of the Limerick appointment were naturally different from that of Down and Connor the previous year, Cullen's role in the making of both appointments was remarkably similar. As in the case of Down and Connor, he certainly emerges as the central figure, and his essential tactic was one of delay. In the end, moreover, he was as diffident about Butler's appointment as he had been about Dorrian's. In the case of Down and Connor, however, he had not known Dorrian and had been obliged in the circumstances to give him the benefit of the doubt, whereas in the Limerick appointment he apparently did know Butler and did not like him, because he was willing to believe almost anything about him. Given, therefore, the large number of votes Butler had received as *dignissimus*, the nearly unanimous report of the bishops in his favor to Propaganda, and the great partiality of the bishop of Limerick for him, Cullen's problem was how to block his appointment. Because Cussen, the second on the *terna*, was not a viable candidate in view of his age, Cullen was obliged to plump even more enthusiastically for O'Reilly than he might have otherwise been inclined to do. Some ten years before, for instance, when he had heard that O'Reilly might be a candidate for the then-vacant see of Killaloe, Cullen had been no less discerning in assessing O'Reilly's deficiencies for Kirby than the father general of the Society of Jesus had been for Barnabò.[30] Cullen was, moreover, too experienced an ecclesiastic really to have expected either that the father general would allow so formidable a precedent as the appointment of O'Reilly would have set for the Society or that the pope would finally approve such an appointment, even on the recommendation of Propaganda, in the face of the father general's veto. In his strong endorsement of O'Reilly, therefore, Cullen was undoubtedly making a virtue of necessity; his real purpose was to secure a delay in the hope that the demise of the bishop of Limerick would allow for the election of a new *terna*, which might be better managed by his friends and supporters in Limerick.

The problem, of course, was that the bishop of Limerick refused to oblige, and when the procedural wheels were again set in motion, after Monsell's interview with Barnabò, Cullen was perplexed about how to proceed. His straw candidate, O'Reilly, had never been a real possibility, and his only viable alternative, that Propaganda might

29. Ibid., fol. 460 (misnumbered 450).
30. K, November 30, 1850.

now order a new *terna* without waiting for the demise of the bishop of Limerick, had just been precluded by Monsell's warm endorsement of both Butler's qualities and his opinions. In arguing for a new *terna*, Cullen not only would have been obliged to contradict Monsell's testimony but would have had to produce some further proof of Butler's alleged lack of clerical zeal and unorthodox opinions on the education question, beyond the mere hearsay he had relied on up to then. That was why Cullen continued to delay as long as possible, hoping that providence would provide the opportunity for a new *terna* in the death of the bishop of Limerick. When time finally ran out and Cullen was constrained to admit to Barnabò, on March 29, that a coadjutor must be provided, his endorsement of Butler was as cautious as it was guarded. By pointing out that all he could really add in favor of Butler was that he had acted well in promoting the pope's collection in Limerick, without explicitly withdrawing any of the things that he had said about Butler previously, Cullen was again, as in the case of Down and Connor, taking as little responsibility for the appointment as he prudently could.

In recommending Butler to the pope on June 3, however, the cardinals of Propaganda also recommended a change in the procedure of appointing bishops in Ireland.[31] The immediate cause of their recommendation, of course, was the irregular report submitted by the Cashel bishops on the Limerick *terna*. The question of reform had, in fact, been raised by the bishop of Kerry in his reply to Barnabò's circular of June 21 of the previous year, which had asked the Cashel bishops to submit their individual opinions of the candidates in the Limerick *terna*.[32] Moriarty had suggested that in the future, after the bishops had met together to discuss the *terna*, they be obliged to report their views individually to Propaganda, rather than forward a collective report. Moriarty argued that the collective reports of the bishops often resulted in a unanimity that was more apparent than real and cited the example of the recent meeting of the Cashel prelates. When the cardinals had met in September and decided to recommend a delay in the Limerick appointment, they also recommended that Barnabò write the archbishops of Armagh and Dublin to ask their opinions of Moriarity's suggested reform.[33] In his reply to Barnabò's letter of October 2, written on October 12, Dixon warmly endorsed Moriarty's proposal.[34] In order to avoid undue delay, however, in the

31. A, vol. 225, fol. 460 (misnumbered 450).
32. A, vol. 224, fols. 421–22, Moriarty to Barnabò, July 2, 1860.
33. Ibid., fol. 409.
34. A, vol. 225, fol. 466 (misnumbered 456).

forwarding of the bishops' individual reports to Propaganda, Dixon suggested that the metropolitan or, failing him, the senior suffragan collect all the reports, signed and sealed, and forward them to Rome within a prescribed period of time. When Cullen replied a month later to Barnabò's letter, he also endorsed Moriarty's proposal, but he was somewhat more specific and practical about ways to avoid any unnecessary delays.[35] "This plan," he assured Barnabò on November 10,

> seems very sensible to me because each bishop will be able to say more freely what he thinks, and it will allow a greater freedom of action to the Sacred Congregation. In any case in order to avoid useless delays, it would be well if this proposal was adopted to prescribe that the metropolitan hold a meeting of the suffragan bishops right away, to confer on the election, and that each of the said suffragans ought to give his views to the Sacred Congregation within ten days after the meeting. It seems to me that in this way the Sacred Congregation would receive without delay the most certain and the most confidential news for directing her in the important business of the election of bishops.

Yet when the cardinals met on June 3 to make their recommendations to the pope, they did not endorse the proposal of the bishop of Kerry as amended by Cullen's practical suggestions.[36] Instead, they recommended that between the meeting of the clergy to elect a *terna* and the meeting of the bishops to report to Propaganda on that *terna*, an interval of at least ten days be allowed to elapse. The pope approved their recommendation on June 9, at the audience at which he approved the appointment of Butler.[37] But why did the cardinals reject Moriarty's proposal as endorsed by Cullen and Dixon, and perhaps even more important, why did they recommend that the bishops of the province be required to wait at least ten days before they met to report to Propaganda? Undoubtedly, the cardinals rejected Moriarty's proposal because they finally realized that it was based on a false assumption. In the accepted procedure to provide for Irish sees, which had been in force since 1829, the purpose of the bishops' report was to advise the cardinals of Propaganda about the merits of the three candidates commended by the clergy in order that the cardinals might make a responsible recommendation to the pope. Moriarty's proposal assumed that the procedure was faulty and that it must therefore be modified. The cardinals, however, realized that the report of the

---

35. Ibid., fols. 466–67 (misnumbered 456–57).
36. Ibid., fol. 460 (misnumbered 450).
37. Ibid.

Cashel bishops was irregular not because the procedure was faulty but rather because the bishops had not followed the required procedure. The remedy was not to modify the procedure but instead to see that it was properly carried out by the bishops. Finally, Moriarty's proposal was also inherently self-defeating, for if the procedure had to be modified every time it was abused, there could be no such thing as procedure, and the result could only, in the last analysis, be administrative chaos.

Still, while it is clear that the cardinals of Propaganda had a very strong grip on the distinction between means and ends, why did they then modify the procedure in the way that they did? Though the irregularities involved in the report of the Cashel bishops obviously upset the cardinals, they were apparently even more concerned about the collapse in time between the meeting of the clergy to commend a *terna* and the meeting of the bishops to report on it. The clergy and the bishops, it will be recalled, had met on the same day, May 2, in Limerick. Although such a proceeding was not strictly irregular according to the decree of Propaganda of June 1829, it was certainly open to grave abuses. The gathering of the clergy and bishops on the same day might result in undue pressure of one group upon the other. Moreover, if the bishops met on the same day as the clergy, they would hardly have time to consider maturely the merits of the candidates, and if they did not know the candidates, or knew them only slightly or by reputation, they would have no time to make the inquiries that would at least allow them to form a responsible opinion. Finally, even if the abuses did not materialize, the bishops' meeting so soon after the clergy would certainly give the appearance of undue haste in a matter where due deliberation and decorum was of the utmost importance, and thus the dignity, at least, if not the integrity, of the proceedings would be compromised. That is why the cardinals recommended that a period of ten days ought to be allowed to elapse between the two meetings.[38]

The promotion of both Dorrian and Butler proved to be a giant step in the strengthening of the bishops as a body in the 1860s. Besides being men of great energy, independence of character, and religious zeal, they were also essentially at one with their episcopal colleagues on all the important questions affecting the policy of the body—denomi-

38. L, Barnabò to Leahy, September 6 and 9, 1861.

national education, pastoral reform, and Fenianism. In their appointments, therefore, no discordant element was introduced into the body, and the harmony and unity so necessary to the effective functioning of the bishops as a body was further enhanced. Given their independence of character, moreover, as well as the history of their appointments, neither Dorrian nor Butler could be designated Cullen's protégés and dismissed in the episcopal body as his mere nominees. At the same time, however, they both soon acquired a very healthy respect for the apostolic delegate, as they almost immediately became embroiled in difficulties with their respective principals, the actual bishops of Down and Connor and Limerick, who were reluctant to yield to them the powers necessary to reform their dioceses. Both Dorrian and Butler, therefore, quickly learned to appreciate Cullen's invaluable support and influence at Rome.

Though Dorrian and Butler were both to prove to be outstanding bishops, they could not function in the body, nor could the body itself function, if it did not meet as a body. Before Cullen had come to Ireland in 1850 as primate and apostolic delegate, the bishops had been meeting regularly every year for some twenty years. After Cullen's arrival, and down until 1859, the bishops had met less and less as a body, and when they had met they found themselves more and more constrained by procedure. This had been a deliberate policy on Cullen's part, and it had had the strong approval and backing of the Roman authorities. During the 1850s, in fact, the procedure in the convening and the conducting of episcopal meetings had been fundamentally modified. Before 1850 the meetings had been informal; they could be convened on the requisition of an appropriate number of bishops; they were presided over by each of the four archbishops in rotation; and no individual bishop was necessarily bound by the decisions reached by the body. After 1850 the meetings of the bishops were synodical in form, convened only on the authorization of the prefect of Propaganda, and presided over by the apostolic delegate. The cardinal prefect also usually outlined the agenda in his letter of authorization, and all the decisions arrived at had to be submitted to Propaganda for its authoritative approval, which, in effect, made the decisions binding on all the bishops.

Besides being narrowly constrained procedurally the general meetings became fewer and fewer in the 1850s. The nadir was finally reached between 1856 and 1859, when the bishops did not meet at all as a body, and many of them began to fear that they would indeed be extinguished as a functioning corporate entity. The great change that took place in 1859, when the bishops met in August and again in

October to discuss the education question, was less a change in the form of the meetings than a basic recognition that the bishops as a body had a legitimate function in the governing of the Irish Church. Although the meetings and their agenda were still authorized by the cardinal prefect and presided over by the apostolic delegate, the decisions reached by the bishops were no longer formally submitted to Propaganda for approval unless the bishops chose to submit them. When Cullen, therefore, in the winter and early spring of 1860, proceeded to bypass the bishops as a body in his effort to secure a unanimous reply to Cardwell's letter on the national system of education, some of the bishops might be forgiven for thinking that the apostolic delegate was attempting to upset the modus vivendi recently arrived at and was once again trying to subvert the corporate character of the episcopal body by reverting to the proceedings of the 1850s. As has already been noted, however, this step was less an attempt by Cullen to subvert the bishops as a body than an effort to manipulate them to secure unanimity on the education question, for shortly after he had gotten his way, he wrote Kirby explaining that a meeting of the body was necessary and asking him to speak to the cardinal prefect about it. Circumstances delayed the meeting until April of 1861, but in the next decade the bishops would meet formally as a body on an average of about once a year to discuss and deal with the more significant and pressing problems facing their Church. These formal meetings were supplemented by the more informal meetings of those bishops who assembled each year in October at Maynooth, for the boards of bishops that governed the Maynooth and Paris colleges. Each board consisted of the four archbishops and some two suffragan bishops from each province—in all, nineteen bishops.[39] All the bishops who were members of either board and any other bishop who might have reason to be present apparently attended, and the meetings of the Paris board, which usually took place the day after those of the Maynooth board, often took on the appearance of a general meeting.

As the episcopal body acquired a greater awareness of itself in the early 1860s through its more frequent meetings, the bishops also acquired greater self-confidence in their dealings both with Cullen and with Rome. An interesting example of this rising self-confidence occurred early in 1863 when Cullen raised the question among the bishops of presenting an address of congratulations to the Prince of Wales on the occasion of his impending marriage. Before introducing the

39. The reason why there were only nineteen instead of twenty was that there were only seven suffragan bishops provided by law for the Maynooth board.

subject generally to his brethren, Cullen took the precaution of writing to Kirby to ask him to sound Barnabò on the project. Kirby presented the proposal in the form of a memorandum to Propaganda quoting from the letter of Cullen, which asked whether an address was thought appropriate and, if so, whether it should be done by province or diocese, as it was not just then convenient to convoke a general meeting of the bishops.[40] Cullen had also added that MacHale would undoubtedly oppose the proposal. Barnabò apparently approved and authorized Cullen to proceed as he thought best.[41] Several days after he had written Kirby to sound Barnabò, and before the cardinal prefect could have replied, Cullen had also written Dixon asking him his opinion. Dixon replied on February 9 that he thought an address a good idea and offered to have one drawn up and circularized among his suffragans (C). After he had received the Roman clearance from Kirby, Cullen wrote Dixon again, asking him to circularize his suffragans as he had promised, and Cullen also broached the subject of an address to the other two archbishops. In general, the replies were very disappointing. MacHale apparently refused outright.[42] Dixon, who was still favorable, replied on March 7 that his suffragans were not unanimous on the subject (C). Two of the nine, the bishops of Meath and Ardagh, had refused to sign the address, and a third, the bishop of Clogher, had not replied. The reaction of the archbishop of Cashel, moreover, was very negative.

Cullen had written Leahy on March 5 about the proposed registration-of-marriages bill then pending before Parliament, and in the course of his letter he gently introduced the subject of an address. "I think the Bishops of this province," he informed Leahy, "will send an address to the Prince of Wales. It has not been agreed to as yet, but many are anxious we sd do so, and I suppose it sd do no harm. Probably great numbers of addresses will be sent, and it might be strange if some of the Cath. laity and clergy were not amongst those who compliment his R. Highness" (L). The vehemence of Leahy's reply must have certainly startled Cullen. "It should and would," Leahy explained firmly on March 10, "ever be a matter of regret to me to differ in anything with Your Grace, & so it is in an address you plan to propose from the Bishops of Ireland to the Prince of Wales" (L). "The

---

40. S.R.C., vol. 34, fol. 612, n.d., but Cullen's letter to Kirby was February 5, 1863.

41. K, Cullen to Kirby, February 26, 1863: "The Prince of Wales' marriage will take place on the 10th March. If we address him, we shall merely wish him every happiness, and the grace of God to become a true believer."

42. Patrick J. Corish, "Political Problems, 1860–1878," in A History of Irish Catholicism, gen. ed. Patrick J. Corish (Dublin, 1967), 5:11, n. 27.

Ecclesiastical Titles Bill," he reminded Cullen, "stands in the statute book. Again we are legally & in reality on the pan. Were we to sign such an address in our proper character, or any of us to go forward in our proper character to present it [it would] not be received." "To be silent, therefore," Leahy maintained, "is in my opinion the only dignified course left us. By remaining silent we shall not provide our enemies with an opportunity to insult us. We shall be much more respected by our enemies & by our own people than if we come forward with an expression of loyalty in circumstances quite uncalled for on our part and for which we would get no manner of credit with either the one or the other and by which we could not do the least good to our poor suffering country." "I need not say," he noted further, "how much of a mockery it is to make any show of rejoicing while our poor countrymen are many of them starving or on the verge of starvation & others in thousands flying from our shores to any part of the world where they can find the necessaries of life all the while that a heartless wicked government is laughing with delight and steadily pursuing that anti-Catholic and anti-Irish policy the direct effect of which is to root the Catholic population out of this land."

Leahy's reply obviously caused Cullen to have some serious second thoughts. "As yet," he reported to Kirby on March 11, after explaining the differences of opinion among the bishops, "we have not come to a final determination, but probably I will send the address from this province and Dr. Dixon from his. Our address is a spiritual lecture for the prince wishing him every happiness, but telling him to protect the poor and act justly" (K). In writing the next day, March 12, to the bishop of Elphin, whom he had persuaded to present an address of his own, Cullen explained that there was no immediate hurry about presenting their addresses. "For my part," Cullen added, giving some insight into his motives in the matter, "I think it very desirable to send the address if for no other purpose [than] to show that we are not to be put down by F. Lavelle & his brotherhood" (G).

By the time Gillooly replied to this letter, he too had begun to have second thoughts about the prudence of presenting an address, and he wrote Cullen a most interesting and revealing letter. "From what your Grace has mentioned to me," Gillooly explained on March 16, "and from what I have learned from other quarters, there appears to be great diversity, & opposition of opinion amongst the bishops regarding the address to the Prince of Wales, and as far as I am concerned myself, I cannot yet make up my mind to forward the address I contemplated" (C).

It is so detrimental to religion to occasion division within our own body—and to exhibit our divisions to the world, that I am inclined to think our *uniform* silence will be productive of less temporary inconvenience as regards the Government—and of more permanent advantage to religion, as a means of preserving union & harmony—our greatest want—in our respective ecclesiastical Provinces. A good understanding & unity of action between each Metropolitan & his suffragans, is of such vital importance that every sacrifice consistent with *duty* sh^d be made to establish & maintain it.

"If they divide on a political question like the present one," he warned, "such division will lead to others in politico-religious questions and the bond of union which has been gaining strength for the last few years, may be abruptly severed again—and there can be no doubt but the Government & the Press—and the extreme sections of our Irish & anti-Irish parties will give worldwide publicity to our divisions and make use of them to the detriment of our religious political interests."

Cullen replied to this very sensible and statesmanlike letter by return of post on March 17, agreeing that it would be better perhaps to wait just a little longer about their addresses "to see whether any division wd be occasioned by presenting them" (G). There were apparently more objections, because when Cullen wrote Kirby ten days later, not only was he very irritated, but he even scolded Kirby, who had also not been in favor of the project. "About the address to the Prince," he reported on March 27, "finding so many Bishops hostile we have suspended it for the present in order not to give any excuse for divisions" (K). "However," he added unrepentantly, "in all probability an address would do good and much good—as to what you state that we would lower ourselves were we to send it without our titles, it is to be observed that all the letters sent to Government for the last 150 years are signed without titles, and hundreds of petitions have been sent to Parliament during the present century, always without titles. It is a thing that is done every year, and if there be anything degrading in it, the degradation is pretty old and well established."

It would certainly be most interesting to know exactly how many of the bishops besides the archbishops of Cashel and Tuam and the bishops of Meath, Clogher, and Ardagh were opposed to presenting an address. In a hierarchy that then numbered twenty-eight regular bishops and two coadjutors, five bishops in opposition would not have unduly alarmed Cullen. In fact, however, the archbishops of Cashel and Tuam probably could have found more bishops in their respective provinces opposed to presenting an address than in favor of it. Though any exact estimate is highly suppositious because of the personal loyalties and pressures involved, if the bishops and coadjutors were left to themselves, probably some twelve bishops and one coadjutor would have opposed the address.[43] This division would have resulted, then, in some thirteen bishops out of thirty being in opposition, and this was too formidable a minority for Cullen to attempt either to manipulate or to coerce. Moreover, the issue was certainly not worth it in itself; it was indeed perhaps the worst possible issue for the bishops as a body to take as their ground in any effort to demonstrate that they were not intimidated by Father Lavelle or the Fenian Brotherhood. Cullen wisely and prudently, therefore, though certainly with no good grace, decided to give up his project of an address to the Prince of Wales.

Meanwhile, in the midst of the upset over the presenting of the address, the episcopal body had been increased to thirty-one by the appointment of a coadjutor to the bishop of Kilmore, James Browne. Browne, who had been bishop of Kilmore for some thirty-four years and was now in his late seventies, had written Barnabò on April 1, 1862, to request from the pope the aid of a coadjutor.[44] Barnabò had then written Cullen, who replied that Browne did indeed need a coadjutor, and though he did not know the clergy of the diocese very well, he was certain that Browne's metropolitan, the archbishop of Armagh, Joseph Dixon, would not fail to present the Propaganda with an exact examination of the merits of the candidates commended by the clergy of Kilmore.[45] For some reason that is not entirely clear, the meeting of the clergy was not convened for more than six months. When it was finally held in Cavan on November 26, Francis O'Reilly, parish priest of Killann, was returned as *dignissimus* with eleven votes; Nicholas Conaty, parish priest of Castlerahan, was *dignior* with nine votes; and John Maguire, parish priest of Kinlough, was *dignus* with six votes.[46] In reporting the results of the election of the *terna* to Kirby on November 28, Cullen explained that he did not know anything about the candidates or their merits (K). "It was said that F. Smith of Rome," Cullen added interestingly, referring to Kirby's former vice-rector in

---

43. Besides the archbishops of Cashel and Tuam and the bishops of Meath, Clogher, and Ardagh, those who would have probably opposed the address were Waterford, Cloyne, Ross, Clonfert, Achonry, Killala, Kilmacduagh and Kilfenora, and the coadjutor to Limerick.

44. A, vol. 227 (1863), fol. 26, "Ristretto con Sommario sulla scelta di un Coadjutore pel Vescovo di Kilmore nella Provincia di Armagh in Irlanda, 23 Febbraio 1863" (fols. 20–27).

45. Ibid.; Cullen's letter is not dated.

46. Ibid., fols. 26–27.

the Irish College, "w^d have been on the list. Perhaps it is as well that he is not." When the bishops of the province of Armagh met two weeks later to report on the *terna* commended by the clergy of Kilmore, they unanimously declared in favor of the second on the list, Nicholas Conaty.[47]

In the meantime, matters had been complicated by John Brady, who had served many years before as the bishop of Perth in Australia and who had been living quietly in retirement in his native diocese of Kilmore since 1853. Soon after he learned that Browne's request for a coadjutor had been approved, Brady wrote to Cullen, attempting to win his approval for his own candidacy for Kilmore. "I should like and indeed I have been long since praying," Brady explained on June 2,

> for permission to dedicate the remainder of my days to some useful mission in Ireland. I humbly believe had I your Grace's sanction or that of the holy see I would be able to promote even in Ireland but especially in the diocese of Kilmore three very grand objects.
> 1st the cause of our holy Father—Peter's Pence.
> 2. the Propagation of the faith
> 3. the Catholic University, & c. & c. & c. [C]

Apparently Cullen did nothing to encourage Brady, but shortly before the election of the Kilmore *terna* was scheduled to take place, Brady set out for Rome. He arrived there on November 19, as Moran explained to Cullen on November 22, and asked Kirby to put him up at the Irish College (C). Kirby refused because he thought that Brady was not in good odor at Propaganda, and the bishop had then to find his lodgings at the Vincentian house in Rome.

When his name did not appear on the *terna* forwarded by the Kilmore clergy to Rome, Brady must have been sorely disappointed. He still had, however, a further contribution to make to the appointment of a coadjutor, for shortly after the meeting of the bishops of the province of Armagh on December 10, reporting unanimously in favor of Conaty, Browne wrote to Brady asking him to translate his letter into French and present it to Barnabò.[48] Brady did so, forwarding the letter on December 16 with a covering one of his own that strongly endorsed all that Browne had said.[49] Browne had written Brady because he felt that the report of the bishops on the Kilmore *terna* had not been full enough, particularly in explaining why the *dignissimus*, Francis O'Reilly, would not do and why the *dignior*, Nicholas Conaty, would

47. Ibid., fol. 27.
48. Ibid., fols. 24–25.
49. Ibid., fol. 24.

do as his coadjutor. In his letter Browne explained that O'Reilly was really the representative of a family faction (*une Clique O'Reilly*) that had controlled the diocese during the episcopacy of his predecessor, Farrell O'Reilly, and that was still very influential in the diocese.[50] In his covering letter to Barnabò, Brady also explained that the O'Reilly family had long been the ruin of the diocese of Kilmore, and the reason why Conaty had acquired only second place on the *terna* was that he had for many years loyally supported the present bishop in his efforts to maintain clerical discipline in the diocese. The cardinals of Propaganda, who met on February 23, 1863, to consider the commendation of the clergy and the report of the bishops, unanimously recommended Conaty for the coadjutorship of Kilmore, and the pope authoritatively approved their recommendation on March 1, 1863.

Perhaps the single most remarkable thing about this appointment was how little Cullen apparently had to do with it. This was all the more remarkable because since his arrival in Ireland as archbishop of Armagh and apostolic delegate in early 1850, he had been the central figure in almost every episcopal appointment made in the Irish Church. What was certainly curious about the appointment was that Barnabò, after his initial inquiry asking whether Browne needed a coadjutor, did not write Cullen again for his opinion about the proposed *terna*. Cullen had, of course, pointed out to Barnabò that he did not know the Kilmore clergy very well and that all might be safely left in the capable hands of the archbishop of Armagh, and he even reiterated his lack of knowledge about the candidates to Kirby when the *terna* was finally commended. Still, Cullen's professed diffidence had never before prevented Barnabò from writing him and asking him to make particular inquiries, and the question remains, Why did he choose to take Cullen at his word on this occasion? On the other hand, Cullen could have had no marked objection to Conaty, for if he had, he would never have been so diffident. Though Conaty did not certainly prove in the long run to be made out of the same episcopal stuff as Dorrian and Butler, he was nevertheless a good, pious, and conscientious man, who was generally at one with his brother bishops on the great and contentious questions of mixed education, pastoral reform, and Fenianism, and the bishops as a body were certainly strengthened by his appointment.

---

50. Though O'Reilly is a very common name in the diocese of Kilmore, its representation among the forty parish priests was remarkable: some ten of them were O'Reillys. Seven curates, moreover, in a body of forty-eight, were also O'Reillys (I.C.D., 1863, pp. 157–58).

Early in January 1864 John Cantwell, the bishop of Meath, also finally decided to apply to the pope for the help of a coadjutor in governing his vast diocese.[51] Cantwell, who was over seventy years of age and in declining health, certainly needed a coadjutor, and the pope quickly approved his request. Because Meath was, after Dublin, the wealthiest diocese in Ireland, and because both its bishop and its clergy had long enjoyed a formidable reputation for their involvement in nationalist politics, the appointment of a coadjutor there was bound to create an extraordinary interest in Ireland. Moreover, Cantwell had been one of MacHale's staunchest supporters in the episcopal body in late years, and so Cullen could also be expected to take a more than passing interest in the appointment. Kirby had obviously early informed Cullen that Cantwell had applied for a coadjutor and that the pope had approved, for he reported to Kirby on February 19, "Dr. Cantwell has not got as yet the letters from Rome authorising him to get a coadjutor, but the priests are all in great movement about the matter" (K). Several weeks later, on March 4, Cullen informed Kirby that Cantwell was about to hold a meeting of his clergy to select a *terna* (K). "He wrote," Cullen noted, "a few days ago to Dr. Dixon that he expected very soon to hold a meeting of his clergy, but stated that the matter was a profound secret." "I went down last week to Navan," he added dryly, "and I found the secret was in the mouths of everyone, clergy and laity are agitating the question. The persons spoken of are a Mr. Nulty, P.P. of Trim, a very plain man, Father McCabe, a Vincentian, Lord Fingall's son, [and] Dr. Farrelly of Maynooth. Who will be elected, I know not, but the place would require a very active determined man."

Cantwell finally summoned his clergy to meet in Mullingar on April 5, but on March 30, while visiting with Cullen in Dublin, he became so seriously ill that he was unable to attend the meeting, and Dixon presided instead. On the day of the meeting Cullen wrote Kirby explaining that Cantwell was still with him in Dublin and that they were both awaiting the result of the election by telegram from Mullingar (K). Soon after the telegram arrived, Cullen closed his letter by reporting that Thomas Nulty, parish priest of Trim, had received twenty-five votes as *dignissimus*; Neal McCabe, the Vincentian, was *dignior* with seventeen; and John O'Hanlon, prefect of the Dunboyne Establishment at Maynooth, was *dignus* with ten. Lord Fingall's son, Father William Plunkett, a Redemptorist, received only five votes,

51. A, vol. 228 (1864), fol. 384, "Ristretto con Sommario sulla elezione di un Coadjutore pel Vescovo di Meath nella Provincia di Armagh in Irlanda, 22 Agosto, 1864" (fols. 380–91).

and Michael McElroy, parish priest of Tullamore, four. "I hope," Cullen concluded, significantly ignoring Nulty, "Father McCabe may be elected by the Pope—Dr. O'Hanlon is too crotchety. However a great deal will depend on the recommendation of the Bishops." The bishops of the province of Armagh, who met on April 21, declared unanimously in favor of Nulty.[52] They explained that McCabe, the second on the list, was not pleasing to Cantwell and that he did not have any pastoral experience. They added that though O'Hanlon, the third name on the list, was a learned priest, he was not in good health.

Meanwhile, Cullen had on April 9 written the bishop of Elphin, who was a Vincentian, asking him what he thought of McCabe, as he knew him well (G). Cullen explained that though McCabe had given great satisfaction at St. Peter's Phibsborough, a Dublin city parish administered by the Vincentians, he had also heard that the superior of St. Peter's, Thomas McNamara, did not like him. Gillooly replied on April 12 that though McCabe was a good priest and zealous missionary, his Vincentian colleagues did not think that he had the requisite talent for governing (C). "With regard to my rev[d] friend," Gillooly explained, "about whom you inquire, there is I believe but one opinion and that most favorable of his piety, humility, zeal and devotedness. His talents and acquirements are also considered most respectable and considerably above average. In the pulpit and confessional and in his ministrations to the sick and the poor, he has been uniformly assiduous and successful." "Of his *administrative* talents," Gillooly added, turning cautiously to the debit side of the ledger,

a less favorable opinion is entertained by those who know him best in that respect, and whose duty it has been to observe and judge the acts of his administration. On this point I cannot myself form an opinion from my own personal experience, but from several facts communicated to me by our common friends, from the reliance I place on their unbiased judgement of him, and from my own knowledge of his general character and dispositions, I do believe him to be deficient in the qualities of an *administrator*. It appears that he has not been prudent or successful in the management of temporal matters. That he is impulsive, and wanting, especially in important affairs, in calmness and steadiness of purpose, that he is apt to pursue a favorite to the the neglect of other and more important duties, and that where those under him need direction and control, he either neglects to exercise it or fails in doing so prudently and effectually. I have no

52. Ibid., fols. 385–86.

reason to think that he has manifested those defects frequently in grave matters, but he did so occasionally, and they appear to be inherent in his character.

"On the whole," Gillooly concluded, "I would fear to see him in a position of such difficulty & importance as the one in question, and that independently of other considerations & interests, for which I shd very much regret his appointment. All this I say to your Grace in the strictest confidence, and solely to assist *yourself* to form an opinion."

When Cullen wrote Barnabò on May 1, some ten days after the bishops had reported, he was therefore not as enthusiastic about the appointment of McCabe as he had been earlier.[53] Indeed, he appeared to suggest that perhaps Nulty might be the best choice after all, even though the diocese of Meath needed a strong and reforming hand and Nulty, because of his close association with Cantwell in governing the diocese in recent years, would not be able to effect the necessary reform. "From what I have heard of the three candidates under consideration," he explained to Barnabò, "I imagine that the first ought to be chosen. He has good qualities and the Bishop is all for him. The only thing that can be said against him comes from his being too much the friend and creature of the Bishop, that he will walk in his footsteps, and allow things to remain as they are." "The second candidate in this respect," he pointed out, "would be much more preferable, but his brethren, the missionaries of St. Vincent, think that because of the lack of prudence in governing, he would do harm rather than good in the diocese." "Without doubt," Cullen concluded, deftly shifting all responsibility, "the Sacred Congregation will know how to choose the best amongst them."

Cullen obviously realized that Nulty's significant plurality in the voting on the *terna*, and his unanimous endorsement by the bishops of the province, made his appointment all but inevitable. There was, therefore, little point in opposing it, especially because the second on the list had been virtually vetoed by Gillooly and there was now no one to oppose to Nulty. However, when Cullen received a letter some ten days later from Terence O'Reilly, parish priest of Dunderry in the diocese of Meath, charging that there was insanity in Nulty's family, he must have regretted that he had not been more negative about Nulty and more positive about McCabe in his letter of May 1 to Barnabò. In any case, Cullen forwarded O'Reilly's letter to Barnabò on

53. Ibid., fol. 386.

May 10.[54] Apparently he also advised O'Reilly to speak to the archbishop of Armagh, for Dixon wrote Kirby on May 13 that he had just spoken to a Meath priest who reported that there was insanity in Nulty's family on his father's side (K). Though Nulty's father, Dixon added, was not himself affected, the Meath priest had charged that Nulty's brother was considered strange or odd in his manner. "I consulted a most worthy ecclesiastic in this country," he further explained, "without mentioning to him the name of the parish priest who came to mention this matter to me. This good priest, whom I consulted told me that he could say nothing of his own knowledge about the matter; but that such statements should be carefully examined; and he advised me to ask the Cardinal Prefect to put off the consideration of the appointment in Propaganda for some weeks until I could get an opportunity of clearing up the matter." "I hope to have an opportunity," he then concluded, "in the course of a very few weeks of prudently satisfying myself regarding the real state of this unpleasant affair."

When Kirby presented the contents of Dixon's letter, Barnabò obviously wrote Cullen asking him for his advice, for Cullen replied on May 27, repeating the charges made against Nulty and recommending that Dixon be formally asked to investigate them.[55] Cullen also prudently advised the cardinal that he thought that it would be better if he did not figure in the case at all. Dixon must not have received his mandate from Propaganda before the middle of June, because he did not complete his formal investigation until the end of the month. When he finally wrote Barnabò on July 3, he reported that the charges against Nulty were completely unfounded, and two days later he forwarded Kirby the supporting documents, authenticated by himself, to be submitted to Propaganda.[56] "In this matter of the Coadjutorship of Meath," Dixon assured Kirby in his covering letter of July 5, "I have no leaning to any man, or prejudice against any other, but I am most anxious of course that His Eminence should not mistake what is false & unfounded for what is true in this matter" (K). "In this affair," he added most pointedly, "vague rumours appear to have been eagerly seized for the purpose of opposing the appointment of Fr. Nulty. The *real* ground of opposition to him being that he is an exceeding great favourite with Dr. Cantwell; and those who were dissatisfied with Dr. Cantwell's rule of the diocese, because I suppose, they thought their

54. Ibid., fols. 386–87.
55. Ibid., fols. 187–88.
56. Ibid., fols. 389–91.

own merits overlooked, dread a continuance of this rule by Fr. Nulty. Moreover, it must be borne in mind that the curates of Mullingar would get the credit of many of the acts of Dr. Cantwell, as his advisors. Now Fr. Nulty was for a long time a most confidential curate of Dr. Cantwell's in Mullingar." "You will see by the conclusion of my letter to His Eminence," Dixon finally noted, "that I am ready to carry out confidentially any suggestion that His Eminence will think fit to make to me."

Cullen was very disappointed by the upshot of the investigation of the charges against Nulty, and the result was a most intemperate letter to Kirby impugning the integrity of the whole investigation. He reported to Kirby on August 6, "There was an investigation as to the question of insanity in his family held at Kells. It is curious that the two priests engaged to carry it on had insanity in their own families. Father Nicolls[,] P.P. of Kells[,] one of the commission[,] has two brothers in the madhouse, the other[,] Father Leonard[,] P.P. of Oldcastle[,] had a brother who some time ago killed himself in a fit of insanity. Of course they ought to be very indulgent on such questions" (K). "As to the charge about Nulty's uncle having been hanged for murder," Cullen continued, adding yet another dimension, "perhaps it may have been refuted by saying that the person hanged was not his uncle. His name was Fagan, the wife of this man was sister to Father Nulty's grandfather. He and the wife were sentenced to death for murder, but the wife being pregnant was not executed. The charge may be true, and yet denied by a suppressio veri." In spite of Cullen's apparently very deep antipathy to Nulty, the cardinals of Propaganda, who met on August 22 to consider the commendation of the clergy and the report of the bishops, decided unanimously to recommend his appointment, and on August 28 the pope gave his authoritative approval.[57]

Kirby wrote Cullen on August 30 to announce the appointment of Nulty. In his reply, Cullen was most revealing about his real motives concerning the appointment. "I hope it may be all for the better," he explained stoically to Kirby on September 4. "However I fear he will not do much to improve the diocese. He will in all probability let the priests go on with a great deal of wild extravagance and folly as they have done for the last few years. God grant that it may not be so. I suspect also that he will be a faithful follower of the West, but as I said I hope everything will be right" (K). Indeed, Cullen had objected to Nulty in the first place because he was afraid that he would, like Cantwell, prove to be a loyal supporter of MacHale in the episcopal

57. Ibid., fol. 383.

body. Cullen was also strongly of the opinion that the Meath clergy needed to be politically tamed, and that was what he meant when he wrote Barnabò in early May that the diocese required reform and that a strong hand was necessary. If Cullen had concentrated on the need to check the political propensities of the Meath clergy, his chances of blocking Nulty's appointment at Rome would certainly have been improved. In his anxiety to check Nulty, however, Cullen seized too eagerly on the rumors of supposed insanity in his family, and obviously misplayed his hand at Rome. When the charges of insanity were effectively demolished by Dixon's investigation, the cardinals of Propaganda had little choice but to recommend Nulty to the pope. Indeed, the large plurality of the clergy in favor of Nulty, the unanimous endorsement of the provincial bishops, and the cardinals' own general disposition to propose a coadjutor pleasing to the coadjutus rendered their recommendation inevitable, as there was no responsible case made against Nulty. Cullen's own intemperate outburst in early August about the investigation conducted by Dixon was yet another sign that he realized he had overreached himself in his efforts to block Nulty's appointment.

Whatever his real feelings or disappointments in the matter, Cullen soon had to put the best face possible on what was now a fact that had to be lived with. The beginning of that difficult adjustment was his attendance at the consecration of the new coadjutor on October 23, in the cathedral at Mullingar. The consecrating prelate, of course, was Dixon, and the customary sermon on the occasion was preached by the coadjutor to the bishop of Down and Connor, Patrick Dorrian, to a vast congregation that included about a dozen bishops and some hundred clergy. Cullen was not present at the usual consecration dinner held that evening because he had a cold and did not want to venture out at night. In explaining all this to Kirby in a long letter in Italian the next day, October 24, he also reported that at the dinner, as guest of honor, Nulty had proposed the customary toasts: first one to the pope, which he did very well, and then one to Dixon, who took precedence among those present as the primate of all Ireland. "He then proposed," Cullen noted more dryly, "the name of Monsignor McHale who was present—hardly was this toast proposed, all the priests rose and shouted long live Monsignor McHale for a long time, and made a very great display for him" (K). "In any case," he added more petulantly,

they were not all nor even the greater part for him, but the most violent were for him, and they always seem to constitute the whole meeting—Monsignor McHale made a long speech that no one was able to understand but he spoke of the enslavement of Ireland, and it appeared that he wished to speak of spiritual enslavement. As he spoke very obscurely, however, no one minded what he said. How things will go in Meath it is difficult to guess. Those who were present said the coadjutor conducted himself very well—but one cannot know whether he will be able to resist the mob with which he has to deal, one resolute act alone would put all in order—let us hope he will declare himself for the good. Meath is a very Catholic diocese, and it would be well that the priests there take a good turn.

"Monsignor Derry," Cullen further reported, naming the bishop of Clonfert and MacHale's most loyal supporter among the bishops, "was present. He made a speech saying that he stood between Tuam and Meath as between two poles and he was adjusting himself to what was taking place in those two dioceses." "I have never seen," Cullen finally concluded, "Monsignor McHale in better health. He seems a young man although he is 76 years of age." When Dixon had occasion to write Kirby a short time later, he attempted, in his own honest, if diffident, way, to soften the effect of the clergy's demonstration on behalf of MacHale at the Meath dinner. "Dr. Cullen's health," Dixon loyally assured Kirby on November 7, "is very firm. I need not tell you that as a politician he does not stand near as high in popular favour as Dr. MacHale; and what great political measure has poor Dr. MacHale ever been able to bring about?"

The occasion for this letter of Dixon's to Kirby was his concern over yet another appointment of a coadjutor in his province, which had been pending for some time in Rome. Very early in 1864, in fact, Dixon had become so troubled about the strange conduct of the bishop of Clogher, Charles McNally, that he took the most unusual course of writing to a prominent parish priest of that diocese asking his confidential opinion about the state of the bishop's health and the necessity of providing him with a coadjutor. The Clogher priest replied on January 16:

Though most reluctant to put on paper my answer to your Grace's question—still in obedience to my ecclesiastical superior, and for the greater good of religion I will do so in the most conscientious manner I can.

I would have done so sooner but that your Grace allowed me time to make inquiries. This I did with all the caution I could and the result of my inquiries is—that I find it to be the firm conviction of the Dean, Archdeacon McMeal, Dr. Donnelly, Rev. E. McKenna, President of our seminary, and of every zealous good priest in the diocese, that the interests of religion in Clogher absolutely require the *immediate* appointment of a zealous and efficient coadjutor.

The grounds of this conviction are—1. That the poor Bishop's confirmed bad health and I am sorry to add, the state of his mind, have quite unfitted him for the last 12 months for the administration of the diocese: and in consequence we have had no conferences—no meetings of the priests, save one or two, and the things which took place at them were of the most painful nature. And indeed, this is the case whenever he takes part in any public ceremony. For instance—some few weeks ago he presided at the profession of a nun in the convent at Monaghan, and had your Grace witnessed the poor old man's conduct on the occasion, you'd have been pained to the quick.

2^{ly} The sacrament of confirmation has not been administered, and we have had no retreat for the priests.

3^{ly} His awfully disagreeable manner and his unguarded sallies of bad humour have made him quite inapproachable even on most important diocesan matters.

4^{thly} His conduct latterly has been so strange, and his oddities and eccentricities so outlandish, as to give good grounds to the people of Monaghan, for speaking rather freely about the state of the poor man's mind.

5^{ly} Some priests here were speaking some time back of the propriety—and they say the necessity of laying before your Grace the state of the diocese—but they got over their scruples—by saying, that your Grace from the frequent opportunities you have had of meeting our good Bishop, must know, as well as they could inform you, how the diocese is administered. [K]

"I will burn your communication," the Clogher priest then assured Dixon in conclusion, "as soon as I shall send this, and since I received it, I observed the most extreme caution."

"The poor Bishop," Dixon explained to Kirby on January 28, on enclosing the above letter, "may be said to be *hors de combat*, and I am not aware there is any vicar general in the diocese; so that, to a great extent, every priest in that diocese, is at present, in a great measure, his own master" (K). "I was speaking to the Archbishop of Dublin yesterday on the subject," he continued,

and he agrees with me in thinking that the following is the feasible plan of making a commencement in the urgent business. We could not let Dr. McNally know that we are moving in the matter. Hence the advice to him to get a Coadjutor, must appear to originate with Rome: and if His Eminence Cardinal Barnabo will write a kind letter to him, to the following effect, I think he will comply instantly with the advice. His Eminence could say that they heard in Rome with great regret, of his continued ill health, and that considering how severe the labours of a diocese must prove to one in his state of health and that [of] his advanced age, it would gratify the Holy Father very much if he (Dr. McNally) would address a supplication to His Holiness for leave to take the usual preliminary steps without delay for the appointment of a Coadjutor. His Eminence might suggest to Dr. McNally as a reason against delay, the advantage of having the names to be forwarded, selected under his own superintendence. The names contained in the letter of the Clogher priest, need not be mentioned to anyone.

"This is indeed," he advised Kirby in conclusion, "an extremely urgent affair."

Dixon then wrote Barnabò on February 5, confirming all that he had written Kirby.[58] Barnabò apparently wrote McNally almost immediately, for Cullen informed Kirby on February 19 that McNally had visited with him the day before and that he was reduced to a mere skeleton. "I fear," Cullen added, "he will die traveling. He has been here twice since Christmas. I am glad the Cardinal has proposed to him to take a coadjutor, but I think he will scarcely do anything at all, a poor coadjutor *avrebbe la vita d'un cane* [would have the life of a dog]" (K). Indeed, McNally continued to procrastinate. "Of Dr. McNally's proceedings," Cullen reported to Kirby on April 5, "I have heard nothing, but as yet he has held no meeting to elect a coadjutor. The poor man is a great torment to his priests" (K). "He had a great office for Dr. Hughes," Cullen explained, referring to the late archbishop of New York, who was a native of the diocese of Clogher, "and had his priests to dine with him after. At dinner, he introduced some extraordinary whisky which was to be given only to a few of his select

58. Ibid., fol. 442, "Ristretto con Sommario sulla scelta di un Coadjutore con diritto di successione per Monsig. Carlo MacNally Vescovo di Clogher nella Provincia di Armagh in Irlanda, Novembre, 1864" (fols. 438–45).

friends, but he happened to go out, and whilst he was out, all the priests got at the reserved ware, and enjoyed the rare treat. When he returned, on perceiving what had happened, he turned the whole body out. He has all about him in terror, he is now so fretful and capricious."

Finally, on May 12, McNally wrote to the pope asking him for the aid of a coadjutor, and the pope promptly complied.[59] McNally called for a meeting of his clergy to commend a *terna* on July 2, in Monaghan. Patrick Murray, professor of theology at Maynooth and a native of the diocese of Clogher, received fifteen votes; James Donnelly, precentor and parish priest at Roslea, received ten votes; and James MacMahon, chancellor and parish priest of Carrickmacross, rounded out the *terna* with eight votes.[60] A month later, on August 2, the bishops of the province of Armagh reported in favor of the *dignior*, James Donnelly. "We have sent our letter to Rome recommending Dr. Donnelly's appointment," Dixon explained to Kirby on August 12.

> The Bishops unanimously refused to recommend Dr. Murray's* appointment. Dr. McNally is most anxious to have Dr. Mac-Mahon appointed: but he is not as good a preacher as Dr. Donnelly. Dr. Donnelly stands second on the list by the votes of the clergy, and Dr. MacMahon third: and there is no reason for passing over Dr. Donnelly, who is an admirable little man, and, I have no doubt, made a favourable impression on you, when you met him in Rome. We have kept all this a secret here for the present. But what I beg of you most earnestly is: that you would implore of His Eminence Cardinal Barnabò to have the appointment of the Coadjutor of Clogher made with the least possible delay. To speak plainly, Dr. McNally is fitter to be the inmate of some quiet asylum than to occupy his present position. His mind is becoming weaker every day; and his extravagant eccentricities, which make Protestants laugh, are well calculated to draw tears from reflecting Catholics. [K]
> *The state of his (Dr. Murray's) health being so uncertain.

"There is another reason," Dixon then confided, "why the Cardinal ought to be anxious to hasten this appointment. How can this poor man in his present state of mind be fit to administer the revenues of the diocese? It is much to be feared that he may create excessive embarrassments for his successor on this head." "In a word," he finally concluded, "His Eminence never did a greater charity for any diocese,

---

59. Ibid., fol. 443.
60. Ibid., fols. 443–44.

since his first connection with Propaganda, than he will do for the diocese of Clogher by having Dr. Donnelly appointed forthwith, and the administration of the diocese transferred to his hands: for indeed it is painful to see the administration of the diocese in the hands of poor Dr. McNally."

Several days before, however, Cullen had written Barnabò about the results of the Clogher clergy's commendation. "Having had occasion yesterday," he explained on August 8, "to see Monsignor Dixon, Archbishop of Armagh, I had a conference with him on the state of the diocese of Clogher, respecting which he is very afflicted."[61] After assuring Barnabò that a coadjutor was indeed necessary, Cullen then further explained that Dixon was very anxious that he be chosen without delay.

As for the persons proposed, all the Bishops were agreed about excluding Father Murray, professor at Maynooth and as all must have known him in the College, they must have good reasons for what they have decided. That professor is certainly a man of talent, and writes well enough as to style, but some years ago he wrote rather in favor of mixed education, and when the Government in 1855 sent a commission to the College to investigate the state of the College of Maynooth, he said many things which ought not to be said in the presence of Protestants. In any case, I have heard he is very repentant about what he then said, and that he has changed his opinions in a fit direction. As Monsignor Dixon, who lived in the College with him for so many years, however, is decidedly hostile to his promotion, it would not be well to make him a Bishop, more so that Monsignor McNally thinks very badly of him.

As for the other candidates, I have little knowledge of them but I believe that the Bishops have had serious reasons for preferring Father Donnelly, who is the second, to Father MacMahon, who is third. Both are very respectable priests, but Father Donnelly seems to be more fit for administration.

"Monsignor McNally however," Cullen added finally in conclusion, "is entirely favorable to MacMahon, but in his present state, no weight ought to be given to his wishes, or rather whims."

Cullen did not write Barnabò again about the Clogher appointment until he reported the death of McNally some three and a half months

61. Ibid., fols. 444–45.

later, in late November. On October 24 Cullen wrote Kirby that McNally had just received the last rites and had written to him (Cullen) that day to ask him to hurry Barnabò about providing him with a coadjutor (K). In asking Kirby to say a word to the cardinal as McNally had requested, Cullen added that it was very "probable and almost certain that before the end of this week the poor Bishop will be dead, whence it is not necessary that the appointment of a coadjutor be hurried." Cullen proved to be somewhat premature in his prediction, for McNally did not expire for nearly a month more. When Cullen wrote Barnabò on November 22, the day after McNally died, he explained that the appointment to Clogher could now be made directly, without the complication of a coadjutor.[62] The cardinals of Propaganda, who met the very day Cullen was writing Barnabò, proceeded to recommend Donnelly to the pope as coadjutor to Clogher.[63] Dixon had also written Kirby that same day, November 22, informing him of McNally's death and asking him to inform Propaganda in order to save the authorities the trouble of having to make up new briefs.[64] The whole matter was finally settled, in any case, when the pope appointed Donnelly bishop of Clogher on December 11, 1864.[65]

Cullen's real views about the Clogher appointment are very difficult to determine. Indeed, in the light of the evidence available, they must remain to a very large degree a matter of conjecture. Though it is clear, for example, that Cullen was determined to block Murray's appointment, it is also clear that he did not display any great enthusiasm for Donnelly's promotion. After his veto of Murray, in fact, Cullen remained studiously passive in his correspondence—most surprisingly, even in his letters to Kirby. Cullen certainly realized as well as Dixon did that a coadjutor in Clogher was necessary, and yet he did nothing to hurry the appointment. The question, of course, is why, and the answer to that question appears to be that he did not quite trust Donnelly. Apparently he was afraid that Donnelly, like Nulty, might prove to be a supporter of MacHale in the episcopal body. Still, after just having overreached himself in the Meath appointment, Cullen prudently decided to be more cautious in the Clogher case and to rest content that he had successfully blocked Murray. In the event, neither Nulty nor Donnelly proved to be a supporter of MacHale, and because they were essentially in harmony with Cullen and their brother prelates on the important questions of denominational educa-

---

62. S.R.C., vol. 34, fol. 1353.
63. A, vol. 228, fol. 440.
64. S.R.C., vol. 34, fol. 1357.
65. A, vol. 228, fol. 440.

tion, pastoral reform, and Fenianism, the unity of the body was very much enhanced by their promotion.

On October 17, 1864, shortly before the appointment to Clogher was finally made, the bishop of Killaloe, Michael Flannery, one of the youngest and most able of the Irish bishops, was obliged to apply to the pope for a coadjutor with the right of succession.[66] For more than a year and a half Flannery had been suffering from an acute mental depression that had become progressively worse and had finally totally impaired his ability to function. Toward the end of 1863 he had been persuaded to take his doctor's advice to find some relief by traveling abroad. He visited France, where after an initial rally his depression only deepened.[67] By the end of January 1864 Cullen became so concerned about Flannery's condition and his prolonged absence from his diocese that he felt constrained to write to Barnabò explaining the sad situation.[68] Barnabò immediately wrote Flannery's metropolitan, the archbishop of Cashel, asking him to report on the circumstances of the case. Leahy replied by return, on February 18, that Flannery was suffering from an acute melancholia and that there appeared to be little hope that he would ever recover.[69] He could, Leahy added, neither say his office nor celebrate mass. The diocese of Killaloe, moreover, was currently being governed by two vicars-general appointed by Flannery. Though the vicars, Leahy pointed out, had done their best under very difficult circumstances, some action should be taken by Rome to regularize the situation.

In the meantime, Cullen had come apparently to the same conclusion.[70] He advised Kirby on March 4, "I wish you would mention to the Cardinal the state of Killaloe. Dr. Flannery is in Paris in a state of melancholy and will do nothing, if they could get him to Rome he might recover" (K). "Get them," he then urged Kirby, "to appoint an administrator or to provide in some way for the place." Barnabò was persuaded to invite Flannery to Rome; he apparently arrived in early April and stayed some six weeks with Kirby in the Irish College.[71] On

66. A, vol. 229 (1865), fol. 126, "Ristretto con Sommario sulla elezione del Coadjutore pel Vescovo di Killaloe della provincia di Cashel in Irelanda, 28 Marzo, 1865" (fols. 122–32).
67. K, Cullen to Kirby, December 11, 1863.
68. S.R.C., vol. 34, fol. 1062, January 28, 1864.
69. Ibid., fol. 1072.
70. K, Cullen to Kirby, February 19, 1864.
71. K, Cullen to Kirby, April 1, 1864.

May 26, in reporting an audience Flannery had with the pope, Kirby explained to the bishop of Elphin that the pope had treated Flannery with gentle consideration (G). The pope had told Flannery, Kirby further reported, "*Noli temere* [Do not be afraid]. What have you to fear? If God be for us, who can be against us? If anybody should be afraid it is I, against whom *tutti i briconi* [all the rascals] are conspiring—*eretici schismatici revolutionari e tutti* [heretics, schismatics, revolutionaries, and all]. And still I am not afraid. *Corragio dunque Monsignore* [Courage then Monsignor]." Kirby then confided to Gillooly that even after the pope's exhortation, he had failed to discern any essential improvement in Flannery's condition, and indeed, when the bishop of Killaloe left Rome, he appeared to be as disturbed as when he arrived.

On leaving Rome, in fact, Flannery did not return to Ireland. He returned instead to Paris, where he took up residence with the Lazarist community at San Sulpice, with whom he continued to live in seclusion until he died in 1891. When Flannery did not return to Ireland, Cullen wrote Kirby again, asking him to explain to Barnabò that something must be done about the diocese of Killaloe.[72] He further suggested that Barnabò be advised to write the archbishop of Cashel in order that the necessary measures be taken to provide Flannery with a coadjutor. Barnabò wrote Leahy on July 8, explaining that Flannery had just been in Rome and that it was the opinion there that he was competent to rule his diocese, but that the authorities would like to have Leahy's opinion in the matter (G). Leahy replied on July 20 that he thought a coadjutor was most necessary because Flannery was not likely to recover, and the clergy and laity of Killaloe required the attention of an active and zealous bishop.[73] On August 14 the secretary of Propaganda, Annibale Capalti, explained the whole situation to the pope, who decided that the archbishop of Cashel should be advised to induce the bishop of Killaloe to ask the Holy See for a coadjutor, or at least an auxiliary, and Barnabò wrote Leahy in this sense on August 23.[74] Leahy visited Paris in late September or early October and persuaded Flannery to write the formal letter suggested by the pope. By this time, however, the authorities had apparently become more concerned about the situation, for Barnabò finally wrote Leahy on October 12 that it had now been decided to proceed with the appointment of a coadjutor, and he asked Leahy to make the necessary arrangements to convene the Killaloe clergy in order that they might select a *terna*.

72. A, vol. 229, fol. 226, Kirby memorandum quoting Cullen's letter of June 1864.
73. Ibid., fols. 126–27.
74. Ibid., fol. 123.

In the meantime, amid all the rumors, the Killaloe clergy had be-gun to grow restless. On September 29 a Killaloe priest, Patrick Moran, the parish priest of Kilmurry in West Clare, wrote to his old friend, Bartholomew Woodlock, the rector of the Catholic University, a long and interesting letter that was obviously intended to be shown to Cullen (K). Moran reported that the news about Flannery's health was very disheartening and that because it was likely they would have a coadjutor very soon, party feelings were running rather high in the diocese. "A stirring active section," he explained to Woodlock, "are determined to have F. Power of Killaloe. They speak openly & above board on the subject. Another section must have F. Kelly of Kilrush. Their respective friends will support both these to the last." "I feel quite assured," Moran further reported, "that there are several good priests in the Diocese who feel no interest whatever in the result of these factious movements, & who would gladly hail the advent of some good Clergyman who would have no connection whatever with either the one or the other" (K). "Would to God," he hinted, "your great Archbishop sent us one of his own choice. I would pledge myself for the hearty welcome he would receive. We do sincerely hope that his Grace will *recommend us one before it is too late.*" "I fear it is great presumption in me," Moran confessed in conclusion, "to write in this manner—but I trust that his Grace & you will impute to me no other motive than the sincere & earnest desire of having the holy will of God carried out & the interests of the Church promoted." Wood-lock must have replied that it was best to leave the matter of a coadju-tor in the hands of the archbishop of Cashel, for Moran explained to Woodlock on October 3 that Leahy was in favor of Father Power of Killaloe because he did not want to place himself in opposition to a strong party (K). Moran then reassured Woodlock that there were many good priests in the diocese who would be pleased to have Cullen recommend and that they "would heartily welcome *one* either from *Dublin* or *Rome.*" "Should his Grace," Moran then added more pru-dently, "not interfere, may I ask as a favour that neither Dr. Leahy or [*sic*] anyone else shall be made aware of my name or suggestions."

In the event, Cullen did decide to interfere, but only indirectly through Kirby. "I enclose," he reported to Kirby on October 7, "two letters written to Dr. Woodlock by a Pat. Moran who appears to be a good priest" (K). "Perhaps in this case they might appoint Dr. Murphy of Hyderabad an administrator until Dr. Flannery recovers," Cullen suggested, referring to the former vicar apostolic who had been unable to return to India for reasons of health and who was then resident in Ireland awaiting a new assignment by Propaganda. "However," he added more diffidently, "I do not know Dr. Murphy sufficiently, its clergy there [Killaloe] are factious and a strong hand will be required." Barnabò had already anticipated Cullen's suggestion, as Cullen was probably aware, and had written Murphy asking him if he would accept a coadjutorship in Ireland.[75] Murphy had declined, and this refusal undoubtedly, taken in conjunction with the delay in securing a formal request from Flannery for a coadjutor, was what had prompted Barnabò to write Leahy on October 12, instructing him to proceed with the arrangements for the selection of a *terna*.

By the time Leahy received Barnabò's letter, he must have realized that Cullen was interfering in the Killaloe affair, for when he replied on October 24 he made it clear to Barnabò that he thought the usual procedure in the choosing of a coadjutor should not be rescinded, as had happened when Flannery had been appointed some seven years before, because it would only reawaken the considerable disquiet among the Killaloe clergy that had been aroused on the previous occasion.[76] Meanwhile, Flannery's letter of October 17 had been received in Rome, and on October 30 the pope gave his consent for the appointment of a coadjutor.[77] Barnabò wrote Flannery on November 14, authorizing him to proceed in the usual way to the election of a *terna* (L). Several days later, on November 16, Barnabò also wrote Leahy, informing him that the election of a coadjutor had been authorized and instructing him to keep an eye on the arrangements in order that all might proceed smoothly (L). At this point Flannery forwarded Barnabò's letter to him to Leahy, explaining that he gave him full power to carry out its instructions.[78] Because the customary procedure in the appointment of a coadjutor in Ireland involved the convoking of the clergy by the bishop of the diocese, who would then preside at the meeting to commend a *terna*, Leahy understandably had serious misgivings about the correctness of his convoking and presiding at a meeting of the Killaloe clergy. Barnabò's letter of November 16 to him did not explicitly authorize him to take this step, and Flannery's delegation of power to him was of doubtful validity both in itself and in light of Flannery's mental condition. Leahy therefore wrote Barnabò again on November 29.[79] He enclosed a copy of Flannery's letter authorizing him to proceed in the matter and explained

75. S.R.C., vol. 34, fol. 1285, Murphy to Barnabò.
76. Ibid., fol. 127. For the appointment of Flannery see Emmet Larkin, *The Making of the Roman Catholic Church in Ireland, 1850–1860* (Chapel Hill, N.C., 1980), pp. 403–10.
77. S.R.C., vol. 34, fol. 123.
78. L, Flannery to Leahy, n.d.
79. S.R.C., vol. 34, fols. 127–28.

that as Barnabò's letter of November 16 had only authorized him to assist Flannery, he now wanted to know if he was authorized to proceed on his own responsibility in convoking and presiding at the meeting of the Killaloe clergy. Barnabò replied on December 15 that he was to take complete charge in the matter (L).

Accordingly, Leahy convoked the Killaloe clergy on January 25, 1865, in Nenagh.[80] Of the forty-nine votes cast for five candidates, Nicholas Power, the parish priest of Killaloe and vicar-general, received thirty-two. Timothy Kelly, the parish priest of Kilrush, received fourteen votes; John Kenny, the parish priest of Ennis and vicar-general, John Egan, the parish priest of Birr, and James Ryan, the parish priest of Burges and Youghal, near Nenagh, each received one. When the bishops of the province of Cashel met in Thurles on February 14 to report on the candidates selected by the clergy, they were unanimous in recommending the first on the list, Nicholas Power, to Propaganda.[81] In his proxy to Leahy, Flannery had also expressed his preference for Power. The cardinals of Propaganda, who met on March 28 to consider the commendation of the clergy and the report of the bishops, were also unanimous in recommending Power to the pope, who on April 3 authoritatively approved the appointment.[82]

After his initial and indirect interference in early October in suggesting that the vicar apostolic of Hyderabad might be appointed administrator of Killaloe, Cullen does not appear to have interceded again. He certainly realized that the Killaloe clergy had given him all the credit for the suspension of the regular procedure in the appointment of Flannery in 1858 and that they were still very sore on the subject. He was therefore anxious not to give his enemies and critics any cause to raise another furor against him for interfering in the affairs of dioceses and provinces not his own. When he learned the results of the Killaloe election, in fact, he immediately realized that the appointment of Power was inevitable. He wrote Kirby on January 31 that he supposed Power would be the successful candidate, and Kirby submitted this tacit approval in a brief note to the authorities at Propaganda, which was then reproduced in the documents in the *ponenza* on the Killaloe appointment to be read by the cardinals of Propaganda.[83] The appointment to Killaloe and Cullen's part in it, therefore, were certainly in keeping with the pattern that had developed over the previous five years in the making of episcopal appoint-

80. Ibid., fols. 128–29.
81. Ibid., fols. 130–32.
82. Ibid., fol. 125.
83. Ibid., fol. 132.

ments in Ireland. Cullen's caution and diffidence were manifest, and in spite of the alarm raised by the archbishop of Cashel with regard to the possible suspension of procedure, the choice of the clergy and the bishops had been endorsed once again at Rome. Power was, moreover, a sensible and prudent man, who proved not only to be an effective administrator but also to be at one with his episcopal colleagues on all the important questions of the day facing the Irish Church.

In fact, the cumulative effect of the six episcopal appointments made between 1860 and 1865 was to strengthen the independence and corporate character of the bishops as a body. The chief casualty in the strengthening of that independence and corporate character was Cullen's hitherto very considerable influence at Rome in the making of Irish episcopal appointments. The most curious thing about the waning of this aspect of Cullen's influence at Rome, however, was that it was apparently less the result of any conscious attempt by the Roman authorities to limit it than a consequence of his unusual diffidence in accepting his share of the responsibility for the making of the various appointments. Indeed, this uncharacteristic diffidence became progressively more apparent over the period. In both the Down and Connor and Limerick appointments, for example, he was very careful about endorsing the prelates who were eventually appointed. In the Kilmore appointment he virtually withdrew, and when he then attempted to reassert himself in the Meath appointment, he handled it so badly that he failed to prevent Nulty's promotion. The immediate consequence of his failure in Meath was that he had to rest content with his veto of Murray in the Clogher appointment, when he probably would have liked to prevent Donnelly's appointment as well, and to acquiesce in the appointment of Power in Killaloe, when he certainly would have preferred someone else. By early 1865, then, Cullen had clearly come to the conclusion that his influence at Rome in episcopal appointments was now limited to the capacity to prevent the worst.

The other side of the coin of Cullen's diminished influence at Rome, of course, was that Rome had become more circumspect, not to say constitutional, about using its power in making Irish episcopal appointments. This was certainly made evident in Rome's increasing respect for the procedures involved in making episcopal appointments, which had not been much observed in the 1850s, when Cullen's influence had been all but paramount at Rome. Between 1860 and 1865, for example, no new *terna* was called for by Rome, though Cullen would certainly have been pleased with one in the Limerick affair and probably would have appreciated one in the Clogher case.

The various commendations of the clergy, moreover, were respected at least to the extent that in every case the appointment went to either the first or the second candidate on the list. Finally, and most important, the reports of the bishops had obviously come to have much greater weight with the cardinals of Propaganda in the making of their recommendations to the pope. The apparent exception in the Limerick case actually proved the rule. The Cashel bishops, it will be recalled, had not observed the customary procedure in making their report, and the cardinals of Propaganda had called them to account, but the fact was that the report eventually produced by the Cashel bishops was very favorable to the *dignissimus*, George Butler, whom the cardinals unanimously recommended to the pope. Moreover, rather than change the procedure for the bishops' report on the *terna*, as had been recommended by David Moriarty, the bishop of Kerry, as well as by Dixon and Cullen, the cardinals decided instead not only to confirm that procedure but to dignify it by insisting that a proper interval take place between the commending of a *terna* and the report on that *terna* by the bishops of the province. The basic lesson to be learned, then, from the making of the various episcopal appointments in the Irish Church in this period was that Rome, by endorsing and upholding the procedure involved in those appointments, was less inclined to act arbitrarily, and therefore functioned more constitutionally, in dealing with the Irish Church.

Ultimately, the most important result of Rome's increasing observance of procedures in governing the Irish Church, as evidenced in the making of episcopal appointments, on the one hand, and Cullen's diminishing influence in those appointments, on the other, was the strengthening of the independence and corporate character of the bishops as a body. Perhaps the outstanding characteristic of the six men appointed in this period was their independence. This is not to say, of course, that they were all men of outstanding ability, but they all did prove to be men of considerable energy and zeal. They all proved to be, moreover, sound on the important questions of denominational education, pastoral reform, and Fenianism, and none of them, despite their general and pronounced bias in favor of nationalist politics, turned out to be an open supporter of MacHale in the episcopal body. In fact, one of the more curious ironies of Cullen's diminished influence at Rome was his increased standing with the episcopal body. Though it would be certainly going too far to say that the majority of Cullen's episcopal colleagues either liked or even trusted him, they did, both as individuals and as a body, have a very healthy respect for him, and as a body, at least, they had apparently even come to fear him less. The reason for his increased standing with the body during this period was that on all fundamental issues in the Irish Church, he and they were in general agreement, and the six recent appointments had introduced no discordant element. What disagreements there were, such as on the presenting of an address to the Prince of Wales, were usually a matter of tactics, and on such occasions it was Cullen who backed down. Perhaps the most significant sign of the developing independence and corporate character of the episcopal body, as well as of Cullen's increasing standing with the body, was the position he persuaded the body to take up with regard to Fenianism. The bishops as a body could have derived very little pleasure from assuming this most thankless and unpopular stand. Still, they freely endorsed Cullen's lead with regard to the Brotherhood, signifying thereby both his leadership and their own independence as a body.

Part II

The Problem of Politics

JOHN MACHALE, ARCHBISHOP OF TUAM
(courtesy of the President of St. Patrick's College, Maynooth)

V

The Revolutionary Challenge

August 1863–December 1864

At their meeting in August 1863 in Dublin, the Irish bishops not only had condemned the Brotherhood of St. Patrick by name but also had passed a number of private resolutions concerning the public conduct of both Lavelle and Jeremiah Vaughan, the parish priest of Doora, in the diocese of Killaloe. Though MacHale had joined in the unanimous condemnation of the Brotherhood, he had refused to countenance the bishops' action as a body with regard to Lavelle, and the resolutions of the bishops were forwarded therefore to Rome for the consideration of Propaganda. The bishops had resolved:

1. As two clergymen—namely, the Rev. Mr. Lavelle, of the Diocese of Tuam, and the Rev. Mr. Vaughan, of the Diocese of Killaloe—are reported to have by published letters or speeches, identified themselves with the Brotherhood of St. Patrick, and as their example and authority are calculated to induce the laity to join this unlawful association, we pray their respective Ordinaries to insist that these clergymen shall publicly abjure all membership with the aforesaid Brotherhood; that they shall condemn it, as it has been condemned by the assembled Prelates, and that they shall retract whatever they may have said or written in its defence.

2. Certain letters, dated Partry, Corpus Christi, 1863, and April 18th, 1863, published in newspapers with the signature of

the Rev. Mr. Lavelle, having been submitted to the assembled Prelates, they have condemned them as containing doctrines false, scandalous, and pernicious, subversive of ecclesiastical and civil authority, and calculated to excite to sedition and agrarian crime. They require that if the Rev. Mr. Lavelle cannot disavow the authorship of these letters, he shall publicly retract them and subscribe their condemnation.[1]

MacHale had raised no objection to the first resolution, of course, because it was only an exhortation and in effect left him free to act as he thought best with regard to Lavelle. The second resolution was an entirely different matter, and MacHale had fought it tooth and nail for nearly four hours in the face of the whole episcopal body, supported only by his suffragan John Derry, the bishop of Clonfert.[2] The real significance of the second resolution was that it asserted that the authority of the bishops as a body meeting formally was superior to that of any individual member of the body. That was why MacHale objected so strenuously, and also why Cullen and his episcopal colleagues had no choice but to refer the whole matter of Father Lavelle's conduct to Rome. Shortly after Cullen submitted to Barnabò his long report of August 30 about the bishops' meeting, he also wrote Kirby explaining what had to be done. "It will be necessary," he maintained on September 4, "for the Propaganda or the Pope to compel Father Lavelle to stop in his mad career. Dr. MacHale supports him through thick and thin, and will do nothing without an express command" (K).

Indeed, the express command was not long in coming. As soon as Cullen's report of August 30 arrived at the Propaganda, it was referred to the pope, who decided that he would personally write to MacHale about Lavelle in the sense decided on by the bishops at their meeting in Dublin.[3] The pope's letter, which was dated September 24, ordered MacHale to suspend Lavelle, who was not to be restored to his priestly functions until he had publicly retracted his letters and retired to a monastery to make a retreat as a proof of his sincere repentance.[4] The letter was not sent off from Propaganda until October 2, and Kirby, who read it there that day, immediately reported the more relevant parts of it to Cullen. "The Pope," Kirby noted, "mentions in his let-

1. S.R.C., vol. 35, fol. 107.
2. A, vol. 228, fol. 99, "Ristretto con Sommario sull' adunanza tenuta dai Vescovi Irlandesi a Dublino nel mese di Agosto del 1863, Marzo 1864" (fols. 96–110).
3. S.R.C., vol. 34, fol. 820. See memorandum by Annibale Capalti, secretary of Propaganda, n.d., explaining that Cullen's report of August 30, 1863, was referred to the pope on September 6, 1863.
4. S.R.C., vol. 35, fols. 130–32.

ter the '*improbam agendi rationem*' [shameful reason for acting] of Lavelle in the Irish Coll. of Paris, on the occasion of McMn's funeral, on his wicked & seditious speeches & letters, especially his doctrine about the killing of oppressive Landlords &c." (C). "He then directs," Kirby then added, "that he [MacHale] at once suspend him from the adm. of the parish et a divinis peragendis [and from his sacred faculties], that he publicly retract & reprobate the wicked things he had written, & that he shut himself up in a retreat for some time. If he duly repent & submit, He the Pope will not refuse to take his case into consideration. If what he orders be not fulfilled, He then says 'Scito nos suprema nostra auctoritate circa eundem presbyt^m opportuna consilia esse suscepturos' [Know you that we by our supreme authority are going to see that opportune counsel is taken concerning this priest]." In a postscript of October 3 to this letter, Kirby then explained to Cullen that Barnabò had given him the pope's letter with permission to send him a copy.

"I am much obliged to you," Cullen replied on October 9, "for the Pope's letter. Poor Dr. McH. brought this business on himself. He would not listen to anyone. It must be an afflicting thing to get such a lecture from S. Peter. I hope Lavelle may obey, but he has got so much encouragement and so much money by violence that it is hard to calculate on what he will do" (K). "What a blessing," he concluded, "that we have a Pope: without one, scandals would never cease." Some ten days later, however, when Cullen wrote Kirby again, he was somewhat less assured. "I believe," he reported on October 20, "nothing has been done about Father Lavelle, at least publicly. Dr. Mac-Evilly writes that probably his Grace will privately suspend him and then privately restore him, writing at the same time that he had carried out all the instructions given to him. Of course anything done privately will not repair that scandal" (K).

On October 24, however, a letter of Lavelle's dated October 16 appeared in the *Connaught Patriot*, a weekly journal published in Tuam and reported to be under the patronage of MacHale and his clergy.[5] Though Lavelle did express his regret for taking part in politics without the consent of his bishop, he continued to insist that the Brotherhood of St. Patrick was not an oath-bound, secret society and that its ends were not immoral. He did not, moreover, offer a word of apology for his attacks on Cullen and the other bishops. Two days after Lavelle's "retraction" appeared, MacHale wrote the pope explaining that

---

5. Ibid., fol. 114. See also Kirby memorandum, n.d., reporting Lavelle's letter, which had been republished in the *Freeman's Journal*, of October 26, 1863 (ibid., fol. 93).

he had complied with his instructions regarding Lavelle.[6] He had suspended the offending priest, who had made the necessary retreat and published the required retraction. He had then restored Lavelle, as he believed he was authorized to do, to his priestly functions.

Hardly had the pope received this assurance from MacHale when Lavelle published yet another letter on October 31, this time in the *Irishman*, a reputed Fenian organ. The letter denounced the apostolic delegate in unmeasured terms. The technique adopted by Lavelle for conveying his denunciation can only be described as ingenious. It appears that the *Tablet*, an English Catholic weekly that was published in London but that had been published in Dublin in the 1850s by Frederick Lucas, had once again raised the old canard that the very promising movement to establish an independent Irish party in the House of Commons in the 1850s had been betrayed in the great moment of promise by a gang of place hunters, and that a large number of the bishops and clergy had sided with those who had betrayed the good cause. Two of the more prominent politicians, the *Tablet* further argued, who had attempted to sustain the cause, Frederick Lucas and Charles Gavan Duffy, had after the great betrayal paid dearly for their loyalty. Lucas, it was charged, had died in 1856 of a heart broken by a long and fruitless duel both at home and at Rome with Cullen, and Duffy then became so discouraged that he soon abandoned Ireland for Australia, where he realized a brilliant and successful political career. Needless to say, the rhetoric of the *Tablet* left a good deal to be desired as far as historical truth was concerned, and Lavelle wrote a letter in response. Though the editor of the *Tablet* published this letter, he asked Lavelle to justify the claims he made in it. But when the editor received Lavelle's second letter, purporting to justify his remarks, he refused to publish it, maintaining that it was nothing less than a libel on the Irish bishops in general and on Cullen in particular.

"The following," Lavelle had maintained in his second letter to the editor of the *Tablet*, which was now published in the *Irishman* on October 31, and which was dated October 6 from Mount Partry, "are the words of the *Tablet*, to which I referred in my former letter:— 'Treachery, selfishness, cowardice, and imbecility will never make wise, brave, patriotic, and honest work. The parliamentary phalanx was broken. A large number of the bishops and clergy abandoned the enterprise, and sided actively against those who were willing to continue or renew it. Lucas died of a broken heart, and Duffy left the country in despair . . . The causes that were operating in 1852 still

6. A, vol. 228, fol. 105, October 26, 1863.

went on in 1856, and have been working ever since.' Of course, you will stand by those words in their plain and obvious sense, and, therefore, by any deduction which can be logically drawn from them." He went on:

> Clearly, then, *some* persons are therein charged with "treachery, selfishness, cowardice, and imbecility," or in other words, proved themselves by their conduct "treacherous, selfish, cowardly, and imbecile." With those vices and crimes, "a large number of bishops" are expressly connected. To them, and to each and every one of them, the epithets—the "fearful epithets"—must, therefore, apply. It is notorious, to all Ireland at least, that foremost among the bishops referred to stood his Grace of Dublin, the Most Rev. Dr. Cullen. Therefore, to him, among others, must the obnoxious "fearful epithets" apply. Therefore, is he pronounced by the *Tablet* guilty of political treachery—in other words, a political traitor, and, therefore a "political Judas." Behold my proof of thesis No. 1.

"Now," he proposed, "for No. 2: that the *Tablet* charged Dr. Cullen with 'murdering Lucas' and driving Duffy into exile."

> Its precise words are, "Lucas died of a broken heart, and Duffy left the country in despair." Now, sir, is not Lucas "dying of a broken heart, and Duffy's flying the country in despair," put down *as the result* of the "treachery, selfishness, cowardice, and imbecility" denounced above, and of their immediate consequence, the "rupture of the parliamentary party?" It was the "treachery," &c "that broke Lucas's heart." Therefore, it was the man who committed the "treachery" who broke that heart. Dr. Cullen is declared guilty of treachery. *Ergo*, he broke Lucas's heart, and *ergo*, "murdered Lucas." Again, it was those who "sided actively" against Lucas and Duffy that broke their heart, or made them "fly the country." It is notorious that Dr. Cullen was the "bishop" who *most* "actively sided against" both. Therefore, and again, according to the *Tablet* has he broke their heart or made them quit their country. Surely, if I break a man's heart I am guilty of his murder, and if I make a man quit his country, I am the cause of his exile. It is only a change of names for one and the same thing; unless, indeed, we are to apply to the present case the adage, "Killing no murder."

"I have now done," Lavelle then concluded, after another column and a half of this specious, if ingenious, logic chopping. " 'As a truthful man,' " he archly assured the editor, "I have reproduced your words. As a man of common sense, I have given them my interpretation. I exempt you from the foul meaning of attributing 'willful murder' to Dr. Cullen or anyone else. In intimating that Lucas died of a broken heart, in consequence of Dr. Cullen 'actively siding against him,' you never wished to convey that his Grace proposed to himself that terrible consequence. You merely stated a fact. I repeated your statement in other words. Let the public judge between us; and if I have done you wrong, as a man of justice, I profess myself ready to make you all due reparation." "If you pledge your word of honour," he closed finally, repeating his charges once again, "that Dr. Cullen was not included in, even among the foremost of those bishops whose antagonism broke Lucas's heart, or that you intended the statement *other* 'bishops,' and not in any way for him, I shall sincerely cry peccavi [I have sinned]. Until you emphatically do so, I think I have established my case to the satisfaction of every sensible and impartial man."

"I send to Dr. Moran today," Cullen informed Kirby dryly on November 3, "a copy of the Irishman in which you will find some gems of Father Lavelle. He has discovered that I am a new Judas, a traitor etc. From this you will see what fruit has been produced by the Pope's letter" (K). "It would be time," he then suggested to Kirby, "for Propaganda to do something unless they wish to let a little priest trample on them." That same day Cullen also wrote Barnabò, enclosing copies of both the *Connaught Patriot* and the *Irishman*[7] and explaining that Lavelle's letters were doing great damage by exciting the people to disobedience and weakening their faith, as well as giving great advantage to their enemies.[8] When Cullen wrote Kirby again some two weeks later, he was still obviously very upset. "I fear the Pope's letter has only made things worse," he explained on November 17. "Father Lavelle has just turned it into ridicule. He has just written enough to show that he wished to humbug. His letter to me published in the Irishman which I sent shows that he has changed or withdrawn nothing. However after stating that the Archbishop of Dublin is a new Judas etc. he adds that with great humility he submits all his important writings to the Holy See. Well oportet ut scandala veniant [it is necessary that scandals come about], and when they come, it is hard to remedy them" (K). "Dr. McHale's letter to the Pope," Cullen added, "was only ad faciem faciendum [putting a good face on it]. He evidently wished to do something, and to do nothing at the same time.

---

7. See S.R.C., vol. 35, fols. 112, 114, for copies of both papers.
8. Ibid., fols. 92, 117, November 3, 1863.

The pope's authority ought not to be trifled with, as it has been in this case."

The pope obviously felt the same way because he wrote MacHale on November 26, not only expressing his astonishment that the archbishop had restored Lavelle to his priestly functions without his express permission, but ordering him to suspend Lavelle once again, and explicitly reserving to himself the right of restoring the offending priest.[9] "I have just recd your letter of the 28th November," Cullen reported to Kirby on December 3, "and I am glad to hear that they are determined to put an end to Father Lavelle's doings. Every day brings proofs that he ought to be checked" (K). "I have this week," he explained, "received the Boston Pilot which gives an account of a convention or meeting of deputies from Fenian Brothers at Chicago. The chief of the society or as they call him the Head Centre is a certain O'Mahony. This is the same man who brought over McManus's remains, and who was that that time head of the Fenians as he states himself in one of his late speeches, though at the time of his visit to Ireland, it was pretended that he came merely to pay an act of respect to McManus's memory." "The villains," Cullen then added,

> appear to be quite ruthless, and they expose their poor dupes here to the halter, by publishing the treasonable objects of the society. If they were to prevail, we would have libertà alla Mazziniana. But I think their object is not to invade Ireland, but to get poor Irish fools to fight for America. The Government of the United States would not spend a dollar for our sake, or to free Ireland— our poor people however are easily duped, and they think Napoleon and Lincoln are their sincere friends. But such old foxes know very well what they are at. They are playing their own game, and if there be a fat hen they will have it for themselves.

"I have got a copy," Cullen reported again about a week later, on December 11, "of the last letter from the Vat[ican]. to Dr. McH. He gets an express order to suspend ab off° et benef. [from office and benefice] our friend in Partry. I hope the Pope will get no more trouble on this matter. He has other things to trouble him—but the evil in Ireland could not be checked in any other way. Probably however Lavelle will continue to do mischief suppresso nomine [anonymously]" (K). In suspending Lavelle for the second time, MacHale apparently advised the administrator of Partry to proceed directly to Rome and present his case in person to the pope and the authorities.

9. Ibid., fols. 90–91.

"Father Lavelle," Cullen informed Kirby on December 29, "passed through Dublin about a week ago on his way to Rome, provided, as he said, with letters highly commendatory to the Pope. I hope the unhappy man may do penance but he ought not to be absolved, or allowed to leave Rome, until he shall have published his retractation. If he got off, or if he be not obliged to make a clear and distinct retractation of his writings he will be worse than ever" (K). "I think it was wrong," Cullen added finally, for good measure," for Dr. McH. to throw the onus of punishing him on the Holy See."

Lavelle arrived in Rome on January 2, 1864, where he enlisted the aid of the influential Monsignor Talbot, private chamberlain to the pope, and the well-connected Dom Bernard Smith, former vice-rector of the Irish College, in convincing the pope and Cardinal Barnabò that he was sincerely repentant.[10] "I saw C. Barnabò yesterday," Kirby reported to Cullen on January 15, "who told me that F. Lavelle had been with him on the evening before. The Card^l. gave him severe reproaches for his wicked conduct. He went thro' all the series of his misdeeds, shewing the horrid character of them, & the mischief to which they naturally tended. The Card^l. says that he acknowledges his errors fully & submits entirely to Rome" (C). "I urged," Kirby added, "both on the Cardinal & Secretary the necessity of having him make a full & explicit reparation for the scandal he has given & for the calumnies & oltraggi [insults] that he has committed. I hope he will do it. He is to make a retreat." "It is very likely," he finally assured Cullen optimistically, "at all events that the lesson he will receive will have the effect of making him abandon a like career for the future."

Lavelle first made a retreat and then wrote the retraction necessary to secure the lifting of the suspension imposed by the pope. His retraction, which was dated January 25, 1864, from the Retreat of Saints John and Paul, Rome, deserves to be quoted in full:

> Frankly acknowledging that in my political writings I have fallen into excesses and said things which either of themselves or by the interpretation given them have caused scandal to the faithful and especially the following—1 that I wrote and acted in quite an improper manner as regards the funeral of McManus—2 that carried away by an excess of zeal I employed a rash and unfortunate expression, unbecoming my sacred state, and inconsistent with that meekness which should ever characterize the

10. Patrick J. Corish, "Political Problems, 1860–1878," in *A History of Irish Catholicism*, gen. ed. Patrick J. Corish (Dublin, 1967), 5:14.

language of a priest in reference to the bigotted Irish landlords, who so cruelly persecute their unprotected Catholic tenants in hatred of their race and religion and for other unworthy motives—3 of having said things offensive to some of the dignitaries of the Church in Ireland and especially of Dr. Cullen[,] Archbishop of Dublin—4 that I have improperly written in defence of the Brotherhood of St. Patrick, in reference to which I hereby entirely submit to the recent judgement of the Irish Bishops, as I have already to the orders of my own Archbishop, that I should cease being a member thereof. Nor shall I in future belong to it, or any other such association. I therefore retract all these unbecoming[,] offensive or otherwise improper publications and excesses, in the hope that this open and candid retraction may counteract whatever harm they may have caused. And I am resolved (and promise) to avoid such things in future, and abstain from political discussions in the papers.

Therefore begging Your Holiness's pardon, which both the parental clemency of Your Holiness and my own sincere regrets make me confidently hope to obtain together with the apostolic benediction I remain your Holiness's most affectionate son and servant.[11]

"I have recd F. Lavelle's retractation today," Cullen reported to Kirby on February 12, "It is not anything, particular, he retracts the errors in his *political writings*, as if he had published something great. I think no great good has been obtained, but it is better to say nothing of it, until [we] see how he will go on" (K). "I have heard," Cullen informed Kirby a week later, on February 19, "that Father Lavelle is at home for the last ten days. He has as yet published no retractation. I hope he won't publish the form he drew up in Rome, it was very badly done and contained an attempt to justify himself. I have got a copy of the retractation from Propaganda, but I do not think it would be creditable to those concerned to have it said that they approved such a document. If Father Lavelle does not publish, I will not" (K). The longer Lavelle delayed in publishing his retraction, however, the greater was the currency given to the rumor that he had triumphed over Cullen at Rome. On February 26, for example, the bishop of Galway, John MacEvilly, wrote Kirby that he had just received the day before a letter from a clerical friend and parish priest in the neighbor-

---

11. S.R.C., vol. 35, fol. 74. A copy was forwarded by Barnabò to Cullen on February 3, 1864. See S.R.C., vol. 34, fol. 1070, Cullen to Barnabò, February 12, 1864, acknowledging receipt of Lavelle's letter.

hood of Tuam, who reported, " 'The rumour extensively circulated here, is that Father Lavelle has returned in triumph from Rome, where he has *non suited* Dr. Cullen' " (K).

MacEvilly then went on to assure Kirby that he did not believe a word of it. "It is absurd to suppose," he explained, "that the H. See would give such a man as Father Lavelle even the appearance of a triumph over the Delegate Apostolic, who has done more for the cause of religion in this country and for the H. See, than any Bishop or number of Bishops since the days of Laurence O'Toole." "However," MacEvilly added,

> I must tell you, the *Tuam [sic] Patriot* of Saturday week expressly stated that "Father Lavelle was that day in Tuam on his return from Rome, that his case was triumphant, and that he would issue an address in the national cause," and this was copied into other papers. On last Saturday—the 20th inst. an article or leader appeared in that day's issue of the *Patriot* of the most defiant and insulting tone as regards the H. See, that I ever saw published in any paper even of the most extreme Orange tendency. It called on the laity to resist the instructions of Propaganda. This article was *never written by the Editor of the Paper*. It was manifestly written to order and published in a Catholic paper, the acknowledged organ of the clergy there, it is calculated to do immense mischief.

Cullen was also acutely concerned about the great damage Lavelle and the Fenian press were doing to ecclesiastical authority in Ireland. "Father Lavelle," he reported to Kirby on Friday, March 4, "is at home more than a month. As yet he has published nothing, but it is announced in the Connaught Patriot of Tuam that important documents are to appear immediately from the pen of Lavelle. I shall send the paper if I get it, the same paper is fierce against Cardinal Barnabò, and it gives notice to the Pope to mind his own business. I sent an article from it to Cardinal Barnabò to amuse him" (K). "Our Fenian brothers," he further explained, going on to refer to a weekly paper the Brotherhood had launched in Dublin the previous November, "are doing all the mischief they can. They publish here a most wicked and insolent paper called the 'Irish People.' It is more Protestant than Catholic, and it is very hard on priests, Bishops and Pope. It is supported by American money, but I suppose it will not last long."

The next day, Saturday, March 5, Lavelle finally published in the *Connaught Patriot* a modified version of the retraction he had made in Rome. To the surprise of all, however, not to say to the consternation of many, he also published a long memorial, dated January 27, 1864, which he maintained he had presented to the pope shortly before he had left Rome. The memorial was also published again the following week, March 12, in the *Irishman*, where it was prefaced by a letter from Lavelle that can only be described as condescending toward the pope and the Roman authorities and full of self-pity regarding himself. "I shall only remark," Lavelle explained on February 22, after asking the editor to publish the enclosed letters, "that in *Rome* I met with nothing but kindness and consideration in all quarters of authority. The Cardinal Prefect, Barnabo, and the Chief Secretary, Monsignor, Capalti, I must say, agreeably surprised me by their courtesy, affability, and accessibility, almost at all times. Of his Holiness it would be idle to speak. His worst political enemies (for personal he could have none), must bow to his admitted virtues. If they were all left alone and not worried, as they are, by interminable complaints and misrepresentations, I think it would be much better for all concerned." "I can now say," he then added in conclusion, "*Liberavi animam meam* [I have cleared my conscience]. My faults—*and for one who has written and spoken so much they are neither so many nor so serious*—I freely admit. What has most pained me, I confess, is that my enemies in Ireland, while picking out every objectionable feature in my words and deeds, totally ignored my unceasing and, through God, successful efforts and my great sacrifices in defence of the faith against the proselytiser, and the poor man against the oppressor, in order to effect my ruin. Were they to live a hundred years they shall hardly labour or suffer as much for faith and humanity as I have done."

But all this was as nothing compared to the audacity of the memorial itself. "Most Holy Father," Lavelle began, "Having now accomplished the will of your Holiness, and satisfied my own conscience by a simple, straightforward, and candid retraction of my obnoxious publications, it only remains for me to offer the following explanations thereof." "Truth and justice," he affirmed, "as well as my own character, require so much at my hand; for, up to this, your Holiness has been furnished only with a one-sided and a garbled history, judging by which it is no wonder you should regard me in the light of a bad man and an unworthy priest. Now, I most humbly and most respectfully pray your Holiness—'*Audi alteram partem*' [Hear the other side]." He elaborated:

I have been accused

1st. Of having been spending a kind of vagabond life for the purpose of propagating a certain political society.

2nd. Of having assisted and "preached" at the obsequies of a certain "heretic" of the name MacManus, and posted my letter on his obsequies on the walls of Dublin.

3rd. Of having been a member of a wicked secret society, "a nefarious gang of conspirators called after the name of St. Patrick."

4th. Of having threatened to rise up and destroy the tyrannical landlords of Ireland.

5th. Of having uttered seditious language against the English regime in my unfortunate country.

6th. Of having written other things that caused scandal to the faithful.

7th. Of having written offensively against Dr. Cullen.

8th. Of having been the cause of the quarrels in the Irish College of Paris.

Lavelle then proceeded in nearly three full columns, and more than thirty-five hundred words, to vindicate himself against these accusations by either denying them or pleading mitigating circumstances. In the process he reiterated every charge and pronouncement he had made in the press and on lecture platforms over the previous three years, and the implication was not only that he had been wrongly accused but that he had really been in the right all along. The evil genius behind all the accusations, of course, was Cullen, who appeared in the infamous role of Rome's informer. The climax of the very well structured and articulated diatribe was the refutation of the seventh accusation, concerning Cullen. It is quoted from at some length here because it contains the essence of the nationalist and patriotic case made against Cullen in the previous ten years:

With the great bulk of the Catholics of Ireland, and nearly all the Catholic bishops, priests, and people of England, I regard Dr. Cullen as the concurrent and efficacious cause of the spoliation of the Pontifical States, and of that complete ruin that has for the last few years overtaken my unhappy country, and is now at its climax. The memorial presented to your Holiness by that great and good man, Frederick Lucas, gives the history of the origin of these melancholy events. He sank of a broken heart in his contest with Dr. Cullen—which is, in reality, mine to-day. The history is briefly told; it is simply this: —that Dr. Cullen "actively supported" the treason (for such it is universally called) of those faithless and perjured members who, in face of their solemn promises, and even their public abjuration of God and their plighted agreement with the bishops of Ireland, abandoned the poor people, sacrificed their rights and vital interests, and sold themselves for a few wretched places and offices, or some contemptible egotistical patronage to that English faction which boasts at its loudest pitch that it has secured the robbery of your Holiness, sapped the foundation of the patrimony of St. Peter, and thus brought about the "unity" of Italy. Everyone knows that, had the "independent Irish members" remained faithful to their engagements, they had it in their power to dictate terms to any government of England—the power to keep the Whig government from robbing your Holiness, devastating Italy, and depopulating Ireland. This power, which the poor people conferred on them at immense sacrifices, they betrayed for their own selfish ends; and Dr. Cullen put his seal to the act of treason.

In the next one hundred years this rendition of the great betrayal of the independent Irish party in the 1850s would become the pure milk of nationalist rhetoric. It was in the 1860s, however, that this nationalist myth was given its clerical dimension, and no one did more than Lavelle to integrate that dimension into the ongoing myth. Just as there had been patriots, such as Lucas and Duffy, who had been willing to make the supreme sacrifice either in martyrdom or in exile for the good cause, so there had been and still were ecclesiastics who would uphold that cause in the face of all subversion. And there had been none more persevering, loyal, or true in the good cause than the great patriarch of the West, the Lion of the fold of Judah, the ever patriotic archbishop of Tuam, who, though he was apparently being worsted in the ongoing struggle for power in the Irish Church by Cullen, still retained the loyalty and affection of the Irish people and priests both at home and abroad.

"But let me frankly speak out," Lavelle then assured the pope; "the fact is, Dr. Cullen wants to rule the Church of Ireland. There must be no voice, no policy there but his, and this in the face of bishops who have borne the weight of the day and the heat"—an allusion to Mac-Hale and his few supporters among the bishops—"who have been fighting Ireland's unequal battle during forty years of pastoral stewardship, with fidelity, dignity, genius, patriotism, honour, and perseverance, and on whose words millions and millions of Irishmen throughout the world hang with breathless attention and respect. Such are the men whom Dr. Cullen would now supplant and displace, and that by a policy which finds favour only with the selfish and corrupt few, but which in the end must yield to the irresistable power of truth, honour, patriotism, and numbers." "I speak these things," he further assured the pope, "to your Holiness in all candour. They may be thought bold, but a kind father would rather know the thoughts of his son, though they might not be his own, than be misled as to that son's disposition and character. To sum up, then, since Dr. Cullen took to himself the helm of Irish politics and the Irish Church, both the Church and the nation have been drifting to an unseen abyss."

"I have thus, with all candour," Lavelle then confessed, "revealed myself to your Holiness. I well know, and all Ireland does, how much of your Holiness's confidence Dr. Cullen *is said* to enjoy; and, consequently, I have not concealed from myself the risk of speaking with the liberty I have done. But I felt called upon to state the truth. I looked upon it as a sacred obligation to put your Holiness in possession of the facts." "Hitherto," he explained, "Dr. Cullen has shown your Holiness only his side of the picture. You have now mine and that of the Irish people. Dr. Cullen's pastoral zeal I have not questioned, but I consider his political zeal not entirely according to knowledge. One thing at least is certain; that since he began to put his programme in force things have gone from bad to worse in our unhappy country. Therefore, while I regret every offensive line I ever wrote against him, I cannot alter my opinion of his suicidal and destructive policy." "All my indiscretions," Lavelle then complained in concluding, "have been magnified and exaggerated: My services have been studiously concealed. For having had the misfortune of offending Dr. Cullen, I have suffered enough; for having saved hundreds of 'little children,' and completely averted and driven back the proselytizer, I have yet to receive the smallest human reward. Thus, in my case, retributive justice is all on one side." "Now, therefore," he finally concluded, "while for my faults I ask the forgiveness of your Holiness, I ask for my toils and services some recognition, and for my sufferings some recompense and consolation."

What indeed is to be said about this incredible performance by Lavelle, in which he had the audacity, at the end of a sustained and vicious denunciation of the pope's apostolic delegate, to ask the pope for a reward for his services—and this, no less, in the public press? When Cullen read the memorial he could hardly believe his eyes. "It is a most wicked document," he informed Kirby on March 8, "in which he renews all his former outrages and endeavors to defend himself. It would be well to inquire whether he ever presented the memorial to the Pope, or whether he put the Pope's name before it to excite attention" (K). "I send it today," he noted in conclusion, "to Cardinal Barnabò. Get it to [*sic*] read it."[12] When he wrote Kirby again the fol-

---

12. S.R.C., vol. 35, fols. 53–54, Cullen to Barnabò, March 8, 1864.

lowing week, Cullen still could hardly bring himself to believe that the document was authentic. "I suspect strongly," he reported on March 13, "that the memorial was an afterthought prepared at home, though it bears the date of Rome. This may have been done as the people willingly read anything having the Pope's name attached to it, and written in Rome" (K). "However," he noted, "this is only a conjecture, but you can find out the truth in Rome."

The truth, however, was even more bitter, for the memorial had indeed been written in Rome. "Yours of the 8th has just arrived," Kirby informed Cullen on March 16; "I enquired at once of Card^l. Barnabò how the case stood about F. Lavelle's memorial to the Pope. The Card^l. said that he (Lavelle) presented no memorial to the Pope, nor to himself. But whilst he was on his retreat he drew up a document in French, directed to the Pope and purporting to be his memorial to him and explanations on his case. But after his signing his retractation, he gave it up to Father Vincent the Passionist, and the latter gave it simply to Card^l. Barnabò on the 6th of Feb^o. who laid it by in oblivion, as he was supposed to have retracted all by his act of submission" (C). "The Card^l. gave me permission," he reported further, "to read the original which I have brought here from Sig. Rinaldini, and Dr. Moran is now collating it with his published memorial in the Patriot. It is clear from the original in French that he never intended it for the Pope; in the original there is not a word of the short memorial, his 'Preface,' which precedes the long one. There is no such thing at all in the original. The letter is also without date; it says merely January—64." "Dr. Moran," he assured Cullen, "will send you the changes which occur in it as also in the published retraction, in which amongst others, he makes his promise of not writing in the newspapers conditional, i.e., unless with the approbation of his ordinary, which condition is not of course in the original."

To all appearances, therefore, it certainly seemed that Lavelle had scored a great triumph and, what was worse, that it was secured through the ineptness of the Roman authorities, which was patent for all to see. The bishop of Kerry, David Moriarty, asked Kirby on March 11, "Have you seen Father Lavelle's last Manifesto in the Tuam Herald?" (K). "It is a most scandalous thing," he then declared, "to allow any Bishop to be publicly abused in the manner in which he abuses Dr. Cullen. His last publication exceeds all the past. He gives it as the memorandum presented by him to the Holy See. You should get a copy of the paper and put it into the hands of the Cardinal Prefect." When the bishop of Elphin had occasion to write Kirby three days later about a troublesome priest of his own, he was also scandalized. "I suppose," Gillooly noted at the end of a long letter on March 14, "you are already aware of the late proceeding, of Father Lavelle. You dealt too softly with him in Rome. I foretold to Dr. Cullen that he would act precisely as he has done, on his return if he were not obliged, *previous* to the removal of censures to make a satisfactory *amende* and retraction *in this country*. There is an obstinate will [i.e., MacHale] sustaining him—and the program of both appears to be—to appeal to the blind prejudice and passions of the people through the Democratic Press against their opponents in Dublin and Rome" (K). "We are in truth," he concluded darkly, "living in evil days—and though beset with dangers from without, it is still true that our greatest dangers are within our own body. Pray for us dear Dr. Kirby—and get as many good souls as you can to join you."

Cullen was, of course, more acutely embarrassed by the whole proceedings than any one else. "I send you a letter," he informed Kirby on March 15, "from Dr. Butler [bishop of Limerick] just to show you what impression Father Lavelle's letter had made, of course I won't take any notice of him either directly or indirectly" (K). "As to publishing the Cardinal's letter to me regarding him," Cullen added, referring to Barnabò's letter of February 3, in which he had enclosed Lavelle's retraction, "it would do more harm than good. Anyone reading the Cardinal's letter would say that he was very easily imposed on when he speaks of the ottime disposizione del Abt. Lavelle [excellent inclinations of Father Lavelle], or that he was afraid of getting into a dispute with him and let him off very quietly conferring some few favours on him to make him behave like a good child." "I have sent you," he then explained, "a pastoral on St. Patrick in which I showed the benevolent disposition of the Fenians, it is a sad thing that such vagabonds should get any encouragement."

In his pastoral for St. Patrick's Day, which was dated March 7, Cullen once again gave a real indication of the kind of stuff of which he was made and showed that he was not about to be intimidated by the charges made against him in the press by Lavelle or his friends, for he finally took the grim step of denouncing the Fenian Brotherhood by name.[13] "I shall now merely add one word of caution against secret societies, and the so-called Fenians or Brothers of St. Patrick," Cullen warned in winding up his pastoral.

> Such societies are only calculated to sow discord in the country, and to weaken it, turning away the people's minds from every useful undertaking, and directing them to schemes of armed re-

13. Patrick Francis Moran, ed., *The Pastoral Letters and Other Writings of Cardinal Cullen* (Dublin, 1882), 2:248–51.

sistance and violence, and to utopian projects, which never can be realised. The promoters of such societies, and those who recommend them in the public press, are false friends, agents of evil, who come among you in sheep's clothing, under the pretense of being children of St. Patrick. They promise to render their dupes happy and independent; but far from being able to realise such promises, they would implicate those who listen to them in misery and difficulties in this world, and perhaps leave them without faith or religion, or any hope of happiness in the world to come. It is a folly to expect good results from secret conspiracies and from deeds of darkness.

"For all these reasons," Cullen then explained, "I exhort, in the most urgent terms, and with true paternal solicitude for their welfare, the faithful of this diocese to avoid all connection with the aforesaid societies and brotherhoods and not to frequent their meetings or to read their newspapers; and I call on those who have had the misfortune to join them, to abandon them immediately, to make reparation to those whom they may have scandalized or led astray by their example, to do penance for the past, and be reconciled to the Church of God."

Cullen also forwarded a copy of his pastoral to his uncle, Father James Maher, parish priest of Carlow-Graigue, for his opinion. "The extracts from the rules of the Fenians, and the London Liberator," Maher pointed out candidly in reply on March 18, "published in the appendix to the pastoral for St. Patrick's day, ought to be a sufficient warning to all the young folk of Ireland to keep clear of those societies. But Father Lavelle and the 'Irish People' and other journals that support his views are much more read now than episcopal warnings" (K). "These firebrands," he then warned, "will corrupt our poor young people, and do more harm than all the proselytyzing societies in Ireland." "It appears," Maher further noted, "that Lavelle may do as he likes. The rein is thrown loose upon his neck, to gallop on fast as he pleases to the Devil. The character of Rome in this transaction is somewhat lowered in public estimation. When the Roman authorities took the case in their hands, they ought for their own sake bring it to a more respectable termination. They know what a bad priest can do in Italy: and they ought to check the growth of such an evil amongst our poor docile religious people." "I hope our Bishops," he concluded interestingly, "will soon meet to take counsel together as to the best means of guarding against impending evils."

The news of the crisis created by Lavelle's retraction and memorial to the pope did not reach Rome until the middle of March. By that time, however, Cullen had already persuaded the authorities that the developing political situation in Ireland might now involve Rome in more serious action than even the effective disciplining of the ubiquitous Father Lavelle. When the Brotherhood of St. Patrick had been publicly condemned by the Irish bishops at their meeting the previous August, Cullen, in his report on the meeting to Barnabò, had explained that he did not believe the case required any further action from Rome. By early January 1864 Cullen had become much more alarmed, especially after the Fenians launched their own newspaper, the *Irish People*, in Dublin in late October 1863. In early February, therefore, Cullen wrote to Barnabò to alert him to the developing and potentially more menacing situation. "I have written to your Eminence many times," he explained on February 5,

> about the Brothers of St. Patrick, and the evil that they do. In dealing with their brotherhood, I find that there are two societies, one which calls itself the Brotherhood of St. Patrick and the other the Fenian Brothers or Fenians.
>
> This latter brotherhood is very extensive in the United States. Their rules state that the object of the brotherhood is to overthrow the English government in Ireland and to establish a republic. These rules were published in the newspapers a few months ago, and I sent copies of them to Rome. In America they can form such associations without risk, and thus, as they say, they do not have any oath. Here in Ireland those who sought to overthrow our government would be liable to be hanged, and thus they seek to save themselves by swearing to be faithful to their promises. Many of these Fenian Brothers have come to me to be absolved, and I have found in every case that they have sworn loyalty to the Irish republic, and true obedience to the officials of the same. The brothers of St. Patrick are united with the Fenians, and they meet together, but the brothers of St. Patrick claim to act legally, and assert that they do not take oaths. Many of them, however, have assured me that they swear and I believe it is true. But however that may be, the members of the two brotherhoods are united among themselves, and thus they are responsible for each other's acts. I mention these things because I know that Father Lavelle always sought to make believe that the brothers of St. Patrick do not form a secret society. Here it appears that the Freemasons do all publicly. But yet they are

regarded as subject to the censures fulminated against secret societies.[14]

"Perhaps it will not be out of place," Cullen further explained, "to observe that the brothers of St. Patrick or the Fenians have founded within the last few months a newspaper in Dublin."

> The spirit of that paper is very bad: it seeks to discredit the Holy See, and puts forth the assertion that the Popes have always encouraged and supported the English in persecuting Ireland. As to the clergy their writers then say that being provided with houses, churches, schools and seminaries, they now believe they can abandon the people, and throw them into the hands of the government. This newspaper of which I am speaking and which is called the *Irish People*, is maintained by contributions from the Fenian Brothers of America. Since it has hardly been in existence four months, it has not yet had time to do much harm, but I fear that little by little it will produce bad results. There are two or three other newspapers in Dublin of the same color, all of recent origin, and all Mazzinian and Garibaldean in their politics.

By the time Barnabò received this letter from Cullen, the Propaganda authorities were already in the last stages of preparing the *ristretto con sommario*, or *ponenza*, that would consider the action taken by the Irish bishops at their meeting the previous August and that would then be submitted to the cardinals of Propaganda at their general *congregazione*, or meeting, in March, for their recommendations to the pope.[15] Indeed, Cullen's letter of February 5 was the last document included in the *sommario* before the *ponenza* was set up in type. The questions, or *dubbi*, proposed to the cardinals in the *ponenza* were three.[16] They had to decide, first of all, whether laymen should be given a voice in the governing of the Catholic University; secondly, whether something more should be done to arrest the damage being done Ireland by the brothers of St. Patrick; and thirdly, whether some action should be taken to require Father Vaughan, the Killaloe priest, to withdraw from that society. The conduct of Father Lavelle, of course, was not referred to the cardinals, because the pope had taken the case into his own hands. When the cardinals of Propaganda did finally meet on March 30, they had to postpone the Irish business on their agenda to their next meeting because of the pressure

14. A, vol. 228, fols. 109–10.
15. Ibid., fols. 96–110.
16. Ibid., fol. 99.

of other business.[17] They did not meet again until May 30, and by that time the situation both in Rome and in Ireland had been transformed.

In the meantime, Cullen continued to urge the suspension of Lavelle on the Roman authorities as the only solution to the checking of that priest's political activities. Cullen reported to Moran on April 12, "I wrote my opinion two or three times to the Prop. about F. Lavelle. They ought not to correspond with him at all. The only plan w^d be to give an order to Dr. McHale to suspend him, and to leave him suspended until relieved by Rome" (C). "Dr. McHale is not a man," he added, mistaking his man completely, "to resist when he is ordered to do a thing—though he talks very loudly until the moment arrives. According to all appearances Lavelle has been encouraged by him in his misdeeds. It would be a good penance on him now to make him punish him (Lavelle) for what he had been encouraged to do." "If he be suspended," he then further assured Moran, "he will lose all his influence. I do not think that he has any party to support him. The Fenians support him merely to be able to say that they have ecclesiastics at their side. Their writings and their articles in newspapers show the spirit that animates them. Their articles against Rome have been most violent. This is so much the better. Wolves in their own clothing will do less harm, than if they came in sheeps' clothing." "I have not seen the Connaught Patriot of last Saturday," he finally noted, "but that of Saturday in Easter week had a fierce attack upon me, and wound up by saying that if I had any feeling I ought to resign and leave the country."

By the time this letter had reached Rome, the pope, who was obviously very upset about what Lavelle had done on his return to Ireland, had already decided what action he would take. He wrote MacHale again on April 18 and ordered him for the third time in less than seven months to suspend Lavelle.[18] In his letter the pope also specifically complained that Lavelle had published a garbled and mutilated version of the retraction he had made in Rome; that Lavelle had circulated in the newspapers a memorial that supposedly had been presented to him but that he had never received; and that Lavelle continued to encourage societies that had been condemned by the Irish bishops. The pope also reserved to himself the right to restore Lavelle. In the meantime, however, the incredible Father Lavelle had actually succeeded in further complicating matters by adding a theo-

17. Ibid.
18. S.R.C., vol. 35, fols. 34–35. See also A, vol. 228, fols. 115–16, "Appendice alla Ponenza di Marzo 1864 sull'adunanza tenuta dai Vescovi Irlandesi a Dublino nel mese di Agosto 1863, 30 Maggio 1864."

logical dimension to the disciplinary one. In writing to Kirby on April 15 to explain that he had just sent a very lengthy report on the Fenians to Barnabò, Cullen pointed out that he had also enclosed a copy of the *Connaught Patriot*, which contained a long letter from Lavelle on secret societies (K). "He endeavours to show," Cullen reported, "that the Fenians do not come under the Bull of Leo XII.[19] To incur the censure the society must be secret, secondly, bound by oath, third[ly,] intent on destroying Church and state. Now he says the Fenians are not hostile to the Church, but they are only anxious to overthrow a most wicked tyranny. If the *et* [i.e., Church *and* state] in Leo XII's Bull be taken conjunctively, it would appear there is no censure against societies who endeavour to subvert the Church but respect the throne. Does not that appear absurd?" "Get us some decision on this point," he demanded finally. "However the Fenians appear to incur the censure for by fomenting revolution, they injure and assail both Church and state."

In his long letter to Barnabò that same day, April 15, Cullen had in effect asked for a formal decision from Propaganda about whether the Fenians incurred ecclesiastical censure as a secret society.[20] "I took the liberty," he explained to Barnabò, "of writing a letter a few days ago about the Fenian Brotherhood, which has been established in the last few years in Ireland, begging your Eminence to give us some instructions about the way in which that brotherhood ought to be dealt with. In order to facilitate the examination of this question, I have made a compendium of their rules which were published about Christmas of last year."[21] In reviewing the rules of the Fenians, which had been published in the United States, Cullen went over much the same ground as in his previous letter to Barnabò, written February 5: that the Fenians wanted to overthrow the English government, that they were sworn to that end, and that they were hostile to the American bishops who opposed them. He further argued that the objects of the Fenians in Ireland and America were identical and that the rules published in the United States, where there was no danger of prosecution, were a correct measure of Fenian sentiments in Ireland.

19. Quoted in Corish, pp. 16–17. Corish goes on: "At this stage it is necessary to summarize, however briefly, the ecclesiastical legislation against unlawful political organizations. It rests on four papal bulls, *In eminenti* of Clement XII (28 April 1738), *Providas* of Benedict XIV (18 May 1751), *Ecclesiam* of Pius VII (13 September 1821), and summing up the three preceding, *Quo graviora* of Leo XII (13 March 1825). *In eminenti* had condemned Freemasonry, and imposed on its adherents an excommunication reserved to the Holy See: the later pronouncements had extended this condemnation and censure to 'similar occult societies.'"

20. S.R.C., vol. 34, fols. 1158–61.

21. See ibid., fol. 1165, for the rules translated into Italian.

Cullen also enclosed an original letter from Lavelle to a publisher in Britain, which proposed to have ten thousand copies of his memorial to the pope printed.[22] The letter, Cullen pointed out, proved not only just how perverse Lavelle really was but also that he was hardly as poor as he claimed, because he was prepared to pay the publisher cash down for the ten thousand copies. Cullen then proceeded to cite MacHale for writing a letter to the promoters of a Fenian fair in Chicago (which had been condemned by the bishop there) and enclosing three autographs for auction at the fair. Cullen professed to be surprised not only that MacHale would put himself in opposition to another bishop but that he would go so far as to support openly a society that was avowedly dedicated to the overthrow of the English government. "However that may be," Cullen added, "it is certain that these acts of Monsignor McHale and the letters that he has written to the head centre of the Brotherhood give occasion to our Fenians to pretend that they have the sanction and the authority of a great and learned Prelate on their side, while the Bishops who condemn them are mere slaves of the government, or fanatical and ignorant men."

After then citing Lavelle for his letter in the *Connaught Patriot* maintaining that the Fenians did not fall under the censure described in the bull of Leo XII, Cullen attempted finally to explain to the cardinal why it was so difficult to convince the Irish people that the Fenians deserved the censures of the Church. "I cannot conclude without saying," he pointed out,

that it is difficult to make the people understand that it is reasonable on the part of the Bishops to condemn secret societies, while our government publicly patronizes them and gives the greatest honors to their supporters and defenders. The Freemasons here are completely sanctioned, and the greatest gentlemen, and the employees of the government are enrolled. Mazzini is patronized in London and the English people went mad about Garibaldi, rendering him honors they would not give to the greatest general, or to an emperor. Lord Palmerston, the prime minister, and his colleagues, Lord Derby, head of the Conservative party and his followers, from whom the Catholics of England expect every good, compete among themselves to see who will appear more friendly to the unfortunate Filebuster who has done so much harm to the world. Meanwhile, the newspapers speak of him as if he were some kind of divinity, or another redeemer of

22. Ibid., fol. 1163, Lavelle to Fowler, March 22, 1864.

the world. It will be difficult to find in history an example of such folly as England has exhibited on this occasion.

Now matters being so, it is not surprising that the poor Catholics begin to think that secret societies are not so very bad, and that if their promoters in Italy and in other countries are deserving of such triumphs, it cannot be a reprehensible thing to want to introduce them in Ireland. It is not easy to reply to those who speak in this way, but yet for the good of religion it is necessary to raise one's voice against secret societies, and to take the regrettable position of guarding [against] the claims of those who promote those societies, and promote through them the hatred of religion.

Cullen noted finally in conclusion, "I sent under separate cover the Tuam newspaper, which contains the letter of Lavelle on secret societies in order that your Eminence has to hand all the documents concerning this affair."

The case made by Cullen against the Fenians in his letters to Rome and in his recent pastoral, which appeared so obvious to him, was apparently somewhat less conclusive to a considerable number of Irish ecclesiastics, high and low. "The differences of opinion among ecclesiastics here," David Moriarty, the bishop of Kerry, informed Kirby on May 1, "as to the meaning of the papal bulls on the subject is causing much mischief. Dr. Cullen and others declare that Fenians and members of the Society of St. Patrick incur censures ipso facto. Others and even Bishops say no, because these Societies though against the State are not against the Church, and the bulls require that the Society shd be not only secret but opposed to Church and State" (K). "Since the beginning of the Phoenix Society," Moriarty explained, referring to a precursor of the Fenian society in West Cork, "I have made the joining of any Secret Society bound by oath a reserved case and I commanded the priests not to give absolution until the Society should be renounced in foro externo, in scriptis, et coram testibus [in public, in writing, and in the presence of witnesses]. I have found this plan very effective." "My dear friend," Moriarty further observed, and with considerable justice, "some of us by our abuse of Govt, drive the people into disaffection and the spirit of rebellion. We cannot blame them if they are more logical than canonical in their conclusions." "I have brought upon myself," he noted in conclusion, "much obloquy by taking another path. Time will tell."

When the cardinals of Propaganda did eventually meet on May 30, they decided to submit the question whether the Fenians incurred censure as a secret society to the Holy Office, or Inquisition, which was the appropriate congregation in such matters.[23] In reply, the Holy Office referred Propaganda to a decision it had made on August 5, 1846, which was confirmed by Pius IX and which declared that all societies that conspired against either Church or state, whether secret or not, were censured by the Church. On June 7, 1864, Propaganda informed Cullen of the Holy Office's decision, explaining also that if he had any difficulty applying this ruling, he should consult the Holy See again and supply the necessary details.[24] This was, in truth, not only a disastrous decision for Cullen personally but also one with very serious implications for the Irish Church. He had asked Propaganda whether the Fenians fell under the censure of the Church and had been told instead only what kinds of societies fell under such ecclesiastical censure. Cullen, who was apparently the only Irish bishop who had formally condemned the Fenians by name, was therefore put in a very awkward situation. Whatever was done about the Fenians in a uniform way, moreover, was left by Propaganda to the Irish bishops as a body. Given the outright resistance that would be offered by such bishops as MacHale and Derry, as well as the passive resistance of those such as Keane and O'Hea, the likelihood of the bishops' collectively arriving at a public condemnation of the Brotherhood was very dim indeed.

But, it may well be asked, why did Rome equivocate about condemning the Fenians? First of all, Rome was traditionally very reluctant to proceed to specific censures, especially by name. The mode preferred was the implicit rather than the explicit. Secondly, the cardinals of both Propaganda and the Holy Office could not have been unaware that Cullen's brief involved the condemnation of the Irish Fenians on American evidence. Although the cardinals might not have been very upset about the difficulties posed by Anglo-Saxon views on guilt by association, they certainly would have been concerned by another aspect of the case; namely, not only were they aware of the very real differences of opinion among the Irish bishops, but, even more important in this situation, they were aware that the divisions among the American bishops about the expediency of condemning the Fenians were, if anything, even more serious. Finally,

23. A, vol. 228, fols. 114–15. The question of Father Jeremiah Vaughan was not included because he had submitted to the bishops' decision with regard to the Brothers of St. Patrick. See S.R.C., vol. 35, fol. 26, for a memorandum on the subject from Patrick F. Moran to Rinaldini, April 30, 1864.

24. A, vol. 228, fol. 437, "Appendice alla Ponenza di Febbraio 1864 sopra un provvedimento da prendersi pel bene della religione nella Provincia Orientale di Scozia." See also Corish, p. 20.

Rome had been attempting in recent years to strengthen the role of the bishops as a body in the governing of the Irish Church, and the Fenian crisis must have seemed an ideal opportunity for the authorities to encourage the bishops to defend their own authority as a body. Whatever may be said about the prudence, if not the wisdom, of Rome's policy in dealing with the Fenian crisis, it was certainly hard on Cullen, who had to endure the continued invective and calumny of the Fenian press in general and Father Lavelle in particular.

In the meantime, MacHale gave no indication that he had received the pope's letter, for he neither suspended Lavelle nor wrote the pope acknowledging its receipt. "Father Lavelle," Cullen reported to Kirby on May 13, some three weeks after MacHale should have had the pope's letter, "has been in Dublin three days past and is probably here still. He is not suspended as yet[;] at least it would appear so" (K). "The whole affair looks like a comedy," he complained.

> Dr. MacEvilly writes to me that Dr. McHale sent a note to the curate of Partry to be presented to Lavelle, but when the note arrived Father Lavelle had disappeared. It is supposed that private notice was sent to the delinquent to decamp before he could be suspended. At least this is the version Dr. MacEvilly gives. Dr. McH. will bring trouble on himself by employing such stratagems. Of course if he wished to suspend Lavelle he could have called him to himself without letting him know the purport of the Pope's letter. It is now said that Lavelle will now go to America without being suspended. I sent copies of the Pope's letter about him to Canada and the U. States.

"It is better," Cullen cautioned Kirby in conclusion, "not to give any written report in this matter [to Propaganda], until we know things more accurately."

When MacHale did not acknowledge receipt of the pope's letter, Cullen was authorized to forward him a copy of it. He reported to Kirby on May 24, "I sent a copy of the Pope's letter to Dr. McH. about F. Lavelle, which is beautiful and forcible. Since it reached, Lavelle published a long letter stating that he could call God to witness that he did not know whether he was suspended or not, and complaining that proceedings had been taken against him, over his Bishop's head. These are his words" (K). "Since the publication of that letter he has gone to Glasgow," Cullen explained,

> and applied to Dr. Murdoch [vicar apostolic of the western district of Scotland] for permission to lecture. Dr. Murdoch at first replied that he could not say yes or no, as Lavelle had done much

mischief on his former visits in Glasgow—but after having heard
of the Pope's letter he addressed a letter to his clergy telling them
to caution their flock against going to listen to a priest who
had acted perfidiously towards the Pope, and whose conduct was
such that His Holiness had ordered Dr. McHale to suspend
him.[25] Lavelle had published an answer to the Bishop which I
have not seen, but those who have read it say that it is full of
quibbling, and that he endeavours to make people believe that
there is no letter about him from the Pope.[26] If I can get the letter
I will send it.

"Since I wrote the above," Cullen then explained at the end of his
letter, "I have got a no. of the Glasgow Free Press containing Lavelle's
letter, and some of Keane's[27] bright writing—I send it to you by this
post. Show it to the Propaganda. You will see that Lavelle calls into
doubt the existence of the Pope's letter, and broadly asserts that he is
not suspended. It is all a piece of trickery. Of course, Dr. McH. has a
finger in it." "I sent the Pope's letter," he concluded, "to Dr. Murdoch,
in order that he might know how to receive Lavelle." In thanking
Cullen several days later, on May 26, for forwarding him the pope's
letter, Murdoch reported, "Father Lavelle is still here, and doing much
mischief; holding himself up as a calumniated and persecuted priest,
and persecuted because of his patriotism" (K). He went on:

> The Nationalist party have of course taken him by the hand, and
> I believe he is reaping a pretty good harvest in the money way. I
> do not grudge him the money, but I must lament the bad feeling
> he is stirring up propagating amongst the people. I regret to in-
> form your Grace, that a certain number of my priests from Ire-
> land, are abettors of the irreligious Free Press. The editor of that
> paper, lately sent a long indictment against me to Rome, and it
> was backed by a memorial signed by 22 out of my 96 priests. I
> have thus been put on my defense at Propaganda. By private ac-
> counts—as yet I have nothing official—I understand the editor
> and his clerical friends have been out and out condemned by the
> Holy See.

25. S.R.C., vol. 34, fol. 1193. See memorandum, Moran to Rinaldini, June 2, 1864.
See also ibid., fol. 1194, *Glasgow Free Press*, May 21, 1864, quoting Murdoch's letter,
dated May 16, 1864, reprinted from *Glasgow Herald*.

26. See ibid., fol. 1194, for Lavelle's letter, dated May 18, 1864, to the editor of the
Glasgow Herald.

27. The reference is to Augustus Keane, the editor of the *Glasgow Free Press*, who
was a former student of the Propaganda.

Three weeks later Cullen could only report helplessly to Kirby that Lavelle was continuing his career of mischief in Scotland by collecting money and creating schisms. "Dr. McHale," Cullen noted on June 17, "never suspended him. Perhaps he thinks he could not suspend once he got out of his diocese. But as we [sic] was ordered to act auctoritate apostolica [on apostolic authority], that reason does not appear valid" (K). By this time, however, MacHale had also received from Barnabò a copy of the Propaganda rescript of June 7, in which the recent ruling of the Holy Office regarding secret societies was included.[28] That very astute and pugnacious man must have certainly realized that the Fenians had been given a new ecclesiastical lease on life and that Rome was most reluctant to proceed to a specific condemnation. This reasoning explains why, during the next six months, MacHale was to push his advantage with regard to both the Brotherhood and Lavelle with every resource at his command.

Indeed, MacHale's audacity was breathtaking. The bishop of Galway had informed Cullen on June 14,

The refusal to carry out the Pope's mandate in regard to Father Lavelle amazes everyone here. I heard yesterday from a Tuam priest who called to see me, that even after his curate had received the Archbishop's suspension to be served on Father Lavelle, he (L.) returned to the parish and said Mass in the mountainous district of Partry, and wrote to the curate he would call to see him on Sunday after Mass, which he took care not to do. The truth is although "he never heard of the document until he saw it with Dr. Murdoch," he was fully aware of the fact of his curate having it, and he thus put him off his guard by saying he would call to see him. [K]

"I am told," MacEvilly further confided, "Dr. MacHale in his tour round the diocese lately said not a word of L. except at Claremorris, and then he very freely gave utterances to his ideas on the propriety of all the clergy rallying round Lavelle, and it is said to be in contemplation to get up a collection for him among the priests." "This some of them," he assured Cullen, "will never consent to do, as they regard it as a downright resistance to the H. See, but others will, who will not see the bearing of the affair, and the matter if carried out at all will be managed so as not to lead to any discussion among the clergy. But

28. Ibid., fol. 1208, MacHale to Barnabò, June 19, 1864, acknowledging receipt of rescript.

matters are coming to a nice pass, when the direct mandate of Christ's Vicar is disobeyed publicly with impunity."

Some ten days later, when a considerable number of the bishops met at the usual biannual meeting of the board that governed Maynooth College, MacHale was apparently still full of confidence and in the best of spirits. "Dr. McHale," Cullen reported to Kirby on June 28, "appeared quite cheerful at the Maynooth Board. He never referred to Lavelle, nor did anyone speak of him" (C). "The Pope's letter to his Grace," Cullen added, "has been published in America, but the newspapers here are so much afraid of Lavelle, that they w^d not venture to insert it. He has established quite a despotic power over the press. I believe he is collecting a good deal of money in Scotland and England. What is worse, he will do much mischief among the poor Irish. However, I think his career will not be long. The people will not support him, when it is known that he is suspended, and almost every one knows that at present." "When I had written the preceeding page," Cullen then explained, "I received a Scotch newspaper containing a letter of F. Lavelle which I enclose. I think it exceeds everything he had previously written in cool impudence. He says he knows nothing about the Pope's letter to Dr. McH., yet he is able to say that it was not a rescript. The poor fellow is also so innocent that he does not know why anyone should find fault with him." After he had sent off this letter to Kirby, Cullen was still apparently incensed; he finally decided to publish the pope's letter of April 18 to MacHale, ordering him to suspend Lavelle. He therefore forwarded it to the *Catholic Telegraph*, where it appeared on July 2.[29]

For the greater part of July MacHale vacationed in France in company with his nephew, Thomas MacHale, professor of theology at the Irish College in Paris, while Lavelle over the same period continued to lecture in Scotland and England. "I send you," Cullen reported to Kirby on July 19, "a paper containing an account of the meeting held last night of the brothers of St. Patrick. A letter from Lavelle was read in which he says he is not suspended. He speaks against Rome in a tone of bitterness" (K). "The meeting consisted," he noted, "of not more very probably than a dozen of poor people—they are generally tradesmen. They are not making any progress in Dublin—Dr. Leahy however tells me that they are very numerous in Tipperary. Their papers wrote against the collection for the Pope, but the result was the collection is much larger this year than usual. I think it will be nearly £2,000, at all events it will be £1,600[,] a large sum in these days of distress." "Many," he then assured Kirby, "are beginning to say what is

29. Corish, p. 19. See C, Kirby to Cullen, April 23, 1864, for pope's authorization.

true that it is a great scandal that the Archbishop does not carry out the Pope's instructions. Cui bono Pontifex [a Pope for whose advantage?] if his orders may be disobeyed."

The report about a memorial to the pope on behalf of Lavelle from the Tuam clergy began to gain greater currency. "I have received a letter," Cullen informed Kirby on July 28, "from Dr. MacEvilly—a document, he says, has been sent round to the priests of Tuam for their signature, addressed to the Pope. The first part is a plea for Father Lavelle, and petitions His Holiness to restore him—the second is an invective contro quel birbone l'arc⁰ di Dublino [against that rascal the archbishop of Dublin], the third a eulogy of the Patriarch of the West the lion of Judah. Of course the priests must sign it. It will be curious to see how they defend Lavelle" (K).

Some ten days later Cullen informed Kirby that Lavelle had moved on to England. "Father Lavelle," he reported on August 6, "is working like a fallen spirit in England. He will do great mischief among the poor Irish. The whole of his lectures is directed against me—but he will damage the authority of all the Bishops and of the Pope. He preaches revolutionary doctrines openly" (K). "I think," Cullen charged, "Dr. McHale is afraid of him. His Grace has probably written many letters of encouragement or sympathy to him, and he knows that Father Lavelle would publish them all and inflict great disgrace on his name were Dr. McHale to move in the matter. I am sure his Grace feels Lavelle a thousand times more than I do." "For my part," he declared, "I do not resent his abuse, the only thing I regret is that he is doing mischief among the poor Irish, and weakening their faith. From some letters published under Lavelle's name in America, it would appear that he intends crossing the Atlantic. He will scarcely return to Ireland lest he should put Dr. McHale under the necessity of suspending him. It is fortunate that the Prop. has written to the Bishops in America."

Meanwhile, at the pope's express command, Barnabò had written MacHale on July 15 enjoining him to act on the pope's instructions in his letter of April 18 and to suspend Lavelle immediately. MacHale replied on July 25 that he would write to the pope personally about the matter, and he did so that same day.[30] In his letter to the pope, MacHale stated that he was at that moment about to write Lavelle to inform him that he was suspended by the express order of His Holiness from all his functions as a priest.[31] Having thus complied with his orders, MacHale further explained to the pope that he thought it

30. S.R.C., vol. 34, fol. 1260.
31. Ibid., fol. 1270.

was his duty to mention that he did not nor could he foresee what the consequences of such a proceeding would be. He then complained that the pope's letter of April 18 to him was not dispatched immediately from Rome and therefore was considerably delayed. Indeed, what was even more extraordinary was that the contents of the letter were common knowledge in Dublin many days before he received it, and shortly after, the letter was actually published in Latin in the American and English newspapers. Finally, to his extreme mortification, it was even published in his own cathedral town of Tuam. He would like to know, therefore, by whose authority this was done. From all this, MacHale concluded, he was sure the pope could well appreciate the spirit that animated those who did such things. In reporting all this to Cullen on August 11, Kirby explained that Propaganda would reply to MacHale "in the name of H. H. & will acquaint him, that all that has been done in this matter has been done by the express orders of the Pope himself. And that more copies than one were sent from Rome of that letter, for the express purpose of *ensuring its publicity*, and this by orders of the Pope himself" (C).

On learning of this official communication to MacHale, Cullen was somewhat heartened. "I hope Dr. McHale," he explained to Kirby on August 21, "will after the last letter take some steps against Lavelle. It is too bad to oblige the Holy See to occupy itself so often with that unhappy priest. One word from Dr. McHale two years ago ordering Lavelle to stay in his parish and not to act as vice president of St. Patrick's Brotherhood would have saved himself and that priest from great evils" (K). "Where Lavelle is at present," Cullen then confessed, "I know not. He was lately in London. He has announced a lecture in Dublin on St. Laurence O'Toole. My opinion is that to avoid receiving any letter from Dr. McHale, he will start for America, and still continue to proclaim that he is free from every suspension." Cullen was mistaken, however, for by this time Lavelle had already returned to Ireland. MacHale had apparently not only notified Lavelle of his suspension but also advised him that it would be prudent for him to return to his parish of Partry and live there quietly until such time as the pope should lift his suspension.

Though Lavelle had, in effect, been removed from the scene, Mac-Hale decided that he would now himself begin to occupy center stage. He made his debut auspicious by giving Lavelle yet another public indication of his confidence in him in spite of suspension by the pope. While on holiday in France during July, MacHale had received £100 on behalf of Lavelle from Father P. E. Moriarty, pastor of the Augustinian Church of St. Mary's, Chestnut Hill, in Philadelphia. Moriarty had collected the money at a public lecture he had given on May 23 in Philadelphia, entitled "English Rule in Ireland." Moriarty had then forwarded the £100 with a copy of his lecture on June 15, and Mac-Hale acknowledged the receipt of both on July 15 from Fecamp in France. After his return to Ireland, MacHale decided to publish his correspondence with Moriarty and sent both his letter of thanks and Moriarty's lecture to the *Connaught Patriot* in late August. By doing so, of course, he not only gave his explicit and wholehearted endorsement to the sentiments expressed by Moriarty but also implicitly approved Lavelle's recently expressed views on the legitimacy of British rule in Ireland. He had written Moriarty:

> Seldom have the questionable rights of subjects to the enjoyment of good government been so clearly placed within the rule of strictest orthodoxy, as they have been in your recent interesting lecture. Although the topics which you addressed to your auditory were from several reasons long familiar to myself, yet I found in them a freshness of view and a charm of illustration which vigorous intellect alone can give, and which free and intellectual hearers are sure to appreciate.
>
> Yet it would seem as if the duties and rights of the governors and governed were to be regulated by the varying meridians of the countries they inhabit. For whilst our rulers extend to the subjects of all the other governments of the world the right to revolt beyond what religion or reason would sanction, so jealous are they of the superior excellence of their own government that to arraign it of tyranny or injustice would be deemed wickedness or infatuation. Such is the practical result by which the fine theories of the British Constitution are often illustrated.[32]

Moriarty's lecture, which ran to some eight thousand words, deserves attention because it was a classic example of that clerical-Nationalist rhetoric which was so important in the nourishing and sustaining of Irish identity in the middle years of the nineteenth century.[33] The theme was simple—seven hundred years of misery and woe in Ireland were the result of English tyranny. The solution was even simpler—that tyranny must be brought to an end, and the means included, if necessary, violent revolution. Moriarty argued that because all the authority and power of civil governments come from God, and because God communicated that authority and power di-

32. Ibid., fol. 1281.
33. S.R.C., vol. 35, fols. 165–72.

rectly to the people, they, as his instruments and ministers, bestow it on the ruler of their choice, who governs in their interest and for their good. When that ruler or government becomes tyrannical, however, the people have not only a right but a duty to rebel against it. When all friendly redress through ordinary legal means becomes impossible, "resistance is lawful, revolution is holy; aye sanctified by the will of God, who wishes a man to sustain and preserve, not merely for individual interests, but for the common welfare, those benefits for the endowment of which society was originally established."

After thus establishing the relationship between popular sovereignty and the right to revolution, Moriarty went on to argue that England had no right to rule in Ireland for two reasons: first, the Irish people had never given their consent to English rule in Ireland, and this was the real significance and meaning of Irish nationality; and second, the history of the English occupation of Ireland was a brutal record of oppression, exploitation, and extermination, which was summed up in a single word—tyranny. "England entered Ireland," Moriarty charged, "not at the call of the nation, but under the impulse of passions most revolting to humanity and religion. There she lived . . . not by the consent of even an oppressed people, but solely in pursuit of criminal purposes; and up to the present moment she has not even pretended to legalize crime, but unblushingly has avowed her whole end and purpose to be the torture and extermination of those whom she unceasingly named aliens in blood, language, and religion. Such has been, and is still, the relation between England and Ireland."

The rest of Moriarty's lecture was concerned with an illustration of England's perfidious role in Ireland. The litany included the destruction of a culture and a civilization, the attempt to pervert the faith, the ruin of manufactures, the restriction of exports, the enactment of the penal laws, and the expropriation of the soil by an alien aristocracy. "All that is native to Ireland," he maintained, "all that is social, loyal, and moral is essentially Celtic and Catholic. Has she ever surrendered her faith? No! is the response from all christendom. Neither has she surrendered her nationality, nor her legal right to the invader; for that undying Catholicity is to her social organization what the soul is to the human body." "Poets used to dream," Moriarty noted in concluding, giving an example of that "charm of illustration" mentioned by MacHale in his letter of thanks, "about a trident sceptre in the hands of Albion, but in fact, her sceptre is the 'Crowbar,' her crozier is the 'Soup Ladle.' Sign painters should not symbolize her enthroned on the sugarbarrel and bale of cotton. Her *see* is a meal-tub; her *throne* a coffin. Whatever *Charter*, Bill of Rights, or Act of Settlement, she may pretend for claims of legal government, its clauses are such as I have enumerated—printed with type of blood and tears." At the conclusion of the lecture the vast assemblage was reported to have "knelt down and prayed with the learned lecturer" for Ireland.[34]

"I enclose a line," an obviously scandalized Cullen explained to Kirby on Sunday, September 4, "from Dr. McHale which appeared in the Dublin papers of yesterday, it is addressed to Father Moriarty of Philadelphia, who delivered a lecture in favour of Lavelle. That lecture was most revolutionary, and Mazziniano almost—yet Dr. McHale praises it to the stars. He receives money for Lavelle and calls it 'a noble offering, the fruit of your zeal and eloquence, and of the piety and patriotism of the people of Philadelphia.' It is piety and patriotism in his Grace's language, to praise and support a priest, whom the Holy See has declared worthy of censure" (K). "I think the authority of the Holy See," Cullen then added, "was never so set at naught as it is in this case. Dr. McHale makes himself the agent to receive money for Lavelle, and compliments those who give it, though that priest is censured by the Pope—would it be worse to send subsidies to Passaglia[?]" Cullen then noted that Lavelle had returned to his parish of Partry and had written a letter to the *Freeman's Journal* from there that had appeared the day before. "I have heard," Cullen reported, "that he still says Mass, to one of the priests in Dublin when here the other day he said, *I am in statu quo* indicating that Dr. McH. had not suspended him. The whole affair will do great mischief. It will be said that Rome is afraid of the Lion, though with others the[y] would be severe enough."

"I have written today to the Cardinal," Cullen reported five days later, on September 9, to Kirby, "giving him an account of Lavelle's doings.[35] I sent him an article of the Connaught Patriot which is quite Jansenistical or Gallican. The Pope's censures may be treated as waste paper, and disregarded, respecting however the Pope's name as he acted under false impressions. The Councils are over and superior to the Pope—he decides ex cathedra when he announces the decision of a Council, and is only then infallible. The Pope's letter to Dr. McHale is an improper Roman ukase—etc." "Dr. MacEvilly says," he added,

---

34. The bishop of Philadelphia, James F. Wood, was apparently a good deal less edified by Moriarty's lecture and suspended him. Whether this suspension was the result of Moriarty's having been cited by Cullen to the Propaganda authorities is difficult to say, but Moriarty publicly and humbly retracted all that was offensive to his bishop and "other dignitaries of the Church" on December 6, 1864 (S.R.C., vol. 35, fol. 172).

35. S.R.C., vol. 34, fols. 1325–26. Cullen's letter to Barnabò, however, is dated September 8, 1864.

"that this article was written by Lavelle, and probably, it was. He learned enough of Gallicanism in Maynooth to do mischief." "I fear," he confessed, "Dr. McHale will resist authority. His letter to Dr. Moriarty of Philadelphia shows that he is enthusiastic for Lavelle." "Perhaps," he prudently cautioned Kirby, "it would be better not to drive him to extremes, lest he should give some public scandal." Apparently even Cullen was somewhat intimidated by the lengths to which MacHale was obviously prepared to go in supporting Lavelle, and in the next six weeks there was a curious hiatus in his correspondence with both Kirby and the authorities at Propaganda concerning Lavelle. Indeed, he mentioned Lavelle to Kirby only once, and then briefly. "Father Lavelle," he reported on October 4, "is said to be suspended—an verum sit nescio [I know not whether it is true]. He is however as active as ever. He has within the last month written a letter in defense of Keane of Glasgow" (K).

Though MacHale had suspended Lavelle, in spite of all the rumors to the contrary, he obviously had no intention of abandoning him to his enemies. In fact, the redoubtable archbishop of Tuam was only gathering his second wind. On November 2 the Tuam clergy presented him with an adulatory address in which they endorsed the position he had taken with regard to Lavelle.[36] Cullen was unable to obtain a copy of the address for more than a month, but when he did get it he wrote Kirby breaking his silence about the administrator of Partry. "I have got the address of the clergy to Dr. McHale," he reported on December 9.

> It is drawn up in the name of all the clergy of the province of Tuam. It extols his Grace to the stars. At the end there is a paragraph expressing regret that the Pope has misunderstood his political opinions, and compelled him to visit with censures *for undue interference in politics a clergyman who has certainly done good service in extirpating heresy and proselytism.* These are the words. They then add that all Lavelle wrote of a political nature cannot be justified, but might well be tolerated. They say not a word of his having been V. President of the Brotherhood, of his doings in England and Scotland. [K]

"Dr. Gillooly," Cullen further noted, "says that no priest in his diocese [Elphin] will sign this address. I suppose that all the priests of Tuam and Clonfert will."

MacHale had continued, meanwhile, to keep up a great head of

36. S.R.C., vol. 35, fols. 173–74.

steam on behalf of Lavelle. "I see in one of the last papers," Cullen complained to Kirby on November 6, "that Dr. McHale received about seventy pounds for Lavelle from John O'Mahony[,] Head Centre of the Fenians in America. This remittance shows the connection of that priest with the Brotherhood. It appears to me that Dr. McHale puts himself in a strange position by making himself or letting himself be made receiver general for Lavelle and the correspon[t] with the Fenians" (K). "However," he cautioned Kirby again with regard to the Propaganda authorities, "it is better not to speak about these matters until we see what turn things will take." By the time Kirby received this letter, Barnabò had already written MacHale again, on November 10, and at the pope's express order, to suspend Lavelle without any further equivocation. MacHale replied on November 24 that he would write personally to the pope.[37]

On November 29 the clergy of the archdiocese of Tuam finally petitioned the pope on Lavelle's behalf. The petition was signed by 88 of the 104 priests of the archdiocese. "In the diocese of Tuam," Mac-Evilly informed Kirby on December 4, "a memorial has been *hawked* about from house to house of priests by Rev. Mr. Reynolds, P.P., Claremorris [chancellor of the diocese] in favor of Father *Lavelle ostensibly*, but its real object is to attack Dr. Cullen. It also contained a paragraph in praise of Dr. MacHale's administ[n] but this latter point was expunged" (K). "It is signed by most of the priests," MacEvilly charged, "thro sheer fear. For to my knowledge (and no one living knows the diocese of Tuam so well) not 6 out of the 100 priests of that diocese, if left free would have anything to say to it. Some have refused altogether to their own cost and they *will pay* for it. It is said, it is done unknown to Dr. MacHale, but everyone knows the contrary to be the fact." "Is it not then," he lamented, "a sad state of affairs, that one or two clerical knaves can frighten mostly an entire diocese to do a thing against their conscience, to lay a Memorial before the Vicar of Christ, which they know to be untrue[?] For they know well that at this moment Lavelle is *privately* celebrating, etc. notwithstanding the document served upon him—whether suspension or not I can't say." Mac-Hale had, in fact, taken this petition as the occasion to write the pope a long personal letter, dated December 5, in which he enclosed the petition and entered a spirited defense of his own recent conduct. He protested his loyalty to the Holy See and maintained that he had carried out all of the pope's orders concerning Lavelle. He also defended his late subscription to the *Connaught Patriot*, as well as his letter to

37. S.R.C., vol. 34, fol. 1359.

Father Moriarty, and complained again about the unscrupulous machinations he had had to endure throughout the whole affair from quarters that had not even hesitated to publish the pope's letter to himself.[38]

Needless to say, the pope's reaction was not positive. In forwarding copies of the petition and MacHale's covering letter to Cullen on Christmas Eve, Moran reported that a few days before, "the Pope gave them both to Cardinal Barnabò, and wrote on the back with his own hand the following substance of a reply to be sent to Dr. McHale from Propaganda" (C). "I have it now before me," he explained, "and whilst I kiss the good Pope's handwriting I give you word for word his whole sentence: —'Propaganda. A Monsignor Arcivescoco di Tuam affinche voglia persuadersi che il Lavelle un cattivo mobile capace di piu di una falsità [Propaganda. To the archbishop of Tuam so that he may be convinced that Lavelle is an unconstant wretch capable of more than one untruth]." "This inscription," Moran added dryly, "might be put on Lavelle's tombstone, and it is the whole notice that the Pope wished to be taken of the Connaught parturition."

But why, it may well be asked, did MacHale insist on creating and then sustaining so serious a crisis by refusing for some three months to act on the pope's direct order to suspend Lavelle, and then continuing for four months more to support and defend that priest, implicitly at least, in the public press, as well as encouraging his clergy to appeal to the pope on his behalf? As in the crisis he had precipitated in Rome nearly ten years before, in the winter of 1855–56, to see MacHale "as simply a strong-willed and irascible man, who would have his own way without counting the cost, is not to take the whole measure of this interesting and difficult man."[39] Any answer to the question raised here, however, is certainly complicated by the fact that it is rooted in what had happened to MacHale's influence in the Irish Church in the previous ten years. Between 1852 and 1860 Cullen had systematically broken up MacHale's very considerable power base among the bishops as a body. By 1860 he had reduced MacHale's episcopal following to only three or four in a functioning body of twenty-eight bishops and two coadjutors. This reduction had been largely effected by Cullen's very considerable influence at Rome over episcopal appointments. In compensating for his loss of power, MacHale, and especially his lay political supporters, had taken every opportunity on public platforms and in the press to enhance their influence in

38. S.R.C., vol. 35, fols. 153–57.
39. Emmet Larkin, *The Making of the Roman Catholic Church in Ireland, 1850–1860* (Chapel Hill, N.C., 1980), p. 301.

the country with both priests and people by undermining Cullen's image as a patriot bishop, labeling him a Whig and Castle bishop in politics. The result was that in the popular mind, at least, MacHale had emerged as the archetypal patriot bishop, who stood, in contradistinction to Cullen, for an uncompromising hostility to the English connection and against any ultramontane intrigue in the national Church.

The Lavelle crisis, therefore, was a splendid opportunity for Mac-Hale to amplify and fulfill that symbolic role he had created for himself in the minds of the priests and people. MacHale certainly believed that the hostility of the Roman authorities to both Lavelle and himself was the result of Cullenite machinations and that his own efforts to carry out the pope's orders regarding Lavelle had been further complicated by the prejudices created against him at Propaganda by Cullen's misrepresentations. The result was that the pope had misunderstood both his motives and his political opinions. MacHale's case was essentially that since the pope was not in full possession of the facts, because of the various misrepresentations and misunderstandings, the only recourse in the interests of conscience and justice was to give him all the facts. MacHale was questioning not the pope's right to order him to suspend Lavelle but rather the information on which that order was predicated. He therefore wrote the pope in late July explaining the case, but meanwhile, he argued, his enemies not only had misrepresented him at Rome but had not even scrupled to publish the pope's letter to him in the newspapers, thus incredibly complicating a difficult and delicate situation.

MacHale's case was just plausible enough to pass muster if one considers only the letter of the law, and it was yet another example of his astuteness in dealing with the Roman authorities and the pope when ordered to do something he really did not want to do. If one considers the spirit of the law, however, his equivocation was certainly subversive of the pope's authority. The weak point in MacHale's case lay in its chronology. If the pope was not in full possession of the facts, MacHale must have realized it on the day he received the pope's letter of April 18, and he should have responded with an appeal immediately in so important a matter. His waiting some three months to apprise the pope that he was misinformed, and his statement to the pope that he was only then writing Lavelle to tell him he was suspended, constituted, to say the least, a profound act of disrespect, if not of actual disobedience. His continued public endorsement of Lavelle by receiving and thanking Father Moriarty and then O'Mahony for money for him amounted to scandalous conduct, especially in the light of his own appeal to the pope, by appearing to prejudge the pope's decision in the case. It is little wonder that the pope was reported to be very angry when he received MacHale's letter of December 5 defending the whole of his recent conduct.

But where did MacHale find the necessary courage to proceed so audaciously to the apparent brink of schism that even so inveterate and determined an enemy as Cullen was intimidated? MacHale well understood that his power in the Irish Church was now a function of his influence with the priests and people, and he was, through the whole Lavelle crisis, playing to that gallery. His reception on October 23, at the consecration dinner of the coadjutor to the bishop of Meath, Thomas Nulty, where he was accorded a tumultuous standing ovation—and this at the height of the Lavelle crisis—was a true indication of where he stood in the affections of the Irish clergy. Even such a loyal supporter of Cullen as the archbishop of Armagh, it will be recalled, who had witnessed this demonstration on behalf of MacHale, had felt obliged to write to Kirby and ask somewhat petulantly what indeed MacHale had ever been able to accomplish on the political level that was significant. The answer to Dixon's rhetorical question was that MacHale had actually achieved a great deal. By assuming the public political posture he did during the Lavelle crisis, MacHale did much to prevent the Fenians from driving any really effective anticlerical wedge between the priests and the people; for while the Fenians might denounce individual prelates, as they did Cullen, and with a vengeance, they were unable in the face of MacHale's stand for Lavelle to tar the Church and the clergy as a whole with such a brush. By taking this stand, moreover, MacHale never allowed his episcopal colleagues to forget that they had a temporal as well as a spiritual mission to their people. Indeed, during the Lavelle crisis the great majority of MacHale's episcopal colleagues, including Cullen and Dixon, finally came to the conclusion that if they were to save their people from the revolutionary politics of Fenianism, they and their clergy would have to play a more active role in promoting constitutional politics.

VI

The Constitutional Response

January 1864–June 1865

The conversion of the great majority of the bishops to a more active role in politics, as had long been advocated by MacHale, was perhaps the most significant result of the Lavelle crisis. Ever since the collapse in early 1861 of the petition movement to secure a referendum on the Repeal of the Act of Union, constitutional politics in Ireland had been in the doldrums.[1] In January 1864 John Martin and The O'Donoghue, who both had been prominent in the petition movement, tried to put new life into constitutional politics by launching the Irish National League. In spite of the league's single-plank platform—Repeal of the Act of Union—it did not prosper. Very few politicians of any promi-

---

1. In September 1862, for example, Father Jeremiah Vaughan undertook to nominate three gentlemen to meet with three nationalists to form a committee to launch a national organization. In December 1862 Vaughan finally wrote G. H. Moore, inviting him to meet with John Martin, Father John Kenyon, and himself in Dublin on January 7, 1863, where they would take counsel with William Smith O'Brien and a few others to see what could be done, given the present prostrate political condition of the country. At the meeting it was apparently decided to convene a conference of constitutional nationalists for March 3, and Moore was appointed to circularize some sixty of them, which he did on February 10. The conference was apparently private and adjourned without anything concrete being achieved, except to leave historians an interesting list of those who were considered influential in constitutional nationalist circles (including some thirteen priests and ten journalists) and a number of letters in the Moore papers that not only throw a good deal of incidental light on the "personalities" that made up the constitutional nationalist movement but perhaps do more than anything else to explain why so little was achieved (see Moore Papers, National Library of Ireland, 894, fols. 715–26).

nence or influence joined the league, and only MacHale among the bishops endorsed it. Though Martin and O'Donoghue persisted in their efforts to arouse interest in constitutional reform, the policy of the Fenians continued to prove more attractive, especially after the founding of their weekly newspaper, the *Irish People*, in late October 1863. During 1864, therefore, a number of bishops became increasingly concerned about doing something to check the general political apathy and despair that were making their people such ready recruits for Fenian organizers.

The difficulties in mobilizing the bishops as a body for political action were very considerable, however, and they were well illustrated by the problems encountered by the archbishop of Cashel, Patrick Leahy, in early 1864. Leahy had been long convinced that if the late alarming increase in emigration was ever to be checked, a good land measure giving the tenantry greater security in their holdings was absolutely necessary. He had also more recently come to the conclusion, through the influence of William O'Neill Daunt, a political reformer and ardent Repealer, that the time was ripe to strike a fatal blow against the established Church in Ireland. In late 1863, therefore, he decided to attempt to arouse public opinion with a petition movement to promote Tenant Right and the disestablishment of the Irish Church in the next session of Parliament. At a meeting of the board of the Catholic University in late 1863, Leahy urged Cullen to have the forms of the the petitions printed up and sent to all the bishops for distribution to their priests, if they were so inclined, for their people's signatures. Cullen agreed, but when the University board met again on January 26, 1864, nothing had been done, and the parliamentary session was about to begin.[2] Leahy again broached the subject to Cullen, who explained that he had discussed the matter with a number of his clergy, who had not approved of the project; he did not explain why. Leahy had then urged the matter again on Cullen and returned home under the impression that Cullen had agreed to have the petition forms sent to the bishops.

Leahy apparently then decided to write to the bishops of his province, asking them for their views on stirring up public opinion over the land and Church grievances. "It is a disgrace to Ireland," David Moriarty, the bishop of Kerry, assured Leahy on February 1, "not to raise her voice against the Ch. Establishment" (L). "It seems the fate of this country," he added, referring obviously to the recent launching of the Irish National League by Martin and O'Donoghue, "to have all

2. L, Leahy to MacHale, March 20, 1864.

her agitations based on falsehood and aimed at impossibilities. What we could do and ought to do we will not do." "Yet," he cautioned Leahy,

I think that the clergy had better leave to the laity the leadership in this crusade, but we can work it on a terzo [as third parties]. I do not look upon the Establishment as a religious evil, nor as a money grievance, but as a disgrace and as an impediment to the Irish union [i.e., the act of Union] and equality of Catholics and Protestants, and therefore a great political evil.

We should pour in petitions and send about lecturers to heat up the public mind on the subject.

I would ask the appropriation of the income of the Establishment to the support of the poor—thus relieving the poor rates in equal measure for landlords and tenants and giving both an equal interest in the change.

"Let me suppose," he conjectured for Leahy, "the agitation fail in its purpose yet a greater good will be obtained—namely an increased and intensified hatred of Protestantism."

"As to Tenants' Rights," Moriarty declared just as firmly, "I think it a delusion." "Deasy's bill," he explained, referring to a land act passed in 1860, "seems to me to have done all the legislature could do and yet it is a dead letter. All mortgage settlements, securities, public credit, in all their ramifications depend upon land dernier ressort. It is dangerous to stir the foundation of all property." "In any case," he noted more practically, "we should not go before Parliament asking a measure—we should take the measure with us, and it should be such as would prove itself to the judgement, not of editors or agitators, but our most eminent real property lawyers." "I see that Sergeant now Judge Shee," he suggested in conclusion, citing the former member for county Kilkenny, who had introduced several land bills in Parliament in the 1850s, "refers the Kilkenny people to a bill of his and regrets it was not passed into law. He is a man who knew what he was about, and the demand he suggests is a definite one." Moriarty's reply was perhaps more significant for the complications it raised for Leahy than for the qualified endorsement it provided for going into action. What the situation would be when nearly thirty bishops and coadjutors had been consulted, and what the difficulties would be in hammering out a comprehensive policy that the bishops as a body could endorse, may be easily imagined.

Cullen, however, continued to drag his feet about sending the petition forms to the bishops, and finally after three weeks of waiting, Leahy decided to proceed on his own. He sent the forms to the bishops of his own province, who had all consented to distribute them among their priests. Leahy also wrote to MacHale asking him to support the good cause. The archbishop of Tuam, however, was not sanguine about the success of the proposed petition movement. MacHale agreed on March 8 "how desirable it would be that the two subjects mentioned in Your Grace's letter should be expressly taken up by all the Catholics of Ireland. And yet strange to say there is such apathy regarding both that you could scarcely hope at present for any assured or vigorous cooperation" (L). "I am borne out in these remarks by Dr. Derry," he explained, referring to the bishop of Clonfert, "who happens to be here just now, who says that he fears he would not be successful in enlisting the active support [?] of his clergy and people. Were I to consult the other Prelates of this province I doubt not but I should receive an answer similar to his Lordship's impression." "I merely state the fact," MacHale further noted, "of the indifference and the difficulty of moving the inert mass [?] of a people once so ready at any call from the Bishops and clergy. The poor tenants at will have suffered so much that they are afraid to resort even to petitions for a rightful land enactment lest they should suffer still more from landlords." In a reference to the editor of the *Tipperary Advocate*, Peter Gill, who had just been successfully sued for libel by a landlord, Mac-Hale ironically pointed out to Leahy, "There cannot be a more significant test of the state of public feeling than the Gill fund to indemnify him for his losses in exposing the injustice inflicted on the tenant class. However I will preface the matter next week at a conference of the clergy."

When MacHale did not write after meeting with his clergy, Leahy wrote him again on Palm Sunday, March 20, attempting to persuade him to take some action and enclosing the petition forms on the chance that he might "on second thought" distribute them to his priests and perhaps persuade his suffragans to do the same (L). Mac-Hale replied on March 26 that he had little to add to his former letter except to say that he had spoken to his clergy on the subject, and there was no difference of opinion among them on the issues treated by the petitions (L). "But," he added, "respecting the utility of more petitioning, there is a strong adverse feeling. The inefficiency of the Irish representatives, even of the the Catholic members with but very few exceptions, is referred to in justifying the general [?] indisposition to petition." "To succeed in obtaining any important concession," Mac-Hale further explained, "mere petitioning is not sufficient and this want of any earnest exertions in some of ourselves to carry out our frequent resolutions on the most important subject of National education is looked on as a most discouraging objection." "But above all," he noted in conclusion, "the increasing desire to leave the country which has seized the people so absorbs every other failing that they appear indifferent to all hope of any temporal relief from whatever quarter especially since the clergy have so long stood aloof from any practical, earnest and efficient defence of their dearest secular interests."

Though both Cullen and MacHale refused to take up the petition movement for their own reasons, Leahy continued to persevere and in company with his suffragans designated April 3, the first Sunday after Easter, as the day for signing the petitions in their province. On March 23 the bishop of Limerick, George Butler, wrote to William Monsell, M.P. for county Limerick, who was spending Easter in Rome, "We are getting up petitions through the county and through Munster in support of Dilwyn's motion on the 'Est^d Church grievance' which is to come off after Easter. These petitions will be signed throughout this Diocese on low Sunday. It is important that you should be in London to receive these petitions. We are also to send petitions for 'an equitable Settlement of the Land question.'"[3] "Dr. Leahy," he further reported, "is very active in these movements, having written the forms of petition himself, and written to the Munster Bishops to invite their support of the movement. The Depopulation of our Country is progressing at an awful pace and we must not appear to be taking it too easy. The Bishops & Clergy & our public men should, in the face of such an evil, be trying some remedy." "I have conferences next week," he assured Monsell in conclusion, "and I will tell the Clergy to send their petitions to you at the House of Commons."

At his conferences the following week, after urging his clergy to press forward with the petitions on the established Church and the land question, Butler made use of the occasion to take exception

to some statements recently made by some newspapers, which went so far as to say that the bishops and clergy were quite indifferent as to the present political state of Ireland, and, in fact, rather counteracted the efforts of the people who sought amelioration than encouraged or assisted them.

These statements furthermore, endeavored to impress strangers with the notion that the bishops of Ireland prevented their clergy from taking their place among the people, and aiding,

3. S.R.C., vol. 34, fols. 1127–28.

assisting, and directing them as of old, in struggling against op-pression. His lordship knew that both these assertions—viz, that the bishops and clergy were indifferent, and that the *bishops in-terfered with the parochial clergy and prevented their political activity*—were both of them known to the clergymen present to be *calumnies,* perhaps believed to be so by those who uttered them. But however untrue it may be, or however honest some may be who say it, it becomes us, his lordship said, to give it the contradiction of facts. *We are not contented with the English government in Ireland;* we have neither love nor liking for its dealings with the Irish race; and we would look upon *any strug-gle which would raise our country to the dignity of a nation, or secure for our people equitable and honest legislation, as an ef-fort that every good man is bound to aid and encourage.* And I tell you, gentlemen (said his lordship), *stand by your people and the people's cause in every way not sinful and which is prudent.*[4]

"Save them from secret societies," Butler exhorted, "—not because secret societies are against the English government, but because secret societies are against reason, religion, and the Holy Catholic Church. In speaking of these same secret societies, too, do not run away with the notion that the members are all corrupt or bad Catholics. Many of them are devoted Irishmen and pure patriots, who have seen no hope for Ireland but violence, and who laboured under a sad misconception of a Catholic's duty." "We cannot be astonished, gentlemen," Butler then added,

that people who have lost all hope betake themselves to the ranks of violence—or even imprudent and rash endeavour.

The country is being depopulated, and its resources are drained by English laws and English policy. *Petition seems to have been in vain, and insult is returned when claims are fully preferred. As long as things are allowed to go on in this way and a man sees no future for his country but to become a grass farm to England, it is not to be wondered at that in greater numbers than we can imagine people are preparing for the last extremity.* At all events, gentlemen, I not only sympathise with those who feel the injustice and wrong their country has suffered and is

4. Ibid., fol. 1141. See also fol. 1140, Patrick Lavelle to Barnabò, April 13, 1864, reporting Butler's and O'Brien's speeches. All the italics in this and the following quota-tions are the result of Lavelle's underscoring the newspaper account of their speeches to heighten their effect on Barnabò. The speeches were originally printed in the *Limerick Reporter,* n.d.

enduring, *but I shall always be glad to see you working ardently, yet prudently, for her regeneration and improvement.* And I wish this to be as extensively known as your voices and efforts may carry it.

The following Sunday, April 3, at Newcastle West, the archdeacon of the diocese of Limerick, Richard O'Brien, elaborated on Butler's theme. "Ireland in my opinion," O'Brien boldly maintained, *has never been so disloyal as she is at this very hour.*" "And pray," he further assured his listeners, "remember I am not now speaking of Fenians and Socialists, and Red Republicans; I am speaking of the bone and sinew, and *honest, principled, and hard-working people of this island,* and those belonging to this island who are now in England and Scotland. *That people, the whole people*—morally—are, I assure all whom it may concern, *thoroughly and entirely disaffected* to the government of England." O'Brien then pointed out,

It is hard to hear the 'Constitution' so constantly boasted of. *What share have we of it?*

To a man perishing of hunger on the flagway, you may as well say there is an excellent hotel lying across the street. We have freedom to vote for members of parliament, provided we are prepared to *undergo a scourging from the agent* (unless where, perchance, such a man as the Earl of Devon is landlord, or Edward Curling is the landlord's representative). We have freedom to vote in *boards of guardians, provided we can outnumber* the more numerous representatives of our government masters. We have freedom of commerce, provided we can traffic on nothing. We have freedom of conscience, *provided we pay £96,000 a year* to rear up parsons, and *£600,000 or £700,000 more* to rear up the parsons' long families, when they choose to marry. We have freedom to live upon the land and improve the soil, provided we give *the sweat and life of three or four* generations to the landlord whenever he calls for "his property." In fact, we have "liberty" in every way only [i.e., except] in one—that is, the power of exercising liberty—on which principle a man in a strait waistcoat may be called perfectly free. Let it not be supposed that we are contented, and let it not be supposed that on this point both priests and people are not perfectly united, and ever will be.

"If we and our flocks oppose the Fenians and others," O'Brien explained, "*it is not because they are opposed to the English government.* Certainly not; but because they are opposed to the law of God.

The man who takes an oath to obey whom he does not know swears rashly; and the man who swears to do something which is not yet defined, does the same. He made the sacred name of God bind himself to what may be evil, and what therefore cannot in him be good. He commits a horrible crime, not perhaps, in the object he may have in view, but in his manner of accomplishing it. He sins against reason and the religion of his fathers and his country. I may admire respect and even share his sentiments, but I must condemn the manner he works, because God does not and cannot approve." "I believe we can never be prosperous," O'Brien then summed up in conclusion, "until we have the power to make our own laws. I believe we never can be loyal—never can be otherwise [than] disloyally affected to England— as long as English arms, mere brute force, compel us to work like slaves for unfeeling landlords, or to be expatriated like felons, and as long as we are mocked by a freedom of conscience which is exercised under a fine of one million per annum, besides the abuse we receive from the strange gentlemen whom we pay."

The political line laid down by Butler and O'Brien was the pure milk of clerical-Nationalist rhetoric on the constitutional side. That line was still what it had always been from the days of Daniel O'Connell—that there was no real difference among Irishmen about ends, only about appropriate means. What distinguished this rhetoric of the 1860s from that of the 1850s, and even the 1840s, was not simply that it was being heard less often but rather that it was increasingly bitter, and this was in itself a fair measure of the growth of Fenianism in the affections of the people, as well as of a deepening clerical concern over that growth. In any case, though the petition movement launched by the clergy of Munster had succeeded somewhat in raising the political temperatures of the people and priests of that province, there is little evidence that it had any real practical effect either in Parliament or in the country at large. There was, however, another and more important factor at work in making the bishops and clergy more aware of their temporal obligations to their people. In spite of a relatively good harvest in 1863, the Irish people were continuing to emigrate in very great numbers during 1864. The concern about emigration permeates all the clerical rhetoric and correspondence at this time. Even Cullen, who was less prone than most to hysteria on the subject of emigration, could not refrain, in winding up a long letter to Barnabò on other matters, from attempting to explain the causes of that disturbing social phenomenon.

"I have mentioned above," Cullen noted on March 18, "that we have already lost three million people. It appears that almost all the great landlords intend to remove the poor labourers and the small tenants in order to introduce cattle on their property. After England adopted free trade in 1845, grain was imported from America and various parts of Europe at a much better price than it can be grown in Ireland—but not up to now for what England can bring in cattle from far off countries. Therefore, everyone in Ireland seeks to convert to pasture to supply meat to England, and the landlords in the avidity for making money do not hesitate to sacrifice the population."[5] "It seems to me however," Cullen added, "this project will not be successful because a very large part of Ireland is not suitable for conversion to pasture, and if it is left uncultivated it will become a desert or marsh. Probably the landlords (who are mostly Protestants and who have obtained their property by confiscating the property of Catholics) in the desire to get rid of poor Catholics will ruin themselves. However that may be, Ireland has, after so many persecutions, risen so many times, it may be hoped that she will also recover after the present crisis." When, some three weeks later, T. W. Croke, a former student of the Irish College in Rome and now president of St. Colman's College in Fermoy, in the diocese of Cloyne, wrote Kirby, he too was deeply troubled by the effects of emigration. "As to the State of the Country," Croke reported on April 8, "it is in the last degree deplorable. No one can say what is to become of it. Emigration will leave us soon, I fear, without any Catholic population at all. Sixty four thousand people left Queenstown by *one* line of Boats, between the January of '63, and the January of '64! That's terrible. We must only hope and believe, notwithstanding, that Providence has something good in store for us yet" (K).

A month later the bishop of Ardagh reported to Kirby from Longford in much the same vein. "Poor and prostrate Ireland," Kilduff explained sadly on May 7, "is bleeding at every pore. You will learn from the Newspapers the wholesale emigration that is taking place from her shores. The young & vigorous, the bone & sinew of the land, are hurrying away as from a place stricken with a plague, leaving behind them the aged & the infirm. The effects of this state of things are becoming plainly visible in the thinned Congregations in our Churches and Chapels & in the ruin of a large number of trading and mercantile classes in our principal towns" (K). "But all that," he added even more sadly, "counts for nothing when we consider the spiritual ruin to which, according to the most accredited accounts, so many of the poor Emigrants are hastening in thus despairingly crossing the

---

5. S.R.C., vol. 34, fol. 1244.

Atlantic." "A large number of them," he informed Kirby in conclusion, "writes an illustrious American Bishop from whom I rec^d a letter on yesterday, become lost to morality, to Society, to religion, and, finally to God. Such is our condition: Won't you pray for us?"

The "illustrious American Bishop" referred to by Kilduff was John Joseph Lynch of Toronto. Not only had he written Kilduff; he had also apparently circularized all the Irish bishops and forwarded a copy of his letter to the pope with a covering letter.[6] In reporting all this to Kirby on May 12, Lynch explained: "The devil could not conquer the Irish on their own sacred soil, [so] he, helped by his best friends and supporters[,] the cruel oppressors of the poor[,] has transferred the battleground[,] and he conquers thousands that would be saved did they die in Ireland" (K). "I am distressed exceedingly," he assured Kirby. "The Irish Bishops make incredible efforts to rescue from the jaws of the wolf a lamb torn from them by proselytizers and there is no effort made to obtain just laws to protect the poor & keep them in Ireland." "Act the part my dear Lord [sic]," he begged Kirby in conclusion, "of a St. Philip Neri that went straight to the Holy Father and asked him not to let his children be massacred. I have written a short letter to the Holy Father. The loss of souls alone afflicts me." When the archbishop of Armagh received his copy of the circular he was appalled. "You have received a copy of Dr. Lynch's frightful circular from Toronto," Dixon wrote Cullen on May 7 (C). "I fear nothing will do for this country but a new Catholic association with a catholic rent. If such a body could be properly conducted, it would apply a remedy to many of the evils that are ruining the Country."

Whether Lynch, who was apparently as naive as he was well-meaning, realized it or not, he was in effect reporting the Irish bishops to the pope for not making greater temporal efforts on behalf of their people.[7] Though both Kilduff and Dixon obviously missed the more practical consequences of Lynch's letter to the pope, Cullen did not, and almost immediately he took occasion to cover the exposed Roman flank. In writing to Barnabò on May 20, to thank him for sending him a copy of the pope's recent letter to MacHale suspending Lavelle, Cullen took the opportunity to explain to the cardinal prefect the complexities as well as the difficulties involved in the problem of emigration.[8] "I am sorry to say," he reported, "that the people are

6. Ibid., fol. 1262, Lynch to Pius IX, May 12, 1864. The letter to the Irish bishops is not included in the Propaganda material, but his circular to the Irish clergy on the deplorable consequences, spiritual and temporal, of Irish emigration is included.

7. See C. Lynch to Cullen, June 9, 1864, in which letter Lynch tries to explain away some of the more critical statements in his circular.

8. S.R.C., vol. 34, fol. 1178.

fleeing Ireland in great numbers. Every day the boats leave full of emigrants. The poor people go totally unprovided of the necessities of life, and then endure incredible misfortunes in America. Our government however does not give the least protection to these poor people." He went on:

If the King of Naples and the Pope had treated their subjects as the poor Irish are treated, England would have been full of indignation, and the English newspapers would have been hurling insults against the sovereigns who did not protect their people. They do not say a word however in favor of the Irish people, but so great is their hatred of the Catholic religion, that they appear to exult in the destruction of the poor people. The emigration this year is principally from the provinces of Cashel and Tuam, from Dublin very few are leaving. It is clear that just now Ireland will lose a great deal, but I have the greatest hope that religion will not lose anything, the losses that we now suffer will be repaired.

"Within the last three hundred years," he assured Barnabò, "the population was almost totally destroyed five or six different times; however it always recovered again, and has always demonstrated an amazing vitality. I hope things will turn out as they have turned out so many other times, that is for the present the Irish will form new Catholic congregations in England and in America, while Ireland will remain completely Catholic."

In spite of the promise of another good harvest in 1864, the exodus continued at an accelerating pace during the summer and fall. "The emigration is continuing," Cullen explained to Kirby on June 30, "—principally however from Munster and Connaught. Very few are leaving from this diocese: but from other parts three thousand per week are leaving. At this rate almost *150,000* souls will be lost in a year."9 "Our harvest," he reported, "promises very well—the wheat, and the rest of the corn, and most of all the potatoes are very fine. So perhaps next year we shall not have to suffer too much. However all that Ireland produces goes to England and the wretchedness only remains amongst us here." All the reports of the impending harvest continued to be good, but apparently nothing could now check the exodus. Thomas English, the adminstrator of the bishop's parish in Waterford, reported to Kirby on July 9, "The crops are very fine this year. Yet the tide of emigration goes on unchecked. Already some of the rural parishes have been reduced to one half of their population"

9. Ibid., fol. 1222.

(K). The following day, English's neighbor, the bishop of Ossory, wrote Kirby from Kilkenny attempting to account for the sad situation. "We are all," Edward Walsh informed Kirby on July 10, "very peaceble [*sic*] in this locality, but can[']t say that we are happy or contented. The farmers are very poor and consequently cannot employ the labourers and this with the encouragement from Amarica [*sic*] accounts for the Exedus [*sic*]" (K).

When Cullen wrote Kirby again at the end of July, however, he noted that the continued good weather was now posing its own problem for Irish farmers, and especially the graziers. "The weather," he reported on July 28, "is very dry, the fields (grass) as burned as the Campagna, but the crops, wheat, oats, potatoes, flax are all very fine" (K). "Lord Carlisle," he noted bitterly, naming the lord lieutenant, "has been continually preaching that Ireland is not fit to be anything but the mother of herds and flocks, and that the population ought to be thinned." "Perhaps God almighty," he added more hopefully, "wishes to show that this country has not been made for beasts, and that it is not to become a place of pasture to supply fat beef to London. The graziers, who are generally Catholics will suffer, but in the end they will be benefitted. The landlords have raised their rents enormously, so that the graziers gain little. If the grass does not grow the rents must be lowered." "I think all the money of Ireland goes to the Jews of London," Cullen declared in conclusion. "The landlords and bankers live in London and live extravagantly—the Jews fatten on them—but intanto [meanwhile] Ireland is starved."

A month later the situation had considerably worsened for the graziers. "The country here is as parched as the Campagna," Cullen informed Kirby on August 21 (K). "Water is carried to the cattle in the fields and in many places it is necessary to give hay to the cattle. There was no such drought within the present century." "The harvest," he further reported with obvious satisfaction, "is splendid—the people will have plenty of everything, but those who feed cattle will suffer. It will be all for the better for the country at large." The weather did not finally break, in fact, until early September. "The present prospect of the grazing districts is awful," the bishop of Meath reported to Kirby on September 20, from Mullingar, "arising out of the long continued absence of rain which however during the last fortnight has fallen in great abundance. The condition is even worse in England, but there they are able to bear their losses" (K). In concluding his letter, Cantwell then apologized for not being able to send as large a sum in Peter's pence as usual but explained that the general impoverishment of his people made any larger sum impossible. In the north of Ireland, however, where tillage was the mainstay of the farmers, rather than pasture, the reports were quite different. "The season," the archbishop of Armagh informed Kirby on September 30, enclosing nearly £500 in Peter's pence, a 20 percent increase over the previous year, "is beautiful and the country is prosperous—particularly in Ulster, where the flax crop is so abundant and remunerative" (K). The weather apparently turned fair again at the end of September and remained so until the third week in October, when the rain returned with a vengeance. "The weather was fine," Cullen explained to Kirby on November 6, "until about the 20th October. Since then we have had torrents of rain, quite as bad as you would have at Tivoli and the whole country was flooded" (K). "I think we shall have no distress this year," he further assured Kirby, "but the prices of corn are so low that the farmers will all suffer. The price of meat is exorbitant and hence notwithstanding the drought, those who have cattle are making well."

Whatever effect the harvest had on the more substantial farmers in either tillage or pasture, the ineluctable fact was that as a class the laborers, cottiers, and marginal farmers continued to emigrate at the rate of more than a hundred thousand a year. There can be little doubt that it was this continuing stream of emigration, taken in conjunction with the alarming spread of Fenianism, that finally convinced the bishops as a body that they must take up a more active role in Irish politics. They apparently took this crucial decision during the third week of October. Every year at that time a very considerable number of bishops came up to Dublin from the country to attend meetings of the various college and university boards of which they were members, which usually met on consecutive days. The Maynooth board consisted of the four archbishops and seven suffragan bishops, while the boards that governed the Catholic University and the Irish College at Paris each included the four archbishops and eight suffragan bishops. In theory, therefore, the four archbishops and twenty-three suffragan bishops in a regular hierarchy of twenty-eight would be tantamount to a full, if informal, gathering of the body. In practice, because some of the bishops served on more than one board, the number present, barring illness or infirmity, would be usually about twenty. Given the growth of their concern about both emigration and Fenianism during 1864, however, it was more than likely that the attendance at the successive boards in October was a very full one.

In any case, the bishops' decision had certainly been made by the first week in November, for John Blake Dillon informed William O'Neill Daunt on November 4 that a new political agitation was "contemplated by all the Bishops and a large number of laymen."[10] Dillon was apparently the key figure in effecting this new alliance between the bishops and the lay politicians, which was soon to be launched formally as the National Association. Dillon was a very able and gifted man who had had a most interesting career in Irish politics. In 1843, as a young man, he had associated with Charles Gavan Duffy and Thomas Davis to found the *Nation*, which soon became the organ of the Young Ireland party. He had then participated in the Young Ireland rising of 1848 and, after escaping to France, made his way to the United States. He remained there until 1852, when he finally returned to Ireland. After his return, Dillon gave up revolutionary politics; eventually he entered the Dublin Corporation, where he served as an alderman for some years. He had joined the petition movement for Repeal in 1861, but when John Martin and The O'Donoghue launched the Irish National League in early 1864, he did not participate. Sometime between 1861 and 1864, therefore, Dillon had come to the conclusion that the single-plank platform of Repeal was not a realistic program in the context of what was then Irish constitutional politics.[11] He preferred instead to concentrate on such issues and grievances as Tenant Right, the Established Church, and mixed education in his effort to launch a new national and constitutional political movement.

Dillon's most remarkable achievement during this period was the winning of the confidence of the bishops, and most especially that of Cullen, who was particularly averse to former Young Irelanders and none more than those who were Catholic and had been educated at Trinity College. What probably carried very great weight with Cullen was that Dillon had given good evidence in recent years of his abandonment of both revolutionary politics and mixed education. With regard to the latter, for example, he had sent his highly gifted son William to be educated at the Catholic University. With regard to the former, Dillon had publicly confirmed his developing conservatism in the Irish political spectrum by taking a very prominent part in the effort to raise a monument in Dublin to the greatest of all the Irish constitutional politicians, Daniel O'Connell. The O'Connell National Monument Committee, with Dillon in the vanguard, had launched a

---

10. E. R. Norman, *The Catholic Church and Ireland in the Age of Rebellion, 1859–1873* (London, 1965), p. 139, quoting *Daunt's Journal*, November 5, 1864.

11. He probably made this decision in early 1863. See Dillon to G. H. Moore, February 24, 1863, Moore Papers, 894, fol. 723.

drive in September 1862 to collect the £20,000 necessary to erect a memorial worthy of the great man.[12] By early December of 1863, and in the aftermath of three successive bad harvests, the committee had collected over £5000; in February 1864 it decided to hold a national collection on March 17, St. Patrick's Day. When that collection realized another £2000, the committee then resolved on May 18 to proceed to lay the foundation stone on August 8. All the bishops were invited as a matter of course to assist at the ceremonies, but they do not appear to have responded with any great alacrity. Cullen, for example, was something less than enthusiastic about the whole affair, though as archbishop of Dublin, he could hardly have avoided being present on such an occasion. "The foundation of the O'Connell monument," he informed Kirby on July 28, "is to be laid on 8th August. The Lord Mayor lays it. There will be several Bishops present. I intend going if there be no danger of a row.[13] A dinner is to be given the same evening to which I will not go—probably there will be a row there" (K).

On the appointed day, in any event, Cullen and eight other bishops marched in the procession and participated in the ceremonies.[14] The demonstration as reported in the public press was both imposing and orderly, and the very large number of people in attendance from all over Ireland and abroad must have impressed a great many of those present that the Fenians had not yet acquired a strict hold over the national aspirations of the people. While the O'Connell demonstration was undoubtedly a significant step in educating a considerable number of the bishops about their political responsibilities, it was still only a step. Some of the bishops who were more politically advanced than their brethren concerning Ireland's national aspirations were not very impressed with the nationalist credentials of the organizers of the demonstration and viewed some of them, at least, as mere political opportunists. Patrick Dorrian, the coadjutor to the bishop of Down and Connor, for example, explained to Kirby on August 10, "The procession in Dublin passed off well. I did not go, because I believed there was too much *Whiggery* with some of the leaders, and I look upon Whiggery as the Evil Genius of Ireland—a few offices for traitors and starvation & oppression for the rest of the Catholic people" (K). By the middle of October, however, even so pronounced an enemy of "Whig-

---

12. I.C.D., 1864, pp. 318–20. See also John O'Hanlon, *Report of the O'Connell Monument Committee* (Dublin, 1888), pp. ix–xxix.

13. A "row" for Cullen was a euphemism for a confrontation with MacHale.

14. *Freeman's Journal*, August 10, 1864. The other bishops present were Dixon, Leahy (Cashel), McNally, Butler, Keane, O'Hea, Gillooly, and Leahy (Dromore).

gery" as Dorrian had become convinced that some effort must be made by the bishops to launch a constitutional movement on behalf of a desponding people.

By that time Cullen had also been finally persuaded that something must be done, and in a carefully worded reply to a letter from the lord mayor of Dublin, Peter Paul MacSwiney, he made his commitment. "In reply to the circular," Cullen explained on October 11, "dated from the Catholic university October 3ᵈ and signed by your Lordship and several Catholic laymen and clergymen, I beg to say that I think it most important that something should be done to rescue this Catholic country from the position of political subjection and religious inferiority in which it now lies" (C). He outlined his position:

> In my humble opinion the first step to be taken should be the appointment of a small working committee that would examine the requirements of the case, determine what steps should be taken at present, and prepare the way for an association, if such a body be necessary or can be worked in the present times.
>
> Though there are undoubtedly many most important questions connected with the welfare of Ireland, such as the condition of the small landholders, the taxation of the country, the exclusion of Catholics from offices of trust and emolument, and above all the education question, yet I fully concur in the suggestion of the circular, that it is better to limit the movement now contemplated to one matter alone, and that the established church.
>
> It is probable that a large majority of the whole population of the three kingdoms will be unanimous upon that subject. Certain it is that no one can defend so great a nuisance with any appearance of plausibility. If that institution so long the source of all the evils of Ireland were once overthrown, the party hostile to us would become weaker, and would not have the same self interest in opposing and maligning everything Catholic as they have at present, whilst the people of Ireland and their friends would take courage, and unite in seeking for other advantages and rights.

"I beg to assure you, my dear Lord Mayor," Cullen added, "that I will be very happy to cooperate in every way I can in any movement which you and the gentlemen whose names are signed to [the] circular shall recommend or initiate." "In conclusion," he cautioned MacSwiney, "I beg to state that you cannot [expect] that all, even our friends, will be unanimous on any course you may propose. But if a fair support can be obtained for a regular agitation against the Established Church, I do not see why that agitation should not be immediately undertaken. If matters be conducted with prudence and moderation, those who are now indifferent or apathetic will soon see the advantages to be obtained by the movement & join in it."

As Cullen had suggested, a small organizing committee was formed, consisting of Cullen, the lord mayor, Dillon, and Alderman R. J. Devitt. Cullen obviously broached the subject of forming an association to the bishops when they met in Dublin to attend the various college boards in the third week of October, and the great majority of his colleagues apparently signified that they were willing to support the proposal. By the middle of November the organizing committee had completed its work, for Cullen, in reply to a letter from the senior member of Parliament for county Leitrim, John Brady, in regard to electoral matters, explained on November 15 that a "project for the establishment of an association has been just set on foot, to commence an agitation against the Established church. If this project be successful I suppose the proposed association will be looking after the election of M.P.s. I dare say something final will be determined regarding this proposal in a few days" (C). "It wd be well," he concluded, enunciating once again his most basic theme, "to have all parties go forward in harmony." Several days later, after all the particulars had been settled by the organizing committee, Cullen and Dillon finally decided how to launch the new agitation. A requisition was to be circulated calling for an aggregate meeting in Dublin to inaugurate the new association. Even before the requisition was finally circulated in early December, rumors were rife that a new association was being formed. On November 23, in fact, Cullen and Dillon had sent up a trial balloon at a meeting of the friends and patrons of St. Brigid's Orphanage at the procathedral in Marlborough Street. With Cullen presiding and the lord mayor present, Dillon denounced the established Church and proselytizing with great energy and then announced that the organized power of the Irish people would soon be brought to bear on the question.[15] Several days later the influential editor of the *Nation*, A. M. Sullivan, announced that the association had been virtually launched. "A new Association," he explained on November 26,

has been in the process of formation for some time past in Dublin having chiefly for its object the abolition of the Established Church. All the movements have been kept private, except from

15. Norman, pp. 139–40.

some few members of the clergy and laity here; for you will be glad to learn that, so far from being opposed to legitimate political action, it is mainly to his Grace the Archbishop and his clergy that this endeavor to reconstruct an Irish Parliamentary Party for the obtaining of Irish Measures, is owing. Alderman Dillon and the Lord Mayor are the only Laymen (beside Mr. Devitt) who, so far as my knowledge extends, have been admitted to any share in the confidential deliberations up to the present; but the sanction of three Archbishops, has, I believe, been obtained for the work in hand. . . ."[16]

Several days later Dillon apparently wrote a number of the bishops that the organizing committee was about to circulate a requisition addressed to the lord mayor of Dublin to summon an aggregate meeting to launch the new association. "I am glad to see," the bishop of Elphin replied on November 30, "your Committee is beginning to act. As the success of the aggregate meeting is of extreme importance to the future action of the Assoc—— I w^d recommend you not to find too early a day for it—but to leave the friends of the movement time enough—say until the 20th Dec—to publicise and recommend its objects and to procure a large number of influential signatures to the requisitions. The Meeting might be held in Xmas week when country gentlemen w^d have more leisure and disposition to repair to the Metropolis" (G). "I wish to know by next post," he efficiently requested of Dillon, "whether you have sent Circulars to the P Ps of this diocese & to our principal lay Gentlemen or if you expect me to solicit signatures throughout the diocese. I think the immediate action of the Bps through their clergy in favor of the requisition wd give a most favorable impulse to the Movement & without such action many even of the clergy will keep back in suspense." "I will myself," he assured Dillon in conclusion, "on receipt of your reply send a circular to our clergy."

"I have only time," Dillon responded the following day, December 1, "for a few hurried lines in reply to your letter rec^d this day. The spirit manifested in it is highly encouraging and indeed on the whole we have so far received as much encouragement as could reasonably be hoped for" (G). "For the purpose of the requisition," he advised Gillooly, "I think it will not be necessary for you to take any further trouble than merely to ask any influential persons who may fall in your way to authorise us to append their signatures." "It would hardly do," he added shrewdly, "to have too large a proportion of Clerical

16. Ibid., p. 140.

signatures to the requisition and for that reason we have not circulated it generally amongst the Clergy. When the Association shall have been formed you will have an opportunity of giving it a fair start by recommending the Priests of the Diocese become members, and judging from your letter, we may hope that you will not be slow to afford us such aid." "We have fixed on the week after Xmas for the Meeting," he reported in conclusion, "in thus anticipating your Lordship's wish."

When the requisition for the aggregate meeting was finally circulated for signatures a short time later, the most surprising thing about it was that the object of the proposed association was not to be limited to a one-plank platform of disestablishing the Protestant Church, as had been early envisaged by Cullen, but involved "a reform of the law of landlord and tenant, securing to the tenant full compensation for valuable improvements; the abolition of the Irish Church Establishment; and the perfect freedom of Education in all its branches."[17] The requisition was signed by a very large number of local worthies, a considerable number of the clergy, and twenty-four bishops in a hierarchy of thirty-two. The most serious deficiency was that the vast majority of Catholic and Liberal M.P.'s did not sign, as only a half dozen affixed their signatures.[18] The name most conspicuous for its absence among the bishops was that of the archbishop of Tuam.[19] Dillon had personally written MacHale in early December asking him to sign the requisition, but he had refused. His letter is quoted here nearly in full not only because it is an interesting and important document in itself but because this was the considered view of the most influential and formidable political foe of English rule in Ireland. He wrote to Dillon on December 6, the day after he had assured the pope that he had suspended Lavelle for the third time:

I am in receipt of your respected letter and the accompanying requisition to the Lord Mayor. . . . With regard to the objects

17. *Freeman's Journal,* December 30, 1864, quoted in Norman, p. 140.
18. The M.P.'s who signed the requisition were Lanigan (Cashel), Dunne (Queen's), O'Reilly (Longford), Blake (Waterford City), Maguire (Dungarvan), and Greene (county Kilkenny).
19. The bishops who did not sign the requisition were MacHale (Tuam), Feeny (Killala), Fallon (Kilmacduagh and Kilfenora), Kelly (Derry), McGettigan (Raphoe), Browne (Kilmore), Walshe (Kildare and Leighlin), and Flannery (Killaloe). Of the seven bishops who did not sign besides MacHale, four were either ill or infirm (Feeny, Fallon, Browne, and Flannery); two were from the far north (Kelly and McGettigan) and were seldom involved in purely political matters; and only one (Walshe) explicitly refused to sign because he had scruples about doing so (see C, Walshe to Cullen, December 18, 1864). The point is, of course, that the bishops as a body had in effect endorsed the proposal to establish a National Association.

(stated in the requisition), there can be no question of their great importance, and the only wonder is, how the representatives of Ireland, at least those of the popular constituencies, have been so long and so generally silent on the legislative requirements of the country, up to the eve of the dissolution of Parliament. But, though there is no question regarding the importance of the objects, not so with the agency proposed to carry them into serious and practical effect.

The zeal to found an association at this crisis reminds us of the great Association founded in 1851; and from its fate, and the consequences which followed, one may draw a lesson in estimating what would be, probably, the result of the projected association.

No association now to be formed for the good of Ireland could surpass or probably equal that Association in the number of its members, in the pledges by which the fidelity of Parliamentary candidates was sought to be secured, or in the unusual solemnity with which its first meeting was inaugurated. The sequel need not be told. It is written in the present prostrate condition of the country, and the dispersion of its people.

Yes, after allowing, in latter times, their own share to bad harvests, this state of things is brought about by the breach of the covenants then made; by the treachery of representatives then, unfortunately, trusted; by the acquiescence of entire, and principally corrupt, municipal constituencies;[1] in the scandalous violation of engagements of which they were the witnesses, if not the securities; and, finally, the ominous silence of a large portion of the once popular press, at first rather loud in its censures of the political apostasy, but gradually adopting a more tolerant tone, until it subsided into a gentle condemnation of this hideous national betrayal.

Nay, more: these infamous men, who betrayed the best interests of the country, were not content with being silent on their misdeeds, but had the hardihood, together with their supporters, to assume the language of complaint and to arraign the conduct of the clergy and people who labored to carry out the policy to which all classes of society were then so clearly committed.

Are we, then, justified in expecting from the association now contemplated more favorable results?

---

[1]Such as Athlone, where the traitor Keogh was re-elected, and Sligo, which returned the arch-traitor Sadleir.

I am not insensible to the lamentable condition of the country, or to the necessity of great and generous exertions to save the people from utter extermination. Nor am I indifferent to the observations regretting the want of union, and expressive of a wish that all past errors and mistakes should be forgotten. The long continued reluctance to unite with convicted delinquents, and the speedy failure following on every attempt to create such an association, are matters of deep significance. They show what a shock has been given to public confidence, which must be restored ere there can be a hope of forming any effective confederation. This caution in trusting projects so often delusive, through the dishonesty of those who betrayed the people, is creditable to the virtue of the nation.

Finding how much they were deceived and injured by public men, the people should naturally expect from those who had been parties to the injury and deceit a sincere and sorrowful acknowledgment of their errors, as well as a sincere pledge of their resolve not to repeat them, before they could again be invested with the country's confidence. This should be the first necessary preliminary to the construction of any national association.

But it may be said that there was no such delinquency as is assumed, and that, therefore, there is no need of apology or reparation. I have no doubt but this is the opinion of several who would wish to take a prominent part in the association. The avowal of that opinion would be creditable to their candor, and not less useful in enabling the people to shape their own course, than the confession of having pursued a wrong career.

Giving, then, credit for sincerity in their views to this large section of the community who can see nothing faulty in what has been done, and who have not a word or feeling of reproach for the most notorious of dead or living delinquents, what is to be expected from an association in which these opinions might prevail? Nothing, in all consistency, but that those who hold them are prepared to play over again the same old game, in which they could see no harm.

To sanction such a result, and it would be the probable one, I am not at all prepared. I cannot enter into alliance with any who manifest no regret for the violation of former solemn engagements. To have been once deceived is in no way discreditable. It only argues a too generous confidence in the faith and integrity of our fellow-men. But to be deceived again by entering into unconditional fellowship with any who had been unfaithful to their trust, would expose one to the reproach of being a willing party to the deception.

Such are my views on the important subject of the requisition, and which I feel due to you, to myself, and to the country, thus to explain in reply to your communication. If I thought that against a large section of men who look solely to their narrow, individual interests, careless of the fate of the great mass of the people, you and some others in whom I have confidence could muster a sufficient force to be at your post, to watch and to baffle their selfish designs, I might then be induced to give any little influence I may have to the experiment; but, aware that the self seekers are always more ingenious in devising, and more active in prosecuting their schemes, than those who generously labor for the common weal, I must respectfully decline affixing my signature to the requisition. . . .[20]

Shortly after Dillon received this reply, the bishop of Down and Connor, Cornelius Denvir, was persuaded to write MacHale asking him to reconsider. The hand was the hand of the bishop of Down and Connor, but the voice was apparently the voice of his coadjutor. MacHale's reply was as succinct as it was devastating. "Your Lordship's kind and respected letter," he reported to Denvir on December 18, "has just reached me. It is not to the objects of the Association in that any objection is made. But I rather fear that, instead of sincerely and earnestly laboring for the attainment of those laudable objects, some will make use of them to forward their own selfish purposes. This fear is founded on recent experience, which has sunk deep into the minds of the people; nor is there any peculiar reason to hope that a similar deception will not be again practised."[21] "In looking over the published list of bishops (who had signed the requisition)," MacHale concluded insultingly, "I missed your Lordship's name out of the number. Wishing you all the blessings of the coming great festival. . . ."[22]

Less than a week after writing Denvir, MacHale forwarded the letter he had sent to Dillon on December 6 to several Irish newspapers to be published. He added insult to injury by including among those papers the *Irish People*, notorious as the particular organ of the Fenian Brotherhood in Ireland. The letter was published in the *Freeman's Journal* on December 22 and in the *Irish People* on December 24, the

20. Bernard O'Reilly, *John MacHale, Archbishop of Tuam* (New York, 1890), 2:536–39.

21. Ibid., pp. 541–42.

22. The fact was that Denvir had signed the requisition.

Thursday and the Saturday, respectively, before the Thursday, December 29, when the aggregate meeting to launch the National Association was to be held. The timing of the publication of MacHale's letter, of course, was designed to throw cold water on the whole effort. Still, a week after the aggregate meeting MacHale's old friend William O'Neill Daunt wrote asking him to reconsider his decision. "With regard to the particular elements of weakness," Daunt argued on January 6, 1865, "apprehended by your Grace, I wish respectfully to say a word or two. Firstly, I have reason to know that all the prelates who have joined the movement are thoroughly in earnest; and whatever may be your thoughts with reference to any particular or individual, there is, I submit, no reasonable doubt that the episcopal body will preserve the movement in its straightforward character and working. Next, I will remember that some members of the body then formed were so injudicious as to hint a desire of recovering for the Catholic Church a portion of the Ecclesiastical State Endowments."[23] "This was enough to destroy all chance of help from the British Voluntaries," Daunt added, referring to the English Liberation Society, whose avowed purpose was to make all churches in the United Kingdom purely voluntary associations. "But I took care at the Aggregate Meeting to give full emphasis to our thorough voluntaryism, and our total repudiation of this source of weakness."

In his reply a week later, MacHale added yet another dimension to his refusal to support the association. "You were, I believe," MacHale observed to Daunt on January 13, "the only one who ventured, in that Assembly, to refer to the great injury inflicted by the Union, and to the necessity of repairing it as the only efficient means of repairing the other grievances which engaged the attention of the Meeting."[24] "You observed fairly," he noted further, going on to refer to the Irish National League founded by John Martin and The O'Donoghue in early 1864, "that, though a member of the League, you deemed it not incompatible with your duties as such to aid in the present movement. It does not appear that there was any reciprocal response to the effect that those who would aid that Association would not deem it incompatible with their duties to advocate, through a similar convention, the restoration of a native legislature." "It is unnecessary," he continued, adding yet another betrayal to his earlier one, "to enumerate the obvious causes of the deep distrust in the recent movement. They are found in the studied forbearance from any reference to the

23. O'Reilly, pp. 539–40.
24. Ibid., pp. 540–41.

treachery already practised on the Irish people. One of the deepest, however, is the restriction of our country's misery to subordinate grievances, without daring even to allude to the prolific parent of wrong, from which all the rest derive their noxious vitality. Without, however, discussing this cause more at length, it is an obvious fact that there is no confidence in the present agitation."

Daunt apparently responded as soon as he received MacHale's letter. He explained on January 13 that he had just received the strongest assurances from the Central Committee of the English Liberation Society that it had agreed to support most heartily and actively the association's efforts to disestablish the Irish Church.[25] "Whether the movement be illusory or not," Daunt maintained, "must depend on the hierarchy, clergy, and people of Ireland. Your Grace, if with us, will be a tower of strength, and will potently help to infuse life and vigor into our councils and our acts." MacHale, who replied the next day, remained adamant, but Daunt persevered. "Only one word," he assured MacHale, "in answer to your Grace's kind letter of the 14th instant. It is this: —Granted the causes of distrust. I submit to your Grace that the true way to remove such distrust, to neutralize treachery, and thereby to render the Association operative for its good (though subordinate) objects, is for those who command the public confidence to join it, and to give it the strengths of their talent and virtue."[26] "Conceive of the effect upon the public mind," he begged of MacHale, "if the Archbishop of Tuam appeared in the ranks of the movement as a leader, carrying a resolution against place-hunting." Daunt then added in conclusion, "I shall not now intrude further on your Grace's time than to implore you to consider well whether much of what you desire would at once be supplied by your own adhesion and that of the numerous patriotic men who would follow your example."

In this correspondence with Daunt, it should be noted that Mac-Hale had shifted his ground in his refusal to support the association. In his letters to Dillon and Denvir, he based his refusal on his conviction that the leadership of the association was not to be trusted, though the objects of the association were laudable. In writing Daunt he maintained that there was really only one object worthy of a national agitation, and that was the Repeal of the Union, which was really the origin of all Irish grievances. By then insisting that the studied refusal of the leadership of the association to commit themselves

25. Ibid., p. 542.
26. Ibid., p. 543.

to Repeal was simply proof positive that they could not be trusted, MacHale cleverly covered the charge of inconsistency that might be leveled against him. In effect, he was arguing that the leadership was not only not to be trusted but too moderate. Although these were the written justifications for MacHale's refusal to support the association, there were perhaps even deeper reservations that affected his decision. What he undoubtedly disliked most about the leadership was the prominent part Cullen had taken in promoting the new movement, and especially his very prominent role at the aggregate meeting. Daunt had put his finger on the heart of the matter when he unwittingly asked MacHale to imagine himself "in the ranks of the movement as a leader, carrying a resolution against place-hunting."

MacHale never had any intention of appearing "in the ranks" of any political movement, much less consenting to be merely "a leader" in any such movement. What remained of MacHale's power and influence in the Irish Church depended on his remaining *the* leader of the clerical component of any national movement in the minds of the priests and people. That is why, for example, he set such impossible terms in his letter to Dillon. Those terms could not, in fact, be fulfilled without making MacHale morally *the* leader of the clerical component of the association. The point was not so much that MacHale demanded that those delinquents who had betrayed the movement in the 1850s must now publicly admit that they had erred, and also promise never to do it again, as rather that those (such as Cullen) who had no "word or feeling of reproach for the most notorious of dead or living delinquents" by their continued silence had demonstrated that they "are prepared to play over again the same old game in which they could see no harm." What MacHale was inviting Cullen to do, of course, was to denounce the delinquents of 1852 and thereby admit that his silence in the intervening twelve years had been a mistake. Any such acknowledgment from Cullen not only would have completed his political ruin in Ireland but also would have seriously compromised his religious and moral influence. MacHale was much too shrewd a political warrior to expect so humiliating a surrender from Cullen, and his letter to Dillon therefore was simply yet another of his political manifestos designed to enhance and magnify his image as the archetypal patriot bishop.

In the meantime, Dillon had been attempting to complete his arrangements to launch the association. "The Archbishop of Cashel & Dr.

Keane," he reported to Gillooly on December 19, "have promptly accepted our invitation to be present to speak. Your Mr. Digby writes to say he will attend and play any part that may be assigned to him. I foresee we will have plenty of good speaking" (G). "I think," Dillon added politely, "we shall set you down for the resolution on Education with Major O'Reilly for a seconder. You know the perplexities which beset one on that subject." "I fear not a few good men," he explained, "will be driven from our ranks if we show uncompromising hostility to the National Board. With that danger in view, in my humble judgement, we shall direct our attacks for the present against the superior education, in which I include the Model Schools. I have endeavoured to avoid the peril of framing a resolution which *ought* to command universal assent. I send you a copy and trust it will meet your approbation." "I need hardly tell your Lordship," Dillon confided further, "that for myself individually I regard Mixed education as radically false & mischievous and if I am disposed to tolerate the National Board for the present it is because its primary schools can hardly be called mixed at all. At least in three provinces out of the four." "It would be bad policy," he warned finally, "by going further than is absolutely necessary on this subject to diminish our chances of obtaining the other great objects we have in view." Cullen had also been working very hard to launch the new association. "The Archbishop of Dublin is taking a very active part," the archbishop of Armagh reported to Kirby on December 18, "in inaugurating a new Catholic association for Ireland" (K). "You will soon hear plenty about it through the newspapers," Dixon assured Kirby. "I trust that it will rouse the drooping spirits of the people and be the means of confirming substantial benefits on the country."

The National Association was finally launched on December 29, 1864, at the Rotundo in Dublin.[27] The lord mayor took the chair, and Dillon and Richard Devitt, a Dublin town councillor, were appointed secretaries to the aggregate meeting, which numbered some five thousand people. There were also present among the dignitaries seven bishops: the archbishops of Dublin and Cashel; the bishops of Elphin, Ardagh, Cloyne, and Ross; and the coadjutor to Meath. The lord mayor opened the proceedings by formally announcing the objects for which the association was to be formed—namely, a measure of compensation for improvements made by tenants, the disendowment of the established Church, and the setting up of a system of denominational education for Catholics. After the secretaries had read the usual

---

27. *Freeman's Journal*, December 30, 1864.

letters of greetings and godspeed from those who were unable to attend, Cullen rose to move the first of the resolutions. Instead of confining himself, however, to the subject of his resolution—the patent injustice of the Church establishment—Cullen took occasion to make what was, in effect, a keynote address. In a speech that took more than an hour and a quarter to deliver and ran to some thirteen thousand words in print, he proceeded to define at considerable length each of the objects for which the association was about to be formed. Significantly enough, Cullen also rearranged the order of the objects as they had been announced both in the requisition and in the introductory remarks of the lord mayor at the beginning of the meeting, thereby implicitly raising the question of their priority. He began with a discussion of the education question, which took up a little more than a quarter of his address, then turned to the land question, which took up something less than a quarter, and then devoted the remaining half to the subject of his resolution, the established Church.

In his opening remarks, Cullen took great care to emphasize that the association would unite rather than divide Irishmen and Catholics. Because the objects of the association were so evidently just and reasonable, there could be no real difference of opinion about them, and they were not, therefore, really either political or party matters. "It is barely necessary," he explained, "to announce such propositions in order to secure their adoption; they are evidently recommended by truth and justice, as well as by the circumstances of our country. They leave no room for any discussion or for serious dissension. They have no connection with party politics; there is nothing personal in them."[28] "If they be properly understood and explained," he further assured his audience, "I do not see how any rational man, it matters not what party he belongs to, can refuse to accede to them, and to aid in carrying them into operation." Cullen then proceeded to explain the education question properly. He actually said little that he had not said many times before. He demanded freedom and equality (which was for him a euphemism for denominationalism) of education for Catholics. Cullen deliberately chose, moreover, to concentrate his fire on the national system of education, apparently ignoring Dillon's view that such an attack was not sound political tactics at that moment. "As far as Government is concerned," Cullen declared uncompromisingly, "its encroachments must be resisted. Government control ought to be limited to the right of providing for the proper and

28. Patrick Francis Moran, ed., *The Pastoral Letters and Other Writings of Cardinal Cullen* (Dublin, 1882), 2:283–84.

careful expenditure of the funds alloted by the public for education. The Government has no right to interfere any further in educational matters, nor is it useful that they should neglect the great political affairs of the nation, and the discharge of their other necessary duties, in attempting to manage things not within their proper sphere."[29]

In turning to discuss the land question, Cullen was a good deal less dogmatic and considerably more wary. "It is one," he noted cautiously, "surrounded with inextricable difficulties, but its settlement is of vital importance to all classes: it is a subject in which everyone who loves his country, and who is animated with a spirit of Christian charity, and feelings of mercy towards the afflicted, must take a deep interest."[30] The condition of the country, he maintained, was nothing less than deplorable: the loss of population in twenty years was three million; emigration still continued; agriculture was in a very backward state; high rents, no leases, and low prices for cereals were likely to result in even greater poverty; trade was declining, and many towns were either in decay or had disappeared; manufactures were nonexistent, and even the production of flour and oatmeal had fallen so that the mills were idle and there was greater unemployment. "Hence," Cullen noted, "a general poverty prevails: the country merchants, the small shopkeepers, the small farmers, many classes of tradesmen, and all of the labouring classes, are in a normal state of distress."[31] What was the reason for Ireland's prostration and misery? The cause, Cullen charged, was three hundred years of English misrule, persecution, and confiscation.

But whatever the cause, the real question now, Cullen maintained, was what was to be done. God, he was confident, would not abandon his people.

> But whilst putting great confidence in God, it is meet that we should use all just and constitutional means to obtain relief from the evils that press on us. I say just, and legal, and constitutional means: for it is foolish, it is wicked, to speak of having recourse to violence and bloodshed, or to expect anything good from illegal combinations and secret societies. On every occasion when our people were led to deeds of violence, or induced by false friends to raise the standard of revolution, the evils of the country were exceedingly increased. It happened so in the end of the last, and the beginning of the present century; and the recourse

29. Ibid., pp. 292–93.
30. Ibid., p. 294.
31. Ibid., p. 295.

to force, which some mistaken patriots adopted a few years ago, only divided and weakened the country, and left us not only an easy prey, but an object of contempt to the foes of our native land. I say, then, that those who invoke the aid of foreign armies; those who talk of civil war, resistance to established authorities, and revolutionary movements are the worst enemies of Ireland and its ancient faith.[32]

"It is our duty and our interest, my Lord Mayor," Cullen then declared firmly, "to walk in the footsteps of our great Liberator, Daniel O'Connell. By peaceable means and by force of reason, without violating any law, he broke the chains which bound Ireland for so long a period, and obtained Catholic Emancipation."

Still, the question remained what was to be done. The evil results of centuries of misrule could not be remedied in a day, but if the tenants were given the right to compensation for valuable improvements, that at least would be a beginning. "Such a measure," Cullen admitted, "will not remove all grievances, but it will be a commencement; it will encourage industry and secure considerable employment for the people."[33] At this point, Cullen then surprisingly proceeded to make what for him was a most radical suggestion. He cautiously endorsed a proposal made by John Bright, the celebrated English Radical and arch-exponent of the doctrine of Free Trade, that the final solution to the land question in Ireland must eventually lie in the establishment of a peasant proprietorship. "Perhaps in accordance with Mr. Bright's letter," Cullen suggested, referring to a letter of encouragement from Bright read by one of the secretaries at the commencement of the meeting, "something more effectual may be done hereafter; and free trade as it is established in regard to almost everything else, may be extended to land. It certainly would be a great advantage to increase the number of those who hold property in fee." Some such step, Cullen argued, was apparently necessary, because many of the landlords were either unwilling or unable to fulfill their elementary social and economic functions in Irish society. Some were absentees, others were on the verge of bankruptcy, and some were deeply hostile "to the ancient inhabitants of the country whose property was confiscated in their favour, and to whose religion they entertain a hereditary dislike." Though there were also many good landlords, who were interested in the welfare of their people and whose property and influence should be preserved, he further maintained that the general state of the coun-

32. Ibid., pp. 296–97.
33. Ibid., p. 298.

try was such at present "that if by free trade in land the number of landed proprietors were increased; if a system like that of Belgium and many parts of the Continent, where almost every man holds the fee-simple of his field, were introduced; if confidence and certainty of enjoying the work of his hands were given to the tiller of the soil[,] [t]he prosperity and security of the country would be greatly promoted."

In finally turning to the subject of his resolution, the established Church, Cullen entered into a long historical account of that Church from its beginnings during the Henrician Reformation in the sixteenth century. On examination, Cullen came to the conclusion that the established Church was founded in iniquity, had survived by intimidation and violence, and was fruitful only in its bigotry and intolerance. And what had been the long-term results of so much bigotry and violence? "The late census tells us," he reported, "that every effort to introduce Protestantism has been a complete failure, and that, notwithstanding so many persecutions and sufferings, the old Catholic faith is still the religion of the land, deeply rooted in the affections of the people." Cullen then pointed out that the members of the established Church numbered fewer than 700,000 and that of the 2,428 parishes that made up that Church in 1861, 199 contained no members, 575 had fewer than 20 members, 416 fewer than 50, and 349 fewer than 100; that is, 1,539 parishes in all had fewer than 100 members. The establishment had, in fact, "no support save in the protection of the State, of which it is the creature and the slave"; he urged that it "ought not to be any longer tolerated in this country—that it ought to be disendowed, and its revenues applied to the purposes of public utility."[34] Cullen then put his resolution to the meeting:

34. Ibid., pp. 319–20. It is interesting to note that Cullen's concluding remarks, as recast by himself and later edited by Moran, vary considerably from the original account in the *Freeman's Journal*, which read: "Moreover, you will admit that it [the established Church] has been the persevering enemy of civil and religious liberty, that it called for penal laws in every century from the days of Elizabeth to the passing of the Ecclesiastical Titles Act; that it never failed to oppose every proposal for the relaxation of such laws, not only in the days of Strafford and Clarendon, but even when there was question of emancipation in the midst of liberality in the present century; that it inflicted great evils on Ireland by depriving the mass of the people of all the means of education, by persecuting schoolmasters, and seizing on and confiscating schools, and, finally, that it has always been the fruitful source of dissensions in the country, and never more so than at present, when Protestant ministers have established a sort of traffic in the souls of poor children, hoping, by educating them in error, to prop up the tottering Establishment and increase its members, and when, with the aid of gold from England, they are carrying on a most insulting system of pecuniary proselytism, a system founded on bigotry and intolerance, and distinguished by its hypocristy [sic] and a total absence of Christian charity."

That the entire ecclesiastical revenues of Ireland amounting to upwards of £580,000 annually, are appropriated to the maintenance of a Church, which (according to the latest census), counts among its members only 691,872 persons—being less than one-seventh of the entire population of this island. That this singular institution was originally established, and has always been maintained by force, in opposition to reason and justice, and in defiance of the will of the great majority of the Irish people. That we, therefore, resent it as a badge of national servitude, offensive and degrading alike to all Irishmen, Protestant and Catholic alike.[35]

After Cullen sat down amid continued cheers and applause, his motion was seconded by Ignatius Kennedy and passed unanimously.

In his very long and able address, Cullen had indeed framed a most comprehensive charge for the meeting, and all of those who proceeded to move and second the remaining resolutions concerning the other objects of the association did not basically deviate from the fundamental line he laid down. In moving the second resolution, on the disendowment of the established Church, William O'Neill Daunt was mainly concerned with making certain that all the property made available by such a disendowment would be devoted to secular rather than religious purposes, thus ensuring that all the various churches in Ireland would become voluntary associations. In this way the budding parliamentary alliance between the English Liberation Society and the National Association, which Daunt had worked so hard to establish, would be made more effective, and disestablishment all around in Ireland eventually achieved.

After Daunt's motion was seconded by Kenelm Digby, and passed unanimously, the archbishop of Cashel, Patrick Leahy, rose to propose the first of two resolutions on the land question. Leahy, who addressed himself to the injustices of the present land system, was, like Cullen, very cautious and moderate in his remarks. "What has anyone," he asked, "a better right to consider his own than the labour or capital a tenant employs in improving his land?"[36] Any system that did not allow such a tenant compensation, he further maintained, was inherently unjust. Leahy then emphasized the fact that the bishops had decided to enter the political arena because they were ministers of justice as well as of peace and were therefore obliged to consider the

35. *Freeman's Journal*, December 30, 1864.
36. Ibid., quoted in Norman, p. 148.

welfare of their people, especially as they were being swept away by emigration before their very eyes. Indeed, if they did nothing in the present crisis they would forfeit the confidence of their people.

Leahy's motion was seconded by John Francis Maguire, M.P. for Dungarvan and proprietor and editor of the *Cork Examiner*, who proceeded to raise explicitly the question raised implicitly by Cullen in his ordering of the objects of the association. By firmly declaring that the land question was the preeminent question because the survival of the Irish people as a people depended on the settlement of it, Maguire left little doubt where he stood regarding the priority of the objects of the association. After Leahy's resolution had been passed unanimously, the bishop of Cloyne, William Keane, proposed the second resolution on the land question. In urging that a legislative measure be called for to compensate tenants for their improvements, Keane also stressed the urgency of the land question before all others and labeled it "the question of questions."[37] After thus endorsing Maguire's stand on the difficult question of priorities, Keane then went on to refer to the even more touchy issue of the pledge breaking that had wrecked the Tenant Right movement in the 1850s. What they now needed, Keane maintained, were good men who would not betray the public confidence. Even twenty good men, united and determined, could do the people's work in Parliament. Keane's resolution was seconded by Edmond J. Synan, an unsuccessful candidate for Parliament for county Limerick in the late general election; it was also passed unanimously.

The resolution on the education question was then proposed by Gillooly and seconded by Myles O'Reilly, M.P. for county Longford. Both Gillooly and O'Reilly deplored the interference of the state in educational matters. They demanded that Ireland be treated like England and given a denominational system of education. This too was passed unanimously, as was the next resolution, formally thanking all who had worked in the interests of Ireland in promoting the association, which was moved by W. K. Sullivan, professor of chemistry at the Catholic University, and seconded by John Lawlor, the mayor of Waterford. Finally, after more than five hours, Richard Devitt rose to propose a resolution to found the National Association. The resolution included the rules of the association, which were to serve as its constitution and which numbered eleven in all:

> That an association be now formed for the purposes indicated in the foregoing resolutions, that its title and fundamental rules shall be as follows:

37. *Freeman's Journal*, December 30, 1864, quoted in Norman, p. 149.

1. The association shall be called the National Association of Ireland. Its objects shall be—1st. To secure by law to occupiers of land in Ireland compensation for all valuable improvements effected by them. 2nd. The disendowment of the Irish Protestant Church, and the application of its revenues to purposes of national utility, saving all vested rights. 3rd. Freedom and equality of education for the several denominations and classes in Ireland.

2. The Association will seek to realize its objects by convincing, as far as possible, all men of their fairness and utility, by fostering a rational and intelligent patriotism, by uniting the people for mutual aid and protection, and by placing in representative positions, both imperial and local, men from whose principles and character they may anticipate a disinterested and effective support.

3. The Association will not support any political party which shall not in good faith co-operate with it in establishing by law the tenants' right to compensation, or in procuring the disendowment of the Established Church. Neither will it recommend, or assist in the election of, any candidate who will not pledge himself to act on the same principle.

4. No member of the Association shall be bound by, or answerable for, any opinion expressed, or language uttered by any other member at any of the meetings thereof.

5. The affairs of the Association shall be managed by a Committee, who shall appoint such officers as they may deem necessary, shall fix the times and places for holding public meetings, and shall appoint a chairman to preside at each meeting.

6. The Committee shall also have power to make bye-laws for the regulation of their own proceedings and of the general business of the Association, provided that such bye-laws shall accord with the general scope and objects of the Association, and that no such bye-laws shall contravene any of these fundamental rules; and provided that such bye-laws shall be passed at a meeting of not less than ten members.

7. At the public meetings of the Association it shall be the duty of the Chairman to prevent violent or illegal discussion; and if any member shall, in defiance of the Chairman, persist in such discussion, the Chairman shall thereupon have power to declare the meeting adjourned, and shall bring the conduct of the member so offending under the notice of the Committee at its next meeting.

8. The Committee, at a meeting to be especially convened for that purpose, shall have power to expunge from the list of

members and associates, the name of any person so offending; and the person whose name shall be so expunged shall thereupon cease to be a member of, or an associate, as the case may be.

9. The accounts of the Association shall be audited and published at such intervals as the Committee may deem expedient—such intervals not to exceed six months.

10. Every person approving of the objects of the Association, and accepting its rules, whose admission shall be moved and seconded at a public meeting thereof, may be admitted and remain a member, on handing in to the Secretary an annual sum of one pound, and may be admitted and remain an associate on paying an annual subscription of one shilling.

11. These fundamental rules shall not be abrogated, added to, or in any respect altered, unless by the vote of the Committee passed at two successive meetings (called by special notice for the purpose) and confirmed by the Association at a public meeting thereof.[38]

James Canon Redmond of Arklow seconded the resolution, and it was passed, as all the others had been, unanimously. The customary vote of thanks to the chair was then proposed, and the aggregate meeting was finally terminated after a grueling six hours.

The following day, December 30, when Cullen wrote Moran, he was still obviously elated (C). "We had a great meeting," he reported, "to form a new association yesterday. Dr. Leahy, Dr. Keane, Dr. Kilduff, Dr. Nulty, Dr. O'Hea, Dr. Gillooly attended. There was an immense crowd." "Everything went on," he explained, "most orderly. Some few Fenians attempted to give annoyance, but the people put them out. I denounced the same Fenians very strongly, and got great cheering from the crowd—so it is clear the party has no power in Dublin. When I was about to begin to speak the whole assembly took off hats, and stood up and cheered for several minutes. This was an answer to the Fenians. I made a long speech and read several extracts from your work on the Reformation." "I will [have] the speech printed," he added, "but I must compose it over again. O'Neill Daunt made a very good attack on the Prot. church, but terminated most foolishly by a eulogy on Smith O'Brien. Maguire M.P. made an excellent speech—Dr. Keane brought in a little young Irelandism, and seemed to be anxious to get a good cheer. The people cheer everything that is menacing to the English government, though it may be sheer nonsense. It is hard to do anything right." "Dr. McHale," Cullen com-

38. Ibid., quoted in Norman, pp. 150–51.

plained finally in conclusion, "was crying out for a long time for an association. The moment the Lord Mayor undertook the matter, he comes out with a letter against it. He will never join an association until Keogh and Co. do penance for their past transgressions."

The most striking thing about the aggregate meeting, of course, was the masterful way in which Cullen dominated the proceedings. His hand may be easily discerned in both the setting out of the objects and the drawing up of the rules of the association. A consideration of the objects, for example, reveals the clever way in which Cullen orchestrated them to meet his own views. The original requisition had listed the land, the Church, and the education question in that order. The aggregate meeting, however, dealt with the Church first, then the land, and finally the education question. In his keynote address Cullen set up yet another order, treating the education question first, then the land, and finally the Church. When the rules were presented to the meeting, the order came full circle, as the objects were again listed as they had been in the original requisition. The question, of course, is why the order of the objects was changed for the aggregate meeting, and then why Cullen rearranged them again in his address.

Cullen was obviously determined to speak first in order to lay down the law at great length on the objects of the association for those speakers who were to follow him, for if they did not want to contradict him personally, and in public, they would have to follow the line he had presented. He was so determined because he realized that the land question was potentially the most divisive one among the objects of the association as far as the Catholic body was concerned. In his remarks to the aggregate meeting on that question, therefore, he devoted the greatest part of his time to a review of the woes and miseries of Ireland that would have warmed the heart of even Father Lavelle and to a denunciation of revolutionary means and Fenianism in favor of the constitutional methods of O'Connell. His recommendation of a peasant proprietary, while most surprising, was undoubtedly an unguarded afterthought prompted by John Bright's letter to the meeting, because Cullen never apparently mentioned the subject again during the life of the association. Indeed, ever since he had been reported to Rome some fifteen years earlier, during the Tenant Right agitation, for his allegedly questionable views on the rights of private property, he had always been most cautious about the land question. Given, then, that he was determined to speak first, and that he was also determined to subordinate the land question, the original order of the objects in the requisition had to be changed. But why didn't Cullen choose to begin by proposing the resolution of the education question, which he would have found even more congenial than the one on the Church establishment? He did not because such a move would have stamped the association Catholic rather than national, and Dillon was already very concerned, as he had explained to Gillooly, that the association should not appear too obviously clerical in its formation. The order in Cullen's address to the meeting was thus determined by the order of the objects at the meeting, because he had to end up with the Church question in order to introduce his proposed resolution; he began therefore with the education question, thus appropriately sandwiching the land question.

Cullen's fine hand can also be discerned in the drawing up of the rules of the association, and most particularly in the third rule, which maintained: "The Association will not support any political party which shall not in good faith co-operate with it in establishing by law the tenants' right to compensation, or in procuring the disendowment of the Established Church. Neither will it recommend, or assist in the election of, any candidate who will not pledge himself to act in the same principle."[39] What was most interesting about this rule was that it was the operative rule for the achieving of the objects of the association. What was most significant about it, however, was that it said absolutely nothing about the third object of the association, the education question. The reason, of course, was that the bishops in general, and Cullen in particular, were determined to prevent any lay or even clerical initiative in the association on a question they had come to view as peculiarly their own.

If there were any doubts about the real order of priority of the objects of the association in Cullen's mind, they were certainly dispelled, at least for his clergy, in the pastoral he sent them on January 23, on the occasion of the approaching Feast of St. Brigid. In enclosing a recast copy of the address he delivered at the aggregate meeting, Cullen explained that the "three important questions which occupied the attention of the late meeting, are of deep interest to every Irish Catholic. The first regards education, on which the future welfare of our religion chiefly depends."[40] Cullen then at considerable length indicted the charter schools, Trinity College, the Queen's Colleges, and the national system in that order. "Having said so much," he then briefly noted, "on the first object proposed to itself by the new Association, I shall merely say, in reference to the protection of the tillers of the soil, that no one can look with indifference on their sufferings,

39. Ibid.
40. Moran 2:322.

and that it is a great work of charity to make every exertion to prevent their total ruin." Cullen then proceeded to devote a paragraph of some 150 words to the third object of the association—the disendowment of the established Church—before concluding.

"As so many respectable laymen," he advised his clergy cautiously, "have undertaken to conduct the business of the Association, and so many priests and bishops have already given in their adhesion to it, it would afford me great pleasure to see as many of you as can spare time, take part in the good work, and aid in carrying it on by your influence, in obtaining associates and members, and by your counsels and contributions."[41] "In promoting this undertaking, of course," Cullen warned, "none of us can be expected to neglect any of our duties, or to do anything inconsistent with the ecclesiastical state." "It will be necessary also," he then added, "to be directed by the decrees which all the Bishops of Ireland adopted in the year 1854, for the guidance of clergymen in reference to temporal matters—decrees which were approved by the Holy See. I enclose a copy of them, which you will find were framed with great moderation and wisdom."[42] These concluding remarks to his clergy were undoubtedly intended for Roman consumption, for Cullen's priests were at least as much aware of the decrees of 1854 as any body of clergy in Ireland. Indeed, Cullen was very cautious about the association in his correspondence with Rome. After the aggregate meeting, he hardly ever mentioned it in his letters to Kirby or Moran, and in his correspondence with Barnabò he referred to it only once, and then only indirectly and very early. "A few days ago I profited from a great meeting which was held here in Dublin," he reported to Barnabò on January 6, 1865, "to elucidate the greatest dangers to the Church and to Ireland [i.e., the Fenian menace]. All the people gathered, there were about five thousand persons present, greatly applauded my words; so much so, that one may hope, that in Dublin evil influence will not make much progress."[43]

Given the considerable amount of time Cullen was to devote to the affairs of the association during the next six months, his ignoring it in his correspondence with Rome was certainly curious. His ambivalence was, in fact, deeply rooted in the reservations he had always had about participating in politics. The key to understanding his position is to appreciate that his one priority in all Catholic action was unity. Anything that would divide the Catholic body, unless it was a matter

41. Ibid., p. 326.
42. For text of the decrees see Emmet Larkin, *The Making of the Roman Catholic Church in Ireland, 1850–1860* (Chapel Hill, N.C., 1980), p. 498.
43. S.R.C., vol. 35, fols. 173.

of principle, was to be avoided at all costs. Politics, therefore, was the great danger, and especially for the clergy, because the people were deeply divided about both ends and means, and active participation by the bishops and clergy must inevitably result in their taking sides. For example, when the matter of an association was first broached to Cullen by the lord mayor, Cullen's view was that the object should be limited to securing the disestablishment of the Protestant Church in Ireland, because that was an issue on which the Catholic body was united. Indeed, up until the drafting of the requisition for the aggregate meeting, the single-plank platform of disestablishment appeared to have been agreed on by all. The proposal to extend the objects of the association to the land and education questions probably came from Dillon, and was supported by the other members of the organizing committee, in the interests of broadening the political base of the association. Cullen ironically had to defer to the recommendation in the interests of that unity and harmony of which he was the arch-exponent. In doing so, however, he must have had very serious misgivings, not only because he thought the land question was potentially a most divisive one, but also because he was convinced the education question was the business of the bishops alone. This divided mind is what accounts for his extraordinary performance at the aggregate meeting, as well as for his laying down the law to his clergy in his pastoral several weeks later. Cullen's effort to remain in control of the association and provide it with leadership, however, would be undermined in the long run by his misgivings and reservations, because they weakened the commitment on which his control and leadership eventually depended. It was that very lack of commitment, in fact, which resulted in his so seldom mentioning the affairs of the association in his correspondence with Rome.

Indeed, the National Association launched with such energy and enthusiasm in the last days of 1864 was very slow in gathering momentum in the early days of the new year. Cullen reported to Kirby on January 31 that it was getting on very slowly (K). "It is hard," he then noted characteristically, "to keep laymen right especially on the education question." A week later the energetic coadjutor to the bishop of Down and Connor, Patrick Dorrian, was more expansive in attempting to explain to Kirby why there was so little enthusiasm for the new association. "It was unfortunate," Dorrian maintained on February 6, "that the Priests were for a time withdrawn from politics. For people were thus driven in despair to combine illegally, when they saw that nothing was to be done but sell them for sops to place-hunters" (K). "The new Association," he assured Kirby, "is sound at heart, but the country will be long in coming to *believe that*, after having been so often betrayed. However, I hope it will work its way and do good in time."

A test of the association's strength in the country was, in fact, not to be very long delayed. A by-election was to be held in late February to fill the county Tipperary seat vacated by the recent resignation of The O'Donoghue.[44] On February 14 the archbishop of Cashel circularized his clergy about the upcoming by-election (L). "Mr. Moore of Mooresfort," Leahy announced, "issues a new address and stands for the County on the principles of the National Association." "We must not," he advised his clergy, "let the County Tipperary pass out of our hands. Do the best you can at once with the Electors. I request your presence at a meeting of the Clergy, to take measures for upholding the independence of the County, which will be held here at the Sacristy of the Cathedral next Friday at twelve o'clock." Apparently not all of the Cashel clergy were able to attend the meeting on Friday, February 17, for Leahy had to brief his clergy immediately after the meeting with another circular. "At the meeting of the clergy held this day," Leahy reported, "it was unanimously resolved to support Mr. Moore at the coming election" (L). "Address the people on Sunday," he advised, "in the Chapel yard or in a convenient place. Call on the Electors to vote for Mr. Moore. Please have the Placards sent you put up on the Chapel Gates in time for the people to read them on Sunday." The reason Leahy was so concerned about mobilizing his clergy was that his candidate, Charles Moore, was opposed by the editor of the nationalist *Tipperary Advocate*, Peter Gill, who not only was the popular candidate but was strongly supported by the Fenian element in Tipperary, which was rumored to be very numerous. When the Conservatives in Tipperary were reported to have thrown their electoral support to Gill, the challenge to the Cashel clergy began to look very serious indeed. "Gill," Leahy informed his clergy grimly in yet another circular on Monday, February 20, "is now taken up by the Tories, and his election expenses paid by them, in the hope to put us

44. The borough of Tralee had become vacant when the sitting member, Thomas O'Hagan, the Irish attorney general, accepted the post of chief justice of the court of common pleas in Ireland. O'Donoghue decided to contest the Tralee seat, which he won against Joseph Neale McKenna, 115 votes to 79, and therefore he gave up his seat for county Tipperary. Technically, of course, one cannot resign from the House of Commons, but must apply for the office of the Chiltern Hundreds, which as an office of profit under the crown is incompatible with holding a seat in the Commons.

down and carry the County" (L). "Do your best with the people on Sunday," he exhorted. "Help to make the voters come to the poll on Monday."

The real difficulty in the election, however, had apparently less to do with the Fenians, or even the Tories in alliance with them, than with the lukewarmness with which the Cashel clergy viewed Moore's candidacy. Shortly after his return from the Tipperary by-election, John Blake Dillon wrote the bishop of Elphin explaining what had happened and how he became involved. "In going down to Tipperary," he assured Gillooly on March 3, "it was my intention to act merely in a professional capacity, and to keep clear of hustings oratory and the like. When I arrived at Clonmel I found the mob excited to the highest pitch in favour of Gill and against 'the candidate of the Archbishop,' as Mr. Moore was generally called" (G). "Many of the Priests themselves," Dillon reported, "half sympathised with the Fenian revolt against their own order, and the Tory landlords gave all their influence to Gill with the avowed purpose of detaching the people from the Priests and inflicting a death-blow on the influence of the latter." "Under the circumstances," he further explained, "I resolved to throw myself into the melee, and I spoke to the people not only at the hustings, but wherever I could find a crowd. I also spent a couple of days driving through the County, visiting the Priests and dissipating as far as I could, all delusion respecting the true character of the contest." When the poll was announced on February 27, though Moore had beaten Gill by more than two to one, receiving 2,134 votes to Gill's 930, the unusually low poll in an electorate of some 9,000 was a disturbing indication that the electorate as well as the clergy was not enthusiastic about "the candidate of the Archbishop."[45]

Before his visit to Tipperary Dillon had made yet another effort to enlist MacHale's support for the association. Dillon had met G. H. Moore by chance in Dublin about February 10, and they had discussed MacHale's refusal to join, which they both obviously attributed to the estrangement between him and Cullen. They apparently agreed to approach their respective archbishops to see whether a reconciliation could be effected. "I lost no time in writing the Archbishop of Tuam," Moore reported to Dillon on February 13, "and speaking to him on the subject which we lately considered and discussed together" (C). "I entirely agree with you," he assured Dillon, "in thinking that a sincere and cordial understanding between him and the Archbishop of

45. Brian M. Walker, ed., *Parliamentary Election Results in Ireland, 1801–1922* (Dublin, 1978), p. 100.

Dublin would be of inestimable benefit to the People and the Church of this our common Country. I am happy to be able to add that I am quite satisfied it will not be the fault of the Archbishop of Tuam, if such a understanding cannot be arrived at. With regard to the mode in which such a consummation may best be brought about, it would be presumption in one to express an opinion: —but I can scarcely doubt that in a matter of such importance those distinguished ecclesiastics will find a proper mode of communicating with each other, should they think such a conversation desirable." "If I could be of any service," he further assured Dillon in conclusion, "in effecting so desirable an object, I should consider myself highly honored; and I beg you to believe that I entertain no personal feeling towards either of those eminent prelates, except a wish that both may be equally an honor to their Church and their Country."

"Your letter rec^d this morning," Dillon reported to Moore on February 15, "is so well calculated to facilitate the accomplishment of the object we both desire, that I shall show it to the Archbishop without waiting to ask your permission."[46] "I shall certainly be greatly disappointed," Dillon explained,

> if I do not find him well disposed to make every reasonable advance and concession to His Grace of Tuam. I have the best reasons for knowing that *at present* the Archbishop of Dublin is as much alive, as any man can be, to the necessity for immediate & *energetic* action on the part of *Priests* and Laity. In principle I do not believe there is a shade of difference between the two Prelates. The objects of the Association are equally approved of by both. Its rules and the absence of all professional place hunters from its ranks afford a guarantee that an honest & independent policy will be adhered to. Under these circumstances if these two eminent Prelates will not unite for the common good it will be a grievous calamity.

"I sincerely feel," Dillon assured Moore warmly in conclusion, "that you could not render a more important service to the Country, than by endeavouring, as you are, to bring about this reconciliation. You will probably hear from me again on the subject in a week or few days. In the meantime, depend on my most earnest cooperation."

Dillon was apparently unable to see Cullen, and as he was obliged to leave for county Tipperary on February 16, he forwarded Moore's letter with a covering one of his own to the archbishop. "I had an

46. Moore Papers, 728, Dillon to Moore, February 15, 1865.

accidental meeting with the writer of this letter," he explained, shortly before he left for Thurles, "recently in Dublin, and the result was a strong impression on my mind that he is very well disposed" (C). "I believe Your Grace," Dillon added, "has some reason to be dissatisfied with certain things which have been said or done by him in past times. But I really believe that he is now disposed to cooperate with us cordially & harmoniously, and from the conversation I have had with him I have not the slightest apprehension that he would try to commit us to unpracticable or extravagant views." "I am not prepared," he assured Cullen politely in conclusion, "to suggest any step to be taken by Your Grace towards a *political* reconciliation with the Archbishop of Tuam, and so will content myself with assuring Your Grace that such a reconciliation would be hailed by the Country with genuine delight, and would certainly be of incalculable advantage to our Association." Unfortunately for Dillon, Cullen apparently decided to do nothing about his initiative to effect a reconciliation. When Dillon therefore did not write Moore again, as he had promised, that very proud and sensitive man apparently concluded that he had been used and dropped, and he was so deeply offended that he became from that moment on a mortal enemy of both Dillon and the association.

One of the reasons why Dillon was so very anxious to secure MacHale's support for the association at that moment was that the first monthly meeting was scheduled for February 20, and the announcement of MacHale's adhesion would have greatly helped to inspire public confidence. When the meeting was held, however, it was evident that the association was not prospering, particularly as far as the laity were concerned. There were only 200 members present, a great proportion of whom were clergy, and when the membership figures were announced, the difficulty was made manifest. The full members of the association, that is, those who had subscribed one pound, numbered only 305; and the associate members, those who had subscribed one shilling, were 748. When it is realized, moreover, that the Irish clergy numbered more than 3,000 strong in 1865, and that the number of clergymen in the association probably did not amount to more than 300, the lack of enthusiasm even among the clergy is apparent. Even Moore's victory over Gill in Tipperary a week later, on February 27, was something less than heartening to the more politically discerning, for the unusually low poll was certainly an accurate barometer of the lack of clerical and lay enthusiasm for both the association and its candidate.

Worse was yet to follow, and particularly for Cullen. A month later a by-election was occasioned in county Louth by the appointment of the sitting member, R. M. Bellew, as a poor-law commissioner. As soon as Cullen heard the news, he wrote the archbishop of Armagh, whose spiritual jurisdiction included county Louth, to recommend Sir John Gray, the proprietor and editor of the influential *Freeman's Journal*, as the proper person to contest the seat on the association's interest. "My own opinion, and the opinion of the Clergy here in Drogheda," Dixon assured Cullen on March 26, "is, that the Clergy and Catholic Body in Louth ought to be very grateful to Sir John Gray for coming forward on the conditions mentioned in your Grace's note" (C). "I am writing to the Dean," Dixon added, referring to Michael Kieran, the influential parish priest of Dundalk, "to know if the Clergy in any part of the county are thinking of another candidate. I shall communicate to you please God the substance of the Dean's answer to my note." The dean's answer was apparently not very reassuring. A new and aggressive political factor, it appears, had recently emerged in county Louth in the person of a twenty-eight-year-old Catholic barrister, Philip Callan. Callan was an admirer of the political views of G. H. Moore, The O'Donoghue, and the archbishop of Tuam,[47] and in this election he threw his support to Tristram Kennedy, a Protestant land agent of advanced nationalist political views, who had represented county Louth from 1852 until he was defeated, in a four-cornered contest for the two county seats in the general election of 1857, by a rabid Conservative, John McClintock, who had then lost the seat in the general election of 1859.

When Dixon wrote Cullen again about a week after his previous reply, the news he had to convey about the acceptability of Gray's candidacy was not very pleasant. "I fear—between ourselves," he explained to Cullen gently on April 3, "that the Catholic electors of Louth under their leader young Mr. Callan of Cookstown have thrown away a grand opportunity by not calling on Sir John Gray to be their candidate" (C). "However," he added stoically, "as Kennedy is the only person now to contest the county with McClintock we must make the most of the chance." "I have consented," he confessed, "to write a

---

47. In early 1863 Callan had been one of those constitutional nationalists circularized by Moore to attend the conference convened in Dublin on March 3, to consider the launching of a new nationalist organization. Callan had to decline the invitation on March 1, because he was then engaged in attending his obligatory law lectures at the Inner Temple in London. He also explained to Moore in the course of his letter that he had no hope for Irish politics unless a political society were to be formed by "known & trusted leaders like yourself, The O'Donohue [sic], & the Archbishop of the West." "The priests," he then advised Moore in conclusion, "are the only *power* in the country, with honest National feelings—and will gladly lead the people in a new struggle cheered on perhaps by the 'inspiration of a glorious future'" (Moore Papers, 894, fol. 725).

few lines in his [Kennedy's] favour, which I have allowed the Dean to publish, if he thinks proper. And I think it is better that the Association would support him if asked to do so, as if it were to hesitate in the circumstances, his chance of success, such as it is, would be worth nothing." The association did endorse Kennedy, and when the poll was finally declared on April 15, the margin of victory, as predicted by Dixon, was a narrow one: Kennedy won by only 79 votes in a poll of nearly 2,000—1,002 to 923.[48]

In order not only to appreciate what happened but to understand its significance, however, it is necessary to comprehend the complex political situation in county Louth. First of all, the electorate consisted of some 2,500 voters, mainly Catholic tenants of largely Protestant landlords. The Conservative-Protestant landlords could command about 1,100 votes among their tenants, whereas the Whig and Liberal-Protestant landlords could control about 1,000 votes. The remaining 400 votes in the county were usually cast in the Catholic and nationalist interest. For a generation after 1832, the Whig-Protestant, Catholic-nationalist coalition generally shared the representation, and the Catholic clergy, with Dean Kieran in the vanguard, proved to be a very effective makeweight in that coalition. In the early 1850s, however, the effort to set up an independent Irish party in the House of Commons had resulted in a serious split in the Catholic body in Louth, as elsewhere in Ireland, and the deep divisions had extended to the clergy as well. Those politicians who remained loyal to their Liberal connections in British politics were denounced by the advocates of independent opposition as "Whigs," who deserved to be driven from public life. When the senior member for county Louth, therefore, C. S. Fortescue, was appointed a junior lord of the Treasury and had to stand for reelection in 1854, the advocates of independent opposition decided to oppose him.[49] Fortescue had a very narrow electoral escape, managing to hold his seat with a majority of only 150 votes, after a very hard fought contest in which the Catholic clergy were deeply divided on the merits of the candidates.[50]

At the general election in 1857, however, the Whigs had their revenge: they entered, besides Fortescue, another candidate, R. M. Bellew—a well-connected Catholic Whig who had sat for the county from 1832 to 1852, when he had retired—thereby splitting the vote and allowing the Conservative, John McClintock, to replace Kennedy,

48. Walker, p. 101.
49. Larkin, pp. 226–27.
50. Walker, p. 300. The results were C. S. Fortescue, 914; J. M. McN. Cantwell, 766.

who was an ardent advocate of independent opposition, in the representation of the county.[51] This election was also a very bitter one, with the clergy once again taking sides. In the general election of 1859 the coalition was patched up, but Kennedy had to seek his political fortune in King's county, where he was defeated as a Liberal. The independent nationalists, however, had only been contained and not digested, for when Bellew resigned his seat in 1865 to accept the poor-law commissionership, they were rallied by Callan in an effort to regain their share of the representation in county Louth. The Whig landlords in Louth wisely decided to accept a compromise, and undoubtedly the peacemaker in that effort was Dean Kieran, who was anxious to reunite the Catholic body, and especially the clergy, in the county. No one apparently appreciated the dean's advice on this occasion more than the archbishop of Armagh, for he was not only willing to approve of Kennedy's candidacy but prepared to endorse it publicly, if necessary, in writing.

The real significance of the by-elections in Tipperary and Louth, however, was that they were an indication of the limits of both episcopal and clerical power in Irish politics. In Louth, for example, neither Cullen nor Dixon was able to impose Gray on the constituency, and in Tipperary it took an extraordinary effort by Leahy to rouse his clergy to make a poor effort on behalf of Moore. If they were determined, the bishops could obviously prevent their clergy from indulging in extravagant political behavior, but they were not able to persuade them to do their will in politics if the clergy were not predisposed to do so. In the operation of the political vehicle, in other words, the bishops, vis-à-vis their clergy, were able to apply the brake, but they were never able to get real control of the steering wheel. This was, moreover, the position of the clergy vis-à-vis the people in Irish politics. Yet while all this does something to explain how the clergy in Louth and Tipperary were able to resist the political views of their bishops, and perhaps even to explain how the electorates in particular constituencies were able to resist and check the views of their clergy, it does not really explain why the clergy were generally so apathetic about the association. This apathy is all the more curious because the unhappy social and economic circumstances of recent years, which had produced a revolutionary political situation, had made the need for a vigorous constitutional response obvious.

The question why the clergy did not take up the cause of the Na-

51. Ibid.: C. S. Fortescue, 1,376; J. McClintock, 1,089; R. M. Bellew, 894; T. Kennedy, 406.

tional Association with greater enthusiasm than they did is obviously a very difficult one. Ascertaining a negative in the motives of even an individual is hazardous enough, but attempting to do so in a body of three thousand is nothing less than presumptuous. Still, there are a number of things that are clear, even if they are not necessarily cumulatively conclusive. First of all, a very considerable number of clergy were not pleased with the objects of the association. The view of these clergy was best articulated by the archbishop of Tuam, who felt that there was really only one remedy for Irish grievances, and that was the Repeal of the Act of Union. Secondly, there was another and perhaps even larger group among the clergy who were also unhappy with the objects of the association, but for a different reason. These clergy were perhaps best represented by the coadjutor to the bishop of Meath, who was disturbed that there was no order of priority among the objects of the association, and most particularly that the land question was not given preeminence among those objects. Indeed, a great many of the clergy, and even a considerable number of the bishops, were convinced that the real question facing the country was the land question, especially in the light of the dreadful exodus that was taking place before their very eyes. "The prospects of our poor country," the bishop of Galway, John MacEvilly, informed Kirby, for example, on March 10, "are very saddening indeed. The poor tenants persecuted by landlords and unprotected by law are bent on emigrating in shoals. May God comfort them. I hope the new Association in Dublin, which I have earnestly enjoined the people in my Lenten pastoral to support, may be the means under God of procuring the removal of the leading grievances under which we labour. To say we are yet emancipated is sheer folly" (K).

The coadjutor to the bishop of Meath, Thomas Nulty, on the other hand, was a good deal less sanguine about the policy being pursued by the association. In his Lenten pastoral, therefore, he advocated a more aggressive line. When Cullen read Nulty's pastoral, he was not very pleased. "Part of it," Cullen explained to Kirby on March 10, "is very good, but then he denounces the M.P.'s for having prostituted their influence to the Whig Government as a rule—he accepts however the two M.P.'s for Meath, two most useless men, who do nothing whatever for the country. He also exhorts the priests to publish in every way possible all evictions etc." (K). "The priests," Cullen further pointed out, "are very much inclined to go astray in their denunciations. It is the good landlords they generally denounce. They scarcely ever say a word against the very bad, and anti-Catholic ones. Probably Dr. Nulty's advice will do no good." "Where the priests are kind and prudent," he finally assured Kirby, "they can generally prevent evictions—but where they are violent, they provoke the landlords."

The tide was rising, in the country and within the association itself, in favor of giving precedence to the land question among the objects of the association. "I wish," Dillon requested of the bishop of Elphin on March 18, "you would read and consider a letter addressed to me in this day's Nation, and signed a *Catholic Layman*" (G). "I suspect," he explained, "the writer is Mr. McCarthy Downing of Skibbereen. The opinions expressed in the letter may be regarded as widely prevalent; and I confess if the rules of the Assoc^n were now to be framed I sh^d urge the adoption of the course pointed out by the writer. Personally I attach little importance to these forms, but it is impossible not to perceive that a very large section of those who ought to be our foremost supporters are dissatisfied because the land question is placed on a level with the other two." "Amongst the disaffected," he reported, "are to be reckoned Dr. Nulty and all his Priests, and even Dr. Dorrian expresses strong dissatisfaction. We are now in the dilemma of being obliged to ignore their feeling and dispense with the aid of those who share it on the one hand, or of Exhibiting a certain degree of vacillation and unsteadiness on the other." "I wish your L^{d}ship w^d consider this matter," Dillon suggested, "and give me (at your leisure) the benefit of your advice."

Whatever Gillooly's advice may have been, the majority of the executive committee of the association was opposed to any modification of the rules. In an attempt to make its position clearer on the land question, however, the committee circulated to the membership on April 11, under Dillon's signature as chairman, a list of Suggestions for the Amendment of the Landed Property (Ireland) Improvement Act, 1860 (C). In his explanatory letter covering the Suggestions, Dillon was most cautious in making a case for the improving, solvent tenant and in assuring the membership that it was not the purpose of the association "to transfer property from one class to another, but rather to stimulate improvement, and to furnish motives for the creation of property, which, under present conditions, may never be called into existence" (C). The result was that the Meath clergy and their coadjutor bishop, who held "advanced views" on the land question and who also had a long tradition of ultra-nationalist politics, became even more dissatisfied with the association's stand both on the land question and on the political means advocated for a solution to it.

In order to soften this criticism, the executive committee of the association then agreed to a conference with its critics. "Dr. Nulty asks," Dillon informed Gillooly on April 15, "that the Conference should be *after* the 20th inst. Both Dr. Dorrian and Dr. Keane say they cannot be absent from home during the first week of May, and the latter wishes the 27th in order that he may have time to return. I shall wait to hear from Yr. Lordship before I definitely fix on the 27th as I am especially anxious that you should be present" (G). "Do you know," Dillon asked, "Mr. McCarthy Downing? He has been writing to me earnestly urging this Conference, and says he is so doing with express sanction of Dr. O'Hea and many of his Priests. If there be no very decided objection I should like to have him present." "This Conference," he assured Gillooly in conclusion, "if well managed will bring a large accession of strength."

The conference was eventually called for Friday, April 28, in Dublin. "The object of the meeting," Nicholas C. Whyte, the secretary of the association, informed Cullen on April 25, "will be to consider some proposals for modifying the rules of the Association so as to render them more universally acceptable" (C). This was certainly a victory for those who hoped to force a more aggressive and popular policy on the association. Patrick Dorrian, the coadjutor to the bishop of Down and Connor, reported to Kirby on May 2, "We had a conference on Friday in Dublin with the Committee of the National Association and the Meath clergy and the coadjutor Bishop; and the Archbishop of Dublin, Bishops of Cloyne, Ross, Elphin, and myself to bring about some amalgamation by a proper understanding of its Rules" (K). "I am happy to say," he assured Kirby, "the result is most satisfactory. It is a perfect amalgamation. The Independent policy is fully recognized, but not factious opposition. Opposition, however, to any Government which will not make the land a Cabinet Measure—No seeking of *favours*—and, as far as the policy of [the] Association can go, the Minority of M.P.'s to be bound by the Majority. This will make us all right, please God!"

Dorrian, however, proved to be too much of an optimist. At the conference it had been agreed that rule three, which had been adopted at the aggregate meeting on December 29, should be revised. It was in fact to be expanded into two new rules:

III. That this Association pledges itself to the policy of entire and complete parliamentary independence, and that—inasmuch as the reform of landlord and tenant is a question of pressing exigency, and can only be accomplished by its advocates in parliament voting, on all questions involving confidence in the Ministry, in opposition to government which will not adopt and make a Cabinet question a measure effectually securing compensation to the occupier of the soil for all improvements by which the annual letting value is increased—this Association will not support any candidate who will not pledge himself to adopt that course.

IV. That the acceptance of place or the solicitation of favours from government is incompatible with an independent attitude towards the ministry; and therefore it shall be a recommendation from this association to all Irish constituencies to bind their representatives to accept no place and to solicit no favour from any government which, by the foregoing rule, they shall be bound to oppose; and to bind their representatives further, to take counsel with the party in the House of Commons who hold the same principles, and to act in accordance with the decision of the majority.[52]

The new rules were leaked to the press in an obvious effort to prevent them from being further revised before they were, as rule eleven in the original rules required, submitted to a full meeting of the association for approval. The executive committee refused to be intimidated by the leak, however, and did, in fact, further revise rule three to read:

This Association pledges itself to the policy of complete Parliamentary Independence, and will support no Candidate for Parliament, who will not pledge himself to vote for all the objects of the Association, and further, to vote (on all questions involving confidence in the Ministry) in opposition to any Government that will not adopt and make a Cabinet Question a satisfactory measure to Tenant Compensation; that question being deemed by the Association of pressing urgency.[53]

This revision of new rule three was basic in two fundamental ways. Firstly, in its original form, new rule three, by ignoring the other objects of the association—the established Church and education questions—had turned the association effectively into a Tenant Right organization, and the revision corrected that anomaly. Secondly, rule three had defined a satisfactory tenant right measure as "compensation to the occupiers of the soil for all improvements by which the annual letting value is increased," thus tying compensation, in effect, to any increase in the rent and introducing a principle that was, at least as far as a British Parliament of landowners was concerned, subversive of

52. *Freeman's Journal*, June 20, 1865. See McCarthy Downing's speech.
53. C, Whyte to Cullen, May 6, 1865.

the right of property. As revised, the rule called for a "satisfactory" measure of tenant compensation, which would allow the adherents of the association in the House of Commons greater flexibility in dealing with so thorny a question as the rights of private property. The executive committee of the association then forwarded rule three, as revised, and rule four to the membership on May 6 by circular. The new rules apparently pleased no one. The Meath priests and those who advocated a forward policy with regard to the land question felt that they had been deceived, and Cullen was so displeased that he decided to resign from the association.

In writing to Gillooly on Monday, May 8, Cullen presumed that Gillooly had already seen the proposed new rules, which he had only just received himself, because they had also been published in the *London Register* on Saturday (G). Cullen pointed out that the letter which had accompanied the rules in the *Register* maintained that the association "now represents all the most advanced liberal opinions in Ireland." "I suppose the writer, who is probably Cavanagh [sic]," Cullen added dryly, referring to J. W. Kavanagh, professor of mathematics in the Catholic University, "takes in the Brothers of St. Patrick and the Fenians." "I think the new rules cannot be defended," Cullen declared firmly. "The association has not sufficient power to exact pledges from more than a dozen M. P.'s and if it commences to domineer over them, we shall lose the few good men we have." "The new rule," he then pointed out, referring to the added fourth rule, "is well calculated to throw everything into the hands of our enemies, and to keep the majority, the Catholics from occupying the places to which they have a full right." "I see so many objections against the changes that have been made," he added finally, "that I could not recommend anyone to adopt them. At the same time I do not wish to get into disputes. I have therefore sent in my resignation to the secretaries, and I will thus save myself from promoting the principles of independent opposition which I heartily condemn."

Cullen, however, had safer and saner second thoughts about resigning and decided instead to bide his time by entering a long and studied protest with the secretaries against the proposed changes in the rules.[54] "I have had," Cullen explained, "the amended form upon which you ask my opinion of the resolutions of the 28th of April

54. C. The memorandum is undated. See also G, Dillon to Gillooly, June 12, 1865.

before me for some days. Unwilling to reply till my many occupations should have allowed me to give the subject the mature consideration which it deserved I have been obliged to defer my answer till now." He elaborated his objections:

In the first place, let me say that I am sorry that any changes in the original rules of the association, even in the form of expression, should have been thought necessary, —On the one hand, the interchange of views which took place at the Conference on the 28th of April, between some members of the General Committee and the gentlemen from the Country who desired explicit expression of the Committee's views, satisfied me that there was no real difference of opinion on the subjects discussed; on the other I felt all along that any alterations of the language in which the fundamental principles of an Association such as ours, had been expressed, was calculated to expose us to the charge of instability and fickleness of purpose, and thus while affording a seeming triumph to our enemies, to render many even of the adherents to our principles timid and apprehensive, lest perchance even the very principles and conditions upon which alone they had joined the Association were actually, or at any future period might be altered.

"This much premised," Cullen further explained, "I proceed to make a few observations on the altered form of the resolutions as they are now before me."

In general, Cullen noted, he approved of the changes that had been made. Though they did not yet fully convey the opinions expressed at the aggregate meeting, they did now approach more nearly the full sense of that meeting than those which were drawn up, "confessedly in a hurry, in the last moments of a very protracted conference," and then circulated to the public. In particular, Cullen agreed that the parliamentary policy of the association should be one of complete independence of both English parties. He was pleased also that in the amended modifications the words "parliamentary Independence instead of *Independent opposition*" continued to be used. "The latter phrase," Cullen noted,

is I think open to misconstruction or has at least been, rightly or wrongly, understood as meaning a blind and indiscriminate opposition to every measure, irrespective of its merits emanating from a government like the present. This interpretation has it is true been disavowed by leading public men both of the Clergy and Laity, but it is equally true that the phrase in question has been used and extensively circulated as the watchword of an extreme, impracticable and morally unsound line of parliamentary action, and as the single criterion by which alone the sincerity of public men—no matter how independent their position or how undoubted their integrity and virtue—and the uprightness of their conduct should be judged.

"For similar reasons," Cullen further assured the secretaries,

I am happy to see the proposed test of the sincere application of the principle of a correctly understood Parliamentary Independence—that of an obligatory hostile vote to a government adverse to those interests which the Association considers paramount—expressly limited to questions of pure confidence in the Ministry of the day—thus explicitly recognising, the uncontestable right, nay, as it appears to me the bounden duty of members of Parliament to exercise their trust according to their conscientious view of the merits even of those questions upon which close, and what are called in the less scrupulous language of mere politics, party divisions may be anticipated between the adverse factions of the House.

"The next point of your modified resolutions," he then added, "upon which I shall offer an observation is the enumeration of the objects to which the previously stated policy of the Association shall be applied, which I am happy to find now so distinctly to comprise all its originally proposed objects, as completely to set at rest the doubts and even the misapprehensions to which apparent limitation of its effects to one object, however important, as expressed in the first form of your resolutions had given rise."

After thus prudently stressing the positive in regard to the revision of rule three, which had prevented the association from being turned into a mere Tenant Right organization, Cullen finally turned to what was really troubling him about the revised rule:

I fear, however, that even yet there is room for a misapprehension of the very opposite tendency and which would give rise to a misinterpretation of the resolution as it now stands, equally at variance with the well known good sense and practical mind of its leading members as the former misunderstanding was at variance with their well known sincerity and firmness of purpose— for as the resolution now stands, it would appear not alone to place the Association itself as such in an attitude of indifference to the merits of a Candidate for Parliamentary honours, who might perchance adopt what a particular Constituency might consider the most important two-thirds of the Association's programme—but further to oblige it [the association] to refuse its confidence to Members of Parliament, possibly too Members of its own body (for as the Association increases in members and influence it will undoubtedly number many such amongst its members), who would refuse to aid, for the time being, in expelling a Government from power, which with the serious intention of giving at least a large Installment of Justice to Ireland, might resolve to confer on the country the two most inestimable blessings—objects two [sic] of the earnest desires of the Association— the Subversion of the Prot. Church as by Law Established & the Freedom of Education from State Control—I am convinced that it never entered into the minds of those who drew up the resolution, which I am discussing as it now stands, to recommend a course of action so inconsistent and self-contradictory to the Association.

"I hope, therefore," Cullen added, "that before its final adoption at a general meeting a distinct and formal declaration, so formal & distinct as to prevent all danger of subsequent misunderstanding, may be given upon this head—and that it shall likewise be understood that the line of action traced out by the resolution applies to the Association as such and not to its members in their individual capacity." "That the Association," he further explained, "as a body should refuse an active support to all who do not embrace its full programme may be fair and reasonable. That wherever the Association feels itself able & thinks it right to interfere actively, no member of it should thwart or oppose its action is to be expected, but beyond this—that its members shall not be allowed to do the best they can in and out of Election times for promoting according to their conscientious judgement the general good, is not I think admissable."

Cullen then turned his attention to a careful analysis of those clauses that made up new rule four, adopted at the conference on April 28. "In the spirit which dictated its first clause," he noted, referring to the admonition that the acceptance of place or the solicitation of favors from the government was incompatible with an independent attitude toward the ministry, "I entirely agree, for nothing can be more deserving of public reprobation than the conduct of the man who accepts the confidence of the people, enters Parliament as representative of certain views, which he at least has professed to entertain in common with his constituents, and then barters the confidence so placed in him, and his now deliberate convictions, for the consideration of personal advancement or gain." "Still," he then added, entering his caveat, "there is a distinction—one fully recognized by the Conference, altho perhaps, from the general adverse usage of Parliamentary life not easily realised in practice between the corrupt solicitation of favor from or the exercise of patronage on behalf of a Ministry, and, the undoubted right, which in common with every other class of their countrymen, Irish Catholics have to an active and proportionate share in the administration of the country." "I think therefore," he then advised, "that your condemnation, otherwise so just, of the policy of seeking for personal interest or advantage on the part of Irish representatives, would be better expressed in words which would convey the distinction just explained between the demand for our rights and the corrupt craving for what is understood as mere government patronage."

"I wish, too," he further noted, turning to the second clause of rule four, the one exhorting the constituencies to exact pledges from their representatives in regard to government patronage, "that in recommending a mutual understanding of each other[']s views and principles between the Candidate for Parliamentary honours and the constituency, terms less indicative of distrust towards the former and of over-confidence on the part of the latter, and mere verbal engagements were used." "The best guarantee," Cullen explained, "for the effectual and honest discharge of the parliamentary trust, and of fidelity in parliament to the principles enunciated on the Hustings is the high personal character for religious and intellectual worth of the objects of their choice. Let constituencies look to this as the primary element in their selection and they will do much to maintain a high character of Parliamentary representation. Apart from this, mere verbal engagements no matter how emphatically entered into will prove of little value—the largest and readiest to promise are not infrequently the first to betray their pledges."

"I come now, before I conclude," Cullen finally pointed out, reaching the third clause of rule four,

> to the last point in your resolutions on which I feel obliged to offer any observation—that in which, for the sake of securing unanimity of action on the part of the popular representatives, you wish the constituencies to enforce upon them the rule of acting according to the decision of a majority of those who profess the principles of the Association. The object of this provision appears to be to ensure such unanimity of action as becomes an united party on the part of Irish representatives. Nothing cer-

tainly is more desirable, as unfortunately hitherto nothing was more wanted than such unanimity. It should not however be enforced in matters of detail by means which are at variance with that freedom of conscientious discretion, subject to which it was well understood at the Conference, that all restrictions imposed by the Association's rules should be understood. Now I think we can no more tie down the conscientious discretion of an individual member in a matter of detail to follow the course decided upon by a majority professing to hold the same principles as himself, than we can oblige him to an indiscriminate adverse vote on all questions not of confidence in the Ministry. The Authority to legislate, vested indeed by the Act of the people in their representatives comes from God, and each member[']s share of it forms in consequence not only a trust but a duty involving his personal responsibility, the discharge whereof he cannot in consequence by justly asked to delegate to any person or majority of persons.

"I hope therefore," he suggested, "that some other form of expression may yet be devised which shall bring this portion of your rules also into harmony with the unanimously expressed sentiments of the Conference to respect conscientious discretion of members in the discharge of their duties." "Let every fair means in fact be used to secure unanimity of action amongst Irish Popular representatives," Cullen then exhorted the secretaries, "and above all that without which all other means must of necessity fail—namely, the selection of Members to serve in Parliament whose personal character for integrity, religion and knowledge gives fair ground to hope that they will maintain in Parliament their public professions on the Hustings, but let us not by advancing any extreme or unsound test of public morality, the effect of which will be to banish from the service of the Country those whom we most need, and by giving occasion to unfair cavil and misrepresentation break up that union in which alone consists our strength."

"You will I trust," Cullen warned in conclusion,

excuse me for having trespassed at such length upon your patience but under the circumstances I could not do otherwise—occupying however unworthily a position, which induces many, from the respect they have for it—to attach great importance to every expression of opinion that emanates from it, and having both by example and exhortation invited those over whom I am supposed to exercise influence to join an Association for the attainment by practical and constitutional means of three objects which in common with its projectors I deemed of paramount importance to the country, I owe it both to myself and them to state how far I can accept the modifications of your rules proposed to be sanctioned in your approaching general meeting—that is in the sense only which as explained is compatible with the original purposes and rules of the Body.

What Cullen was saying, of course, was that if the rules were not further modified at the upcoming general meeting of the association to suit his understanding of them, he would in all likelihood be obliged to resign. But why did he change his mind about resigning immediately? Undoubtedly he did so because the government had just announced that it would dissolve Parliament and hold general elections in July. He certainly understood that if he persisted in resigning at that critical moment, and if the association were not successful at the general election, his political enemies, clerical and lay, would place the electoral disaster at his door and denounce him with even greater vehemence than they had in the 1850s as a Whig and Castle bishop. He therefore wisely entered only his formal protest, and prudently decided to wait and see what the full meeting of the association, required for any ratification of the modified rules, would do.

The meeting, which had been scheduled for June 5, had to be postponed until June 19. The reasons for the postponement, Nicholas Whyte, secretary of the association, explained to Gillooly on June 10, "were the knowledge that the attendance from the country would be very small and the fact that the proposed changes in the Rules of the Association had failed to elicit any response from those whom we were let to believe only waited for the change to join us 'en masse'" (G). "Should the meeting of the 19th inst. prove a failure," Whyte reported, "it is felt here that the fate of the Association is sealed. It will proclaim far and wide the apathy of the Country and will shew Parliament and the Govt that the grievances we talk of so loudly either are not really felt in Ireland or we are incapable of uniting for their redress." "Knowing your Lordship's feelings and opinions on the subject," he noted in concluding, "we entreat you to attend this meeting if possible and to endeavour to secure the attendance of some gentlemen from your district whose presence would excite the confidence of the people." "The Committee beg to remind your Lordship," Whyte added finally, "the important effect a large meeting at the present juncture may have on the approaching elections."

Several days later Dillon also wrote Gillooly urging him to attend the meeting. "I look forward with great apprehension," he confessed on June 12, "to the next meeting of the Association to be held on this day week. Indeed I think it will be better to hold no meeting if the influential friends of the Assoc^n will not attend. I have written Dr. Keane and Dr. Leahy urging them to come, and that they and Yr. Lordship sh^d have a private consultation previous to the meeting. If this be not done I see no prospect of escape from the perils which beset us." Dillon's apprehension had so increased by June 16, the Friday before the meeting on Monday, that he had decided against submitting the revised rules to the meeting. "I shall have no difficulty," he assured Gillooly on June 16, "in satisfying you of this when we meet and shall defer a full explanation until then. Under the circumstances I think the best thing I can do for the Association as well as for my own character, is to grapple with the difficulty boldly and explain how it has arisen and why I am driven to that course. This I can do without making an attack on any person or giving anyone just ground for offence" (G).

By this time, however, Gillooly had already decided that he would be unable to attend. As he explained to Cullen on June 15, he had arranged before the day of the meeting was appointed to hold a large and important conference of his clergy at which he had to be present (C). "I don't know," he further explained, "what your Grace has since done with reference to the amended rules—they are I suppose to be discussed & either approved or rejected on the 19th." "I have been thinking over that matter," Gillooly confessed, "and I am still convinced that it w^d be more prudent to allow the amended rules to be ratified. They will not be acted on to any extent detrimental to our interests, and if now opposed by yr. Grace, the Assoc^n will be virtually dissolved—to, I believe, the great disappointment & vexation of several of the Bishops who are cordially attached to your Grace & anxious to cooperate with you in eccles^l matters." "Such a disruption," Gillooly warned, "w^d I fear be productive of much permanent evil, and I hope your Grace will pardon me if I beg of you to prevent it." "I had no desire myself," he assured Cullen in conclusion, "for the change made or for the Conference that led to it, but once made with the sanction it received at the Committee meeting & in the Country, and published & discussed as it had been, it ought in my opinion to be upheld, and if the opposite course be pursued, all the consequences imaginary as well as real, will be attributed to your Grace."

In his reply on June 17, Cullen regretted that Gillooly would not be able to attend the meeting, but he was still very sore on the subject of the rules and not very sanguine about the future of the association (G). In Cullen's opinion the leaders of the association had gone astray, especially after McCarthy Downing had written his anonymous letter criticizing them in the *Nation* in March. "Since then," Cullen maintained,

> the three great objects of the Association have been practically given up, and nothing discussed but independent opposition—As yet this question is not settled, and even were it settled no good w^d result from it. None of the men whom we w^d wish to see in Parliament wish to pledge themselves to a course which they cannot persevere in, but every worthless candidate will pledge himself to any and everything, and then do nothing.
>
> Since the question of independent opposition was introduced, only two new members have joined the Association. In the meantime expenses go on and debts are contracted. I believe that not one single priest from Meath joined the Association since or before the Conference in which they had their own way.
>
> I have never gone since that Conference to the Association and as I do not like wrangling I will not go any more until its principles are finally settled.
>
> My opinion is that the question of independent opposition had disjointed the Association in such a way that it will have to dissolve itself in a few weeks. I have repeatedly told Dillon that this would be the result. In his desire to gain a large accession of members I think he has lost both the moderate party and the ultras to please whom he was not inclined to go far enough.

Cullen then added in conclusion, after explaining that in order to avoid any public difference of opinion he too would not attend the meeting on Monday, "If the Priests of Meath or others come up, and assist in obtaining the three objects of the Association, I wish them every success, but it seems to me that they intend doing nothing themselves, and that their great object is to compel others to adopt their way of thinking on independent opposition and other theoretical questions, the discussion of which will do no one any good."[55]

Therefore, when the general meeting of the association finally assembled on June 19, in the Pillar Room of the Rotundo in Dublin, the only prelate present was Nicholas Conaty, the bishop of Kilmore. The chair was taken by Alderman MacSwiney, the former lord mayor of Dublin, who proceeded to review for his auditors the achievements of the association to date, and to reassure them that they might "fairly

55. Dillon had already come to the same conclusion about the Meath clergy. See G, Dillon to Gillooly, Sunday [June 4, 1865].

look forward with hopeful hearts to the future."[56] "If true to the principles of their great departed chief," MacSwiney then added, referring to Daniel O'Connell,

> it was impossible for them to err or go astray. False teachers were among the people, entrapping them to their ruin and swearing them to carry out the wildest and most senseless doctrines; therefore, it behooved the friends of order and of society to denounce the miscreants who thus trade on the credulity of the people, who blacken the character of their pastors in order that they may undermine their faith, and thus make them an easy prey to the spy and the informer (cheers). It behooved all who felt an interest in the country to rally round the National Association of Ireland, the only Association which in their day was calculated to unite the prelates, the priests, and the people of Ireland (hear, hear).

"Every man," MacSwiney then further advised, "should ask himself this question, were the objects of the association deserving [of] his support? If so, why should the mere working of a rule—if the rule itself were right—deter him from joining the Association?" "For his part," he declared, taking up Cullen's line, "he looked to a man's character for honour and integrity as far more valuable and reliable than all the pledges that ever were framed and glazed for the study of needy adventurers. He was for sending men into parliament upon whom he could depend for an honest vote—he was for returning men who could act together for the good of the country, who could afford to be independent of Whig or Tory government, and who would vote against either the one or the other when the programme of that Association would be unheeded or ignored by them (cheers)."

The secretary of the association, Nicholas Whyte, then read letters from four bishops, Leahy (Cashel), Gillooly (Elphin), O'Hea (Ross), and Dorrian (coadjutor, Down and Connor), expressing their regrets that diocesan duties prevented them from attending the meeting. Whyte next presented a list of some 120 names, the great majority of whom were priests, who had applied for membership in the association, and on the motion of Dillon they were formally admitted. Whyte further proposed that the 998 gentlemen who had applied since the last meeting of the association be also admitted as members, and his motion was unanimously adopted. Dillon then proposed that the executive committee of the association be enlarged by some 50 members, the

56. *Freeman's Journal,* June 20, 1865.

majority of whom (28 of 53) were clergymen. After this increase in the committee was also unanimously adopted, Dillon introduced the address that was to be presented to the electors of Ireland on behalf of the association in the upcoming general election. "Here is the practical course we recommend," the address announced.

Let a committee of electors be formed in each county and borough. Let all electors favourable to the objects of this association be invited to join it. Let us consider the claims and the characters of the present representatives, and if they have been faithful to their trust, let them not be hastily rejected or condemned. Let all due allowance be made for the apathy of the country, and the want of an organized plan of action by which many a well-disposed representative has been paralysed and rendered useless. But let there be no tolerance of deliberate treachery, no trafficking with corruption, no respect or forebearance towards the man who will presume to ask the suffrages of the people without clearly and explicitly informing them of the grounds on which he does so.

"If the object of your selection," the address then further advised, "should be a local gentleman whose principles are known to you, and whose character is a guarantee that those principles will be advocated with honour and fidelity, your choice will be wisely made." "But in no case," the address warned, "where the power of selection is in your hands, dispense with a clear, explicit and written avowal of adherence to the principles of the Association." "The necessities of the country," the address then finally added, "and the danger which threatens the existence of our people point to a reform of the law of landlord and tenant as a measure of paramount urgency and importance. In all cases where it is possible you will do well to have an understanding with your representatives that they will oppose every government which will not incorporate that measure with its policy, or at least afford it a sincere and efficient support." The address then concluded with a pious exhortation against "the system of bartering parliamentary votes for patronage and personal favours. . . ."

Before moving the adoption of the address, Dillon begged the indulgence of the meeting while he made some remarks in regard to the recent reconsideration of the rules of the association. He explained that in the interests of unity, those who were dissatisfied with the rules of the association as not expressing the principle of independent opposition strongly enough had been invited to a conference on April 28 with the executive committee of the association. After some five hours of intense discussion and debate, with some twenty or thirty people all taking active part in the reconstructing of the original rules, Dillon explained, he had come to the conclusion that if the new rules were presented to the public in their present form, the committee's reputation for both good sense and literary composition would be considerably compromised. The new rules had, in fact, almost immediately been leaked to the press, and the association had then been congratulated by the *Irish Times* for having abandoned the agitation against the established Church and taken up the cause of Tenant Right instead. The committee, realizing that there was some justice in the *Times's* remarks, decided to amend the new rules and circulate them to all those who had attended the April 28 conference for their approval. The result was that some of those who had attended the conference declared that there had been a breach of faith by the committee in regard to the rules that all had previously agreed to.

"What I desire this meeting and the public to understand," Dillon further explained, "is this, that, for the present, the committee are placed in this dilemma—either we must submit those rules to this meeting in the exact words in which they were framed at the conference, or we must not submit them at all, for, if we submit them in any altered form, however slight the alteration may be, we expose ourselves to the charge of having departed from a solemn compact and violated good faith." "Now," he pointed out, referring to the criticism of the *Irish Times*, "I have already alleged one reason why we cannot submit the rules without alteration. I shall specify another, and it is not the only other, reason for doing so." "One of those rules," Dillon noted, indicating that the full effect of Cullen's long memorandum of early May to the secretaries of the association had not been lost on him, "recommends that our representatives should be bound by a solemn pledge that they will take counsel with one another, and that each will act in accordance with the decision of the majority." "The object aimed at by the rule," he then added, "is unquestionably good, viz., that members of parliament returned through the influence of this Association should act together as a party. But to accomplish this object it is not necessary to exact from each individual a pledge that he will act with the majority of the party in all cases, even when he believes them to be wrong. We are all agreed as to the value of systematic co-operation amongst our representatives, but valuable as it is it would be purchased too dearly by a violation of conscience." "Well," Dillon asked, "what are we to do?" "I leave this question," he then proposed, "to be answered by the good sense of the country, confident that it will approve and justify the course we are taking here to-day, and will pronounce that we are acting both rationally and honourably in postponing the consideration of these rules until there is further opportunity for discussing them. In the meantime I flattered [sic] myself that the true principles of parliamentary independence and political rectitude are put forward with sufficient clearness in the address which I have read to the meeting (cheers)."

Before the proposed address could be put and voted on, a step that would in effect have resulted in the postponement of a consideration of the rules, as recommended by Dillon, T. McCarthy Downing, a leading proponent of Tenant Right in the association, took the floor and insisted that the new rules approved at the conference on April 28 be considered by the meeting and not postponed. Because the conference had been a representative one, McCarthy Downing maintained, and because the changes in the rules had been endorsed by the archbishop of Dublin and the five other prelates present, as well as all the laity who attended, except one person, it would be tantamount to an act of disrespect to that consensus not to consider the rules. He therefore read the new rules three and four to the meeting; adding that he had also been apprised of the committee's amendment to rule three, he read that as well and then declared that he, for one, was willing to accept the rules as amended, because if they did not face up to the question of the change in rules at that meeting, he believed that it would be "the funeral day of the National Association." What McCarthy Downing obviously did not know was that Cullen did not really favor any change in the original rules, much less the various amended versions of them, and that if the new rules three and four, amended or not, were endorsed by the meeting, the likelihood was that Cullen would resign from the association and quietly forbid his clergy from taking any further part in it. Such a result on the eve of the general election would be a political disaster of the first magnitude, and the demise of the association prophesied by McCarthy Downing would be fulfilled in a way that he did not anticipate.

In a last-ditch effort to secure a postponement of a decision about the change in the rules, Dillon spoke again at some length, emphasizing that what was at stake was the issue of a pledged party with the minority being bound by the majority. "In asking for the postponement of the consideration of the rules," Dillon assured the meeting, "they [he and his associates] were actuated by nothing whatever but a desire to satisfy all reasonable objection to the rules and to unite the country so as to bring about that result which his friend Mr. Downing so eloquently depicted, and which was so much to be desired—namely an association comprising the whole popular strength of the country, and concentrating it upon the legislature for the attainment of the national objects they all had in view (applause)." In the meantime, someone had apparently been able to explain the political facts of life concerning Cullen to McCarthy Downing, for in his reply to Dillon he explained that "he had been urged to say that for the purpose of unanimity, and in order to keep within the association those distinguished prelates to whom he had alluded, he ought to move that the resolutions passed at the conference should be adopted, subject to such alterations as a committee to be appointed might afterwards make." He therefore concluded by moving the following resolution: "That the resolutions agreed to at the conference on the 28th of April last, be affirmed, subject to such amendments as a committee hereafter to be appointed may deem necessary, preserving the principles therein enunciated."

Before the special committee called for in McCarthy Downing's motion could be convened, however, a number of those bishops who assembled every spring in the third week of June at Maynooth to attend the various college boards met on June 21 and informally discussed the proposed amending of the rules of the association. "On Wednesday at Maynooth," Dorrian reported to Kirby on June 27, "a little private talk amongst a few of us showed good symptoms. Drs. MacHale, Derry, Keane, Nulty promised to meet at ten o'c. next morning at Coffey's Hotel [with] Alderman Dillon: and, on our [the bishops'] reaching Dublin, the Alderman and myself went at 10 o'c at night to Dr. Cullen who kindly consented also to be present next morning at Coffey's Hotel. The result was most satisfactory." The six prelates and Dillon had drawn up the following amended set of rules:

I— The association pledges itself to the policy of complete Parliamentary Independence, and the electors shall in all cases be urged to bind their representatives, not only to vote for all the objects of the association, but also to oppose any government which shall not incorporate with its policy, or otherwise efficiently support, a satisfactory measure of tenant compensation—that measure being deemed one of pressing exigency and paramount importance.

II— That as it is impossible to give an honest and efficient advocacy in parliament to measures, and at the same time to incur personal obligations to a minister who is opposed to those measures, the electors should bind their representatives to accept no place or honour for themselves, and incur no personal obligation to any minister who shall not support a satisfactory measure of tenant compensation.

III—That there should be an understanding between the electors and their representatives, that the latter should take counsel together, so as to secure a general uniformity of policy and a combined action for the ends of the association.[57]

The amended rules were then presented to the special committee, which included Dillon and the six prelates with the addition of Gillooly and Kilduff, and the committee approved them unanimously. "The names as given in the Freeman," Dorrian assured Kirby on June 27, "are the right ones, as are also the rules there proposed to be substituted" (K). "Dr. MacHale," he further reported, "would at once join the Association, he said, if the Association consisted only of those there present, but he would watch [to see] if it followed the policy now agreed upon and then act accordingly. I suggested that he might, perhaps, take some opportunity of stating that he fully approved of the Programme and policy as now at that conference agreed upon. He replied that he would do that at some proper time." "Dr. Cullen," Dorrian explained, "made the point about place-seeking, by suggesting the word 'honour' should be added, still more palatable. The agreement and cordiality was refreshing."

The new conciliatory spirit proved to be very short-lived, however. The day after he returned to his diocese, MacHale wrote a letter, dated June 24, to be read at a June 27 banquet of clergy and laity in honor of the former Young Irelander Charles Gavan Duffy, in which the archbishop reopened all the old wounds. Duffy, who had been prominent in the Tenant Right League and the independent Irish party of the fifties and who had emigrated to Australia in 1855 in political despair, had returned to Ireland for a visit. "Though public Tributes, as they are called," MacHale explained to the assembled banqueters, after regretting that he could not be present, "have become so common as to be indiscriminately bestowed on the worthless and the deserving, the claims of your guest are entirely apart from selfish considerations. Far from associating himself with those faithless men who made public promises only to break them to their own shame and to the injury of their constituents, his public virtue was conspicuous amidst treachery and corruption."[58] "To men of this stamp," MacHale then insisted,

57. Ibid., June 24, 1865.
58. Ibid., June 28, 1865.

"the parliamentary career of Mr. Gavan Duffy and a few others was a reproach; whilst to honest candidates for senatorial honours, it will furnish a lesson for imitation. Nothing short of the pledge of independent opposition, in all its plenitude and vigour, can save the country, with the exercise of greater vigilance on the part of the electors to see this pledge carried out by their representatives."

What was even worse, at the banquet itself (with Dillon presiding as toastmaster), George Henry Moore, former M.P. for county Mayo and a leading proponent of the policy of independent opposition since its inception, deliberately went out of his way to provoke a scene when he responded to the toast "Our Native Land." He denounced at great length, as had MacHale, those who had betrayed the people's cause after the general election of 1852, and he did not spare those bishops and clergy who had not kept political faith with the people in that crisis.[59] "The cause of Ireland," Moore maintained bitterly, "was dead in 1855. The men who did the deed walked red handed through the land, and were now engaged, he was told in a work of reparation, the only parallel for which, in fact or fiction, was the case of the famous Chinese jugglers, who were so dextrous that they could cut off a man's head on the street and put it on again without his knowing it (laughter)." "The running account between the Irish people and the English government," Moore added, "was not yet closed, nor the balance settled either way. But how stood the account between Ireland and the Irish people?" "Mutual forbearance, mutual toleration," he then declared even more bitterly, "between class and class, creed and creed, opinion and opinion, but no forbearance, no toleration, no parole, no compromise, no capitulation, no quarter in dealing with those vile principles and those dishonest men who, from the first ages of Irish history, have stood in the way of the rights and the honour of their native land (loud cheers)."

In proposing the next toast, "the Hierarchy and clergy of Ireland," Dillon did not choose to pour any oil on the troubled waters. In pointing out that the toast was a time-honored one on such occasions, Dillon noted acidly that he

was the less disposed not to comply with the custom now because he had just heard an eloquent invective against that body. He admired as much as any man the eloquence and ability of that performance, but frankly he declared that he questioned its wisdom and its policy (hear, hear and cheers). He looked back into the history of his country, and if the religion of their forefa-

59. Ibid.

thers had come down to them unsullied and uncorrupted, if the moral elevation of their race had been preserved intact, he wished to know to what influence those great blessings were to be attributed (hear, hear and cheers)? Where would they be that day but for the hierarchy and clergy of Ireland, and looking forward in the future, and putting aside vague generalities, what had they to rely upon if it was not the confidence and affection of the people for their hierarchy and clergy, and the intimate union between the two (hear, hear)[?] Individuals amongst them may have gone wrong, but while he admitted that, he would not be one to impute moral guilt.

Dillon then admitted that even he might have gone wrong sometimes, but when he asked who was always right he was interrupted with cries of "hear, hear" mingled with cries of "question." Realizing that he had gone too far, he closed by pointing out that he "would have given them the toast without one word of comment, but for the observations of Mr. Moore."

Dillon then proceeded amid loud cheers to propose the toast. He was, however, interrupted by Moore, who was not a man to let anyone else have the last word. "This was not," Moore pointed out, "the proper place to enter into a vindication for what he had thought proper to say, for what he said was vindicated by every man's knowledge of the facts (hear, hear). But when his friend spoke of vague generalities, he thought it would be better, instead of a general assault on what he said, [if] Alderman Dillon had stated what facts, what allegations he had made that were untrue (hear, hear and cheers), or what conclusions he suggested were not justifiable (cheers)." After the toast was finally drunk, it was responded to by Robert Mullen, the parish priest of Castlepollard in the diocese of Meath, in what was described as a "forcible" speech. Mullen, who denounced any attempt that might be made to return Whig members to Parliament, concluded by saying that he would "as soon vote for the d——l as for a Whig (cheers)." To make matters even worse, in reporting the banquet four days later, on July 1, the influential editor of the *Nation*, A. M. Sullivan, who had been present, attacked the association and denounced Cullen with a greater vehemence than was customary even with him. Such was the sad state of disarray of constitutional politics in Ireland on the eve of the general election of 1865.

VII

The National Association

July 1865–September 1866

Before proceeding to examine the part played by the National Association and the bishops and their clergy in the general election of 1865, it is first necessary to analyze at some length the differences that took place over the rules of the association, because they are important to any understanding of the development and significance of Irish politics and the emerging political system. Three stages may be easily discerned in the discussion over the rules. The first was the adoption of the rules, and most particularly rule three, at the aggregate meeting on December 29, 1864. The second was the revision and expansion of that rule into new rules three and four, which took place at the conference held on April 28 and the ensuing days. The third culminated in the further revision of rules three and four by the special committee appointed for that purpose on June 22. The original rule three adopted on December 29, it will be recalled, required the association *not to support* any political party that would not promote tenant compensation or disendowment of the established Church, nor would the association recommend or assist in the election of any candidate who would not pledge himself to act on this principle. Two things upset the critics of this rule in general, and the Meath priests in particular: first, the M.P. so pledged was obliged not *to oppose*, but only *not to support*, any political party that would not promote its position with regard to the land and the Church; and second, the land question was not given precedence over the Church question.

After the conference on April 28, therefore, it was decided that rule three should now require the association not only not to support any candidate who would not vote for *all* its objects but also not to support any candidate who would not vote against the ministry of the day (on all questions involving a vote of confidence) that would not make tenant compensation a cabinet measure. The significance of this change, of course, was that the M.P. was now required *to oppose* the ministry on all questions involving the survival of the government, a position that greatly enhanced the policy of independent opposition and also gave precedence to the land question over both the Church and the education questions. In the additional rule four of April 28, moreover, the association was to recommend that all the Irish constituencies bind their M.P.'s to accept no place or favor that might compromise their independence of the ministry, and to take council with the *party* in the House of Commons who held the principles of the association, and to adopt and act upon the policy approved by the majority. The significance of rule four was that it assured the existence of a third party in the House of Commons pledged to the principles of the association, as well as the binding of the minority of that party by the majority in all matters of policy. Depending on one's point of view, rules three and four of April 28 either fundamentally modified or reasonably clarified what the means and ends of the association were to be. In effect, these new rules provided for making the land question the chief end of the association; the adoption of a policy of more systematic opposition was to be the means to that end. What would keep the effective instrument of that means, the party, safe from corruption was the pledge not to accept any form of patronage, be it place or favor. Finally, what would give the party its discipline and its effective political cutting edge in the House of Commons was that the minority would be bound by the majority.

The special committee of the association that convened on June 22 to reconsider rules three and four proceeded to modify each of those rules in a fundamental way. Though the committee confirmed that the end of the association was primarily a satisfactory measure of tenant compensation, and the means to that end a more systematic opposition, *the electorate* rather than the association was now *to bind its representatives* with regard to the approved ends and means. The M.P.'s were thus made responsible to their constituents rather than to the association for their political behavior. This alteration in rule three further weakened any hold the association might have on those M.P.'s who accepted its endorsement because the association did not really exist as a constituency organization, except in the persons of a few local notables, namely, the bishops and their clergy. Though this was undoubtedly a great theoretical gain for the concept of popular sovereignty, the practical effect would only be to increase clerical control in the constituencies in the name of the association. Rule four was modified in an even more fundamental way. The obligation not to accept place or favor was retained, but the M.P.'s were now only to take counsel together (the word "party" not even being mentioned), and above all, the clause about the majority binding the minority was dropped altogether. This would make the organizing of a disciplined, purposeful, third party in the House of Commons a virtual impossibility and would, in effect, draw the teeth of any policy involving independent opposition.

A further consideration of the radical and the conservative revisions of the rules of April 28 and June 22, respectively, also reveals a great deal about the political values and principles of the various groups that made up the constitutional political spectrum in Ireland in the early summer of 1865. At least five discernible political groups in that spectrum can be initially identified according to their ends. On the extreme left were those who were best represented by MacHale, and who may be designated as Repealers. To the right of the Repealers stood the Meath priests and their coadjutor bishop, who were essentially representative of those who thought the land question was the real and urgent one. In the center were the promoters of the National Association, best typified by Dillon, who were committed to all the objects of the association. To the right of the Associationists were the Cullenites, who thought a proper solution to the education question was the real end of all Catholic political action. Finally, on the extreme right was a more heterogenous group of professional politicians, who made up the great bulk of those fifty-five Irish M.P.'s designating themselves as Catholic and/or Liberal and whose ambition was high office, or places and honors for themselves, or simply favors for their friends. They were perhaps best represented on the highest level by William Monsell, M.P. for county Limerick, and on the lowest by John Ennis, M.P. for the borough of Athlone. They were generally designated as Whigs by their enemies and as Liberals by their friends.

The groups, moreover, were identifiable not only according to their ends but also, though less specifically, according to their means. Both the Repealers and the land reformers were ardent supporters of the policy of independent opposition as the appropriate means for achieving their ends. The promoters of the association and the Cullenites advocated instead a policy of parliamentary independence, which did not involve "factious opposition" and which did not preclude tactical political alliances in the House of Commons with other groups or parties aiming to remedy existing Irish grievances. Cullen, for example, was hostile to the policy of independent or "factious opposition" because he realized that it must inevitably lead to a policy of parliamentary obstruction, which would make the structuring of any tactical political alliance to remedy Irish grievances a virtual impossibility. Moreover, a legislative body faced with the threat of systematic obstruction would undoubtedly have to take measures in self-defense, measures that would inevitably result in the expulsion of the obstructionists from the House of Commons; and this was a consequence that could only make the position of Irish Catholics worse than it already was. The Whigs or Liberals, who wanted to enter as fully as possible into the British political system and enjoy its fruits and rewards, of course could not subscribe to a policy of independent opposition, or even to too strict an interpretation of the policy of parliamentary independence.

In the last analysis, what is finally revealed by this examination of the means and ends of the various groups that made up the nationalist-Liberal political spectrum in Ireland is that a distinct Irish political system was in the process of emerging. This emerging Irish system, moreover, was fundamentally different from the dominant British political system in a number of significant ways. First of all, and most fundamentally, whether one's politics in Ireland were revolutionary or constitutional, the concept of popular sovereignty was paramount. Indeed, for most Irishmen the ultimate and the only source of legitimate political authority was the Irish people. Even when the rules of the association were modified in a conservative way on June 22, it will be recalled, the authority of the electorate was at the same time theoretically increased. The second basic way in which the Irish political system was distinct from the British system of its day was in its concept of representation. Repealers, land reformers, Associationists, and even the Cullenites, if Cullen perhaps be excepted, all subscribed to the view that an M.P. was really a delegate rather than a representative. In their view an M.P. was to go to Parliament instructed and pledged to his constituents' will, rather than, as was the case in the Whig or Liberal tradition, as a representative who was free to do what he thought best for the general interest as developing and unanticipated circumstances required. A third fundamental feature that distinguished the Irish system from the British was that the Irish, like the Americans, had a penchant for putting things in writing in order to define their political views and procedures. The "objects" and "rules" of the association, and their various modifications, were an obvious example of this Irish need for greater political concreteness in the form of "constitutions," or written documents.

The practical result of these Irish conceptions of sovereignty and representation, and the penchant for fundamental documents, was that the Irish political system was not only different from the British in its workings but also paradoxically, at one and the same time, both more radical and more conservative as a system than the British. The paradox can be resolved if the Irish system is considered first in its British political context and then in its own right. If the Irish system is compared to the British, which in 1865 was dominant, it was essentially radical, but if it is considered simply in itself, it was basically conservative. The radicalism of the Irish system, interestingly enough, was a function less of its ends in 1865 than of its means. If the ends of the five political groups that made up the nationalist-Liberal political spectrum are examined, for example, only the Repealers were interested in fundamental, or root, change—the Repeal of the Act of Union. The land reformers, the Associationists, and the Cullenites were all really involved in grievance politics, which was soon to become the essence of the Gladstonian Liberal program for Ireland. These three groups were, therefore, at least in their ends, essentially reformers. The Irish Whigs and Liberals were committed to the even more traditional patronage politics of the group or interest that had been on the wane in the British system since the late eighteenth century.

The radical essence of the Irish system in 1865, then, was to be found in its means rather than its ends, and particularly in the policy of independent opposition, with its insistence that an M.P. was a delegate rather than a representative. More important for the future, however, was the Irish system's radical potential in the British political context. In a short time, when all the various political groups would finally subordinate their grievance and interest politics to the end of the Repealers in a policy called Home Rule, and then find a political leader in Parnell, who could crystallize that end in his person, the radical means would have found their complementary end.

At the same time, if the Irish system is considered in itself, it was basically conservative and, from a British point of view, even reactionary. The reason, of course, was that the basic communal nature of a preindustrial Irish society, which expressed itself politically in a consensual way, was at fundamental odds with the Liberal and individualistic political ethic that had made great strides in Britain in the course of the nineteenth century. Indeed, it is not too much to say that both MacHale and Cullen, like the great majority of the Irish bishops, instinctively hated what British Liberalism and its concepts of progress and freedom came to represent in Ireland. The welcome they gave Pius IX's *Syllabus of Errors* early in 1865, for example, was as sincere as it was enthusiastic, and none was warmer in his appreciation of it than that inveterate enemy of Whiggery and West Britonism, the coadjutor to the bishop of Down and Conner. "I look upon the Encyclical and accompanying *Syllabus*," Dorrian had assured Kirby on February 6,

> as the most glorious event of modern times. Here in Ireland I hope our discussions must soon be brought to a close. The *Whigs* and their Catholic Supporters must now see the ground taken from *under* their feet by the condemnation of their views on the questions of Education and the Temporal Power. All, who wish to be right, will *now* have no excuse. And I hope Bishops and Priests will be faithful. We want to be *more consistent*.
>
> I have explained these points in all the Churches of Belfast. And yesterday when I was expected in St. Patrick's for that purpose, it was reported that 600 Fenians were determined to shew their defiance by walking away if I should make any allusion to Secret Societies. [K]

"Thank God," Dorrian added significantly, and with obvious relief, "they stood their ground and seemed to give way under my remonstrance."

What made the Irish political system conservative, of course, was the power and influence exercised by the Irish bishops and priests in the system. Their political sway was, in fact, so very considerable that it was absolutely necessary to the success of any political movement at the national level. The most serious problem from a constitutional point of view was therefore how to give the bishops and priests their effective weight in the system without either compromising their ecclesiastical state or allowing them to impose too much on their lay political colleagues, who must, in the last analysis, assume the basic responsibility for the system. The solution to this problem was to be found eventually in the emerging Irish political system, but the working it out in a practical way was as slow as it was painful. The bishops and clergy had for a very long time been attempting to establish on the constituency level a mode in which the professional character of the priests would not be compromised by their participation in politics, while at the same time they would be able to devote a full measure of their power and influence to the political cause at heart.

This mode was worked out in a piecemeal way over a long period of time in various constituencies, and it is therefore difficult to describe briefly in a coherent way. The result, however, was that in the choosing of parliamentary candidates, the clergy gradually ceased to caucus with the laity in the local political clubs and met instead as clergy, when they decided as clergy on their candidate, the majority binding the minority; thus they presented the laity with a united front. Under such a procedure, the laity might split on who was to be the candidate, but the clergy never. In this way the clergy were saved from unseemly confrontations with each other on the hustings and were assured that their considered judgment regarding the appropriate candidate would receive all due consideration from the laity if they wanted their support.

What was even more significant, however, was that this procedure, which was being worked out on the constituency level, now also began to become more evident at the national level. The change was made clear both in the founding of the National Association and in the procedural difficulties encountered by the association in its first six months. The bishops had decided as a body to help launch the association and had negotiated as a group with the laity in its formation. The real indication that the procedural mode practiced in the constituencies had found its way to the national level was made evident in the series of conferences and meetings on the proposed modification of the rules in April and June. The bishops who attended the conference on April 28 obviously attended as a representative group, and when Dillon asked the bishops to attend the general meeting, on June 19, he suggested very significantly that they ought to have "a private consultation previous to the meeting," at which they would presumably agree to the course they would pursue collectively at the public meeting. Though this private meeting did not materialize, another did a few days later, when a representative group of bishops met at Maynooth and again the next day at Coffey's Hotel in Dublin. Even more significantly, the modifications in the rules that the bishops decided on were those presented to the meeting of the special committee of the association, and there passed unanimously. In this way the bishops on the national level, by imitating the clergy on the constituency level, worked out a procedure which guaranteed that there would be no public and unedifying political disagreements that might jeopardize the unity and harmony of the episcopal body.[1]

1. We had a glimpse of this developing procedure in the way in which the bishops had proposed to incorporate the laity in the governing of the Catholic University.

Such was the general political situation in Ireland in July 1865 when Dillon and his friends in the association were preparing to try their political strength in the approaching general election. Because there has been no systematic study of that general election it is very difficult to measure the degree of success the association had in Ireland in returning members to Parliament. Though many of the candidates were willing to subscribe to all of the objects of the association, they were not all willing to commit themselves to its rules, which would oblige them to support a policy of parliamentary independence. How many of these candidates, therefore, or even those candidates who could endorse some of the objects, if not all, received informal support from influential members of the association, as individuals, is also very difficult to determine, given the present state of research on the subject. Dillon, however, had little doubt about the course that should be pursued in such situations. "In my opinion," he informed Gillooly on June 3, "our obvious policy is to exert ourselves *individually* to return the best man we can return under the circumstances of each case, even though the Association cannot directly interfere" (G). "An illustration of this policy," he pointed out, "is to be found here in the County of Dublin, where Captain White [the recently declared Liberal candidate] openly avows himself in favour of our views on the land question & on Education, but will not (from motives of policy) declare himself openly against the E. Church. The members of the Assoc[n] here are I think all agreed that while we cannot openly adopt him as the candidate of the Assoc[n], we ought to give him all the support we can each in his individual capacity."[2]

In any case, there were probably not much more than a dozen members, in an Irish representation of 105, who were returned to Parliament on the whole program of the association.[3] What is more certain

2. The individual members of the association, and especially the clergy, were very prominent in supporting Captain White in county Dublin. Indeed, in an almost impossible electoral situation, White did surprisingly well. The sitting conservative members for the county were Captain T. E. Taylor, who had held his seat since 1841, and I. T. Hamilton, who had been elected in 1865 in succession to his father, J. S. Hamilton, who had held the seat since 1841. The results of the election were Taylor, 2,100; Hamilton 2,083; White, 1,646 (Brian Walker, ed., *Parliamentary Election Results in Ireland, 1801–1922* [Dublin, 1978], p. 102).

3. Those returned on the association interest included Sir Patrick O'Brien (King's county), *Sir John Gray* (Kilkenny borough), *J. B. Dillon* (county Tipperary), C. Moore (county Tipperary), *E. J. Synan* (county Limerick), J. F. Maguire (Cork borough), J. A. Blake (Waterford borough), *R. Armstrong* (Sligo borough), *D. J. Rearden* (Athlone borough), *T. O. Stock* (Carlow borough), R. J. Devereux (Wexford borough), T. Kennedy (county Louth), Major M. W. O'Reilly (county Longford), and J. Brady (county Leitrim); italics indicate candidates returned for the first time. At least another dozen Irish members were certainly sympathetic to the objects of the association, though it was not yet

is that of those dozen, and especially those elected for the first time, nearly all owed their return to the exertions made by the clergy, high and low, on their behalf. The upper limit of clerical political zeal in this general election was undoubtedly displayed in the boroughs of Athlone and Sligo by Laurence Gillooly, the bishop of Elphin. Not only was the sitting member for Athlone, John Ennis, a wealthy Catholic merchant with banking interests, detested by all shades of nationalist opinion as a corrupt and place-hunting Whig, but he had also had the recent misfortune of falling foul of the bishops on educational matters. The bishops of Elphin and Ardagh, who shared spiritual jurisdiction in the town of Athlone, therefore decided in the interests of the association to throw their combined influence in the borough, which was very considerable, against the sitting member.

When a clerical friend of Ennis wrote the bishop of Elphin to intercede for him, Gillooly wasted little time in coming to the point. "I regret exceedingly," he explained to Father F. Murphy, "that I cannot comply with the request you have so kindly made in the interest of your friend Mr. Ennis. The Bor. of Athlone has been demoralised by the bribery practiced by his Agents—and already in preparation for the coming election a regular system of Corruption has been established by them without any disguise or concealment beyond what the law may strictly require."[4] "In Parliament," Gillooly added, "the few votes given by Mr. E. were not such as to recommend him to those who have Irish ["the people" crossed out] interests at heart. By one of his Votes—on the Model School question, he separated himself from his Cath^c fellow Members and took advantage of his position to proclaim opposition and defiance to the Bishops and Clergy of his Church, approving what they had publicly & repeatedly condemned, aiding & abetting what they had strenuously opposed, denying the right they assumed of guarding the faith & morals of the Cath^c youth of Ireland." "Such is the notoriety," Gillooly concluded, "he has acquired in Parl^t—it cannot be forgotten nor will it at the next Election; and if the counsel of the bishops who have jurisd^n in Athlone cannot prevail against money & Corruption, it will be their duty at least to condemn such agencies & to protest against the Parliamentary delinquencies of your friend."

Accordingly, Gillooly and John Kilduff, the bishop of Ardagh, proceeded to gird themselves for political battle. Their correspondence

---

clear to what extent they were committed to the whole program, or indeed whether they thought that program went far enough.

4. G, copy, n.d. [late June 1865]. Father Murphy was probably the member of the Society of Jesus assigned to the Church of St. Ignatius in Gardiner Street, Dublin.

not only gives an interesting insight into the conduct of elections in mid-nineteenth-century Ireland but also demonstrates the very real power and influence of the Irish bishops when aroused and determined. "We are committed, fully committed," Kilduff reported to Gillooly on July 5 from Athlone, "to share in the infamous degradation of having the Borough of Athlone continue in the slough of Whiggery and the barest venality or to share in the *imperative duty* of rescuing it from its present state of degradation and venality so odious & so shameful" (G). "Mr. Ennis is alarmed!!" Kilduff exclaimed, explaining, "The O'Donohue [sic] called and asked permission to have his Father-in-law retract past political errors, and to issue an address in conformity with the avowed principles of the N¹ Association. I had no idea till we counted our forces, that we were so sure of Victory, provided no apathy or division weaken or disunite us." "Mr. Rearden's references," he assured Gillooly, referring to the candidate selected to oppose Ennis, "as to genuine honesty of purpose are now, after receipt of Telegrams and as appears from other sources, quite satisfactory, and more than up to the mark."⁵ "Yr. Ldp. shd," Kilduff then advised Gillooly, "write by *immediate* return of Post the strongest letter you can pen to our mutual friend the Archdeacon [Martin O'Reilly, the parish priest of St. Peter's in Athlone], in support of Rearden's canvass. I will write a similar letter to the Priests of St. Mary's notwithstanding I have already more than done my part by verbal exhortation." "A bright era is," he finally concluded, "I have no doubt, about being opened for the Immaculate Borough."

As soon as Gillooly received this letter he wrote to his archdeacon. "I am happy to learn this morning," he informed O'Reilly on July 6,

> from His Ldp. Most Rev Dʳ Kilduff that the Electors of St. Mary's, Athlone, are, like those of your Parish, deeply dissatisfied with the Parliamᵗʸ Conduct of Mr. Ennis—and determined to be no longer misrepresented by him. The selfish, uncatholic & unpatriotic course he has pursued in politics ever since his first

5. Just how D. J. Rearden came to the attention of Kilduff and Gillooly is not clear. He was apparently an Englishman of Irish extraction living in London; he issued an election address to the electors of the borough of Galway that appeared in the *Freeman's Journal* on July 4, 1865, in which he promised "to strictly adhere in all respects to the principles of independent opposition laid down by the Catholic and National Association of Ireland, to any and every Government who do not carry into effect by Act of Parliament the measures above mentioned, and shall heartily devote myself to the Commercial prosperity and general interests of your town." Though it is only conjecture on my part, Rearden's "references" were probably supplied by the bishop of Galway, John MacEvilly, to his good friends the bishops of Elphin and Ardagh, when it became apparent that Rearden had no chance in Galway borough.

election in your borough, has inspired me & all interested in the character of your town, with regret & indignation: And I am happy that the time has at length arrived for punishing & protesting against his political delinquencies—and retrieving your own character. Dr. Kilduff is satisfied with the qualifications of Mr. Rearden, who presents himself for your Election in opposition to Mr. Ennis—and relying as I do with perfect confidence in his Ldp's judgement & patriotism in this matter, I hasten to make known to you my approval of Mr. R's Candidature—and to request you—your Curates to unite with his Ldp & his clergy and with the honest Electors in both parishes, and to use every lawful exertion to secure the return of Mr. Rearden. [G]

Meanwhile, Gillooly had already written to assure Kilduff that he would be in Athlone on Saturday, July 8, to canvass personally for their adopted candidate, Denis Rearden. Kilduff replied on Thursday night, July 6, from Longford, "I am delighted to learn that Yr. Lsp. will be in the Immaculate Boro' on Saturday. Be sure to be up by early train. Before leaving Athlone I took care to see that St. Mary's will be true to its colors" (G). "James Murtagh told me yesterday," Kilduff then reported, referring to an old friend and schoolfellow, "on the Bridge of Athlone that he w^d support. I know that Mr. Ennis' party will work heaven & earth to secure him to their side, but he will be complimented by Yr. Ldp's visit & he will be too stern to go back on his promises to me." "I don't know if Yr. Ldp. is aware," Kilduff further explained, "that I do not attach so much value to the six votes the Murtagh's have in the Boro as I do to the *powerful* influence they have over their customers & creditors, the Publicans and Bakers of Athlone." "I have been speaking to several on this day," he assured Gillooly in conclusion, "about the Contest on which we have entered. They said unanimously that nothing which has occured for years back w^d teach the Government such a lesson as the ejection of John Ennis from the Boro of Athlone."

In the event, Ennis was soundly defeated by Rearden, 107 votes to 60.[6] This formidable demonstration of clerical power in Athlone was not, however, the whole measure of Gillooly's political influence in this general election. He was also instrumental in helping to defeat the sitting member for Sligo borough, Francis MacDonagh, a "Liberal-Conservative Protestant" who was a follower of Lord Derby. In early June Dillon had written Gillooly about the possibility of starting a candidate of their own for Sligo borough. "On my arrival from London

6. Walker, p. 101. The Conservative candidate, George Handcock, received 21 votes.

this morning," Dillon explained on June 3, "I was informed by my friend Mr. Harkan that he was about to visit Sligo for the purpose of conferring with Your Lordship as to the possibility of returning for the borough of Sligo a representative who (if not everything we could wish) would be a very decided improvement on your present representative" (G).

By the following day Dillon had learned that the prospective candidate, Serjeant Richard Armstrong, a Dublin barrister and a Protestant, was a good deal more amenable to the program of the association than he had first thought. Dillon informed Gillooly on June 4, "Mr. Harkan will probably hand you a note from me in the course of today" (G). "The circumstances of your borough," Dillon explained, "are peculiar in this respect[—]that without Ld Palmerston[']s support it is impossible to succeed and this should be kept in mind by the electors as well as by the Candidate. I believe the Serjeant to be a man of liberal mind, and sincerely favourable to *all* the measures we demand; but to prevent mistakes on this point I think Mr. Harkan ought to convey to him that a full exposition of his views & intentions on these questions of land tenure, Church & Education ought to be given in the shape of a private letter to Yr. Lordship before you can commit yourself to this candidature." "In fact," Dillon further advised, "while on the one hand it is prudent to avoid as far as possible any open declaration that might endanger the result of the election; on the other hand it is fair and right to drive a hard bargain with the Candidate in private, so as to have no doubt as to what he will really do."

"There is another matter," Dillon added, attempting to start yet another political horse in the interests of the association, "about which I wish to consult Y^r Lordship. While recently in London I learned that young Kenelm Digby is prepared if he gets any encouragement to offer himself for the County of Sligo. I need not say that he would stand on our principles. There is no doubt that he would be an excellent member of Parliament. He has some property in the county and will spend any money that may be required." "Altogether," Dillon maintained, "I think it would be difficult to find a more desirable candidate, and if there be a fair chance of success I think we ought to take him up. The present members are so inefficient that the Tories themselves ought to be ashamed of them and undoubtedly [?] when they learn that a good man is in the field prepared to fight hard and to spend freely, one of them may shrink from the contest." "A little audacity in those cases," he advised finally, "is often most useful and I strongly recommend that Mr. Digby should be encouraged to offer himself."

Though Gillooly apparently thought that there was little chance of success for Digby, and did not therefore encourage him to contest county Sligo, he did promote the candidacy of Serjeant Armstrong in the borough of Sligo. On June 8 Armstrong wrote Gillooly the required private letter endorsing the objects of the association (G). In his reply the next day, Gillooly not only assured Armstrong that his undertaking was satisfactory but also offered him some very shrewd political advice if he hoped to be successful in Sligo (G). "You will of course be called upon," he warned Armstrong, "by friends & opponents to give public expression to your Pol.[l] opinions and you will, I am sure be prepared, to do so in due time with honesty and precision as befits a public man." "It w[d] not however be prudent," he advised, "to announce your opinions in very strong or explicit terms, especially on the Church question, previous to your canvass—and it was in that view that I expressed myself satisfied for the present with your private profession of your Pol.[l] creed. There are several dissenters & liberal Prot[ts] here amongst the Electors who will not question you closely on y[r] opinions, & who, if not influenced by party spirit, will be rather pleased with your equality principles. After your canvass you will be able I hope to shape your Address with honesty as well as prudence."

When Gillooly finally received Armstrong's election address, however, he was not very pleased. "Your intended address is, I am sorry to find," he informed Armstrong bluntly on July 2, "exceedingly vague & defective and unless I am greatly mistaken will not fail to produce amongst the great majority of Liberal Electors of Sligo, a strong feeling of disappointment & dissatisf[n]" (G). "The address in a word," Gillooly then concluded, "does not read as an honest trustworthy profession of opinion nor does it contain any definite engagement with the Constituency and I therefore consider it more advisable for your [words illegible] to convey to you at once my opinions of it and to suggest the advisability of remodeling it whilst yet there is time to do so."

Armstrong submitted the required amendments to his address to Gillooly by return of post. "Pardon my phraseology," Armstrong noted further, in his covering letter, on July 4, "when the spirit & meaning are right—& pray bear in mind that while I would in Parliament act & speak up to the letter & in the spirit of my address, to be more pointed (in my humble judgement) would render my appearance on the hustings perfectly hopeless" (G). "However," he then added more softly, "I am in your hands, & as I will not go a step further unless you have entire confidence in me & say to me 'go on,' I trust an early hour on Thursday will decide, so that if possible I may be able to go to work with my whole heart, or else retire as unable to come up to your Lordship's expectations." Armstrong's address, as revised, was still not very substantial. He was guarded about Tenant Right, vague about denominational education, silent about the established Church, hopeful about an Irish parliamentary party, and specific only about the efforts he would make to secure better stipends for the medical profession for their ministrations to the destitute and poor.[7] In his interview with Gillooly on Thursday morning, however, Armstrong was apparently able to convince the bishop of his sincerity of purpose, for he continued to persevere and on July 15 defeated the sitting member for Sligo borough by the narrow margin of 165 to 153.

Meanwhile, Gillooly had given further example of his increasingly aggressive political temper when Sir Robert Gore Booth, one of the sitting Conservative members for county Sligo, asked him on July 7 for his "vote and interest" at the approaching election (G). Though Gillooly had already decided that he would not encourage Kenelm Digby's offer through Dillon to contest county Sligo, he did take occasion in his reply to Booth to read him a very stiff lecture on his past political conduct, as well as to issue a stern warning about the future. "I beg to acknowl^g the receipt of your letter," he noted on July 10,

> in which you request my vote & influence at the approaching Election—and express a hope that your votes in Parl.^{t} have given satisfaction & that there will be no opposition to your Election. Altho' in this last point your wishes are likely to be realised, owing chiefly if not entirely to the peaceful & kindly feelings of the Catholic clergy of the County, I feel it is my duty to make known to you the great dissatisfaction created amongst them & their flocks by the votes you have given lately on Mr. Monsell's County Oath's Bill and previously on several divisions affecting the liberty of our Church—and the interests of the Tenant class. Those votes are incompatible with the admission of your claims to civil & religious equality—they evince a disposition to maintain the domination of a class & creed—and to foster those unhappy dissensions which are the weakness & the shame of our Country. They present a most painful contradiction to your kind & generous conduct as a Landlord—and all who esteem you in this latter capacity—as I do myself—earnestly desire that you s^d. in your political views & in your parliam^{ty}. votes exhibit the same just & conciliatory spirit and cast off the unreasoning prej-

7. *Freeman's Journal*, July 8, 1865. The letter is dated July 3, 1865.

udices which have led you, perhaps unconsciously, to give pain
& offence & to perpetuate unjustice. [G]

"It is & has always been," Gillooly assured Booth in concluding, "my
earnest wish & study to foster kindly relations between Landlord &
tenant, and no consideration except that of strict public duty could
move me to sanction what w^{d} sow divisions & anger between them. It
is therefore my earnest desire that the conduct of our County members in the next Parliament may efface the dissensions of the past, and
remove the painful necessity which must otherwise arise of opposing
at any risk their future reelection."

If this letter had been written by MacHale it would hardly cause
any surprise, but Gillooly was one of the staunchest supporters of
Cullen's views on clerical participation in politics in the episcopal
body. Gillooly had kept a very low profile in Irish politics since his
consecration some ten years before. His conversion to a more aggressive political posture with the founding of the National Association,
and his efforts on its behalf in the general election of 1865, were to
become more generally representative of the bishops in the next fifteen years. In fact, it is not perhaps too much to say that after 1865
the bishops were once again gradually politicized, as they had been in
the 1820s in the interests of Catholic Emancipation and again, though
only partially, in the early 1840s in the interests of Repeal.

A fundamental distinction, however, has to be made in regard to
this increasing episcopal participation in politics, and that is between
principle and procedure. Episcopal participation on the level of principle involved endorsing the issue or issues, whereas on the procedural
level it was really a question of attending to the "nuts and bolts" of
politics, or electioneering. In 1865 the great majority of the bishops
endorsed the objects of the association, but what gave that general
election its particular intensity was that an increased number of the
bishops were very active on behalf of their chosen candidates in the
constituencies. As has already been pointed out, the key to this
greater, and eventually more effective, clerical and episcopal participation in politics at the constituency and national levels, respectively,
was to be found in the ability of the priests and bishops to establish an
identity in politics distinct from that of the laity. By being able to
coalesce as a group or body, so as to be able to act politically as such,
the priests on the constituency level and the bishops on the national
level were able to prevent their being reduced to mere individuals in
the emerging Irish political system, and thus were able to lay the
foundations for the basic consensual nature of that emerging system.

As far as that system was concerned at the national level, however, there were two other basic elements besides the bishops as a body that had to be in their effective places before the system could become operative: the leader and the party. After the death of Daniel O'Connell in 1847, no leader had managed to succeed the great man. His son John, William Keogh, George Moore, and The O'Donoghue had all successively aspired to the leadership, but none had been able in the last analysis to sustain themselves in the affections of the Irish people. Part of the reason why they had not been able to do so was certainly their personal and political deficiencies, but part, and undoubtedly the greatest part, had to do with the nature of the office, or role, itself. Leaders, like clan chiefs, emerged. They did not inherit the office, nor were they appointed or even elected. They were, in fact, the product of an unspoken consensus. O'Connell had been the leader, in effect, because his ascendancy had been self-evident. Before an Irish political system could really become operative, therefore, another leader would have to emerge out of a national consensus. Until that leadership could be better defined, and satisfactorily institutionalized, moreover, there would always continue to be an awkward hiatus in the succession.

The concept of party had fared institutionally somewhat better than that of leader after the death of O'Connell. Though his Repeal party had disintegrated soon after his death, an independent Irish party had been structured in the early 1850s that had a continuous if increasingly tenuous existence until the general election of 1859. The attributes thought to be necessary to an Irish parliamentary party, at least in their ideal state, had been fashioned during the fifties. In effect, the members of the party were to be pledge bound, the majority was to bind the minority, and the party was to remain independent of all English ministries and governments. In the minds of many Irishmen in the early 1860s, the inability to live up to these political precepts had been the real reason for the ruin of the independent Irish party in the 1850s. The demise of that party, moreover, made the efforts to effect those precepts all the more necessary if a viable Irish party was ever to emerge in the House of Commons. In any case, the general election of 1865 not only resulted in a renewal of the commitment of the bishops as a body to constitutional politics but also marked a further development in those other two elements necessary to an effective national political consensus—the leader and the party.

Though there was little doubt that John Blake Dillon possessed all the necessary personal qualifications for leadership—courage, integrity, energy, determination, and intelligence—as well as some very considerable political abilities—loyalty, tact, patience, presence, timing, and a talent for organization as well as for writing and speaking—whether he had that one thing most necessary, the power to capture the political imagination of the Irish people, had yet to be demonstrated. The first step in that necessary quest was to secure a prestigious Irish seat in Parliament. There was perhaps no more prestigious seat in Ireland than in the very Catholic and nationalist county of Tipperary. As Dillon had explained to Gillooly on March 3, just after he had visited Tipperary to support the association's candidate, Charles Moore, in his effort to win the by-election there, he had been asked by the clergy everywhere he went "why I was not the candidate selected by the Archbishop, and the explanations I gave on that point went far to reconcile them to Mr. Moore. I was asked by many would I consider to stand for Tipperary at the general election, on condition of being returned free of expense, and I evaded a direct answer by saying it would be time enough to make up my mind whenever the offer should be made" (G). The "explanations" made by Dillon to the Tipperary clergy were, of course, that he was not a wealthy man and depended for his support on his income as a barrister. He could not afford, therefore, either the expense of contesting a seat or the subsequent loss of professional income consequent on the winning of it.

There was yet another problem besides the financial to be overcome before Dillon could be returned for the prestigious county Tipperary seat. The senior member for the county, Laurence Waldron, who had held the seat since the general election of 1857, gave no indication that he was ready to retire from Parliament. Waldron, however, did not enjoy the same esteem among the clergy in Tipperary as he had in the general elections of 1857 and 1859. When the archbishop of Cashel had asked him in January 1865 his position with regard to the objects of the National Association, Waldron has assured him in a long letter of January 19 that there was really no difference between his views and principles and those advanced by the association (L). Despite this indirect invitation from the archbishop, Waldron apparently did not join the association, or if he did, he certainly took no prominent part in its affairs. Waldron had also had the misfortune of antagonizing Cullen as well as Leahy in educational matters when he became a commissioner of national education in 1860.

When Waldron wrote Leahy in late May asking the archbishop for an interview to discuss the approaching general election, Leahy replied on June 2 that he could not grant him an interview, but that he would give him his support in the upcoming election. Waldron responded on June 5 that he regretted he could not see Leahy but it was consoling for him to know that they were agreed on political essentials (L). When Waldron sent the archbishop a copy of his proposed electoral address at the end of June, however, Leahy wrote expressing his disapproval. In his reply on July 2, Waldron indicated regret that his address did not meet with Leahy's approval, but stated that he was obliged to express his opinions frankly and concluded by hoping that the election in Tipperary would proceed calmly (L). By this time, however, Leahy had received a most interesting and significant letter from Cullen. "Some friends called on me today," Cullen informed Leahy on June 30, "to state that they are most anxious to get Mr. Dillon returned for Tipperary. It appears that Gill will oppose Waldron and Moore, but that if Moore were to coalesce with Mr. Dillon and pay his expenses there would be no contest" (L). "Mr. Moore," Cullen added, "could afford to expend a few thousands as he is worth nearly a million of ready money. It would be no harm to give Mr. Waldron a lesson. He is quite opposed to us on educational matters, and altogether he is a wrongheaded man." Cullen concluded more diffidently, "I mention these matters to Y^r Grace—but at the same time I must say that I know so little about the state of things in the country that I can venture to give no opinion of my own."

The situation Cullen had outlined did in fact materialize. When Waldron learned that Dillon would be a candidate for Tipperary, he undoubtedly realized that he had no chance of being returned; he wrote Leahy on July 7 to thank him for all his help in the past and to inform him that he had decided to retire permanently from politics (L). In his letter to his constituents explaining his decision to retire, however, Waldron could not prevent a small note of bitterness from creeping in. "As a contest for the County of Tipperary," he noted on July 10, "now appears to be inevitable between the supporters of Mr. Gill on the one side and the other sections of the Liberal party on the other and as I find that efforts have been sedulously made to withdraw from me support on which I think, I was fairly entitled to calculate I have determined to retire."[8] Though Peter Gill, the editor of the *Tipperary Advocate*, did decide to contest Tipperary again, and was supported on the hustings by Father John Kenyon, he placed a very poor third in the voting. He received only 930 votes, whereas Moore and Dillon received 2,722 and 2,662 votes, respectively, which was yet another very impressive tribute to the power and influence of the Irish clergy, when united, in constitutional politics.[9]

8. Ibid., July 11, 1865.
9. Walker, p. 104.

The return of Dillon for Tipperary was also a giant step in his own political career. Not only did he obviously possess the confidence of the bishops, but he was also respected, if not esteemed, by nearly every shade of Irish nationalist opinion as a man of real political integrity. The basic question now was whether he could secure the confidence of the Irish people by putting together a parliamentary party, which he could turn into an effective political instrument in the House of Commons. The task was not going to be an easy one because of the heterogeneous nature of the political commitment of the more than fifty Catholic and Liberal Irish members returned at the general election. Dillon could not count on much more than a dozen members who were fully committed to the objects and rules of the association. There were perhaps another two dozen Irish members who were committed to a partial or conditional support of the association program, and another dozen who were not amenable to any policy of parliamentary independence because they were aspirants to office or place under the Liberal government. The key to forming an Irish party committed to an active policy in the House of Commons was to be found obviously in how many of those two dozen partially or conditionally committed members would coalesce with the dozen or so hard-core association supporters.

In the second week in October, therefore, a concerted move was made in various quarters, apparently on Cullen's initiative, to suggest the convening of a conference of the Catholic and Liberal Irish members in order to determine the policy to be pursued when Parliament met in February 1866. "I will (DV) tomorrow," Sir John Gray, the editor and proprietor of the *Freeman's Journal*, promised Cullen on October 12, "write a paragraph advising a conference of the Irish Members on the Church, Education, land & Finance questions" (C). "I do not think however," he added, "it would be prudent for me to *originate*. Some men are very weak and therefore very jealous. I will avail myself of the suggestions of some 'correspondent whose opinions I report.'" "I am not very sanguine as to the result," Gray confessed.

Many good men will *not* come. Many *can* not come. Some will be afraid to come to be worried perhaps by men who are not responsible. If there are *few* it will be a sign of weakness, and an occasion for a triumphant howl from the enemy. Has your Grace calculated the numbers that can be relied on? —I mean for coming. Will *Monsell*, Brady, Sir J. Power, Cogan, Barry, Armstrong, O'Loghlin[?] Can Stock, McKenna & others[?] *All* these men *will* I think and *must* if pressed vote on Land, Church, Education &

with your friends. I would before irreversibly binding the liberal members to a meeting venture to suggest that the pulse of such men as Monsell be felt so as to *ensure* against failure.

Again—would you suggest a conference *of* the Members, or a conference *with* the Members, and if the latter a conference between what body and the Members[?] Would it be *the Ass^n*, the Committee of the Ass^n, a deputation from the Committee or the Archbishops and Bishops, or a general gathering such as that which met in *1852* where the wildest theories were propounded by some of the Ulster men[,] amongst others, the Revd. Mr. Bell, the present lecturer on Fenian policy!

"All these matters," he advised Cullen, "I think ought [to] be duly weighed by your Grace before a Conference *be fixed* or even resolved upon. A public conference and the angry discussion that would arise if any man who pleased might come and talk would be a dangerous experiment NOW." He suggested in conclusion, "A conference of the Irish Members if only 20 were present to hear the views of the Bishops and a few others selected by them as consultants would in my humble judgement be of *infinite service.*"

Cullen apparently replied by return of post, for Gray wrote him again on Sunday, October 15, from North Wales, where he was spending the weekend (C). "I have run over here for two days," Gray explained, "but you will see that I have commenced the subject of the conference in an article published on Saturday which I wrote before I left Dublin on Friday evening. I am much gratified at learning from your note that you prefer a private conference and that you think 30 or 40 will be present. Much work for the Country could be 'cut out' at such a meeting if all men enter the room resolved to think of the Country only and to sink self." "I hope your Grace," he added, "will feel that I dealt cautiously with the question of the Conference and that the article is so written that it in substance accords with your views or at least leaves your views open for adoption as fully as if it had been formed with them before and not after writing it." Cullen had also written those bishops with whom he had some influence, urging them to encourage the Catholic and Liberal Irish members within their spiritual jurisdiction to attend the proposed conference. The bishop of Waterford, Dominic O'Brien, for example, replied on October 15 that on receiving Cullen's letter he had immediately contacted John A. Blake, one of the Waterford city members, who promised to attend the conference; he would write now, O'Brien said, to the other city member, Sir Henry Winston Barron, and the county member, John Esmonde, to urge the same course of action on them (C).

Cullen also apparently wrote Gillooly, for he too wrote the Catholic and Liberal members within his spiritual jurisdiction. "There is at present," Gillooly explained on October 13 to The O'Conor Don, the junior member for county Roscommon and a Catholic landlord of some prominence, "an anxious desire throughout the Country amongst those who best understand its wants and honestly seek to promote its interests, that our Catholic and Liberal M.P.s should meet in Dublin to agree on the policy to be pursued by them with reference to Irish affairs in the approaching Session and to adopt practical means of acting together in parliament in fulfillment of the resolutions they may adopt" (G).

> No one understands better than you the importance & necessity of this course and no one will I am sure more cordially lend his aid to secure its adoption. It is thought that the beginning of Novr w^d be the most suitable time for the meeting, and many here are anxious to publish the requisition for it next week. About 15 or 20 names of Members will be attached to the requisition—and I write to you just now to request that you will authorise me to have your name attached to it. The names will be put in Alphabet^l order. The Conference will be exclusively composed of M.Ps and it is understood that no pledge of what is called Indep^t opposition will be proposed or taken by them on the occasion.

In a long and windy reply on October 15, O'Conor Don proceeded to give Gillooly more advice than satisfaction (G). After explaining that he could not attend the proposed meeting because he had already arranged to visit America before Parliament met, he added that the proposed requisition was not to his liking and that he would have preferred "a different form altogether." As Gillooly had asked for his suggestions, however, O'Conor Don pointed out that he thought the proposed conference should be private rather than public, with the proceedings not published in the newspapers. He felt that a public conference would "lead to dissension and disunion and to consequent weakness of parliamentary action." O'Conor Don, who was really a very able and clever man, was obviously attempting in this reply to Gillooly to let one of his more important constituents down as easily as possible. When Gillooly had asked him nearly a year before to join the National Association, for example, O'Conor Don had replied on December 7, 1864, that though he approved of the objects of the association he could not join it (G). An association, he explained, would make a lot of promises, but few of them would ever be fulfilled. In any case, because he had to spend a great deal of time in London, he could not devote the time the association would require. Gillooly was apparently no more successful with the senior member for Roscommon, Col. Fitzstephen French, a Protestant landlord who had held his seat as a Liberal since 1832. It may be presumed, however, though their replies do not appear to have survived, that Gillooly had greater success with the two new members for the boroughs of Athlone and Sligo.

Gillooly's efforts were only the prelude to a more concerted effort to convene a conference of the Catholic and Liberal Irish members, for on October 18 the suggestion was generally endorsed at a meeting of the committee of the National Association. Nearly all those who spoke encouraged the calling of a conference, and none was more forward in his endorsement than Cullen. "Our grievances are so great and palpable," he explained, "that I trust a sense of justice will at length induce parliament to listen to us, and grant all we demand, and in order to effect this it is necessary our members should act in concert."[10] "How are we to get them united?" he then asked.

> I think by the conference which has been proposed in many influential quarters. It has been proposed to bring them together and let them deliberate upon the questions to be brought forward in parliament, and deliberate also on the course of action to be adopted. They are all men of intelligence and men of education, who are accustomed to business, and when they come together to discuss these questions in a friendly way there is no doubt they will determine on what is to be done. It is to be regretted that they are not very many, but still their number is sufficient to produce a great effect and exercise great influence in parliament. I trust, then, that they will meet and discuss the questions of the church and of tenant right, and the objectionable oaths that are taken by Protestants and Catholics, and that then they will determine upon what they can effect to succeed in parliament, and adopt a system of action which will give them force to enable them to render great service to the country (applause).

In the course of his remarks at the meeting, Dillon also addressed himself to the proposed conference of Irish members. "It has been suggested," he noted, "that a conference of Irish members take place. I most ardently wish to see such a conference meet in Ireland, but I did not permit that wish to prevail with me so far as to originate the idea in this Association." "I thought it better," he explained,

10. *Freeman's Journal*, October 19, 1865.

that it should grow spontaneously in the public mind and in the mind of the representatives themselves, and accordingly the idea has been put forward and vigorously pressed, and from communications made to myself by a good many of the representatives, I have no doubt we shall have a very influential meeting of members of parliament in Dublin within a month. I trust and believe that the members will meet with a due sense of the responsibility of their position. The country will look to them for guidance, for independent honest action in parliament. On the other hand neither we here in this Association nor any other parties in the country have the slightest desire to impose on them any unreasonable condition or to fetter their action in the slightest degree. They come to deliberate and to decide upon what shall appear to their unbiased judgement the best course to adopt in their capacity as representatives. I trust that they will arrive at a substantial agreement between themselves, and that can only be effected by a disposition on the part of each representative to yield to the feelings and opinions of others.

Dillon added most significantly in concluding, "If I could persuade the members to act as I think best, I would be in favour of laying down a certain programme of measures, and of going with these measures to government, and saying that upon the condition alone of giving us these measures, would they have our support." "Other members," he noted finally, "may take a different view of the case. I certainly don't say I should attempt to impose my views upon other members. I can only express an earnest hope that when the members come together there will be a substantial opinion amongst them, and that they will present a solid front when they enter the House of Commons [hear, hear]."

The real significance of Cullen's and Dillon's remarks, of course, was that they prefigured the eclipse of the association as an effective political organization. Both Cullen and Dillon recognized that the political initiative had now fallen to those Catholic and Liberal Irish members who might choose to meet together before Parliament convened. If they wanted that conference to be more than a rump of the dozen or so hard-core Irish members obliged to the association, they had to face up to the fact that the program of legislation and the means devised to implement it by the Irish members could not be dictated by the association. That is why, for example, Cullen most pointedly recommended that the proposed conference deal with the Church, Tenant Right, and objectionable-oaths questions, and did not even mention the education question. He wanted no lay initiative on that question which he and his brother prelates were not in a position to control. Dillon went even further by pointing out that the initiative for a conference of the Irish members was spontaneous in the country and did not originate in the association, and that although he certainly had his own views about a program and a party in the House of Commons, he was not prepared to attempt to impose his views on his fellow Irish members. In all this, of course, Dillon was making a virtue of necessity, because the association simply did not have the power to do more.

The waning of confidence in the association as a viable political force was even more in evidence in the remarks of the others who chose to speak at this committee meeting. The archbishop of Cashel, for example, confessed that the association had "not had the success that its friends would wish to have" and attributed the lack of success to the fact that there were still "many good Irishmen" who had not thought fit as yet to join it. In referring to the proposed conference of Irish members, Richard J. Devitt, a Dublin town councillor and a founding member of the association, expressed the hope that the Catholic bishops "would do a great deal in inducing the members of their respective districts to come to Dublin to take counsel together," thus not only testifying to where any real power yet remaining in the association had come to rest but also explaining why "many good Irishmen" had not yet joined it. In closing the proceedings, Alderman MacSwiney struck the final mournful note by plaintively explaining that he believed the association had done good work, given the limited resources at its command, and that "every intelligent man in Ireland must feel the necessity of supporting that or some such kindred association. If another body possessing the confidence of the hierarchy, clergy, and people, to a larger extent than their Association could claim, be promoted, why, by all means, let them give place to it; but, in the absence of any such body, it is clearly the duty of every patriotic Irishman to sustain and rally round the existing organization."

By the middle of October, therefore, it had become obvious even to those who had been most forward in launching and promoting the association that it had failed to capture the political imagination of the country. The reason it failed to do so, of course, was that it lacked *national* credibility. Almost immediately on its founding, the association became so identified with Cullen and his clergy that it became more generally known as "Cullen's Association" and was viewed as a clerical rather than as a genuinely national organization. Besides its clerical complexion, the association had the misfortune of also being identified as essentially a Dublin phenomenon, so that it was not considered to be really rooted in the country. To make matters worse, no layman of any national eminence, except Dillon, was prominent in the affairs of the association, and both the clergy and the local Dublin politicians thereby acquired a greater visibility in its affairs than they might ordinarily have had. Because the hoped-for national consensus backed by the united political will of the public did not emerge, the real power and influence in the association remained essentially in the hands of those bishops who had originally committed themselves to making it work.

When even that hard core, which consisted of Cullen and about a half dozen more, began to soften, in the disagreements that took place over the rules and the priorities, it became all too evident that the future of the association as an effective national constituency organization was very dim. Its fundamental weaknesses had been mercifully masked by the political activity of the bishops and their clergy in the general election, but when the electoral dust had settled, it soon became even more evident that except for what influence the local bishop and his clergy could still exert, the association as an effective force in the constituencies was dead. Soon after the general election, in fact, the telltale signs of the association's dissolution began to emerge. By late September one of its most enthusiastic early supporters among the bishops, Patrick Dorrian, the former coadjutor and now the actual bishop of Down and Connor, explained his own disappointment to Kirby. "For my part," Dorrian confessed on September 28, "I cordially hate Whiggery and believe that the indirect support, its Patrons receive from some of us, is *the* great folly of our policy. If a Bishop supports at an Election a man who has supported the Ecclesiastical Titles Bill or one who has contributed to Garibaldi's Fund, what must be the consequence?" (K). "Our Nat[l] Assoc[n]," he pointed out, "has failed to touch the *heart* of the country from its' [sic] too great and too evident leanings towards the great liberal party, instead of being TRULY *independent*." "The Fenians," he concluded, "were valueless but to do harm; and, wherever we look, we see no power but in the Union of the Bishops. May God bring IT about!"

Whether the failure of the association to touch the heart of the country was indeed attributable, as Dorrian maintained, to the tendency of Whiggery among the Irish bishops is a moot point, but the bishop of Down and Connor was soon given a very good example of that want of unity among the bishops about which he had also complained. The irony was that it could hardly be described as coming from a quarter that was Whiggish in its tendency. Thomas Nulty, the coadjutor to the bishop of Meath, who had been the leading figure in the effort to have the rules of the association revised in April in order that the Meath clergy might be accommodated, met with his clergy in Navan on November 6 and finally launched the long-deferred Meath Tenant Right Society.[11] Worse was yet to come, however, for on November 29 the new society met at Navan and published an address in which the proposed conference of the Catholic and Liberal Irish members, which had been finally scheduled for Dublin on December 5, was denounced as "a Freemasons' meeting" because its deliberations were to be private. The address further declared the land question to be the only legitimate political question of the day, lyrically adding, "and in this dark hour, the next, *mayhap*, before the dawn, but an hour big with the destinies of Ireland, for good or ill, we turn our eyes to the west, where still lingers—far, we trust, above the horizon—that sacred star whose entire course has been so steady and so auspicious, to which we have so long looked up with streaming eyes—and never looked in vain—for the light that guides and gladdens a bewildered nation—we look up to the oldest and best friend of Ireland—the great Archbishop of Tuam."[12]

The disillusionment of Dorrian and even the defection of Nulty, however, were as nothing compared to Cullen's continued ambivalence regarding the association. Though he had done his best among his episcopal colleagues during the general election to secure the return of candidates pledged to the principles of the association, he apparently came to understand very quickly that the political future now lay with those Catholic and Liberal M.P.'s who could be persuaded to give the association's principles substance through legislation in the Imperial Parliament. After the general election, therefore, he never again wasted any real time or energy on the association. Indeed, he soon reduced it to a mere forum to be used to keep public opinion up to the mark on those objects he had most at heart, the disestablishment of the Protestant Church and the education question. The association became, in fact, for the rest of its existence, little more than Cullen's personal propaganda machine, which he apparently could turn on and off at will. For example, when he appeared at the association meeting on October 18, after an absence of nearly six months, it was less to breathe new life into the organization than

11. Ibid., December 4, 1865. A meeting had, in fact, been held in Navan on April 26, 1865, at which a resolution was passed calling for the establishment of a Meath Tenant Right Society. The resolution had apparently not been acted on because the full meeting of the National Association to revise its rules had been called for April 28, 1865.

12. Ibid.

to endorse the proposed conference of Irish M.P.'s and to warn anyone who might be so inclined that unauthorized lay initiatives on the education question were not welcome.

The state to which the association had been reduced was made amply clear about a month later in a somewhat pathetic circular letter addressed by Dillon apparently to all those bishops who had originally signed the requisition inaugurating the association. "Your Lordship will have seen by the newspapers," Dillon explained on November 24, "that our efforts to procure a conference of Irish members have met with a fair amount of success. Twenty-four members have expressed their willingness to attend, and the number will probably be increased to thirty. Any reasonable measures put forward by such a body will be certain to receive favourable consideration at the hands of the Government. English opinion inclines more to a redress of Irish grievances at the present juncture than at any former period in our history. A fierce struggle for power between the two great English parties is universally anticipated" (C). "All these signs on the political horizon," he assured the bishops,

> encourage the belief that Providence has afforded us an opportunity for achieving, by a comparatively short and easy effort, reforms which (under less favourable circumstances) might cost the labour of many years.
>
> It is because I clearly see this great opportunity, and am apprehensive that it may pass away from us, that I am tempted to urge your Lordship not to give up the good work in the inauguration of which you assisted a year ago. Neither our representatives, nor even the Government, can carry the important reforms we require, unless the country exhibits an earnest desire for them.
>
> Assuming that the approaching Conference will agree on measures which will merit our support, it should be the business of our association to send forward numerously signed petitions in favour of such measures at the commencement of the session. For this purpose some (though by no means large) funds will be required. Probably £500 or £600 would enable the association to do all that will be required of it, and to exercise a decided influence on the course of legislation during the next year.
>
> If the friends of the association will now fail to exert themselves in its behalf, not only will all the good work, of which it is capable, remain undone, but our enemies will point to its failure as an evidence that the country is indifferent regarding the objects for which it was established.

"To prevent these disastrous results," Dillon further explained, "I take the liberty of urging your Lordship to continue your patriotic efforts on behalf of the association. If great popular excitement or large pecuniary contributions were required, I should hardly desire to engage your L^{d}ship in so weighty an undertaking. But we require only very moderate funds, and such occasional expressions of interest and good will from the clergy and laity as will afford some evidence that the association fairly represents the opinions, and expresses the wants, of the Catholic intelligence of Ireland." "Above all things," he exhorted in conclusion, "I desire to impress on your Lordship that any effort in behalf of the Association will lose more than half its value if it be not made *at once.*" But why, it may well be asked, did Dillon write so uncharacteristic a letter, especially when he must have understood better than anyone else that the future of the association as a viable political organization was very dark? The reason, of course, was that he was desperately attempting to preserve what was left of his narrowing political base in order to be able to exercise some political leverage at the upcoming conference of Irish members. His own following of about a dozen or so members who had been returned on the program of the association at the general election would certainly provide him with considerable influence at the conference, but only so long as they acted in concert. If they could be held together they could provide Dillon with the necessary nucleus around which the less-committed Catholic and Liberal members might coalesce to form an Irish parliamentary party in the House of Commons. If it became apparent, however, that the bishops, and particularly Cullen, had abandoned the association, the prospects for evolving a common program and a party to implement it would be a good deal more dim than they already were.

In any case, when the conference did meet in Dublin on December 5 and 6, there were only twenty-two Catholic and Liberal members in attendance.[13] The chair was taken by Col. F. S. Greville-Nugent, the senior member for county Longford; the secretaries were Tristram

13. Ibid., December 8, 1865. The M.P.'s who attended were Sir James Power (county Wexford), Sir Patrick O'Brien (King's county), Sir John Gray (Kilkenny borough), The O'Donoghue (Tralee borough), Col. F. S. Greville-Nugent (county Longford), J. B. Dillon (county Tipperary), T. Kennedy (county Louth), G. Bryan (county Kilkenny), M. Corbally (county Meath), G. Barry (county Cork), W. P. Urquhart (county Westmeath), C. Moore (county Tipperary), Major M. W. O'Reilly (county Longford), E. J. Synan (county Limerick), J. F. Maguire (Cork borough), J. A. Blake (Waterford borough), J. Bagwell (Clonmel borough), R. Armstrong (Sligo borough), R. J. Devereux (Wexford borough), T. O. Stock (Carlow borough), D. J. Rearden (Athlone borough), and B. Whitworth (Drogheda borough).

Kennedy, the junior member for county Louth, and Dillon. The deliberations were private, and at the end of the two-day meeting a series of fourteen resolutions was published under the names of the twenty-two members present. Some days later it was reported that four other members, including The O'Conor Don, had also subscribed to the resolutions.[14] The first seven resolutions were a resounding endorsement of the three objects of the association—Tenant Right (resolutions one and two), Church disestablishment (three and four), and denominational education on the university, primary, and secondary levels (five through seven).[15] A committee of seven was appointed to draw a bill "to provide adequate compensation for all tenants' improvements" to be submitted to a general meeting of the Irish members and, when approved, introduced in the House of Commons, "the support of the government claimed for it as essential to their acquiring the confidence of the Irish people." The established Church was declared to be an intolerable grievance, and it was proclaimed the duty of the government to settle this question on the basis of equality. After noting with pleasure that negotiations were just then pending between the bishops and the government on the University question, the conference called for a denominational system on the primary and secondary levels.

Resolutions eight through twelve were respectively concerned with oaths, productive improvements (fishing, harbors, draining), the grand jury laws, the cattle plague, and reform of the railway system. Resolution thirteen read, "That, inasmuch as the 'advanced' section of the English Liberal party largely share our political views and sympathise with our efforts, we are anxious to cooperate with them in anything calculated to advance our common interests, and hope for their assistance in the promotion of measures beneficial to Ireland." And finally the fourteenth resolution, while warmly welcoming a general extension of the franchise, recommended that if such a measure were extended to Ireland it should be accompanied by "safeguards necessary for the security of the voter," which was another way of saying that the broadening of the franchise in Ireland would not be of much use without the secret ballot.

Though it is obvious that Dillon was very successful in persuading the conference to endorse a comprehensive program of reform for Ireland, and largely on the basis of what had been advocated by the asso-

---

14. Ibid., December 11, 1865, quoting the *Dublin Evening Post*. The report from the *Evening Post* mentions only The O'Conor Don (county Roscommon) by name, but the other three were likely Jonathan Pim (Dublin borough), W. H. F. Cogan (county Kildare), and John Brady (county Leitrim).

15. Ibid.

ciation, he was a good deal less successful in getting the Irish members to commit themselves to any specific means to effect those salutary ends. In a word, he had secured a program but had not succeeded in creating a party. The crucial resolutions as far as means were concerned were the first and the thirteenth, and both were subversive of the idea of an Irish parliamentary party. By merely pointing out in the first resolution that a good Tenant Right measure from the government was essential to securing the confidence of the Irish people, the Irish members signified that they were not prepared to oppose the government as a body on the issue. By advocating in their thirteenth resolution an alliance with the "advanced" section of the Liberal party, they were, in effect, relegating themselves to being the tip of the radical tail of that party. Just as the speeches made at the meeting of the committee of the association on October 18 carried with them the portent of doom for the association, the resolutions of the Irish members at their conference on December 5 and 6 signified the end of the hope for an effective independent Irish party in the House of Commons for more than a decade.

———————◆———————

Dillon, however, bravely continued to persevere. Shortly before Parliament was to open he spoke at a meeting of the National Association in Dublin, making a most provocative speech about the relationship between Fenianism and Irish grievances. What gave his remarks their bite was that for the previous three months large numbers of Fenians had been tried and sentenced to long terms of penal servitude, and Irish public opinion had become, if anything, only more hostile to the British connection. "Let it not be supposed," Dillon explained on January 23 to the crowded meeting, at which a large number of the clergy were present,

> that I seek to exaggerate the extent or the power of the confederacy which has been formed in this country and in the United States (loud cheering) for the overthrow of the British government in Ireland. What a statesman will not fail to see underlying all these outward manifestations of treason and repression of which the public have grown tired, are these few pregnant facts —that a great military and naval Power, destined, in all probability, to become, at no distant day, the greatest power on earth, has sprung suddenly into existence within ten days' sail of the Irish shores (cheers); that those in whose hands mainly rest the guidance and control of that Power are animated by the deepest

resentment against England (cheers); that this resentment is inflamed and stimulated to activity by the presence of ten million citizens of Irish blood; and, finally, that deep and widespread disaffection pervades the population of at least three of the provinces of Ireland. (Renewed cheering.)[16]

"It seems to me," Dillon then added, "that the conditions of disturbance and of change are here in abundance; whether it is to be a beneficial change or not will depend, under heaven, on ourselves. (Hear, hear.)"

Our social system as it now stands is not calculated to bear the impending shock; the tree that would defy the tempest must strike its roots deep into the soil. Yes; we want change, and radical change, in this country. Should our people be summoned to war, let us make sure this time that they shall fight in defense of homes that they can call their own, and of altars freed from insult and dishonour. (Loud cheers.) We want change, but we want neither Jacobinism, nor anarchy, nor spoliation—we want rather to advance with safe and steady steps towards the goal we have in view under the guidance of religion and intelligence. (Cheers.) And if religion and intelligence will not respond to the appeal which the country makes upon them—if at this moment, when the clouds are gathering dark around us, the helm is to be abandoned to recklessness and folly, then is the prospect before us a gloomy one indeed.

"Take the transactions of a week," he then noted by way of example, "and, what are they? Arrests, more arrests, until the gaols are becoming too full to hold any more, until we begin to doubt whether Swift's plan for the insane might not be conveniently applied to Irish disaffection; whether it might not be found more practicable to put the loyal portion of the community into gaol and leave the disaffected at large. (Laughter.)"

"On the other hand," Dillon added more pointedly, "you find in the history of the week just past such a fact as this—a gentleman in Tipperary purchases an estate in the Landed Estates court in 1864. There are about thirty tenants on it—solvent, industrious tenants, whose forefathers had probably lived there for generations, and had created much of that property which was sold as the legal property of another. Regardless of all this—regardless of their rights, regardless of

---

16. *Times* (London), January 25, 1866. See also the *Freeman's Journal*, January 24, 1866.

their sufferings, this purchaser serves the fearful notice to quit; and although they have paid their last November rent, he proceeds with his ejectment. (Hear.)" "Here is the key," Dillon then assured his listeners, "to all this Irish disaffection by which the people affect to be so bewildered. The law robs and exterminates the people; the people naturally hate and defy the law. (Cheers.)" "For my part," he boldly concluded, "I shall content myself with saying that such laws do not deserve to be respected, and that the perpetrators of such outrages as I have just described are greater enemies of law, of peace, and prosperity in Ireland than those heroic though mistaken men who have been sent to penal servitude during the last six weeks. (Loud cheers.)"

"The most remarkable thing in the speech," the Dublin correspondent of the London *Times* shrewdly noted of Dillon's effort, ". . . was his reference to Fenianism, and the extraordinary manner in which it was received in an association over which archbishops and bishops preside, and in the presence of a number of Roman Catholic priests." Even before he arrived in London for the opening of Parliament, therefore, Dillon's reputation as a man of extreme political views had preceded him. Indeed, in the next several months the company he would find most congenial in the House of Commons was among the English radicals, and especially John Stuart Mill and John Bright. He first made the acquaintance of Mill on the evening of February 8 in the division lobby, when the House divided on The O'Donoghue's proposed amendment to the queen's speech calling attention to the widespread disaffection in Ireland and the government's duty to take measures to remove the causes for it. "Only 25 voted in favour of O'D's amendment," Dillon reported to his wife on February 9, "and amongst them were John Bright and J. S. Mill. I spoke to the latter, and after a few words['] conversation I said that there was a gentleman well known to him, who was my particular friend—C. G. Duffy. I then mentioned my name. He shook hands very warmly and said I was just the man whose acquaintance he most desired to make, that he had been reading my evidence about the land question."[17] " 'You have been roundly abused lately,' " Dillon added, quoting Mill in reference to Dillon's recent Dublin speech, " 'but I suppose you don't mind that' and he went on to say that my speech contained nothing which was not said during the debate [on the queen's speech] and listened to by the house with tolerable favour." "In point of fact," Dillon further explained to his wife,

17. Dillon Papers (D), Trinity College Library, Dublin. Dillon's letters to his wife are not dated; internal evidence has been used to place them.

the tone of the debate was encouraging[,] especially Gladstone's speech. I was sitting nearly opposite him and he spoke fairly *at* me, looking straight at me and I at him. I suppose he saw that I was drinking in every word he said. He is certainly a *great man—* far greater than I had supposed. Fancy Jonathan Hen with the musical voice and intonation of the Chief Baron, & you may form some idea of Gladstone. He is *fearfully* persuasive, and much of his power is certainly due to his elevated moral character.

"Mill said to me," Dillon assured his wife in conclusion, "that his [Gladstone's] speech portends good things for Ireland, and—'what he says he means.' "

Almost as soon as he had arrived in London, in keeping with the priorities set by the association the previous June in its rule changes, Dillon began to prepare a land bill that was to be introduced that session. On February 5 he forwarded a copy of his bill to Cullen. "I send your Grace," he explained, "a copy of the Tenant Bill. Although Mr. Gladstone has pronounced it 'fair and moderate' I have little hope that the landlords will be satisfied with it. However, if the Governm^t should take it up, there is a fair prospect of its being carried through the House of Commons" (C). "What I fear most," Dillon confessed, "is that a clamour may be got up in Ireland by those who will think it too moderate. These people little understand the difficulties we have to encounter. To say nothing of the Governmen^t or the House of Commons, it would be impossible to get our own *Tenant right* members to adopt a more decided measure that the present." "You must not suppose, however," he assured Cullen, "that I think the present bill has little in it. I honestly think it a fair settlement of the question, and firmly believe that in twenty years it would give to Ireland a tenantry practically independent of their landlords." "It w^d be most desirable," he advised Cullen shrewdly in conclusion, "that we should have a general meeting of leading members of the Assoc^n in Dublin on Tuesday fortnight."

Two weeks later, however, Dillon was still attempting to get the Irish members to agree to his land bill. "I am very busy," he reported to his wife on February 19, "drafting a land Bill for the Irish members—i.e. about 25 of them. We meet tomorrow at 2 o'c. when 'My Bill' will be considered in detail. It is now in the hands of the printer" (D). "If they will agree on it," he added hopefully, "it stands a fair chance of becoming law." The Irish members, as Dillon had warned Cullen, were not easy to satisfy. "I was engaged a good deal yesterday," he reported again to his wife on February 25, "and will be again to-day in trying to get the Irish members to agree to a decent land bill" (D). "I fear," he confessed, "I shall have hard work to succeed. They always pretend that their only objection is the impossibility of carrying it in the House. But it is plain enough that they have no desire to carry anything that is worth having." "Your friend Sir Rowland," he added, naming Rowland Blennerhassett, the junior member for Galway city, "agreeably disappointed me. He attended most diligently. I think he was attracted by J. S. Mill who was present on my invitation. He (Mill) said nothing, but whispered to me 'I see what a difficult business you have in hand, but I was prepared for it by reading your evidence.' "

In the meantime, Dillon had finally made the acquaintance of the archbishop of Westminster. Every Tuesday evening in the parliamentary season, Manning held a political soiree at which prominent politicians and journalists were very much in evidence. Dillon had been invited to attend by an influential Irish Catholic journalist, J. Cashel Hoey, then subeditor of the *Dublin Review*, which was owned by Manning. "A most pleasant talk," Dillon reported to his wife on Wednesday, February 21, "with the Archbishop last evg. He rec^d me most cordially and we had a great deal of talk. He evidently prefers our political principles to the Ultramontane principles of the Tablet. I told him that some English Catholics were too apt to confound our 'liberal' party in Ireland with Continental 'liberals.' He said he understood the distinction very well" (D). "He alluded to my speech in Dublin," Dillon added, "and said that he saw nothing in it but a bold enunciation of the truth—'something like what Mr. Bright w^d say, in a similar case.' " "Altogether," he concluded, "I like him very much, and I think we would agree very well."

The following week, on February 27, at the usual weekly meeting of the committee of the association in Dublin, Alderman MacSwiney reported that he had just returned from London that morning after having met with Dillon and that it had been decided to convene a general meeting of the association on March 13 to discuss the proposed land bill drawn up by Dillon and his parliamentary colleagues.[18] The general meeting had to be postponed to the following week, however, because Dillon wanted to participate in the debate on the proposed bill to modify the oaths all members of Parliament were obliged to take, which Roman Catholic members found particularly obnoxious.[19] The meeting finally took place on March 20, with Dillon

18. *Freeman's Journal*, March 1, 1866.
19. Ibid., Cullen to MacSwiney, March 14, 1866.

present, and it was not an easy one for him to manage.[20] Matters were made immediately difficult when the secretary, Nicholas Whyte, began to read the letters sent by those who were not able to be present. After reading an immoderately short and tepid letter from Michael O'Hea, the bishop of Ross, in support of Dillon's proposed bill, Whyte then read a letter from The O'Donoghue, which advised the association to defer consideration of the bill drafted by his parliamentary colleagues to an aggregate meeting. "I have tried," O'Donoghue explained,

> to persuade myself that it might do good, but have failed in the attempt. I look upon the bill as utterly worthless, because it confers no rights on the occupiers, and because the landlords can render it completely inoperative. A mere permissive bill such as this is of no use. I have no faith in the power of public opinion to save the tenant farmers from injustice. Experience has proved its inefficacy. According to my judgement the land question can only be settled by the legislature enacting "That no man in the possession of an agricultural holding shall be dispossessed as long as he pays a fair rent. If the landlord and tenant cannot agree as to the rent, in which case the rent to be determined by a valuator or valuators appointed by the state." I may be told "the English Parliament will never sanction such an enactment." The reply I give to this statement is that the refusal of the English Parliament does not alter the fact that the settlement I propose is just, and the only one adequate to meet the requirements of the occupiers of land. Had we a Parliament in our own College-green a land bill such as I have indicated would be at once carried.[21]

"I will only add," O'Donoghue concluded, "that I think the National Association ought not to adopt the bill which is to be considered tomorrow without calling an aggregate meeting of the association, and of all Irishmen willing to come and give us the benefit of their advice on a matter affecting the dearest interests of those agricultural millions who are the strength and hope of Ireland."

In answering the objections raised in O'Donoghue's letter, Dillon made a most able and telling presentation. He began by reading a letter from T. MacCarthy Downing, who before the general election had been highly prominent in securing the preeminence of the land

20. Ibid., March 21, 1866.
21. Ibid., O'Donoghue to MacSwiney, March 19, 1866.

question among the objects advocated by the association.[22] Though Downing recommended that the association adopt the proposed bill, he explained that he thought it was only the bare minimum of what they had a right to expect, and that he had not much hope that the present Parliament would accept even that. In beginning his remarks, Dillon took Downing's generally desponding tone as his point of departure. He confessed that though Downing's view appeared to be the prevailing one just then, he was somewhat more hopeful. The Irish members of Parliament, at least some thirty-five of them, had since Parliament assembled "devoted themselves honestly, energetically, and disinterestedly to the service of their country." Their English friends in Parliament, especially the radical wing of the Liberal party, in the persons of Mill, Bright, and W. E. Forster, had done good work in helping to shape public opinion in England on the questions of interest to Ireland. As to Irish public opinion, the large number of petitions that had been sent from Ireland on the land question, which involved some 150,000 signatures, had made a distinct impression on the House of Commons. Moreover, the government was thoroughly with them on the land and established Church questions. The great difficulty was with the education question, where the government was hampered by the strong opinions held against denominational education and, for understandable reasons, by the rank and file of the Liberal members of Parliament. Still, he did not despair, because he thought that since they were fair and just men, they would, in the end, appreciate that Irish circumstances were not English and that a different solution to the problem was therefore involved.

Dillon then turned to the thorny question of persuading the meeting to endorse his proposed land bill. "I am very anxious, as I have stated," he explained temperately, "that this bill should be thoroughly understood in the first place, and that if it is not deemed satisfactory by the country that the country should let us know that, because I think the greatest merit of any measure that can be passed on this subject of landlord and tenant is that it shall be accepted by the country as a fair settlement of the question." He continued:

Now, if the question were whether this bill is the best possible arrangement that could be made on this subject—if the question were whether any one of us, if possessed of supreme power, would adopt this mode in preference to all others of settling the question, I would deem it difficult to maintain that this is the precise settlement (hear, hear). But this is essentially a question

22. Ibid., McCarthy Downing to Dillon, March 19, 1866.

of compromise. The O'Donoghue says it is not such a bill as ought to be accepted, and the reason is that it confers no right on the occupier. Well, now, Sir, I flatly deny that, and say that it confers most important rights upon the occupiers of land, and I say that if this bill had been in operation for the last fifty years the occupiers of the land would have as much interest in the land at least as the proprietors have in it. It is rather a sort of libel—without meaning any offense—upon the people of Ireland to say that a bill which confers upon them the right of compensation for all improvements they may make on the land without imposing upon them the necessity of serving any notice upon the landlord, or instituting any proceeding in courts of quarter sessions or elsewhere, is not an improvement. The man who says the tenant can gain nothing by that law says in fact that the tenants are hopelessly lazy, because if the tenants can apply themselves to the improvement of the soil they must derive great advantages from the bill, which gives them full right to compensation for improvement. He [O'Donoghue] speaks of it as a permissive bill. Well, I clearly do not understand what that means. If he means that the tenant is bound, before he commences any improvement, in respect to which he would be entitled to compensation, to obtain the permission of his landlord, the bill is not bad. But that is not the bill; on the contrary, I consider the chief merit of this bill to be that the tenant, without asking the permission of his landlord, or without giving any information of his intention to make any improvement, may by simply making it get the right to compensation. My friend, The O'Donoghue, adds that he thinks the only bill worth anything would be one involving this principle, that there should be a perpetuity of tenure to every occupier of land, or that the rent should be valued by impartial valuators. If we were discussing this matter as a question of political economy it might be all very well to talk in that way, but we are here as politicians not as philosophers (hear, hear). But surely The O'Donoghue would be the last to say if he were here that there would be a shadow of a chance of getting from the Imperial Parliament a bill like that.

"If we want measures," Dillon finally pointed out, "that can be carried only by revolution, and if we will accept no measure short of that, our only plan is to become revolutionists. On the other hand, if we want to carry any measure by the ordinary course of applying to the legislature, our plan is to adopt any measure that there is a fair chance of carrying through the legislature; and might not that be the best measure that we would have a reasonable chance of carrying? That is the principle that guided us in the arrangement of the present bill."

After a long and interesting discussion of the meaning and the merits of the proposed bill, in which Dillon ably continued to defend it as the best measure that could be then obtained, Alderman James Plunkett of Dublin finally asked whether, since the government was said to be preparing its own land bill, it might not be better to defer approval of Dillon's measure until the government's bill was available, because it might indeed prove to be a better one. Patrick O'Reilly, the parish priest of Drumlane (Belturbet) in the diocese of Kilmore, pointed out that though the proposed bill was not all they would prefer, it was essential that at that juncture the association strengthen the hands of its representatives in Parliament by endorsing their work, and he proposed the following resolution:

> That having fully considered the land bill drawn up by the conference of Liberal Irish members as now submitted to this meeting and also the ample explanations of same as given to us by Mr. Dillon, M.P., we are of opinion that whilst its provisions fall far short of those which might legitimately be demanded by the occupiers of the soil, nevertheless we endorse this bill, but only as the minimum of the tenants' just demands, a minimum less than which should not be supported by our members or accepted by the people of Ireland.

The resolution was seconded by A. J. McKenna, the proprietor of the *Ulster Observer*, and was passed unanimously.

Dillon had indeed handled a very difficult situation with great tact. He not only had secured the endorsement of his bill but had by his temperate and firm statement of the case contained The O'Donoghue without alienating that proud and testy man. When, for example, the association met again some two weeks later, on April 3, both Dillon and O'Donoghue were in attendance, and they appeared to have made up their differences: the latter emphasized that the association should now throw its full support behind the English people in their effort to extend the franchise through the medium of the Liberal party in Parliament. What occasioned O'Donoghue's exhortation was that the Earl Russell's government was having an increasingly difficult time in finding the necessary votes to sustain its efforts to carry its proposed reform of the franchise through the House of Commons, and the continued support of those Irish members committed to the program of the association was becoming absolutely necessary for the survival of the government. At this point a good many Irishmen, and especially those who were advocates of the idea of independent opposition, thought that this was the opportune moment for the Irish members to exact a pledge from the government to support the objects of the association; if it refused, the Irish members should vote against the government and put it out of office. On their return to London after the Easter recess, therefore, Dillon and O'Donoghue had a difficult decision to make. Alderman Plunkett, who had long been an advocate of independent opposition, had precipitated the crisis for them by getting up a requisition to convene a special meeting of the association for April 17, in order to consider the present and future prospects of those questions the association was founded to promote. Though the meeting was postponed to the following day, some of those members of Parliament who were prominent in the affairs of the association were not able to be present. Dillon, however, wrote to the secretary, Nicholas Whyte, a long and able letter, dated April 14, that was read at the meeting.

"I am glad to find," Dillon assured Whyte, "by your letter, received this day, that the Committee are about to meet on Wednesday; and I entirely approve of the terms of the requisition which calls the meeting. It leaves them at full liberty to take all the circumstances of the situation into calm consideration, and I am greatly mistaken if their common sense will not unreservedly approve the course which both The O'Donoghue and myself have made up our minds to adopt."[23] "That course," Dillon explained,

is to give an unconditional support to the extension of the franchise bill. I say unconditional *in this sense*, that we have not gone to Mr. Gladstone and demanded the *formal pledges* from him in respect of Irish measures as the price of our votes; but not in the sense that we are entirely in the dark as to what the Government are likely to do. The reasons by which I would justify this course, and for which I submit that the committee ought to give it their express sanction, are as follows: —1st—this is not merely a question of confidence in a Whig Government, but a question on the decision of which depends the future political status of the true Liberal party in England. Should this bill become law, that party will rule the state. The importance of the crisis is fully and keenly felt on both sides. Setting aside the merits of the question, it becomes necessary that Ireland should make choice of friends and allies, and upon the wisdom of that

23. Ibid., April 19, 1866.

choice the destiny of our country will depend for many a year to come. —2d.—It is my opinion (though I speak on this point with less confidence) that if we were at liberty to regard this question as merely a question of confidence in the Government, a rational regard to the true interests of the country would decide us against voting them out of office. I shall freely express my true opinions on this subject, although I know I do so at the risk of having my motives misunderstood or misrepresented. Since the meeting of Parliament Mr. Gladstone has on three or four occasions referred to Ireland, and as to the mode of governing that country has expressed opinions very deliberately formed, in words very carefully weighed. He has more than once admitted that the discontent of the Irish people is the natural result of the misgovernment to which they have been subjected. He has said that the future government of that country ought to be different from the past or *the present*, and that Irish questions ought to be dealt with in accordance with the views and sentiments of the Irish people. If it be said that these are only vague expressions thrown out to raise hopes that are never to be fulfilled and to catch the votes of credulous Irish members, I am able to refer, not merely to the general character of Mr. Gladstone (which I believe to be above such acts), but also to the measures of his Government and his own recent acts.

"The Association," Dillon then explained, after reviewing the government and Gladstone's recent efforts, "has put forward four claims—the reform of the land laws, the removal of obnoxious oaths, freedom and equality in education, and the disendowment of the Established Church. The Government concede the first two in full, and at once give an installment of the third; and as to the fourth, ask us to wait a little, as its hands are full, bidding us in the meantime 'God speed.' " "If any man will tell me," Dillon eloquently concluded, "that, as a member of the National Association, I am bound to take the earliest opportunity to put that Government out of office, and for that end to inflict a grievous injury on the working classes of England, and to alienate and outrage the only party in the House of Commons from which we can expect any aid or sympathy, I can only say that his arguments will be very cogent and persuasive if they convince me that his conclusion is not unwise, unpractical, and absurd."

After the chairman, Alderman MacSwiney, endorsed the views expressed in Dillon's letter, Plunkett proceeded to explain why he had requisitioned the special meeting. "He was not," Plunkett declared, "one of those who believed that much was to be got by coaxing. He felt that it was by coercion and extortion, justice was to be obtained from the Government." Plunkett then proposed the following resolution for the consideration of the meeting:

> Resolved, that as the two great English parties have agreed to treat the division on the Reform Bill as a vote of confidence or no confidence, and as the present Government have not done anything to redress the grievances of this country, we are of opinion that the independent Irish members ought to vote against the Government unless they get sufficient guarantees that the land laws will be so reformed as to give the occupiers of the soil in Ireland full compensation for their improvements.

"It was not," Plunkett then further explained, "by begging or whining that anything was to be got from the ministry. Redress was only to be had by extorting it from the necessities of the ministry, and such need as they were in seemed to give a fitting opportunity to exercise pressure on them in the interests of Ireland. Mr. Gladstone calculated on a majority of 20 to carry the Reform Bill. He (Alderman Plunkett) firmly believed that if even 12 Liberal members, upon whom the Government counted in the division, threatened to vote against them, the Government would be got to look at Irish questions in a very different spirit from that which now animated them."

When Plunkett moved his resolution, however, he could not find a seconder and had to confess that it appeared he stood alone. In the embarrassment, the chairman attempted to ease the awkwardness by complimenting Plunkett on his "patriotic and honest speech," but it was Canon P. D. O'Regan, the parish priest of Kanturk in the diocese of Cloyne, that finally put the sense of the meeting best. "There is much, indeed," the canon confessed, referring to the several historical precedents cited by the alderman in favor of a policy of independent opposition, "in the observations of Alderman Plunkett to which I would most cordially subscribe, but I think the question must narrow itself to the present time, and that is whether it be wise or not to sustain the Government on the Reform Bill." "Some ten days ago," O'Regan explained, "I forwarded a petition from my own parish calling upon our members to sustain the Government upon that movement, and I abstained altogether from troubling them to make any ungenerous compromise as to giving to the English people all the aid in our power to assist them in time of need (hear, hear)." In finally closing the special meeting, the chairman again assured Plunkett that if indeed "the Government do not act as they proposed to act in respect to these, that the resolution of Alderman Plunkett will be endorsed by every true Irishman, and the time may soon arrive when every member of this Association will be asked to adopt another resolution and that is—that there is no hope for this country except in a native legislature governing this country, and in demanding that Ireland should manage her own affairs (applause)."

When Cullen read the account of the meeting of the association, he wrote Dillon congratulating him on his letter and encouraging him to persevere in the good work. "Many of the Irish members here," Dillon replied on April 21, "have expressed their approbation of my letter to the Nat[l] Associ[n], and indeed I find amongst them a very sincere desire to do all the good they can" (C). "Since I came into personal contact with them," he further explained, "I have learned fully to appreciate the mischief done by systematic *denunciation* in Irish politics, and I have often congratulated myself that I earned the reproach, cast upon me by the Nation, of being 'too amiable.'" "Sir John Gray," Dillon then added in a postscript, "showed me a letter he addressed to Yr. Grace suggesting that some pressure ought to be brought to bear on Stock—member for Carlow. I have heard it rumoured that a scandalous negotiation is on foot, the terms of which are that in consideration of his vote for the Tories, the petition against his return would be withdrawn. I heard this merely as a rumour and *would be very sorry that my name should be mentioned in connexion with it.*" "At all events," he assured Cullen again in conclusion, "I entirely concur with Sir John that every possible pressure should be brought to bear on Mr. Stock."

Apparently Stock was not the only Liberal member whose support of the government was doubtful, because several days after receiving Dillon's and Gray's letters, Cullen was constrained to write Thomas Nulty, the bishop of Meath, urging him to do his best to keep his two county members up to the mark in the approaching vote of confidence. "I write by the first mail this Evening," Nulty assured Cullen on April 26, "in accordance with your wishes to Mes[rs] Corbally & McEvoy deprecating strongly the return of Derby & Whiteside to power & have every hope that my letter will decide their votes against lending any help towards inflicting so great a calamity on our unhappy country" (C). Indeed, the general expectation was that the government would have a majority of about twenty in the test of strength on the Reform bill. When the moment of truth came the next evening, however, April 27, they squeezed through with a majority of only five, 318 to 313.[24] Seven Irish Liberals voted against the government, one of whom was Stock, and three abstained, one of whom was Corbally. If

24. *Hansard Parliamentary Debates*, 3d ser., 183:152.

all the Irish Liberals had done their duty, the government's majority would have been twenty-two. In any case, the government had survived, and three days later, April 30, the Irish members finally brought in their long-awaited land bill for its first reading.[25]

Before the land bill could be read a second time, however, the political situation had been further complicated for the Irish members. On May 4 the government refused to consider the modification of the nondenominational character of the national system of education that had been requested by the bishops in their memorial presented some four months before, in the middle of January.[26] The bishops in general were very annoyed at the government's response to their memorial, and none was more upset perhaps than the bishop of Elphin, who wrote Cullen asking him to convene a general meeting of the bishops immediately in order that some appropriate action might be taken. Cullen seems to have scotched this suggestion, but when Gillooly read the terms of the government's proposed land bill, he was even more upset. "I hope to have the pleasure," he informed Cullen on Friday, May 11, "of seeing your Grace on Monday, and I write now to request you to read over the New Tenant Compen^n Bill—that some steps may be taken at the next weekly meeting of the Nat^l Assoc^n to express their disappointment & disapproval on the land question; as on the two others, the Ministry is acting with ignoble weakness, which should be denounced & resented" (C).

At their meeting in Dublin on Monday, May 14, Cullen was apparently able to persuade Gillooly that it would not be prudent to embarrass Dillon and his colleagues in their efforts to secure beneficial legislation from the government by calling on the association to denounce that government. Gillooly therefore, at the meeting of the association the next day, May 15, after a long speech in which he was very critical of both the government's land bill and its recent refusal to come to terms with the bishops' educational demands, proposed that because the land bill was open to such grave objections, a special meeting should be called for the following week "for the purpose of further considering its provisions and conferring with our Parliamentary representatives."[27] The effect of the postponement, of course, would be not only to increase the pressure on the government to meet the reasonable demands of the Irish members but also to allow Dillon to be present.

In his criticism of the land bill at the meeting, Gillooly had focused

25. Ibid., 214–31.
26. See Chapter IX, pp. 469–70.
27. *Freeman's Journal*, May 16, 1866.

on the obscure language of a number of clauses, the most important of which was the twenty-ninth, which read, "No tenant shall be entitled to compensation under this act in respect to any improvements which the owner may have compelled him to make, or restrained from making in pursuance of any contract in writing regulating the terms of the tenancy." "I know," Gillooly had explained, "from the opinion of a very respectable journal in this city, that this clause is supposed only to regard written contracts existing previous to the enactment of this bill, and that the purpose of the clause is to prevent the bill from having a retrospective effect. I hope this is the meaning, but . . . if it is the meaning, it is expressed very obscurely indeed, and everyone interested in the country must deplore that in framing a clause on which all the advantages of the Land Bill most depend, the promoters of it have not used language more clear and more definite." "I can say with certainty," Gillooly then assured his audience, "that if the tenant be not secure against private contracts imposed upon him by the landlord and secured in the enjoyment of his improvements, the country will regard the bill as utterly worthless (hear, hear)."

In the meantime, Dillon had apparently been besieged on all sides about the unsatisfactory nature of the government's land bill. "My heart is literally broken," he confessed to his wife on May 14, "writing letters chiefly defending the Tenant Bill from all sorts of objections raised against [it]. I write [sic] long letters today to Dr. Cullen, Dr. Leahy and Father Tom O'Shea" (D). "There is to be a debate on tomorrow about Education," he then explained, "on which I ought to speak—but really I am so fagged by writing long letters that I don't feel able to put my ideas in order. I am now scribbling away hardly knowing what I write so I must go out to get a mouthful of air." Dillon did not, in fact, speak in the education debate the next day, but he did make a short and effective speech in the debate on the second reading of the land bill on May 17, in which he attempted to reassure the Irish landlords that they had nothing to fear from the bill.[28] In the first place, he argued, the bill gave no compensation except when a tenant was evicted, and so long as the tenant was left in possession of his tenancy, no claim could arise. Second, tenants with leases for more than thirty-one years would have no claim to compensation at the expiration of their lease, the presumption being that they had either

28. *Hansard*, 183:1097–1102.

exhausted their improvements or been adequately compensated for them in the interim covered by their lease. Third, by clause twenty-nine, "the landlord had the power to stipulate that any specific improvement should not be made by the tenant, and, if made, that he should have no claim for compensation. This provision would oppose an effectual bar against attempts at making improvements which would be unreasonable and out of place. It was sometimes said that this would legalize a general agreement against all improvements whatever, but this was an unfair interpretation of the clause." "The landlord," Dillon finally explained, "had a fourth effective security in the provision that the limit of compensation was to be the increase in the letting value of the land as fixed by an impartial valuator." "To insist on the necessity of an expressed consent by the landlord preliminary to any improvement," he added, adverting to the chief amendment to the bill proposed by the Conservative opposition, "was equivalent to saying that no legislation whatever ought to take place, since an agreement between landlord and tenant might of course be made at any time without legislation at all." Dillon then concluded his remarks by warning the government that its acceptance of such an amendment would prove ruinous to the bill.

Shortly after the adjournment of the debate, Dillon crossed over to Dublin in order to be present at the special meeting of the association requested by Gillooly. The meeting, which took place on May 25, was obviously a very carefully orchestrated affair.[29] The chair was taken by Alderman MacSwiney, and the secretary read a number of letters from members who were unable to be present. The most important of these was from MacCarthy Downing, urging the acceptance of the government's land bill, not as a final settlement but as an installment of justice. MacSwiney then called on Dillon to explain those clauses, particularly clause twenty-nine, which had caused so much concern at the recent meeting. In responding, Dillon begged to be allowed to say a few words regarding the recent conduct, which had been much criticized by the supporters of the policy of independent opposition in Ireland, of those Irish members who were representatives of the views of the association in Parliament. He defended their decision to support the government on the Reform bill, noting interestingly that the alliance he and his colleagues were thereby supporting was not one between the Irish members and the government per se but rather one between them and the English Liberal party, whose interests and sympathies were in the main identical with their own. In a word, Dillon

29. *Freeman's Journal*, May 26, 1866.

was arguing that he and his colleagues were buying futures in the British Parliament by supporting the Reform bill.

He then turned to the criticism of his detractors in Ireland: "The names—I may well call them the honoured names—of Lucas and of Duffy have been used against us, and it has been said how differently they would have acted under similar circumstances. Now, Sir, it so happens that Mr. Duffy was in London during the entire of the great debate on the Reform Bill, and I had many opportunities of consulting him as to the course which I ought to pursue. I first put him the question without intimating any opinion of my own. He answered without hesitation that I ought to vote for the Reform Bill." "The reasons which he assigned," Dillon explained, "he has himself so well expressed in a letter which he afterwards addressed to me that I prefer giving them in his own words. It is a document which well deserves attentive consideration, especially from those who seem to consider that independent opposition consists in assailing friends and foes without discrimination, like a drunken man at a fair (hear, hear)." In his letter, dated May 4 from Paris, Duffy had assured Dillon not only that he too would have voted for the Reform bill had he been in Parliament but that he now had some serious reservations about the vote he and his colleagues had delivered against the Conservative government on the celebrated occasion in 1852 when Disraeli's budget was defeated by some ten votes, a vote that had been ever since the signal example among those who supported the policy of independent opposition of both the wisdom and the effectiveness of that policy.

After thus effectively disarming his opponents with Duffy's letter, Dillon proceeded to review the work of those M.P.'s pledged to the objects of the association. He explained that he thought both the education and the established Church questions had made good progress during the recent session, and he briefly outlined what had been achieved. He then turned to the question that "the great majority of the people of Ireland" regarded as the "vital" one. Dillon declared unequivocally:

> I am satisfied that if this bill [i.e., the government's land bill] becomes law, leases or compensation would become the rule, which would regulate the great bulk of transactions between landlord and tenant, and that evasion of the law and spoliation of the tenant would become the rare, the odious, and the transient exception (cheers). I understand the respected Bishop of Elphin has expressed some doubt in connexion with the 29th clause, as if it legalised agreements which but for it would not be legal. The present law officers have stated, and I have no doubt of the cor-

rectness of the statement, that the clause in question can have no such effect. It merely provides that if an agreement, which would be otherwise legal, is made for the purpose of preventing the tenant from making any specific improvement, the tenant violating that agreement shall not be compensated for that specific improvement. For example, if a landlord, in letting his land, stipulates that no additional dwelling shall be built on the land, and if the tenant afterwards builds a house in disregard of that contract, he will be precluded by the 29th clause from obtaining compensation for that house. But this does not render legal any contract manifestly made with the fraudulent intention of evading the general operation of the act.

"Judging from the determination hitherto displayed by the Government," Dillon then explained, "I am induced to hope that it will pass the House of Commons without material alteration. But I have little hope that it will escape the House of Lords, except in so mutilated a form as to render it entirely worthless." "What will the tenantry of Ireland," he asked, "do in that event (hear, hear)?" "There is a suggestion," Dillon advised, endorsing a most remarkable course of action, "which appeared in the London *Times* some few months since, and which has been reproduced in a very remarkable article in the last number of the *Dublin Review*, which is well worthy [sic] the consideration of the Irish tenant farmers at the present crisis." He elaborated:

That suggestion was, that in the event of its proving impossible to settle this question by legislation, it might be effectually settled by means similar to those adopted by the artisans of England for adjusting the relations between themselves and their employers; that is to say, by a great agricultural union (cheers), comprehending the great bulk of the tenant farmers of Ireland, and as many of the landlords as would be willing to cooperate. Such a union, extending into every parish in Ireland, ruled by a committee sitting in Dublin, acting strictly within the law, aiming at nothing but justice, enforcing its rules by no deeds of violence, but by the same species of moral sanction which secures obedience of the rules of Trades' Unions (cheers)—such a union would, in my opinion, as in the opinion of the London *Times*, set the question of tenant right in Ireland at rest speedily and for ever.

"Perhaps," Dillon finally confessed, "my apprehensions may prove groundless, perhaps this bill may pass, and may be accepted by the landlords as a fair settlement of this vexed question. If so, I believe it will satisfy the tenants of Ireland, and may be for the country the starting point of a new career of prosperity, contentment, and peace. If it should be otherwise, I believe the bulk of the tenant farmers of Ireland can hold their ground only by means of some such combination as that which I have above referred to (cheers)."

Though no formal resolution was proposed endorsing Dillon's views, the chairman, on behalf of the meeting, offered sincere thanks to him for his "clear and valuable explanation" of the land bill. Dillon then crossed over to London to resume his parliamentary duties, but in an apparent effort to keep public opinion in Ireland up to the mark on the land bill, the debate on which was to be resumed immediately after the government completed the committee state on its Reform bill, he returned to Dublin to attend the weekly meeting of the association on June 12. In his remarks to the meeting Dillon reiterated the remarkable advice he had given some three weeks before about forming a national agricultural union to regulate relations between landlords and tenants if the House of Lords refused to pass the land bill in its integrity.[30] Before the debate could be resumed on the second reading of the land bill, however, the ministry was unexpectedly defeated on June 18, when the opposition carried an amendment to the government's proposed Reform bill by 315 votes to 304.[31] The defeat was the result of the defection or abstention of a large number of Liberals, among whom some eight Irish voted no and six abstained. The following day a disappointed and disheartened Dillon reported the sad news to his wife. "You will see by the papers," he explained on June 19, "that we got a regular pounding last night. The Ministry resign this evg—and I presume the Tories come in" (D). "Several Irish liberals," he then added, "including McKenna, Bowyer, Blennerhasset [sic], McEvoy voted with the Tories.[32] Irish prospects here look now so gloomy that I now feel half tempted to give the thing up." "I hope to start for Ireland," he concluded, "before the end of the week."

By the end of June Lord Derby had replaced Earl Russell as prime minister, and by the middle of July his government was in place. The new Conservative ministry then attempted to wind up the business of the session. Dillon and a number of the Irish members returned to London for the August 2 debate on the second reading for the continuing of the suspension of the Habeas Corpus Act in Ireland.[33] They were unsuccessful, however, in preventing the continuance of the suspension of the act, and Parliament was finally prorogued on August

30. Ibid., June 14, 1866.
31. *Hansard*, 184:639.
32. Ibid. Bowyer, in fact, abstained.
33. Ibid., 1910–83.

10, when Dillon returned to Ireland for a well-earned holiday and rest. A month later, on September 10, he was taken ill, and several days later it became evident that he had been stricken with the dreaded cholera. The attack was a very severe one, and though he rallied briefly on Saturday morning, September 15, he died shortly before eight that evening.

Needless to say, Dillon's death at the age of fifty came as a profound shock. "A more sad bereavement," the editor of the *Freeman's Journal* announced on Monday, September 17, "could hardly befall this country at the present crisis than to be deprived, as she has been by the will of Providence, of the most gifted, the most trusted, and the most loved of those who devoted themselves to the service of the people and the improvement of their condition. No man in our day enjoyed a position of greater influence or of greater or more deserved confidence than *John Dillon.*" "His unselfish career," continued the editor, "is too familiar to his countrymen to require detailed notice at an hour of deep affliction, when men mourn over an irreparable loss, and must of necessity think rather of the void that loss will create, and of the impossibility of adequately filling it, than of the early antecedents of a man whose return to Irish politics has been so recent, and whose progress to the first position has been so rapid, so legitimate, and so unenvied by those who worked with him and knew his worth." "As the leading lay member of the National Association," the editor then added,

his loss will be deeply felt. Other able and gifted men no doubt remain, but no man will hesitate to say that there is not left either in the Association or in the Irish representation a man who combined all the qualities possessed by *John Dillon*—the gentleness of manner—the practised skill as a speaker—the readiness as a writer—the persuasive firmness, and the unbounded confidence of all the members of his party in his honour, in his zeal, and in his singleness of purpose. These qualities enabled him to keep men together, and to bring them to sink minor differences for the sake of a great public purpose. Patient and conciliatory in council, Mr. *Dillon* won men round to his views, or banished hostile dissent without exciting the envy and jealousy of any person, and every man who took part in Irish Parliamentary politics looked forward to the time when, by the gradual exercise of the qualities which won the confidence of friends and the respect of foes, he would be able to cement the Irish representatives into a compact united mass, able to enforce good measures for the country, and to resist bad ones.

"Alas," he concluded, "Providence ordained that it should be otherwise, and the gifted and gentle member for Tipperary, whose ambition it was to live to carry out a good Tenant-right Bill—who laboured assiduously to frame that bill—who did so much to induce the late Government to accept that bill—and in this success but indicated the future triumphs which the exercise of the same patient, laborious work could achieve—now rests from his labours, and sleeps that long sleep of death from which the last trumpet alone can recall him!"

Because history has rather to do with what actually happened, or perhaps even with what people thought really happened, than with what might have happened, there is little profit in lamenting the "lost leader" in the case of John Dillon. Still, no more promising an Irish politician had emerged since the death of O'Connell nearly twenty years before, and something must be said about the impact of his sudden loss on the developing Irish political system. Indeed, Dillon's death was a severe blow to that system, and most especially to the concept of leader, which was more difficult to institutionalize than that of the party or the bishops because it depended on the emergence of a unique individual, rather than on the consolidation of a body. In his brief political career Dillon had certainly demonstrated that he had the potential for leadership in talents and abilities, but whether he possessed the supreme gift of being able to capture the political imagination of the Irish people only time and circumstance would have revealed. His other gifts, however, were considerable, and by understanding them one can better appreciate not only the nature of the loss in his demise but the complexity as well as the fragility of the emergent and indigenous Irish political system.

First of all, and most important, Dillon possessed the ability to articulate the consensus; in other words, in moments of crisis he was capable of producing the formula on which all could unite. Secondly, Dillon also understood that it was the leader's task not only to set but to maintain the priorities on the national agenda, and not to allow them to be trenched upon by the other elements that made up the consensus. Thirdly, Dillon realized that the bishops and their clergy had a legitimate place in the consensus, and that they must be accorded their real and effective weight in the political system if that system were ever to become operative and remain truly representative. Finally, he appreciated that it was not by vying or competing with his parliamentary colleagues that he would become leader, for that gift was not within their competence to bestow. He would become leader only when his authority was recognized, and thereby legitimized, by the Irish people as a people.

In the nearly two years that encompassed the beginnings of the association and Dillon's death, he gave consistent proofs of his considerable potential for leadership. At the general meetings of the association on April 28 and June 19, for example, it was Dillon who finally produced the formula in the election address on which all could unite in fighting the general election. In insisting that the land question be given first priority before the general election, moreover, and then taking that question into his own hands by preparing a land bill for the consideration of Parliament after the election, Dillon set and maintained the priorities. When there was then criticism of his land bill from The O'Donoghue, as well as of the government's subsequent bill from the bishop of Elphin, Dillon again articulated the consensus on which all eventually united. Even more impressive, perhaps, was his performance in persuading the association to endorse his lead in supporting the Liberal government in its efforts to reform the franchise and effect an alliance, if not with the ministry, with the Liberal party and the English democracy in the persons of Gladstone, Mill, and Bright, thus laying the foundations for what would soon become an Irish-Liberal alliance. As far as the developing Irish political system was concerned, however, Dillon's most significant achievement was winning the confidence of the bishops as a body, a process that led to their being gradually politicized to a degree that had not prevailed since the political heyday of O'Connell.

Still, as gifted a politician as Dillon was, there had been loss as well as gain for the developing Irish political system. It must be acknowledged that his abilities had been demonstrated only in the circumscribed political arena of the association, which had not captured either the political imagination of the Irish people or even the support of more than a small minority of the clergy. Among the Catholic and Liberal members of Parliament, moreover, he had been able to create only a program and not a party, and he soon learned, both in his efforts with his own land bill and eventually in the defection of those Irish members who brought down the Liberal ministry, that salutary ends without effective means tend to piety and then venality in politics. In the last analysis, however, it was Dillon's and the association's inability to rally any political enthusiasm at the grass roots that raised the more fundamental questions about what it was possible to achieve in constitutional politics in this period. The fact that neither the objects of the association nor their endorsement in the program agreed upon by the Irish members at their conference made any impact at the grass-roots level is an ample indication that these were not the issues, taken together or individually, on which the Irish people were pre-

pared to take up a national agitation. Though Dillon showed a remarkable prescience in the late spring of 1866 in realizing that the land bill,
even if passed by the House of Commons, probably would not survive
the Lords, it is more than doubtful whether indeed the Irish tenant
farmer would have responded—given the unparalleled agricultural
prosperity over the next ten years—to his appeal for a national agricultural trades union, such as eventually emerged in the Land League.

What cannot be blinked, therefore, is that in the middle 1860s Irish
politicians, including Dillon, misread the political signs, and the association as an effective vehicle for carrying a national agitation never
had a chance. The basic mistake of the politicians in this period was
not that they assumed that there was a fundamental cause-and-effect
relationship between the land-tenure system and emigration, because
there was, but rather that they assumed that the members of the tenant-farmer class, and especially the more affluent among them, were
really interested in having that system reformed to save the laborers,
cottiers, and marginal farmers from having to emigrate. Since the
Great Famine of 1847, and the vast clearances and evictions following
it, the stronger farmers and graziers had been moving from strength to
strength economically, and the irony was that the disastrous harvests
of the early 1860s had further improved their economic position by
again clearing the bottom of the social pyramid. Because the increasing prosperity of this class depended on its ability to shift from tillage
to pasture in order to respond to the British market, where prices
favored meat and dairy products rather than cereals, the continued
clearing of the cottiers and marginal farmers so that their holdings
might be consolidated into larger and more economic units became all
the more necessary. The alternatives for those whose holdings were
consolidated were to become either laborers or emigrants, and the vast
majority chose the latter alternative for both social and economic reasons. Given the strong farmers' unprecedented prosperity and their
increasing standard of living, which depended in large part on a continuing emigration, it was virtually impossible to interest this crucial
social and political class in a reform of a land-tenure system that was,
in effect, serving them well.

Indeed, because this class of strong farmers had little or nothing to
fear from evictions, Dillon's bill for compensation for improvements,
which would become operative only if the tenant was dispossessed,
held no advantage for them and therefore little interest. When it is
also understood that for these farmers the question of the established
Church amounted to little more than a nuisance or another indignity,
rather than a serious grievance, and the educational system, inasmuch

as they participated in it, was for all practical purposes as satisfactory and denominational as they could desire, it becomes clear that the program of the association was not really very appealing to them as a class. What would prove of great concern to them was to be made abundantly clear in the late 1870s, when they were severely shaken by a sharp decline in agricultural prices that threatened to reduce radically their incomes and standard of living; at that point they were immediately mobilized for economic action in the Land League on a national scale. All of this, however, was still a long way in the future, and the main point to be made here is that the National Association failed because it had virtually no appeal for a class that was coming to count for more and more in the developing Irish political system.

If the association had little to offer the better-off tenant farmers, moreover, it had even less to offer that class which had some very real grievances during this period, the laborers, cottiers, and marginal farmers. Indeed, if anyone articulated and represented the needs of this class, it was the Fenian Brotherhood. It was no accident, therefore, that the strength of the Brotherhood was to be found in this class, and most especially among those who were the better off among them, the artisans and the laborers, who were able to earn a money wage. In and of themselves, however, no matter how inclined members of this class might have been toward revolution and the establishment of a Fenian Republic, they had not the effective weight in numbers, without a substantial section of the tenant-farming class, to make a revolution, let alone consolidate it. And with each succeeding year their future as a class became bleaker as emigration decimated their numbers. The fact was, then, that the Brotherhood, though it had the advantage of a constituency, had actually no more of a political future than did the association.

VIII

Fenianism

January 1865–March 1868

At the very moment the National Association had begun to limp toward its end in the autumn of 1865, the Fenian Brotherhood, though few appeared to realize it at the time, was also in the first stages of its disintegration as a viable revolutionary conspiracy. The beginning of the Fenian eclipse was somewhat masked by its remarkable success during the first eight months of 1865. The continued depression in agriculture through 1864, and the consequent emigration of some 100,000 people per year, had provided the Fenian recruiters with sufficient evidence of the baneful effects of British rule in Ireland. The regular and more ample flow of money from America and the increasing effectiveness of the *Irish People* as a propaganda instrument had also enabled the Brotherhood to expand and strengthen its organization in Ireland. With the end of the Civil War in America in April 1865, moreover, not only could the organization in Ireland count on a greater supply of funds for recruiting and arms, but also in the subsequent demobilization of the Union and Confederate armies, a very large number of experienced Irish-American veterans of that bloody and hard-fought conflict could be expected to place their considerable professional expertise at the disposal of an Irish Republic "now virtually established." Indeed, the head of the Brotherhood in Ireland, James Stephens, had been insistent during 1865 that that year was to be the "year of action" in Ireland for the Brotherhood. At the very moment when the Brotherhood appeared to be at the height of power, and its prospects most hopeful, however, the British government decided to make 1865 its own year of action. On the evening of September 14 it carried out a series of concerted raids in Dublin, Cork, and the provinces, suppressing the *Irish People* and arresting a very large number of the leaders of the organization. Though the government's blow was not immediately a mortal one, it inaugurated a series of repercussions at the leadership level that resulted in the eventual demise of the Brotherhood as an effective national conspiracy.

While at the height of its power during the first eight months of 1865, however, the Brotherhood gave the Irish Church as much cause for concern as it did the British state. If Cullen and his friends in the Irish Church had hoped that the suspension of Father Lavelle in the summer of 1864 would result in his silence and the easing of the propaganda war against them in the Fenian press, they were sadly and sorely disappointed. The Fenian press, especially the *Irish People*, continued to abuse the bishops and priests it found most obnoxious, as well as to insist that the correct policy for the clergy to pursue was "no priests in politics." Lavelle had hardly been suspended, in fact, when Cullen was obliged to report to Kirby, on December 9, 1864, that he feared "our Fenians are spreading" (K). "The Irish People," he then added, "their organ[,] is as bad as a Mazzinian paper." Less than a month later he wrote Barnabò to alert him to the continuing danger of Fenianism. "I am sorry to say," he reported on January 6, 1865, "that our Fenians are trying to spread throughout the country and they do great harm wherever they penetrate. The government does not molest them because they don[']t do any harm to anyone other than the Catholic clergy, against whom the most frightful calumnies are made."[1] "If the Fenians," he warned Barnabò, "acquire influence among us, religion will be ruined, and the Mazzinian doctrines will accomplish what the Anglican heresy has never been able to effect. Let us hope however that the bad grass will not take deep root."

Some seven weeks later a scandalized Cullen had to write Barnabò explaining that Lavelle had once again broken out in the press and was doing his best to nourish that bad grass. "In a newspaper called the *Connaught Patriot*, of last Saturday, the 18th instant, published in Tuam," Cullen reported on February 24, "there appears a letter from the celebrated Father Lavelle written with the usual insolence, in which he announced that the bishop of Philadelphia, Monsignor Wood, has received a letter from Propaganda in which he is advised— '*Feniani non sunt inquietandi*' [the Fenians are not to be disturbed]. In

1. S.R.C., vol. 35, fol. 173.

the same paper there is a long article demonstrating that the above such are declared free of any charges, and all Catholics can freely join that Fenian society."[2] "As Father Lavelle," Cullen further explained, "is so often inaccurate in his assertions, I thus question the truth of what is now published. To avoid any doubt, however, I beg your Eminence to let me know if the news given by Lavelle has any foundation. I hope that it is a fabrication." "Our Fenians," he assured the cardinal, "are unmasking themselves more and more every day. Their newspaper, the *Irish People* has become a sink of iniquity. Every week it publishes the most atrocious articles against the clergy and the Catholic religion, and it can not be otherwise, since some of the editors are either Protestants, or open apostates."

In writing to Kirby that same day to alert him that he had written Barnabò, Cullen showed that he was not only scandalized but also worried about the increasing effect of Fenian propaganda (K). "If the Propaganda," he warned Kirby, "confirm the Fenians, we shall all have to quit the country. Their organ the Irish People is full of venom against the Church, and pours out torrents of abuse and calumnies on priests and Bishops. It would be strange to tell us the *birboni di tal fatta si devono lasciar fare* [rascals of such stamp ought to be left alone]." "Some of the writers of the Irish People," he further explained, "are, I am told, Protestants—some are apostates. I heard from Dr. Butler of Limerick the history of one of them[,] by name O'Leary. He and another brother went to study at the Queen's College, Galway.[3] The second brother ruined his health by dissipation, and fell into a consumption. When his death was approaching his friends did everything possible to induce him to reconcile himself with God—in vain, his faith was gone. His mother, a pious woman, went then to Limerick and brought to Tipperary where the young man was dying a Redemptorist to attend him—but without any effect. The young man died like a Turk. The other brother is now a writer for the Fenians." "See what Governments get," Cullen finally noted, drawing the moral from his story, "by giving an infidel education. Those educated at its expense in the Godless Colleges turn against it, and proposed [sic] revolutionary principles. Well I dare say all that will be overlooked, because these good Government pupils are most intent on overthrowing the Catholic faith."

Though there proved to be no basis in fact for Lavelle's assertions that Propaganda had given tacit approval to the Fenians, a number of

2. Ibid., fol. 206.
3. His Christian name was John, and his brother's name was Arthur.

the American bishops apparently decided that they also had had enough of the Brotherhood, for eleven of them petitioned Propaganda to declare formally whether Catholics were permitted to belong to the organization.[4] Propaganda replied on July 13, referring the American bishops, as it had referred Cullen some twelve months before, when he asked for a similar decision, to the rescript of the Holy Office of August 5, 1846, which described the kinds of societies condemned by the Church.[5] The authorities also assured the American bishops that there was no truth in Lavelle's assertion that they had advised the bishop of Philadelphia to leave the Fenians alone. The real significance of this decision, of course, was that for the second time in a year the Roman authorities refused to condemn the Fenians formally by name. The very day, in fact, that Propaganda wrote the American bishops, the archbishop of Armagh, Joseph Dixon, had written Barnabò requesting that Propaganda formally condemn the Fenian front organization in Ireland, the Brotherhood of St. Patrick.[6] Barnabò, however, seems to have done little more than also refer Dixon's letter to the consideration of the Holy Office. Rome had obviously decided that whatever action was to be taken against the Fenians or the brothers of St. Patrick would have to be taken at the local or national level by the bishops concerned.

Cullen apparently learned or realized very soon which way the mind of Rome was turning on the question of Fenianism, for after he reported Lavelle to Barnabò on February 24, he did not mention the subject of Fenianism again in his correspondence with the cardinal for some six months, that is, until the British government finally decided to move against the Brotherhood. Though he did not write the cardinal directly, however, Cullen continued to keep both Patrick Moran, the vice-rector of the Irish College, and Kirby informed about the dangers of Fenianism, and it may be presumed that they both prudently passed on the necessary information verbally to the authorities at Propaganda. On March 2, for example, Cullen explained to Moran that the Fenians were out once again in their true colors, abusing and insulting the clergy in Tipperary for supporting the National Association's candidate, Charles Moore, in the by-election there, instead of

4. Patrick J. Corish, "Political Problems, 1860–1878," in *A History of Irish Catholicism*, gen. ed. Patrick J. Corish (Dublin, 1967), p. 21.

5. Ibid., pp. 21–22. Monsignor Corish has provided an excellent analysis of this document.

6. S.R.C., vol. 35, fols. 368–69. Barnabò had also written Patrick Leahy, the archbishop of Cashel, regarding the rules of the Brotherhood (L, July 13, 1865). See Leahy's reply, S.R.C., vol. 35, fols. 388–89, August 10, 1865.

the pro-Fenian editor of the *Tipperary Advocate*, Peter Gill (K). Cullen could not refrain from adding that the Tipperary clergy were only getting what they deserved, because some of them had been "rather bitten with young Irelandism." A week later, in a letter to Kirby written on March 10, Cullen denounced the current deluge of cheap, bad books in Ireland and then again returned to his theme: "The Fenians also are doing a great deal of mischief by attacks on all good priests. The *'Irish People'* is most wicked. The writers are, some Protestant, some infidel, others Catholic so-called. They are nearly all from Tipperary" (K). "I hope," he wrote Kirby again on March 17, "S. Patrick will look down upon us, and set things to rights. We have great difficulties to contend with and great efforts are made to shake the faith. . . . The *Irish People* and the Connaught Patriot are as bad as ever" (K).

In his effort to keep the Propaganda authorities well informed indirectly through Kirby and Moran, Cullen did not neglect to forward some of the more flagrant breaches of clerical discipline that appeared in the press. When the *Irish People*, for example, published a letter purporting to be written by "The Irish and Irish-American Students" at the Collegio Brignole, a seminary at Genoa, giving an account of their festivities on St. Patrick's Day and explaining how much they enjoyed reading the *Irish People*, Moran reported it to Monsignor Rinaldini, an undersecretary at Propaganda, who then wrote the rector at Brignole asking for an explanation.[7] Later that month, on April 25, Cullen forwarded Kirby a copy of the *Connaught Telegraph* of April 22, which contained an exchange of letters between Lavelle and Major Myles O'Reilly, M.P. for county Longford and commander of the pope's late Irish Brigade (K). Lavelle had taken the opportunity of the correspondence to pen a diatribe of four full columns of close print on the perfidy of English rule in Ireland.[8] Cullen also reported in this same letter, for good measure, that Father P. E. Moriarty, the Augustinian who had been suspended the previous year by the bishop of Philadelphia for a most revolutionary lecture, had just repeated the offense.

In spite of all of Cullen's efforts at Rome, however, MacHale apparently managed to persuade the pope and the Roman authorities to restore the suspended Father Lavelle. MacHale and his suffragan, the bishop of Clonfert, John Derry, had arrived in Rome in early May to fulfill their *ad limina* visit, required at least once every ten years. On April 26, while they were on their way, Lavelle had written Barnabò to

---

7. S.R.C., vol. 35, fols. 220–22, Moran to Rinaldini, n.d. See ibid., fol. 304, May 29, 1865, for the rector's reply that the charges were false.

8. Ibid., fol. 10. This exchange was covered by a note from Moran, n.d., ibid., fol. 9.

ask that his faculties be restored.[9] Barnabò undoubtedly explained to MacHale and Derry what they already knew, that the case was entirely in the hands of His Holiness and that Lavelle should write directly to the pope. Lavelle did so on May 27,[10] and apparently MacHale's intercession was successful. Cullen wrote Kirby on July 16, reporting that he had just received a letter from John MacEvilly, the bishop of Galway (K). "He states," Cullen explained, "that Father Lavelle is again acting as parish priest of Partry. Probably Dr. McHale got permission in Rome to restore him. He cannot now do much harm. Nothing has been published about the matter." Though Cullen tried to put the best face possible on Lavelle's restoration, and was certainly relieved that it had not received any publicity, he must have been sorely disappointed that his own influence had not prevailed.

The real question, of course, is why Rome continued to temporize with regard to Fenianism, especially in the light of the recent petition of the American bishops and Cullen's insistent, if indirect, warnings. On more careful analysis, however, the situation from Rome's point of view had not much changed in the year that had elapsed since the authorities had equivocated about Cullen's first request for a decision on Fenianism. The two new elements in the Fenian equation were more apparent than real. The petition of the American bishops only underlined how divided the American hierarchy was on the subject, for a petition from eleven in a hierarchy of nearly fifty was hardly a testimony to the enthusiasm of the body. Cullen's continued warnings, moreover, had perhaps an adverse effect, for as Fenian influence increased a condemnation became proportionately more dangerous, and that may be part of the reason why he ceased writing Barnabò directly on the subject altogether. Then, too, when MacHale and Derry were in Rome, they must have had some very hard home truths to tell the authorities about the dangers of alienating the Irish people from their clergy. They must have explained not only that the disaffection of the people was very deeply rooted but that they had a better understanding of the real situation than did Cullen or those prelates who were under his influence, and that the information Rome was receiving about Ireland therefore was entirely and dangerously one-sided.[11]

9. Ibid., fols. 250–53.

10. Ibid., fols. 302–3. See also Lavelle to Barnabò, June 28, 1865, ibid., fols. 329–32.

11. Though the evidence is very slight, MacHale apparently had made some effort to collect testimonials in Ireland that would improve his credibility in Rome. See K, Dominic O'Brien, bishop of Waterford, to Kirby, May 10, 1865, for a report of a testimonial being circulated on behalf of MacHale in the area of Dungarvan by Jeremiah Hally, the parish priest of Dungarvan.

Indeed, if the testimony of one of Kirby's more recent students in the Irish College is to be believed, the Roman authorities were well advised to forgo any condemnation of Fenianism at that moment. James O'Leary, who was teaching at St. Colman's College in Fermoy in the diocese of Cloyne, informed Kirby on July 28, "This country is rapidly pining away. The people are going to America in [great] numbers. A few weeks ago thirty-two young men left Fermoy, one of the most advantageously situated towns in the south of Ireland. All people are downcast and hopeless, have lost their confidence in the Bishops, except in a few and care not for the Association. They cannot understand and will not understand the condemnation of societies against the state whether secret or otherwise" (K). "The best and most virtuous of the Irish," he then added sadly, "are gladly leaving their homes, and going where they may be corrupted. Fathers at home say that if the Irish are spreading the faith they likewise fill the brothels. The poor people leave without leaders and fall on the way. Yet hundreds are leaving every week. Ireland is becoming a sheep walk. Those who remain (as a rule) are either Cautholics, that is half-protestants, or else poor people many of whom there is good reason to know have not frequented the sacraments since the publications against the St. Patrick's Brotherhood or the Fenians appeared." "'Tis a sad thing," he noted finally, "to see the people separating from the priests and souls remaining in sin because as they say Bishops violated the articles of '52 to which they put the sign of the Cross." "Let us pray," he concluded more piously, "that God may save our faith and fatherland."

The British government in Ireland, meanwhile, in the person of Her Majesty's viceroy, Lord Wodehouse, had become more and more alarmed about the seriousness of the Fenian conspiracy. From information gathered through its spies and informers, who had penetrated the Fenian network, and from documents that had fallen into its hands during the summer of 1865, the government had become convinced that the Fenians were preparing to strike. It hoped, however, if the opportunity offered, to be able to strike first. As Lord Wodehouse explained to Earl Russell, the foreign secretary, on September 1 from Dublin, "I certainly agree with you that the Fenians are not to be despised. They mean mischief and if they can get arms and leaders from America may attempt an outbreak which would cause bloodshed and confusion."[12] "We have been most vigilantly watching them for

12. Russell Papers, 30/22/28, Public Record Office, London.

months," he reported, "and if we can get, as I hope, evidence enough of their treasonable design, we shall strike them a blow, but they are very *wary*, and the difficulty is considerable of obtaining tangible proofs, tho' I am quite prepared to run some risk of exceeding the law, if necessary."

"The Irish law officers," Wodehouse assured Russell, referring to the attorney and solicitor generals, "are both of them acute and courageous men, by whose advice I can be safely guided; and I have great confidence both in the commander in chief and the inspector general of police, so that I trust we shall be able to deal successfully with this conspiracy, for such it undoubtedly is." "I have written to the Duke of Somerset," he further assured Russell, naming the first lord of the Admiralty, "to suggest that two or three gunboats or other small armed vessels should be sent to Cork to cruise along the south & southwestern coast. I see no reason why some Irish desperadoes who have been trained to arms in the American civil war should run over in steamers with arms to some place like Skibbereen—and raise an insurrection in Cork & Kerry where the people are quite disposed for evil." When the government, through one of its informers, intercepted a week later a very imprudent letter from James Stephens, supreme head of the Fenian Brotherhood, it finally decided to take action. In a letter of September 8, instructing the Fenian circle at Clonmel in county Tipperary to elect a center, or colonel, and send him up to Dublin to be confirmed, Stephens went on to exhort his Clonmel brethren, "*There is no time to be lost. This year*—and let there be no mistake about it—must be the year of action. I speak with a knowledge and authority to which no other man could pretend, and I repeat, the flag of Ireland—of the Irish Republic—must this year be raised."[13] The government struck in Dublin, in Cork, and in other parts of the country on the evening of September 14, arresting a large number of the most prominent Fenians. The raid on the premises of the *Irish People* proved to be particularly damaging because the police found a number of incriminating documents, which allowed the government to bring most of those arrested speedily to trial and inflict very severe punishments.[14]

As soon as he read the accounts of the Fenian arrests in the press on Monday morning, September 17, Cullen hastened to write to Barnabò to inform him of all the latest developments.[15] Before proceeding to the details, however, he explained why he had not continued to write

13. Desmond Ryan, *The Fenian Chief* (Dublin, 1967), p. 207.
14. R, 30/22/28, Wodehouse to Russell, September 17, 1865.
15. S.R.C., vol. 35, fols. 414–15.

to Propaganda about the Fenian menace during the past year. "After having written so many times to Rome," he noted,

> and having published very many letters warning the people of the danger to which they exposed themselves by joining that society, seeing that it was not possible to obtain any condemnation from Rome, and that the evil was spreading in Ireland, I resolved not to think any more about the business, and to let things go from bad to worse, consoling myself by saying *liberavi animam meam* [I have cleared my conscience]. When matters appeared hopeless to me, behold everything was mended in a moment. Friday night last, the octave of the nativity of the Madonna, the government finally determined to put an end to the Fenian leadership. That evening at ten o'clock the police went into action in Dublin, and in a few minutes twenty-two leaders of the conspiracy were arrested in one of their meeting places, and then conducted to jail. Other arrests were made in other parts of the city, so that almost all of the most daring and most involved among the Fenians are now in the hands of the government. I have often mentioned a wicked paper called the *Irish People* that was published by the Fenians and directed principally against the Catholic clergy. That paper had the same fate as the Brotherhood. Before midnight on Friday the police broke down the door of the printing office, arrested all the employees who were getting the paper ready for the following morning, seized all the correspondence, and carried away the type, the presses, and everything that they found in the place. All Dublin is very happy with what the government has done, and not a citizen moved to defend the unhappy Fenians who some few days before were proudly boasting of having hundreds of thousands of associates.

"Among the Fenians arrested in Dublin," Cullen then further explained, "some are Protestants, some are students of the Cork Queen's College, others are Catholics that lost the faith in America. It appears that no priest is involved and none among the respectable Catholics. As to Dublin, as far as the regular and secular clergy [are concerned], we are happy that we have done as much as was possible to save the people from that harm some are now suffering. The exertions made by the clergy, seem to me, to be the reason why our citizens, the very fewest excepted, have not suffered and in fact almost all those arrested are from the south of Ireland." "I hope for the future," Cullen concluded, "no more will be heard of Fenians in Ireland. It may be that they will continue to do harm in America, and that Father Lavelle, or the Augustinian Father Moriarty will have more authority with them than the Catholic Bishops, but at least we shall be able to be at peace in this poor country, which has been prey to other endless evils, but which would be totally ruined by a Mazzinian revolution, which the Fenians were preparing here."

Some two weeks later, however, in writing Barnabò again, Cullen was obliged to modify his earlier report slightly with regard to the number of priests involved with the Fenians. "I discovered," he explained on September 29, "that an Augustinian friar living here in Dublin, and a priest from America, resident here also were associated with that infamous newspaper, the *Irish People*, which continually wrote against religion and the Catholic clergy."[16] "I am determined," he assured Barnabò, "to punish these two priests severely. The regular is more to be blamed than any other, because he ought to know that the first victims of revolutions are the friars and their monasteries."

Meanwhile, in writing Kirby on September 27, Cullen not only went over much the same ground as in his first letter to Barnabò but could not resist noticing that for all their vaunted boasting, not one Fenian made any resistance when arrested; he wondered what Father Lavelle would have to say now about his "pets" (K). Cullen also added that a few priests, but only a very few, had been subscribers to the *Irish People*. Some ten days later, on October 8, Cullen reported that Father Lavelle's organ, the *Connaught Patriot*, had been suppressed and its editor, Martin O'Brennan, arrested (K). "Nearly two hundred Fenians," he explained, "have been arrested. In the statement of Mr. Barry, the crown prosecutor, it is asserted that the Fenians wish to establish an Irish Republic, and that they propose to confiscate all property of the country, and to massacre the gentry and the Catholic clergy. I have heard that Dr. Leahy of Cashel and I were specially marked out—thanks to God they have been checked in their wicked projects." "In one of the letters seized on[,] a Mr. O'Keefe, writer for the Irish People," Cullen added, referring to a half-demented and well-known eccentric in Dublin journalist circles, "said that the Irish revolution should be a facsimile of the first French Revolution and that the people of Ireland should be prepared for it by the *pen of some new Voltaire*."

"There were no respectable persons engaged in this conspiracy," he then assured Kirby.

The head, James Stevens [*sic*], a desperate infidel[,] was an auctioneer's clerk from Kilkenny. He took part in the campaign of

16. Ibid., fol. 401.

1848 at Ballingarry. Having escaped he spent several years among the infidels of Paris, and became as bad as any of them. This time he has not been arrested, but it has been reported he has become informer. There are three or four other informers, two of whom, *Warner* [and] Pettit are, I believe, Orangemen. Four or five soldiers were implicated—if found guilty, probably they will be shot.

As to the others, some few will perhaps be hanged or get twenty years penal servitude—what unfortunate fellows to bring ruin on themselves and families and disgrace upon their country.

It is well for them [*sic*] however that they have been checked in their career and have not been allowed to ruin religion, and to fill the country with bloodshed.

I think no priest is likely to be implicated unless the Tuam editor [O'Brennan] tells stories about his friends.

It is hard to know whether Fenianism will now die out. They may keep it up in America, and if so, it is probable that it will continue to work underhand here. There was never so villainous an attempt to ruin religion in poor Ireland—God and the Blessed Virgin and St. Patrick have preserved us.

Cullen could not resist a final crow: "Almost all the *gentlemen* who took part in McManus's funeral four years ago are now in prison. I was denounced on all sides for opposing that funeral. The proceedings of the last month prove that I was quite right."

Cullen was so convinced that he was right, in fact, that he chose just that moment to address a pastoral letter to his clergy denouncing the Fenians root and branch. The pastoral, which was dated October 10 and which ran to some fifteen printed pages and five thousand words, was yet another of his very able and interesting polemical performances.[17] It is worth examining in some detail because it was the most comprehensive of the many charges Cullen delivered to his clergy and flock on the subject of Fenianism in the 1860s. He began his charge by evenhandedly denouncing both Orangeism and Fenianism as two "moral evils" that were the result of "human folly and wickedness." Indeed, Orangeism was the logical parent of Fenianism, because the example given by those in high places in Ireland in participating in the orgies of Orangeism was a source of scandal to others and a justification for their joining in such dangerous combinations. "As long as persons enjoying power or influence are allowed to form

17. Patrick Francis Moran, ed., *The Pastoral Letters and Other Writings of Cardinal Cullen* (Dublin, 1882), 2:388–404.

secret or dangerous societies," Cullen then asked pointedly, "how can the humbler classes be condemned for following their example?"

"As to what is called Fenianism," he maintained,

> you are aware that, looking on it as a compound of folly and wickedness wearing the mask of patriotism to make dupes of the unwary, and as the work of a few fanatics or knaves, wicked enough to jeopardise others in order to promote their own sordid views, I have repeatedly raised my voice against it, since it first became known at the time of McManus's funeral, four years ago, and that I cautioned young men against promising or swearing obedience to strangers with whom they were altogether unacquainted, putting themselves at the mercy of plotting spies and treacherous informers, and risking their lives and liberty, and endangering the lives of others, in attempting to carry out projects, hopeless in themselves, which doing no good to any class, might involve the country in ruin and bloodshed.

Cullen then went on to pose a series of rhetorical questions concerning the Fenians: Who were they? What was their purpose? And how did they propose to achieve it? He answered his first question by asking another series of pointed questions about the credentials of the Fenian leadership; if this matter had been rationally considered, he maintained, no man of any sense would have joined their ranks. As to the real purpose of the Fenians, Cullen charged that if what was said about them was true, their goal was nothing less than the destruction of the faith of the people and the extermination of both the gentry and the Catholic clergy. Concerning the means of the Fenians, Cullen exhorted his clergy to save their flocks from the "Contamination of all secret societies" and to remind them that such societies were condemned by the Church for being "dangerous to the State or the Church, whether bound by oath or not."

Now that the structure of Fenianism had been demolished by a "few policemen," with not a hand raised in its defense, there would be no harm, Cullen then proceeded to explain, in the interest of eradicating it completely, in reviewing its proceedings and tendencies to show the "simple people" its folly and absurdity. First of all, in promising the return of a golden age to Ireland, the Fenians not only played into the hands of Orangeism by preventing the consideration of the real grievances of the country but, by the building of these castles in the air, also turned the people from useful and industrious pursuits. Secondly, by their vain boastings and menaces, the Fenians had made the Irish ridiculous in the eyes of everyone. Thirdly, Fenianism, because of its inability to gain any hold on the inhabitants of the country, who had not sympathy with revolution or violence, had lacked the element essential to its success. Finally, the Fenians had not even observed the basic dictates of prudence. They had instead advertised their conspiracy in every way they could on both sides of the Atlantic. "About to strike a blow," Cullen pointed out, "even in a bad cause, and risk their lives, were they in earnest, they would have matured their plans in silence, and acted not after the fashion of foolish children, prattling about everything, but with thought, and like men conscious of having assumed a work of danger and great responsibility."

After reviewing the proceedings of the Fenians, in fact, the only conclusion one could come to was that, if the leaders be excepted, they had been duped by wicked and designing men, and they were therefore to be pitied and treated with leniency. Indeed, when one considered the example given in recent years on the highest levels of church and state in England in the praising of Garibaldi and revolution in Italy, was it not natural for Irishmen to ask, "If a revolution be so praiseworthy elsewhere, why not get one up at home? If it was a glorious thing for Garibaldi to collect a fleet at Genoa, and invade a country which was living in peace with all other states, and dethrone its king, why should not a head centre of the Fenians in America collect an army, and endeavour to overthrow the government of this empire? If Garibaldi was a hero for his exploits, why should not a valiant colonel of his own stamp, the great head-centre of the Fenian movement, have a right to walk in his footsteps? Why should he not be applauded by all England?" "If equal justice were to be shown to both sides," Cullen asked finally, "should not London and the English nobility and dignitaries of the Protestant Church, and the press of England, and the Orange press of Ireland, be as loud in the praises of the disciple as they were in extolling his revolutionary master?" The moral that Cullen drew for his clergy from the English example, of course, was that they could not allow a bad example to serve as justification for what was wrong in itself and that, as ministers of the gospel of Jesus Christ, they were bound to preach "humility and obedience, to encourage a love of peace, to inculcate patience and forebearance in the time of trials and sufferings, and to prevent the spread of secret societies, and to check everything revolutionary."

But did that mean they were obliged to sit like dumb dogs under the lash of the oppressor, without complaining and without seeking justice? Certainly not. Though they must recommend obedience to established authority, that did not mean that they were the enemies of rational liberty or that they did not love their country. Their grievances were so obvious, Cullen argued, that a reasonable and earnest constitutional agitation would undoubtedly obtain everything necessary for the welfare of their people from the government. Indeed, it was in the government's interest to do justice, for justice would put an end to Fenianism, and the Irish people would be a source of strength rather than weakness to the empire at large. As for patriotism, Cullen declared, it was a noble virtue, but no one could "love his country properly who neglects his religion, and sacrifices the welfare of his own soul for all eternity." Cullen then concluded this long and able pastoral by explaining that he had only just received an allocution of the pope to the sacred college of cardinals dated September 25, in which His Holiness had renewed the various excommunications of his predecessors against Freemasons and all such secret societies. Cullen asked his clergy, therefore, to explain the allocution to their flocks and to emphasize the grave dangers that accompanied such societies. "When such dangers shall have been pointed out," he noted in conclusion, "the faithful will, undoubtedly, be most thankful to God for having given such a check to Fenianism, and having brought its designs to light, thus preserving thousands of good people from the troubles and evils into which they might have been incautiously led, had the public authorities allowed that system to exist any longer, or to continue to exercise its baneful influence on the country."

Several days before he could have read Cullen's pastoral indicting the Fenians, Kirby received another letter from his former student James O'Leary, a teacher at St. Colman's College, containing quite a different point of view. "I have passed through the country during vacation," O'Leary explained on October 5, from Fermoy, "and it is wretched in the West. We shall ere long have civil commotions and God grant that the hierarchy would not be so active against the people" (K). "NEUTRALITY," he advised, "is a splendid policy as the people do not ask more, and priests owe nothing to a heretical Government." "There was never," he further assured Kirby, "so powerful an element against England. Every town in Ireland has its rebellious subjects—so Liverpool, London, Glasgow and all America. It is an uprising of the Irish race against Saxon domination. There is no *irreligious* tendency in it *whatever may be said.*" "I met twelve officers in Queenstown," he reported interestingly, "who had been colonels and captains in the American army. Four of them were educated in Tuam [St. Jarleth's] Seminary as aspirants to the church, and three had brothers priests in America. Rise they will and if opposed by the Hierarchy will make no difference between Government officials and Clergymen. The English correspondents in America give the number of them as a *moderate estimate* at 300,000. Would to God they could smash the first heretical power on the globe and destroy the great bulwark of the Devil!" "I have met Fenians in every part of Ireland," he finally informed Kirby, "and none of them dreamt of rising, if the Americans do not effect a landing."

Kirby's other correspondents were naturally a good deal more circumspect than Father O'Leary when writing to Rome about this subject. John O'Beirne, a curate in the bishop's parish of Templemichael in the diocese of Ardagh, wrote Kirby more characteristically on October 8 from Longford: "The Fenian Movement will try the zeal and energy of the Priesthood in Ireland more than anything that ever occurred" (K). "'Tis a most insidious enemy of religion," he explained, "it aims at the influence of the Clergy principally. It wishes to separate the Priests from the People and was busily engaged in sowing the seeds of rebellion against clerical authority when detected." "But now that it is unmasked," he concluded, "it is to be hoped with God's assistance that it will come to naught." Giving both Fathers O'Leary and O'Beirne all due credit for the sincerity of their sentiments as expressed in their letters to Kirby, it is nonetheless probable that the real feelings of the great majority of the Irish clergy were not reflected in the views of either priest. The matter was undoubtedly a very complicated one, and perhaps the letter of a young curate in the town of Tralee in the diocese of Kerry was actually a good deal more representative. "Fenianism," Florence McCarthy had assured Kirby on September 26, "is nipped in the bud by the Government, and justly, as it is a most irreligious organization" (K). He added most revealingly, "No arrests have been made in this town up to this, although I must assure you that we are all Fenians in spirit as is every true Irishman—ab sit, —however that any true Catholic would encourage the means that the Fenians have recourse to."

Whatever curious psychological ambivalence the Irish clergy manifested in distinguishing between the ends and means of Fenianism, there was certainly little of it revealed at this time in the mind of the most important man in the Irish Church. Cullen continued to be Fenianism's most implacable foe both at home and at Rome. He now regularly wrote both Barnabò and Kirby to keep them informed of the latest details. "Here," he wrote the cardinal on October 9, "many are much alarmed on account of the Fenians. However the whole business may be considered ended with the arrests that have been made of two or three hundred of the leaders."[18] He included a number of details

18. S.R.C., vol. 35, fol. 405.

that, as we have seen, he had already shared with Kirby: "From their documents it is evident that they were determined to confiscate the property of the rich, and massacre the Catholic clergy. It is said the archbishop of Cashel and I were to suffer first among others. I have seen one of the letters written on this business by one O'Keefe, and he said that all should be an imitation of the first French revolution, but for success in such a project, it was necessary to begin to prepare the people by distributing propaganda written in the style of Voltaire. In sum, all the leaders appear to be unbelievers." "These unfortunate men," Cullen further reported, "have put together a good kind of pike or lance and similar weapons that are now of little value. Ten or twelve days after the first arrests the government has sequestered about £6,000, that is 30,000 scudi which the conspirators received from America. From this it is seen that the Fenians in America are not idle. I hope that the bishops will unite to condemn them." "Among those arrested," Cullen noted finally with some satisfaction, "was the editor of the Tuam paper called the *Connaught Patriot*, who for four years has never published an issue of his paper without inserting an article against me full of the most vile calumnies. Recently he began to write against the government, and now he lies in jail charged with the crime of high treason. I fear that our government will hang many of these unfortunate men."

"Thank God," Cullen reported to Barnabò again on October 13, "we appear to have been liberated from the snares of the Fenians. Their head here in Dublin, James Stephens, spent seven or eight years in Paris with revolutionaries and unbelievers, and became truly impious there. He then spent some time in America and then he became a disciple of Mazzini. There was not the smallest hope that he could succeed in his conspiracy against England, but it is certain that he did and can do great damage to religion."[19] "Those who first encouraged him and other similar rogues," Cullen added, referring obviously to the archbishop of Tuam and Father Lavelle, "ought now to open their eyes to the evil that they wished to do to Ireland. It will not be out of place to observe that the English who condemned the Italian governments for their harshness toward the Carbonari, now deal with our foolish conspirators with the greatest rigor." A month later Cullen had some good news to report about Stephens. "The head of the Fenians," he informed Kirby on November 15, "J. Stephens, has been arrested. He is said to be an open infidel" (K). "In Ireland," he explained, "the society will cease its operation at least in public. However they may

19. Ibid., fol. 408.

begin to assassinate the people a la Mazziniana. Ere yesterday two policemen were fired at, but though struck by the bullets they were not much hurt. They were the men who had arrested Stephens, and seized on the Irish People."

Several days later he wrote Kirby again. "The Fenians," he reported on November 19, "will be tried tomorrow week. The leaders will be transported probably for life. In Ireland the system at least as far as it is directed against Government will be given up, but I fear very much that the editors of the wicked paper the Irish People will be let go on against religion provided they do not assail Government. Stephens, the head of the Fenians, would not plead in the court. He said he acknowledged no English rule in Ireland" (K). "In America," Cullen then complained, "Fenianism is going ahead. I see Dr. Moriarty of Philadelphia has delivered a lecture most revolutionary in its favour. However when the people see that their money is producing no effect they will suspend the supplies, and the bubble will burst." Only ten days after Stephens had refused to acknowledge English jurisdiction in Ireland, however he effected his escape with the aid of several Fenian prison warders who had taken wax impressions of the necessary keys. Needless to say, the government officials were badly shaken, especially because the event revealed that their own apparatus had been penetrated by Fenian agents. With Stephens free once again, the rumors and alarms about an imminent Fenian rising, which had been persistent since the first arrests in September, began to appear much more menacing.

"Do not be surprised," James O'Leary of St. Colman's College warned Kirby on December 7, "if in two months you should hear of war in Ireland. It is stated that there are 1,000 men in this district of Fermoy. I do not doubt it. There is not a town in Ireland that has not some American officers in it" (K). "On yesterday," he reported, referring to the rumors that the British army in Ireland had also been infiltrated by Fenian agents, "there were twenty rounds of cartridges given to the men of the barracks, but it is certain that many a round of them would—and we know not when—[and] may [yet] be driven through the officer who gave them by Fenian soldiers." "All the mechanics, clerks, smiths, shoemakers, labourers, farmer's sons etc.," he further assured Kirby, "are in the organization, perfectly quiet, knowing their officers, having no communication with any who could in any way implicate them and merely waiting for the landing of a nucleus from America and the word of command." "Priests," O'Leary explained,

did they wish to prevent the progress of the movement are powerless and would only bring themselves into angry relationship with their flocks. Our Bishop ordered his priests not to denounce. He thinks it the most formidable element England ever encountered. One thing is certain whatever be said[,] that it is not an *anti-Catholic* movement. All the Americans in the country are Irish who served in the American War and have been sent over by O'Mahony, a Catholic and native of Mitchelstown, County Cork. They all attend Mass and think like the very Irish. Stephens[,] whose escape has produced among the upper classes and Protestants a favourable feeling in their [*sic*] regard[,] heard Mass every day while he was in prison.

In fine, on their move, with what success the God of battles will determine, one thing is certain[,] that the Irish portion of the army is banded in their ranks—through the prisons, *the coast guards*, the magazine-keepers, the police, the soldiers, and the civil service men. The American officers say that they have the consent of the American government in coming into the country. Their object is to take Ireland and Canada and make them the property of the Irish race. As soon as the St. Lawrence is frozen, 200,000 American Fenians are to marshall at different points and pass into the Canadian territory. I have heard that Roberts, the Vice President of the Fenians[,] is worth 7,000,000 of dollars, that Morrison is worth about the same, so of many many others.

A Christian Brother from New York who called here looking for subjects for his order said that were it not for the clergy every *Irish-American* would be in the movement. Father Hickie, who is collecting for the Catholic University, wrote to Dr. Croke three days ago and says that (1.) Fenianism is the furor of the Californians, (2.) that he is getting nothing himself because they (the people) say the priests in Ireland are opposed to the Fenians and they do not want to support Dr. Cullen's University; (3.) that in his opinion it is a movement of all the Americans.

"Whatever come," O'Leary assured Kirby in conclusion, " 'honor et gloria Deo et Mariae.' "

The government was just as concerned as Father O'Leary about the possibility of an insurrection at this time, but obviously for different reasons.. Writing from Dublin on December 10, Wodehouse informed Russell, who had succeeded as prime minister upon Lord Palmerston's death in late October, "I have written to the Duke of Somerset strongly urging that a certain number of ships be left for our protection during the winter."[20] "I am sorry to say," he explained, "that the spirit

20. Russell Papers, 30/22/15.

of disaffection is again much increasing. Our spies & informers warn us of an outbreak which is to take place shortly and some of the statements are so curiously coincident from different quarters that I am more inclined now than I ever was before to believe in its possibility. The signal is to be the arrival of a filibustering expedition, and it is a curious fact that both from one of our best sources of information in Ireland and from our detectives at Liverpool we received a simultaneous statement that a pilot or pilots had gone to the United States to bring over the filibustering expedition."

By the end of the month Wodehouse's views on the subject of a Fenian insurrection were, if anything, even more grim. "I am very glad the two regiments are coming immediately," he confessed to Russell on December 28, in obvious relief, "We have a number of American Irish prowling about Dublin and the disaffected parts of the country."[21] "Unfortunately," he then pointed out,

> these men have become so cautious that it is very difficult to get evidence sufficient to warrant their arrest. One would naturally suppose that after the contemptible figure which the Fenians have made both here and in the U.S., the whole organization would dissolve in inextinguishable laughter, but I fear the disaffection has too deep roots be be so quickly got rid of. Great watchfulness will I am sure be needful for some time to come; and though the alarm of the loyal gentry and merchants may seem preposterous in England, it is not without some excuse.
>
> The remembrance of the massacres which disgraced Ireland in 98 and previous rebellions has sunk deep in Irish imagination, and the views and designs of the Fenians are so distinctly revolutionary that it is not surprising that the loyal landowners should fear a "Jacquerie"[;] if any serious outbreak occurred, I have no doubt it would quickly assume that form, and that dreadful atrocities would be perpetrated.

"At the same time," he concluded more reassuringly, "my firm belief is that no such outbreak will occur, if reasonable precautions are taken. Meanwhile the general distrust which prevails is doing incalculable harm to the country."

In the meantime, in the face of all the rumors and menaces, the government had proceeded to put the arrested Fenian leaders on trial. Cullen reported to Kirby on December 3, "I sent you yesterday the Freeman with the Fenian trials. Read the attorney general's speech,

21. Ibid.

and you will see how wicked they were. The Blessed Virgin has preserved us from a great calamity" (K). "Luby, the first who was tried,"
he explained, naming one of the chief editorial writers of the *Irish
People*, "has been sentenced to twenty years *di galera con lavoro
forzato* [penal servitude at hard labor]. He is son of a parson—his uncle
is Fellow in Trinity College. They are all apostates. You recollect Mrs.
Luby, the Ursuline nun. She was their aunt." "O'Leary," he added,
referring to a colleague of Luby's on the staff of the *Irish People*, about
whom he had previously written Kirby, "is on trial [at] present. His
brother who was at school with him in Cork [correctly, Galway]
Queen's College died an infidel. I suppose this man on trial is like his
brother an infidel—what nice leaders for our good people." O'Leary
was also convicted and also received twenty years' penal servitude at
hard labor, as did Charles Kickham, another editorial writer for the
Irish People. Jeremiah O'Donovan Rossa, the business manager of the
paper and perhaps the most successful of all the Fenian organizers,
received the most severe sentence of all, penal servitude at hard labor
for life.

The Fenian leaders, who conducted themselves with considerable
dignity at their trials and who received their sentences manfully and
stoically, won the grudging admiration of many of those who were
most condemnatory of their views about revolutionary political action. Cullen, however, refused to be moved and remained as adamant
as ever. "The unfortunate Fenians, who were arrested by the government last September," he reported to Barnabò on December 10, "are
presently on trial. The leaders have already been sentenced to twenty
years at hard labor. Those trials prove that Fenianism was a conspiracy
more against religion than against the state. The writings published
by the Fenians were designed to bring down religion, and to discredit
the clergy, in order to be able afterwards to assail with greater success
the civil authority."[22] What is certain," Cullen then added for good
measure, "is that almost all the leaders of Fenianism have been educated in the Protestant Dublin University, in the Queen's Colleges,
and in the normal and mixed national schools. The youth of the
Christian Brothers' schools, of the Catholic colleges, and of the Catholic University, have not taken any part in this movement, and none of
them have been compromised."

While Cullen's *ex parte* statements about Fenianism certainly need
to be taken with a large grain of salt, he did apparently sense what was
really at stake for the Irish Church in the Fenian conspiracy. The

22. S.R.C., vol. 35, fols. 452–53.

Fenians were in their quarrel with the Church attempting to drive a nationalist wedge between the clergy and the people, and Cullen was determined that this effort was to be resisted at all cost. W. K. Sullivan, professor of chemistry and dean of the faculty of medicine at the Catholic University, also pointed out the danger when he was asked by his good friend, William Monsell, for his considered opinion on the real meaning and impact of Fenianism in the country. "It is almost impossible," Sullivan explained on January 12, 1866, "to give you any rational opinion of Fenianism. One set of persons magnify and distort the affair—and another sneer at the whole thing. My own opinion is simply this—the real number of *actual* Fenians is considerable but nevertheless they form only a small percentage of the people; that there will probably be no outbreak in Ireland, that 9/10 of the farmers, tradesmen and shopkeepers in Ireland, of Irish birth in Great Britain and America are thoroughly discontented, and so far sympathise with the objects of Fenianism that if the latter were successful for one month the whole people would join them."[23] "This is the worst feature of the business," Sullivan further explained, "because if Fenianism as a conspiracy be extinguished, Fenianism as a sentiment remains. The upper classes of Catholics have in a great measure separated themselves from the Priests, while they have, or at least the *lower* part of them, have used them for influencing the peasantry to return them to Parliament, so as to get on the bench &c." "The peasantry now find," he maintained, referring to the failure of the National Association, "that they have lost by the political agitation, and accordingly are either preparing to emigrate, or silently waiting the result of the Fenian Movement. In either case a wide breach has taken place between them and the Clergy which I fear will only widen more and more every day as the country becomes more and more Americanized."

Meanwhile, on New Year's Day, 1866, the bishop of Cloyne, William Keane, took the occasion of forwarding some £260 Peter's pence to Kirby to explain the growing complexities of the political situation in Ireland (K). Essentially, his analysis had much in common with Sullivan's. "In the political world," he informed Kirby sadly, "things are almost everywhere confused and menacing. A prophet alone can foretell the denouement. The Fenian trials are going on for some weeks in Dublin and Cork, ending in conviction and penal servitude for almost all the prisoners." "If the English Government," Keane warned, "won't try to pass good laws for Ireland, and therby make the

23. M, 8318 (5).

people happy and contented at home, there will be always discontent and disaffection, and, from time to time, conspiracies and outbreaks." "Since the clergy ceased to have," he explained, "the appearance of working, and, as it was called, agitating for the people, the discontent was becoming more dangerous and more revolutionary. The people were beginning to feel and to say, that the priests, who were always their friends and their guides, no longer cared for them, no longer sympathized with them, no longer took any trouble to redress their grievances. Distrust and estrangement have been perceptible for some time. I need not say what sad consequences would follow if the people lost their confidence in the clergy." "In truth," he noted gravely in conclusion, "as long as the Irish continue to have well-grounded causes of complaint against England, the priests must sympathize and cooperate with them. Though among the many clergymen in Ireland, one or two or more may sometimes be guilty of an imprudence in speech or in action, that can be corrected, and, in any case, it is a mere trifle compared to the value of the hold which the clergy, as a body, ought to have on the esteem, on the confidence, and on the affections of the people."

Kirby must have responded to this letter with a gentle remonstrance, for the bishop of Cloyne returned to the subject with even greater vigor in his next letter. "The great question of the day," Keane assured Kirby unequivocally on February 6, "is that of 'Fenianism.' It is destined to exercise an extraordinary influence on the future relations between priests and people" (K). "The mass of the people," he explained,

> down to the very children going to school, are either Fenians or sympathise with the Fenians, not because they wish to give up the faith or to neglect their religious duties, but because they hate England, the enemy of their country and of their creed, and of our Holy Father and of everything Catholic, and because the Fenians are opposed to England.
>
> For some years past, several complaints were made by the people against what they called the inactivity and neglect of the priests. In plain words, it was said over and over again, that "the priests don't care about us any longer. They and the upper class Catholics who expect places, are well enough off, and they no longer feel for the suffering farmers and the working people."
>
> This language and these sentiments have prepared many to adopt or to encourage conspiracy against a Government that refused redress.

"If once the masses," Keane warned Kirby in conclusion, "throw off the respect they always had for their priests, then will come the real Irish difficulty for England and for all concerned."

By the time Kirby had received this very candid and sensible letter, however, the British government had decided on another course than the conciliation Keane had recommended as the remedy for Irish disaffection. On February 15 the government asked Parliament to suspend habeas corpus in Ireland and rushed a bill through both houses to that effect in less than twenty-four hours. The following day, February 16, with the ink on the royal assent hardly dry, the government struck once again in Ireland. That same day, and obviously before he had heard of the mass arrests carried out by the government, Cullen was informing Kirby that the situation was steadily growing more serious. "Fenianism," he reported, "is becoming more alarming. This day week a man named George Clarke was murdered within seven minutes['] walk of my house. Before he died he gave the names of three persons who were with him when he was assailed. Still not one of the whole lot has been found as yet. This shows how mysterious the whole business is. Clarke was in Rome with the brigade, but having become discontented he returned home after a few days. Latterly he appears to have been a B as they call a captain of the Fenians. It was suspected that he was peaching, and four or five Fenians took him out to walk, and murdered him most brutally. What a fine system to be encouraged by Lavelle" (K). "It is greatly to be feared," Cullen then added, "that a system of assassination like that of the Italian Carbonari will now be introduced. The quantity of arms introduced into Dublin was really extraordinary." He noted finally, "There is also here a set of American rowdies who probably are managing everything. They don't drink, and keep their secrets well. They also have lots of money, so that they are not very desirable visitors."

Indeed, what had promoted the government to strike when it did was that it had become particularly alarmed about the large numbers of Irish-Americans in the country. There were at least some 500 known to the police, about 160 in Dublin and the remainder in the provinces.[24] There were also several Fenians in Dublin who had recently come over from England and Scotland, and more were known to be arriving every day. In addition, the police had discovered three Fenian arms factories in Dublin and suspected that there were a number of others. The chief difficulty facing the government, as Wodehouse had pointed out to Russell the previous December, was that it

24. Leon O'Broin, *Fenian Fever* (New York, 1971), p. 44.

had not been able to proceed under the ordinary course of law against the suspected American and British Fenians. With the suspension of habeas corpus, however, the government was enabled to make some 650 arrests within a week. "We are here," Cullen informed Kirby on February 23, "in hot water with the Fenians—within the last four or five [days] probably a thousand persons have been arrested, nearly all Americans, or adventurers from England or Scotland" (K). "I have heard," he added, "that among the prisoners there are Freemasons, Methodists and Swaddlers—what fine liberators for the island of saints." "There is a great alarm here," he noted further, "but I am confident that nothing will occur to disturb the peace."

Cullen was more right than even he knew. Several days before, on the evening of February 20, what was left of the Fenian executive decided to postpone any immediate action in Ireland for the present. Stephens, John Devoy (the chief organizer of Fenian circles in the British army), the two Irish-American members of the Fenian Military Council who had not been arrested, and four of the most important Dublin Fenian centers had met to decide what was to be done. Devoy argued for an immediate insurrection before the wholesale arrests completely destroyed their network in the British army and in the country, but he was overruled by Stephens and the others. Devoy was arrested the following day, and early in March 1866 Stephens was finally smuggled out of Ireland via Scotland and England to France. He was accompanied by Col. Thomas J. Kelly, the Irish-American chief of staff of the Military Council, who was soon to become Stephens's second-in-command. They arrived in Paris in the middle of March and there made arrangements to sail to New York, which they reached in early May.

Stephens's departure left the movement in Ireland, in effect, leaderless for nearly a year. When his equivocation in the United States on the opportuneness of raising a rebellion in Ireland finally resulted in his being deposed as head of the movement in December 1866, the leadership that replaced him found itself in a very difficult situation. By deposing Stephens for his equivocation, the leaders had committed themselves to an immediate insurrection in Ireland as a matter of honor, and they now had to go ahead regardless of their state of real readiness and without even a cool consideration of their prospects for success. The rising that eventually took place in March 1867, therefore, was really more a gesture of defiance than a serious effort to shake British rule in Ireland. The inability of the Fenians to maintain themselves in the field, and the unwillingness of the great mass of the people to commit themselves to what was patently a *beau geste* in a lost cause, resulted in the rapid disintegration of the movement as an effective and widespread revolutionary conspiracy. Indeed, the role of the Fenians in the Irish political spectrum would change dramatically after their failure in 1867. The hard-core, physical-force party among them would become with each succeeding year a tinier and tinier revolutionary sect, while the more thoughtful and able among them would take up their places in ever-greater numbers on the extreme constitutional left, where they would learn to play the game of radical confrontation with real skill and an increasing effectiveness. Still, it will not do, perhaps, even in the interests of this most salutary development, to anticipate the narrative too much—especially the account of the Church's part in helping to contain Fenianism's more violent propensities.

With Stephens in the United States the focus of the Fenian agitation shifted to that country, and little was heard about the dangers of Fenianism in Ireland for nearly six months. Shortly after his arrival in New York, Stephens was obliged to attempt to resolve a very serious split in the American movement that had resulted from a difference of opinion about where the American Fenians might best strike a blow at British power. An influential section of the American Fenians, led by William R. Roberts, a very wealthy Irish-American merchant, argued that British power could best be laid low by a Fenian conquest of Canada. The founder and head of the Brotherhood in America, John O'Mahony, on the other hand, continued to support the original Fenian commitment to action in Ireland. In this stance, he was supported throughout by Stephens, who had written O'Mahony some very intemperate things about Roberts and his supporters, which did nothing to help his efforts at peacemaking when he arrived in the United States. To make matters worse, in early April, shortly before Stephens arrived, O'Mahony attempted to steal some of the thunder of the Roberts wing by seizing the Canadian island of Campobello off the east coast of Maine. The raid was a complete fiasco and cost the already-depleted Fenian treasury some $40,000. Shortly after his arrival, therefore, Stephens forced O'Mahony's resignation and took over the American organization.

In an attempt to unite all the American factions, Stephens then undertook an organizing tour of the United States. He had hardly begun his tour when the Roberts wing invaded Canada at the end of May. Though the invasion proved to be yet another Fenian fiasco, it at least allowed Stephens to argue that he had been right about a rising in Ireland all along. After his return to New York in September, Stephens continued to maintain that the fight would be made in Ireland and that it would be made before the end of the year. At Jones's Wood, New York, for example, he assured his audience on September 22, "No matter what others say, take my word I will be in Ireland, and the people will strike a blow for liberty."[25] Some five weeks later, at his last public appearance in New York, Stephens dramatically announced to the fifty thousand Fenian sympathizers present that he was returning to Ireland. "My last words are," he again assured his audience on October 28, "that we shall be fighting on Irish soil before the 1st January and that I shall be there in the midst of my countrymen."[26]

In Ireland, meanwhile, the Conservative government of Lord Derby, which had succeeded on the fall of Russell's Liberal ministry in late June, not only had released most of the prisoners and repatriated the Irish-Americans who had been arrested under the suspension of the habeas corpus Act in February but also had prudently extended the suspension in early August, before it was due to expire in September, in order to be able to deal summarily with any renewed Fenian effort. Indeed, by the middle of November the Conservative government was as alarmed about the developing Fenian threat as the Liberal ministry had been the year before. A retrospective report of the permanent undersecretary at Dublin Castle, Sir Thomas Larcom, reviewed the situation in this way:

> Fenianism began to revive throughout the country, especially in the South and West. Money was being collected; penny a week subscriptions were being taken up ostensibly "for a distressed family" while raffles were frequently held and lectures given under the same pretense. Revolvers were being sold at 15/- and rifles at 12/- each. It was reported that arms were being imported on an extensive scale, packed as merchandise. Fenian emissaries from England and America were again pouring into the country. The "Public House" by night and the streets by day were filled with strangers of their class. Local agents were again active. Serious fears of an insurrection were very frequently entertained, and applications by the loyalists for military protection were again received from many towns and districts.[27]

Moreover, reports from the American papers appearing in the Irish press advertised the fact that Stephens was about to leave for Ireland, if indeed he was not already on his way.

25. Ryan, p. 247, quoting the *Irishman* (Dublin), October 13, 1866.
26. Quoted in O'Broin, p. 87.
27. Ibid., p. 81.

By the end of November the government had decided to move against the Fenians once again. Nicholas Power, the coadjutor to the bishop of Killaloe, reported to Kirby in some alarm on November 25, "There are numerous Fenian arrests daily, and great agitation throughout the country—they will attempt something desperate, and blood will be shed" (K). Cullen, who had been created a cardinal by Pius IX in June and who had returned to a triumphal reception in Dublin in August, had also become very much concerned about the Fenian danger. "We are all in alarm again about the Fenians," he reported to Kirby on November 27 (K). "The Fenians are returning from America and it appears they are conspiring through the country. The government is prepared so I think the unfortunate Fenians will only get themselves hanged or shot." Patrick Moran, who had returned from Rome in March to serve as Cullen's secretary, reported to Kirby from Dublin on December 4 that the Fenians promised a rising before the first of January and that the government had been sending more troops to Ireland, mainly English and Scotch (K). "I fear," he added ominously, "some of the Irish regiments have been totally corrupted by Fenianism." On December 11, however, Moran accused the government of creating the Fenian scare in order to prepare the mind of Parliament, which was to open its session in February, for a renewal of coercion (K). "I think there is no danger whatever," he explained, "of any revolutionary movement in this country for the present, unless England may get into any difficulties with America."

Early in the new year Cullen had apparently arrived at the same conclusion. "Fenianism," he reported to Kirby on January 2, "appears to have taken its departure with the cholera. I think we shall hear little more of it" (K). "The Government," he explained, "has filled the country with troops and stationed war vessels along the coast. This will do no harm, but there was no necessity for such warlike preparations." "The people however," he added, "though not Fenians are discontented and have a thousand reasons to complain." When he wrote Barnabò early in February, Cullen was still of the opinion that Fenianism was all but dead. "It seems," he explained on February 8, "that Fenianism is now completely defunct in Ireland, at least it is not much spoken of, and the government has now made up its mind to set free from jail all the Fenians that were detained. These poor people have suffered a very cruel imprisonment for their madness, and I hope they will be wise for the future."[28]

Cullen, was, however, very much mistaken. About the middle of

28. S.R.C., vol. 35, fol. 971.

December 1866, Stephens had called a meeting in New York of some thirty of the chief Irish-American Fenian officers in the United States. When these officers learned that Stephens wanted once again to postpone any immediate action in Ireland, they decided there and then to depose him as the head center of the American organization, a position he had assumed when he had forced O'Mahony to resign the previous May. Before the end of the year he was also deposed as the chief organizer of the Irish Republic and replaced, in effect, by Col. Thomas J. Kelly, his former second-in-command, who was a most determined and dangerous man. Kelly gathered what money he could and proceeded immediately to England to prepare for an insurrection. On February 10, shortly after his arrival there, Fenian representatives from the four provinces of Ireland met with him in London and set up a provisional government. Previous to Kelly's arrival, the Irish organization had fixed on February 11 as the day for the rising in Ireland, but it was now postponed until March 5, and the provisional government proceeded to make final preparations for the insurrection.

On February 15, however, a premature Fenian rising took place in the neighborhood of Cahirciveen in Kerry. The Fenians who took the field had apparently not been informed about the postponement of the rising. "We have had," Cullen informed Kirby dryly on February 22, "a Fenian outbreak last week in Kerry. It appears there were only about 35 armed men in the field to overthrow the British Government" (K). "As soon as the soldiers appeared," Cullen reported, "the armed and unarmed men dispersed, and have not been since [*sic*] ever since. One poor Catholic policeman was shot. The Fenians hearing he was a Catholic sent two men to call the priest. After he had attended the wounded man, the priest went to the police barracks and told the policemen to be on their guard. He then told the Fenians not to attack the police, as he had given them notice that they were to be attacked. You never heard of so peaceable a revolution as this." Cullen further reported, referring to the bishop of Kerry, "Dr. Moriarty made a furious attack on the Fenians at Mass and concluded by saying that eternity was too short and Hell not hot enough to punish their wickedness. He is very much blamed for so foolish an exaggeration."

The government, meanwhile, was fully apprised through its spies and informers of the proposed Fenian rising scheduled for the evening of March 5, Shrove Tuesday. "Here we have all sorts of reports," Cullen wrote Kirby on Ash Wednesday morning, March 6, "about Fenianism and disturbances. Last night the streets were paraded by horse and foot and artillery. It was said that 800 Fenians had assembled at Portobello just close to Rathmines and it was feared that they were about to attack the City. The precautions are very useful—but I think there was no danger of an outbreak. In Dublin there are probably twelve or fourteen thousand troops and a large body of police. All the Fenians of Ireland would not be able to stand for five minutes before the rifle cannon and needle rifles with which the garrison is provided" (K). "I have just now heard," he then reported, "that the railroad between Dublin and Cork was torn up last night and the telegraphic wires cut. Troops have been dispatched to Tipperary, and great precautions taken. I suppose all will end like the Kerry movement. However it is a sad thing to have the country disturbed by a set of reckless madmen—men who would rob us of the only treasure we have[,] our religion."

Father Lavelle has latterly resumed his former work. He wrote since Xmas a long letter to Dr. Manning in which he maintains most absurd and dangerous doctrines. This letter was published in the newspapers. It is now printed as a pamphlet and circulated in Dublin. There is no printer[']s name so it is as you say in Rome *publicata a la macchia* [published clandestinely]. In a paper of New York, the *Irish People*, he has lately given the world a furious letter against me, and he has published other documents in the Connaught Patriot. Indeed all the leading articles of that paper are against me or rather against Rome and everything Catholic.

"Whilst I write," Cullen then continued more excitedly, "intelligence has arrived that a large body of Fenians assembled last night at Crumlin just outside Rathmines—the soldiers marched out and arrested some sixty or seventy—the others are said to have gone towards Kildare. They appear to be all tradesmen from Dublin or adventurers from America." He went on:

In Drogheda there was an affray between them and the soldiers— some lives lost, the railroad towards Cork is interrupted. Still I think it will all blow over in a few hours. The men who assembled at Crumlin were armed some with guns and pikes and others with shoemakers['] knives—what arms to oppose rifle cannon. The mischief done however will be incalculable. The country will suffer materially and spiritually.

This moment I have learned that about 130 of the clerks in the different large shops of Dublin went out last night and joined the Fenians. They marched to Glencullen (Mrs. Fitzsimon's place) and attacked the police and took them prisoners. Before morning the soldiers were out, and just now near 200 Fenians have been marched in as prisoners. At Kilmallock the bank was attacked—it is said about a 1000 are up in County Louth. So the rising is pretty general.

"God help this unfortunate country," Cullen concluded, "thus ruined by madmen. It appears some lives were lost last night. Pray for the poor people."

Several days later, Cullen wrote Kirby another long letter expanding on what he had already said. "Lest you should be in any alarm about our affairs here," he explained on March 8, "I write a line to state how things stand. For several days we had reports here of approaching disturbances. I did not believe that anything would occur. However, trying to save our poor people, I inserted in the pastoral for Lent a paragraph on secret societies and said all I could against them.[29] I sent the pastoral to you" (K). "However," he added sadly,

> my words were not listened to. On the evening of Shrove Tuesday, three or four thousand men left Dublin to assemble at a village called Tallaght about five miles from the City. Some of them had guns, some revolvers and others pikes. It appears there were some American trained soldiers to command and organise them. It appears that every step they took was known to the police—and the soldiers were at Tallaght almost as soon as the Fenians. Before the arrival of the soldiers some skirmishes had taken place with the police, and a Captain Burke and ten policemen had assailed and dispersed about a thousand of their opponents. No resistance was offered to the troops, who took about 200 or 300 prisoners and dispersed the rest of the unfortunate people. The prisoners are generally taylors, shoemakers, and very poor tradesmen. The Captain Burke just mentioned is an excellent Catholic, and he and his men all went to confession the day before the affray in order to prepare for the worst. They all escaped safe and sound.

"The unfortunate Fenians," Cullen further reported, "generally attempted to go to confession—but they were always told that unless they gave up their insane projects, they could not get absolution. Here I suppose we shall have no more disturbances." "I hope in a day or two," he then added more confidently, "everything will be right again. It is fortunate that the farmers and farm labourers have taken no part

29. Moran, 3:57–62, February 22, 1867. This provides a very convenient summary of Cullen's and the bishops' admonitions regarding secret societies and the Fenians during the 1860s.

in the movement. About Tallaght outside Dublin not a single man from the whole district joined the Fenians." "I have given you," he then assured Kirby in conclusion, "all the news I could collect up to 3 o'clock Friday the 8th of March. . . . Here in Dublin you would not suspect from going about that anything had occurred. I was through the whole city today and at some schools and convents and I never saw the people quieter. Probably what has happened may do us good."

James Walshe, the bishop of Kildare and Leighlin, wrote to Kirby the next day, March 9, from Carlow: "The Newspapers will have already acquainted you with the Fenian raid—these wretched people have been duped into a most Criminal Lunacy—they will entail ruin of every kind upon themselves and grievous injury thru the country—" (K). "Many years," he assured Kirby, "will be required to restore the confidence so wantonly so rudely so wickedly shaken by this Lollard Movement—We all here are—thank God—perfectly quiet and I hope & believe may continue so—." Two days later, on March 11, David Moriarty, the bishop of Kerry, wrote Kirby in the same vein: "We are now quiet in this part of the country, but believe me Fenianism has wrought more evil to religion in Ireland than all the Proselytism ever attempted" (K).

That same day the *Cork Examiner* published Moriarty's formal excommunication of the Fenians. "Hitherto," Moriarty explained in the circular to his clergy, "many of the clergy deemed it unwise to speak of Fenianism from their altars on account of its almost total absence from their parishes. Some considered that by doing so they would give to the few members of this condemned society, who might be in their midst, an unmerited importance" (K). "Though we do not believe," he continued, "that the conspiracy is either widespread or dangerous in the rural districts, yet the events which have recently occurred in this country are so notorious, that silence on the subject is no longer advisable, even in those parishes which may be the most free from this moral pestilence. You will, therefore, inform your flock that all persons joining the Fenian society, whether sworn or unsworn, incur a Papal excommunication." "You will explain on this occasion," Moriarty then further advised his clergy, "the consequence of Excommunication, so that those who may have yielded to the temptation, or who may yet be tempted, may know that they have to choose between Fenianism and membership with the Church of Christ. You will also remind your flock of the deep sinfulness of taking or keeping an unlawful oath, making the sacred name of God a bond of iniquity."

"The rising," Cullen confessed to Kirby on March 12, "was more extensive than I ever imagined it could be. From Drogheda to Dublin and from this to Kerry there were outbreaks through the country at certain intervals. The Fenians were not able to offer resistance any place to the troops, but they appeared to hope to worry the soldiers retreating from place to place" (K). "Here about Dublin," he reported, "many of the Fenians had good primer rifles but they did not know [how] to manage them, and they threw them away. It is hard to know where the arms came from, as they could scarcely be introduced without the knowledge of the custom house people." "The heads of the Fenians," Cullen explained,

> must have been very active in swearing in their dupes. Yesterday I saw a poor boy of a most respectable family who was sworn by Stephens himself two years ago whilst he was at school. The boy had fled from his family to join the Fenians, but was caught after some time and brought back to his father who presented him to me to see if I could make any impression. He told me how he had been sworn in etc. and promised to give up his folly for the future. This fact shows how dangerous a man Stephens is, since he got into most respectable shools. . . .
>
> A Commission has just been appointed to try the prisoners. Some of the unfortunate will perhaps be severely punished, but Stephens and the real delinquents are out of the reach of the law. It is just the same as in Italy: the unfortunate agents suffered but the leaders, the Mazinnis and Garibaldis[,] all remain safe.

"All the priests and Bishops," Cullen then assured Kirby, "have acted very well in the present emergency[,] doing everything possible to keep the people from going mad. The police or constabulary who have acted so well are generally Catholics. The farmers and their workmen have all kept aloof from the Fenians." "Lord Naas," Cullen finally concluded, referring to the Conservative chief secretary for Ireland, "stated in the House of Commons that 29 National school masters had joined. This ought to convince our rulers that education without religious control is well calculated to promote revolution."

Cullen's first accounts of the Fenian rising, which were apparently taken largely from the newspaper reports, were a fairly accurate description of what actually happened. Still, when he had some time to reflect on the events of those exciting days, he found the whole of his recent experience something less than its parts. "Your letter to Dr. Moran," he informed Kirby on March 18, "reached [us] on yesterday St. Patrick's day. I perceive from it you have received stirring accounts about the Fenians" (K). "The whole affair," he explained, was very foolish and insignificant but you know that those who have bad consciences are subject to great fear, and that fear magnifies every little appearance of danger. Here in Dublin the whole rising passed off between ten o'clock Shrove Tuesday night, and three on Ash Wednesday morning. Two unfortunate men were killed, and a half a dozen wounded. All the others took to flight, but I dare say about three hundred have been made prisoners. Fourteen policemen under a Mr. Burke (all Catholics and all good Catholics) put the whole body of Fenians to flight and captured numbers of them. The number of the Fenians was greatly exaggerated at first, but it is probable there were seven or eight hundred of them. The night of this adventure was quite dark, and the belligerents could not see one another. Ever since that memorable night we have had awful weather—snow and hail and rain and a severe frost have followed each other in succession and this day 18th March S. Gabriele [it] is snowing heavily ever since morning. The unfortunate Fenians who escaped from the police at Tallaght where the affray took place must have all been destroyed in the mountains by the terrible weather which we had during the last fortnight.

"Great numbers of the Fenians," Cullen then reported, elaborating on a point he had made in one of his earlier letters, "went to the Churches to go to confession before they set out on their mad exploit. Of course the priests told them that as they were going to expose their own lives to danger, and to take away the lives of others, they could not be absolved. The unfortunate fellows however would not listen to reason or remonstrance."

"A pastoral of mine," he further explained, "was read on Quinquagesima Sunday [March 3, the Sunday before the rising] in which I said a great deal on the matter, but of course the wise counsels of Stephens and Father Lav[elle] were preferred." He continued:

> In a little pastoral for St. Patrick's, I reverted to the subject. I expressed a hope that the dupes would be treated with mercy. However I fear some of them will be hanged. They are charged with high treason having been taken with arms in their hands, fighting against the Queen, and the penalty is death. If Stephens and the leaders were caught no one would be sorry for them.
>
> The risings in Drogheda, Limerick, Tipperary, Cork etc. all terminated as quietly as that of Dublin. One policeman was killed at Midleton, one was wounded at Killarney—the Government has sustained no other loss. The soldiers have never had to

fire a shot, but they have suffered great hardship from the inclemency of the weather.

The whole affair was a piece of most solemn madness. It will be turned to a good account by the Protestants to persecute poor industrious Catholics, and to get everything in the country into their own hands.

Cullen then reminded Kirby again,

Dr. Moriarty's saying that eternity was not long enough, and Hell not hot enough for the Fenians has given great offense. I wish he could be called to an account for it. He is now publishing a letter to the clergy of Kerry in which he praises the *parsons* as models of every virtue, whereas we all know that they are the greatest enemies of everything good. I just happened to see a proofsheet where these outrageous praises are given—as it was shown to me in confidence I cannot write to Dr. Moriarty about it—but if I get it any other way, I will write to him. I well send a copy as soon as I get one. Dr. Moriarty was first an ardent young Irelander, now he has gone into the opposite extreme. In the Connaught Ranger of last week there is a fierce letter against him signed Patrick Lavelle. The worst of the letter is that it tells a good deal of truth.

"I fear," he confessed in concluding his long résumé, "that from time to time we shall have foolish outbreaks of Fenianism. The leaders must get something done to keep up their funds in America. *D'altro* [On the other] side they are quite safe themselves, just as Garibaldi and Mazzini were when conspiring against Naples and Rome—*Qui seminat ventos mettet tempestates* [Who sows the wind, reaps the whirlwind]."

As Cullen had surmised in his earlier reports of the Fenian rising, a number of the Fenian leaders were tried, convicted, and sentenced to be executed for high treason. In the immediate aftermath of the rising the government set up special commissions for the trials of the captured Fenians in Dublin, Cork, and Limerick. In all, 169 Fenians were tried. Of that number, 7 were acquitted, 52 were convicted, and 110 pleaded guilty.[30] Three of those convicted of high treason, Col. Thomas F. Bourke, Patrick Doran, and Capt. John McCafferty, were sentenced to be hanged, drawn, and quartered. Upon a recommendation of mercy from the jury, Doran's sentence was commuted to life

30. O'Broin, p. 179.

imprisonment, but the executions of Bourke and McCafferty were fixed for May 29 and June 12, respectively. Several of the other Fenians prominent in the insurrection received sentences of fifteen years' penal servitude; the remainder received varying lesser terms. The government was immediately besieged on all sides with pleas of clemency for those sentenced to be hanged.

Among those who interceded for the condemned men was Cullen. On May 10 he had written Kirby that the trials of the Fenians were then going on, and "some have been sentenced to death. I hope no one will be executed" (K). "There is," he further explained, "a whole host of informers, vile scoundrels, who were serving both sides." On May 25, in company with his secretary, Patrick Moran, and one of his vicars-general, Laurence Forde, Cullen took what was for him an unprecedented action. He called at the viceregal lodge to plead with the viceroy, the marquis of Abercorn, for the lives of the condemned men. Three days later, on May 28, the executions were stayed and the sentences commuted to life imprisonment. Though it is undoubtedly too much to claim that it was Cullen's intercession alone which saved the condemned men, it is certain that he received a very large share of the credit, at least in the public mind. There were, in fact, serious legal misgivings in the mind of one of the trial judges, and enormous diplomatic pressure had been brought to bear by the U.S. government because of the state of Irish-American public opinion. There was also, of course, the government's concern about the turn Irish public opinion would take if the executions were carried out. As Cullen explained to Kirby on June 6, shortly before his departure for Rome to help celebrate the eighteen-hundredth anniversary of the martyrdom of Saints Peter and Paul, "There was great alarm here lest disturbances s^d occur if the Fenians were executed & I c^d not be well absent if anything occurred" (K).

During the summer of 1867, the dangers of Fenianism appeared to subside once again. The reprieve of the condemned men had certainly eased the tension that had been building up in Ireland since the rising, and the continued suspension of habeas corpus made it very difficult for Fenians to pursue any forward policy there. The center of their activity therefore shifted to England, as the year before it had shifted to America, and Manchester became their headquarters. In late July or early August the self-appointed new Fenian leader, Colonel Kelly, called a convention in Manchester and had himself duly declared the chief executive officer of the Brotherhood. On September 11, however, before he was able to renew operations in either England or Ireland, he was arrested in Manchester with Capt. Timothy Deasy on a charge of vagrancy. While in custody Kelly was identified, and the government was delighted that it had finally captured the leading and perhaps the most dangerous Fenian of them all. The government's delight was short-lived: when Kelly and Deasy were being conveyed from the courthouse to jail a week later, some thirty Fenians armed with revolvers rescued the two prisoners. Though the prisoners made good their escape, a policeman was killed, and several of the rescuing party were captured by the police. Five of those arrested were immediately tried, convicted, and sentenced to be hanged for the killing of the policeman. One of the condemned men was pardoned, and another had his sentence commuted to life imprisonment. The other three men, William Allen, Michael Larkin, and William O'Brien, were hanged in Manchester on November 23, 1867.

The execution of the "Manchester Martyrs," as they soon came to be popularly called, created an enormous outburst of sympathy for them in Ireland. T. D. Sullivan, the brother of the editor and proprietor of the *Nation*, wrote a ballad in their honor, "God Save Ireland," which remained the unofficial Irish national anthem for the next fifty years. The Sunday a week after the executions, December 1, a mock funeral procession held in Cork drew great crowds of sympathizers.[31] The following Sunday, December 8, funeral processions were held in other parts of Ireland in imitation of the Cork example. The processions in Limerick and Dublin were particularly impressive. In Dublin between twenty thousand and thirty thousand people were reported to have marched, sporting green sashes and singing seditious songs.[32] "I see," W. K. Sullivan, professor of chemistry at the Catholic University, wrote William Monsell on December 10, "that you have had a great funeral procession in Limerick also."[33] "The one here," he assured Monsell, "was unquestionably the most remarkable demonstration I ever saw. Not only were the numbers who took part in it more than double those who marched at the McManus funeral but the dreadful weather was such [as] to test the sincerity of everyone who took part in it. That unfortunate Manchester business has advanced the revolutionary movement in a way that all the efforts of the secret organizers could not have done in two years." "I am greatly afraid," he added,

31. Ibid., p. 203.
32. Ibid., p. 205.
33. M, 8318 (5).

"that in a few years more the priests unless they join in the movement heartily will be thoroughly separated from the people. If some of
the things I hear be true, there is a curious and truly dangerous relation growing up between the clergy and the people."

A fund was soon organized for the support of the families of the
dead men, which was then followed by a ground-swell demand for
solemn requiem masses for the repose of the souls of the "Martyrs."
Needless to say, Cullen was appalled by this manifestation of public
sympathy, though he had himself privately expressed the opinion that
Allen, Larkin, and O'Brien were honest men when compared to the
Garibaldians being encouraged by the British government.[34] "I am
sorry," he reported to Barnabò on December 11, "that here our affairs
are becoming very dark. It seems that Fenianism is increasing in
strength. Last Sunday the members of that society paraded in great
numbers through the streets of Dublin. It seems to me that those who
are responsible for our affairs do not act wisely."[35] "On the one hand,"
Cullen explained, "they treat the Fenians with the greatest rigor, on
the other, praise the Garibaldians, and permit the publication every
day of the greatest eulogies of revolutionaries in Italy and elsewhere.
Such a system serves only to provoke the people." Some days later
Cullen returned to the subject again in another letter to Barnabò. "It
appears," he noted on December 16, "that the government was not
wise in executing these men. It has excited among all a great sympathy for them, and reprisals are threatened. Here in Dublin there was a
parade in their honor at which there were perhaps 50,000 people
present."[36] "Meanwhile," he then added, "the Fenian leaders have
made every effort to induce the clergy to have high masses to justify
them. The newspapers announce that the clergy have consented to
the demand in many places. I do not know if it is true. In this diocese I
have advised the priests to pray privately if they wished for the repose
of their souls [per li giustiziati], but not to celebrate high masses,
which are asked for not out of devotion, but for political motives. In
fact those who are engaged in this business are often Protestants, and
generally Fenians who have no respect for the precepts of the Church.
Certainly things are confused enough, and very serious evils may
arise." "It appears," Cullen concluded sadly, "that others having sown
the wind for us, we shall reap the whirlwind."

Less than a week later Cullen reported to Kirby that another dimen-

34. K, Cullen to Kirby, November 22, 24, 1867.
35. S.R.C., vol. 35, fol. 1322.
36. Ibid., fol. 1329.

sion had been added to the demand for high masses for the executed men. "There is," he explained on December 20, "a great deal of work about the three poor men who were executed in Manchester. An attempt is been [*sic*] made to raise a large sum for their families—A Protestant Mr. Martin proposes that everyone in Ireland should give one penny—Dr. McHale approves the proposal and sends five pounds" (K). "It appears," he further explained, "the unfortunate men died penitent and it is all right to pray. But masses and prayers are sought for to make them appear heroes and martyrs and to encourage Fenianism." "I believe," he declared firmly, "they were Fenians themselves, and they were executed for having killed a policeman whilst rescuing two Fenian prisoners. It appears to me to be a great mistake to *canonise* such men. Yet a High Mass was celebrated for them at Cong on the 17th and Father Lavelle [officiated], and a High Mass is to be sung today in the Cathedral of Tuam. I send you a Connaught Patriot in which you will see the advertisement. I fear great mischief will be done."

The lead given by Lavelle and MacHale in the diocese of Tuam was quickly imitated in other dioceses, and high masses for the "Martyrs" soon became the rage. "The Nation," Cullen complained to Kirby on January 7, "a very dangerous paper edited by A. Sullivan[,] a Catholic, a very mischievous publication[,] announced that there were masses and offices in 18 churches of Dublin for the unfortunate men executed at Manchester" (K). "I let the clergy know," he explained, "that it was right to pray for them, and to say mass privately for them, but that no public manifestations should be made to approve their conduct." In writing the bishop of Elphin several days later, on January 12, Cullen complained that the report in the *Nation* "was a pure fabrication" (G). "It was put in circulation," he explained to Gillooly, "to induce other dioceses to imitate Dublin. I did not hear of the publication until it was not worthwhile to contradict it. I dare say the matter is now all over—and there will be no more about it." Indeed, a week later Cullen reported to Kirby that the public displays were apparently finished. "The rage for masses or public offices for the Manchester Fenians appears to have subsided," he noted on January 19 (K). "At least there is nothing about the matter in the papers." "It was very foolish," he concluded unrepentantly, "to have any display in approbation of their conduct, though it was a very good thing to pray for their souls."

By the time Cullen had written this letter, however, the rage for high masses for the executed Fenians had already involved him in yet another imbroglio—this time, surprisingly enough, at Rome. "Cardinal Antonelli told me this morning," Odo Russell, the unofficial representative of the British government in Rome, informed Lord Stanley, the Conservative foreign minister, on January 7, "that about forty Fenians had been discovered among the Irish Catholics who had come to enlist in the Papal Army. They were very unruly and had endeavoured to get up a Fenian demonstration and mass in favour of Allen and Larkin at Sant' Andrea della Fratte, but the Pontifical authorities had been in time to prevent it and had sent the forty Fenians back to Ireland—which I was sorry to hear."[37] Russell noted in concluding, obviously referring to MacHale, "His Eminence also informed me that he had ordered the Propaganda to reprimand an Irish bishop, whose name he did not tell me[,] for having encouraged Fenian demonstrations in his diocese."

It appears that the small number of Irish who volunteered to remain in the papal service after the defeat of the papal army at Castelfidardo in September 1860 were eventually incorporated into the Franco-Belgian Zouaves. When Garibaldi launched another campaign in the fall of 1867 to deprive the pope of what was left of his temporal power, and the Zouaves particularly distinguished themselves in the fighting, the excitement created in Ireland was reminiscent of what had taken place in 1860. Cullen immediately undertook a very successful collection in Dublin for the pope, and the other Irish bishops generally imitated his example. Kirby apparently suggested that the pope could use men as well as money, but Cullen, who had been badly burned on that score in 1860, was naturally very cautious about involving himself in the problems of another papal brigade. While admitting on October 24 that the Zouaves had covered themselves with glory, and that there were many in Ireland who were willing to volunteer, Cullen explained to Kirby that the expense involved was very great and, further, he did not think it was wise to introduce "discordant elements" into the papal army (K). The volunteering, therefore, should be left to the French and Belgians, who had the added advantage of speaking French. When Garibaldi was decisively defeated by the papal forces at Mentana on November 3, the excitement in Ireland was greatly increased. In the month of November, for example, the collection in Dublin amounted to £2,500, and on November 17 Cullen took advantage of the enthusiasm by holding a large meeting in Dublin in support of the pope. Similar meetings were soon held in the rest of Ireland, and in spite of Cullen's reluctance to encourage volunteering for the pope's service, a number did set out for Rome. "This morning," Cullen's secretary, Patrick Moran, reported to Kirby on Decem-

37. F.O., 43/101.

ber 20, "about 20 young Irishmen started for Rome. I gave some of them letters for you" (K). "I hope," he added, "that they will not [be] a disgrace to us. I hope they will remain incorporated with the Franco-Belgian Zouaves and that no distinct Irish corps will be formed." In all, it appears that upwards of fifty Irish volunteers set out for Rome before the end of the year to serve the pope.

When Odo Russell then informed Stanley on January 7, 1868, that some forty Fenians had been discovered among the recent recruits, and that they had all been sent back to Ireland, the foreign secretary apparently did not reply immediately. When he did, on January 17, it was most urgently, by telegram: "Obtain if possible from Antonelli names of the Fenians sent home and particulars as to possible destination. Also of any known in Rome. MacAuliffe who wrote to Mr. Severn is known, and can, if he will, give useful information. He should not be neglected but urged to give it at once. If returning someone would be sent to meet him at Paris."[38] The reason for the delay in sending appropriate instructions to Russell was that the British consul in Rome, Joseph Severn, was not on good terms with Russell and had not informed him that he had forwarded a copy of McAuliffe's letter to Stanley. When Stanley received McAuliffe's letter through Severn he obviously referred it to the appropriate authorities at the Home Office and learned that he had a valuable informer in Rome. McAuliffe had explained to Severn:

> I have been acting for the Government at Manchester and London in connection with the Fenian Movement. I came to Paris a month ago to attend a meeting of an extraordinary nature. Mr. Inspector Williamson of Scotland Yard came to Paris to accompany me back to London—but circumstances over which I myself had no control prevented me from returning with him.
>
> I was asked to come to Italy on behalf of the organisation to confer with the continental revolutionists of Europe by which means I have worked out all European information in connection with the Fenian Movement.
>
> I have on former occasions given the Government more important information than any man in Europe—but all that is nothing to what I can give now. My present information will be the fall or rise of the Government. I wrote twice to Inspector Williamson of great Scotland Yard, who is the principal officer acting for the Government, one was from Florence and the other

38. Ibid., January 17, 1868, 4:45 P.M.

from Rome. I also wrote Mr. Greenor the home Secretarie's [sic]
Man and had no answer from him, those letters must all be lost.
I'll call tomorrow and talk to you over matters.

Bourke or Casey of London and Thompson and Hagan of Manchester can't be convicted without my evidence.

The state of things in Rome at present is astonishing, there is
[sic] 17 more here who can be easily reached for Murder over the
Manchester and London affairs, but this is all unknown to the
Papal Government, they would be glad to give up those men if
they knew of it as they know they are connected with the Continental revolutionists.[39]

"I'll tell you more tomorrow," he assured Severn in conclusion; "don't
let anyone see this if you don't want to have me murdered in Rome
and all my work lost. I can put my hand upon Kelly and several important men." Severn, however, had declined seeing McAuliffe, as he explained in his covering letter of January 8 to Stanley, because "the
immediate object of the letter was not concerning my Consulate or
myself."[40]

About a week later, after he had heard of the expulsion of the recent
recruits, Severn was more expansive regarding the Fenian-Zouave connection in Rome. "It seems," he reported to Stanley on January 14,
"that the Roman Police discovered lately that most of the Irishmen
who came to enlist in the Papal service as Zouaves, came for the sole
object of learning military exercise and their frequent desertions were
the cause of the discovery."[41] "Several," he further explained,

have since been expelled from Rome. A young Irishman[,] James
O'Connor (who was in the employ of a Stationer)[,] attempted
lately to get up a funeral mass for the three Manchester crimi-
nals, but the Papal authorities prohibited this scandal and to-day
O'Connor is to be exiled and goes to Florence.

He appealed to me for protection but on my communicating
with Monsignor Randi the Governor I found that this Irishman
was actually the Fenian Agent and so I advised him as the only
thing left to make a confession to the Monsignore as to the
Fenians who had reduced him to this vicious position but this I
find he declined to do as he said it would have obliged him to
betray more than a hundred persons.

39. Ibid., 43/102, John F. McAuliffe to Severn.
40. Ibid.
41. Ibid.

Of course I refused all protection on my part, indeed the Monsignore wished me to do so and communicated with me confidentially.

"I am glad to assure your Lordship," Severn then noted in conclusion, "of the Papal rigour against these criminal proceedings. The greater part of the above information I have received from good authorities on whom I can rely but has been given me confidentially."

A short time later, on January 20, Russell informed Stanley by telegram that McAuliffe and O'Connor had been expelled from Rome and were probably in Florence.[42] The next day he reported to Stanley that he had asked Severn to secure all the information he could about the Fenians from the governor of Rome, and that Cardinal Antonelli had promised him reports from the Ministries of War and Police.[43] "With respect to the forty Fenians," Russell added, "who had come to enlist in the Papal Army, Card. Antonelli told me that they were from Glasgow and that they had proved to be Irishmen and so unruly and unmanageable that they had to be sent back to Glasgow, from whence they came, at the expense of the Papal Government, —his Eminence promised to give me a list of their names." The following day, January 22, Severn wrote Stanley again.[44] On being requested by Russell to find out all he could about Fenian activities in Rome, Severn had at once sought an audience with Monsignor Berardi, the undersecretary of state, with whom he was in more friendly communication than with Monsignor Randi, the governor of Rome. "The Monsignore assured me," Severn reported, "that he would at once proceed and find out these persons as he considered that Fenianism endangered Rome as much as London. I then suggested that many of them might possibly be Irish Priests, and the Monsignore answered 'so much the worse for they shall have the severer punishment.'"

By this time, however, reports of the expulsion of the recently arrived recruits for the Zouaves had reached Ireland. "I hope the Irish," Cullen wrote Kirby on January 19, "are getting on better in Rome. Their position is rendered difficult by their want of knowledge of the language—it will become worse if they be placed under English officers" (K). "If it would do any good," he assured Kirby, "I would write about this matter. However no one here has been consulted about anything." A few weeks later, on Febuary 3, Cullen reported not only that the number of volunteers had slowed to a trickle but that he did

42. Ibid., 43/101.
43. Ibid.
44. Ibid., 43/102.

not suppose any others would go, except those who could pay their own way. When he wrote Kirby again on February 16, matters had obvously not improved (K). "I have had," he explained, "a couple of letters from Lord Denbigh [the Earl of Denbigh, a leading English Roman Catholic peer] in reference to the Irish Zouaves. He asks me to send an Irish chaplain in all haste, as things are going on very badly. Of course I will do no such thing until I get instructions from Rome." "It would be well," he then advised Kirby, "to speak to Cardinal Antonelli on the matter. I was never consulted about it at all by anyone and I do not know how the case stands. Several young lads went from Dublin—I believe they were engaged by a Mr. Duffy but who he was I know not. I suppose Lord Denbigh supplied the money, but he never wrote to me about those young men, and Mr. Duffy never called here." "Lord Denbigh's first communication with me," he further explained, "was written to induce me to undertake to pay for 1000 rifles, and 500,000 rounds of ammunition. The sum required being about £5,000. Fortunately we had sent all our funds to Rome, and I could not promise anything for the rifles." "The whole affair," Cullen concluded, "*è un vero pasticcio* [is a real mess]. Try to set things right if you can. I send Lord Denbigh's letter. Show it to Cardinal Antonelli if you wish."

Cullen reported again on Thursday, February 20:

I sent you on Sunday last a letter from Lord Denbigh giving a sad picture of the Volunteers in Rome. Father Delaney, S.J. was here yesterday. He says that things have been fearfully mismanaged. He throws the blame on Monsignori Stonor and Talbot. He says that De Charette made furious attack on the Irish and that Stonor was by his side whilst De Charette was doing so. He also says that the first 20 men who returned were marched felons between two rows of armed men to the station. Father Delaney adds that the Irish were not Fenians and they had nothing to do with the Mass for the Manchester Fenians. I requested Father Delaney to put all in writing and he has promised to do so—if I get a good case I will send it to Cardinal Antonelli or the Pope. Of course Father Delaney's name is not to be mentioned. I should have stated above that he is persuaded that the men were left without beds and some days without sufficient food.

"Perhaps it would be well," he advised Kirby again, "for you to call on Cardinal Antonelli, and tell him that the men are good. Father Delaney says they are excellent, especially the lads from Dublin." "They all," Cullen added, "went out enthusiastically for the Pope. What will they come home? Probably filled with hatred of everything Roman. They will produce a bad impression, and this impression will be widely felt as the men are from every part of the country. Father Delaney says that Monsignor Stonor did everything possible for the few English, whilst he did nothing for the Irish." "Try if you can to remedy matters," he then advised Kirby.

"The accounts we have received about our Zouaves are frightful," Moran explained to Kirby two days later, on February 22, while enclosing £200 for the pope (K). "I think," he added, "you should not stand aloof. If Mgr Stonor and Father Formby be allowed to interfere they would quite suffice to *imbrogliare* [confuse] twenty regiments." Moran assured Kirby in conclusion, referring to Cardinal Antonelli by his code name, "His Eminence intends to write a strong letter to Don Giacomo in a few days on the subject." When Kirby did not receive any notice of this promised letter in the next few weeks, he apparently asked Cullen why he had not written, for Cullen replied on March 22 that Father Delaney had not drawn up his promised report and that he had no basis therefore on which to act (K).[45] Cullen then explained that he had heard that matters had now improved, but he asked Kirby to do what he could, in any case, because if the volunteers returned home with sore feelings, the effect could only be bad in Ireland. "Our Peter's pence," he explained, "has run dry since the accounts of the Zouaves arrived. We got from June to January about £6000—since the beginning of the year scarcely anything."

Though the Fenian threat in Rome was undoubtedly a good deal less important than it was thought to be at the time, and the reaction of the Roman authorities was certainly excessive, the significance of the whole affair lay less in what was so than in what the Roman authorities thought was so. Up to this point Fenianism had been just another of those abstract questions with which Rome had to deal. The English clergy in Rome and Odo Russell certainly exercised themselves in their own interest in seeing more in the Fenian threat in Rome than there actually was, but in fact the threat was now brought home to the Romans, and when it came time to deal with Fenianism again, and the question was formally raised by the Irish bishops as a body, the Roman authorities would be a good deal more amenable to strong action than they had been in the past.

While the opinions of the Roman authorities toward Fenianism had

---

45. C, undated memorandum, "The Irish Zouaves, 1867–68, William Delany, S.J." Internal evidence indicates that the memorandum was composed about March 20, 1868. Cullen obviously received this memorandum after he wrote Kirby on March 22.

undoubtedly hardened as a result of their recent brush with it, the attitude of the great majority of the Irish bishops and clergy, if Cullen and Lavelle be excepted, continued to remain a good deal more ambivalent. It is this ambivalence, rather than the limited amount of evidence available on the subject, that makes any general assessment of the attitude of the bishops and clergy toward Fenianism so very difficult. Though Cullen's general antipathy toward the Brotherhood was certainly approved by the bishops as a body, it is a good deal less clear that either the body or the second order of clergy as a whole approved the expediency of his condemning the Brotherhood by name. What is clear, however, is that though a large number of the clergy and a few of the bishops may have sympathized with the Fenians, not one of the clergy, except Lavelle, nor any of the bishops, was prepared to support the Brotherhood publicly under his own name, and very few of the clergy, if Cullen's information was correct, were even covertly involved with the Fenians or their press.[46] Given that the Dublin clergy numbered more than four hundred, the two Dublin priests mentioned by Cullen in writing to Barnabò were—like Lavelle himself—really the exceptions that proved the rule of the lack of clerical involvement with the Brotherhood. In the crisis for the Church promoted by the Fenians between 1865 and early 1868, therefore, the bishops as a body had managed to keep a grip on their clergy as far as any public involvement was concerned, but they also realized, especially in the aftermath of the executions in Manchester, that the more prudent policy would be to attempt to ride out the storm by leaving well enough alone. In the meantime, they had also been spending a very considerable part of their time and energy as a body on a subject that was a good deal closer to their hearts—the question of higher education.

46. In the whole vast collection of Fenian papers and documents now housed in the Irish State Paper Office in Dublin Castle, there is apparently only one correspondence of any significance involving a priest. This is a series of letters from Christopher Mullen, a young curate in the parish of Taghmon, near Mullingar, in the diocese of Meath, to J. MacDonnell, who was apparently a member of the council of the Brotherhood of St. Patrick and a Fenian and who seems to have been involved in attempting to launch a number of Fenian-sponsored newspapers between May 1863 and December 1864. Perhaps the most revealing thing about Mullen's letters is how naive he was. By his own inadvertent admission he was obviously looked upon by his fellow priests as a foolish young man whose romantic enthusiasms were likely to get him into trouble, and his bishop, John Cantwell, had prudently prohibited him on the pain of suspension from visiting Dublin, in order to curb his propensity for appearing at political meetings. MacDonnell and his friends apparently found Mullen useful in collecting funds for their journalistic ventures and finding subscribers for them. See *Fenian Briefs*, State Paper Office, Dublin Castle.

Part III

Consolidation

WILLIAM E. GLADSTONE, PRIME MINISTER
(courtesy of the Victoria and Albert Museum, London)

IX

The University Question

May 1865–June 1868

After the cardinals of Propaganda had decided in the spring of 1864 against the expediency of any lay representation on the governing board of the Catholic University, the question of higher education for Irish Catholics remained dormant for nearly a year. In early May 1865, however, Bartholomew Woodlock, rector of the Catholic University, decided to make an attempt to reopen the question with the government. He crossed over to London, in company with David B. Dunne, professor of logic and metaphysics and secretary to the faculty of philosophy and letters at the Catholic University, and attempted to secure an interview with William E. Gladstone, chancellor of the Exchequer, through the good offices of Henry Edward Manning, provost of the cathedral chapter of the archdiocese of Westminster. Manning, who would soon be informed that he had been chosen by the pope to succeed the late Cardinal Wiseman as the archbishop of Westminster, wrote Gladstone on May 6, requesting an interview for a delegation led by Woodlock and urging him to use his influence with his cabinet colleagues to help secure legislation for a charter for the Catholic University.[1] Gladstone received the delegation on May 12,[2] and in the discussion that followed he gave every indication that he was open to

---

1. Gladstone Papers (Gl), British Library, Add. MS. 44248, Manning to Gladstone, May 6, 1865. See also W, Manning to Woodlock, May 6, 1865.
2. H. C. G. Matthew, ed., *The Gladstone Diaries* (Oxford, 1978), 6:355.

a settlement of the question that would be satisfactory to "the body of Roman Catholics" in Ireland.[3]

What Gladstone was alluding to, of course, in referring to "the body" of Irish Roman Catholics, was the dissatisfaction still felt by a section of the Irish laity, represented by a number of influential Irish Roman Catholic members of Parliament closely associated with the government, who resented the refusal to allow lay representation on the governing board of the Catholic University. Therefore, in reporting the interview of the delegation with Gladstone to Cullen, Woodlock once again introduced the question of lay representation on the University board and asked about an amelioration of Rome's policy regarding such representation. "Dr. Woodlock," Cullen informed Kirby on May 21, "has asked me to get Cardinal Reisach [the cardinal prefect of Studies in Rome] and Cardinal Barnabò to read the enclosed sketch of a Constitution for the C. University, and to learn from them whether it would be approved it if were adopted by the Bishops or the majority of them. Dr. Woodlock is afraid that Dr. McH. would oppose it" (K). "Some sort of constitution," Cullen explained, "must be adopted before any recognition can be obtained from Government. I have not examined Dr. W.'s plan, but he says it is a copy of the Sapienza—laymen are very anxious to get a share in the management of the University—Dr. Woodlock thinks they get something in his plan, but not too much." "The Bishops meet at Maynooth," he reminded Kirby, referring to the Maynooth and Paris boards, "on the 20th June. It would be well to have an answer before then."

Obviously, Cullen was writing Kirby on behalf of Woodlock only for the sake of writing, for his admission that he had not examined Woodlock's proposal was no recommendation at all to the busy cardinals of the Curia that they should take it seriously. What Cullen really wanted, of course, was for the whole matter of lay representation to be left as it was until further developments should dictate either a reconsideration or a reaffirmation of Rome's previous decision. In the next several months, however, Cullen would find it more and more difficult to keep all the various strands of the question of higher education in his own hands because of a number of lay and episcopal initiatives in the matter. The first of these was taken shortly after Cullen had written Kirby by The O'Donoghue, M.P. for the borough of Tralee, who gave notice in the House of Commons in late May that he would introduce a motion for a charter of incorporation to be granted to the

3. W, Dunne to Woodlock, n.d., recalling the substance of their interview with Gladstone.

Catholic University. The difficulty posed by O'Donoghue's initiative was that the members of the governing board of bishops of the Catholic University had the previous October taken Myles O'Reilly, M.P. for county Longford, into their confidence regarding their views about securing a charter for the University, thereby commissioning him, in effect, as the representative of their point of view in Parliament.

Woodlock, who with Dunne returned to London again for the introduction of O'Donoghue's motion and the full-scale debate that would follow on it, apparently smoothed over any ruffled feelings O'Reilly might have been prone to for O'Reilly agreed to support O'Donoghue in the debate. Before arriving in London Woodlock had also taken the precaution of briefing O'Donoghue in writing, with Cullen's express approval, about the views expressed by the bishops of the University board to O'Reilly the previous October.[4] In any event, O'Donoghue introduced his much-modified motion on the evening of June 20: "That an Address be presented to Her Majesty, representing to Her Majesty that conscientious objections to the present system of University Education in Ireland prevent a large number of Her Majesty's subjects from enjoying the advantages of a University Education and praying that such steps may be taken as will remedy this grievance."[5] In opening the debate, O'Donoghue pointed out that of the 1,837 students enrolled in the Queen's Colleges of Belfast, Cork, and Galway, and in Trinity College in Dublin, only 268 were Catholics.[6] Catholic parents were reluctant obviously to send their sons to these institutions, and the lack of a charter in the one institution they could conscientiously subscribe to inhibited them there as well, because their sons could not acquire the accredited academic degrees necessary to their professional advancement. The remedy, O'Donoghue argued, was to grant a charter to the Catholic University. Not only was it up to the required academic standard, but precedents existed in charters granted to Catholic institutions of higher learning both in Canada and in Australia.

Sir George Grey, the home secretary, undertook to reply for the government.[7] Though he refused to consider the granting of a charter to the Catholic University, because he thought that it was unwise to multiply the number of institutions conferring degrees, Grey did pro-

---

4. W, Cullen to Woodlock, June 18, 1865.
5. *Hansard Parliamentary Debates*, 3d ser., 180:541, also quoted in E. R. Norman, *The Catholic Church and Ireland in the Age of Rebellion, 1859–1873* (London, 1965), p. 198.
6. *Hansard*, 180:542–47.
7. Ibid., 549–56.

pose to enlarge the powers of the Queen's University, of which the three Queen's Colleges were the constituent bodies, by revising its charter in order to allow it to grant a degree to anyone who could pass its examination for such a degree. This was, in fact, the system in effect in England, where the London University served as the examining body for a large number of constituent colleges. Having thus secured the government's promise to take some action in the matter, O'Donoghue agreed to withdraw his motion. After the debate Woodlock returned to Dublin, leaving Dunne to hold a watching brief with regard to their interests. The following day, June 21, Dunne wrote Woodlock reporting yet another lay initiative, this time taken by William Monsell, M.P. for county Limerick.

"Have had a long conversation," Dunne explained, "with Mr. Monsell. He saw Mr. Gladstone last night after we parted. Mr. Gladstone urged him to lose no time in putting before Government *our* plan of how the views enunciated by him can be best carried out so as to secure the principles we have in view. Mr. Gladstone seemed to think it desirable that this should be done *at once*, before [sic] public attention will be concentrated upon it, and so opposition may be directed, and the action of government hampered" (W). "I think I gathered from Mr. Monsell," he further reported, "that the favourable section of the Cabinet are desirous of having something settled at once which will not be liable to recall, while they have the ascendant, and before Palmerston and Peel can mar anything. Peel was savage last night. He intended to speak; but Sir George Grey, *per-emptorily prohibited him*." "Now Monsell says," Dunne explained, "you must within the next six days have a plan ready to submit. He suggests to send it to him as a private letter—thus the University will not be compromised, nor will the Bishops. He can communicate it as his own which he has reason to believe will be acceptable, etc. etc." "There will be no necessity," Dunne then finally noted, "for anyone now to be in London. Had the plan been ready it might be advisable that I should stay on. But not being so, he says it is best that I go over to assist in getting it on. Our work is now in Dublin. And he implores [us] to have everything as perfect as possible i.e. as *complete*."

Several days later Myles O'Reilly wrote Cullen, reporting his recent conversation with Sir George Grey and also urging that the views of the bishops of the University board be put into writing for the government. As the tone of O'Reilly's letter indicates, he was already aware that his commission as the representative of the bishops of the University board in any negotiations to be conducted with the government might be in jeopardy. "It seems to me," O'Reilly explained to Cullen on June 26, "it would be very desirable to have a paper drawn up embodying in some detail the mode in which we would wish the Senate, as regards the Catholic element, constituted; and the scope & mode of its action; and that either I, or whoever you prefer, should privately submit this when carefully revised, to the government" (C). "I say 'I or another,' " O'Reilly added, "because it would not do to have more than one in correspondence with gov^t as they w^d naturally cull out of each correspondence the points more favorable to their views." "If you approve of this," O'Reilly proposed in conclusion, "& w^d communicate with Dr. Woodlock, I would go over the details with him & draw up the best paper we could, then to be submitted to you & the University board for correction."

Cullen was obviously much embarrassed by O'Reilly's letter, for by the time he received it, he and Woodlock had already committed themselves to Monsell's initiative. "I was anxious to see Dr. Woodlock," Cullen explained somewhat lamely to O'Reilly on June 20, "before I should write to you. He appears to me to contemplate the erection of a new body to be called the National University. He thinks the government is disposed to have one half of that body Catholic and his hope is that the Catholic University will be incorporated so as to be able to possess property and to affiliate Catholic colleges through the country so that all would be able to get their degrees in the new University. I think what you proposed was not the establishment of a new University, but of a jury d'examen which would give degrees to students from any recognised colleges."[8] "Before I saw Dr. Woodlock," Cullen noted, coming finally to the point, "he had written Mr. Monsell on the plan which I have mentioned. I do not understand the case well, and unless the government make some proposal, or let us know what they wish, it will be difficult to know what can be done on our side. If you should happen to be in town next week, I could get Dr. Woodlock to meet you and see what is best to be done."

O'Reilly was plainly mortified at thus being thrown over by Cullen and Woodlock for Monsell, but his reply to Cullen several days later was both dignified and a portent of the future. "As the University board have selected Mr. Monsell," O'Reilly pointed out on July 4, "as their representative with the government; it is not for me to interfere: & I should be the less inclined to do so: as I think the proposal you mention as having been made thro' him; rather as a return towards the error, (as it was considered at the meeting of the board I attended), of *numerical* representation of Catholics instead of *official* representation: the latter I believe essential; but I am aware that Mr. Monsell

8. Peadar MacSuibhne, *Paul Cullen and His Contemporaries*, vol. 5 (Naas, 1977), p. 22.

does [not] so view it" (C). "He told me," O'Reilly explained, "he thought the government would have the choice of the Catholics they would put on the Senate: and he suggested that two bishops sh^d be of the no. & that he thought your Grace & Dr. Moriarty w^d be a good selection. I said I thought the *principle* of the gov^t selecting Catholics to put on the board was a fatal error an[d] that in that case I w^d value very little the concession of even one half the senate being Catholics." "I do not think," O'Reilly finally added, "there is the difference you think between me & Dr. Woodlock as to the University. It is a settled point that the University is to be like the London University, not a teaching but an examining one. It is to consist of a Senate who will appoint examiners & subjects of examination. The difference is that Dr. Woodlock wishes that no students sh^d be allowed to stand an examination for degrees who had not studied in either a Queen's College or Catholic University. Mr. Gladstone suggested that all students sh^d be allowed to present themselves for examination: & I told Dr. Woodlock I w^d prefer his plan but did not think it w^d be carried."

What O'Reilly was politely telling Cullen, and with considerable justice, was that the reasons offered by him for preferring Monsell in the negotiations with the government were inconsistent and specious. As O'Reilly pointed out, having one-half of the body of the Senate Catholic would actually be a deviation from the principle of official representation (i.e., by virtue of the senators' offices in the constituent colleges that would make up the University) as against mere numerical representation, laid down by the bishops of the University board at their meeting the previous October, and the supposed difference between Woodlock and O'Reilly about the necessity for a collegiate residence to qualify for examination was more apparent than real. If O'Reilly was upset, however, by being displaced as the bishops' representative in Parliament in educational matters, his good friend Richard More O'Ferrall, M.P. for county Kildare, was aghast at the possible consequences of Monsell's initiative. "I believe," O'Ferrall assured Cullen on July 5, "there never was a period since the agitation of the veto, of so much danger to Catholic interests. The Government are ready to purchase, and we have people willing to treat, but as long as the Bishops are no party to a treaty, there is no danger. When the Government state their plans, the Bishops will give their opinion, without being influenced by any acts, opinions, or engagements entered into by any individuals, lay or clerical. I believe I am right in stating that this will be the course adopted by the Bishops."[9]

9. C, quoted in Norman, p. 203.

In the meantime, Cullen had taken up the stance of watchful waiting. "You have seen the debate on the Catholic University," he wrote
Kirby on June 27 (K). "How the matter will terminate I know not. The
Government seems disposed to incorporate the University as a College, giving it the right to possess property etc., and then to establish a
National University which will not teach but merely confer degrees.
Belgium and France have something of this kind." "The Government," he concluded more suspiciously, "has not communicated anything officially so we do not know what they will do. Probably the
whole business may be an electioneering trick." What Cullen was referring to, of course, was that the present Parliament was approaching
the end of its statutory life of seven years, and a general election had
been scheduled for the middle of July. A promise to do something for
Catholic higher education was a prudent political move by a Liberal
government that hoped to cut very substantially into the aberrational
Conservative majority acquired at the previous general election in
1859 in Ireland. That this rather obvious Liberal tactic had some electoral value, at least, was made evident when even so inveterate a
Whig-hater as the bishop of Down and Connor, Patrick Dorrian, proceeded to write Kirby in a more politically optimistic vein than was
usual with him. "I think there is a prospect," Dorrian confessed on
June 27, "of obtaining an arrangement about the University that will
not lower its *Status*, leave education fully in the hands of the Bishops—chartering *them* for all property purposes etc. etc. as a corporation—and give the University a proper and safe representation on the
Examining Senate" (K). "But," he concluded, alluding to the approaching general election, "we had better say little."

Shortly after receiving O'Reilly's and More O'Ferrall's letters of July
4 and 5, respectively, and before the general election, Cullen had made
up his mind on how he was going to proceed. On July 7, therefore, he
wrote Barnabò a long letter about the recent developments with regard to University education.[10] He explained the unofficial proposal of
the government and noted that the plan would be of great advantage
to the students of the Catholic University, because it would allow
them to acquire those degrees so necessary to the successful pursuit of
their civil and professional careers. He added that though the government had not yet put its proposals in writing, and it was difficult
therefore to form an accurate judgment, the system offered did not
appear to be worse than the system presently in effect in Belgium. "If
the government is acting in good faith," Cullen then advised, "it

10. S.R.C., vol. 35, fols. 358–59.

would perhaps be expedient to enter into negotiations with them, and see if it is possible to put into execution the plan now proposed without compromising religion." "In any case," he warned Barnabò, "there is danger of dissension between the bishops and other Catholics over this business. Many have declared themselves favorable to this new scheme while others condemn it. This very day a letter of Monsignor McHale has appeared in the papers, in which without declaring his views openly, [he] makes it clear that he is determined to resist the new project." "Perhaps in these circumstances," Cullen further advised, coming finally to his point, "and to avoid discussion among Catholics it would be well to hold a meeting of the bishops. I know that such meetings in recent years have not resulted in much good, but yet in dealing with a question that concerns all Ireland, it is desirable that all the prelates should hear the views of their colleagues. If the meeting is not held in a regular manner, and with the authority of the Holy See, there is danger that more harm than good will be done." "I submit these things to your Eminence," Cullen explained in conclusion, "so that it may be decided whether a meeting of all the prelates is necessary, and to hear what they may think about the business now pending. If it is desired that a meeting be held, it will be necessary to give precise instructions that it be held canonically. Otherwise Monsignor McHale will see to it that nothing can be concluded."

The cabinet, meanwhile, had met on July 6, the day before Cullen wrote Barnabò, and decided to defer any action on Irish university education until after the general election.[11] The elections, which were over by the third week in July, increased the government's majority from about forty to sixty, with a gain of some seven seats in Ireland. At a meeting of the cabinet on July 24, therefore, the ministers decided to proceed with the plan of chartering the Catholic University as a College within the framework of a new University.[12] That same day Monsell, who had returned to his home in county Limerick for the general election, wrote Woodlock from Tervoe about the urgent need to press on with the negotiations. He complained that he had not yet received the plan, which was to be drawn up by Professors Dunne and Sullivan of the Catholic University and which he had requested of Woodlock more than a month before. "I have written to Sir George Grey," he explained to Woodlock, "to beg him to get powers from the Cabinet to deal with the question. I hope we shall not be driven to have an exclusively lay Senate" (W). "Would you get Dr. Cullen," he requested, "to look at the constitutions of the ante-reformation Col-

11. Cabinet Paper, November 25, 1865, quoting Grey to Wodehouse, July 7, 1865.
12. Ibid., quoting Grey to Wodehouse, July 25, 1865.

leges of Oxford? Surely there the corporate body was the Rector & Fellows but the visitor had ample powers—or take the constitution of Maynooth—there we have a precedent that might well be followed." "It will be such a pity," he lamented, "if our negotiations are broken off on what after all is but a practical difficulty. Could faith & morals suffer by six laymen being associated with six bishops in the governing body or by making your own body [i.e., the University council] controlled by the four archbishops, the governing body?" "I hope to see Dr. Moriarty to-morrow," he noted in conclusion; "I think that you and I should go together to see the Archbishop of Cashel."

At this point the government dispatched to Ireland Henry A. Bruce, vice-president of the committee of the Privy Council on education and M.P. for Merthyr Tydvill in Wales, recommending that he contact Monsell, who invited him to Tervoe for an informal conference on the question of university education during the first weekend in August. Monsell also invited the bishops of Kerry and Limerick, David Moriarty and George Butler, respectively, as well as Thomas O'Hagan, judge of the court of common pleas, and Aubrey de Vere, poet and a prominent convert to Catholicism. Bruce arrived at Tervoe in company with Woodlock, after having had discussions in Dublin with Sir Dominic Corrigan, a prominent Catholic physician (and brother-in-law of Woodlock) who had long been partial to the Queen's Colleges, and with Professors Dunne and Sullivan of the Catholic University. Woodlock, meanwhile, had called for a meeting of the University board in Dublin on Monday, August 7, and he and Butler interrupted their stay at Tervoe to attend the meeting. As only three or four of the twelve members of the board were able to be present that Monday, and as they could not authorize Woodlock and Butler to speak in the name of the whole body, it was decided that Cullen, who had recently received the requested permission from Barnabò, should convene a general meeting of the bishops on August 22, to decide what was to be done. Woodlock and Butler then returned to Tervoe, where they resumed their discussions with Bruce after explaining that they were not in any way authorized to express the sentiments of the bishops as a body.

Woodlock, who made a long memorandum of his conversations with Bruce on August 9, noted that he had explained that whatever the bishops as a body would do,

there was one thing they w^d never do: viz., approve or countenance, or even *appear* to countenance, the mixed system, as embodied in the Queen's Colleges.

Mr. Bruce said: there was no question of their doing so. The

Gov^t was willing to abolish the present Queen's Univ^y and establish another in its stead. That this new Univ^y might even be called by a new name: *The Royal Irish Univ^y*: He also said: that it was intended that neither the Q. Colleges, nor any other institution sh^d have any connection with the new Univ^y: that its examinations & degrees sh^d be open to all comers.

I remarked: that then no advantage w^d be given to our Univ^y wh w^d not be common to all Colleges & even to every individual. [W]

"A long conversation then ensued," Woodlock explained,

on the advantages of maintaining the Collegiate system in connection with the Univ^y, for the purpose of securing that the candidates for degrees sh^d not only have the requisite knowledge, but also have had a careful training. In the course of this conversation Mr. Bruce asked: did others wish for a monopoly, or for protection agst. our own Colleges?

I said: that I did not ask for privileges; for otherwise under [the] system now proposed we w^d be set to contend unaided agst. the Queen's Coll. with their endowment.

He said: that the endowments as far as they were Exhibitions, scholarships &^{c} might be thrown open to all the students of the new Univ^y without distinction of the place where they w^d pursue their studies. And that as far as the Professors &^{c} were concerned, it was all the same to them whether their salaries were paid by an endowment or by private benefactions.

I remarked: that the contest would still be very unequal: we were heavily weighted, while these Colleges had several advantages ex.gr. their buildings, Museums, libraries &^{c} wh. we had to provide for ourselves, while they were provided for the Q. Coll. at the public expense.

He said: But it w^d be hard to deprive them of the advantages they had already obtained.

I said: The equality might be restored by endowing our Univ^y.

He then explained the intentions of the Gov^d with respect to this new Univ^y Senate: viz. that it sh^d consist of 30 Members: of whom 5 w^d be *ex officio*: 5 to be always named by Gov^t, but by mutual agreement. The 5 *Ex officio* members w^d be: the two Cath. Primates: the two Protestant Abps: & the Moderator of the Synod of Ulster.

I remarked: that this did not seem equality: as there would be 3 Protestants agst. 2 Catholics: & especially considering that on acct. of the privileges still enjoyed by Trinity Coll., this new Univ^y was chiefly for the benefit of Catholics & Presbyterians.

Mr. Monsell said: that there might be a third ex officio Catholic member: ex. gr. the President of Maynooth. To this Mr. Bruce seemed to agree.

With respect to the 20 (or 19) members not ex officio nor Gov^t nominees Mr. Monsell said: the question might arise as to the mode of nominating them, when a vacancy would occur. That the nominations might be made in one of three ways: 1st by Gov^t: 2^{ndly} by election by the Graduates: 3dly by the election by the surviving Catholic (or Protestant) members of the Senate.

Mr. Bruce seemed to think it w^d be difficult for the Gov^t to give up its right to nominate.

I said: that I thought the 3rd mode the least objectionable: of course I could not say whether the Bps w^d be satisfied with any of the three. I added: that I thought the first mode most objectionable: that the 2nd could not be adopted till there was a large number of graduates, say for ten years: and that in the meantime, if any of the suggested modes were adopted, the third might be taken.

"With respect to the charter of the Cath. Univ^y College," Woodlock noted, turning to the most difficult problem of all,

it was asked: whether the Bps. w^d leave the government of it to the Rector & Professors, subject to their visitorial powers: and the example of the ante-reformation Colleges in Oxford was cited.

I replied: that in the Oxford Colleges the founders & benefactors established such rules as they thought best: & these rules not being contrary to morals, nor to the faith wh. all then professed, were accepted: and that I did not think it fair to ask the Bishops to make the rules otherwise than as they deemed best in a College which they founded & supported. And moreover, that the ante-reformation Colleges were almost entirely clerical, and consequently might be governed by other rules than ours. That I felt sure the Bps w^d not allow their powers to be limited to mere visitation.

"In a subsequent conversation (this morning)," Woodlock added, "I endeavoured to show Mr. Bruce the inconvenience & injury to the students and Colleges which w^d result from not requiring the testimonium from the Head of the College, that the candidate had fulfilled the requirements of the College. The result w^d be, as is found to be the case with candidates for the London Univ^y that everything, even those things wh. we, as Catholics, deem of paramount importance, w^d be neglected, except what would be required by the Univ^y, and would be prepared by *cramming* for a few weeks—instead of extending the education over the whole time spent in the College. Mr. Bruce seemed to think, that the testimonium of the head of the College or School might be required from all students going up from a School or College." "I also said to Mr. Bruce," Woodlock finally noted, turning to the crucial question of the proper mode in which any future negotiations were to be conducted, "that, as the Gov^t has expressed its desire to meet the wishes of the Bps & Cath. people of this country & to make the new Univ^y such as to enjoy their confidence, it was absolutely necessary, that their opinions & wishes sh^d be ascertained *in an authentic way*: and that I saw no better way to do so, than that adopted by Lord Chelmsford, and the Committee on the marriage-laws; viz. that he (Mr. Bruce) should write to one of the Abps or to me as the official of all the Bps, informing me of the intentions of Gov^t, and asking the Abps or me to ascertain officially & communicate the opinions & wishes of the Prelates on the Gov^t proposal, & on the mode of carrying it out." "Mr. Bruce," Woodlock concluded, "seemed to think that the plan adopted by Lord Chelmsford & the Committee in question might be an excellent precedent."

As the last point of Woodlock's memorandum indicated, he had come to have some very serious second thoughts about the advantages of Monsell's acting as an intermediary between the government and the bishops and himself. Indeed, by the end of his visit to Tervoe, he was prepared to recommend that Monsell be eliminated from the negotiations altogether. The reason for his change of heart was of course less the rising tide of lay resentment, as expressed by O'Reilly and O'Ferrall, than the developing uneasiness excited among the bishops by the rumors of such lay initiatives independent of the approval of the episcopal body. Woodlock had been quickly apprised of that uneasiness when he wrote the bishop of Clonfert, John Derry, asking him as a member of the University board to attend the meeting scheduled for Monday, August 7, which would consider the "New Government Scheme of University Education." Derry, in his reply on August 1, explained that he and his clergy would begin their diocesan retreat on that Monday, and it would be therefore impossible to attend the meeting (W). He then asked Woodlock to send him a copy of the scheme he had referred to in his letter. "I have, as yet," he explained, "no knowledge whatever of the nature of that *Scheme*: and even were

I present at next Monday's meeting I would be very unwilling to consent myself to any action regarding it, without more thoughtful examination of its bearings than I could expect to make immediately on learning its terms." "I have also, as you are aware," Derry added for good measure, "a very decided opinion against the Competency of the University board to deal decisively with the question. I do not believe the Board was constituted with power to do so."

Woodlock replied by return of post, for Derry rejoined on August 3 and gave full vent to his feelings about the dangers of unauthorized negotiations. "I shall expect your promised favour," he assured Woodlock, "—and on receiving it, shall give it all the consideration I am able to give to any document, for I believe nothing so serious has occurred these twenty years as a negotiation such as now seems to be carried on by the Government by and with some unknown parties as to the terms on which Degrees may be conferred on Catholics and the machinery by which a new scheme for dealing with the education of Catholics may be worked" (W). "The present unsatisfactory (to use [the] mildest epithet) state," Derry maintained,

> of everything connected with the education of Catholics in Ireland would never have existed, if like in 1815 an unauthorized negotiation had not emboldened government in 1830 and afterwards in 1845 to found and endow the Mixed System.
>
> I very respectfully suggest to you, dear Monsignor, to give in *the very language of the Government* the proposal that is made on their part. Don't trust to the *views*, or *expectations*, or *inferences* of the chosen negotiators. Of course, if the communication has been directly with yourself as Rector of the Catholic University there can be no mistake about its meaning: but if it has been through intermediate Channels, believe me it will behoove you to be thoroughly on your guard.

"The Government," Derry then pointed out, "knows well enough our hierarchical position. It occasionally acts on that knowledge. Its powerful Commission for Administering the Laws for the Relief of the Poor is every day obliged to deal with us as Bishops. Its Commission for inquiry into the [nature?] and operation of the Laws concerning marriage has addressed itself to us."

> I do therefore look upon the course adopted by the Government in the present crisis of University Education—passing the Bishops by and having recourse to officious Agents—as not ominous of much good.

I believe one great danger to the Catholic University was averted by the decision of the Sacred Congregation which refused to allow its governing body to consist of Lay gentlemen and Bishops. But I apprehend that a pet idea of some Parliamentary Patrons of Catholic University Education—that Bishops have little if anything more to claim than a negative interference in regard to it, but their role is to be rather that of watchmen than of Governors—

Derry then concluded, "I do certainly advise you—as you have been please[d] to ask my opinion on the point—to send to all the Bishops of Ireland copies of whatever statement you do present to the Board."

After the conference at Tervoe, however, and in spite of Derry's warnings, Woodlock foolishly decided to prompt yet another lay initiative by writing Myles O'Reilly. "I am sorry to tell you," he confessed to O'Reilly on August 12, "that I am not at all satisfied with the turn our business is taking. I have seen Mr. Bruce at Tervoe and I fear the friends of the Queen's Colleges, in fact Dublin Castle influence will have it all its own way. They seem disposed to give us the London University system with three colleges endowed—to contend against us."[13] "It has occurred to me," he suggested, "that it might be a useful thing if Sir G. Grey could be seen before the bishops meet on the 22nd: Would it be possible for you to see him? I know you will do so, if at all possible, and if you think it would serve us, I would go also if you and the bishops thought it desirable." "The Archbishop of Cashel," Woodlock concluded, "will, I think, write to you on this point. His Grace agrees with me that it would be most desirable."

O'Reilly's refusal was prudent, dignified, and to the point. "I am very sorry," he commiserated on August 14, "you do not now see your way to a better issue of your negotiations but I hope you may ultimately succeed better than you seem at present to anticipate. I wish I could see that I should do any good by going to look for Sir G. Grey now, but I cannot see my way to it. . . . I have very little personal acquaintance with him and as an individual my representations to him would I fear bear little weight in influencing the decision of the government, even if accompanied by you in a non-official capacity."[14] "No doubt when the bishops meet," O'Reilly concluded shrewdly, "they will decide as to the basis on which they will negotiate, and send up some proposals which they can have laid in an official man-

13. MacSuibhne, 5:23–24.
14. Ibid., p. 24.

ner before Sir G. Grey who may at present be looked upon as the acting head of government."

By this time, however, the archbishop of Tuam had complicated matters even further. On August 9 MacHale received Cullen's circular letter of August 8, convening a general meeting of the bishops for August 22 and enclosing Barnabò's mandate and agenda for the meeting. Immediately he wrote Sir George Grey asking him for some further information about the government's intentions regarding university education for Irish Roman Catholics.[15] Grey replied on August 12 that the principle on which the government would act had been enunciated in his speech on O'Donoghue's motion in the House on June 20, but the details could not be made public until they had been submitted to and approved by the cabinet.[16] Although Cullen apparently had no knowledge of MacHale's initiative, he already knew enough to make him uneasy and apprehensive about the approaching meeting of the bishops. "It is to be hoped," he explained to Kirby on August 14, "we may do no harm. I fear we shall do no good. We do not know what the Government wish to do and there is no great chance of our agreeing about anything" (K). "Dr. McHale," he complained, "has not done anything for the C. University for the last thirteen years. He condemns everything, but gives nothing, and will take no part—he verifies the old proverb, the best hurler is always in the ditch. It is very easy to condemn, but it is not easy to see what is right." "If something be not done at present," he warned, "the Queen's Colleges will go ahead. The students say they are thrown back if they do not get degrees. With near £30,000 a year to bribe the students, the Queen's Colleges can make a great stand. The division among the Bishops and Dr. McHale's opposition give ground to the people to withhold their subscriptions—four dioceses gave nothing this year and eight or ten gave little. Some of the priests say that Dr. McHale is right in opposing the University, and then they tell the people not to contribute." "This," he cautioned Kirby more prudently in conclusion, "is only for yourself."

Cullen reported to Kirby on August 25,

We had our meeting on Tuesday, Octave of the Assumption, fifteenth anniversary of the opening of the Synod of Thurles. All the Bishops in Ireland attended except Dr. Feeny of Killala who is fond of staying at home, and Dr. Cantwell whose place was sup-

15. *Parliamentary Papers*, 1866, 55:243–59, no. 1.
16. Ibid., no. 2.

plied by Dr. Nulty. Our meetings lasted two days. We had a long discussion upon the University education and the Government projects.

In the end it was determined to authorize the four archbishops to treat with Sir George Grey, and to learn of him what the Government plans and its details are, and when they have learned all that, that the Bishops should meet again. We adjourned the late meeting until such time as the desired information could be obtained.

From this you will perceive that we did nothing. The head of the Education Board of England and the Vice President of the Privy Council, Mr. Bruce, was in Dublin and ready and anxious to give us the information we required—but Dr. McHale and a few others would not consent to treat with him, so that nothing could be done. Dr. Butler however waited on Mr. Bruce and got in writing a sketch of what the Government wishes to do. Their project is to suppress the present Queen's University—and to institute a Royal Irish University. This University is not to teach, but merely to appoint subjects for examinations, and to select examiners, and to confer degrees on all such candidates as the examiners shall find fit—degrees are to be given only in medicine, law, and arts.

The Senate of the University is to consist of sixteen Catholics and sixteen Protestants. The Government is anxious to have some Catholic Bishops in the number, and it will allow the Bishops to present or recommend the Catholic members.

A question here arises[:] would it be expedient or lawful for Catholic Bishops to confer the above degrees on heretics[?] On the other side would it not be well to have some bishops present to watch and protect Catholic interests[?]

It was agreed at the meeting also that the Archbishops should treat about the model and training schools of the National Board and endeavour to get them suppressed. [K]

"When I sent the letter of the Propaganda to Dr. McHale," Cullen further explained, "he immediately wrote to Sir G. Grey, and got a reply from him stating what the Government was going to do." Cullen elaborated:

The first day of the meeting he asked me whether I had any official communication of the intentions of the Government, and when I said I only knew of what was going to be done by the declarations in Parliament and reports, he complained about the unsatisfactory state of the question, and said he would say nothing on the matter. The next day after all the Bishops had spoken, he trotted out his own letter to Sir George Grey, and the reply dated a fortnight before the meeting and read them—he read a complimentary letter he had received from the Propaganda. This brought about a dispute between him and Dr. Butler. He had condemned the Bishop of Limerick for entering into this question with Mr. Bruce. Dr. Butler now asked had he not as much right to speak with Mr. Bruce as Dr. McHale had to treat with Sir G. Grey.

"All our proceedings," he added dejectedly, "will simply end in nothing—Dr. McHale's object is to prevent anything from being done, and to put an end to the Catholic University." "I will write to the Cardinal in a day or so," he promised in conclusion. "It is clear we can do no good in treating with the Government, as Dr. McHale will be ready to say he does not agree with the other archbishops in what they propose. The Government will then say settle your own differences before you come to ask favours from us."

That same day Patrick Moran, Kirby's vice-rector, who was in Ireland on holiday and was visiting with Cullen in Dublin, also wrote Kirby about the bishops' meeting. "The deliberations," he reported to Kirby on August 25, referring to the first day's meeting, "lasted til five, and all were invited to dine with the Abp. at Clonliffe. All accepted the invitation except Dr. MacHale. However Dr. Moriarty got a little ill and did not go, and Dr. Derry also sent an apology as some business required his attendance" (K). "All the others," he added, going on to name two Irish prelates, one retired and the other visiting, "with Dr. Whelan and Dr. Murphy of Hyderabad, joined the dinner party. The priests of Marlboro St. and the vicars etc., were also there. Some very good speeches were made, and subsequently all adjourned to take a cup of tea in the sitting room. There was no punch, and everything was as orderly and becoming as could be desired." "The deliberations," he then noted, turning to business and conveniently summing up the proceedings,

were resumed on Wednesday at 11 o'c a.m. and continued again til 5 p.m. when the Bps. terminated, having resolved 1st, that a committee of their number should wait on Sir G. Grey to learn officially what measures they could receive from the Government; 2ndly, it was resolved that no compromise should be allowed: that the Queen's Colleges should be unequivocally condemned, and nothing allowed that should be in any way a mixed education. 3^{rdly}, that whilst the evils of the Model schools and National schools were also condemned, any step towards the recognition of the Catholic rights to an equal share in the educational grants would be accepted, etc, etc.

"You will be glad to learn," Moran then assured Kirby, "that the Bishops seem quite orthodox on the point of keeping the Catholic University in their own hands, and in not allowing the laymen to get any hold of the Board. At the meeting of the Bishops, everything went on very peaceably. Dr. MacHale was very quiet the first day, but on the second he made a great display of a letter received by him from Cardinal Barnabò on the subject of education, and approving in the most eulogistic strain of Dr. MacHale's course in some particular questions." "Tell Rinaldini," Moran advised, naming the undersecretary of Propaganda, "that such letters do a great deal of harm, and several of the Bishops expressed their surprise that Rome should allow such weakness, in writing this to one who is the only dissentient from their body, and whose labours seem all directed to impede the University and every other good work that the others seek to carry on." "Dr. Butler of Limerick," Moran further reported, "in reply gave Dr. MacHale a good lesson; and as Dr. MacHale had said everything should be done as it was in Maynooth, Dr. Moriarty gave Maynooth such abuse as he alone could give. He said amongst other things, that if you wanted a model of blundering and mistakes you should point to the Board of Maynooth, and as for discipline, he added, I have been seriously deliberating on withdrawing all my students from it entirely, and sending them to Paris and Rome." Turning to their mutual friends in Dublin Moran then assured Kirby, "Dr. Forde [the influential vicar-general of the Dublin diocese] is as usual and quite orthodox about the University Board. I met David Dunne; he is quite strong, and is now the factotum of the University, being, as they tell me, of great service to Mgr. Woodlock with whom he cooperates in everything. He seems however tinged with the opinion of Dr. Woodlock about the lay Board."

The following day, August 26, when Cullen sent Barnabò his promised report of the meeting, he appeared somewhat less pessimistic than he had been immediately after the meeting about what might eventually be achieved.[17] "After having examined what was known of the Government's plan," Cullen reported, "the bishops seeing that it was not possible to make a judgement about a plan not yet well defined, it was decided to charge the four archbishops to ask the govern-

17. S.R.C., vol. 35, fols. 391–92. See also K, Cullen to Kirby, August 27, 1865.

ment for an exact statement of the concessions that it wishes to make to us, and to explain in greater detail what it proposes." "It was then decided," he noted further, "to adjourn our meeting until a reply was received from the Government. I shall then call the bishops together again. The four archbishops were also charged to propose to the government the suppression of the national model schools that are mixed and which do us much harm." "I shall write," Cullen then promised,

> more at length about this business in a few days, but meanwhile I shall beg your Eminence to write again ordering that the new meeting be held as the last was held [i.e., canonically]—it may be that such an order may not be necessary, but it must be ready to answer Monsignor McHale who appears very disposed to prevent us from arriving at a happy result. I beg you moreover to tell me your sentiments on the proposal to enroll the bishops with Protestants on the Senate of the new University. It seems that there is a similar mixture in the council of education in France. Many believe that the bishops would be able to do good in that new office—but the union of light and darkness appears to me so repugnant that I am not much in favor of such a union for education, but for the granting of academic degrees, I shall not say anything adverse.

"It may be," he advised in conclusion, "that the secretary of state in London will give us an interview very soon. I should be much obliged to your Eminence if you would consent to give me a list very soon about what ought to be done."

When all the various reports and accounts of the bishops' meeting are taken into consideration, what emerges is that the position the bishops had worked out as a body on the education question on all its various levels in 1859 was not about to be compromised by them. Indeed, their position in the interim had, if anything, actually hardened. They were still determined about demanding denominational education on all levels, and the Queen's Colleges, the model schools, and even the national system were no more acceptable than they had been in 1859. As far as the Catholic University was concerned, moreover, they were apparently now even more determined not to brook any interference from the laity in the governing body. What really distinguished the bishops as a body at this meeting, however, was their decision to appoint a committee to deal directly with the British government in the person of the home secretary, Sir George Grey. In refusing in the first instance to treat with Bruce in Dublin at their meeting, and in deciding in the second instance to bypass the Irish government in the persons of the viceroy, Lord Wodehouse, and the chief secretary for Ireland, Sir Robert Peel, the Irish bishops were, in fact, asserting their right as a body to negotiate with the cabinet through their respective intermediaries. The bishops thus not only asserted their corporate identity in the de facto political complex but also showed a determination to establish their right to be consulted at the highest level of government in educational matters, and thereby they took a giant step in consolidating their position as a body.

On August 27 Cullen wrote Sir George Grey requesting the interview for the four archbishops resolved on by the bishops at their meeting.[18] In his reply the next day, Grey agreed to an interview but added that it could not be conveniently held until November because Parliament was not in session and most of his colleagues were still in the country.[19] When Lord Palmerston, the prime minister, then suddenly died on October 18, and the government had to be restructured, there was a further delay in arranging a meeting; finally it was scheduled for late November. "I came over to London," Cullen reported to Kirby on November 30, "with Dr. McHale, Dr. Leahy, and Dr. Dixon to treat with the Government about education. Sir George Grey received us today. We laid our grievances in the strongest terms before him and his colleagues in the Ministry, Mr. Cardwell, Mr. Gladstone, and Mr. Bruce. We showed how Trinity College and the Queen's Colleges were placed in a position to exercise a baneful influence by their wealth and attractions over Catholics whilst we were left without the power of giving degrees or holding out any attraction to students—Sir G. Grey gave us good hopes that something would be done for us" (K). "We also spoke about the National System," Cullen added, "and condemned it very strongly. They appear disposed to listen to us at present. God grant that they may do so." "Dr. Manning," he then noted, referring to the new archbishop of Westminster, "has just called on us returning a visit which we paid him yesterday. He was not at home. He is most anxious to cement a union between the Irish and English clergy if possible." "Of course," he assured Kirby, "we are all anxious to be united but dummodo [provided] we unite on fair terms."[20]

18. *Parliamentary Papers*, 1866, 55:243–59, no. 3.
19. Ibid., no. 4.
20. See Shane Leslie, "Irish Pages from the Postbags of Manning, Cullen, and Gladstone," *Dublin Review* 165 (1919): 163, for Manning's terms. "My belief is," he wrote Cullen on December 8, 1865, "that the bishops in England would desire to avoid con-

Several days later, on his return to Dublin, Cullen wrote Kirby again about his recent visit to London. "Our interview with the ministers," he explained on December 3, "is likely to do good. We put our claims on Catholic grounds, and insisted upon getting fair play for Catholics. We urged the granting of a charter to the Catholic University, and also an endowment, and the suppression of the mixed system of education. We got good promises. God grant they may be fulfilled" (K). Cullen also wrote Barnabò that same day, reporting his visit to London, but did not enter into any details.[21] A week later, however, he wrote Barnabò again. "In my last letter," he explained on December 10, "I mentioned that the four archbishops had visited the home secretary in London to discuss the Catholic University and the national system of education. We were very well received, but nothing was decided. After our conference the secretary made some kind remarks and then said, [']put all that you desire in writing, we shall examine your scheme, and then we shall do as much as possible to satisfy you.[']"[22] "In order to determine what ought to be done in these circumstances," Cullen reported, "the bishops will meet again on the 19th of this month here in Dublin. From what we have been able to gather from the words of the ministers who received us we are hoping that the mixed system will be abolished in Ireland, which would be a great blessing." "I shall write in greater detail after the meeting of the bishops," he promised in concluding.

The day before the meeting, however, Cullen wrote Barnabò again. "Availing myself of the authority given me by the Holy Father," he reported on December 18, "I have convened the bishops for Tuesday, 19 of this month, in order to determine what further steps we ought to take in regard to the education question. The government has declared itself disposed to make important concessions to us, but not to concede all that would be required to make education in this region fully Catholic."[23] "There will be some difficulty on this point among the bishops," he explained to the cardinal. "The greater part are disposed to accept everything that is a step towards the recognition of our rights, believing that it is not possible to obtain at a stroke all that we desire. Monsignor McHale appears disposed to accept nothing, if

---

tact with all political parties and to maintain a perfect independence, requiring of all Governments two things: (1) A cessation of the Anti-Roman policy in Italy; (2) justice to Catholics in the full sense, especially in education and the treatment of our prisons and poor."

21. S.R.C., vol. 35, fol. 440, December 3, 1865.
22. Ibid., fol. 452.
23. Ibid., fols. 451, 454.

the government does not give us a system totally Catholic. He will not be happy until the government overturns the present national system from top to bottom, and he seems to seek the same fate for the Catholic University. I do not know if he will come to our meeting, but in any case we will seek to do the best we can, and I hope that we will meet at least without doing harm to religion."

Cullen's newfound optimism regarding the various aspects of the education question, except for his usual forebodings about MacHale, must have been partially prompted by a piece of news he learned while he was in London conferring with Grey and his cabinet colleagues: his inveterate enemy in the Irish administration, Sir Robert Peel, was about to be succeeded as chief secretary for Ireland by Chichester S. Fortescue, M.P. for county Louth, whom Cullen liked and respected. Though Fortescue was an Irish Protestant, and known to be in favor of the principle of mixed education, he was not accounted a fanatic. He apparently contacted Cullen early on to ascertain what might be done about one of the proposals in Bruce's "Memorandum," which had been objected to by the committee of the cabinet appointed to deal with the Irish education question. The troubling proposal was the fourth, which provided for the representation of Catholic bishops on the senate of the proposed Royal Irish University by virtue of their office as bishops. The cabinet committee apparently objected not only because it thought the *ex officio* principle bad in itself but also because the proposal involved admitting that ecclesiastics had an inherent right to control over education. "The only point of any importance," Fortescue assured the new prime minister, Earl Russell, on December 20, while the bishops were still meeting in Dublin, "remaining to be decided before the new charter for the 'Royal University of Ireland' can be completed, is whether the charter shall provide for two R. Catholic Bishops (and of course two Bishops of the Established Church), having seats in the Senate."[24]

"The committee of the Cabinet," he reminded Russell, "as you will remember, were opposed to such a provision, though desirous that seats in the Senate should be offered to the Bishops. I have been trying to ascertain whether they would accept such an offer, and am satisfied they would not." "They say they have confidence in the present government," he explained, going on to refer to the Irish attorney general in the last Conservative government, "but not in a Whiteside Gov^t, w^h may succeed it, and that their position in the Senate w^d be neither secure nor dignified, unless ensured to them by the charter." "Now I

24. Russell Papers, 30/22/15, Public Record Office, London.

am convinced," he warned Russell, "that a breach with the R.C. Bishops on such a point as this will go far to destroy the success of our whole plan—and I earnestly trust that you and the cabinet will not allow this to happen. The object is to give confidence to the several denominations in the working of this mixed & undenominational University, by admitting a few representatives of the religious bodies into the Senate. The presence of two R.C. prelates among a body of 30 or 32 Senators, will have that effect beyond anything else so far as the R.C.'s are concerned, while I don't see how it can do harm in other ways." "If we think," he asked cogently in conclusion, "that, under the circumstances of this country, they ought to be there, and are ready to place them there, can there be any vital objection to recognize that fact by the terms of the charter itself?" "I think, Wodehouse," he added in a postscript, referring to the viceroy, "is prepared to take this view & is sending to Sir G. Grey a letter of mine on the subject." In the event, the cabinet accepted Fortescue's advice and agreed that two Catholic bishops should be in the senate by virtue of their office.

"We have just finished our meeting," Cullen informed Kirby on December 22 (K). "Dr. McHale," he then explained, "did not attend and did not write to me explaining his absence, but it was stated by Dr. Derry that his Grace had a cold—for my part, I was glad he did not come." "At our meeting," he reported, "we drew up a long petition to Sir G. Grey asking a charter for the Catholic University and an endowment, and we framed a form of charter, which would leave all power in the Bishops. As to the new University proposed by the Government, we said nothing to condemn or approve it, but we stated that it could not be admitted if it sanctions mixed education for the Queen's Colleges." "The great difficulty in the case is," Cullen pointed out, "can Bishops take a place on the Senate of the University—some said they might, others said not. But the wish was that the Holy See decide the difficulty—regarding the National Board, we asked for separate schools, and Catholic books for Catholics, and also training schools for Catholics. Our whole object was to get Catholic schools for Catholics." "Altogether," he noted approvingly, "we did our business very fairly. Dr. Woodlock is getting the papers printed, petitions, charters and all—I will send them in a day or two to the Propaganda—and a copy to you." "The question now is," he noted shrewdly, "shall we get anything from the Government? I fear not—if not, it is possible that our University will fall—as many Bishops and priests won't make collections and Dr. McHale prohibits them in his diocese."

Cullen also wrote Barnabò that same day, December 22, to explain that he would send a full account in a few days.[25] On December 24, therefore, he forwarded a very long, detailed, and able account of the meeting to Barnabò.[26] After reporting that the meeting had been attended by three archbishops and twenty-three bishops and that the absentees were the archbishop of Tuam and the bishops of Meath, Killala, Kilmacduagh, and Killaloe, Cullen noted that the absence of the four bishops was explained by their incapacitation owing either to age or to illness. "The meeting," he further reported, "was entirely taken up with the question of higher and lower education, and it was decided to send a memorial to the government explaining our position and asking them to concede to us what we have a right to." He elaborated:

> Regarding higher or academic education, we have demonstrated that nothing as yet has been done for Catholics, while to the Protestant University of Dublin income and property of immense value have been conceded to the members of the Established Church who are very few compared to Catholics, and the Queen's Colleges and University are also richly endowed, which being condemned, serve only the Presbyterians, and who do not count much religiously. Hence we have asked that the right of conferring university degrees be given to the Catholic University, and that a sufficient endowment be conceded to the same.
>
> This last demand was necessary, because having the Protestant University and the Queen's Colleges vastly endowed, they exercise an influence that we can not possibly resist if we are obliged to depend on collections for the maintenance of our University. Our difficulties are further increased in that Monsignor McHale prohibits every collection in his diocese for the University and many parish priests availing themselves of his example do not ask their parishioners for anything for the Catholic University.
>
> The power of conferring degrees is also necessary because there are many careers to which the candidates are not admitted without degrees or certificates of study from a legally recognized University. In truth matters are so arranged in favor of the government Universities, that those who do not go to them are exposed to heavy burdens. For example if one wishes to become a lawyer he can take his diploma after three years of study of the law, if he has taken any degree in the Protestant University, but

25. S.R.C., vol. 35, fol. 457.
26. Ibid., fols. 459–62.

if he has been a student in the Catholic University, and has not a legally recognized degree, he cannot take a diploma until after five years of legal studies, and without paying for the law lectures, and for the diploma, an amount very much greater than that paid by the others.

"After having demanded," Cullen pointed out, "what would be necessary to place us in a condition of equality with Protestants, we come to the plan that the government has put forward, and to the concessions to which for the present they wish to limit themselves." He detailed the plan:

The project of the government is

1.⁰ to abolish the Queen's University

2.⁰ to institute a new University called the Royal Irish University, or something similar

3.⁰ to limit the functions of this new University to examining students, and to the granting of academic degrees, or rather to choose every year examiners, who after the necessary proof, will determine which students are worthy of degrees in law, medicine, and the arts, the degrees thus conferred in the name of the University. From this it is seen that the new University will be something like the jury d'examen that they have in Belgium, and perhaps that exists in France.

4.⁰ that the Senate of the new University will be composed of thirty-two persons, sixteen Catholics and sixteen Protestants. In the first instance the Senate will be chosen by the Government, however we have been assured that the Catholics will be nominated after having consulted our bishops. Afterwards the Catholics would choose the Catholics if one of their places were vacated and the Protestants would do the same. There would not be elections however in every case of vacancy because the government proposes that there be certain persons who by virtue of their office should always be members of the Senate. These persons are not yet settled but the president [*sic*] of the council of education in England proposes that they be two Catholic archbishops, two Protestant archbishops, the head of the Presbyterian Synod, and the president of Maynooth College.

"These few transactions," Cullen noted, "will give an idea of what the government proposes to do with regard to the Senate of the proposed Royal University. The government however has not given us anything in an official form, because, I suppose, they do not wish us to examine what they propose, and the ministers do not wish to make firm promises in order not to compromise themselves with Parliament. In sum, up to now this business is treated privately and without anything from the ministers, as such, being put in writing."

"In dealing with the government's proposal in our letter to the secretary of state," Cullen then assured Barnabò,

the bishops confined themselves to saying "we acknowledge in the plan of the government a proof of its good will to concede to our flocks an instalment of justice in educational matters to which we are entitled; but if a proper endowment be not given to the Catholic University, and if the Queen's Colleges are not reconstructed, we can not regard the said plan as satisfactory to the Catholics of Ireland." We have also said that "we shall be grateful for the changes proposed by the government provided they are made in a way that does not meddle with Catholic education, and tend to renew the inequalities that exist between Protestants and Catholics.["] In expressing these sentiments, however, I deemed it a duty to condemn or to renew our condemnation of mixed academic education, on which the Queen's Colleges are founded, and which in conformity with the repeated declarations of our church, we regard as intrinsically dangerous to the faith and morals of Catholics.

Afterwards the bishops said that they were convinced that the government wishing to make an act of benevolence towards Catholics will not refuse when they will come to execute their plan, to accompany it with various concessions which they enumerated.

The first is that the Catholic University in the quality of a college be given in connection with the new University all the rights of a civil corporation, leaving the education in the hands of Catholics, and under the authority of the bishops who founded it.

2 that an endowment be given to the Catholic University.

3° that all the scholarships already existing and all the public prizes according to learning, be accessible to the student[s] of the Catholic University, or that new scholarships or prizes be instituted in favor of the said students.

4. that the Catholic University will have the power to adopt as its students the young men who study in other Catholic colleges, being examined and registered as belonging to the University. It must be observed that this condition would be very advantageous to Catholics. We have many private colleges, where the young men would be able to study without exposing themselves to dan-

gers to which they would be subject in a large city, and then being examined by professors of the Catholic University, would be able to take their degrees in the legal University.

5 & 6 that the exams are conducted in a way as to say or do nothing against the Catholic Church, and

7° that the system of the Queen's Colleges be changed.

Together with this letter to the government it is proposed to submit the form of the act of incorporation which we are asking for the Catholic University, leaving the same in the hands of the Catholic bishops.

"I shall send under separate cover the following documents," Cullen promised. "First, the address of the bishops to the home secretary, regarding higher education, and the copy of the proposed recognition of the Catholic University, as well as another address to the same minister requesting changes in the system of national education. I am having printed for private use all these documetns, and I hope they will be ready two or three days after the holidays."

"When your Eminence will have read this long letter," Cullen assured the cardinal, "you will have before you a brief exposition of all that we have done at our recent meeting. It seems to me that when you will have read the printed documents, which I hope to send in a few days, you will see that we have not admitted anything, or asked anything that could be prejudicial to our religion. In writing to the government, however, we have passed over in silence a question of importance and which will be necessary to introduce in putting into execution the plan of a new University." He explained:

As I said the government proposes that the Senate of the said University ought to consist of sixteen Protestants, and that some of the Catholics be bishops or priests. As for this union of Catholics and Protestants regarded in itself, it may not always be avoided in countries such as this, and then it may be that the Catholics placed in such an office will be able to do something to protect and promote the interests of Catholics, and to remove from Protestants a little some of that influence they have always enjoyed up to the present in educational matters. Besides being only a question of examinations in law, medicine and arts or rather being only a question of deputizing examiners in such faculties, it appears very evident that the Catholics, supposing that they are in the Senate, will not be constrained to do anything contrary to religion or that tends to promote mixed education in the schools, on the contrary the reason for which they will take office will be akin to having occasion to encourage purely Catholic education, and to impede the progress of mixed schools. For this reason the bishops in general are not able to see any sufficient reason for not taking places in the new Senate, if they were chosen.

"On the other side, however," Cullen noted, "there arose some doubts." He outlined the principal reservation:

According to the plan of the Government the powers of the Senate will be confined to examining the students of the Catholic University and the three Queen's Colleges. The young Catholics, who in spite of ecclesiastical authority make their studies in the Colleges already condemned many times, at the end of their course, will have the right to demand degrees from the new Senate, and if the bishops were members of it, consenting to the said demand would appear to approve the conduct of the said young men and to encourage mixed education in the condemned colleges. This reflection has made a great impression here on some bishops. Perhaps it would be possible to reply here that the new Senate will not give degrees to anyone because he has studied in the Queen's Colleges rather than in the Catholic University, but will confine itself solely to conferring honors on those who are distinguished for their progress in knowledge, in a word, that the knowledge or the ability of the student will be rewarded, and not his disobedience to the church, which will not officially come before the Senate.

"Whatever may be said of this answer," Cullen again assured the cardinal, "the bishops are determined not to accept any place in the Senate of the proposed University, if the Holy See shall not have first declared that the accepting of such posts is lawful or at least tolerated." "I hope that your Eminence," Cullen concluded, "will examine the question as soon as possible because if something is not done before the meeting of Parliament on February 1, next, nothing will be done this year. We shall not send the letters to the secretary of state until your Eminence will have read them. If what you will deign to write contains nothing disapproving, we shall send them to their fate."

On December 29 Cullen forwarded to Barnabò a copy of the memorial on the university question he had prepared in the name of the bishops for Sir George Grey.[27] In sending a copy to Kirby that same

27. Ibid., fol. 470.

day, Cullen amusingly assured him that there was nothing in it "contra fidae or mores" and asked him to have Barnabò give it approval as "Nihil obstat quominus mittatur [Not containing anything that would prevent it from being forwarded]" (K). He also asked Kirby to have news of its approval telegraphed to him to expedite matters, and Barnabò did as he asked on January 8, 1866.[28] Meanwhile, on December 31, Cullen had sent copies of both the memorial on university education and the memorial on the national system of education, which had been drawn up by the archbishop of Cashel, Patrick Leahy, to a number of the bishops for their opinions and advice (G). When he learned that Barnabò had no objection to the memorial on university education, Cullen had both memorials printed, and on January 10 he distributed them to the bishops for their approval. On January 12 Cullen informed the bishop of Elphin that notice had just reached him from Kirby that the pope had read and approved both memorials (G). Kirby was also of the opinion, he informed Gillooly, that the pope favored having bishops sitting in the senate, but he was still awaiting the official approval of the proposal. MacHale had refused to sign the memorials, but Cullen had written him again informing him of the pope's approval and was awaiting his reply.

On January 14 Cullen finally forwarded to Grey both memorials and a petition to the queen for a charter of incorporation for the Catholic University as a College, without MacHale's signature.[29] The bishops' memorial regarding the system of national education was, in effect, yet another demand that the system be so modified as to make it essentially denominational.[30] The system under the control of the Board of National Education, the bishops pointed out, could be divided into two classes, the ordinary, or primary, national schools and the model, or secondary, schools. The primary schools were essentially of two kinds, those that were exclusively Catholic or Protestant and those that were mixed. The bishops maintained that the first kind, which were denominational in fact, should be made so in law. In the second kind, the mixed schools, the chief problem was guarding against the spirit of proselytism, and the remedy was to return to the original rules, which had been modified by the national board over the years since the inception of the system to the great detriment of the Catholic pupils in the system, particularly in the most Presbyterian

28. Ibid., fol. 471.
29. *Parliamentary Papers*, 1866, 55:243–59, no. 7. See also Patrick Francis Moran, ed., *The Pastoral Letters and Other Writings of Cardinal Cullen* (Dublin, 1882), 2:450–62.
30. *Parliamentary Papers*, 1866, 55:243–59, no. 7, enclosure 1.

areas of Ulster. The second class, the model schools, was even more objectionable because the Catholic bishops and clergy had no control over any aspect of the education offered in them. Nothing would, in fact, satisfy the Catholic bishops, clergy, and people but that those schools be abolished altogether and their buildings utilized as reformatories or denominational training schools for teachers, which were sorely needed and would be of great national benefit.

The greater part of the bishops' memorial on university education was taken up with their grievances concerning the opportunities for the higher education of Irish Catholics.[31] They pointed out the privileged position Protestants and Presbyterians enjoyed in Trinity and the Queen's Colleges in regard to endowments, exclusivity, and academic degrees, and the inferior position of the Catholic University in regard to those privileges. To remedy the patent inequality, the bishops pointed out that the Catholic University College should receive a charter of incorporation from the state, be suitably endowed out of public funds, and be empowered to affiliate colleges and schools to itself; they argued further that prizes and scholarships should be made available to all on the basis of merit. The bishops also recommended that the "tests of knowledge," or the examining function of the proposed new University, should be conducted in such a way as to avoid even the appearance of connecting them with a system (i.e., the Queen's University and Colleges) which their system of religion condemned, and they urged that those tests should also be secured against "the exercise of any influence hostile or prejudicial to the religious principles of Roman Catholics." Finally, the bishops demanded that the Queen's Colleges be rearranged on a denominational basis— that is, Belfast for Presbyterians and Cork and Galway for Catholics.

In asking for a charter of incorporation of the proposed Catholic University College, the bishops had proposed in their memorial a draft of a charter that they thought would be suitable.[32] Among the more important elements outlined in it were that the four archbishops of Armagh, Dublin, Cashel, and Tuam were to be by virtue of their offices perpetual governors of the College. In addition, the bishops, eight in number, of Clonfert, Ardagh, Waterford, Kildare, Elphin, Ferns, Killaloe, and Dromore were to be life governors. The four archbishops were also to be the visitors of the College, and their authority was to be supreme "in questions regarding religion or morals and in all other things in the College." The governors, perpetual and life,

31. Ibid., enclosure 2.
32. Ibid.

were to have full power to appoint and remove "the Rector, Vice-Rector, the Professors, and other members of the Faculties, the Tutors and Masters, as also the Secretary, and all officers, agents and servants of the said College." There was also to be a council of the College, which was to consist of the rector, vice-rector, five deans of faculties, a dean of discipline, and three other members of the corporation. The last four members of the council were to be appointed by the governors, and five members of the council were to constitute a quorum. Finally, the four visitors were to be the trustees of all property belonging to the College, and the governors were also to have the power of appointing the treasurer or treasurers. In a word, the bishops, as represented by the governors, were to have absolute control of the College.

On January 16, two days after he had forwarded the memorials and the petition for a charter to Grey, Cullen sent three copies to Kirby. Besides complaining that MacHale alone of all the bishops had refused to sign, though he had written to him twice, Cullen also reported that he had heard the government was disappointed because the bishops had not asked for a mixed senate. Several days later, on January 20, Cullen wrote Kirby's vice-rector, Patrick Moran, reporting that he had sent the memorials the week before but had not as yet received any answer (K). "I fear," he confessed, "we shall get very little for all our trouble. However, we have, I think, put a fair statement of our grievances and our claims before them, and if nothing can be done now, something may be obtained hereafter."[33] "The Government," he pointed out shrewdly, "is probably afraid to get into difficulties with the English and Scotch Liberals who are ready enough to assail the Protestant Church, but who are quite opposed to Catholic education." "Kindest regards to Dr. Murray, Dr. Quinn (if they be with you)," he then added most interestingly, naming the recently consecrated bishops for Maitland and Bathurst in Australia, respectively, who both had been Dublin priests and alumni of the Irish College in Rome, "and to Dr. Kirby—get the whole of them to call on the Cardinal and to make him say an expediat aut liceat ut episcopi locus accipiant in senatu N. Universitatis [whether it is expedient or lawful for bishops to accept a place in the senate of the National University]. Tell the Cardinal that we shall be split into parties if he do not write *Auctoritate apostolica* [By the apostolic authority] very soon." "The reason," Cullen then

33. See also G, Cullen to Gillooly, January 10, 1866, in which Cullen argued that there was no point in making a strong statement of their principles in the memorials to a government that does not care in the least about those principles. The government wanted to know only what grievances they had to complain of. Cullen thought it better to save principles for their Lenten pastorals.

added in a postscript, "I think, of Dr. McHale's opposition to the proposed Senate of the N.U. is that he imagines that he would not be put on it himself. For my part I would much rather have nothing to do with it—but if I [am] put on it quid agendum [what then]." By the end of the month Cullen had apparently received the required approval, for he wrote the bishop of Elphin on January 31, explaining that the pope had left it to the prudence of the bishops themselves to decide whether they would take seats in the senate. The pope had also advised that the government should not be allowed to pick and choose among the bishops. What he meant, of course, was that though the government would have the right of appointment, the bishops as a body should have the right to nominate those of their body who would serve on the senate.

Cullen had hardly written Gillooly when he received Grey's reply, dated January 30, to the bishops' memorial on university education (W). Grey began by assuring Cullen plainly that the Government had no intention of modifying the Queen's Colleges or the mixed principle on which those Colleges had been founded and were being conducted. The government admitted, however, that there were a large number of Catholics who had a conscientious objection to the mixed principle, and it was therefore prepared to modify the charter of the Queen's University to allow those who had such an objection to take degrees. The government trusted, Grey added, that when that charter was revised, and the composition of the new senate was settled, the equality sought for by the government for the higher education of Catholics in Ireland would be attained.

Grey then turned to the draft of the charter of incorporation of the Catholic University College presented by the bishops. The government was unable, he explained, to advise Her Majesty to grant it in the form proposed. "Without adverting to the other points which will require revision," Grey added, "Her Majesty's Government think it essential that, while due precaution is taken for the protection of Faith and Morals of the Students in such a College, for which purpose the Archbishops might be constituted Visitors, its governing body, if it is to receive a Charter from the Crown, shall not be entirely composed of Ecclesiastics, but should contain a considerable proportion of Laymen." The government was in fact willing to suggest a form of charter that might be properly granted. Grey then took up the remaining points recommended by the bishops in their memorial. The government refused to consider an endowment but was prepared to propose the granting of a sum for burses and scholarships, open competitively to all students without distinction in the new University. The government, however, was adverse to chartering a College with the right to affiliate to itself other Colleges or Schools because this privilege, it felt, belonged properly to a University. Finally, the government agreed that the senate of the new University should be constituted to entitle it to the confidence of all the different religious denominations, and the government was prepared on that basis to entrust to the senate the whole regulation of examinations.

Though Cullen had, characteristically, become more cautious and less optimistic as the decisive day approached, he was still sorely disappointed when he finally received Grey's reply. He had the reply printed immediately and distributed it on February 2 to the Irish bishops. In forwarding a copy to Kirby that same day, he explained somewhat sourly that it did not really disappoint him because he had not expected very much (K). "I do not know," he then confessed, "what we shall do next about the education question. The government will do nothing good. They put us to a great deal of trouble, but after all we get nothing." On February 11, however, after an interview with Fortescue in Dublin, Cullen finally replied to Grey's letter, explaining that the delay had been occasioned by his having solicited the opinions of the Irish bishops.[34] "Having communicated your reply to those prelates," Cullen reported, coming straight to the point, "I regret to say that they are all of opinion that the promises held out to them in that document are far from corresponding to the hope which they had entertained; that the present Government so liberal and enlightened, would have taken some effective step to place them and their flock on a footing of equality with their fellow subjects of other religious denominations in regard to education." "However," he further explained, "they are not willing to give any decided opinion on this matter until they shall have seen the proposed Charter of the new University, and the draft of a Charter for the Roman Catholic University College in the form in which the Government would consider it admissable. May I take the liberty to request of you to give orders that copies of these two documents be sent to me." Grey in his reply had ignored their memorial on national education, and Cullen noted in conclusion, "I have now to add that the Roman Catholic Prelates are anxious to receive an answer to their memorial on national education, which was forwarded on the same day as the memorial on University Education."

Several days later the chief secretary finally forwarded Cullen a memorandum on the draft of each of the proposed charters, and Cullen immediately sent them to the other archbishops. "This moment," he informed the archbishop of Cashel on February 15, "I have rec^d the

34. *Parliamentary Papers*, 1866, 55:243–59, no. 11.

enclosed from Mr. Fortescue" (L). "The new University facilitates the obtaining of degrees," he complained, "and nothing more. All the members of the old Queen's University retain their places on the Senate. The persons selected to fill the Catholic portion are Mr. Monsell, The O'Conor Don, Mr. O'Reilly, Aubrey de Vere, Judge O'Hagan, Dr. Russell, Dr. Woodlock, Professor Sullivan, Lord Dunraven, two Prelates to be selected by their Catholic colleagues and two as yet not named. The proposed charter for the Catholic University is quite incomplete, and, I think, inadmissable." "Mr. Fortescue asks," Cullen noted, "if I have anything to suggest on those documents. Would Y^r Grace tell me what observations I ought to make[?]" "The two printed papers," he finally added, "are *Confidential*. The answer regarding the National Schools will soon be given. I suppose we must hold a meeting of the Bishops to settle matters as soon as possible."

The two documents make interesting reading, and it is little wonder that Cullen was something less than enthusiastic about them. Regarding the charter for the Catholic University, the memorandum read:

Heads of a Proposed Charter of Incorporation for the Roman Catholic University College.
 The Rector and Professors to form the Body Corporate
 The Four Archbishops to be Visitors and Trustees.
 The Rector to be appointed by the Visitors
 Vacant Professorships to be filled up by the Rector and Professors after *concursus*
 The Visitors have the power to reject any person nominated to a Professorship, and to dismiss any existing Professor upon the ground of his having been proved, upon due inquiry, to be justly liable to censure in respect to faith or morals
 The property of the College to be vested in the Trustees [L]

The memorandum concerning the proposed new University read:

 The Charter recites and revokes the original Charter of the Queen's University, and constitutes a University under the name of the Queen's Irish University.
 The body politic, which succeeds to all the powers and liabilities of the former corporation, to consist of a Chancellor, Vice-Chancellor, Senators (including the Senators of the Queen's University), and Students.[35]

35. "Students" appears to be crossed out.

The Senate to consist of thirty-four members, half Protestant, and half Roman Catholics

Five Senators to be always ecclesiastics, namely two prelates of the United Church of England and Ireland, two prelates of the Roman Catholic Church of Ireland, the Moderator of the General Assembly of the Presbyterian Church for the time being.

The first appointment of Senators to be made by the Crown

Future vacancies to be filled by the Crown, the Senate, and Convocation successively—subject to the condition that the successor of a Protestant Senator shall be a Protestant, the successor of a Roman Catholic Senator a Roman Catholic.

With the exception also of the ecclesiastical places in the Senate, which are to be filled as follows: —In case of a vacancy in one of the places filled by an Archbishop or Bishop, such other Archbishop or Bishop of the United Church of England and Ireland, or of the Roman Catholic Church, as the case may be, to succeed, as shall be recommended by the majority in number of the prelates of the said Church and approved of by the Crown.

The Moderator for the time being to be the fifth ecclesiastical Senator.

In case of no recommendation as above, being made within three months, the Crown to appoint an Archbishop or Bishop.

In case of the Moderator declining to act, the Crown to appoint some other Presbyterian minister.

All elections to the Senate to be subject to the approval of the Crown.

The three Queen's Colleges, the Roman Catholic University College, and the Magee College, to be Colleges in connection with the University.

The Colleges to be subject to their own Charters and Statutes, and not under the jurisdiction or control of the University, except as to qualifications for matriculation, degrees, and other University distinctions.

The Senate, with the consent of the Lord Lieutenant, to have power to add to the above mentioned Colleges, or any other Colleges, or institutions, and also to admit to degrees etc., persons not educated in any College in connection with the University on such conditions as they may determine.

Power to the Senate to found Fellowships, Scholarships, Prizes, etc. [L]

"I send you," Cullen informed Kirby the next day, February 16, "the charter of the new University, and also that proposed for the Catholic

University. This last is quite inadmissable" (K). "We could not," Cullen explained, going to the heart of the matter, "support the University if it were taken out of the hands of the Bishops. As it is, it is very difficult to get anything. In some dioceses the P.P.'s tell the people to give nothing. In a large town not very far from Dublin, the priest, a Bishop's curate, told the people that it was not expected that anyone giving silver would contribute more than five shillings. In Naas [in the diocese of Kildare and Leighlin] the P.P. collected fifteen pounds, but he said he would only give six as that was the sum recommended by the Bishop. Che miseria [What wretchedness]. He said the remainder would save him the trouble of a collection next year." "I have just received a new letter from Sir G. Grey," Cullen then reported in a postscript. "He has forwarded our memorial [i.e., the second memorial of the bishops to the government concerning the national system] to the Commissioners of Nat. Education to take it into consideration."

The following day, February 17, Cullen acknowledged the receipt of the government's memorandum on the draft charters, and on the eighteenth he wrote Fortescue again, delivering up his considered opinion (W). "Since I had the honour of writing to you on the 16th inst.," he explained, "I have attentively examined the draft charter for the Catholic University College and consulted the other Catholic Archbishops upon the same matter. Having done so I can now state that I am confident that all the Catholic Bishops will consider it inadmissible. When the bishops presented their memorial to the Government, they expected that something would be done to raise those who had suffered injustice and privation for the past to a level with others. The probable operation of the charter as proposed would be to deprive us of what we have, & to lower our condition. Being accustomed to disappointments we can wait in patience in our present position until the times will become more just and liberal." "As to the Charter for the Queen's Irish University," Cullen added,

> I cannot say whether the Bishops will consent to take any part in it or not, but I think that as soon as we shall have received an answer to our memorial on National Education the Bishops will meet, and decide on the course to be adopted. I shall with your permission make an observation on one of the clauses of the charter in which treating of the way of perpetuating the senate it is stated that future vacancies are to be filled by the Crown, the senate, and convocation successively. As the Lord Lieutenant who represents the Crown must be always a Protestant he might mistake the character of the persons to be appointed, and commit the care of Catholic interests to persons merely nominal

Catholics and very unfit guardians for such interests. Unhappily, it is to be admitted that there are many of this class in France, Italy, and even in Ireland, to whom we would not wish to trust the education of young Catholics. As the election in the second case would be made by a body consisting of equal numbers of Protestants and Catholics and as there might be some of the class just described in this last body, I do not think that Catholics would be well protected by such a system of election. As to the third manner of filling vacancies, I think it still more objectionable as the great majority of the convocation would consist at present and for many years to come of students of the Queen's Colleges who cannot be expected to entertain very kind feelings for the Catholic Church.

"I think all objections could be removed," Cullen suggested in conclusion, "by allowing the Protestant senators to fill up Protestant vacancies, and Catholic senators to exercise the same right in reference to their own body."

Fortescue, who at that moment had his hands full with the Fenian threat and the decision to suspend the Habeas Corpus Act in Ireland, was apparently anxious for some accommodation, at least, on the education question, if not a settlement. To add to Fortescue's problems, Sir Robert Peel, the disgruntled former chief secretary, had complicated matters even further by giving notice in the House of Commons of a question, fixed for February 23, about the proposed alteration in the Queen's University. "I have written this evening," a harassed Fortescue reported to the prime minister from Dublin Castle on February 22, "to Sir G. Grey with a view to Peel's motion on the University charter tomorrow. I trust that he, Lowe [former vice-president of the education board of the Privy Council and M.P. for Calne], & aided by our No-Popery Liberals, who are the great obstacle to doing right things for Ireland, may not be able to embarrass the Gov^t seriously."[36] "We have been expecting," he explained, "for several days an answer from D^r. Cullen to the unofficial communication which I made to him, by arrangement with Wodehouse, as soon as the Cabinet had finally decided on the draft charter.[37] I did not send him the draft,

---

36. Russell Papers, 30/22/16.

37. This is a most curious remark, for Cullen had written Fortescue on February 17, 1866, explaining that the provisions of the charters outlined in his memorandum would not do. Though the copy of this letter preserved in the Woodlock papers has no indication to whom it is addressed, it is presumed to be to Fortescue because Cullen mentioned such a letter three times in his letters to Woodlock: on February 18, 1866, he explained to Woodlock that he had written to Fortescue about the unsatisfactory way in which it was proposed to choose the senate of the new University (W); on February 23,

but a memorandum containing the principal provisions." "Difficulties have been made," Fortescue pointed out, revealing how little he understood his man, "more (I believe) by the other R.C. Archbishops than by himself. They say we have not granted their College charter yet—that their College will still be in a position of great disadvantage compared to the Queen's Colleges, that they have had no answer yet about National Education, —and that the provision for the election of Senators by the Senators and graduates is very objectionable." Fortescue dealt with these criticisms in some detail:

> As to the first objection, the charter of incorporation for the College, (upon which its affiliation to the University does not necessarily depend) will probably be arranged within a few days. I have sent Sir G. Grey the head of one which w^d be accepted.
>
> As for the next two objections, I have treated them as totally inadmissable.
>
> No prospect of Endowment has ever entered into these negotiations, publicly or privately, and if scholarships are to be attached to the University, as I hope will be the case, it cannot, of course, be done by Charter. With respect to the last objection, the only one which Dr. Cullen makes to the University charter, I think there is a good deal to be said. It is said not only by him, but by reasonable R. Catholics, that the present graduates, who are to elect nearly a third of the Senate, are all Queen's College men, the large majority of them Protestants, the rest what the priests and zealous members of the Church consider "bad Catholics," —and that these voters cannot be trusted to choose good Catholic Senators. It is true that if the system succeed, this state of things will in the course of years be reversed, but this is only an additional reason for taking some suitable precaution in the charter.
>
> Again, it is quite conceivable that the Protestant Senators reinforced by one or two R. Catholics might elect a Roman Catholic Senator against the wishes of all the rest; —or which I think

---

1866, he explained again that he had written Fortescue saying that the four archbishops had disapproved of the plan (W); and on February 26, 1866, he forwarded to Woodlock various copies of his *"official* correspondence on the University question—vid. a letter to Mr. Fortescue 17th Febr" (W). The only possible explanation is that Fortescue, for some reason, had not received Cullen's letter when he wrote Russell on February 22. Fortescue went on to quote, in effect, the substance of Cullen's objections, but he may have received that information from Monsell, who had been informed of Cullen's objections by David B. Dunne on February 17, 1866, after Dunne had had an interview with Cullen that same day. See M, 8318 (8), for that letter and also for another to Monsell on February 19, 1866.

more likely, —that the R. Catholic Senators reinforced in the same way might choose some Protestant politician who would be completely subservient to R. Catholic interests. These are possible dangers which ought not to stand in the way of a charter, as now decided upon. But I think they might be properly guarded against. The R. Catholics want to have the R.C. Senators elected by R.C.'s, the Protestants by Protestants, —as was originally proposed by Bruce & Monsell.

I have proposed to Sir G. Grey, that a proviso should be inserted in the charter, —to the effect that a Senator should require for his election, not only a majority of the whole number voting, but a majority of the votes of the religious denomination to which he himself should belong. This would meet the difficulty and give great satisfaction.

"I have given you a long explanation," Fortescue finally pointed out, "without answering the question which you put to me in your letter received this morning. What I meant in my former letter was, that, if the R.C. Bishops refuse to accept seats in the Senate, we ought to leave out that part of the draft charter which provides for the ecclesiastical Senators, and go on with the rest of it; and, if the R.C. College is not affiliated throw the University open to all comers." "At the same time," he assured Russell in concluding, "we ought to have something to show which will put us in the right, and the Bishops in the wrong, for which purpose I have sent Sir George Grey the draft of a letter to Dr. Cullen."

Meanwhile, as he had explained to Fortescue, Cullen had received replies from both Leahy and MacHale to the letter of February 15 in which he had enclosed the heads of the two proposed charters. Both archbishops agreed with Cullen that the proposals were inadmissible; they also felt that the government was not sincere in its desire to settle the education question, and MacHale reiterated his determination to have nothing to do with the proposed senate. In explaining all this on February 18 to Woodlock, who was in London on his instructions, holding a watching brief for the Catholic University, Cullen pointed out not only that he agreed with the other archbishops but also that he had sent to the archbishop of Westminster a copy of Sir George Grey's reply of January 30 to the bishops' memorial, and Manning had observed that it was evident from Grey's letter that the government was attempting to secularize education in Ireland and that he would not be a party to it (W). When Cullen wrote Barnabò that same day, February 23, he was even more pessimistic about their educational expectations.[38] "For the last two months," he explained,

I have been so much occupied in dealing with educational matters, and so entangled with the business of our people that I have not been able to find time to answer the various letters I have been honored with by your Eminence. The worst is that there has not been any good result from so much business. After having made the trip to London, and had a meeting, besides two meetings of the bishops dealing with education, after having written an immense number of letters on the same business, we have not been able to obtain anything. The government has rejected all our demands, and now it has been reduced to saying that if we put the Catholic University in the hands of the Rector and a council of lay professors, it will give to the same the right of possessing property in its own name, but at the same time refuses to endow it or to give it the right of conferring academic degrees, that is, it is trying to make us give up all that we have, without even offering any compensation.

"I imagine," Cullen prophesied in conclusion, "that the negotiations on national education will end up the same way."

By February 22 Cullen had come to the conclusion, as he pointed out to Woodlock, that it would be better now to defer the chartering of the Catholic University to a more propitious time (W). If the proposed charter for the new Queen's Irish University omitted all mention of the Queen's Colleges and the Catholic University, he went on, allowing the new University to be only an examining body, the bishops would probably accept it. If the government, however, insisted on mentioning the two constituent Colleges in the charter, it would be better perhaps to have two good priests in the senate rather than two bishops, because that would obviate any disputes among the bishops about accepting or not. Cullen's point, of course, was that accepting the charter for the new University with the Queen's Colleges officially designated would be tantamount to their recognition by the bishops as a body if their elected representatives were in the Senate, and this situation would undoubtedly result in a quarrel among the bishops. Cullen further instructed Woodlock to tell the government that neither he nor MacHale would accept places in the senate, and then he wrote Leahy to ask for his opinion in writing.

38. S.R.C., vol. 35, fols. 609–10.

When Cullen was interviewed the next day, Friday, February 23, by Monsell, Dunne, and W. K. Sullivan, dean of the faculty of medicine of the Catholic University, he told them, as he had explained to Woodlock, that though he could not speak for all the bishops, he could say that the four archbishops not only declined to serve on the senate but could not accept the charters offered by the government (W). Monsell and Sullivan, at least, if not also Dunne, were apparently very much annoyed and disappointed. "After I had closed this," Cullen explained to Kirby, whom he also wrote on February 23, "Mr. Monsell came to me and gave me a good rating because I would not say the two proposed *charters* which I sent you would be most beneficial to religion. I said if named I would not act on the Senate. He went away very much huffed. I think there is nothing worth accepting in the proposed charters. What is your opinion?" (K).

Over the weekend Cullen apparently resolved any doubts he might have had, for he composed a masterful letter to the Irish bishops on the subject of the recent negotiations. "On the 2nd of the present month," he informed the bishops by circular letter on Tuesday, February 27, "I forwarded to your Lordship a copy of Sir G. Grey's reply to our Memorial on University Education. As yet no answer has been given on the question of National Education; but Sir G. Grey has written to say that he had referred our Memorial to the Lord Lieutenant with instructions to submit it to the Commissioners of National Education, calling their attention to that portion of it which treats of Model and Training Schools. Probably an answer will be given in a short time. I have now to communicate to your Lordship two papers connected with the University question, which I have received from Mr. C. Fortescue" (L).

The first paper gives the outlines of a Charter for the Catholic University, in the shape in which the Government is disposed to grant it. According to this project the Rector and Professors of the University would form the body corporate, and have the right of naming the Professors; even those of theology and canon law do not seem to be excepted.

It is proposed to make the Archbishops Visitors of the University, and Trustees of the property, and to give them a veto on the appointment of professors, the power to appoint the rector, and to remove the rector and professors upon due inquiry. In the Queen's Colleges and in Maynooth, the Visitors are obliged to exercise their power in open court. If it be intended to introduce the same system into the University, the Visitors' control over the officers of the house would be very small indeed. How the property of the University is to be held is not really explained; but I suppose the Archbishops would hold it as Trustees for the corporate body.

As to the Bishops the proposed draft appears to exclude them altogether from any connection with the University. Your Lordship will recollect, that in his letter of 30th January, Sir George Grey informed us that the Government would grant us no endowment for the Catholic University; that no change would be made in the Queen's Colleges; and that other concessions which we asked for would not be granted.

Hence, were we to accept the Charter as proposed, we would agree to surrender the rights we now have without obtaining any advantages or privileges of doing so. The only privilege left to us would be that of collecting the funds for the support of a body over which little control would be left to us.

"As soon as I received the draft of the proposed Charter," Cullen reported, "I sent it to each of the other Archbishops, and having heard their views on it, I wrote to Mr. Fortescue informing him that the Archbishops considered that charter inadmissible, depriving us, as it would, of what we have, and giving us nothing in return. Since then, Mr. Fortescue has expressed his willingness to enter into further communications on the matter with the Bishops, but he has not communicated any new project." "My humble opinion is," Cullen added, "that fear of the opposition of Sir Robert Peel, and other bigots, will prevent the Government from doing anything."

"The second paper which I forward," Cullen further pointed out,

contains the heads of the Charter, by which it is proposed to convert the present Queen's University into the Queen's Irish University. This Charter would give our students a facility of taking out degrees in the new University. Such a measure is desirable; but it cannot be considered a very great concession, as we could have obtained a similar privilege from the London University, had we sought for it, any time within the last ten years. It is to be added, that several Catholic Colleges, both in England and Ireland, already enjoy this power of sending their students for examination to a University, so that the boon now offered to us would only put us on a level with them.

On the proposed Charter for the new University there are one or two observations to be made; the first regards the proposal to give the Catholic Bishops a place in the Senate.

Your Lordship will recollect that in his letter of the 30th January, ult., Sir George Grey entered into an elaborate defense of the Queen's Colleges and mixed education. I fear that the new Charter will be a practical carrying out of these sentiments, and contains a real appreciation of the Queen's Colleges and mixed education.

All the members of the Senate of the Queen's University are retained on the Senate of the new University: the three presidents of the Queen's Colleges will be members of it; the professors of the Queen's Colleges will have the style of Professors of it; the graduates of the Queen's University, nearly all Presbyterians and Protestants, and all students of the Queen's Colleges, are declared graduates of the new University.

The principal office of the Senate of the new University, will be to confer honours and degrees upon students who shall have passed their examination according to the prescribed form. Now, let us suppose that a Catholic student from the Queen's Colleges were to present himself to the Senate to receive honours, and that Catholic Bishops were there to sanction the proceeding by their presence and authority, assisting to confer such honours, would they not be liable to be reproached: "for years you have repeatedly condemned the Queen's Colleges and mixed education; now you come forward to reward a young man who has despised your denunciations, and exposed himself to all the dangers of a condemned system." Were I on the Senate I do not see how I could answer so serious a reproach.

"The other observation I wish to make," Cullen continued, "refers to the mode of filling up future vacancies in the Senate." He elaborated:

The Crown or the Lord Lieutenant, would have the right of filling up the first vacancy among the Catholics (I speak only of them), and, as he must be always a Protestant, he might select a Catholic of the Cavour or Ratazzi class, most hostile to everything Catholic, and injurious without being conscious that he was doing so.

Every second vacancy is to be filled up by the whole Senate; so that a body consisting of one half Protestants, with a mixture of Catholics such as those I have just referred to, or belonging to that school of which there are some already on the Queen's Senate, would have to select our representatives and supporters of our claims.

In regard to election by Convocation, the Presbyterian and Protestant students of the Queen's Colleges, who would constitute nearly the entire body of the graduates of the new University, would have for very many years a large majority at any election. This would be very unfavourable to us, as their numerous exhibitions of bigotry and hatred against Catholicity on late occasions, must convince us that they would exercise their powers in a spirit of decided hostility against our views and interests.

"Being convinced by careful examination of the two Charters," Cullen assured the bishops, "that were we to accept them, as now proposed, we might be placed in a position in which we would seem to have sacrificed our conscientious objections against the mixed system of the Queen's Colleges, without obtaining, by doing so, any solid advantage or any change in the system, I have not hesitated to write to the chief secretary, stating that so far as I was concerned, I would not act on the Senate if placed on it or offered; and I added, that whilst I could not speak for the body of the Bishops, I had received letters from the other Archbishops which gave me reason to assert that they would follow the same course I have adopted, leaving all responsibility in the case on the originators of the measure in its present shape." "It is greatly to be regretted," Cullen added for good measure, "that the government is not able to act more liberally towards us, as I am persuaded that a great and generous concession, in regard to education, would contribute very much to put an end to the spirit of discontent now so prevalent in the country." "It would be easy," he concluded, "to make further observations in this matter, but I will not trouble you with them, as it is probable that the violence of party spirit in Parliament will thwart the Government even in regard to this very little installment of justice which they propose to grant."

In forwarding copies of this letter to Woodlock the following day, February 28, Cullen reported that Myles O'Reilly, M.P. for county Longford, had just seen Fortescue, who had assured him that a satisfactory charter for the Catholic University could be arranged and that the government would agree to omit mention of all the Colleges, Queen's and Catholic, in the charter for the new University (W). He also advised Woodlock to trust only to what he could get in writing from the government. In the next few days the bishops who wrote Cullen and Kirby were apparently all of one mind about the unacceptability of the government's proposals. "We are not likely," the bishop of Dromore, John Pius Leahy, informed Kirby on March 1, "to obtain any concession worth taking from the Government in the matter of education. What they propose about the Catholic University would in my mind lead speedily to its destruction" (K). The next day the archbishop of Armagh wrote Kirby in the same vein. "I believe all our expectations," Dixon explained on March 2, "about concessions in the matter of university education will end in smoke. Such is the bitter hostility to Catholics in the Imperial Parliament that the Government, I suppose, could hardly carry anything through the house, which it would be worth our while to accept" (K).

The half dozen other bishops who took the trouble to reply to Cullen's circular of February 27 were unanimous in their disappointment with the government; several suggested that it was time perhaps for stronger measures in regard to mixed education. "The Queen's Colleges," the bishop of Galway, John MacEvilly, maintained on March 3, "are becoming a dreadful curse to the country, and something should be done to arrest their progress" (C). "Some years ago," he reminded Cullen,

> I took the liberty of suggesting at one of our General meetings, that all parties connected with the Queen's Colleges, pupils, parents, should be excluded from Sacraments. I am of the same opinion still, and I am convinced this course and this only will ever empty the Queen's colleges of Catholics. I know it is a bold course to pursue, but I am convinced that if [it] were carried out bona fide, and zealously in every Diocese of Ireland, the Queen's colleges would be emptied of Catholics before the lapse of five years. No doubt some Catholics would for a time brave all Ecclesiastical penalties, but these would be comparatively few and they would become fewer under the pressure of public opinion every day. And even [if] the same *few* were to continue disobedient, would a worse state of things arise than exists at present when a large number are in a state of antagonism with us? In order to adopt this course with any success, the action should be universal throughout Ireland and carried out with zeal and determination.

"Some time ago," MacEvilly then reported, referring to his cosuffragan, the bishop of Clonfert, "Dr. Derry wanted me to join in making the frequenting of the Queen's colleges a reserved case for this *Province*, but I declined to do so chiefly on the ground that such a course would be perfectly useless unless it were made general throughout Ireland. In point of fact, the majority of pupils frequenting the College here are from other Provinces." "I feel," MacEvilly then confessed, "that the answer sent me by the Cardinal Prefect on this subject in 1857 is to some extent unfavourable to such a course, but I should think the change of circumstances since then, and particularly the late mockery & delusion on the part of the Government, & their determination to force mixed education on us at all hazards would modify His Eminence's views on the subject." "Besides," he suggested finally to Cullen, "he leaves the determination of the question to the Bishop of each Diocese, & hence there is nothing to prevent them combining on the subject."

Cullen, however, was too prudent to allow his disappointment with the government to get the better of his temper by acting on MacEvilly's suggestion. Cullen's purpose was not simply to succeed with the government in his negotiations but rather to make sure that the bishops remained united in that process, for Cullen believed that as long as the bishops remained united the future was theirs on the education question. Such an initiative as that suggested by MacEvilly, therefore, was not to be then thought of, and when Cullen wrote Barnabò on March 6 he emphasized that in the face of all their disappointments, the bishops were determined to maintain their traditional policy with regard to the Queen's Colleges.[39] "Our negotiations on education with the Government are not yet terminated," he reported, "but I believe they will not have any result. Up to now the Government sought to make us approve of the Queen's Colleges, at least indirectly, promising us some trifle in return. I have written to the secretary of state for Ireland that it was useless to propose such things to us, and that we were determined to maintain at whatever cost the condemnation of the Queen's Colleges." "So far," he further explained, "they have not proposed anything to us, and it appears that the Government, although wishing to make some concessions to us, is too weak to resist the anti-Catholic spirit of the nominal Liberals, who are declared enemies of Catholic education, and who wish at any cost to introduce unbelief into the schools of Ireland."

When he had heard nothing further from the government two days later, a sadder but more stoic Cullen finally wrote Woodlock, who was still in London, suggesting that he come home. "The appearances," he explained on March 8, "are that faremo fiasco [we shall fail]. Mr. Fortescue went to London yesterday. He appears well disposed but what can he do[?] I think also that Mr. Monsell and Prof. Sullivan impressed him with the idea that the Government ought not to yield to the Bishops." "Perhaps, in the end," he then suggested, "it w^d be well to get up a deputation, and to ask the Government for a real University with the power of giving degrees and with an endowment.

39. Ibid., fol. 612.

Such a request w^d have been quite as well rec^d as our very trifling demands." "Dr. Leahy writes," Cullen reported, referring to the archbishop of Cashel, "that he fully approves of my letter to the bishops of which I sent you two copies. It w^d be well to give a copy of it to Mr. Dillon & Sir John Gray in order that they might understand our present position. I think the Government injures itself by making an important matter of trifling concessions." "When the people hear that our claims were rejected by the Government," he assured Woodlock in conclusion, "they will still support us."

Cullen, however, had yet another and perhaps even more important reason for not wanting to break with the government just at that moment. He was still awaiting the government's reply to the second of the bishops' memorials, on the national system of education. The government had referred the second memorial to the twenty commissioners who formed the Board of National Education, but the serious illness of the resident commissioner, Alexander MacDonnell, had prevented any immediate action on it. On April 11, after nearly three months, the joint secretaries to the Board of National Education finally wrote the undersecretary for Ireland, Sir Thomas Larcom, on behalf of the commissioners (C). "Concurring cordially and unanimously with the opinions expressed by Sir George Grey on behalf of Her Majesty's Government," the secretaries explained, referring to Grey's letter to the commissioners forwarding the bishops' memorial, "that the system of National Education 'is well adapted to the peculiar circumstances of Ireland,' and has been the means of conferring very great advantages on this country, the Commissioners also 'would regard with sincere regret any step tending to its overthrow.'" "But for many years," the secretaries further pointed out, "although pamphlets, essays, and books have been issued in great numbers, assailing the National Board in various ways, the Commissioners have never replied to any of these publications. They have regarded themselves as an administrative body, whose function is to act, and not to argue; and they have deliberately avoided any attempt at controversy, which conducted by them as a body would demand an impossible identity of opinion." "Continuing to believe," they then added, after explaining that in spite of all the hostile criticism over the past eight years, the number of schools in the system had increased from 5,408 to 6,372, "that the policy that they have heretofore pursued is wise and sound, as it has been successful, the Commissioners beg to be relieved from the necessity of departure from it, by making the observations on the Memorial of the Roman Catholic Prelates, which the letter of Sir George Grey invites them to offer."

Sir Thomas Larcom forwarded this letter to the viceroy, Lord Wodehouse, who then sent it on to Grey on April 18, with a brief covering note of his own (C). "I will merely remark," Wodehouse noted, "that the unequivocal, and increasing success of the present system, furnishes a strong argument against any departure from the main principles on which it is founded." After a further delay of more than two weeks, Grey finally wrote Cullen on May 4, enclosing the letters of the viceroy and the commissioners. In effect, Grey refused to consider any modification in the mixed system as suggested by the bishops in their memorial and agreed with the viceroy and the commissioners that the success of the system was a strong argument in its favor (C). "They will, at the same time," Grey assured Cullen on behalf of the government, "be prepared to consider, with the aid of the Commissioners, whether any additional safeguards can be provided against interference with the religion of the children attending Mixed Schools." In concluding his letter Grey turned to the model schools. The government would have been prepared to consider their usefulness, he noted, but because the bishops had no suggestion to make except their abolition, and because the government was unable to agree to such a course of action, he would refrain from referring to that part of the bishops' memorial.

Cullen, who was very much disturbed by Grey's reply, immediately sent it and the enclosures to all the bishops asking for their comments and suggestions. In his covering letter to the bishop of Elphin, Laurence Gillooly, Cullen pointed out on May 6 not only that Grey's reply was "unsatisfactory" but that the commissioners' letter was "offensive" (G). "I suppose," he added somewhat surprisingly, "we must take active steps now, and make it a reserved case for anyone to be a Commissioner, or to take part in the model schools." When Gillooly replied the next day, May 7, he agreed that the bishops should respond with "prompt & resolute action" before the question should be discussed in the House of Commons (G). He therefore suggested a general meeting of the bishops for the following week, but significantly enough, he refrained from any comment on Cullen's suggestion about making it a reserved case in the confessional to be a commissioner or to participate in the model schools. Indeed, of the twenty bishops whose replies survive, though all but one, Moriarty (Kerry), were also deeply disappointed with Grey's reply, and many indulged in a great deal of passionate rhetoric, only two, Derry (Clonfert) and Dorrian (Down and Connor), were apparently prepared to recommend strong action. The diffidence, not to say ambivalence, of the bishops polled by Cullen was perhaps best expressed in the reply of the archbishop of

Cashel. "The course suggested by your Grace," Leahy assured Cullen on May 7, "would be a bold &, as far as it went, a successful one too" (C). "What step or steps," he added more cautiously, "it behooves us to adopt requires the deepest consideration. We not only have the enemy in front but we have difficulties within our own body, which may embarrass us most seriously when we come to act. If not united ourselves we can do nothing effectual against the common enemy."

The great majority of the bishops, in effect, advised Cullen that some attempt ought to be made to secure a modification of the national board to safeguard Catholic children against proselytizing efforts, especially in Ulster, and to explore the possibilities of reforming the model schools to meet Catholic needs. What apparently rankled a number of the bishops most, however, including Cullen, was the letter of the twenty commissioners (half of whom, it will be recalled, were by statute Roman Catholics), in which the Catholics had declared themselves "cordially and unanimously" in agreement with their Protestant fellow commissioners. "The pronouncement of the Catholic Commissioners," the bishop of Limerick pointed out to Cullen in his reply of May 7, "that 'the Nat[l] system is well adapted to the peculiar circumstances of Ireland' is very damaging to our cause, for it gives a signal proof of what has been so often thrown in our faces— 'that the Educated Catholic laity are against us' " (C). "It is much to be regretted," Butler added, "that the Catholic Commissioners did not abstain from commending in so unqualified a way a system against which their Bishops have laid such grave objections."

Cullen, however, had already anticipated the reaction of his colleagues to the letter of the Catholic commissioners, for on the day he forwarded Grey's letter and its enclosures to the bishops, he also sent them to John Blake Dillon in London, asking him to move to have the correspondence between the government and the commissioners laid on the table of the House of Commons and to secure, if possible, the names of those commissioners who had been present and had approved the letter dismissing their memorial. "The conduct of the Catholic members of the Board of Education is indeed surprising," Dillon agreed in his reply of May 8 (C). "I shall lose no time in moving for the returns which you desire. I have no doubt the names of Commissioners who took part in the proceedings will be refused. I must try to put it into such a shape that the object will not be apparent." Cullen had also apparently suggested in writing Dillon that the Irish members should bring some pressure to bear on the government by threatening to withdraw their support in the special divisions now expected on the Reform bill, which was in the committee stage, for

Dillon wrote Cullen a longer and more interesting letter the following day, May 9, spelling out the constraints of parliamentary political life (C). "After I wrote to you yesterday," he explained to Cullen, "I had a conversation with Mr. Monsell, and he suggested that two or three Irish members should have an interview with Sir Geo Grey. Afterwards I saw Major O'Reilly, The O'Conor Don and Mr. Cogan and we arranged that Major O'Reilly shd solicit an interview for tomorrow afternoon."[40] He assured Cullen,

> I think the members of the Government would be fairly disposed to go a long way to meet us, but it is useless to shut our eyes to the fact that on this question of education they would have to encounter the opposition not only of the Tories but also of a very large section of their own most ardent supporters. The great bulk of the liberals who are so strongly with us on the land & Church questions, on the other hand regard the national education of Ireland with a sort of idolatry. If you ask them, "why not give us the same system that exists in England"—they answer that they are always endeavouring to have the blessings of the Irish system extended to England. Under those circumstances it is nearly certain that if the Government were to exert all its power it would hardly succeed in giving us the denominational system.
>
> Your Grace will therefore see that the ordinary course of bringing pressure to bear on an *unwilling* Government by threatening a withdrawal of support does not apply to the present case. I have not the slightest doubt that Mr. Gladstone, if he had the power, wd make every school in Ireland strictly denominational. Through his aid we may be able to get rid of some of the worst parts of the system—such as the Model Schools and the Stopford rule.[41] But of a radical change in the system I can see no present hope.

"I was disposed to be very angry," Dillon confessed, "when I read the letter of the Com^rs regarding it as a cool and insolent refusal even to discuss the arguments in the Memorial of the Bishops. But on consideration I am disposed to attribute the tone of the document to internal

40. The arranging of this interview, at least as far as O'Reilly was concerned, was apparently a good deal more difficult than Dillon let on. See W, Dunne to Woodlock, May 9, 1866, and [May 10, 1866?].

41. The Stopford rule required that no compulsion could be employed by managers of national schools vested in the board to cause children of one faith to attend the religious instruction of another, but it removed the requirement that managers exclude all children from religious instruction unless their parents asked that they be present. See Donald H. Akenson, *The Irish Education Experiment* (London, 1970), pp. 200–201.

differences of opinion. I think it means no more than this—'we cannot agree as to the Government and the Bishops.' I observe too that the closing paragraph of Sir Geo Grey's letter points to the possibility of reform." "Tomorrow or after," he promised Cullen in conclusion, "I shall send Yr. Grace the result of our interview."

Though Dillon's promised account of the interview does not appear to have survived, nor any other for that matter, the upshot of the meeting was that it was apparently agreed that O'Reilly would move for a select committee of the House of Commons to inquire into what changes might be made in the system of national education "in order to allow greater freedom and fulness of religious teaching in the schools attended by pupils of one religious denomination only, and to guard effectually against proselytism and protect the faith of the minority in mixed schools."[42] In introducing his motion on May 15 (it was seconded by The O'Conor Don), O'Reilly also raised the question of the unsatisfactory nature of the model and training schools in Ireland. In reply, on behalf of the government, Fortescue explained that the first part of the motion could not be acceded to without, in effect, abandoning the mixed principle on which the national system was based, but that in regard to the second part, he was pleased to say the commissioners of the Board of National Education were, *proprio motu*, now considering the means by which the dangers of the proselytism complained of might best be guarded against.[43] Fortescue also promised that the government would soon reconsider the present position of model and training schools in Ireland with a view to modifying them to the advantage of the country. He then concluded by hoping that O'Reilly would not press the House to a division on his motion, and O'Reilly, after a short debate, accordingly withdrew his motion, expressing himself satisfied with Fortescue's assurances.[44]

Before these assurances could be implemented, however, the government was unexpectedly defeated on June 18, by a vote of 315 to 304 in the House of Commons on an amendment to limit the franchise in the government's proposed parliamentary Reform bill.[45] The defeat, it will be recalled, was occasioned by the combined defection and abstention of a considerable number of Liberals, among whom were a large number of Irish. The defeat was all the more galling because the nominal Liberal majority in the House of Commons was more than sixty. The queen was reluctant to accept Lord Russell's resignation

---

42. *Hansard*, 183;1002.
43. Ibid., 994–1010.
44. Ibid., 1029.
45. Ibid., 184:639–43.

because of the threatening situation occasioned by the Austro-Prussian war, and though Lord Derby finally undertook to form a government on June 28, his ministry, particularly the Irish portion of it, was not finally in place until nearly the middle of July.[46] In the meantime, Fortescue did his best to implement the promises he had made with regard to Irish education. On June 19 he wrote the commissioners of the Board of National Education informing them that the government did not intend to extend the present system of model schools because of the patent inability of those schools to produce the number of teachers required to staff the national system of education.[47] The government, he further explained, proposed to place the existing model schools under local management. On June 26 the commissioners met in Dublin to consider the appointment of chaplains of different denominations to each model school and the establishment of denominational boardinghouses for the students at each school.[48] These recommendations were approved on June 30, and some two weeks later they also approved a new rule, which virtually repealed the controversial Stopford rule. The new rule provided that no student who was registered by his or her parents as a Roman Catholic could receive religious instruction from a person who was not a Roman Catholic, and no pupil was allowed to be present at religious instruction if his or her parents or guardians objected.[49]

If the bishops' achievement in regard to the University question during this period is measured by either the time and energy they expended on it or their success in persuading the government to accede to their demands, then it must be admitted that they accomplished very little. If their negotiations are measured by what they contributed to the institutionalization of the bishops as a body, however, then it is evident that they achieved a very great deal. As a result of their general meetings in August and December, they had become more united in their demands, and their opinions had actually hardened as they became more determined to have their way in educational matters. They refused to give an inch on what they regarded as being fundamental—a complete system of denominational education on all levels absolutely under their control. Though this determination had little baneful effect on the elementary and secondary systems, where the bishops, outside Ulster, had achieved a de facto de-

46. G. E. Buckle, ed., *The Letters of Queen Victoria* (New York, 1926), 2d ser., 1:334–54.

47. *Parliamentary Papers*, 1866, 55:213.

48. Norman, p. 229.

49. Akenson, p. 309.

nominational system that was largely under their control, it had a very serious and negative effect on the provision of higher education for Irish Catholics. The bishops' refusal to allow the laity any control in the governing of the Catholic University, given the temper and membership of the House of Commons, made it impossible for any government during this period, Whig or Tory, to grant that institution either a charter or an endowment. This was the price, of course, that the bishops had to pay for their determination, but it must be pointed out that, at least in terms of maintaining the unity and harmony of their body, which was necessary for the protection of the general interests of the Church and the Catholic body in the long run, they found it a relatively small price to pay.

TORIES, JULY 1866–JUNE 1868

When the negotiations between the archbishops and the Russell government over the charters for the proposed new Royal University and the Catholic University College finally collapsed in early March, the government decided to proceed to a solution of the problem in keeping with its own views and aims. It decided, in fact, to proceed in two stages, and without any further reference to the Irish bishops. The first stage was to issue a supplemental charter by royal patent that would allow students not educated in the Queen's Colleges to receive degrees in the Queen's University if they could pass the required examination. The second stage involved the introducing of a bill in Parliament that would give the new graduates the same rights and privileges as the old graduates. This last was necessary because the law officers of the crown were of the opinion that the conferring of such rights and privileges was not within the competence of the royal prerogative. The supplemental charter was drawn up and granted by royal patent on June 25, only three days before Lord Derby accepted office as prime minister. On June 27 six additional members, including Monsell and Sullivan, were named to the senate of the Queen's University. The fall of the Whig ministry, however, had prevented them from introducing their proposed bill. When the enlarged senate of the Queen's University met on July 11 to consider whether it would accept the supplemental charter, which under the terms of the royal patent was optional rather than mandatory, it decided to postpone a decision until the next meeting. Finally meeting again on October 6, the senate decided to accept the supplemental charter by the narrow margin of eleven to nine. When the convocation, which consisted of the faculty and graduates of the University, assembled on October 19, however, this group decided that it was inexpedient to accept the supplemental charter. The senate then proceeded to deny that the convocation had any competence in the matter, and during November began to draw up and publish the regulations necessary to put the charter into effect.[50]

On December 3, however, before the charter went into effect, three Queen's University graduates brought an action against it, and the master of the rolls in Ireland issued an injunction preventing the senate from issuing its new regulations. When the master of the rolls delivered his judgment some four months later, on April 16, 1867, he dismissed the suit on a technicality; he advised the petitioners that his court did indeed have jurisdiction in the matter but told them that their proper course was, in effect, to take a class action on behalf of the convocation, through the attorney general, rather than acting as private individuals. A suit was then instituted through the attorney general, the upshot of which was the issuance of a permanent injunction some ten months later, on February 1, 1868, which forbade the adoption of the charter. Though it had become increasingly apparent since the royal patent had been issued in June 1866 that the charter was a dead letter, the fact that the case was so long in the courts proved to be very useful to a Conservative government reluctant to grasp so prickly a political nettle. On July 20, almost as soon as the new Conservative government was in place, Woodlock wrote Lord Naas, the chief secretary for Ireland, asking whether the government intended to continue the negotiations with the bishops conducted by the previous ministry in regard to university education (W). Naas apparently replied that he preferred to wait and see how the supplemental charter worked out. Nothing further was done until the master of the rolls dismissed the case in April 1867, advising the petitioners to proceed through the attorney general in their suit. In early May in the House of Commons, therefore, Fortescue suggested that the government should now either proceed with the legislation proposed by the late Liberal government the previous year or provide something better. Naas, who replied on May 31, declined to intervene while the matter was still pending in the courts.[51]

Meanwhile, in early May, the ubiquitous archbishop of Westminster, Henry Edward Manning, had had an informal interview with the chancellor of the Exchequer, Benjamin Disraeli, and on May 21 he wrote Disraeli requesting an interview for Woodlock.[52] What Wood-

50. Norman, p. 234.
51. Ibid., p. 238.
52. W. F. Monypenny and G. E. Buckle, *Life of Disraeli* (London, 1929), 5:5.

lock wanted to discuss with Disraeli was his plan for a "St. Patrick's University," which apparently had the approval of the Irish bishops as a body. Woodlock had outlined his plan at an April meeting of the board of bishops governing the Catholic University, and they had, in turn, authorized him to write to all bishops asking their opinion of the proposal. Woodlock therefore circularized the bishops on April 18 (M). "Dr. Andrews," he explained, "V.P. of the Queen's College, Belfast, has just published a pamphlet in which he proposes that Maynooth College should be raised to the rank of a University. He says, that Maynooth ought to be made the Irish Cath. Oxford; that it was originally intended for laymen as well as ecclesiastics: that medical students should, of course, get their professional education elsewhere, but that there is no reason, they should not get their Degrees from the University of Maynooth."

> Now, there is much that is objectionable in Dr. Andrews' plan: but might not something be gleaned from it? For instance, the following scheme has been suggested: —not that Maynooth *precisely* should be made a University; but that a *"St. Patrick's University"* should be created, of which the present Maynooth Board should be the Senate—this Senate to have under it two Colleges; viz. Maynooth College and a Cath. College in Dublin, comprising Arts, Science, Law & Medicine—just as the Queen's Univ^y has its three colleges.
>
> The following seem to be some of the advantages of this scheme: —
>
> 1st There would be no question of creating a new body, but only of extending the powers of an old one
>
> 2^{ndly} That body—the Maynooth Board—has confided to it the disbursement of £26,000 a year of public money.
>
> 3^{rdly} As a matter of fact it meets once-a-year in Maynooth & once-a-year in Dublin.
>
> 4^{thly} It is a mixed body, composed of Bishops & laymen.
>
> 5^{thly} In fine: it enjoys the confidence of the Bishops, of the Gov^t & of the public.

Woodlock noted in conclusion, "This is the plan—it only remains for me now in accordance with the further directions given me by the Board, to beg the favour of a reply at your Lordship's convenience and your suggestions as to the best mode of urging upon the Gov^t this scheme if you approve of it."

At their interview, Disraeli seems to have done little more than listen politely to Woodlock's proposal; the decision to wait upon the judgment of the courts in regard to the supplemental charter, which would be announced by Naas on May 31, had undoubtedly already been taken by the cabinet. Indeed, little more could be done over the next several months, because in early June the archbishops of Dublin, Armagh, and Cashel and nine bishops left for Rome to assist at the eighteen-hundredth anniversary of the martyrdom of Saints Peter and Paul, and they did not return to Ireland until the end of July. Though the bishops must have explained to the Roman authorities that their educational prospects were not promising, the subject that apparently excited the most interest in Rome was the attitude that should be taken by Catholics with regard to the property of the Protestant Church of Ireland, if that institution, as now seemed very likely, were to be disestablished and disendowed. Some Irish Catholics, including Aubrey de Vere and David Moriarty, the bishop of Kerry, had been recently arguing that a portion of the property of the established Church should be used to endow the various other religious denominations in Ireland in proportion to their numbers, but not to support the clergy—that is, for indirect rather than direct aid. The question was whether the mode, which was referred to as "leveling up," was more just and practical than disendowing all the churches in Ireland, or "leveling down." Moriarty had published his views in "A Letter on the Disendowment of the Established Church" the previous March, and Cullen had forwarded a copy to Kirby, explaining that Moriarty's proposal for leveling up was not practical. "I am persuaded," Cullen had assured Kirby on April 5, "that Protestants will never give back the old property of the Church to Catholics—nor will it [sic] give us a fair share. The only chance is to take away all from the parsons, and apply it to public purposes" (K).

Shortly after he arrived in Rome, Cullen had a long conversation with Cardinal Antonelli, the papal secretary of state, on the subject of the property of the established Church. "He says," Cullen reported on June 26 to his secretary, Patrick Moran, "we ought not to accept any portion however small of the property of the E. Church if it [be] offered to us—if we accept anything we become slaves. Let the property be applied for charitable purposes or for the poor—this is his view which corresponds very much with your own" (C). When Cullen finally returned to Dublin on July 29, he found that the situation with regard to both the established Church and the education question had taken a turn for the better in his absence. On July 22 Sir John Gray, proprietor of the *Freeman's Journal* and M.P. for the borough of Kilkenny, had written him reporting a long and satisfactory interview with Gladstone in reference to the established Church (C). Gray reported that Moriarty's letter of the previous March had created the impression in

Gladstone's mind that a respectable minority of Irish Catholics would oppose the disendowment of the established Church, and they in alliance with Irish Church Protestants, Irish Presbyterians, and the Anglicans of England would provide a very formidable opposition. "Mr. G—," Gray explained, "felt great difficulty in 'going in' to support any resolution pledging himself to *immediate action* because of the *divided* opinion indicated above, especially the want of *unity of plan in the Catholic party* in Ireland. He thought it would be dangerous to pledge to any plan till opinion as to allocation [i.e., of Church property] becomes more developed and PUBLICLY EXPRESSED. If this were done and done well, his view would be *A Bill* AT ONCE for the 'approved plan' be it [a leveling] 'up' or 'down.' "

How Cullen learned on his return from Rome that the Conservative government appeared willing to negotiate the question of chartering and endowing a Catholic University is less clear. Perhaps he had been apprised of its change of heart by Manning, who continued to remain on good terms with both Gladstone and Disraeli. In any case, the day after he returned to Dublin Cullen wrote Barnabò suggesting that recent developments on both issues made it advisable to convene a meeting of the bishops. "It seems to me," he explained on July 30, "that it will be necessary to hold a meeting of the bishops of Ireland next September or October. The question of the property of the Protestant Church will be soon proposed to Parliament—it seems also that the government is disposed to establish a Catholic University, or to endow that which we have. It is desirable therefore that the bishops should be agreed on these matters. If your Eminence believes it opportune you might give me suitable instructions and authority for convening the bishops, and I shall be able to hold the proposed meeting with some hope of a happy result."[53] "If the bishops do not come to an understanding among themselves," he warned in conclusion, "there is a danger they will be divided, and nothing good will be done."

Some two weeks after he wrote Barnabò, Cullen apparently received a note from Manning asking him about the difference of opinion among the Irish Catholic M.P.'s in regard to university education, as well as his and the bishops' attitude to that difference of opinion. "I am altogether," Cullen assured Manning on August 17, "in favour of a Catholic University with an independent Charter for itself, and altogether under Catholic control. I think this is the desire of all our bishops with the exception, perhaps, of Dr. Moriarty."[54] "I am aware," he further explained, "that some of the Catholic M.P.'s are opposed to

53. S.R.C., vol. 35, fol. 1180.
54. Shane Leslie, *Henry Edward Manning* (London, 1921), p. 181.

this plan, and that they would prefer the system of London University, with a mixed board, deputed to examine the students without taking into account where they studied. An attempt was made by the late Government by granting what was called a supplementary charter to the Queen's University. That grant pleased no party." "If your Grace," Cullen added, "could suggest any way of proceeding likely to ensure our success, I would be most obliged if you would put me in possession of your views." Several days later Manning wrote Disraeli urging him to disregard the opinions of those Irish members who were hostile to the chartering of a Catholic University, and further assuring him that they did not represent the views of either Cullen or the Irish bishops.[55] He also warned Disraeli of the importance of securing the cooperation of the Irish bishops in educational matters. By the time Disraeli had received this letter, however, the government had already decided to make its move on both issues. In an obvious attempt to buy time, the government announced the appointment of two royal commissions, one to consider the problems presented by the Irish Church and the other to examine the state of Irish primary education.

Cullen reported to Kirby on August 19, "We shall have a Royal Commission to examine into the state of the Protestant Church. Of course the object of the Commission will be to save the Establishment, or to make a little sacrifice giving a small share to Catholics in order to *share* with them the odium now attached to the Protestant Church property" (K). "There is also," he further reported, "a *Royal* Commission appointed to examine into the state of primary education in Ireland. Who the Commissioners will be, we know not as yet. I fear they will be in part Liberal Catholics, votaries of mixed education, and anxious to promote Government views. Undoubtedly the Protestants will try to keep up their own influence." "This Commission," he added, "may do much mischief if it be composed of dangerous men: it may also do good if it can be properly directed. I think the Bishops ought to meet to decide on what course they are to take in regard to both Commissions. I wrote to Cardinal Barnabò on the matter. Probably he will answer me—if we hold a meeting we must determine upon what course we are to adopt and fix what we are to say." "I fear," Cullen confided, "Dr. Moriarty will be put forward by the high Catholics as the representative of the Catholic body—he would perhaps defend mixed education, and propose that Catholics should take a portion of the income of the Protestant Church." "It would be most important," he concluded very significantly, "to have a general declaration of the Bishops as to their views as a body."

55. Monypenny and Buckle, 5:6.

By the end of August Cullen had received the necessary permission from Barnabò to convene a general meeting of the bishops, and on September 2, therefore, he informed the bishops that they would assemble in Dublin on October 1 to discuss the problems presented by the Protestant Church as well as the various aspects of the education question (L). Some two weeks before the scheduled meeting, however, on September 17, Moriarty wrote Cullen explaining that he had been asked by the government to accept a place on the royal commission recently appointed to examine the question of primary education in Ireland, and asking his advice about whether he should accept (C). "I would not venture," Cullen replied on September 19, "to give an opinion to your Lordship on the difficult position in which you are placed by having been asked to become a member of the Commission about to examine the state of primary education in Ireland. However I w^d suggest that your Lordship should defer giving any answer until the meeting of the Bishops. If they sanction y^r acceptance of the office, of course they will assist you, and you will be able to do some good—but if you accept without consulting them, especially as the meeting is so near, very probably they will not be inclined to cooperate with you and you will labour in vain" (M). "It cannot be any great inconvenience," he added shrewdly, "to delay the appointment of the Commissioners for a few days longer with a view of having things done in a more satisfactory manner." "I understand," he further noted, "that Dr. Russell of Maynooth is in the same difficulty as y^r Lordship."

The bishops, who met on three successive days, October 1–3, were not able to consider Moriarty's dilemma until their second day. "Today," Moran reported to Kirby on October 1,

> our Bishops met in accordance with the convocation and the instructions sent from Rome. All were present with the exception of the Bps. of Waterford and Killala, both of whom were excused on account of ill health. They assembled in The Marlboro St. chapel of St. Kevin at 11 o'clock and they just finished at 3½ p.m. The subject for consideration today was the Established Church and three resolutions were agreed to:—
>
> 1st. That they unanimously demanded the disendowment of the Est. Church.
>
> 2nd. That in accordance with the tradition and teaching of the Catholic Church in Ireland they would repudiate every endowment from the state.
>
> 3rd. That as there was no hope that the funds of the Est. Church would be appropriated to their original ends, they would endeavour to secure their application for objects of charity.

Everything was carried out most amicably. Dr. MacHale at first thought they should not express any opinion at all, but subsequently he coincided with the rest. Dr. Moriarty also said something about his former pamphlet-views, but he also withdrew the statement he there put forward and adopted the opinion of the rest. So it was a glorious thing to see all unanimously adopting the principle of sacrifice in order to preserve the independence of their sacred ministry. [K]

"The resolutions," he further explained, "are to be drawn or formalized before the meeting on tomorrow, and under the protection of the Angels Guardian I hope they will [be] all right, and that the deliberations of tomorrow will be as successful as those of today."

The cordiality and harmony displayed by the bishops on their first day was in fact carried over into their proceedings for the next two days, and this became for Cullen, at least, the real achievement of the meeting. When he wrote Barnabò on October 4, the day after the meeting closed, he was most particular in assuring him, while explaining that he would soon send a full report of the meeting, that the bishops were all agreed and united in regard to what was to be done about both the established Church and the education questions.[56] Moran, who wrote Kirby that same day, giving him an extended and detailed account of the three days' proceedings, also emphasized that what really distinguished the meeting was the basic unity displayed by the bishops as a body (K). When Cullen wrote Kirby a week later, on October 10, he was able to offer some further insight into why things had gone so smoothly at the recent meeting (K). MacHale, who had attended only on the first two days, Cullen explained, was as agreeable as he had ever seen him at an episcopal meeting. All the bishops, he then further reported, had not only signed a Latin letter to the pope but had anathematized the Protestant Church and declared that it ought to be disendowed, while also declaring that they would not accept any endowment by the state for their own Church. Cullen assured Kirby, in reference to the advice given by the cardinal secretary of state about this matter to those Irish bishops who had been in Rome the previous summer, "I think we followed out exactly the recommendations of Cardinal Antonelli."

Cullen then turned to the issue that had been potentially, at least, the most divisive for the bishops at their meeting. "The Government," he explained to Kirby,

56. S.R.C., vol. 35, fol. 1247. See also, for the full report promised by Cullen, ibid., Kirby to Barnabò, n.d., fols. 1248–49.

had proposed to make Dr. Moriarty a Commissioner to enquire into the state of National education in Ireland. He consulted the Bishops about accepting. They all told him not to do so. He said himself publicly that he would sign a report condemnatory of the demands of the Bishops. He would probably have gone great lengths with the Government and this was the reason why he was selected. When Dr. Moriarty had heard the opinion of the Bishops he resigned. Dr. Russell who had also been asked to become a Commissioner acted in the same way—so did Lord Dunraven—Dr. Moriarty, Dr. Russell and Lord Dunraven[,] all weak and yielding men[,] were selected to defend the Catholic cause— a poor support. We said nothing about Lord Dunraven, but he would not act without the other two. If some good Catholic layman could be got to act, he might do some good.[57]

"We renewed our former demands for a purely Catholic education," he added, turning to the third day's proceedings, "and we determined to support the Catholic University—probably it was to avoid supporting this institution, that Dr. McHale left Dublin. The question was brought on after his departure." "We condemned the late Fenian movement," Cullen further reported, "and appealed to the Government to redress the grievances of the country in order to restore peace." He added most interestingly, "we deputed Dr. Leahy of Cashel and Dr. Derry to treat with the Government about a Charter for the Catholic University and other educational matters. I proposed Dr. Derry as he is very determined against the mixed system. I will send you tomorrow a short pastoral which I got printed in order to convey the resolutions of the Bishops to the people of Dublin." "You see," he pointed out finally, "we did nothing new or great—but we did some good by preventing Dr. Mor. and Dr. Russell from accepting an office in which they might have done mischief—it is now said that the Government will not appoint any Commission."[58] "So much the better," he added for good measure, "—the Commission was only a sham to create delay."

Though Cullen certainly believed that the containing of Moriarty and the preserving of the harmony and unity of the bishops as a body

---

57. Cullen was apparently misinformed about Dunraven, because he did accept a place on the royal commission.

58. See K, Moran to Kirby, October 4, 1867. Moran's view of Moriarty and Russell, which was, of course, a projection of Cullen's, was that they were both "men whose views on Education would not meet with the approbation of the great body of the B^{ps}. All the B^{ps} unanimously resolved that no B^p or Priest should accept an appointment on this Commission, as it was evidently the intention of the Government to seek to sow dissension & not to allow Catholics their rights."

in educational matters were the great achievements of the meeting, yet another decision made by the bishops was perhaps at least as important as far as the body was concerned. The bishops had deputed the archbishop of Cashel and the bishop of Clonfert to represent them in any future negotiations with the government on the education question. When they had met more than two years before, in August 1865, it will be recalled, the bishops had deputed the four archbishops to represent them in the discussions that had taken place with the government. Why, it may well be asked, did the bishops now choose to downgrade their representation to an archbishop and a bishop, and more especially, why did they elect to exclude Cullen, who not only had been promoted to the dignity of a cardinal the previous year but had been, in effect, the chief architect of episcopal educational policy for the previous seventeen years? The answers to these questions, unfortunately, must remain largely a matter of conjecture, because virtually nothing appears in the various correspondences available that sheds any light on the bishops' motives. Undoubtedly, the bishops were still very sore about the way in which they had been treated by the recent Whig administration in the person of its home secretary, Sir George Grey, and they were determined that any future negotiations were not going to be dignified by so weighty a representation of their body. Whether the bishops also intended to modify Cullen's influence in any future negotiations by not including him as one of their deputies is another question. But whatever their intentions were, their decision not to include him was, in fact, a very significant assertion of their self-confidence as a body.

Shortly after the episcopal meeting, Moriarty, who was apparently as restless as he was able, had an interview with the chief secretary, the former Lord Naas, who had recently succeeded his father as the sixth earl of Mayo; he reported the substance of it to Cullen. "When I went to Lord Mayo," Moriarty explained on October 15, "to decline serving on The Educational Commission, he expressed opinions on the reforms of our system which I wished your Eminence to know and which he gave me leave to repeat to you. He thinks that where the pupils are all of the same religion the school should be denominational, where the pupils are of different religions there should be a conscience clause. He thinks moreover that after a few sittings of the Commission they would report to this effect. This of course was said very guardedly" (C). "However," he then concluded, "I think it right, that your Eminence should know the way things are drifting." Immediately, on October 16, Cullen wrote to the archbishop of Cashel reporting what Moriarty had written and suggesting that Leahy write to Lord Mayo to ask the intentions of the government with regard to the education question (L). Cullen must have been very much annoyed at Moriarty's thus seizing the initiative with the government, especially as this was now the prerogative of those deputies appointed by the episcopal body at their recent meeting.

On receiving Cullen's letter, Leahy apparently wrote to his colleague, the bishop of Clonfert, to learn his views, because on October 23 they jointly wrote Mayo, enclosing a letter of the same date to be transmitted to Lord Derby, the prime minister.[59] They also wrote both the home secretary, Gathorne Hardy, and the chancellor of the Exchequer, Benjamin Disraeli, enclosing copies of their letter to Derby. In their letter to Derby they explained that they had been deputed by the Irish bishops to apply for a charter and an endowment for the Catholic University. Derby replied on October 29, assuring them that he would bring the contents of their letter to the attention of the cabinet at its next meeting (L). The significance of Leahy and Derry's initiative, of course, was that they chose to write directly to the prime minister, and by making Lord Mayo, in effect, the mode of communication, they bypassed the Irish government. The two bishops were as obviously determined as Cullen and the other three archbishops had been two years before to deal directly with the cabinet, and their letters to Hardy and Disraeli were a further measure of their intention to negotiate only at the highest level. Needless to say, given the downgrading of their own representation from the four archbishops to an archbishop and a bishop, their insistence on opening the negotiations at the highest level was yet another indication of their assurance and self-confidence on behalf of the body.

On the whole, Cullen was very pleased with both the timing and the results of the episcopal meeting. "I received," he reported to Kirby on October 31, "a very nice letter from Dr. Manning about our late meeting. He says he will get the English bishops to adopt them [the resolutions] also when an opportunity occurs. It was fortunate we held the meeting so soon, otherwise we would have been divided into several parties, losing all our influence. Dr. Moriarty w^d have been supported by a faction of lay Catholics (K)." "Sir Robert Kane," he explained, referring to the president of the Queen's College in Cork, who had been just appointed to the royal commission on elementary edu-

59. *Parliamentary Papers*, 1867–68, 13:1–10, enclosure 1.

cation in Ireland, "is now a Commissioner and he is a bitter opponent of Catholic education, though himself a Catholic." "However," Cullen added pointedly, "he will not be able to do much harm as he is a layman. A Bishop would have ruined us if he went astray." In the next several weeks the education question was eclipsed by the news of the victory of the papal army over Garibaldi on November 3, at Mentana. On November 22, however, shortly after the initial excitement created by the meetings and collections for the pope, and the requiem masses for those who had fallen in his defense, had subsided, John Francis Maguire, M.P. for county Cork, raised the question of a charter for the Catholic University in the House of Commons by asking Lord Mayo the intentions of the government on the matter.[60] Mayo replied that the question was being considered by the government and that the subject would be shortly brought before the House.

Indeed, Mayo had apparently been turning a number of alternatives over in his mind for some time. As he explained on December 3 to Robert Warren, the Irish attorney general and M.P. for Dublin University, who had written him about the anxiety that had been created in his constituency by his reply to Maguire, there were two possible solutions to the subject of university education for Roman Catholics. First, there was the possibility of creating a Catholic University that would stand to Irish Catholics as Trinity College stood to Irish Protestants. Second, there was the possibility of creating a degree-granting body, which would include Trinity, the Queen's Colleges, and a new Catholic College, leaving to all the Colleges their "distinctive principles of government and teaching, and their property and endowments."[61] Mayo further explained that he favored the second alternative because it would avoid what all acknowledged to be a great evil, namely, the multiplication of universities in one kingdom. He also noted that the second plan would give the race for education on the university level to the strong, adding parenthetically, "we all know who the strong would be."

Cullen was obviously very pleased that he had managed to maintain with such success his first priority, the keeping of the bishops united, in his efforts to secure a complete system of denominational education for Irish Catholics. At this point he turned his attention to his second priority, the keeping of Irish public opinion strong on the unsatisfactory nature of the present system for Irish Catholics. On December 18 he held a meeting of all of the secular and regular clergy

60. *Hansard*, 190:142.
61. Norman, p. 249.

of Dublin in St. Kevin's Chapel in the procathedral in Marlborough Street, at which they were treated to a series of discourses on the dangers and inadequacies of mixed education in Ireland by Cullen and the most learned and eloquent of his clergy.[62] He reported to Kirby on December 20, "Father Curtis, Monsignori Forde and McCabe, Father Burke, Dr. Moran, Dr. Molloy, and others made excellent speeches which you will read in the paper I sent. I hope a very good effect will be produced through the country by those speeches. I think you will like them very well. We shall get them printed in a pamphlet in which it will be easy to read them" (K). The various speeches, in fact, added up to a very able polemical effort; Cullen set the tone with a slashing and comprehensive attack on the whole system of mixed education on all its levels in Ireland, paying particular and extensive attention to the inequities and iniquities of the national system of education.[63]

Leahy and Derry, meanwhile, who had been waiting for Derby's promised reply for some two months, finally wrote the prime minister again on December 23, asking whether the cabinet had come to any decision about the matter raised in their previous letter (L). Derby replied on December 30, explaining that he had brought the subject of their letter before the cabinet as he promised and that it had been decided that the government's intentions on the university question in Ireland would be brought before the House of Commons by Mayo when Parliament reconvened in February (L). Leahy forwarded Derby's reply to Cullen, who responded on January 1, 1868, that it was not very encouraging (L). Cullen then added, however, that he had just heard from Manning, who had seen Disraeli and thought that he appeared inclined to make concessions.

Indeed, when Cullen wrote Leahy, Manning had been discussing the question of Irish University education with Disraeli for more than three weeks. "I have today," Manning had informed Cullen on December 10, "had a long conversation with Mr. D'Israeli on the subject of the Catholic University, & urged on him the justice and expediency of granting a Charter" (C). "He is prepared to consider the proposal," Manning reported,

but he dwelt on two points.

First on the impossibility of carrying it through the House coupled with any proposal of endowment.

This appears to be certain; and also that when once Chartered

---

62. *Freeman's Journal*, December 19, 20, 1867.
63. Cullen's speech is also in Moran, 3:123–43.

the University will hereafter be in a condition to ask for endowment with much better hope of success.

Secondly that he had no hope of carrying it unless in the Constitution & Government of the University some laymen were admitted.

On this I could give him no light, but undertook to inform myself.

"The importance of a Charter," Manning then pointed out, "seems to me very great in every way. It would establish the principle of pure Catholic education which at last would spread through the National Board. The present moment is favourable for gaining it. I do not know whether a new, & reformed Parliament would be equally favourable. I am afraid that it would rather secularize all education." "If your Eminence," he added in concluding, "will kindly instruct me how to proceed I will do so at once. I may add in confidence that Mr. Gladstone would not oppose a Charter."

On December 22 Manning wrote Disraeli that he had just heard from Cullen and would appreciate the opportunity of another interview, which then took place on December 28.[64] "I had a long conversation," Manning reported again to Cullen on December 30, "with Mr. D'Israeli: but I confined my statements to the two points of referring him to the Archbp of Cashel, & the Bp. of Derry [sic]: and also to referring to the University of Louvain as an example of the Government of a Catholic University" (C). "He promised," Manning added, "to write at once to Lord Mayo. The whole tone of his conversation was I think promising." In his reply to Manning, Cullen forwarded a copy of Lord Derby's reply to Leahy, which he did not feel was very promising. "The day I received the [sic] last," Manning assured Cullen on January 14, 1868, "& the copy of Lord Derby's letter, I wrote to Mr. D'Israeli. Yesterday I saw him for a moment. He told me that he had acted on my letter: & said that he would see me again" (C). Though Manning wrote Disraeli the following day, January 15, attempting to arrange the promised interview, it does not appear that they were able to meet for more than a month.

In the meantime, Manning wrote Cullen on January 19 to call his attention to an article in the *Quarterly Review*, which, though apparently in fact written by Robert Lowe,[65] was thought to be by Lord

64. Monypenny and Buckle, 5:6.
65. "What Shall We Do for Ireland?" *Quarterly Review*, January 1868, pp. 255–86. See *Wellesley Index*, 1:750. I owe this reference to Professor Josef Altholz, University of Minnesota.

Cranborne, the future marquis of Salisbury, and which was thought "to represent the sense of his friends, & some of the Govt." (C). "It urges the endowing of the Catholic Clergy," Manning explained, "transparently to purchase & control them. I trust the Bishops in Ireland will be as explicit on this as on the rejection of the endowments of the Establishment. If your Eminence could furnish me with any declaration or document on this subject I could use it advantageously." Cullen wrote reassuringly in reply, for Manning reported on January 24, from Bournemouth, that he was greatly relieved by his letter (C). "I know," he explained, "that the worst & most tyrannical enemies of Ireland & the Catholic Church are now urging endowment of the Clergy to buy them, & ruin their influence, & the union of the people & their pastors. They will even go the length of forcing it, & leaving it to time to take effect. We cannot be too outspoken or too prompt." "I have nothing good," he noted further, "to report about the Charter: and I expect little from these men. What your Eminence says is certain: all places are filling up with partizans, & mischief is laid up for twenty years." Expectations, however, in spite of all the gloomy forecasts, had already begun to build in Dublin. Moran reported to Kirby on January 23, "We are anxiously awaiting the opening of Parliament to hear the Government declaration on the Education question. They are promising to do something but *timeo Danaos* [I fear Greeks (bearing gifts)]" (K).

When the man who would be most responsible for the fulfilling of those expectations, the earl of Mayo, began to collect his thoughts several weeks later, in order to make his presentation to the cabinet before Parliament should be asked to consider the matter, he apparently realized almost immediately that any proposed measure must stand or fall on whether or not it was acceptable to the Irish bishops. "Any plan proposed by the Government," he maintained in the notes he made for his presentation to the cabinet, "for the erection of a University at which Irish Catholics could be educated would, if acceptable to the Irish R.C. bishops, be at least boldly and thankfully received by the R.C. laity, and would be violently opposed by the Protestant Party. Again, anything falling short of an acceptance of the proposal of the Irish bishops would be magnified by them into a grievance—perhaps an insult—and in this line they would be supported by the R.C. laity for party purposes, or to obtain cheap popularity."[66] The alternatives facing Mayo, therefore, appeared to be either to do something that would be acceptable to the Irish bishops or to do nothing,

66. Quoted in Norman, p. 252.

which would please the Irish Protestants. Though in mid-February Mayo seemed to be disposed to do something, the proposals he outlined in his notes were somewhat unrealistic. He proposed, for example, to set up a royal commission empowered by the government to grant a charter directly through legislation, as well as to have Parliament empower municipal corporations, through an enabling act, to erect buildings or grant the use of existing ones and to make grants and to endow chairs. It was also obvious from Mayo's notes that he had reverted to the first of the two options that he had outlined to the Irish attorney general, Robert Warren, the previous December—the creation of a Roman Catholic University that would stand to Irish Catholics as Trinity College and Dublin University stood to Irish Protestants—which at that time he had thought the less acceptable option because it would multiply the number of universities in Ireland.

Whatever the practicability of Mayo's musings, he was soon made very aware of what the Irish bishops thought acceptable by a Statement of the University Question Addressed to the Catholic Members of Parliament, dated February 20, from the archbishop of Cashel and the bishop of Clonfert. After indicating that they had been deputed by the Irish bishops to negotiate with the government and outlining what had transpired in their correspondence with the prime minister to date, Leahy and Derry explained why they were now writing to the Catholic members collectively. "It is easy to see," the two bishops pointed out, "what serious embarrassment would arise in the event of our Catholic representatives accepting at the hands of Government, or even approving, of a measure of University Education for Ireland which their Lordships the Bishops would in the interests of religion feel bound to reject. Hence with a view to securing unity between our Catholic Representatives and the Bishops for the good of Catholic Ireland, we respectfully offer a statement of the principles which have governed and still govern the action of the Bishops in reference to this important question" (L).

The rest of the address, which amounted to some twelve printed pages and four thousand words, was divided into three parts. The first and longest part was essentially a statement of grievances; the second and shortest was an enunciation of those principles that were the sine qua non for any settlement; and the third was concerned with the adopting by the government of practical measures that would make for a satisfactory solution. In the first part Leahy and Derry complained that their grievances were really a house of many mansions. They pointed out that the Catholics of Ireland were, "compared with their Protestant fellow subjects, placed in a position of inequality, and *that* an inequality at once *religious, educational, social, professional, financial and national.*" In the second part the episcopal deputies assured the Catholic members that there were two indispensable tests upon which they could rely as far as the Irish bishops were concerned: "first any measure of Academic Education embodying the mixed principle, would be rejected by them; secondly, any such measure not respecting the authoritative supervision of Bishops in what appertains to the faith and morals of Catholics, would be rejected by them." Finally, in the third part of their address the two bishops argued that all of the foregoing led to the inevitable conclusions that it was therefore necessary in the interests of equality and Catholic teaching that an institution of higher learning for Irish Catholics be both chartered and endowed by the state, and that the advantage of having just such an institution ready to hand in the Catholic University of Ireland would be apparent to all. "Ireland," they then concluded simply, "is a Catholic nation, and has a right to such a Catholic University."

If Leahy and Derry were aware of Disraeli's caution to Manning, relayed by him to Cullen, about asking for an endowment, they obviously decided to ignore it. Even more seriously, however, they explicitly rejected in their address the second of Disraeli's injunctions, about the necessity of leavening episcopal control of the University with a lay element, by denying that there was any need for it. "It has been said," they admitted, "the Bishops exercise in the Catholic University an undue amount of authority, incompatible with the freedom and self-government which a University ought to enjoy. The Bishops, it is true, have the supreme government together with the appointment of the Rector, Vice-Rector, and Professors of the University, according to its original constitution, and as being the persons who collected its funds; but they have never interfered with its internal administration, nor with the teaching of the Professors; nor would they ever so interfere, except in case of necessity." "The authorities of the University, the Rector, the Vice-Rector, the Deans, the Council, the Senate," they assured the Catholic members, "have all the freedom of action which is essential to the principle of self-government; and the Professors have no limit set to the freedom of their teaching, except that they shall not offend against the moral or doctrinal teaching of the Catholic Church." What Leahy and Derry were doing, in effect, was warning the Catholic members off the University question. They were obviously intent on preventing another lay initiative such as that taken by Monsell and his friends in their negotiations with the Russell ministry some eighteen months before. By making their statement as comprehensive as possible, in fact, Leahy and Derry left those Catholic members who might be so disposed very little room for maneuver or negotiations with the government. What they did not appear to realize, however, was that the very comprehensiveness of their statement would also seriously inhibit them in their own proposed negotiations with the government.

On the day the episcopal deputies were thus narrowing their ground, Archbishop Manning was attempting to broaden it in an interesting letter to Cullen. "If the Government," he posed on February 20, "were to propose to Charter the Catholic University without giving endowment would it not be best to accept it? Would not endowment come by force of events?" (C). "And," he asked further, "if they were to propose the admission of laymen into the Government is it not possible to reserve the supreme control of the Bishops over all its system?" "As I am likely to be asked these questions," Manning explained, "I should like to know what you would answer." "The present Govt.," he then added, "could do more than their opponents, because the country would let them, and they are opposed to latitudinarian education. Their Anglicanism makes them denominational." That same day Manning had another interview with Disraeli, who expected soon to succeed the ailing Derby as prime minister. "For reasons which I am not able to state," Manning wrote Cullen the next day, February 21, in a letter marked "*Private*," "I think it is of urgent importance that the Archbishop of Cashel and the Bp. of Ferns [sic] should come over to London, if possible, next week. If both cannot, I hope one will: but both would be better. I hope your Eminence will kindly excuse this, and make it known only to the two bishops, as I think much harm might arise to me by any public notice of this letter" (C).

"In my letter of yesterday," Manning apologized to Cullen in his third letter in three days, "I mistook the Bp. of Ferns for the Bp. of Clonfert. If it were possible for them to be here I think some progress might be made" (C). "I have to thank your Eminence," he added most interestingly, "for your letter of this morning which I read with much interest. It exactly expresses what I hoped." "I have refrained absolutely giving any opinion when asked here," he further assured Cullen.

> But what your Eminence wrote exactly expresses what I should say if I were to speak.
>
> It appears to me that if we could get a purely Catholic University chartered & recognized by law, we should have planted the root of a Catholic education for all classes in Ireland. It wd be the victory of the denominational over the mixed system.

For this end, we might well wait for endowment. A charter plus endowment wd be long resisted. A Charter once gained, endowment must come.

Trinity College & the Cath^c University, side by side, wd be too scandalous a contrast to last long.

As to the admission of laymen, I should not fear any ill effect. Theology, mental & moral Philosophy, History, and Spiritual discipline being reserved what would remain in which the general fidelity of our religion, the authority of the Episcopate, & the public voice of Catholic Ireland would not control any lay officers?

The present moment is most favourable. This country will let the present Govt. do what it, & they would turn out Mr. Gladstone for proposing. And he will not hinder the Govt. if they will propose a Charter on these terms.

"Pray keep me well informed of your wishes," he assured Cullen again in conclusion, "& be sure of their exact expression."

What seems to have happened was that Disraeli told Manning very privately at their interview on February 20 that he was ready to negotiate an arrangement of the Irish University question; therefore Manning wrote Cullen the next day informing him that the presence of Leahy and Derry in London was absolutely necessary. When Manning received Cullen's assurance on February 22 that they were of one mind on the question of endowment and lay representation, he wrote Disraeli that same day to assure him that there was indeed a basis for negotiations:

Since I had the pleasure of seeing you on Thursday I have carefully informed myself as to the two chief points in the Scheme you were so good as to show me: I mean of the Charter without endowment, and 2) the admission of laymen into the Government of the University.

I need not say, that no thought could arise from my inquiry, as to the confidence you were so good as to repose in me.

I believe that the question of endowment would not be proposed; and that the admission of laymen into the Government, saving of course the Theological, moral, & religious matter, would be accepted.

The scheme appears to me to afford an ample basis for conference with great probability of satisfaction to both sides.

And I would strongly urge that it be, when the Cabinet shall see fit, communicated to the Cardinal, & the two Bishops chosen

by the Irish Episcopate to represent them, namely Archbishop
Leahy of Cashel, & Bishop Derry of Clonfert.

They would willingly come over if you so desire: & I should
advise this course as best. I believe that this evidence of good
will on the part of Government would be of great moment at this
time in Ireland.[67]

In the meantime, Cullen had forwarded to Woodlock a copy of
Manning's letter of February 21 that urged Leahy and Derry to come to
London, explaining that he had sent copies to both bishops. "It wd be
most desirable," Cullen added, "that they sd go over—write to them
& endeavour to get them to start at once" (W). At this point Cullen
had another thought, for he dispatched Woodlock to London to hold a
watching brief for him in any eventual negotiations that might take
place with the government and to act as his liaison with Manning.
Woodlock, who left Dublin on the evening of February 24, arrived in
London the next day in the midst of the ministerial crisis that resulted in Disraeli's finally accepting, on February 27, the office of
prime minister. "I suppose," Cullen surmised on Ash Wednesday, February 26, "you can do nothing until the new ministry is formed. Agitate as much as possible in favour of a charter & endowment. [But in]
the end it will be better to take the charter even without an endowment, than to wait any longer" (W). "Dr. Derry," he reported "is angry
with Disraeli because he never answered their letter (his & Dr. Leahy's [of the previous October])." "I suppose," he concluded, "there is
not much to be hoped for. Write & report progress."

Derry, who had written Cullen on February 25, thought it inadvis-
able to go over to London at that moment, and when Leahy wrote
Cullen two days later, on February 27, he reported that neither he nor
Derry thought a charter without an endowment worth accepting (C).
"For my own part," he explained,

I think the Charter, unaccompanied by the endowment, would
not be worth much. So, at any rate, Dr. Derry & myself are just
after saying *in our Statement.* To profess our readiness, almost in
the same breath, to treat of a Charter without an Endowment, —
would it not argue a degree of inconsistency, if it would not be to
stultify ourselves? At least, it seems to be a case of emergency,
such as was contemplated in the deputation of power to Dr.
Derry & myself. I do not think we are able or competent to say
whether or not the Bishops would accept a Charter without an
Endowment. It is a nice, or difficult, point to decide.

67. Mayo Papers, 11170, National Library of Ireland, Dublin.

Leahy then concluded by venturing to suggest that perhaps the bishops as a body might meet to decide the question.

Cullen, however, was in no mood for equivocation. In a reply that was as ruthless in its logic as it was imperious in its tone, he virtually told Leahy that he had no choice but to go to London. "In my opinion," he informed Leahy on February 28, "it wd be very useless to bring the bishops together, unless we get something official to put before them. On this account it appears to me that it would be necessary for your Grace to see the Prime Minister, and to treat the University question with him. You would in this way learn what he proposes, and you wd have an opportunity of insisting on our rights" (L). "As to taking the Charter without an endowment," he added, "this much good might result from it, that we might get the Bishops' authority recognized in the way in which it now stands. If an endowment be given just now, the Government will insist on giving some authority to laymen, a thing which might not be insisted on if the endowment were given to a body already recognized and in operation." "Dr. Derry writes," Cullen concluded implacably, "that he is not at all well. I dare say on this account your Grace will have to go to London alone."

As Cullen was writing this very stiff letter on February 28, Leahy had already come to the conclusion that he and Derry had to go to London; he wrote Cullen that same day asking him to recommend a suitable place to stay while there (C). Therefore, when Leahy received Cullen's letter the next day, February 29, he was very annoyed at being so peremptorily ordered to do the necessary. When Cullen received Leahy's letter about suitable lodgings in London, he realized that he had gone too far and wrote Leahy immediately in his best velvet-glove style, attempting to mollify him. "I hope your Grace," he suggested on February 29, more softly, "will go over to London in time to see the Ministry before they make any public declaration of their plans. When they shall have published what they are about to do, they are too proud to yield" (L). "If your Grace," he added, "could see Disraeli as soon as the Ministry is completed, very probably you wd succeed in inducing him to grant the endowment as well as the charter. However as Lord Cairns, Mr. Corry, and Lord Mayo are now members of the Cabinet, and as they are all very hostile to Irish claims, I fear they may mar any project that may be set afoot to promote the interests of the country. I believe the three gentlemen I have mentioned are all very polite and reasonable in their communications but they seem to be bitter enemies of Ireland and Catholicity." "It is not very agreeable," Cullen pointed out, "to deal with such persons, or with such a man as Disraeli, but to do any good persons must be prepared to suffer a great deal of annoyance and trouble." "If there be no question," he noted further, "to be decided by a meeting of Bishops except this, whether a charter without an endowment shd be received, I think a letter could be written to each of their Lordships asking their opinion. If the Government consent to the endowment as it is to be hoped they will, everyone will be satisfied."

Before he received this mollifying reply, Leahy had already written to Disraeli on February 29, requesting an interview for Derry and himself as deputies of the Irish bishops and enclosing a copy of their Statement of February 20 to the Catholic M.P.'s; he had written also to Cullen on March 1, enclosing a copy of the letter to Disraeli. "I send Your Eminence," Leahy explained coldly and briefly, "a copy of a Letter I have addressed in Dr. Derry's & my own name to Mr. Disraeli. I suppose this will bring him out. Please return it when read, as I have not another clean copy" (C). Leahy had also written Woodlock, apparently on February 28 before he received Cullen's very peremptory letter, to complain about Woodlock's unauthorized presence in London, for Woodlock forwarded Leahy's letter to Cullen. "I return Dr. Leahy's letter," Cullen noted on March 1 (W). "Both he and Dr. Derry appear to be a little *petegoli* as they say in Rome, though the word is not in the dictionary, or as F. Faber calls it, *touchy.*" "If they go on in this way," he added more sharply, "they will do nothing—but mischief. I write to-day to both. Dr. Derry is, I think, worse than Dr. L. If they put themselves on the high horse, of course, they may prevent any good from being done." Cullen then informed Woodlock in a postscript, "I have sent our letter to Sir G. Grey to Dr. Manning and marked pages 11, 12, 15 where all the Bishops say that a charter without endowment would be *unsatisfactory*, but there is not a word to indicate that it would not be accepted. When you see that no good can be done come home." "Do not," he warned in concluding, "propose yr. project of going to Rome to Dr. Leahy or Dr. Derry. They wd oppose it."

When Cullen wrote Leahy that same day he attempted, as he had the day before, to soften the impact of his first letter by patiently and considerately explaining the difficulties of the case, while subtly shifting the responsibility for them to the bishop of Clonfert. "Dr. Derry," Cullen reported on March 1,

> complains that Disraeli has never answered the letter written to him whilst he can find time to communicate with Dr. Manning. I suppose it was a great oversight or a want of politeness on the part of Disraeli not to attend to your letter, yet where a great national good is at stake, I think such matters ought not to prevent the action of those who are looking for their rights. Unfortunately we are at the mercy of the English ministers, without

any power to compel them to do justice or to discharge their duties. They look on us as troublesome petitioners, and I dare say they are not at all desirous to do anything to please us. If we stand aloof, they will have a pretext for doing nothing and they will justify themselves by saying they were not asked to do anything.

As to Disraeli's communicating matters interesting to Ireland to Dr. Manning, it appears quite natural that he should do so—it appears they have been long acquainted, and still keep up some private intercourse—when Dr. Manning wrote urging the attendance of your Grace and Dr. Derry in London, he seems to have acted on some private information he had gleaned in an interview with Disraeli or some other Minister, and his object in writing evidently was to let you know that a favourable opportunity was likely to present itself for dealing with the Government. So far from wishing to take up the matter himself Dr. Manning seems to have been most anxious that those who were charged to act, should avail themselves of a favourable occasion of doing so. I think Dr. Manning deserves our thanks for communicating to us what he learned incidentally, and what very probably was not known to anyone else. [L]

"However," Cullen admitted, "there may be more talk than reality on the side of the ministers at present." "In your letter to the M.P.'s," he then added, turning to the crucial issue, "at page 8 there are two essential conditions laid down without which a charter would on no account be accepted. But neither of those conditions refer to an endowment." "In my opinion," he pointed out, "every effort ought to be made to get an endowment without which a charter would be very sterile—but if after making every effort to get what we have a right to, i.e. the means of supporting the University, we cannot succeed, I would accept the charter alone, and petition the next day for an endowment." "We compromise no right or no claim," he maintained in conclusion, "by accepting a very small installment of our rights, and perhaps the charter might be made an engine for extorting an endowment."

This letter and that of the day before had their desired effect, for Leahy, who was both a vain and a weak man, and if left to himself, especially in a crisis, likely to do the rash rather than the prudent thing, finally caved in. "I am very thankful to your Eminence," he replied on March 2, "for the last two letters you have written. I fully coincide with Your Eminence's views, and will give whatever earnestness I can towards carrying them into effect, with God's help" (C). "I am," he confessed abjectly, "a very poor & weak instrument, and my dependence is upon God. As Your Eminence then has put me in the position of representing, along with my Brother Prelate, the feelings & opinions of the Bishops of Ireland upon an occasion of so much importance, I ask you to pray for us that God by his grace may enable us to acquit ourselves in a manner conducing to his glory & to the good of religion." "As soon as Mr. Disraeli fixes time & place for an interview," he assured Cullen in conclusion, "Dr. Derry and myself will be prepared to start for London." Disraeli did indeed reply several days later, on March 5, through his secretary, C. W. Freemantle, apologizing that the pressure of business had prevented him from replying sooner but saying that he wished to postpone any meeting with them until the matter had been laid before Parliament (L).

Disraeli had, in fact, held his first cabinet as prime minister on March 2 and 3, and the cabinet was almost entirely occupied with the consideration of its Irish policy, which was discussed under four main heads: material improvements, land, education, and the established Church. In reporting the discussion of education to the queen on March 4, Disraeli explained that primary education must wait upon the report of the royal commission, which was then sitting, "but the Cabinet were prepared to recommend a charter to a Roman Catholic University, provided the governing body contained such a decided lay representation as would prevent its being a mere sacerdotal institution."[68] Lord Derby, Disraeli assured the queen, had previously approved of this proposal by Lord Mayo, "not as the best, but the only, practicable solution of the question." Lord Derby had, in fact, written him that day, Disraeli further reported, to say that "it is doubtful whether the R.C. Prelates will accept our offer. If they do not, upon them will rest the responsibility of rejecting fair and liberal terms. If they do, I think our Protestant friends will acquiesce for fear of sanctioning worse." "An application," Disraeli then explained to the queen, "has been made by a deputation of R.C. Prelates from Ireland to Mr. Disraeli to enter into negotiations on the measure before it is introduced to Parliament; but he has declined this offer, though with much courtesy, and expressing his wish, after the proposition has been made public, to listen considerately to any criticism and suggestions made by the Prelates." "The truth is," he concluded, "the House of Commons will receive with prejudice the measure, if the first confidence is not made to itself."

This was a very curious performance by Disraeli, and it calls for

68. Buckle, 1:509–11.

some comment. He had apparently authorized Manning in a very private way to urge the Irish episcopal deputies to come over to London to negotiate a charter for the Catholic University. Why then did he reject Leahy and Derry's request for an interview in so abrupt a manner, and through his secretary, after obviously encouraging them through Manning? The answer appears to be that Disraeli would have preferred to be assured that the Irish bishops would accept the government's proposals about a charter before the matter was proposed for legislation in Parliament, but his cabinet colleagues thought otherwise. He and his colleagues had decided, in fact, in the previous December, when Derby was still prime minister, to have the government's proposals regarding a charter introduced by Mayo when Parliament reconvened in February. But why had Disraeli come to think that negotiations were preferable? He had undoubtedly come to agree with Derby that the government's proposals were bound to be rejected by the Irish bishops. It would be better, therefore, from the point of view of both the immediate survival of his ministry, which was in a minority in the House of Commons, and the approaching general election, to enter into extended and private negotiations with the Irish bishops than to make an immediate proposal to legislate that they might then publicly reject. By introducing even a modest proposal, Disraeli not only would severely test the loyalty of the more fervent Protestants among his own followers but, even more important for political survival, would antagonize those of like mind in the Liberal party, and if the Irish bishops rejected his modest proposal, he would have the alienated Irish Catholic and Liberal members to contend with as well. He would thus realize the worst of all possible political worlds in a House of Commons where his survival depended on not giving the majority arrayed against him an issue on which to focus and unite, and where his political future depended on not giving them yet another issue they could turn to their advantage in the upcoming general election. Disraeli's cabinet colleagues apparently viewed matters differently and thought the greater danger lay in not taking the House of Commons into their confidence. They must have argued that Mayo could be depended upon to make a proposal that would not offend their ultra-Protestant supporters and would at the same time prove just attractive enough to entice the Irish bishops into the extended negotiations Disraeli believed to be tactically necessary. In any case, Disraeli acquiesced and loyally hewed to the line of the cabinet majority in his report to the queen.

When Leahy received the reply Disraeli sent through his secretary on March 5, he was incensed, and all of Cullen's careful efforts to mollify him in the previous week appeared to have gone for naught. "At length," he reported brusquely to Cullen on March 6, "I have heard from Mr. Disraeli. Here is a copy of a letter received today—" (L). "It is well," he added at the end of his enclosure, "we did not put it in the power of this thimble-rigger to say we had endeavoured to force ourselves upon him." Leahy was so incensed, in fact, that he telegraphed Woodlock that same day, "Return to Dublin at once. We don't go to London now" (W).

Given Leahy's state of mind, Cullen wisely decided to leave him to himself for a while. On receiving Leahy's telegram, however, Woodlock wrote to Cullen asking him what he was to do. "My opinion," Cullen replied on March 8, "is that as the Irish debate is at hand you should remain to hear it. In the meantime try to act on our M.P.'s" (W). "I send you," he then added, "Disraeli's letter to Dr. Leahy. Do not show the copy in Dr. Leahy's handwriting to anyone except Dr. Manning. The last sentence shows how much Dr. Leahy was offended. Take a copy of Disraeli's letter and send me back the letter of Dr. Leahy." "I think we ought to accept the charter without endowment," he advised Woodlock. "I think the gt bulk of the Bishops are of the same opinion. However Dr. M^{C}H. will be for not accepting, and also I suppose Dr. Leahy and Dr. Derry, who will have some influence on acct of the commission they got. A greater difficulty will arise if the Ministry propose to grant the charter to a mixed body of Bishops and laymen. Then I dare say the Bishops might reject it." "Don't approve or reject anything," he then warned Woodlock in conclusion; "otherwise Dr. Leahy will be on you." Woodlock replied that he had informed Manning about what the bishops would be likely to do in the event the government proposed no endowment or a mixed body of laymen and bishops. "I am sorry to hear," Cullen replied posthaste on March 10, "that Dr. Manning thinks the Bishops cannot receive the plan proposed by Disraeli" (W). "Come home," he then advised Woodlock, "as soon as you see that nothing is to be done—the sooner the better lest Dr. Leahy s^d take your absence as a transgression against his telegram."

That same day, March 10, Mayo finally took occasion, on John Francis Maguire's motion for a committee of the House on the state of Ireland, to announce the government's Irish policy. In outlining the plan for a new Roman Catholic University for Ireland, Mayo proposed that the University would have a charter with degree-granting powers and a senate consisting of a chancellor, vice-chancellor, four bishops, and the president of Maynooth, all Catholics; the teaching body and graduates would both have a voice in choosing the senate; and the state would provide a small initial grant for scholarships. On reading Mayo's proposals the next day, both Cullen and Manning were very much encouraged. "Our papers inform us this morning," Cullen reported to Manning on March 11, "that Lord Mayo promises us a charter for the university and that the Senate is to consist of a Chancellor, Vice Chancellor, four bishops and six laymen."[69] "As we are likely to have a great deal of discussion on the matter," he alerted Manning, "it would be important to know whether the Chancellor and Vice Chancellor are to be Bishops or not—if they be laymen we would have eight laymen and only four Bishops—it would also be important to know how the laymen are to be chosen. We have some laymen in Ireland who are as hostile to the rights of the church as our open enemies. Probably the choice of government would fall upon men of that class; in which case the education of the country would not at all be safe." "If Your Grace," he urged in conclusion, "can get any accurate information, it would be of the greatest service. I fear that before we know how things really stand, some of our Bishops may make strong declarations against the government proposal before they know what it is, and thus we might be compromised or dissensions might be created."

Manning whose letter crossed Cullen's, wrote that same day. "The Government propose both Charter & Endowment," he reported on March 11 (C). "I trust this will get over one difficulty. The Govt. is willing to treat details, and I think they can be so moulded as to make them possible to accept." "I feel," he added magisterially, "that this is our moment." When Manning received Cullen's letter of March 11 asking for more information, he immediately wrote Disraeli to request an interview. "I have just now," he reported to Cullen on March 14, in a letter marked "CONFIDENTIAL," "had an interview with Mr. Disraeli. I feel no doubt that he sincerely intends to carry his proposal about the University if he can. But his hope of carrying it is by satisfying the Irish Bishops" (C). "Mr. C. Fortescue last night," Manning further reported, "declared that if the Catholics in Ireland accepted the plan, he would not hinder it. I think I can say that this will be Mr. Gladstone's line. If therefore your Eminence & the other Bishops could examine and pronounce upon the plan, this would decide the question, *the House permitting.*" "I will, within a day or two," he finally assured Cullen, "get all the information I can upon the points

69. Manning Papers (Ma), Archives of the Archdiocese of Westminster, London.

your Eminence mentions: & I hope that the constitutional parts of the plan can be modified."

Meanwhile, Woodlock had secured an interview with Lord Mayo, who had given him a memorandum outlining the government's proposals for a charter for the University, and Woodlock immediately forwarded copies of the memorandum to both Cullen and Leahy. Cullen had also written Leahy again in another effort to persuade him to go over to London for negotiations. "I am ready—so is Dr. Derry—to go to London," Leahy replied on March 13, still obviously somewhat sulky, "when a letter comes saying the people there are willing to have an interview. I had a letter yesterday from Dr. Woodlock stating that Lord Mayo had been at great pains to explain to him that Mr. Disraeli's not having at once assented to the proposed interview arose from no discourtesy but simply from his wish to be able to say he had no previous understanding with us. Dr. Woodlock added he had no doubt that I should have a letter today or tomorrow from Mr. Disraeli inviting us to the interview" (W). "Lord Mayo's proposal with respect to the University," Leahy confessed, "is much better than I expected it would be, and the only thing of any worth in the whole Ministerial programme." "It is highly probable I should think," he added shrewdly, "that Mr. Disraeli will not be allowed to retain office long enough to carry the proposed measure." "When I arrive in London," he promised Cullen in conclusion, "I will keep your Eminence daily informed of the progress of the business."

According to the memorandum Mayo gave Woodlock, the existing Catholic University would become an affiliated College of a new Roman Catholic University, to which other Colleges might also eventually be affiliated, and which would be empowered to grant degrees to the students of those Colleges. The government body of the new University was to consist of a senate of twenty members: a chancellor, a vice-chancellor (who would in effect be the *rector magnifico* of the new University), the president of Maynooth, four bishops, six laymen, five members of the various faculties in the affiliated College or Colleges, and two heads or rectors of the Colleges first affiliated. Initially, the members of the senate would be named in the charter granted by the state. Afterward, the chancellor was to be elected by convocation, consisting of the senate, professors, and graduates, and the vice-chancellor was to be appointed by the chancellor. The four bishops were to be nominated by the body of the bishops, the six laymen elected by convocation, and the five members of faculties elected by their faculties. The president of Maynooth and the two rectors of the Colleges first affiliated were to be senators by virtue of their offices. The senate was not only empowered to determine what Colleges might be affiliated but also given the right of confirmation of rectors, professors, and so on in those Colleges. On the subject of an endowment, however, the memorandum was much more equivocal. "Until the colleges are firmly established," Mayo noted, "it may be proper to postpone the question of endowment."[70] "It may, however," he then added, "be necessary to ask Parliament to provide a sufficient sum for the payment of the expenses of examinations for the foundation of a certain number of university scholarships, and the giving away of prizes; and also the payment of the salaries of certain officers and servants of the university, and perhaps some provision for a university hall and examination rooms."

Cullen's initial reaction to Mayo's memorandum was a good deal less enthusiastic than Leahy's. "From the paper you sent," he informed Woodlock on March 13, "it appears that the Chancellor and the six laymen are to be elected by convocation. This elective system would occasion dissensions and agitation, and in the end would put us in the hands of demagogues. The senate should fill up all the vacancies, otherwise there would be no unity in the body. The last paragr. of the circular seems to say that there will be no endowment at present except for the expenses of the university—I suppose that wd include salaries for professors" (W). "Stay where you are until you hear more about the matter," he advised Woodlock in conclusion. Woodlock apparently thought, as did Manning, that it was now or never for the Catholic University; he replied in a long and interesting letter, which underlined not only the immediacy of the crisis but also the necessity of accommodating the demand for lay participation in the government of the University. Woodlock explained to Cullen on March 14,

It will be extremely difficult for Gov^t to pass their scheme thro' the H. of Commons. I saw Mr. Gladstone yesterday; & he said it will be *impossible* for them to do so & to get a grant from the Consolidated Fund. I think if your Eminence & the other Bps, Dr. Keane, Dr. Butler &c. saw your way to *putting the screw* on the Irish M.P.'s, *by writing individually to those with wh. you are acquainted,* it may be carried.

Fortescue's speech is very fair. If the Primate w^d write to him, approving the scheme, & asking him to support it, I think he would do so. A line from your Eminence to Sir John Gray would decide him. Otherwise these sort of men are so bound up with

70. *Parliamentary Papers,* 1867–68, 13:8, no. 8.

party that they will take nothing from Tories. Can they not accept this as the first step towards equality; a step, indeed taken by *levelling up*; but I suppose there is no objection to that process to some extent in educational matters, altho' the Bps have objected to it in ecclesiastical. [W]

"With respect to the election of the Chancellor by Convocation," Woodlock reported, turning to the main point in Cullen's recent letter, "I think Gov^t w^d be induced to transfer it to the Senate. And if we can make them (the Gov^t) appoint your Eminence in the first instance as they ought to do, there might be an understanding or arrangement in the Senate, that the Abp of Dublin sh^d always be Chancellor." He went on:

With respect to the other six [i.e., laymen] it will, I think, be *impossible* to get that provision changed: for it is the one wh. w^d chiefly recommend the scheme to the H. of C. On the other hand it c^d easily be made innocuous—if not, positively advantageous: for by it the best Cath^s in Ireland, clerical & lay, & they only, might be connected with the Univ^y. For, in the first place, the first six will be appointed by Gov^t in concurrence with the Bps, and it is only as they drop off, others, one by one, will have to be selected. Secondly: the Senate itself will belong to the Convocation; also, I suppose, all the Professors of the Univ^y, & of its College or Colleges—and thus the Bp's influence will always have a vast preponderance. 3^{rdly} As large a number as possible of Eccles. students & Priests ought to take Degrees, as among Protestants in Trinity College, & thus clerical influence would always be paramount. Finally, & I think this is a most important consideration: the conditions for becoming members of Convocation ought to be such as very few would fulfil: for instance, under Dr. Newman's old rules, which Dr. Leahy & Dr. Derry accepted in this particular at our meeting in Thurles last January, no one could be a member of Convocation unless he had been *seven years* a student of the Univ^y and had taken one of the *higher* Degrees. This is the rule in Oxford, and also in Trinity College; altho' in the latter it is made nugatory by their granting the M.A. Degree without examination: whereas we ought to require a stringent one for the Degree of Master or Doctor in any Faculty. By these means the Convocation would always consist but of few persons, & these w^d be persons who w^d have rec^d a thorough Cath. Education. The Abp of Cashel or Dr. Forde, who have both of them given attention to this subject, will explain the matter to your Eminence better than I can.

"On the other hand, the H. of C. is as your Em. knows," Woodlock noted, "MAD *on the question of representative institutions;* and this clause of the proposed Charter will induce them, if anything can, to accept the scheme." "Again," he reminded Cullen in concluding, "a line from your Em. to Cogan, Maguire, Monsell, O'Reilly, in fact to any of the Irish Members w^d be most important."

After receiving both this letter and Manning's, containing the news of his interview with Disraeli and asking Cullen to get the Irish bishops to pronounce on the draft charter, on March 15, Cullen was less uneasy about the government's proposals. "Though the charter," he pointed out to Manning on March 15, "is not what we could wish yet I think it might be accepted with some modifications. The chancellor's election ought not to be left to Convocation. As for the election of the six laymen I suppose it might be left to the graduates though it would be safer in the hands of the Senate" (Ma). "I think it wd be better," he further explained, "not to hold a meeting of our bishops until something final is arranged. Dr. MacHale would appeal to Rome against us and stop all negotiations—if things were finally agreed on by Dr. Leahy & Dr. Derry with the Ministers, the Bishops would all agree to them—and the Holy See would not object. But if the things be brought in appeal to Rome, then delay wd be too great."

Meanwhile Mayo had finally written Leahy on March 14, enclosing his memorandum and inviting him to communicate either in writing or in person with regard to it.[71] After consulting with Derry, Leahy wrote Mayo on March 19, informing him that they hoped to be able to meet with him in London during the early part of the following week and listing eight points that might be usefully considered at their interview:

1. There is no provision saving the authority of the Catholic prelates in matters appertaining to faith and morals; nor is the constitution so framed, as far as I can see, that under it such authority could be freely exercised.

2. As a sequel to the foregoing, there appears to be no effective provision for the appointment of professors or other officers sound in faith and morals, or for the removal of such persons as might prove to be heterodox or immoral.

71. Ibid., p. 2, no. 3.

3. Such definitive appointment is vested, not in the Catholic bishops, but in the senate, which is objectionable.

4. The bishops ought to possess the power of at least an absolute negative on such appointments. I am not prepared to say that would suffice.

5. In the constitution of the senate there is too much of the lay element, too little of the clerical.

6. The Chancellor named in the first instance by Government would, I presume, be his Eminence Cardinal Cullen. That would be due to his rank and position in the Catholic church. After the first instance, the Chancellor ought to be elected by the senate, not, as is proposed, by convocation, and ought to be one of the four archbishops. A spirit of party might by-and-by animate the body of the graduates, and a person unfit for the high office of Chancellor might be elected were the office open to all.

7. The number of the Senate is set down at 20; yet from its constitution, one would think it ought to be variable. The number of the Senate is made up of two elements, one invariable, the other variable; the former being 18, the latter being the heads of the affiliated colleges. Were the number to be fixed at 20, it would follow that at no time could there be in the Senate more than two heads of affiliated colleges.

8. A great objection to the proposed scheme is, the want of a suitable endowment.[72]

Leahy forwarded a copy of this letter the same day to Cullen, who immediately upon receiving it, on March 20, wrote Manning to report that he had sent a copy to Woodlock and that Woodlock would show it to him (Ma). Cullen then explained to Manning that he thought the eight points made by Leahy were much too decided to serve as a basis for negotiations. He was pleased, he added, that Manning had written to Barnabò, because this step would ensure that Rome would do nothing until the whole business of the proposed charter had been fully examined by the Irish bishops. Manning had in fact written Barnabò, "riservatissima [most confidentially]," in order to prevent any appeal by MacHale from being entertained by Rome.[73] "In the meantime, however," Cullen reported further, "I have received a message from Cardinal Reisach [prefect of the sacred congregation of Studies in Rome] saying it is of the utmost importance that the Bishops should

72. Ibid., pp. 4–5, no. 4.
73. C, Manning to Cullen, March 19, 1868.

maintain their control over the professors, and expressing his fear, that, if the professors be made independent of ecclesiastical authority, they will become infected with rationalism and Jansenism."

By this time, however, Gladstone had suddenly transformed the whole political situation by finally declaring in the House of Commons on March 16 that the established Church in Ireland must cease to exist as a state church.[74] Since the defeat of the Liberal ministry in June 1866, the Liberals had continued to have a majority in the House of Commons of about sixty, but they had been so dexterously outmaneuvered by Disraeli, especially on the issue of parliamentary reform, that they had been unable to focus on an issue that would allow them to mobilize their majority. When Gladstone declared against the Irish Church, however, it became immediately apparent that he had found the issue that would unite the Liberals, and that the effective power of the Disraeli ministry was doomed. In order to consolidate his position in the House, Gladstone gave notice a week later, on March 23, of a series of three resolutions on the disestablishing of the state Church in Ireland.[75] After an intense and extended debate of some two weeks, the first of the resolutions was approved on April 3, by a majority of sixty.[76]

After Gladstone's initial declaration on March 16, no one was quicker than Manning to sense that any further negotiations for a charter for the Catholic University were useless. Indeed, if Manning had not understood the situation immediately on March 16, he certainly realized it on March 20, when Woodlock showed him a copy of Leahy's letter to Mayo outlining the eight points, which Cullen had correctly characterized as being much too decided to serve as a basis for negotiations. From this point on, in fact, Manning ceased all communication with Disraeli. As he explained to Disraeli some ten months later, on December 2, on the occasion of his resignation as prime minister, "I have felt that a ravine, I will not say a gulf, opened between us when the Resolutions on the Irish Church were laid on the Table of the House. I regretted this, as I had hoped to see the scheme of the Catholic University happily matured; but with my inevitable conviction as to the Irish Church, I felt that I ought not to trespass upon your kindness, which I can assure you I shall remember with much pleasure."[77] At the same time, Manning was apparently both

74. *Hansard*, 190:1764.
75. Ibid., 191:32.
76. Ibid., 471.
77. Monypenny and Buckle, 5:10.

annoyed that the negotiations had been taken out of his hands by Leahy and Derry and also piqued because they proceeded to act at variance with his considered judgment and advice. For all these reasons, therefore, he decided that the sooner he washed his hands of the whole affair, the better.[78]

Cullen was much slower than Manning in realizing the implications of Gladstone's declaration. In the days immediately preceding it, Cullen had been using his best efforts to persuade the Irish Catholic and Liberal members to support the Conservative ministry on a charter, and he was becoming increasingly resentful of those Liberals in general, and Gladstone in particular, who appeared determined to use the issue as a means of bringing Disraeli's government down. Cullen informed Woodlock on Monday, March 16, "I wrote a few lines to you on Friday to show to some of the Catholic M.P.'s. I also wrote to Sir John Gray. Today I have written to Mr. Murphy and Sir G. Bowyer who wrote to consult me" (W). "It will be well," he advised Woodlock, "to make the best terms we can—but our liberal friends appear determined to defeat all our hopes." When he received a letter from Woodlock the next day—obviously before he learned of Gladstone's declaration of the evening before—complaining about Gladstone and his followers, Cullen gave vent to his feelings. "You have very little reason to expect anything from men," he replied to Woodlock on March 17. "[Nolite confidere] in principibus in filiis hominum in quibus non est salus [(Place not your trust) in princes the sons of men in whom there is no salvation]" (W). "I never liked Gladstone," he confessed, "since he wrote his letters against Naples. He first misrepresented things, and then when he was refuted, he refused to retract. This shows that he is not a lover of justice. What trust can we place in him in Irish affairs?" "I suppose his opposition," Cullen concluded sadly, "will prevent the government from going on with the charter."

When Cullen learned of Gladstone's declaration of March 16, he must have realized that his efforts to mobilize the Irish Catholic and Liberal members on behalf of a charter would now be doubly difficult, and he instinctively attempted to compensate by arranging for a meeting of the committee of the National Association, which had not gathered for some four months. At the meeting, which took place on March 20, a long letter from him to MacSwiney was read to the assembled members:

78. Ibid. As he wrote Disraeli some years later, on May 7, 1870, the negotiations "were entirely taken out of my hands by the Bishops who corresponded with you, but in a sense at variance with my judgement and advice."

Will you be so kind as to hand in my subscription to the National Association. During the three or four years that have passed since it was first called into existence that body has rendered good services to this country; and its meetings, the statistical returns regarding the Protestant Establishment which it collected, the reports on the exclusion of every Catholic by the grand juries from almost every office at their disposal, and the addresses which it has published, have contributed largely to place the condition of Ireland in a proper light before the world. Convinced by the evidence of the facts placed before them, English statesmen now generally admit that it is an injustice and an insult to force a Catholic population to maintain a Protestant Church, and they seem determined to put an end to an establishment which has been for centuries the source of all the evils and misfortunes of this unhappy land. They also appear to be convinced that legislation on the land question is necessary, and that something must be done to protect the agricultural classes from the utter destruction that menaces them. As to education, things have made so much progress since the corporations of Ireland and your association commenced to discuss the question that the present Government has appointed a commission to report on primary schools, and has manifested its intention of granting a charter to a Catholic University, a measure which, if properly carried out, will be applauded not only by Catholics, but by all heads of families of every denomination, who are anxious to resume a religious education for their children, in the higher branches of knowledge.[79]

"However," Cullen warned, "those favourable appearances ought not to lull the association into security, or induce it to relax its efforts." "Everyone knows," he then asserted,

that there is a strong party in this country most hostile to everything Catholic, a party that would prefer to see the people immersed in ignorance and barbarity rather than allow them to be instructed in the doctrines of the Catholic Church, professed by the most enlightened and powerful nations of the earth; moreover, a rationalistic school is spreading in England, and those who are infected with its doctrines are anxious to establish a purely secular system of education and to banish God and reli-

79. *Freeman's Journal*, March 21, 1868.

gion from the school. The anti-Catholic party in Ireland and the anti-Christian school in England will unite in opposing our just claims, and endeavour to deprive the children of the country of the advantages of a Christian education and of the blessings conferred on them by the true faith.

"In these circumstances," Cullen finally assured his auditors, "great efforts must be made to preserve our religion, dearer to us than our lives, from the dangers with which it is menaced by a Godless system of instruction, and your association can render good services by uniting the energies of the people to defend liberty of education at this alarming crisis."

Cullen was now obviously determined to get what he could from the Conservatives, because there was no hope of securing anything from the Liberals in the future on educational matters. "I trust," he had written Manning at the end of a letter on March 20, "something may be done before any change of ministers takes place" (Ma). Unlike Manning, however, Cullen did not realize that the chances for a charter were now no better from the Conservatives than from the Liberals. What he did not appear to understand was that Disraeli's government, especially after Gladstone's resolutions of March 23, was only a caretaker ministry until the next general election, and that any controversial legislation was out of the question. Besides these constraints in the parliamentary equation, Disraeli had also to consider the exigencies of party politics. Not only were there now no Irish votes, either in or out of Parliament, to be gained by pressing on with legislation for a charter, but what was even more important, there were actually votes to be lost among the Conservatives' own ultra-Protestant supporters by pursuing such a course. The only real question left, therefore, for Disraeli and his colleagues, was how they were going to disengage as gracefully as possible from the negotiations they had unfortunately initiated with the Irish bishops through Mayo just two days before Gladstone's celebrated declaration of March 16.

After an important conversation with Cullen in Dublin on Sunday evening, Leahy, in company with Derry, crossed over to London the next day, March 23, for their interview on the twenty-fourth. At that interview at the Irish office with Mayo and his cabinet colleague, the earl of Malmesbury, the lord privy seal, the bishops made their presentation, and Mayo then politely asked them to put their views into writing for the consideration of the cabinet. When he did not hear from Leahy the day after the interview, Cullen, who realized now that time was of the essence, immediately wrote to him. "I hope," he began on March 25, "your Grace's interview with Lord Mayo has been satisfactory, and I trust that something final will be arranged about the charter" (L). "Probably," he explained, "if Mr. Gladstone's resolutions be adopted on next Monday, a change of government will take place. The accession of the Liberals though it may bring a settlement of the Church question, it would undoubtedly lessen our chance of getting a charter on fair terms." "It is to be hoped therefore," he then advised Leahy, "that something may be done before the present ministry shall be put out of office. If any arrangement could be made securing the rights of the bishops to control the professors and to exclude bad books, I suppose all other matters could be easily settled. As we are in the hands of two parties equally hostile to us, and ready to leave us as we are unless they can gain something by assisting us, it seems that it would be good policy to take anything that is offered provided no principle be compromised, and the rights of the Church be respected." "But as your Grace and Dr. Derry are on the spot," he noted politely in concluding, "you will be the best judges of what can be done."

On their return to Ireland, Leahy and Derry proceeded to put their views into writing as Mayo had requested; on March 31 they forwarded them to the chief secretary for the consideration of his colleagues.[80] The alterations the two bishops thought desirable or necessary in the government proposals were these: that the new University should be a teaching as well as an examining and degree-granting body; that the affiliated Colleges should be wholly independent of the University, except in matters appertaining to University examinations and the conferring of degrees; that the senate should consist of a variable number, rather than being fixed at twenty, so as to be able to accommodate all the heads of the various affiliated Colleges; that the chancellor should be a bishop, and the cardinal archbishop of Dublin the first chancellor; that the election of the chancellor and the six laymen on the senate should be by the senate and not convocation; and that as faith and morals were the exclusive province of the bishops, the bishops on the senate should have a veto on all books and on the nomination of professors and other officers, as well as the right to remove them if they were adjudged by the bishops to be heterodox or immoral. They added that, appreciating as they did the difficulties the government would have in carrying an endowment just then, and

---

80. *Parliamentary Papers*, 1867–68, 13:3–6, no. 7.

without prejudice to the future, they would press only for a provision for the current expenses, such as salaries, scholarships, prizes, examinations, equipment, and lecture halls.

In this letter the two bishops had obviously climbed down a long way from the letter of March 19 in which they had outlined their eight points, and also from the position they had taken up in their statement to the Catholic M.P.'s the previous January. The influence of both Cullen and Manning on their latest production was apparent. The two bishops said nothing, for example, about the proportion of laymen to clerics on the senate, and they postponed the necessity for an endowment to a more propitious occasion in the interest of obtaining operating expenses.

When Leahy did not even receive an acknowledgement of his letter, he wrote Mayo on April 11 to ask if he had received it. Mayo replied on April 21, explaining lamely that he had thought the letter had been acknowledged and promising that he would submit it to his colleagues as soon as he returned to London from Dublin after the Easter recess (L). When Mayo did finally write Leahy some three weeks later, on May 11, his letter on behalf of his colleagues was devastating (L). The reason why he had taken nearly six weeks to reply, of course, was that in the excitement generated by the debate and voting on Gladstone's resolutions on the established Church, it was not at all clear, especially after the majority of sixty against the government on April 6, that the ministry would long survive. If it did not, there was little point in Mayo's replying because circumstances might soon make the whole question of a charter academic. When it became obvious after the Easter recess, in early May, that the ministry was going to remain in office at least until after the general election scheduled for the autumn, Mayo had no alternative but to answer Leahy. In his letter of May 11 he began by enumerating the alterations suggested by the bishops:

1. That the veto of the Senate of the university over the appointment of the professors and other officers of the affiliated colleges is uncalled for, and ought not to be maintained.
2. That the Chancellor should always be a Prelate.
3. That the first Chancellor should be Cardinal Archbishop Cullen.
4. That the Chancellor should, after the first nomination by the Crown, be elected by the Senate, and not by Convocation.
5. That the election of the six lay members of the Senate should rest with that body, and not with Convocation.

6. That the episcopal members of the Senate should have an absolute negative on the books included in the university programme; and, on the first nomination of the professors, lecturers, and other officers, and that they should also have the power of depriving them of their offices should they be judged by the bishops to have done anything contrary to faith and morals.

Mayo then proceeded to reject categorically each and every suggestion he had listed as being made by the bishops. "The object of the Government," he finally concluded, "was to create an institution which, although denominational in character, would be thoroughly independent, self-governed, and free from any external influence, either political or religious. The proposals made in your letter would strike at the very root of these principles, and I am, therefore, with extreme regret, obliged to inform you that the recommendations contained in that letter cannot be entertained." When he received this letter, Leahy apparently consulted Derry about what should be done and then, on May 16, replied merely acknowledging its receipt.

This was a very shrewd and able performance by Mayo. In breaking off negotiations with the bishops, he chose as his ground, in effect, undue clerical influence in educational matters. He had obviously already decided to publish the correspondence between the government and the bishops, and his letter of May 11 was designed to be the pièce de résistance in this epistolary banquet, the main purpose of which was not simply to place the bishops on the defensive but to put them in the wrong with British public opinion. The letter was, in short, a first-rate election manifesto, especially meant for the "no-popery" element in the British electorate. Leahy apparently forwarded a copy of Mayo's letter to Cullen as soon as he received it, for Cullen wrote Manning on May 13, asking him to find out from Disraeli whether Mayo's letter really meant that negotiations were at an end. "In the course of next week," Manning replied on May 15 from Dover, "I will try to ascertain what the Gov^t intend as to the Charter" (C). "Late events," he explained, "have placed me in a difficulty as regards Mr. Disraeli: & I have not liked to communicate with him lest he should take it as a request & to lay me under a difficulty towards him." "Nevertheless," Manning promised, "I will obtain such information as I can: & report without delay."

When Mayo announced that he would lay his correspondence with Leahy before the House of Commons, Cullen finally realized that the negotiations were at an end. He advised Leahy on May 17, therefore, to write a telling reply to Mayo in order that it might mitigate the effect of the chief secretary's letter of May 11 (L). "Perhaps it would be well also," Cullen added, "to write to the Catholic M.P.'s to tell them that the conditions proposed by Lord Mayo cd not be admitted." By this time it was too late for Leahy to have the last word: the correspondence between the government and the bishops was published on May 19 (L). As far as tactics and political maneuvers were concerned, therefore, Mayo and his colleagues had apparently had it all their own way, and the sad legacy of this enormous expenditure of time and energy was a series of mutual recriminations about who was responsible for breaking off the negotiations, the government or the bishops.

Though the negotiations with both Whig and Tory governments on the education question over the previous three years had ended in frustration for the bishops, with the Tories it was a frustration with a distinct difference. With the Whigs the bishops had been sorely disappointed and angry, but with the Tories they had been treated contemptuously, and they were furious at their humiliation. This humiliation, however, should not be allowed to cloud their real achievement at their general meeting in early October 1867. At that meeting they not only continued to give proof of that harmony and unity on the education question which had so distinguished both their meetings in 1865, but they also laid the foundation in their resolutions on the established Church for the development of the Gladstonian Irish-Liberal alliance and Gladstone's program of justice for Ireland. In refusing to take any part of the endowment of the established Church, and unequivocally demanding its disestablishment and disendowment, the Irish bishops made possible a tactical alliance between Irish Catholics and English Nonconformists, an alliance that allowed Gladstone to proceed to his celebrated resolutions in the House of Commons in March 1868, to his reconstruction of the Liberal party, and to his eventually winning supreme power in the general election of 1868. On the education question, moreover, the bishops demonstrated that, if anything, their line in the interim had actually hardened. They also exhibited a very real self-confidence, both in containing their colleague, the bishop of Kerry, by vetoing his taking a place on the royal commission on elementary education, and in appointing Leahy and Derry, to the formal exclusion of Cullen, to represent their interests in any future negotiations with the government. By early 1868, therefore, the bishops were able finally to write *finis* to an issue that had divided and troubled them as a body for more than thirty years.

X

The Bishops as a Body

May 1864–March 1870

The problems of Fenianism and university education both certainly provided serious challenges to the Irish bishops in their efforts to consolidate their body, and it must be admitted that they responded well to those challenges in maintaining and strengthening their unity. There was, however, yet another challenge to the body that was to prove to be just as serious, and even more difficult to meet, because, unlike the political and educational issues, it was unprecedented. When Cullen was finally raised to the rank of cardinal in June 1866, his position in the Church was transformed both at home and at Rome, most especially with regard to his relationship to the episcopal body. At home he was no longer simply the first among equals and the acknowledged leader of the Irish bishops; he was now by rank superior to his brother prelates and the formal head of the national hierarchy. At Rome what were formerly his privileges were now his rights by virtue of his office. The real challenge for the Irish bishops as a body, however, was to be found less in the fact that he would now be consulted by Rome as a matter of right in all Irish episcopal appointments than in the fact that his voice was now likely to prove to be the determinant one in those appointments. How indeed the bishops would stand up to this new and extraordinary challenge was to prove not only the most interesting but also perhaps the most important question as far as their own corporate character and effective will were concerned.

The story of Cullen's newfound power and influence in Irish episcopal appointments actually begins some two years before he became a cardinal, with the efforts to provide a coadjutor for Patrick Fallon, the bishop of Kilmacduagh and Kilfenora. Fallon, who had had a serious drinking problem for several years, had finally decided to apply to the pope for a coadjutor in May 1864, and Barnabò wrote both MacHale and Leahy on May 31 to ask their opinions in the matter. Barnabò was obliged to consult both archbishops because Kilmacduagh was in the province of Tuam and Kilfenora in that of Cashel. Both archbishops apparently advised the cardinal that Fallon did need help, for in writing Cullen some time later, Barnabò explained that he was endeavoring to have a coadjutor appointed. In reporting this information to Kirby on September 4, Cullen suggested that if he should see Barnabò he should "tell him that it would be infinitely better to give that diocese to Galway" (K). "The diocese of Galway," Cullen explained, "has very few parishes, Kilmacduagh has only ten or twelve, Kilfenora only a similar number; put all three dioceses together and you will have only thirty five or thirty six parishes and less than *100,000* souls, perhaps not *80,000*." "Dr. MacEvilly," Cullen added, referring to the bishop of Galway, "would manage them well. The present Bishop of Kilmacduagh, Dr. Fallon, is become quite useless, he shuts himself up and does nothing. The diocese must be in a bad way." "Speak to the Cardinal," he urged Kirby in conclusion, "as soon as you can do so."

When Cullen apparently heard nothing regarding Kilmacduagh and Kilfenora, he wrote Barnabò again about a month later. "I wrote a line yesterday," he alerted Kirby on October 7, "regarding Kilmacduagh and Kilfenora and Galway. The whole of the three dioceses would not make one proper diocese. There are only thirty-one parishes, about forty priests, and I daresay not more than 60,000 people. Dr. Fallon has scarcely enough to live on. Dr. MacEvilly is also poor[;] their predecessors got on badly enough, but now the times are worse than ever. I think they ought to unite them" (K). "If they consult Dr. McH. or Dr. Leahy," he warned, "they will meet opposition, but if they will do it all at once there will be no more about it. Dr. McH. wishes to have a good many suffragans and this is his ground of opposition." A month later, when he still had heard nothing, Cullen wrote Kirby again. "I suppose," he complained on November 6, "there is no use in writing anymore about Galway and the proposed union of Kilmacduagh etc. I will not refer to it anymore" (K). Two days later, however, on November 8, he wrote Kirby again, asking him to tell Barnabò that things were going very badly in Kilmacduagh and Kilfenora (K). He had just seen the bishop of Elphin that day, Cullen explained, and he had been assured by him that Fallon was in a helpless condition, and a coadjutor, or at least an administrator, was absolutely necessary. An election to choose a coadjutor, he added, would be very difficult because there were very few priests in Kilmacduagh and Kilfenora, and even fewer, if any, would have the qualities required in a bishop. Rumor had it, moreover, Cullen warned, that an effort would be made to choose William Derry, the brother of the bishop of Clonfert, who was not only strongly imbued with the ideas of MacHale but also very much engaged in temporal matters.

Nothing more seems to have been done about Kilmacduagh and Kilfenora until some six months later, when MacHale visited Rome in May and June 1865 to fulfill his required *ad limina* obligations. MacHale obviously persuaded Barnabò that Fallon needed a coadjutor, for the cardinal wrote the archbishop of Cashel on July 14, authorizing him and MacHale to proceed with the selection of a *terna* in Kilmacduagh and Kilfenora (L). MacHale and Leahy apparently had considerable difficulty coordinating their efforts because Fallon was unable to function, and so finally, on February 20, 1866, Barnabò wrote them instructing them to arrange for the convoking of the clergy and the conducting of the meeting. MacHale therefore wrote Leahy on March 13, suggesting that they should each choose a priest, respectively from Kilmacduagh and Kilfenora, to represent them in the likelihood that Fallon would be unable to preside (L). The problem, of course, was that if Fallon could not preside, the prescribed procedure in the appointment of a coadjutor required that his metropolitan do so. Because Kilmacduagh and Kilfenora were in two provinces and subject to two metropolitans, the procedure would require both archbishops to preside jointly. MacHale was anxious to avoid such a situation because having both archbishops present might seem to the Roman authorities to infringe on the freedom of the election. He therefore advised Leahy that perhaps the best solution would be for each of them to select a priest to act as surrogate for him at the meeting if Fallon were unable to preside, and he suggested that each select a priest not from his own diocese but instead from, respectively, Kilmacduagh and Kilfenora. Accordingly, MacHale chose Timothy Shannon, vicar-general of Kilmacduagh and parish priest of Kilmacduagh and Kiltartan, near Gort, and Leahy selected John Sheehan, vicar-general of Kilfenora and parish priest of Ennistymon.

In the event, and after all these elaborate precautions, Fallon was able to preside, so that the surrogates were not necessary. The clergy of both dioceses then met on April 12 at Gort. Of the sixteen votes, Timothy Shannon received five, and John Sheehan and Michael Connolly, the parish priest of Kilcornan, near Oranmore in the diocese of Kilmacduagh, received four each.[1] The other three votes were distributed among three other candidates, one of whom was James Lynch, a Vincentian and rector of the Irish College in Paris. The meetings of the bishops of the provinces of Cashel and Tuam were then scheduled respectively for April 24 and May 3, at Thurles and Tuam. In the meantime, Cullen, who had set his face against a coadjutor's being appointed in Kilmacduagh and Kilfenora, began to canvass assiduously to have the bishop of Galway appointed administrator of the united dioceses. "The Bishops," Cullen's secretary, Patrick Moran, reported to Kirby on April 16, referring to the Cashel prelates, "are to meet on tomorrow week to give their opinion. Some of them intend to recommend the non-appointment of a coadjutor. According to all accounts, the diocese has gone to the dogs entirely, and in addition to the other *miserie* [wretchednesses], there is an utter impossibility of any Bishop being able to support himself there whilst the present Bishop lives" (K). "If the Sac. Congregation," he suggested, "without suppressing the diocese, made an arrangement that during the lifetime of the present Bishop, Kilfenora should be administered by the Bishop of Limerick [correctly, Killaloe], and Kilmacduagh by the Bishop of Galway, it would save both *capre e cavolo* [goats and cabbage] and perhaps before the old Bishop dies some opportunity may present itself of making a better arrangement." Cullen then added in a postscript, "Dr. Moran has told you of the election for Kilmacduagh. The best plan would be to give Kilmacduagh and Kilfenora to Dr. MacEvilly. If not to give Kilfenora to Killaloe etc. etc."

The following day, April 17, Cullen wrote the bishop of Elphin and a suffragan of the archbishop of Tuam, recommending this solution when the Tuam prelates met (G). Apparently he also wrote the bishop of Limerick to give him the same advice, but when the Cashel prelates met on April 24 they confined themselves in their report to recommending unanimously the first on the list, Timothy Shannon, and did not mention the subject of appointing an administrator. The coadjutor to the bishop of Killaloe reported to the bishop of Elphin that after the meeting, on April 25, he had objected to anything being added to or taken away from Killaloe, and the Cashel prelates had refused to discuss Kilmacduagh (G). A week later, on May 4, an obviously determined and undaunted Cullen assured Kirby, "All the Bishops in Cashel were of opinion that Kilfenora and Kilmacduagh ought

1. A, vol. 231 (1866), p. 2, fol. 472, "Sopra un provvedimento da prendersi per la Diocesi unite di Kilfenora e Kilmacduagh in Irlanda, 30 Luglio, 1866" (fols. [469]–75).

to be united with Galway, but they did not write anything on that point—I have suggested to Dr. Butler to write—he said he would—and that Dr. Moriarty would also write" (K). "The three dioceses," he insisted stubbornly in conclusion, "will make one decent diocese—as it is each Bishop is starving."

Meanwhile, Cullen had also written Gillooly again, on April 24, to keep him up to the mark for the meeting of the Tuam prelates on May 3. Cullen suggested that in writing Rome, Gillooly too should point out that Kilmacduagh and Kilfenora "were too poor to support a coadjutor" (G). When the Tuam prelates did finally meet in Tuam on May 3, they were not unanimous in their report to Propaganda, as their Cashel colleagues had been.[2] The bishops of Achonry and Clonfert, like the Cashel prelates, recommended the *dignissimus*, Timothy Shannon, but the bishops of Elphin and Galway, in surprising company with the archbishop of Tuam, recommended the third name on the *terna*, Michael Connolly. The reason why these three bishops preferred Connolly to Shannon was that he was both younger and more vigorous, and he had also pursued a more distinguished course of study at Maynooth. The bishops of Elphin and Galway also noted that Connolly had the virtue of being a total abstainer, though they added that they did not wish to cast any imputation on Shannon in recommending Connolly for this reason. The burning question of the day, that of recommending that the bishop of Galway be appointed the administrator of Kilmacduagh and Kilfenora, was not raised at the meeting; the prelates confined themselves to reporting on the merits of the *terna*. Several days after the meeting, however, the archbishops of Cashel and Tuam received a remarkable letter from the cardinal prefect of Propaganda. Barnabò had written them on April 30, explaining that it had now been proposed that an administrator rather than a coadjutor be appointed in Kilmacduagh and Kilfenora, because the dioceses were so small and poor, and asking the archbishops for their opinions on the matter (L).

The question is, of course, Why did Barnabò suddenly raise this point, especially after he had gone to so much trouble to have a coadjutor selected by the clergy and reported on by the bishops of two provinces? The obvious answer is that he had been finally persuaded by Cullen on the advantages of an administrator rather than a coadjutor. But why did he make such a precipitate decision virtually in the midst of the procedure itself? The answer to this question is that Barnabò had undoubtedly learned that the pope had decided to raise

2. Ibid., fol. 473.

Cullen to the rank of cardinal, and so Barnabò would soon have to deal with his new colleague personally in Rome about the Kilmacduagh and Kilfenora problem. Just when the pope finally decided to promote Cullen is not entirely clear,[3] but the question was being mooted in early March, when Cardinal Antonelli, the papal secretary of state, seems to have advised Odo Russell, the British government's unofficial agent in Rome, about the pope's intentions. "I suspect," Russell informed the earl of Clarendon, the British foreign secretary, by telegram on March 5, "the pope wants to make Dr. Cullen a Cardinal. If so should I advise against it or not?"[4] Clarendon replied the following day, March 6, "We do not wish to interfere in the matter." A month later, however, on April 6, Russell concluded a very long dispatch to Clarendon, reporting an interview with Cardinal Antonelli concerning the complaints of the British government about the conduct of the Irish clergy and their involvement with Fenianism, by noting that "Card¹ Antonelli then went on to speak of Dr. Cullen, of whom he entertains a very high opinion, but he assured me nevertheless that the Pope would not make him a Cardinal for the present."[5] "The present," was apparently of very short duration, for Antonelli, as was customary in promotions to the sacred college, wrote Cullen in early May, informing him of the pope's decision to raise him to the rank of cardinal.

In the midst of the developing crisis created by the question of providing for Kilmacduagh and Kilfenora, and before the news of Cullen's promotion arrived in Ireland, the archbishop of Armagh, Joseph Dixon, died on April 29, at the age of sixty, after a brief bout with typhoid fever. Dixon's death was a very serious blow to Cullen both personally and ecclesiastically, because for nearly fifteen years he had been not only a faithful friend but also one of his most consistent supporters in the episcopal body. Dixon was also very much respected by his episcopal colleagues, for in maintaining his loyalty to Cullen he had not compromised either his personal integrity or his primatial

3. There is some evidence that the question of promoting Cullen was being discussed in late January 1866, for Manning noted on February 3, in a reply to a letter of Monsignor George Talbot, private chamberlain to the pope, "I am glad to hear that Dr. Cullen is to be made cardinal. It is most due" (Edmund S. Purcell, *Life of Cardinal Manning* [London, 1896], 2:392).

4. F.O., 43/96 a.

5. Ibid.

dignity. He was, moreover, much esteemed in the Irish Church at large as a sincerely pious and holy man. "The last three days," an obviously touched and saddened Cullen reported to Kirby on May 4, "I have been in Armagh paying the last marks of respect to our dear friend Dr. Dixon, whose death is a sad loss to Ireland. He died last Sunday having been ill for only eight days of low fever. He never lost his consciousness to the last moment" (K). "As he had a great devotion to St. Catherine of Siena," Cullen explained, "it seems she obtained for him the favour to die on the same day she died (the vigil of her feast) and at the same hour. I sang Mass on Wednesday for him— about 200 priests and eleven Bishops were present, and a great concourse of people. He is buried in the convent of the Ladies of the Sacred Heart, which is dedicated to St. Catherine. Everyone regrets him very much." "I do not know," Cullen then confessed, turning to Dixon's successor, "who will be elected by the clergy." "Dr. Kieran," he predicted, referring to the parish priest of Dundalk and dean of the diocese, "I suppose, is certain—the other two will probably be selected from Maynooth." Ten days later Cullen was somewhat more specific. "Dr. Kieran of Dundalk," he informed Kirby on May 15, "will probably be the first on the list. Dr. Russell of Maynooth and some others are spoken of" (K). "If the Government had a voice," he warned Kirby, "they would translate Dr. Moriarty who sides with them on the education question. He (Dr. Moriarty) has been lately in London for several days treating I believe, with the Government about education and the marriage laws. I have not been able to discover what recommendations he has made."

By the time Cullen had written this letter, his own position in the Irish Church had been radically transformed by the news that he was to be made a cardinal. "I have just received," an obviously shaken Cullen had informed Kirby on May 13, "an alarming letter from Cardinal Antonelli which has left me in such a state that I do not know how to answer his Eminence" (K). "He has informed me," Cullen explained, "(probably you have heard of the matter yourself) that His Holiness has determined to promote me to the Sacred College. Knowing how unfit I am for such a dignity I feel confounded and ashamed at the proposal of His Holiness, and I do not know what to answer. I will try to put two or three sentences together before tomorrow." "Will you call in the meantime," he requested of Kirby, "on the Cardinal and thank him, at the same time telling him what a difficulty he has placed me in. Indeed I never had the remotest idea that such a dignity would [be] offered to me." "Besides speaking to the Cardinal," Cullen added, turning to the more practical implications of the dignity, "I would be obliged if you would get an account of the expenses etc. and let me know all. Cardinal Reisach or any foreign Cardinal will tell you—I am very low in a financial point of view as I have expended everything I could get on schools or in Clonliffe." He noted in conclusion, "I write this line in a hurry—I have not mentioned this matter to anyone as yet, except to Dr. Forde and Canon McCabe."

"I wrote a line ere yesterday," a much more composed Cullen informed Kirby on May 15, "to inform you of the intelligence I had received from Cardinal Antonelli that His Holiness had determined to promote me to the Sacred College" (K). "I thought when writing," he confessed, "that the Cardinal might have mentioned the matter to you—but from your letter to Dr. Moran which came today I am convinced you had not heard of it and from a letter of Cardinal Barnabò of the 4th I conclude that he knew nothing of it. It is better therefore to keep the business private." "Send me a telegram," he then advised Kirby, "when you do receive this and if you wish me to go [i.e., come to Rome] say simply all right—then tell me how much the first expenses would amount to. You can say a thousand *volumes* for sale or anything that way to conceal what is going on." "If you can learn," he then further explained, "when the Consistory will be you could indicate it as the day for the sale 'one thousand volumes for sale 28th of June or 1st July[']' as may be." "I am greatly fretted by this matter," he finally confided, "but what can be done[?]"

"I have received your telegram of yesterday," Cullen reported a week later, on May 22, "for which I feel much obliged" (K). "I fear," he confessed, "it will be difficult to put together £2000. It is a large amount in a poor country, and when it is not for a useful purpose, but merely for state, it is not easy to put it together. I shall see some of the clergy, and try what can be done." "For my own part," he declared, "I would rather give up honours and do something useful in the way of building schools or churches." Cullen then added a postscript in reference to the papal government's funds, in which he had a large sum invested: "If the Consolidate could be sold out all would be right." There is little doubt that Cullen was shaken by the expense involved in becoming a cardinal. Two thousand pounds was certainly an enormous sum of money in Ireland in 1866, equivalent to the amount annually sent to the pope as Peter's pence from the archdiocese of Dublin. In any case, the problem was resolved when the news of Cullen's promotion was made public on May 29, because it was announced at the same time that it was "the intention of the clergy and laity of Ireland to present his Eminence with a testimonial suitable to his exalted rank on his return from the Eternal City."[6] In fact, the testimonial was largely made up by the clergy and the laity of Dublin, who eventually subscribed about £1000 each to make up the required sum.[7]

Cullen, meanwhile, had written Barnabò on May 17, lamenting the loss of Dixon and portending the future.[8] "His death," Cullen explained, "is a very great loss to the Irish Church, because he sought always to maintain the spirit of charity, and to avoid divisions, especially among the bishops, while at the same time he was very firm in maintaining all that was just and necessary for the well-being of the Church. In all the controversies that agitated our Church for the last fourteen years he and I were always in agreement and this union has contributed much to putting an end to those schisms and scandals that prevailed in Ireland for many years before the Synod of Thurles, and gave rise to the public quarrels between bishop and bishop. Thank God that such things have not now been seen for several years." In then turning to the future, Cullen pointed out that the choice of the Armagh clergy would probably fall on the dean of the diocese, Michael Kieran, and the bishop of Dromore, John Pius Leahy, both excellent men. "Here in Dublin," he reported, "some friends of the government are broadcasting the name of Monsignor Moriarty of Kerry as the best candidate that can be found. The real reason for their predeliction for that prelate is that he has declared himself the decided partisan of the government in all the disputes over education. I am persuaded however that the Armagh clergy will not give him many votes." After thus entering this caveat, Cullen concluded his letter to Barnabò by promising to explain all to the cardinal personally when he arrived in Rome in early June to receive his red hat. In writing Kirby the next day, May 19, Patrick Moran covered much the same ground about the Armagh *terna*, but he was somewhat more pointed in his conclusion (K). "The Cardinale," he assured Kirby, referring to Cullen, "will be in Rome when the election will be made, and he will be able to arrange it properly."

By the time the Armagh clergy assembled in the town of Armagh on June 4 to commend their *terna*, however, the news of Cullen's promotion had been the talk of Ireland for more than a week, and they were undoubtedly as aware as Moran of the significance of Cullen's

6. I.C.D., 1867, Annals, May 28, 1866, p. 361. In the end the sum required in Rome came only to about £1000. See C, Forde to McCabe, July 15, 1866.

7. Ibid., June 11, 1866, p. 370.

8. S.R.C., vol. 35, fols. 701–2.

being in Rome when the cardinals of Propaganda considered the appointment to Armagh. Before their meeting, therefore, the Armagh clergy caucused with an efficiency that was legendary in their diocese. Their purpose was twofold: to maximize the number of votes for a single candidate, who would then be their overwhelming choice; and at the same time to construct as tight a *terna* as possible by minimizing the number of stray votes. This tactic not only would leave little room for the bishops of the province in their report to Propaganda, or the cardinals of Propaganda in their recommendation to the pope, to deviate from the obvious choice of the clergy but would minimize the possibility of a stray or a stranger being appointed because of the clergy's inability to focus on their *terna*. The great difficulty in effecting this plan, however, was that the Armagh clergy had long been divided into two distinct camps—the southerners and the northerners. The effects of this division were made plain for all to see when they finally commended their *terna* on June 4 in Armagh. Of the fifty-four votes cast, the southerners returned Michael Kieran as *dignissimus* with twenty-eight votes, while the northerners cast their twenty-six votes for Charles Russell, the president of Maynooth.[9] Each party had obviously counted on the other's splitting, thus allowing its candidate a majority or a plurality of the votes, as well as providing for a rounding out of the *terna*. To resolve the acute embarrassment of having no votes cast for a third candidate, the bishop of Derry, who, as senior suffragan of the province, presided at the meeting, directed that another scrutiny be taken, because the procedure required that three names be commended to Rome. On the second vote one of Russell's supporters voted for James Tierney, precentor of the diocese and parish priest of Tallenstown, thus rounding out the *terna*.

Shortly after the election, on June 10, the candidate of the northerners, Charles Russell, proceeded to complicate matters even further by writing to Kirby, asking him to use his good offices with the Propaganda authorities and the pope to excuse him from consideration for the Armagh appointment on the grounds for which he had been excused some six years before, when he had been returned as *dignissimus* on the *terna* for Down and Connor. At that time Russell had pleaded that the financial liabilities he had incurred in the interests of saving his family would both impair his ability to function as a bishop and, if, as he expected, he was also involved in legal proceedings,

9. A, vol. 231 (1866), p. 2, fols. 464–65, "Ristretto con Sommario sulla elezione dell'Arcivescovo di Armagh in Irlanda, 30 Luglio 1866" (fols. 461–69). See also Ambrose Macaulay, *Dr. Russell of Maynooth* (London, 1983), pp. 227–32.

reflect on the episcopal dignity as well. "I deeply regret," Russell explained to Kirby at this point, "to have to say that what was then but an apprehension became since that time, by the misfortunes and death of my brother, a distressing reality, and although I am gradually discharging the unhappy liabilities which I most imprudently contracted, yet my actual condition is worse now than it was when I made my former petition to the Holy Father."

The most curious thing about Russell's letter to Kirby is that he does not appear to have followed it up with either a letter to Barnabò or a petition to the pope asking to be excused. Kirby did not apparently submit his letter to the Propaganda authorities, for it does not appear either in the general correspondence or among the documents in the usual *sommario* of the *ponenza*, or presentation, submitted to the cardinals for their consideration. The most likely explanation is that Russell had some prudent second thoughts about withdrawing his name when it was pointed out to him, either by Cullen through Kirby or by some of the more astute of the Armagh clergy, that if he withdrew his name, it would be tantamount to leaving the authorities and pope without a choice. The pope would undoubtedly take this as an act of disrespect and probably would take the appointment into his own hands and select a stranger, as he had done once before in Armagh and again only recently in Westminster. Such an argument, if indeed made, must have had considerable effect on Russell, because he was a good friend of Kieran's and did not want him to be excluded from consideration in the Armagh appointment by any untoward act of his. In the last analysis Russell, who was a very sensible and intelligent man, must also have realized that Cullen was very partial to Kieran and would throw his considerable influence at Rome behind his preference; and for this reason as well, therefore, Russell allowed his nomination by the Armagh clergy to stand.

When the bishops of the province of Armagh met at Mullingar on June 19, they were not entirely of one mind.[10] Of the ten bishops present, eight reported in favor of Kieran, one in favor of Russell, and the other in favor of a stranger. The majority endorsed Kieran because of his greater pastoral and diocesan experience. The bishop of Down and Connor, Patrick Dorrian, however, who thought that Russell was the worthiest of the three candidates, but more suited to remaining president of Maynooth, also reported to Barnabò that several Armagh priests had complained to him that Kieran had actually voted for himself in the election, and that he was therefore unworthy of being a

10. Ibid., fols. 465–66.

bishop.[11] Dorrian confessed that he did not know if the accusation were true, and he certainly hoped that it was not, but that he felt it was his duty to report it. The bishop of Kilmore, Nicholas Conaty, on the other hand, thought that a stranger should be appointed.[12] He was particularly disturbed by the factionalism demonstrated by the Armagh clergy in the choosing of their *terna* and was of the opinion that neither Kieran nor Russell would be able to maintain independence of the faction that had voted for him if appointed a bishop.

By the time the report of the Armagh prelates arrived in Rome, Cullen had already been raised to the rank of cardinal. The ceremonies, which took place over some four days and which were reported in great detail in the Irish press, were very impressive.[13] The pope, it was reported, as a special mark of attention and kindness, invited Cullen to receive the official announcement of his elevation, as well as to hold his customary levees, or *recevimenti*, after each day's proceedings, in the magnificent central apartments of the Quirinal Palace. On the first day, Friday, June 22, a private consistory of the sacred college was held at the Vatican at which the pope delivered a short allocution on the merits of the five cardinals-elect, who were waiting to receive official notification of their promotions at their respective residences in Rome. On receiving the news, Cullen set out with the members of his household, among whom, significantly enough, were the two secretaries of Propaganda, Annibale Capalti and Giovanni Simeoni, to visit the cardinal secretary of state at the Vatican. Cullen's train was reported as consisting of thirty carriages, with the servants in their gala livery walking in front and at either side, "all being in accordance with and fully realising the prescribed princely pageant of Rome."[14] Cullen and the other cardinals-elect were then robed in the apartments of the cardinal secretary and presented in private audience to the pope, from whom they received their red hats, the first emblem of their new rank. As the senior prelate, Cullen delivered an elegant Latin oration returning thanks to the pope in his and his colleagues' names. As they left the pope's apartments, each of the cardinals-elect was presented by an attendant with a red *zucchetto*, or skullcap. Cul-

11. Ibid., fols. 466–67, Dorrian to Barnabò, July 2, 1866.
12. Ibid., fol. 466, Conaty to Barnabò, June 30, 1866.
13. *Freeman's Journal*, July 9, 1866. See also C, Forde to McCabe, June 24, 28, 1866.
14. I.C.D., 1867, p. 402.

len then returned to the Quirinal Palace, where he received his congratulations at the prescribed *recevimento*.

During the next two days, June 23 and 24, public consistories were held in the Sala Regia at the Vatican. Before the last of the public consistories, on Monday, June 25, the cardinals-elect had proceeded in state to the Sistine Chapel at the Vatican, where they took the prescribed oath of office. After the body of the sacred college had then paid homage to the pope in the Sala Regia, the new cardinals, each accompanied by two cardinal priests or deacons, paid homage to the pope by kissing his hand; they received in return the customary kiss of peace from the pope, after which they were fraternally embraced by the other members of the sacred college. The new cardinals were then summoned to the foot of the papal throne, where the pope placed their red hats on their heads while reading the prescribed Latin formula, which was to remind them that the color of their hats signified their readiness, if necessary, to shed their blood for the Church. At the conclusion of this ceremony the pope returned to his own apartments, and the sacred college proceeded in procession, as the Te Deum was intoned, to the Sistine Chapel, where the new cardinals prostrated themselves at the foot of the altar. When the Te Deum was concluded, the presiding cardinal recited the prayer Super Electus over them. The new cardinals then placed themselves at the entrance of the Sistine Chapel, where they received the renewed congratulations of their colleagues as they passed out of the Chapel.

Immediately afterward, at a private consistory in the private hall of the Vatican, each of the new cardinals was assigned to a church in Rome from which he took his title. Cullen was named to the *title*, or titular church, of San Pietro in Montorio on the Janiculum, a church rich in Irish associations, being the burial place of the celebrated Irish chieftains of the early seventeenth century, The O'Neill and The O'Donnell. In addition to his *title*, Cullen also received at this consistory his sapphire cardinal's ring, as well as his assignment to the customary four congregations, or departments of state, of the some twenty that made up the Roman Curia, or government. The pope had chosen to have Cullen serve in the congregations of the Index, Sacred Rites, Discipline of Regulars, and, most important and significant of all from the point of view of Irish business, Propaganda. Cullen then returned to the Quirinal, where, in the full regalia of his office, he would receive formally and finally from the ab-delegate of the pope, accompanied by the noble guards, his red hat. He then changed into less formal attire and received renewed congratulations at the last and most gala of his receptions.

Soon after the formal ceremonies were over, Cullen was immersed in the more practical obligations of his new office. Because the cardinals of Propaganda were scheduled to consider pending Irish, English, and Scots business at their next congregation on July 30, Barnabò turned over all the relevant documents on the Kilmacduagh and Kilfenora and Armagh appointments to Cullen and asked him to prepare a *voto*, or opinion, on each for the meeting. Cullen's *voto* on Kilmacduagh and Kilfenora was certainly a true witness both formally and substantially to his newfound power and influence at Rome.[15] The usual procedure at Propaganda was for a *ponenza*, or presentation, to be drawn up by the secretary in the name of the *ponente*, a cardinal appointed by the cardinal prefect to make the presentation to his colleagues. The *ponenza* consisted of a *ristretto*, or synopsis of the case based on the relevant documents, and a *sommario*, or compendium of those documents arranged in chronological order. The *ristretto con sommario*, or *ponenza*, was then printed and distributed to the cardinals of Propaganda to serve as a brief in their considering of the case. In special or difficult cases, the cardinal prefect asked that a *voto* be provided by a *consultore* deemed to be an expert on the matter under consideration. The most interesting thing about the *ponenza* finally presented to the cardinals in the Kilmacduagh and Kilfenora case was that Cullen's *voto* literally became the *ponenza*: his *voto* made up eight of the nine printed pages of the text of the *ponenza*, as the part superseded the whole.

"Having read all the documents," Cullen assured Barnabò in his *voto*, "concerning the choice that ought to be made of a coadjutor to the bishop of the united dioceses of Kilfenora and Kilmacduagh in Ireland, I shall try [first] to give a summary of the same, and second to indicate in my feeble opinion what it would be expedient to do in regard to this affair."[16] He then proceeded with very great effect to demolish the *terna* commended by the Kilmacduagh and Kilfenora clergy and reported on by the bishops of both provinces.[17] He pointed out that the sixteen votes cast were distributed among six candidates and that the *dignissimus*, Timothy Shannon, had received only five votes. Furthermore, though the eight Cashel prelates had reported unanimously in favor of Shannon and had correctly excluded the *dignior*, John Sheehan, from consideration because he was old and ill and too much involved in political matters, they had not really given any

15. A, vol. 231, fols. 472–75.
16. Ibid., fol. 472, n.d.
17. Ibid., fols. 472–73.

cogent reasons why Shannon should be preferred, other than that he had the most votes and that the present bishop, Patrick Fallon, wanted him as his coadjutor. They had not really explained, moreover, why the *dignus*, Michael Connolly, should be excluded. Cullen did not think that Shannon's five votes ought to be made too much of, especially as Sheehan and Connolly had received four votes each, and given Fallon's unfortunate condition, his preference for Shannon ought perhaps to be viewed as a reason against appointing him. In then turning to the report of the Tuam prelates, who, it will be recalled, had split three to two for Connolly in preference to Shannon, Cullen thought that the reasons addressed by the majority were the more convincing, but accepting them would mean that the suffrages of some three prelates were to be preferred to the suffrages of eleven.[18]

"At this point," Cullen observed, turning to what ought to be done, "a question arises, namely whether it would not be expedient to defer for the present the appointment of a coadjutor, and meanwhile to provide for the well being of the two dioceses under consideration by giving the administration of them to the bishop of Galway whose merits and zeal for religion are well known." Cullen then explained that the bishop of Galway had pointed out in 1862 in his *relatio*, or report to Propaganda on the state of his diocese, how poor he was, noting that the income from his diocese could not really maintain a bishop with advantage to religion. The bishop of Galway had also, as recently as May 15, reported to Propaganda that all the Cashel prelates, including the archbishop, were of the view that Galway and Kilmacduagh and Kilfenora should be united. The bishop of Elphin in the province of Tuam, Cullen added, was also of the same opinion, as he was himself and as he had repeatedly recommended to Propaganda over the last five years. He then proceeded to explain why he thought the dioceses should be united. First of all, the Catholic population in each was very small, altogether numbering hardly more than sixty thousand souls. Secondly, there were very few parishes involved; if the dioceses were united, they would include only some twenty-nine parishes, three of which would have to be mensal parishes for the support of Fallon and MacEvilly—still hardly a respectable diocese from either an economic or an administrative point of view. Finally, he noted the wretched poverty of all three dioceses. "As things now stand, unfortunately," he then summed up, "the bishop of Galway is very poor, his income hardly suffices to procure for him the necessaries of life. In

18. Ibid., fols. 473–74.

giving him the dioceses of Kilmacduagh and Kilfenora he would be somewhat better off, although he would still be poor."[19]

"It may be," Cullen advised in conclusion, "that in the present circumstances, while awaiting the answers of the Tuam and Cashel prelates on the union of the dioceses of Galway, Kilmacduagh and Kilfenora, it is not expedient to adopt any final decision on this plan. But meanwhile, the administration of Kilmacduagh and Kilfenora could be given *ad beneplacitum apostolicum* [at the apostolic pleasure] to Monsignor MacEvilly, and thus the good of that diocese would be provided for, leaving open the question of union, until other clarifications are received. Whatever is done, either the appointing of a co-adjutor or an administrator, it would be necessary to suspend all the faculties of Monsignor Fallon, who is totally incapable of governing." When the cardinals of Propaganda met on July 30, Cullen was of course present, and undoubtedly he elaborated verbally on his *voto*. In any case, they adopted his advice and unanimously recommended that the bishop of Galway be appointed administrator of Kilmacduagh and Kilfenora.[20] They also stipulated that Fallon receive a suitable pension and that the question of what was to be eventually done about the united dioceses be reserved in the brief appointing MacEvilly administrator. The pope approved the recommendation of the cardinals on August 5, adding that the appointment of MacEvilly should be *"ad beneplacitum S. Sedis* [at the pleasure of the Holy See]."[21]

At their meeting on July 30 the cardinals also considered the appointment to Armagh, and once again the critical document in the *ponenza* was Cullen's *voto*.[22] The bishops of the province of Armagh, it will be recalled, had not been unanimous in their report to Propaganda on the merits of those commended by the clergy. Eight bishops had reported in favor of the *dignissimus*, Michael Kieran; one in qualified favor of the *dignior*, Charles Russell; and one with the recommendation that a stranger be appointed. In his *voto* Cullen strongly supported the report of the majority of the bishops. He pointed out that Kieran, as vicar-general of the diocese for the last seventeen years, had given great satisfaction both to him, when he was archbishop of Armagh before his translation to Dublin, and to the late archbishop. He had also done wonders in building churches and in providing for the Catholic education of the poor in his parish. After he concluded his review of Kieran's virtues and attainments, Cullen then

19. Ibid., fol. 475.
20. Ibid., fol. 471.
21. Ibid.
22. Ibid., fols. 467–69.

turned to consider the objections made to the appointment by the two Armagh prelates who had refused to subscribe to the majority's opinion and had written separately to Barnabò.

"What the bishop of Kilmore says," Cullen candidly confessed,

about the divisions among the Armagh clergy is too true. The diocese of Armagh belongs in part to the civil province of Leinster and in part to the province of Ulster, the southern part being in the county of Louth in Leinster, while the counties of Armagh, Tyrone, and Derry, which constitute the northern part of the diocese are in Ulster. Now it happens that in Louth the Catholics are numerous and rich, while in the northern part the Catholics hardly equal in number the Scotch Presbyterians and other Protestants among whom they live, and are very poor. Moreover, in the north the Catholics speak a dialect similar to that which is spoken in Scotland, and very different from that which is spoken in Louth, which is the same as that spoken in Dublin. From these and other circumstances there arise antipathies among the different populations of the diocese of Armagh, and the clergy of the northern part are always in opposition to that of the south and vice versa. These divisions then have produced the effect that for the longest time strangers were always appointed to the see of Armagh.[23]

Until Dixon was appointed in 1852, Cullen pointed out, no native of the diocese of Armagh had been appointed there for nearly a hundred years. "At his election," Cullen explained "all the northern priests voted for him, while those of the southern part voted for Father Kieran. I presided at the election, and I was able to observe how matters proceeded, and that each party wanted to be victorious. When Monsignor Dixon was promoted, however, those who had voted against him received him with due respect, and never raised any opposition to him." "I believe," he finally assured Barnabò and his colleagues, "if Father Kieran is now chosen archbishop the same thing will happen."

In then turning to the charge made by the bishop of Down and Connor that Kieran had voted for himself in the balloting for Armagh, Cullen sensibly pointed out that it was more likely that he had voted for the second on the list, Charles Russell, who was an old and good friend of his. "In any case," he noted further, "as the election is over, it would now be impossible to determine with certainty if Kieran had voted for himself or not, because in giving their votes the priests write

23. Ibid., fol. 468.

only the name which they vote for on a ballot, and after the election
the said ballots are burned."[24] "The accusation," Cullen finally maintained, "is reduced to a mere suspicion, which could be put forward
against anyone." At the meeting of the cardinals, however, there was
apparently some discussion of the Armagh case, for Cullen was reported by the well-informed Bernard Smith, sometime *consultore* at
the Propaganda, as having "answered all the objections, praised very
much Dr. K and strongly recommended him."[25] The cardinals unanimously endorsed Cullen's recommendation, and Kieran was proposed
to the pope for the appointment to Armagh.

At this same meeting on July 30 the cardinals also made a recommendation to the pope for the appointment of a coadjutor to the vicar
apostolic of the western district in Scotland, as well as an appointment to the vacant diocese of Hexham and Newcastle in England.[26]
Cullen had long been concerned about the reports he had heard of the
very great spiritual destitution among the Irish who had emigrated
recently in large numbers to Glasgow and western Scotland. By 1866
the great majority of the Catholics in the Glasgow area were Irish-
born, and Cullen had become convinced that what was necessary in
Scotland was a reforming Irish bishop who would correct the loose
discipline among the clergy and the lax practice among the laity. The
cardinals of Propaganda, therefore, rejected the three candidates, who
were all Scotsmen, reported on by the Scots bishops for the coadjutorship in the western district, and recommended instead the appointment of an Irish Vincentian, James Lynch, rector of the Irish College
in Paris, who had received one vote on the recent Kilmacduagh *terna*.
Cullen, who was very partial to the Vincentian community in Ireland
and who had known Lynch for a very long time, considered him not
only a good and holy man but also just what the Scottish mission
needed in the way of a reforming bishop. This intrusion of an Irishman into the Scots hierarchy, moreover, was yet another very significant demonstration of Cullen's new power and influence at Rome.

Shortly after the meeting of the cardinals on July 30, Cullen wrote
his secretary, Patrick Moran, in Dublin, reporting what had happened.
Moran, who later in life, as the cardinal archbishop of Sydney in Australia, liked to refer to Ireland's "spiritual empire," was even at this
time an enthusiastic ecclesiastical imperialist. In a reply, for example,
to the bishop of Elphin, who had written to ask when the new cardinal

24. Ibid., fol. 469.
25. Smith Papers, Archives of St. Paul's Basilica outside the Walls, Rome, memorandum, July 1866.
26. Ibid.

might be expected home, Moran noted on August 7, "Perhaps your Lordship has not as yet received intelligence of the Congregation of Propaganda held on the 30th of July. Dr. Kieran was appointed to Armagh. Dr. MacEvilly receives administration of Kilmacduagh and Kilfenora: —one of your former confrères the Coadjutorship of Glasgow: —and another priest of Irish birth is appointed to the See of Durham" (G). "Of course," he cautioned Gillooly in concluding, "all this is strictly private till the appointments be confirmed by the Holy Father."

Moran's caution, at least as far as Armagh was concerned, was a portent. When the pope was asked to confirm the cardinals' recommendation of Kieran on August 5, he refused. He instructed the secretary of Propaganda, Monsignor Capalti, to write to the bishop of Derry, Francis Kelly, who had presided at the July 4 meeting of the Armagh clergy when the balloting for the *terna* had taken place, and ask him for his views about the charges made against Kieran.[27] Kelly replied on August 21 that those priests who had accused Kieran were still adamant about their accusations, but there was now no way of determining the truth of the charges.[28] When Capalti reported the substance of Kelly's reply to the pope on September 2, the pope was still disturbed and instructed Capalti to write to Cullen and have him prudently reveal to Kieran the charges made against him and invite him to clear his name on oath.[29] In the meantime Kelly had also written Cullen, for Cullen reported to Barnabò on August 31 that the "business of the choice of an archbishop of Armagh has become a little confused. Monsignor Kelly has written me that the priests opposed to the choice of Father Kieran persist in accusing him of having voted for himself, but they do not give, nor is it possible to give any proof of it. Father Kieran however asserts firmly that he gave his vote for Father Russell. It is certain that he wrote Father Russell not to place any obstacle in the way of the clergy who wanted to make him their choice, and then after the election he wrote him again exhorting him to accept the episcopate if it were offered."[30] "In these circumstances," Cullen concluded, "it appears that the accusation circulated against Father Kieran, who without a doubt deserves well of the Church, ought not to have any weight." When Cullen then received the letter the pope had ordered Capalti to write to him, he replied on September 18, testifying that Kieran had orally and in writing in his

27. A, vol. 231, fol. 463.
28. Ibid.
29. Ibid.
30. S.R.C., vol. 35, fol. 813.

presence sworn that he had not voted for himself. In an audience with the pope of September 30, Capalti reported Cullen's assurance, and the pope finally approved Kieran's appointment to Armagh. For some reason that is not yet entirely clear, however, the briefs necessary for Kieran's consecration were very much delayed, and they did not arrive in Ireland until early in the new year.

Meanwhile, the situation in regard to Kilmacduagh and Kilfenora had also become somewhat complicated. Barnabò apparently had some serious second thoughts about how to break to the redoubtable archbishop of Tuam the news that the proposal to appoint a coadjutor had been shelved, and that an apostolic administrator in the person of the bishop of Galway had been appointed instead. Barnabò mentioned his perplexity in writing to Cullen, for the latter replied in no uncertain terms about what he thought ought to be done. "As for matters in Galway," he advised Barnabò on August 31, "nothing can be done with the archbishop of Tuam, and it would be better to publish the choice of Monsignor MacEvilly without delay. Monsignor McHale will not say a word once the thing is done."[31] "After my return," Cullen explained, "I wrote him a friendly enough letter, but up to now, though eight days have passed, he has not answered me. The best way of dealing with him is not to consult him at all." Before Cullen wrote this letter, however, Barnabò had already decided on his course of action. He wrote both MacHale and Leahy on August 24, informing them of the decision to appoint MacEvilly administrator, which, he explained, had been made at the pleasure of the pope. He asked them their opinions on the decision and also on what would be the best course to pursue, in making provision for the united dioceses, when the present bishop of Kilmacduagh and Kilfenora died. This was a very clever way of breaking the news to MacHale, because in noting that the appointment of MacEvilly had been made at the pleasure of the pope, Barnabò was emphasizing that nothing had been finally determined and that the present solution was only a temporary one.

What Barnabò was concerned about, of course, was an adverse reaction among the Kilmacduagh and Kilfenora clergy, which would probably be surreptitiously encouraged by MacHale. By emphasizing the provisional nature of the new arrangement and taking the two archbishops into his confidence about what any future arrangement should be, Barnabò was attempting to soften the impact of the decision on those who would be most opposed to it. As Barnabò had astutely anticipated, the reaction of the Kilmacduagh and Kilfenora

31. Ibid.

clergy was most unfavorable. On September 10 Cullen explained to Kirby that, as MacEvilly had reported, "they are making a great noise in KilmacDuagh against the union with Galway. He thinks Dr. McHale gave instructions to get up a little agitation against the proposal" (K). Cullen then added that he hoped there would be no delay in sending the bull confirming MacEvilly's appointment. The Kilmacduagh and Kilfenora clergy had, in fact, protested the recent decision formally in a petition to Barnabò on September 3, and MacHale had reported to Leahy on September 10 that he had received Barnabò's letter of August 24, informing him of the decision, but would not reply until he heard Leahy's views in the matter (L). MacHale also added that he thought they should take united stand in making their views known at Rome, thereby tacitly assuming that Leahy's views would be the same as his own.

Leahy must have quickly disabused MacHale of that notion, for MacHale had to write Barnabò on his own on September 14, protesting, in effect, the decision already made, as well as any proposal to unite Kilmacduagh and Kilfenora to Galway permanently.[32] When Leahy replied to Barnabò about a week later, he noted that there was little to be said about a decision already made and added that the procedure for the choosing of a coadjutor had been suspended without consulting any of the parties involved.[33] As to the future, he referred Barnabò to a proposal he had made to the authorities at Propaganda eight years before in 1858. He had then proposed that when the present bishop of Kilmacduagh and Kilfenora died, the ancient twelfth-century diocese of Roscrea, which was now part of the diocese of Killaloe in county Tipperary, be reconstituted under its own bishop. The loss of Killaloe would be compensated by uniting the diocese of Kilfenora with it, and Kilmacduagh could then be united with Galway, thus finally resolving the anomaly of having one bishop subject to two metropolitans. Leahy did not explain, however, how the bishop of Killaloe and his coadjutor were to be persuaded to give up a very considerable number of the wealthiest parishes in their diocese in exchange for eight of the poorest parishes in Ireland.

In any case, the briefs appointing MacEvilly arrived in Ireland toward the end of September, and he wrote Kirby a long and interesting letter on October 6, reporting what had happened (K). "I put off this acknowledgement until I could give you a full account of the event of the whole affair," he explained,

32. Ibid., fols. 823–24.
33. Ibid., fols. 827–28.

I am delighted to tell you that everything has gone on most smoothly and satisfactorily. On receipt of the Brief, I at once went to see Dr. Fallon in the first instance, and from his house he and I both wrote to the vicars general of the two dioceses to assemble the clergy at Gort in order to meet me on Thursday last (the 4th). All the priests of both dioceses attended except two, and these begged to be *let off* as their health would not allow them to attend. They all had the greatest welcome for me. Not a symptom of complaint or murmur of any kind. I read for them the Letters Apostolic, showing them "I came in by the door," which was opened for me by Him who holds "the keys of the Kingdom of heaven." They were all perfectly satisfied. I reappointed the vicars general who acted under Dr. Fallon, and I am disposed for a time at least, to act on the principle of *"festina lente"* [hurry slowly].

"I dare say you are aware," MacEvilly then added, "there was an attempt made at agitation in the shape of a protest to the H. See against the arrangements made by them. I got a copy of the protest from parties in the diocese. The truth is, if left to themselves, the priests would never dream of *protesting* or interfering at all." "But all was *suggested* and *counseled*," he charged,

by a certain personage [i.e., MacHale], who should be the first in this province to uphold the authority of the H. See. He told them, "there was no time to be lost to remonstrate with Holy See, and protest respectfully, but *firmly*." —A nice advice to a body of priests, among whom are always to be found some excitable spirits. What "protesting *firmly*" means coming from that quarter is quite evident. It evidently means a threat of resistance, which is conveyed pretty clearly in the 'scandala magnopere pertimescenda" [most terrifying scandals] contained in the Protest, of which I hold in my hands a copy—A greater falsehood was never uttered, than the assertion in the Protest, that the *Laity* were opposed to the arrangements. The very contrary is the fact. The laity are delighted with the whole affair. On this you may depend.

"In my administration of the diocese," he assured Kirby, "I shall consult the H. See in every case of difficulty, and then there can be no fear of going astray. I hope the eyes of the few priests who listened to the suggestions *ab extra* [from outside] will be opened before long. I, of course, never pretended I heard of any such things." In any case, the upshot of the whole affair was that the Kilmacduagh and Kilfenora clergy soon settled down and accepted the new arrangement, which was to prove, in effect, permanent.[34]

———————————

The real significance of the appointments finally made to Armagh and Kilmacduagh and Kilfenora, of course, was in what they revealed about Cullen's new position of influence in the Irish Church. The appointment to Armagh was a good case in point. The delay in making the appointment would make it appear that Cullen's ascendancy in the Irish Church was at least restrained by the authoritative will of the pope, but the actual fact was that the pope's concern was really yet another confirmation of Cullen's power and influence. In the 1850s, it will be recalled, Cullen had also had the absolute confidence of both the pope and Propaganda in Irish affairs. The difference now was that as a cardinal he would be consulted as a matter of right rather than just as a favor, because his new dignity was the highest mark of confidence the pope could bestow on any individual in the Church. As far as the Armagh appointment was concerned, the pope was obliged by virtue of his office and as the conscience of the Church to make every effort that was humanly possible to assure himself of the integrity of the individual recommended. Because a question had been raised about Kieran's integrity, the pope quite correctly wanted to be reassured and instructed the secretary of Propaganda to write to the bishop of Derry for that reassurance. When Kelly's reply did not ease the pope's mind in the matter, he had of necessity to turn to Cullen for that reassurance. The pope was certainly aware that Cullen had already *viva voce* strongly urged the appointment of Kieran at the congregation of cardinals on July 30, but he wanted assurance formally in writing before confirming the appointment. When Cullen gave that formal assurance of Kieran's integrity, the matter was settled as far as the pope was concerned.

Not only was Cullen's position in the Irish Church vis-à-vis the universal Church changed by his promotion, but his position within the Irish Church itself was fundamentally transformed. He was no longer one among equals, or even as the pope's apostolic delegate the first among equals in some matters, in relation to the other Irish archbishops. As a cardinal, he was now superior in rank to his episcopal

34. K, Cullen to Kirby, October 30, 1866.

colleagues. Indeed, his new rank both raised him above his colleagues and, because the responsibilities of his new dignity involved his position in the universal Church, also set him apart from his colleagues.[35] Those bishops, therefore, who had long been resentful of Cullen's inordinate interference at Rome in the affairs of dioceses and provinces not his own, and especially those bishops who might be concerned about the effect his promotion would have on the independence of their body, must have been made very uneasy by the recent demonstration of his power and influence in the appointments made in both Ireland and Scotland. This is not to say, of course, that at the same time the great majority of the Irish bishops were not delighted, as indeed were the clergy and laity, at the marked honor the pope had bestowed on their national church for the first time in its history, or that they did not recognize the basic legitimacy of Cullen's new position as a prince of the Church. Still, how the Irish bishops as a body would stand up to the unprecedented challenge presented by Cullen's promotion would prove to be not only the most interesting but also perhaps the most significant question in the Irish Church in the next decade.

Cullen was, of course, well aware of the significance of his promotion to the sacred college. In the next few years, in fact, there was a very noticeable change in his attitude and his conduct. In his correspondence with Barnabò, for example, there was a difference in the tone of his letters. He now wrote more as an equal and peer and less as a dependent and subordinate. The extreme diffidence that he had displayed over the previous six years in regard to Irish episcopal appointments became a thing of the past. His new assurance and confidence were extended to other things as well. It has already been noticed, for example, that he took a very independent line in early 1868 on the bishops' negotiations with the government over the education question. At their general meeting in early October 1867, it will be recalled, the body of bishops had not deputed the four archbishops, as they had done in 1865, to represent their body in negotiating with the government, but had instead chosen the archbishop of Cashel and the bishop of Clonfert to represent them. Though Cullen had thus been formally excluded, he then proceeded to open negotiations with the government indirectly through Archbishop Manning and to send to London as his personal representative the rector of the Catholic

35. K, William Delany to Kirby, June 9, 1866. Delany asked Kirby to secure a postponement of his *ad limina* visit until 1867, remarking, "After the honour conferred on our Country, by the elevation of Cardinal Cullen to his present exalted post, I suppose we the smaller fry are likely to be indulged in our petitions."

University, to hold a watching brief for him there. The touchiness of the two bishops' representatives during the negotiations with the government was proof enough that they, and probably a number of their colleagues, resented Cullen's interference, but there was little they could say as long as he observed the formalities and did not act directly. What is really significant about his interference is that though Cullen as a cardinal could now take an independent line, he still had to be very careful in dealing with the body of bishops, and their representatives, if he did not want to provoke a reaction that would jeopardize the harmony and unity he had worked so long and so hard to secure.

Cullen's new assurance and independence were also expressed in the way he conceived of his public role. Before he became a cardinal he had seldom appeared at state or civic functions, and he hardly ever had anything to do with state dignitaries, especially if they were English. In his new role as a cardinal, however, Cullen apparently came to construe his public duties more broadly, and even appeared to enjoy them more as well. In late October and early November, for example, he dined with the celebrated English radical John Bright at the invitation of the former Liberal chief secretary for Ireland, C. S. Fortescue, and he asked Gladstone's eldest son, William, to dine with him on his visit to Dublin.[36] This consorting with the hereditary enemy was apparently not much appreciated by at least one of the more politically independent and patriotic of his episcopal colleagues. "If there be here," Patrick Dorrian, the bishop of Down and Connor, complained to Kirby on December 10, "one thing more than another which disheartens me it is our fraternizing with those of our own party who are and have been deadly enemies to the temporal power of the Pope whilst they contend they are the real friends of Ireland but are helping on the Queen's Colleges and the Model School System" (K). "Whilst Prelates in high places," Dorrian charged, "associate with these (no doubt through simplicity and with the best intentions) and pay visits and dine at their houses with the late Chief Secretary or the present John Bright[,] whose principles on the question of education are both so opposed to us, I can have no hope for Union." "You once remarked," he then reminded Kirby, "that by Union we were sure to succeed. Certainly. But we have no union and are perhaps our own greatest obstacles to success. Things are drifting from bad to worse. Nothing will, say some, do for us, but the great liberal Party!"

36. K, Cullen to Kirby, October 30, 1866. In noting that Bright was in Dublin, Cullen added, "He will put down the Protestant Church. I hope he will stop there." For Gladstone's visit see K, Cullen to Kirby, November 6, 1866.

Early in the new year Cullen accepted an invitation to the annual dinner of the lord mayor of Dublin. "On last Tuesday," he reported to Kirby on February 22, 1867, "the Lord Mayor gave a great dinner at which I attended. The Lord Lieutenant [the Conservative viceroy, the marquis of Abercorn] took the first place, and I got the second as Cardinal. The Protestant Archbishop stayed away—there were about six hundred persons present. My health was proposed and received with great applause by Jews, Unitarians, Presbyterians, Swaddlers, Quakers, Protestants and Catholics" (K). "It was a difficult task," he confessed, "to address such an audience. I took up the subject of Charity. I told them that we could not agree on religion or education, but that there were many subjects on which we could endeavour to do good to the country. I pleased the people very much, but I do not know whether I made any *sproposti* [gaffes] or not. The Lord Lieutenant was most polite. I sat between the Lady Lieutenant and her sister Lady Butler. They are sisters of Lord John Russell, and they made themselves most agreeable. They appear to be very humane ladies." "Since the dinner," Cullen further explained, "I got a message from the Lord Lieutenant expressing his great desire to do anything in his power to please our Bishops. My reply will be that we want nothing from the Government except good measures for the country—if they protect the people and give us fair play we shall support them."

Cullen soon had reason, however, to have some very prudent second thoughts about being seen too much in the company of the hereditary enemy. "It is said," he informed Kirby on March 18, during the exciting aftermath of the Fenian rising, "that the proceedings at the Lord Mayor's dinner have done much good" (K). "I was pressed very much," he added, "to go to the Castle, but if I went, I would lose all power of doing good among the poor people. Such gentlemen as the writers of the Fenian papers and such as Father Lav. would hold me up as a Castle hack of the worst character. It is better in these times to do our duty towards the Government, and at the same time to accept no favour or recompense. We can speak more freely by holding this position. The Government Catholics and Liberal Protestants would be glad to get us under Government patronage, but they are not anxious to increase our influence[;] they rather seek to lessen it." Cullen was obviously very aware of the dangers of appearing to be too friendly to the government, but this awareness did not prevent him from doing his duty as he conceived it. When several of the Fenian leaders, for example, were sentenced to death for their part in the rising in 1867, he did visit the Castle at the end of May for the first time in his life to plead for their lives.

Cullen's enlarged conception of his public duties as a cardinal is perhaps best illustrated by his reaction to the state visit made by the Prince and Princess of Wales to Ireland in the spring of 1868. "I have got into an easy way," he explained to Kirby on April 15, "of paying a visit to the Prince. The Lord Lieutenant has invited me to dine with him tomorrow in the Castle at eight o'clock, and of course I have accepted. Dr. Forde will come with me. For my part I would much rather stay at home, but we cannot always do as we wish" (K). "The Prince and Princess," he further reported, "go to the races of Punchestown on two days—on Saturday the Prince will be installed Knight of St. Patrick in St. Patrick's Church. I was invited to attend, but I refused lest the people should think it wrong of me to go to a Protestant Church." "However," he added interestingly, "there will be nothing religious in the matter, and I told the Catholics who were invited that they might go. Next week when the Prince will be a little freer, I will pay him another visit."

"On yesterday[,] Thursday," Cullen reported to Kirby on April 18, "I went on the Lord Lieutenant[']s invitation to dine with the Prince and Princess. There was a large company, forty two persons including the Duke of Cambridge, the Prince of Saxe Weimar, Prince Teck and other members of the Royal family, as well as several noblemen of the first rank in Ireland and England. The Prince of Wales sat opposite the Lord Lieutenant. The Prince of Saxe Weimar sat next the Prince and then I came next. The Princess of Wales sat next the Lord Lieutenant. The Duke of Cambridge next here and then Prince Teck who was opposite me. I suppose I got my proper place as Cardinal. At all events everyone appeared anxious to treat me with the greatest respect" (K). "How things have changed!" Cullen added. "When Cardinal Wiseman came here in 1858[,] ten years ago[,] Lord Eglinton[,] then Lord Lieutenant[,] would not dine with the Lord Mayor because Cardinal Wiseman was to be present, now the Lord Lieutenant invites a Cardinal to meet the Prince and Princess of Wales and several members of the Royal Family." "Before dinner," he further reported, "I met Whiteside [lord chief justice of Ireland] and his wife. He inquired most kindly for you. He was rather amazed when I went over, and said I would be happy to renew our Roman acquaintance. He never spoke to me since I came to Dublin—but being in the same room with him, I thought it well to speak to him. He is a great bigot. The Duke of Manchester who sat next after me at dinner is another bigot—but we became great friends." "There were," Cullen then noted, "some of the Secretaries of State from England at the dinner. I had some conversation with each and told them about the grievances of Ireland. I suppose no good will come out of such things—but we must do what we can." Cullen then requested Kirby to report all this to Cardinal Antonelli, the papal secretary of state, if he should see him.

The state visit lasted ten days, April 15–24, and on the twenty-second, the prince visited the Catholic University. He visited Maynooth the following day, and he and the princess visited the Mater Misericordiae hospital in Dublin on the twenty-fourth, immediately before they left. Cullen explained to Kirby on April 27, obviously much relieved, "Everything passed off most satisfactorily—not a single accident occurred—I was afraid that some unfortunate Fenian might occasion disturbances, but the feeling of rejoicing was so general that no one stirred. Unfortunately the case was not the same in Australia. There the second son of the Queen, Prince Alfred, Duke of Edinburgh was fired at and dangerously wounded. The assassin was an O'Ferrall and declared himself a Fenian. If anything of the kind happened in Ireland, we would have been ruined." Cullen then mentioned again his dinner with the prince and princess and the precedence he was given as a cardinal. "After dinner," he reported, "four or five parsons and their wives were introduced to the drawing room but no one paid the least attention to them. The poor parsons think the world is going upside down when they see Popery in the high places." "About 25 years ago," Cullen further explained, going on to name his predecessor in the see of Dublin, "the Royal Dublin Society blackbeaned Dr. Murray when it was proposed to admit him to the Society as a member. On this occasion the Society invited me to a *conversazione* [party] to meet the Prince and Princess of Wales. I went to it. About 3,000 people were present." "There were two or three hundred," he then noted, "dignitaries of the Protestant Church who looked at my red cloak with horror and amazement. They must have been terribly mortified when they saw me called up to the dais on which the Prince and Princess were placed, whilst all the Protestant clergymen were left in the crowd." "As the rejoicings are now over," Cullen then concluded, "everyone asks *che buono ne verrà?* [what good will come of it?] Probably nothing—things will go on as usual—and the people will be left as they are."

What Cullen's episcopal colleagues thought of his consorting with royalty at the Castle and the Royal Dublin Society is difficult to judge because nothing is said about it in the various correspondences. If the bishops were voting with their feet, however, the answer is obvious. Not one Irish bishop, if Cullen be excepted, attended at any of the public functions, even the Catholic ones, during the state visit. When the prince visited the Catholic University and Maynooth, for example, none of the nineteen bishops who served on the boards governing those institutions, except Cullen, was present to greet him. The more extreme nationalists, such as MacHale and Derry of Clonfert, were undoubtedly upset by Cullen's fraternizing with the hereditary enemy, whereas those of a more politically conservative mind, such as Delany of Cork and Moriarty of Kerry, were probably pleased. Still, these extremes now represented only a small part of the episcopal body, the bulk of whom were moderately nationalist in their sympathies. Indeed, if the bishops had been consulted by Cullen about granting some appropriate public mark of attention to the prince, they probably would have demurred, as they had in 1865 when Cullen proposed that they present an address to the prince congratulating him on the occasion of his marriage. In this case Cullen apparently did not consult anyone, including the Roman authorities, and acted entirely on his own.[37] The significance of this *proprio motu* of Cullen's, of course, was that he was acting both as a cardinal prince of the universal Church and as the archbishop of Dublin, within whose ecclesiastical jurisdiction the whole of the royal visit took place, and not as the leader of the Irish bishops. The Irish bishops as a body, in fact, by ignoring the royal visit, apparently endorsed that distinction unanimously.

In the nearly two and a half years that elapsed between the arrangements made for Armagh and Kilmacduagh and Kilfenora in the early autumn of 1866 and the appointment of a coadjutor to the bishop of Kildare and Leighlin in the spring of 1869, there was only one episcopal appointment made in the Irish Church. This was occasioned by the unexpected death on June 21, 1867, of the youngest bishop in the Irish Church, John Kilduff, of Ardagh and Clonmacnois. The customary meeting of the clergy to commend a *terna* to Rome, which usually took place about a month after the death of the bishop, was delayed in this case because the archbishop of Armagh, who would have to preside at the meeting, had only just left for Rome in company with a number of his suffragans to assist at the eighteen-hundredth-anniversary celebration of the martyrdom of Saints Peter and Paul. The meeting took place, therefore, shortly after the archbishop's return from

37. S.R.C., vol. 36, fol. 168, Cullen to Barnabò, May 15, 1868. Cullen reported the Prince of Wales's visit as if it were simply a matter of fact. He does not appear to have mentioned it earlier in his correspondence with Barnabò.

the Continent, on August 7 in Longford.[38] The Ardagh clergy placed
Peter Dawson, parish priest of Kiltoghert (Carrick-on-Shannon), first
on their list with eighteen votes. Some fifteen years earlier, in 1852,
Dawson had also been returned as *dignissimus* by the Ardagh clergy,
but the pope had appointed Kilduff, who had received only one vote,
because a number of scandalous charges made against Dawson had
raised serious doubts in the pope's mind about his suitability for the
episcopal dignity.[39] The second place on the Ardagh *terna* was taken
by Neal McCabe, a Vincentian and rector of the Irish College in Paris,
who received ten votes. McCabe, it will be recalled, had been selected
as *dignior* some three years before by the Meath clergy in their election of a coadjutor though Thomas Nulty was eventually appointed.
The third candidate on the Ardagh *terna* was James Reynolds, the
president of St. Mel's, the local diocesan seminary, who received four
votes.

When Cullen wrote Kirby about a week later, on August 15, he
pointed out in reviewing the Ardagh *terna* that Dawson was "now
rather old and was very ill last winter" and that McCabe was "an
excellent man and would keep up Dr. Kilduff's good works" (K). The
third on the list, Cullen added, was reported to be "well informed and
a good man." "I believe," he predicted, "the Bishops will recommend
Father McCabe, and he is the best." When the bishops of the province
of Armagh met on August 28 in Dundalk, they reported, as Cullen had
predicted, unanimously in favor of McCabe.[40] In a long letter to Barnabò on August 30, Cullen entered a formal report on the Ardagh
terna, in effect endorsing the report of the bishops but giving no indication that he knew what they had reported.[41] "The first," Cullen
explained to Barnabò,

> was Father Dawson, one of the parish priests of the diocese. He
> was first also on the *terna* in 1852 when there was a question of
> appointing a coadjutor to Monsignor Higgins. In any case he was
> excluded for reasons which can be seen in the *Ponenza* that was
> printed then or in the year following. He is now rather old, and
> the bishop of Elphin, who resides in the same vicinity, assures
> me that he has shown little zeal in administering his parish, and
> that while so many others have embellished their churches, he

38. A, vol. 232, fol. 501, "Ristretto con Sommario sulla elezione del Vescovo di
Ardagh nella Provincia di Armagh in Irlanda, 18 Novembre 1867" (fols. 497–503).
39. Emmet Larkin, *The Making of the Roman Catholic Church in Ireland, 1850–
1860* (Chapel Hill, N.C., 1980), pp. 161–68.
40. A, vol. 232, fol. 502.
41. Ibid., fol. 503.

leaves things in their ancient state. It seems to me that it would not now be expedient to promote him.

The second on the *terna* is a priest of the Congregation of the Mission of St. Vincent, Father McCabe, who is presently rector of the Irish College in Paris. He was in this diocese for a long time, and he always showed himself to be a very good and most zealous priest. I believe that he will be an excellent Bishop, and that he will walk in the footsteps of Monsignor Kilduff if he is chosen to be his successor.

The third on the *terna* is Father Reynolds. This priest was the superior of Monsignor Kilduff's Seminary, whose confidence he enjoyed, and appears well informed and zealous for the good of religion. From all that I have been able to learn, however, everyone thinks that Father McCabe is to be preferred to him.

In any case, Cullen then advised Barnabò in conclusion, "it would be well to provide for the vacant diocese without delay so as not to allow time for tricks or intrigues."

Meanwhile, McCabe had written Barnabò on August 12, explaining that he wished to be excused from consideration in the appointment to Ardagh and offering four reasons in support of his supplication.[42] First, he felt called to live as a simple priest. Second, he knew himself to be lacking in the virtue proper to a priest. Third, St. Vincent, the founder of his order, had recommended that his followers avoid all ecclesiastical dignities. And fourth, he was needed as rector of the Irish College in Paris. The secretary of Propaganda, who drew up the *ristretto* summarizing the case for the consideration of the cardinals, reviewed McCabe's reasons for declining the nomination and remarked that the first three were actually recommendations, because the candidate thereby expressed a suitable humility in the face of accepting so great a responsibility.[43] As for the final reason, that the College in Paris would suffer if he were removed, the secretary admitted that it was a serious consideration but pointed out that in fact the Congregation of the Mission in Ireland had several very good priests who could effectively supply McCabe's place. When the cardinals of Propaganda met on November 18, therefore, the result of their deliberation was an almost foregone conclusion. They unanimously recommended McCabe to the pope, and he authoritatively approved their recommendation on November 24.[44]

42. Ibid., fol. 502.
43. Ibid., fol. 499.
44. Ibid., fol. 500.

In retrospect, the Ardagh appointment was perhaps the most routine of all the appointments made in the sixties. Given his antecedents, his age, and the delicate state of his health, Dawson was an impossible candidate, and the patent superiority of McCabe to Reynolds in experience and ability was also obvious. When the bishops reported unanimously in favor of McCabe, and Cullen independently endorsed that view, the appointment was assured. No one in Ireland, therefore, was either surprised or upset by the appointment, especially as all the constitutional niceties involved in the procedure of the appointing bishops in Ireland had been strictly observed. Such was not the case, however, when the pope appointed James Lynch, the former coadjutor to the vicar apostolic of the western district in Scotland, as coadjutor to the bishop of Kildare and Leighlin on April 15, 1869. The history of this most unusual, not to say unprecedented, appointment in the Irish Church is almost as long as it was complicated. The story actually begins with the appointment of Lynch in August 1866 as coadjutor to John Gray, vicar apostolic of the western district in Scotland. This intrusion of an Irishman into the Scottish hierarchy, it will be recalled, had been a very formidable demonstration of Cullen's new power and influence as a cardinal. The appointment of Lynch, however, also finally brought to a boil that resentment which had long been simmering among the Scots bishops and their clergy against the Irish, who had numerically swamped their Church since the Great Famine of 1847. The national and cultural aggressiveness of the Irish, and especially their clergy, it will also be recalled, had been recently and considerably heightened by the struggle between Gray's predecessor as vicar apostolic, John Murdoch, and those Irish priests who had supported the Fenian *Glasgow Free Press* and Father Lavelle against Murdoch's injunctions, and who had carried their protests all the way to Rome.

When Lynch arrived in Glasgow, therefore, the resentment was not long in manifesting itself. "I regret to write," Cullen informed Kirby on March 22, 1867,

> that Dr. Lynch has gotten into some trouble at Glasgow. He says he has written you, so I suppose you know how things stand when Dr. Lynch arrived in Glasgow. He made an arrangement with Dr. Gray that they should hold a *congresso* [meeting] twice a week and arrange all that was to be done. This was carried out. At the meeting each time Dr. Lynch drew up the minutes—at the following meeting the minutes were read and approved before anything else was done. Dr. Lynch states most solemnly that he never undertook anything that was not authorized in this way,

and he always gave the clergy to understand that he was acting in the name and with the authority of Dr. Gray. Things went on very well in this way until a short time ago when Dr. Gray took into his confidence three Scotch priests who were all hostile to Dr. Lynch, and he appears to have determined to change the former system of holding weekly congressi. They have written to the Cardinal Barnabò charging Dr. Lynch with trying to reverse some decision made by the late Dr. Murdoch regarding an insurance policy of £600 the right to which was in dispute between two districts or parishes. Dr. Lynch says that Dr. Murdoch after his decision[,] shortly before his death[,] suggested an arbitration. He adds that he and Dr. Gray had discussed the matter and that the final decision they had come to was to refer the matter to Rome. There was nothing to be condemned in all that, but it appears some Scotch priest in whose favour Dr. Murdoch's decision had been given became alarmed and wrote a complaint to the Propaganda against Dr. Lynch as if he were upsetting all past decisions in the diocese. The Cardinal immediately sent an injunction to Dr. Lynch not to attempt any innovations. [K]

"Dr. Lynch is a little upset by the whole proceedings," Cullen reported further. "I wrote to him to take matters quietly, and that time and patience would bring all things to order. I told him that Rome could not do anything without hearing both sides of the question, and that it would require some time to settle matters. Not having been ever outside a College where things are settled in a moment, he is not acquainted with the difficulties and delays which necessarily occur in higher tribunals." "Poor Dr. Gray," Cullen noted finally, "is said to be quite unfit for governing, but the Scotch priests in whose hands he has put himself may give great trouble, as some of them are deep enough. Write to Dr. Lynch and encourage him to wait patiently until things will be finally settled."

Kirby obviously did write Lynch as Cullen suggested, for Lynch replied on April 12, enclosing a copy of another letter of Cullen's [K]. "I think," Cullen had advised Lynch on April 10, referring to the anniversary of the martyrdom of Saints Peter and Paul, "it will be very desirable for your Lordship to go to Rome before the Canonization of the Saints" [K]. "It would be well," he suggested, "to collect all the statistics of the Catholics in the vicariate, & to elicit an expression of some of the best missionaries without letting them [know] that you wish to use their declarations in Rome." "It will not be necessary to do anything in regard to the Irish priests, as their opinion is well known," Cullen added, "but letters from Dr. Strain [vicar apostolic of the east-

ern district, who was more partial to the Irish than his colleagues] &
the Jesuit & other Missionaries would be very useful." Kirby then
consulted Barnabò about Lynch's coming to Rome, for in summarizing
his reply in a note on this letter, he wrote, "Do not come now—C.
Barnabò has written & strongly to Dr. Gray." Meanwhile, Cullen had
written Kirby again on March 24, enclosing a letter from Lynch (K).
Cullen assured Kirby that Lynch was determined to be submissive
("*passive se habere*"), but Gray had placed himself in the hands of the
three Scots priests mentioned in his previous letter. Because the Scots
laity were only a handful, however, and the Irish were some 150,000,
the best thing for Lynch to do for the present was to remain quiet and
allow the Scots to make a mess of it.

For the next six months Lynch hewed to his passive line, residing
and working with his confreres, the Vincentians, among the Irish poor
at St. Mary's in Lanark, while keeping both Kirby and Propaganda
informed about the appalling spiritual destitution of the clergy and
laity of western Scotland. Because relations between Gray and Lynch
did not improve over the same period—and indeed, according to Gray
they worsened—in the early fall of 1867 Propaganda finally asked the
archbishop of Westminster to investigate the difficulties that had
arisen and to report what he thought should be done.[45] Manning visited Glasgow for five days in late October, and in his report to Rome
about a month later, he recommended, in effect, that both Gray and
Lynch resign and that George Errington, former coadjutor to the late
Cardinal Wiseman, who had been deprived of his right to succession
as archbishop of Westminster in 1862 at Wiseman's insistence and
who had since been serving as an ordinary parish priest in the Isle of
Man, be asked to undertake the restoration of a regular hierarchy for
the Scots Church, of which he would be the primate and archbishop of
Glasgow. In late February 1868 Cardinal Barnabò finally authorized
Manning to sound Errington on the proposal, and Manning wrote him
in early March. Manning's report of his negotiations with Errington
was apparently positive enough for Barnabò to authorize him to write
Gray and Lynch suggesting they resign. On May 26, therefore, Manning wrote both Gray and Lynch, and they both replied by return of
post that they were ready to place their resignation in the hands of the

45. Vincent A. McClelland, "The Irish Clergy and Archbishop Manning's Visitation
of the Western District of Scotland, 1867, parts 1,2," *Catholic Historical Review* 53
(April 1967): 1–27; (July 1967): 229–50. See also McClelland's "Documents Relating to
the Appointments of a Delegate Apostolic for Scotland, 1868," *Innes Review*, Autumn
1957, pp. 93–99; and Peter F. Anson, *Underground Catholicism in Scotland, 1622–1878*
(Montrose, 1970), pp. 314–21.

pope. When Cullen finally learned what Manning had recommended and Rome had authorized, he was not entirely pleased. "Dr. Lynch," he explained to Kirby on June 16, "has been working like a slave giving missions, and he says that the immorality especially among females exceeds belief. The spirit of John Knox still produces its baneful effects and corrupts everything that comes in contact with it" (K). "The Catholics in Scotland," he reported, "are nearly all Irish—an Englishman or Scotchman will find it difficult to manage them especially when they shall have seen the removal of so good and holy an Irishman as Dr. Lynch." "Perhaps," Cullen suggested, "it will be no harm to have a little conversation with Card. Barnabò on this matter."

When he then learned a short time later, however, that the affairs of the western district had been in effect settled, Cullen's attitude toward Errington's appointment apparently softened. "We were all pleased," Moran assured Kirby on June 24, "with the appointment of Dr. Errington to Glasgow, although we regret the resignation of Dr. Lynch" (K). "It was a pity he did not get fair play," Moran lamented, "as he is undoubtedly, a most worthy man, but from the time of his appointment his hands were tied and he could do nothing. I trust the energy of Dr. Errington will set matters right. It is an immense city with 120,000 Irish Catholics, who are surrounded with all the viciousness and wickedness that can be conceived in that manufacturing city. To meet and combat all this there are I may say no institutions, no religious communities and only 30 priests." "Scotland requires," he advised Kirby, "to be very closely looked after by the Holy See. Some of the good people there are too anxious to take the world quietly and have not energy enough to grapple with the wants of the thousands of immigrants who rush over month after month. I hope Dr. Errington will do a world of good, but until the hierarchy is established and the number of bishops doubled, nothing can be hoped for." On reflection, Cullen had undoubtedly realized that with the creation of a new hierarchy for Scotland, the number of bishops would probably have to be doubled, and a place for Lynch would thereby be easily provided. Cullen had also known Errington for many years, and he both liked and respected him not only because of his very great energy but also because of his very real concern for the Irish poor. In Errington's difficulties with Cardinal Wiseman, moreover, Cullen's sympathies had been all on the side of Errington. All in all, therefore, Cullen realized that the proposed solution in Scotland was, from his point of view, the best that could be had. What Cullen apparently did not realize, however, was that Manning in his report to Rome the previous November had recommended that Lynch, on his resignation, should be translated to an Irish See, and he would not, therefore, be provided for in the proposed restoration and expansion of the Scottish hierarchy.

When Errington then refused to accept the charge of heading a new hierarchy in Scotland, a difficult situation was only made worse. "I now learn," Odo Russell, the British government's unofficial representative in Rome, reported from Rome to Lord Stanley, the foreign secretary in Disraeli's first administration, on November 18, "that Dr. Errington has declined to undertake the organization of the Scotch Roman Catholic Hierarchy entrusted to him by the Pope, —but that although the creation of that hierarchy is put off in consequence the idea has not been given up and will be reserved 'in petto' until Dr. Manning comes to Rome this winter to be consulted about the nomination of another 'Archbishop of Glasgow,' who will accept the mission declined by Dr. Errington."[46] When the announcement of the creation of a new hierarchy for Scotland appeared in the British and Irish papers in early December,[47] therefore, Russell asked the secretary of state, Cardinal Antonelli, whether the report had any foundation in fact, and was assured by the cardinal that it did not. Manning, upon his arrival in Rome in late December, confirmed Antonelli's assurances in an interview with Russell. "The Archbishop admitted," Russell explained to the earl of Clarendon, foreign secretary in Gladstone's first administration, on January 1, 1869, "that a Hierarchy for Scotland had been under discussion of the Propaganda, but on mature reflection had been given up for various reasons, and the Scotch Vicars Apostolic Dr. Eyre and MacDonald appointed Bishops in partibus instead—a 'mezzo termine' [compromise] which was in all respects preferable."[48] "I was also glad to hear the Archbishop say," Russell added, "that the present friendly relations existing between Her Majesty's Government and the Roman Catholic clergy in England precluded the adopting of a measure of so much importance as the creation of a Hierarchy in Scotland without previous notice or understanding."

The "mature reflection" that Russell mentioned signified primarily that the authorities did not want a repetition of what had happened in 1850 when the pope had unilaterally reestablished the Catholic hierarchy in England. The "no popery" outburst that had greeted that restoration of the hierarchy had embarrassed Anglo-papal relations for the following fifteen years, and another such furor was to be avoided at all cost, most especially as Gladstone was at that moment initiating

46. F.O., 43/101. See also S.R.C., vol. 36, fols. 311–15, Cullen to Barnabò, November 6, 1868.
47. *Freeman's Journal*, December 9, 1868, reporting the *Church News*.
48. F.O., 43/103 b.

his program of justice for Ireland by attempting to disestablish the state Church in Ireland. The Roman solution to their Scots problem, therefore, was bound to be in the circumstances a modest one. The old system of vicars apostolic, that is, of titular bishops whose titles were taken from ancient sees that were now in parts unfaithful (*in partibus infidelium*), was to be retained, and the three vicariates of the eastern, western, and northern districts in Scotland were to remain as they were. The western district, however, which was the most heavily Catholic, was to be given precedence with the appointment of a titular archbishop, *in partibus*, instead of a bishop. Charles Eyre, a protégé of Manning's, canon in the diocese of Hexham and Newcastle, and pastor of Newcastle-on-Tyne, therefore was appointed archbishop of Anazarba, apostolic administrator of the western district, and delegate apostolic of the Holy See. A Scots priest, John MacDonald, was appointed bishop of Nicopolis and coadjutor to John Kyle, who had been vicar apostolic of the northern district for more than forty years; John Strain, the bishop of Abila, remained the vicar apostolic of the eastern district.

When all these arrangements were finally announced, and it became obvious that no provision had been made for Lynch, who was still living and working as a mission priest with his confreres in Lanark, Cullen was naturally very embarrassed. Indeed, the new arrangements in Scotland were a mortifying blow to Cullen's prestige. He had not been consulted about the new arrangements, and his influence in Scots affairs at Rome had obviously been superseded by Manning's. If Lynch was not provided for, and soon, he would continue to stand as a painful reminder of Cullen's embarrassment. "I send a letter," a somewhat subdued Cullen informed Kirby on January 10, 1869, "I rec^d from Dr. Lynch—if everything regarding Glasgow has been already settled, I suppose it w^d be useless to put it in or speak about it. Act as you think fit, but there is no use in talking about matters if they be finally settled. Poor Dr. Lynch has had to suffer very severely. I dare say his diocese has scarcely given him food and raiment. I hope the Propaganda will do something for him" (K).

Therefore, when the bishop of Kildare and Leighlin, James Walshe, again approached Cullen in February to ask him to intercede on his behalf at Rome for the appointment of a coadjutor, Cullen apparently saw his opening to provide Propaganda with an opportunity, and he acceded to Walshe's request.[49] Barnabò wrote Cullen in the middle

49. When Walshe had written Barnabò some eighteen months before, requesting that the pope grant him a coadjutor, Barnabò had written Cullen asking him his opinion (S.R.C., vol. 35, fol. 1201, Cullen to Barnabò, August 11, 1867). Cullen had consulted

of March, explaining that the pope proposed to appoint Lynch as
Walshe's coadjutor and suggesting that Cullen break the news to
Walshe. Cullen politely demurred. As he explained on March 24,

> It appears to me that it would be better that your Eminence write
> directly to Monsignor Walshe on this matter, and I am persuaded
> that he would be happier to deal with it immediately with you
> than with any other. I have not begun any correspondence with
> him on the subject of the coadjutorship, and I consented only at
> his request to send his petition for a coadjutor to Rome. If I now
> proposed Monsignor Lynch he would imagine that it was a plot
> on my part to impose on him a person of my choice. If your
> Eminence opened the matter with him this difficulty will not
> arise. There is another thing to be avoided. Father Lavelle and his
> followers, pretending great patriotism, continually write that I
> am seeking to destroy the rights of the Irish Church, and by ex-
> cluding the priests from taking that part in the choice of Bishops
> they have a right to by the permission of the Holy See. These
> charges have not the least foundation, but being continually
> repeated make a certain impression, and one should not give
> cause to the above-mentioned patriots to make people believe
> that the facts which they are asserting can really be verified. It
> seems to me that a letter from your Eminence to the bishop of
> Kildare will avoid every inconvenience. In any case, if you desire
> it I shall be able to visit the bishop after Easter, and treat with
> him about the matter.[50]

Shortly after receiving this letter, Barnabò took Cullen's advice and
wrote Walshe informing him that the pope was disposed to provide
him with a coadjutor in the person of Lynch. On receiving Barnabò's
letter, Walshe decided to write Cullen. "I had the honour," he explained on April 17, "of receiving the enclosed a day or two ago. I
think I ought to respectfully submit to your Eminence the expression
of some thoughts which occur to me on the subject. I rely upon your
kindness to excuse the liberty" (C). "There is no question of the merits of Dr. L.," he assured Cullen. "And, of course, there is no doubt
whatever of the right of the H.F." He went on to explain his reservations:

---

his two other suffragans, Ferns and Ossory, who were of the opinion that Walshe did not
require a coadjutor, and Cullen added that this was also his considered opinion (ibid.,
fol. 1001, Cullen to Barnabò, August 15, 1867).

50. S.R.C., vol. 36, fol. 475.

But I apprehend that the derogation, in this case, from the Rescript of 1829 will cause surprise and pain to the clergy. Such a departure is unprecedented in this diocese—and rarely, as well as I remember, took place elsewhere and then, only, in peculiar circumstances, which to my knowledge do not exist here. Hence in the present case the withdrawal from the clergy of the favour or privilege graciously bestowed upon them by the H. See in 1829, may appear to intimate the displeasure of the Holy Father. They —and their unhappy Bishop—would be sorely grieved by this, for they are not—I am confident—conscious of having done anything to deserve such a penalty. On all occasions they exhibited not only a dutiful, but a strong[,] generous and devoted attachment to the Holy F.

"If the uneasiness, which I fear," Walshe added, "arise, the inconvenience which it would tend to entail would, in my judgement, be greater than what would proceed from a continuance of my administration *without* a Coadjutor. Whether a change at Rome be practicable I know not. It is, however, useless for me to write. But if your Eminence think that the H.F. would countermand the issue of the 'Apostolica Litera' and you deem what I have stated to be of sufficient weight, may I ask your Eminence to write to Rome—if it be not unbecoming that I ask you to do so." "I have not mentioned to anyone," he assured Cullen in conclusion, "the purpose of the Card. Prefect's letter, or of this communication to your Eminence."

In the meantime, the pope had on April 15 formally appointed Lynch coadjutor with the right of succession to the bishop of Kildare and Leighlin. Barnabò apparently wrote Cullen that same day, for Cullen reported the news to Kirby in a letter postmarked April 23: "I fear there will be some trouble there as the Card[1] consulted neither Bishop nor clergy. He appears to have set his heart on getting Dr. L. out of Glasgow. I think he made a great mistake as Dr. L. is the very best [manuscript torn] of man that would have introduced some religion into Scotland" (K). "Some of the students from the Scotch College," he charged, referring to the alumni of that Roman College, "appear to have resolved to persecute Dr. L. out of Scotland and as they knew how to write Italian, they got round His Eminence and prejudiced him against a good laborious missionary who took no notice of intrigues and diplomacy. I hope we shall not have trouble in Kildare." Cullen then added prudently in the margin next to this paragraph, "(don't mention this to any)."

Barnabò also apparently wrote Walshe again, officially announcing the pope's decision, for Walshe immediately wrote Cullen apprising him of the news. "Dr. Walshe," Cullen reported to Kirby on April 27, "has received a letter from the Card. announcing the appointment of Dr. Lynch to be his coadjutor. Dr. Walshe says the intelligence was like a bombshell in the diocese. He expected that the elections w^d be conducted more solito [in the usual manner]—I did not think the matter wd be done so abruptly" (K). "What the priests in Carlow say," he added, "is that to gratify six or 7 Scotch priests who carried on a wicked war against Dr. L., the feelings of a couple of hundred Irish priests have been disregarded." "Of course if Dr. Lynch accepts the office," Cullen assured Kirby, "all the priests will sacrifice their own feelings. Dr. Lynch is known to them all as a most worthy man. Dr. Walshe wrote several times during the last years for permission to get a coadjutor. I always wrote against his petition until last February when he pressed me to say a word in his favour. He is now disappointed, but as I said, if the matter be carried out, I think all will submit." "Dr. Lynch," he noted finally, "is older than Dr. W."

When Cullen wrote Kirby again about a week later, however, it did not appear that the Kildare and Leighlin clergy would prove as well disposed to Lynch as he had predicted. "Some busybody," Cullen explained on May 7, "announced the matter in the *Tablet*, before it was known in Kildare, and the clergy was [sic] very angry that such an announcement should be communicated to a London paper before they know anything about [it]" (K). "To fan the flame of discontent," he added, "someone, I think he must be a disciple of Lavelle or some person who expected to be elected by the clergy of Kildare, put an article in the Freeman treating Dr. Walshe as an imbecile and saying that the patience of the clergy in bearing Dr. Walshe so long was at length rewarded by getting a right Bishop in the person of Dr. Lynch. This article set Dr. Walshe furious. The clergy are also very furious and they threaten all sorts of opposition. They say they will even send a deputation to Rome to oppose Dr. Lynch. All this is very unfortunate—but it is a consequence of the impunity which Father Lavelle has enjoyed, notwithstanding all the misdeeds he has been engaged in." "Dr. Lynch is at Castleknock," Cullen then reported in conclusion, referring to the Vincentian house near Dublin, "uncertain what to do. He will wait to see how the storm will proceed."

Some two months later, when the dust had settled on this remarkable appointment in Kildare and Leighlin, James I. Taylor, the parish priest of Maryborough in that diocese and an old friend of Kirby's, wrote him about the continued soreness of feeling in the diocese. "We have got, I am sure," he reported on June 30, "an exceedingly good

Coadjutor Bishop in Dr. Lynch. But there is among the priests of the diocese a great deal of sullen discontent at the way in which he was put upon them. They set it all down to the Cardinal [i.e., Cullen] & say it was *he* who did it" [K]. Taylor added reassuringly, "At all events—whoever did it has every reason to be satisfied with his act: for a better appointment could not be: Dr. Lynch is a good pious— humble, sensible[,] well informed Man: one who in his own person will give an example to every priest what he should be." The resentment of the bishop of Kildare and Leighlin, however, was apparently even more deeply rooted than that of his clergy. Cullen reported to Kirby some three months later, on September 23, in reference to Vatican Council I, which was soon to be convened, "Dr. Taylor, P.P., Marybor°, spoke to me some days ago about Dr. Walshe of Carlow [*sic*], and suggested that it would be well if the Propaganda would give him [Dr. W.] leave to stay away from the Council. His Lordship is in very bad humour—he thinks I am persecuting him and writing against him to Rome. Of course I never wrote a word against him and never had any reason to do so—so the poor man is under a great delusion" [K]. "Dr. Taylor says," Cullen added, referring to the affair of the coadjutor, "if he be obliged to go to Rome, he will throw all the blame on me. Though I think these suspicions are of very little importance, still Dr. Taylor thinks it w^d be well to let Dr. W. have his own way and remain at home. Dr. Lynch c^d go to Rome and supply his place." "I heard from one of the priests in Kildare," he noted finally, "that an attempt to get up an agitation against Dr. Lynch was lately made, but that it failed altogether."

Though Cullen was very careful in this case to keep clear of all direct responsibility, there can be little doubt that he prepared the way for the appointment of Lynch by interceding when he did at Rome on behalf of Walshe for a coadjutor. What Cullen had not counted on was that Barnabò and the pope would decide to ignore the ordinary procedure and appoint Lynch directly. Cullen had expected, of course, that when the pope authorized a coadjutor for Walshe, he would be able to secure through the influence of his uncle, James Maher, the parish priest of Killeshin, and his old friend James Taylor the parish priest of Maryborough, a place on the Kildare and Leighlin *terna* for Lynch. He also undoubtedly counted on his influence among his suffragan bishops to secure a favorable report to Propaganda for Lynch. He was therefore somewhat unhappy about the way the appointment had been made, not only because he thought that he could have handled it better by working through the ordinary procedure, but also because he certainly realized that Father Lavelle and his friends would once again denounce him throughout the length and breadth of the land for sub-verting the rights of the clergy in the election of their bishops. Why then, it must be asked, did the pope, who certainly must have realized the acute embarrassment such a mode of procedure on his part would cause Cullen, proceed to make the appointment in the way he did? The answer to that question, of course, is that the pope was acting not simply within an Irish frame of reference but to meet what he con-ceived to be the greater needs of the universal Church. Indeed, what the pope most certainly understood was that his own person was now involved in Cullen's standing as a cardinal, and if the preserving of that standing necessitated the making of a provision for Lynch, then the sooner and more authoritatively it was done the better. What must have been made perfectly clear to Cullen's friends and enemies in the Irish Church was that Lynch's appointment, most especially in the way that it was done, was yet another impressive indication that Cullen still enjoyed the absolute confidence of the pope as far as the Irish Church was concerned.

When the archbishop of Armagh, Michael Kieran, who had been ill for some two years with a stomach complaint that was finally diagnosed as cancer, had to apply to the pope for a coadjutor in the summer of 1869, the recent appointment to Kildare and Leighlin was still very fresh in the minds of the bishops and clergy of the Irish Church. The pope consented to Kieran's request, but the day before the Armagh clergy were to meet to commend a *terna* to Rome, Kieran died. "He had convened all his clergy," Cullen reported to Kirby on September 16, the day after Kieran died, "for the purpose of selecting a coadjutor. They are all today in Armagh, and Dr. Leahy of Dromore was deputed to preside at the meeting. I do not know whether the death of the Primate will stop the election. It was a great pity the permission for the clergy to meet was not sent in time" (K). Several days later Cullen wrote Kirby again. "The election for Armagh," he reported on Septem-ber 21, "will take place in about a month or sooner. It is said the *Northerners* will elect Father Harbison the Redemptorist, who is a very good man, but who had a paralyzed arm some time ago, and probably would not be able to confirm" (K). Cullen went on, referring to his chaplain and secretary, George Conroy, who was only thirty-six years old, "The *Southerners*, that is the priests on the south side of the diocese, would have elected Dr. Conroy if the Primate had lived to see his coadjutor elected. He was very anxious to have Dr. Conroy appointed, and I am sure Dr. Conroy though young would make an excellent Bishop." "As Dr. Kieran is now out of the way," Cullen added, "probably the priests will not be much influenced by his recommendations. I do not know therefore what they may do, but perhaps they may turn their thoughts to someone in Maynooth."

The results of the election, however, were not at all what Cullen predicted. When the clergy met in Armagh on October 12, under the presidency of the senior suffragan of the province, they returned Daniel McGettigan, the bishop of Raphoe, as *dignissimus* with twenty-seven votes. The *dignior* was James Tierney, the archdeacon of Armagh and parish priest of Drogheda, who received nine votes. Francis Kelly, the bishop of Derry, who presided at the meeting, was elected *dignus* with five votes.[51] Conroy also received five votes, and four others received one vote each. When Cullen wrote Kirby the next day, his annoyance was exceeded only by his disappointment. "In Armagh," he reported on October 20, "the clergy have elected Dr. McGettigan 25 [sic] votes, Father Tierney 9 votes—Dr. Kelly of Derry 5 votes. Dr. Conroy had also 5 votes but he was not put on the list" (K). "F. Tierney," Cullen added angrily, "is an old man going on a crutch and quite unfit to be a Bishop. The priests that voted for him showed a great want of honesty and principle." "If Dr. Kieran had lived," he assured Kirby, "Dr. Conroy wd have been on the list perhaps 1st. But as soon as his Grace was taken away, the greatest intrigues were commenced against Dr. Conroy, on the ground that he was an Italian monk or something of that kind, and likely to be anxious to promote practices of piety and Roman images. I suppose only some few priests were engaged in the business, but a few noisy people can do a great deal at an election." Kirby translated this letter, and also that of September 21, and submitted them both in the form of a memorandum to Propaganda, which was then included in the *ponenza* prepared for the cardinals of that congregation. "Cardinal Cullen here concludes with those words," Kirby noted in closing his memorandum, "which reveal how he feels about this affair, and about which it seems unnecessary to make any further inquiry. Especially because in this case it would perhaps be a difficult matter for him, or at least a delicate one, to recommend Dr. Conroy, his secretary, in preference to two Bishops."[52] "If the Holy Father," Kirby suggested boldly, apparently thinking of the recent appointment of Lynch, "felt

---

51. A, vol. 236, fol. 180, "Ristretto con Sommario Sulla elezione dell'Arcivescovo di Armagh Primate di tutta Irlanda, Febbraio 1870" (fols. 173–83).
52. Ibid.

inspired to do it of himself, it could be said that the Supreme Pontiff exercised his right."

What must have annoyed Cullen most about the Armagh election was the very clever way in which the clergy structured their *terna* so as to leave him very little room for maneuver. First of all, it was obvious that the northern clergy had caucused and decided to vote *en bloc* for the bishop of Raphoe. When the southern clergy caucused, however, they were apparently unable to focus on a single candidate, and the majority decided to attempt to exclude Conroy by casting their votes in such a way as to take the second and third places on the *terna*. They obviously either miscalculated or had not sufficiently organized their votes, because there was a tie for third place. At this point the Armagh clergy proceeded to give a real demonstration of their political resourcefulness. They moved to exclude Conroy by a most unusual interpretation of the procedure involved in the commending of a *terna*. Normally, both Kelly and Conroy, having tied for *dignus*, would have had their names returned to Rome, but it was proposed that the clergy be polled a second time in order to determine who should round out the *terna*.[53] It was not surprising that Kelly, who was presiding, received forty-three votes to Conroy's five in the second scrutiny. Moreover, by electing Tierney as *dignior*, the clergy had obviously, as Cullen complained, set up a straw man as candidate. The only viable candidates were McGettigan, who had received the overwhelming number of votes cast, and Kelly, who had, in effect, been set up to exclude Conroy. Finally, and most important of all, the fact that the only viable candidates were bishops made it impossible for Cullen to say a word against them, especially as both had proved to be, on Cullen's own testimony in recent years, not only exemplary in the administration of their dioceses and in their personal conduct but also sound on all those issues that the bishops faced as a body.

Indeed, when Barnabò received the commendation of the Armagh clergy in late October, he was reported by Bernard Smith, former vice-rector of the Irish College under Kirby and now a consultor to Propaganda, as having "read me the letter of the Senior Suffragan relating the election—He said the case was settled—A bishop with 27 votes!"[54] When the bishops of the province of Armagh met in Armagh on October 26 with McGettigan and Kelly absenting themselves, they reported unanimously in favor of the two bishops and against both

53. *Scritture originali riferite nelle congregazione generali*, vol. 997, fols. 452–53, J. J. McGahan to Rinaldini, n.d.
54. Smith Papers.

Tierney and Conroy.[55] Their report on McGettigan was, in fact, as full an encomium as it was possible to pen. With regard to Kelly they were also very complimentary, noting that to know him was to love him, but McGettigan was clearly their preference. The bishops reported that Tierney was unfit in ability and health to be a bishop. With regard to Conroy, the bishops noted that he had had no practical experience as a priest on the Irish mission, that the Armagh clergy were not favorably inclined toward him, and that the late archbishop had wanted Conroy to succeed him because they were related.

Given the report of the bishops, it was clear that Cullen, who was about to leave for Rome with the great majority of the Irish bishops for the opening of the first Vatican Council, would have his work cut out for him there in persuading the cardinals of Propaganda and the pope that his thirty-six-year-old protégé and chaplain should be promoted to the see of Armagh. Still, Cullen had not achieved greatness in the Irish Church by flinching in difficult situations. He would, after all, soon be in Rome, where as a cardinal and a member of the congregation of Propaganda he would be able to exert his very considerable personal influence. During his first few months in Rome, Cullen and the other cardinals of the Curia were greatly occupied with the ceremonies and administrative details of the council, and it was very difficult to get any ordinary business done at Propaganda. Shortly after Propaganda resumed its biweekly congregations in the third week of January 1870, however, Cullen took occasion to put his views in writing to Barnabò about the vacant see of Armagh. "As the time is approaching," Cullen explained on January 24,

> when the election of an archbishop of the vacant see of Armagh must be dealt with, I believe that it will not be out of place to make Your Eminence aware that the two bishops, namely of Derry and of Raphoe, who find themselves on the *terna* proposed to the Sacred Congregation by the clergy of the said diocese, are determined not to accept that dignity if it were offered to them. They are both advanced in years, and they have asked me to tell Your Eminence that they have neither the strength nor vigor sufficient to undertake the government of a diocese much divided by factions and very troubled as Armagh is.
>
> I do not know what judgement the bishops of the province have given about Father Tierney, archdeacon of the diocese, whose name is also found on the *terna*, but knowing that arch-

55. A, vol. 236, fols. 180–81.

deacon personally for many years, I can assure Your Eminence that he has not the qualities that would make him fit to be the Primate of Ireland. He is old and ill, eager to amuse himself, and not fond of discipline.

In the first ballot taken when the Armagh clergy chose the three names to present to the Sacred Congregation, Father George Conroy had a number of votes equal to those of the bishop of Derry and his name therefore ought to be inserted in the *terna*, or at least in the report forwarded to the Sacred Congregation, and this was the view of the Bishop of Derry, who presided at the meeting: but the clergy insisted a second ballot be taken, which is in opposition to the rescripts of the Sacred Congregation, and thus the name of George Conroy was undeservedly excluded.

I shall now only add that the late Archbishop, Monsignor Kieran, was very anxious to have the said Conroy for coadjutor, that Conroy was an excellent student at the *Collegio Urbano* [in Rome], and that I can certify that he is a very pious and exemplary priest, having lived with me as secretary for several years. Besides he is an excellent theologian and philosopher, knows Latin, Greek, Italian and French very well and [is] moreover an excellent writer and preacher in English.[56]

"He is," Cullen finally assured the cardinal prefect, "in the best of health and I believe about thirty-five years of age."

That same day, January 24, Cullen also wrote Conroy, who was acting as his liaison in Dublin in diocesan business, informing him that the appointment to Armagh would probably be soon considered by the cardinals of Propaganda.[57] To Cullen's great annoyance, however, the Armagh case had to be postponed several times over the next three weeks because of the pressure of other business. By this time Cullen had been able to read the report of the Armagh prelates and had been asked by Barnabò to put his views formally in writing for the consideration of his colleagues. In a long letter, dated February 7, Cullen therefore mobilized his very considerable powers of persuasion in the interests of Conroy.[58] The burden of his argument was, in effect, that there was no *terna* because the two bishops had given notice

56. S.R.C., vol. 36, fol. 653.
57. Peadar MacSuibhne, *Paul Cullen and His Contemporaries*, vol. 5 (Naas, 1977), p. 47.
58. A, vol. 236, fols. 182–83.

that they would not accept the see of Armagh if offered, and the other name on the list, as the bishops pointed out in their report, was not fit to be a bishop. This left Conroy, who had been unlawfully excluded by the Armagh clergy from the *terna*, as the only candidate. Cullen then proceeded to dispose of the reasons why the Armagh prelates thought Conroy should not be appointed, while at the same time making a case that he should be considered. He admitted, for example, that Conroy had no experience on the Irish mission as a pastor or a curate, but he pointed out that Conroy was a very good preacher and had considerable experience in administering the sacrament of penance. He was, Cullen argued, an excellent writer in English, an accomplished linguist, and well versed in philosophy and theology, which he had taught in the diocesan seminary in Dublin for several years. As to the bishops' maintaining that the clergy of Armagh would not find Conroy pleasing, Cullen cleverly noted that the same clergy apparently thought Conroy worthy of being Kieran's coadjutor when the archbishop was alive, and their change of heart reflected less on Conroy than it did on them. In disposing of the charge that Kieran had favored Conroy's promotion because they were related, Cullen maintained that Kieran had not been prompted by either the kindly dispositions he felt toward Conroy or by the relationship, but rather had realized that there was not one among the Armagh clergy fit to be a bishop.

Cullen's very able letter was apparently the last item included in the *sommario*, or document section of the *ponenza*, before it was set up in type to be presented to the cardinals for their meeting. The *ristretto*, or digest of the case, moreover, which was usually an impartial summary of the relevant material, was in this instance very much a partisan statement. After what can only be characterized as a systematic Cullenite presentation, the author of the *ristretto* finally summed up for the cardinals of Propaganda in the following manner:

> If to all this one adds that Father Conroy belongs to the diocese of Armagh, that he is the only priest there . . . who is considered deserving of governing it, and that this is the firm judgement of his Eminence, the archbishop of Dublin, who was for some years archbishop of Armagh, and being therefore fully acquainted with the clergy, the circumstances, and the abuses to be remedied, is the most competent among the Irish bishops to express the aforementioned judgement, in spite of the contrary advice of the bishops of the province of Armagh. I have now to beg

your Eminences to decide whether Conroy is to be recommended
to the Holy Father for the see of Armagh in preference to the
three subjects placed on the *terna*.[59]

When Cullen wrote Conroy again on February 17, he explained that
Armagh would finally be considered at the next congregation of Propaganda.[60] "I have been reappointed *Ponente* in the case," he reported,
"that is I am to introduce the question to the cardinals who then will
do as they like." "If you be concerned," he then assured Conroy, "in
the election of Armagh *scil. si sors ceciderit in Georgium* [namely, if it
turns out to be George] I will send a telegram saying *you are required
in Rome*. That will tell you that Propaganda has dealt with the case
and the Pope has confirmed it. If you get no telegram, *res infectae
habendae sunt* [matters remain as they are]." The following day, February 18, a very embarrassed Cullen had to write Conroy again and
confess that he had ought not to have written what he had the day
before.[61] Barnabò had just told him, Cullen explained, that the Armagh case would now have to be postponed until the middle of
March. Yet a week later, on February 25, Cullen reported to Conroy
that they were to meet that evening at six P.M. to decide about Armagh.[62] "As soon as the decision will have been confirmed by the
Pope," he assured Conroy once again, "I will send a telegram or if
there be no doubt about the matter I will send [it] sooner." "If you be
appointed," Cullen advised, "the best plan will be to take possession
of the See (but you must have the brief to do that), appoint a vicar-
general and come off to Rome for consecration."

> You will avoid trouble by appointing Dr. Slane, and if there be
> any other very worthy man in Louth you could appoint him.[63]
> Father Levins and Father Macken are well spoken of, but do not
> appoint anyone unless you are certain of his fitness.
>   Dr. Slane will not be long in the way, but the others, if not fit,
> might be a permanent source of annoyance, as it is very ungra-
> cious to remove a vicar-general. Don't give any powers to Fr.
> Tierney even though he may ask you. Perhaps treating of Louth
> you might give powers only *ad tempus* [for a time], or until your
> return from the Council when such powers should cease.

59. Ibid., fol. 178.
60. MacSuibhne, 5:60.
61. Ibid., p. 63.
62. Ibid., p. 66.
63. Felix Slane was the dean of Armagh, a vicar-general to the late archbishop, and as
parish priest of Drumglass (Dungannon) a northerner.

"But you will say," Cullen concluded more prudently, "I am putting the car before the horse, regulating matters which may not occur, so I will say no more."

When the cardinals of Propaganda met that evening, the Armagh affair did not turn out as Cullen had hoped. "I believe," he dejectedly wrote Conroy the following day, February 26, "the Armagh affair is all lost."[64] "Cardinal Barnabò," Cullen explained, "told me the other day that your appointment was certain and I foolishly wrote to you, relying on what he said yesterday; the Congregation met, and the cardinals said they could not get over the recommendations of the bishops of the province in favour of Dr. McGettigan and they selected him accordingly. As, however, he had declared he would not accept, the matter is to be referred to the Pope who will decide the case." "My opinion," Cullen predicted shrewdly, "is that Dr. McG. will accept. You see how things change in a minute. Perhaps it is all for the better." "Don't say a word about Armagh," he then finally added in a postscript. "Things are so changeable that a new phase may arise." An audience with the pope was arranged on March 6 for McGettigan. Before the audience, on March 3, the cardinals of Propaganda met again and discussed what was to be done if McGettigan still refused to accept. The cardinals decided to put their views formally in writing and unanimously recommended that McGettigan be translated from Raphoe to Armagh.[65] They added the proviso, however, that if McGettigan formally declared against accepting the promotion, Conroy should be nominated and the cardinal prefect should be charged with speaking to the Armagh bishops with a view to settling their minds and forestalling whatever touchiness there might be by advising them to allow it to pass. In any case, McGettigan was persuaded to accept, and the pope appointed him archbishop of Armagh on March 6. "He will," Cullen reported to Conroy the following day, "have hard times there and many troubles. He very justly said to me that probably his career would be at an end before he could know all the priests of the diocese or understand the state of things."[66] "As he is now archbishop," Cullen added, "I hope he may have every success."

The immediate question that arises is, of course, Why did McGettigan change his mind? Several days after the appointment, Cullen wrote Conroy reporting a very interesting conversation apparently with the pope's secretary.[67] "The secretary told me yesterday," Cullen

---

64. MacSuibhne, 5:68.
65. A, vol. 237, fol. 176.
66. MacSuibhne, 5:29–30. This letter is misdated there.
67. Ibid., p. 77.

explained on March 10, "that it was Dr. Nulty who made him [Mc-Gettigan] accept. He was here, said the secretary, with his *Angelo custode* [Guardian Angel] to answer for him. I asked who was this angel. Nulty said the Secretary." "The secretary told him," Cullen reported further, apparently referring to Nulty, "that the Pope was much displeased with the *terna* as the bishops by the exorbitant praises given to one left him no room to make a choice." "Dr. Kieran told me," Cullen noted finally, "that the only person he feared was Dr. Nulty. He was right."[68]

The charge that the bishop of Meath was primarily responsible for McGettigan's having changed his mind is obviously a gross oversimplification. All of the bishops of the province of Armagh were then in Rome attending the council, and they were collectively, therefore, in a position to endorse *viva voce* what they had unanimously and enthusiastically recommended in their report about Armagh to Propaganda. From their report, moreover, it was obvious that they were determined on McGettigan, not simply because he was a good, conscientious, and amiable man, but also because they were determined to block the appointment of Conroy. Indeed, their reasons for wanting to do so, though left unspoken, are not difficult to divine. What they undoubtedly resented the most was Cullen's naked effort to impose his thirty-six-year-old protégé and chaplain on them. If it had been a question of just another bishopric their resistance might not have been so resolute, but to have a mere youth, who barely had reached the canonical age required in a bishop, imposed on them not only as their archbishop but as the primate of all Ireland and titular head of the Irish Church, was obviously more than they were willing to bear.

There were, however, other considerations that weighed with the Armagh prelates in their determination for McGettigan, considerations perhaps more important than even their natural and very understandable resentments. If Cullen could have Conroy appointed in spite of the commendation of the clergy and the report of the bishops, it would prove a very serious blow to the procedure involved in the appointment of bishops in the Irish Church, and it would also be fraught with grave consequences for the ongoing role of the bishops as a body in the governing of the Irish Church. The Armagh prelates, therefore, with Nulty in the vanguard, undoubtedly made it clear to McGettigan that the responsibility for preserving the integrity of their body in the face of this particular threat from Cullen now rested primarily with him. The consideration that must have finally influenced

68. See C, Kieran to Cullen, September 10, 1869.

McGettigan the most in making his decision was the endorsement of the view taken by his episcopal colleagues and by the cardinals of Propaganda, in spite of Cullen's strenuous efforts on behalf of Conroy. McGettigan must have understood that the cardinals also realized that if Cullen had his way, the procedure in Irish episcopal appointments, of which the cardinals were themselves an integral part, must be seriously compromised. After the cardinals had recommended McGettigan, therefore, the whole responsibility for sustaining that procedure was laid on him. Indeed, under the circumstances he could not have continued to refuse, and that was why Cullen realized immediately after the cardinals made their decision that the game was lost and shrewdly predicted to Conroy that McGettigan would accept.

There is, however, yet another and perhaps even more significant dimension to the containment of Cullen in the appointment of McGettigan to Armagh. If the appointment is taken in perspective, that is, with all the episcopal appointments made in the 1860s, it appears less the frustration of a dramatic and unsuccessful power play by Cullen than the logical culmination of a long-term policy pursued by the Roman authorities. It will be recalled that in the early 1860s, before Cullen became a cardinal, there were six episcopal appointments in the Irish Church. The basic lesson learned in those appointments was that the cardinals of Propaganda were increasingly inclined to endorse and uphold the procedure involved, and to act more constitutionally, therefore, in dealing with the Irish Church than they had in the 1850s.

When the five appointments made in the Irish Church after Cullen became a cardinal in 1866 are analyzed, it becomes even more apparent that Roman policy, though certainly adjusted to accommodate Cullen's new status in the Church as a cardinal, remained basically the same in regard to Irish episcopal appointments. The appointments of Kieran to Armagh and McCabe to Ardagh, for example, were very routine in procedure. Kieran had placed first on the *terna* and had been endorsed by the great majority of the bishops of the province, and McCabe had placed second and had been endorsed unanimously. The two apparent exceptions in the established procedure were the appointment of MacEvilly as the administrator of Kilmacduagh and Kilfenora and that of James Lynch as coadjutor to the bishop of Kildare and Leighlin. Though the appointment of MacEvilly was certainly a clear break with the usual procedure, as well as an obvious compliment to Cullen's views, it should be noted that the appointment was also part of a consistent and longer-term policy by the Roman authorities of liquidating MacHale's real power and influence in the province of Tuam, and it was not simply, therefore, an arbitrary exception to their own policy. The appointment of Lynch to Kildare and Leighlin, though Cullen was much blamed for it, was really an act of the pope, who in taking the decision into his own hands actually transcended authoritatively the whole procedure, in the interests of preserving his own pontifical dignity in the person of Cullen as a cardinal. Finally, the appointment of McGettigan, who had placed first on the *terna* and had received the unanimous endorsement of the bishops of the province, was only another affirmation, if taken in perspective, of that basic policy pursued by the Roman authorities for more than a decade. The real significance of that policy, of course, was that it allowed for the constitutional containment of Cullen and the further consolidation of the bishops as a body in the governing of the Irish Church.

In the meantime, by adopting the program of the National Association and inaugurating the Irish-Liberal alliance Gladstone had issued a provocative political challenge to the Irish bishops as a body. How they would respond to this new and potentially divisive political initiative is really the story of one of the final elements in their consolidation as a body.

XI

The Liberal Alliance

March 1868–March 1869

One of the most significant events in Irish political history in the last half of the nineteenth century took place on March 16, 1868, when William Gladstone finally declared in the House of Commons that the established Church in Ireland must cease to exist as a state Church.[1] That declaration inaugurated an Irish-Liberal alliance that was to have a profound effect on the emerging Irish political system. On March 23, a week after his declaration, Gladstone gave notice in the House of Commons in the form of three resolutions that he would move to disestablish and disendow the Protestant Church in Ireland.[2] The Irish bishops, it will be recalled, were at that very moment negotiating with Disraeli's Conservative government for a measure of university education that would meet the needs of Irish Catholics. When the Irish-Catholic members of Parliament then voted to a man on April 3 against the government in support of the first of Gladstone's resolutions, it became very evident that there was little political profit for the Conservative government in conciliating Irish Catholics on the education question. The negotiations between the Irish bishops and the government were therefore soon broken off by the government, and both the Irish bishops and the Irish-Catholic members of Parliament were quickly swept up in the Gladstonian Liberal campaign to disestablish the Church of Ireland.

1. *Hansard Parliamentary Debates*, 3d ser., 190:1765–71.
2. Ibid., 191:32–33.

The Irish bishops' newfound enthusiasm for Gladstone and his supporters may at first appear somewhat surprising. Though Cullen, and a good many of the Irish bishops, certainly mistrusted the English Liberals and Radicals on the education question, the general political bias of the bishops as a body was to favor the Liberals as a party. The reason for this curious ambivalence, of course, was that the English Liberals, Radicals, and even Whigs, if the question of denominational education were excepted, were much more amenable to the remedying of grievances and basic reform in Ireland than were the Conservatives. A Conservative ministry in England, moreover, meant a root-and-branch Tory and Orange administration in Ireland, from which Catholics were totally excluded. The simple fact of the matter was that there was no real future for Irish Catholics in either reform or patronage as long as the Conservatives were in power. In spite of the dashing of his hopes for a charter for the Catholic University, therefore, Cullen was delighted with the prospect of the Protestant Church of Ireland's being laid low, and he became one of Gladstone's most enthusiastic supporters in the course of disestablishment.

On March 30 Gladstone moved first that the various acts of Parliament relating to the established Church in Ireland be read and then that the House of Commons resolve itself into a committee to consider those acts.[3] Lord Stanley, the Conservative foreign secretary, moved an amendment to the effect that the question of disestablishment be left to the consideration of the new Parliament soon to be elected. Gladstone's motion was furiously debated over the next four days, and on the day of the evening when the first great test of strength was to be made in the House of Commons, Cullen was in a state of considerable excitement. "Here," he confessed to Kirby on April 3, "we are all on the tip toe of expectation. The Protestant Establishment has been most powerful [sic] assailed every day this week and it is shaken to its very foundations. I hope the B. Virgin on this her festival of the Seven Dolours will compel the M.P.s to do their duty, and to give a fatal blow to the monster" (K). "I published a short circular last week," he explained, "exhorting the people to have recourse to prayer in this emergency, and I think thousands of fervent prayers have been said today calling for the downfall of the Establishment." "Probably," Cullen then promised in conclusion, "you will learn by telegram how things will turn out tonight in the Commons."

Cullen was not to be disappointed, for that evening Gladstone secured majorities of sixty and fifty-six, respectively, against Stanley's

3. Ibid., 469–70.

amendment and for his own motion. In writing Barnabò two days later, Cullen explained that a great victory had been achieved. "For several weeks throughout this country," he reported,

> we have been full of anxiety about the outcome of a question which was discussed in Parliament regarding the Established Church of Ireland. Mr. Gladstone proposed to the House that the incomes which that Church had robbed from the Catholics at the time of the Reformation, and that all the privileges which that Church had enjoyed as the only one recognized by law, should cease. The debate was long and full of excitement. Disraeli and the other Ministers defended the Church with their swords unsheathed, and stated that they wanted to fight to the utmost to preserve it. However, the Protestant Church of Ireland has within it so many anomalies, and so many proofs of the injustices of its origin, that no art could sustain her; and when the time came to vote, 330 members of Parliament declared themselves for the abolition of the Protestant Church of Ireland and only 270 for the maintaining of the same.[4]

"This is the first great blow," he further explained to Barnabò, "that has been given to Protestantism in this country, and I believe that it will not be able to recover from its effect. There will be however a struggle of some years before the resolutions of the House can be executed. It is a question of an enormous sum of money, which has been up to now spent in enriching the clergy, the Protestant bishops, their families and their friends. The sum thus spent amounts probably to five million scudi [£1,000,000], and it reckons out that the capital, or the capitalized value of the property of the Church is equal to a hundred million scudi [£20,000,000]." "The Irish Protestants," he assured the cardinal in conclusion, "will resist in every possible way the proposed spoliation, not for the love of their Church, but because they have no other hope of surviving without the possession of the riches of this world."

When Kirby wrote Cullen on April 11 that the news of the recent victory over the established Church had been very well received in Rome, Cullen was quick to reply. "I was glad to hear," he reported on April 15, "that the vote against the Church (Protestant) in Ireland was so much applauded in Rome. You may tell Cardinal Antonelli that his good advice had a great deal to do in the matter" (K). "Last summer," Cullen explained, "he told me that it would be most fatal for us to

4. S.R.C., vol. 36, fol. 153, April 5, 1868.

take anything in the way of endowment from the English Government. It was in accordance with that advice that I induced the other Bishops to adopt the resolutions of last October which produced an excellent effect. Had we asked for any part of the spoils, nothing would have been done. But all parties seem to have been pleased with the disinterested course we adopted." "The vote in Parliament," he assured Kirby again, "has shaken Protestantism to its very foundations—it will scarcely every recover its former prestige. Even in England the blow given to the Establishment in Ireland will be felt, and its effects will also extend themselves to the United States." "Our poor Protestants," Cullen added, "are greatly downcast. Disraeli has endeavoured to get up a no Popery cry, but without success. The Protestant papers now say that the disendowment of the Church [is] un fait accompli and that they must accept it. However as there is a question of twenty millions of pounds[,] about a hundred millions of dollars[,] I dare say the Protestants will make great efforts to keep possession of so vast a treasure."

Meanwhile, the House of Commons had adjourned for the Easter recess, and the discussion of the first of Gladstone's three resolutions did not take place until April 27. After an intense debate over the next several days, the House finally divided, 330 to 265, in favor of the first resolution.[5] The second and third resolutions were then introduced and accepted on May 7 without a division. "Everything," Cullen assured Kirby on May 10, "has gone well in Parliament up to the present. On Gladstone's first resolution there was a long debate but in the end it was carried by a great majority of sixty-five. The other two resolutions were carried without a division, but a fourth resolution was proposed by some firebrand that Maynooth should also be disendowed, and that the Regium Donum should be taken from the Presbyterians. The Maynooth grant amounts to £26,000. The Presbyterians get £41,000" (K). "The loss of Maynooth," Cullen confided, "would do us very little damage. In Dublin we have Clonliffe which would soon suffice for this diocese. In others they have also large seminaries. The people are not now willing to pay because they hear so much of the large grant to Maynooth but if they knew we were receiving nothing from Government they would be ready to support their own children whilst studying for the Church." "In the last debate," Cullen pointed out, "both Conservatives and Liberals displayed great bigotry. The Scotch Liberals wished to pass a resolution that not a penny of the Church property should be applied to Catholic institutions. Gladstone

5. *Hansard*, 191:1675.

opposed this motion, and it was defeated." "On tomorrow," he added, going on to refer to the repercussions over the recent visit of the Prince of Wales, "another bigot is to ask the Government whether they gave permission to the Lord Lieutenant of Ireland to call me Cardinal Archbishop of Dublin, and to give me precedence over Protestant Bishops and noblemen." "What lawmakers," he concluded contemptuously, "to occupy themselves with such trifles, and to forget the great interests of the country."

When Cullen wrote Barnabò several days later, however, he was less concerned with stressing the successes of the immediate struggle than he was with emphasizing the long-term significance of disestablishment and disendowment for the future of Protestantism in Ireland. "It is very likely," he assured the cardinal on May 15, "that all the property, which it despoiled the Catholic Church of in 1561, more than three centuries ago, will be taken away from that Church. It is also probable that the very great privileges, which the Protestant bishops and ministers enjoy, will be abolished. If Mr. Gladstone succeeds in doing these two things, he will deserve forgiveness for all the evil that he did in Naples."[6] "If Parliament is able," Cullen maintained, "to carry to a successful conclusion the work that it has begun, I expect that the Protestants in Ireland will become Catholics, or else they will go to England or the colonies. If the clergy is deprived of the income they receive, they can only live here with the greatest difficulty." "There are in this diocese," he then explained, "more than 150 fat benefices in the hands of Protestant ministers and perhaps as many chaplaincies or foundations for masses made in Catholic times. If Gladstone's plan be put into execution, all these gentlemen will not have successors, and Protestantism will lose every means of maintaining itself any longer in Dublin. The clergy are very numerous, while the people are very few, so that it will not be possible to maintain as many ministers by means of voluntary contributions." "It seems to me therefore," he assured the cardinal again in concluding, "if the plan now proposed to Parliament and already adopted by the House of Commons be put into operation, in thirty years we shall not have many Protestants in Ireland."

Meanwhile, a week after the House of Commons had passed his three resolutions, Gladstone introduced a suspensory bill on May 14,

6. S.R.C., vol. 36, fols. 167–68. The reference to Naples, of course, was to the celebrated letter to Lord Aberdeen published by Gladstone in July 1851, complaining about the harsh treatment of political prisoners in Naples by King Ferdinand's government, which created a sensation in diplomatic circles throughout Europe and greatly embarrassed the Neopolitan government.

which was designed to prevent the creation of any new interests or appointments in the Church of Ireland until the question could be dealt with by the new Parliament.[7] The suspensory bill was quickly passed through all its stages in the House of Commons, but it was rejected in the House of Lords on June 29 by a majority of ninety-five, shortly before Parliament was recessed. Not only had the earnestness with which Gladstone had pursued his proposals to disestablish and disendow the Church of Ireland kept the whole question before the public for more than three months, but the very stiff Conservative resistance, culminating in the action of the House of Lords in rejecting the suspensory bill, made it inevitable that the upcoming general election would be viewed as a referendum on Gladstone's Irish policy. Disraeli, meanwhile, had announced that Parliament would be dissolved in the autumn when the new registers for the recently enfranchised voters under the Reform Act of 1867 would be in order.

Though Parliament was not to be dissolved until November, there were stirrings in the Irish constituencies almost as soon as Parliament had recessed for the summer. Indeed, Ireland was to be kept in a state of considerable political ferment for nearly six months by the anticipated general election and its aftermath. The main result of all this political excitement was a growing enthusiasm, especially among the Irish bishops and priests, for the new Irish-Liberal alliance. Gladstone's promise to do justice to Ireland by first disestablishing the Church of Ireland, and then treating the thorny questions of Tenant Right and Catholic education in their turn, won him almost universal acclaim from the Irish bishops and their clergy. They did their best, therefore, in every constituency in Ireland where they had any influence, to return candidates pledged to support Gladstone and to oppose any ministry that would not take up his program to do justice to Ireland. The tone for the campaign, which might be better termed a religious crusade, was set in Dublin during July and early August on the occasion of the nomination of the lord mayor of that city. The nomination struggle was watched with more than ordinary interest because it was a real and early indication of how far the most powerful and influential man in the Irish Church was prepared to go in satisfying the requirements of the Irish-Liberal alliance.

The candidate initially favored by the aldermen and councillors of

7. *Hansard*, 192:314.

the Dublin Corporation for the office of lord mayor for 1869 was James Vokes Mackey, a Conservative alderman. Though the corporation had a large Liberal majority in 1868, it had been the custom of the two parties to share the office in alternate years. In 1869 it would be the turn of the Conservatives, and on the first Monday in July the corporation duly nominated Mackey, who would then be formally elected on December 1 as lord mayor for 1869. Unfortunately for Mackey, the *Globe*, a Conservative and Protestant paper, proceeded to maintain that the nomination of a Conservative and a staunch upholder of the established Church in Ireland, by a vote of three to one in the Dublin Corporation, was a true indication of the feeling in Dublin on the question of disestablishment. Cullen then took occasion to write to a prominent Dublin alderman and former lord mayor, Peter Paul MacSwiney, enclosing a contribution toward the electoral work that needed to be done to ensure the return of Liberal candidates in the city and county of Dublin, while at the same time denying the allegations of the *Globe* and giving sanction to the mounting of an agitation against the nomination of Mackey.

"Allow me," Cullen wrote MacSwiney on July 10,

> to forward you £5, as my contribution to the funds of the Central Franchise Association, now taking measures to place the names of such citizens as have a right to the franchise under the new Reform Act on the roll of voters for the city. I trust that by the exertions of this association the friends of justice and equal rights will have it in their power to return members for this city and county determined to disendow the Protestant Establishment, the source of all our evils—to oppose educational monopolies—and to regulate on principles of justice the relations between landlord and tenant, and, I will add, to watch over the interests of the poor, imprisoned and condemned to a melancholy fate in our workhouses.[8]

Cullen then turned his attention to the allegations in the *Globe*. "The *Globe* is undoubtedly wrong," he maintained, "when it states that the vote referred to evidences the feelings of the population against Mr. Gladstone's project. The meetings already held by the wards have given a sufficient answer to that statement." "Would it not be well," Cullen suggested, "to follow up those ward meetings, and also to hold parochial meetings, in order to show still further that the citizens of Dublin are determined not to allow any one to misrepresent their

8. *Freeman's Journal*, July 11, 1868.

feelings or to pretend that they are favourable to a Protestant ascendancy[?]" Before Cullen could take any further part in the proposed agitation, he was laid low on July 16 by a severe and nearly fatal attack of cholera. Though he was not able to attend to any public business for more than two months, a movement was launched shortly after he fell ill by Sir John Gray, the proprietor of the *Freeman's Journal* and himself a Dublin alderman, to have Mackey's nomination disavowed by the corporation.

On July 29 Patrick Moran, Cullen's secretary, reported to Kirby that though a large number of the Liberal aldermen had previously voted to nominate Mackey, the opposition to him now had become so great that there was a very good chance his nomination would be set aside on August 10, when the corporation was scheduled to reconsider its previous actions (K). "It is feared," Moran further explained, "that some of the Liberals will still vote for him being like him Freemasons, & hence pledged to help one another, still the Catholics are very strong and if necessary Vokes Mackey & his grand carriage must be pitched into the Liffey sooner than have an Orangeman Lord Mayor at this important crisis." In the next week ward meetings and parochial meetings, usually presided over by the local parish priest, were called all over Dublin by the electors, and resolutions were passed calling on their municipal representatives to set aside Mackey's nomination. "We have had great agitation here," Moran reported to Kirby on August 5, "about the approaching Lord Mayoralty. You will be glad to learn that on Monday next we will have a majority against Freemason Mackey" (K). Moran wrote Kirby again on the following Tuesday, August 11 (K). "Yesterday," he reported, "the Corporation achieved a great triumph in the ejection of the Orangeman from the Lord Mayoralty. Four or five Catholics were so worthless as to vote for the orangeman, but the others who on a former occasion had voted for him now changed their quarter & voted against him."[9] "The success of the movement," he finally assured Kirby, "is mainly due to the letter of His Eminence & subsequently to the exertions of Alderman MacSwiney and Sir John Gray." In the next several months the Dublin clergy, obviously elated by their victory over Mackey, and with Cullen's warm approval, took a leading part in the affairs of the Central Franchise Association, the local Liberal political machine in Dublin, and contributed significantly to the increase in the number of Liberal voters registered in Dublin.

9. See ibid., August 11, 1868. The vote was twenty-eight to twenty-three to set aside Mackey's nomination. Six Liberals voted with the minority.

The success of the Dublin clergy in revitalizing the local Liberal machine and in upsetting the nomination of Mackey for lord mayor was, in fact, a portent of things to come both in Dublin and in the rest of the country during the general election. Not since the heady days of Catholic Emancipation, forty years before, had the commitment of the Irish clergy, high and low, been either so complete or so determined. The bishops and their clergy were, in fact, politically active in virtually every diocese in Ireland outside Ulster, and even in Ulster there were unusual episcopal stirrings on behalf of disestablishment candidates.[10] What gave the clerical commitment its real force in 1868, however, was not simply its extent but its intensity. In the last analysis it was the attitude of the clergy rather than their mere activity that made the difference, and this was particularly true of the bishops, who had since the days of Emancipation been the critical restraining influence on clerical participation in politics. Indeed, no prelate in Ireland had done more over the previous eighteen years to restrain the Irish clergy in political matters than Cullen, and his newfound determination to support the Irish-Liberal alliance wherever he had any power or influence was perhaps the best example of this change of attitude among the bishops.

Sometime in late August or early September, for example, while Cullen was convalescing from his recent attack of cholera, William Monsell, the senior member for county Limerick and one of the most influential of the Irish Liberals, wrote Cullen, apparently to encourage him to use his considerable influence with the bishop of Galway in promoting the Liberal cause in that town. It appears that one of the sitting members, George Morris, was looked upon by his more orthodox Liberal colleagues as being not only lukewarm on the issue of disestablishment but also much too partial to the Conservative ministry headed by Disraeli. "I will write to Dr. MacEvilly," Cullen assured Monsell in reply, referring to the bishop of Galway, "about Mr. Morris—but I believe he has great influence in the town."[11] "I hear," he then reported, "that Mr. D'Arcy, the great brewer, a very good man[,] will stand for Wexford, so perhaps Kavanagh may be put out, and two Liberals returned. In Dublin nothing can be done unless the franchise be lowered and the freemen set aside." "If there be fair play," he concluded, "I hope the Liberal party will be greatly increased in Ireland."

In the event, the election contest in Dublin, where Cullen initially thought little could be done, proved to be very close and one of the

10. David Thornley, *Isaac Butt and Home Rule* (London, 1964), pp. 38, 44.
11. M, 8317 (3), n.d.

most exciting in Ireland. The sitting members were Sir Arthur Guinness, the brewer and a Conservative, and Jonathan Pim, a Quaker merchant and a Liberal. They both decided to stand for reelection and were joined respectively on the hustings by David Plunkett, a cousin of Sir Arthur's, and Sir Dominic Corrigan, an eminent Dublin Catholic physician. "Here," Cullen reported to Kirby on November 18, "we are all in the turmoil of an election. The nomination for Dublin took place ere yesterday and a most noisy scene it was. Dr. Corrigan the Liberal candidate, formerly a great advocate of mixed education, denounced the Queen's Colleges most vehemently, and declared for a Catholic education. Pim the Quaker went on in the same strain. The Tories declared for the Protestant Church and mixed education" (K). "Today," he added, "the polling is going on—I voted for Pim and Corrigan—I suppose no Cardinal ever voted for a Quaker before. The contest is very close and it is impossible to know who will win—the elections are going on in every part of the three kingdoms." "If the Liberals get a large majority," Cullen pointed out, "the poor [Protestant] Church will soon count her last days. In Ireland it is expected that the Liberals will have an increase of 15 or sixteen votes [i.e., eight seats]."

When the poll was declared the next day, November 19, the voting in Dublin, as Cullen had predicted, was extremely close. Guinness and Pim were returned with 5,587 and 5,586 votes, respectively; Plunkett received 5,452 and Corrigan 5,379.[12] A week later Moran explained what had happened in a long and interesting letter to Kirby. "We had great excitement here throughout the elections," he reported on November 27 (K). "In the City election 2,200 Freemen voted for Guinness and Plunkett. Nevertheless the Liberals brought up their numbers within *one* of Guinness, and gave Pim a majority of about 200 over Plunkett. So Guinness and Pim are for the present our members. Sir Dominic Corrigan did not get so many votes, for some Presbyterians and Protestants who voted for Pim refused to give their second vote for Corrigan. However we expect that bribery can be proved against the Tories, and thus Corrigan will get in. All such cases of election-bribery etc. are now no longer to be tried in Parliament, but in the usual judicial form by our own judges." "Sir D. Corrigan has made a wonderful conversion," Moran added, alluding to the fact that for more than twenty years Corrigan had been one of the outstanding Catholic champions of the Queen's Colleges and mixed education,

---

12. Brian M. Walker, ed., *Parliamentary Election Results in Ireland, 1801–1922* (Dublin, 1978), p. 108.

and has brought around with him to strengthen the Catholic ranks, all those of the *Fitzgerald* stamp who hitherto stood aloof from all our Catholic movements. Corrigan has proved himself a consumate orator, and the bitter opposition with which he has been assailed by all Protestants has done a great deal of good. It has convinced our high Catholics of their folly in relying on Protestant support, and it has unmasked the true character of our soi-disant Protestant liberality in this city. Nothing could be better than the general spirit of devotedness to religion which our good people display. The registration moreover had been terribly mismanaged by the liberal agents, and we lost 800 votes in consequence. We are now trying to reform the liberal organization, and I take a little credit to myself for calling attention to this matter. On probing the matter *a fondo* we found that the so-called liberal agents were many of them Protestant scoundrels who of course betrayed everything into the hands of the Tories: they received their instructions from the English liberal club and we had no authority here over them. Now we are determined to throw overboard both the former agents and the English Club and to look after matters ourselves.

"Throughout the country," Moran noted with real satisfaction, "the Liberal majority has been very great, and probably we will have 65 or 70 Liberal Irish M.P.s in the coming Parliament."

In fact, the Liberals gained eight seats in Ireland, and in the new Parliament they would hold 66 of the 105 Irish seats.[13] The real measure of the power and influence of the bishops and clergy, however, was not simply to be taken by the number of seats won and lost. The upper limit of that power and influence was perhaps best demonstrated in the borough of Galway, where technically there was no loss or gain, at least as far as party representation was concerned. The political tide in the borough had begun to rise about a month before Monsell had asked Cullen to use his influence with the local bishop to secure a more orthodox Liberal representation, when the *Dublin Evening Post*, a Catholic and Liberal paper, made it plain on August 5 that it would be useless to return members who had formally declared in favor of disestablishment and disendowment but who in practice would not commit themselves to put Gladstone in and Disraeli out in the next Parliament, and thus make the declared policy practicable.[14]

13. Ibid., p. 193.
14. Thornley, p. 47.

The *Post* then went on to name the offending constituencies as the boroughs of Galway, Dundalk, and Youghal, where the sitting Liberal members had demonstrated an attachment to the Conservative ministry in the last Parliament. In naming the constituencies rather than the members, the *Post* was, of course, pointing out that the final responsibility for such a state of affairs rested squarely with the electors in those constituencies. Several days later, on August 8, the *Freeman's Journal* followed up the *Post's* criticism with a brief announcement noting that efforts were now being made to find an appropriate Liberal candidate for the borough of Galway.

The main target for all this dissatisfaction was the sitting junior member for Galway, George Morris. Morris's elder brother Michael had been returned as a Liberal member for the borough in the general election of 1865. On the fall of the Russell ministry in June 1866, Michael Morris became solicitor general for Ireland in Lord Derby's third Conservative government, and in February 1867 he was promoted to attorney general for Ireland. In both the by-elections occasioned by his having accepted office, Morris was easily returned. In March 1867 he finally received his political reward when he was appointed a judge of the court of common pleas in Ireland. His brother George was then returned unopposed for his vacated seat. George's Conservative propensities had become so evident by March 1868, when Gladstone gave notice of his three resolutions on the established Church, that the bishop of Galway took the precaution of having an interview with him to assure himself that Morris would vote for those resolutions. Morris did vote for the resolutions, but when the question of his political sincerity was again raised in early August, MacEvilly prudently decided to take further precautions; the *Freeman's Journal* announced on August 27 that a "Galway Independent Club" had been formed under the patronage of the bishop of Galway and his clergy, who were determined "to accept no candidate who will not pledge himself to adopt Mr. Gladstone as his leader, and promise to hurl from power the present no-popery administration."[15]

Some ten days later, on September 5, Morris had another interview with MacEvilly, at which, Morris later claimed, the bishop had assured him that the borough could not be better represented than it was.[16] When Morris issued his election address on September 9, however, he made no mention of the burning issues of the day and pointed

15. Ibid., p. 48.
16. The account of what follows is taken from ibid., pp. 48–50, and the manifestos of both MacEvilly and Morris, "To the People of Galway," which justified their courses of action and were published in the *Freeman's Journal* on October 8 and 13, 1868, respectively.

out instead what he had done on behalf of the town of Galway, while promising to remain independent of all political parties. His address resulted in a great deal of criticism, and three days later, on September 12, he issued a letter augmenting his address and repudiating the misconstructions put on it. He now emphasized that he would support Gladstone on disestablishment and that he was in favor of both Tenant Right and denominational education. This was apparently not enough, however, for on September 18 MacEvilly and his clergy met at his residence and issued the celebrated College House resolutions. In the first they demanded a pledge from the candidates on the questions of the Church, the land, and education. In the second they resolved to refuse their support to any candidate who would not pledge both to support Gladstone's resolutions on the established Church and "to assist in hurling from office, any, and every ministry, which will refuse to make the said resolutions cabinet measures." Copies of the resolutions were sent to both Morris and the senior member for Galway, Sir Rowland Blennerhassett. The latter immediately replied that he would accept the resolutions, but Morris did not reply. At a second meeting at his residence on September 28, MacEvilly and his clergy resolved that the silence of Morris was tantamount to a refusal to accept their resolutions, and they accordingly declared him "an unfit person to represent this Catholic borough at the present juncture in Parliament."[17] The meeting then resolved to adjourn until October 2, when the clergy hoped to be able to select a candidate who would pledge himself to act in accordance with their resolutions.

The candidate endorsed by MacEvilly after the meeting on October 2 was the Viscount St. Lawrence, a Protestant and the eldest son of the earl of Howth. St. Lawrence had early become a candidate for county Louth, but he withdrew from that contest because there were two other Liberals in the race, and a contest between them might result in a Conservative's winning one of the two seats. Morris withdrew from the Galway contest on October 5, after having had some hard things to say about MacEvilly and his clergy.[18] MacEvilly rejoined in a long letter on October 6, giving a brief history of the whole affair from his point of view. Morris replied on October 10 and pointedly asked MacEvilly what had prompted him to change his mind after assuring him on September 5 that all was well with his candidacy. The unspoken answer to Morris's question, of course, was that it was Cullen who had effected MacEvilly's change of heart. The fact was, however, that MacEvilly, given Morris's conduct, had little

---

17. *Freeman's Journal,* September 30, 1868.
18. Ibid., October 7, 1868.

choice but to repudiate him. At their interview on September 5 Morris undoubtedly gave MacEvilly the verbal assurances that he needed, and MacEvilly naturally reassured him in turn. When Morris then equivocated in both his election address and his addendum to it, MacEvilly could do little else than issue the College House resolutions. Indeed, it might even be argued that in publishing the resolutions MacEvilly had provided Morris with an easy way out of his dilemma. When Morris did not then immediately and unequivocally adopt those resolutions, as did Blennerhassett, he placed MacEvilly in an impossible situation, and the bishop was forced to declare him an unfit candidate "at the present juncture." Still, whoever or whatever was ultimately responsible for MacEvilly's change of heart, it is certain that Cullen received a very large share of the credit for Morris's being set aside.

MacEvilly's political problems in the borough of Galway, however, were not settled with the withdrawal of Morris, for another candidate now entered the contest. Martin Francis O'Flaherty was apparently a former Young Irelander and was a favorite of the local Fenians. As well as being the popular candidate, therefore, he probably could also count on the support of Morris and those of his followers who were influential in the town. In order to avoid the turmoil of a contest, MacEvilly on October 31 convened a meeting of the clergy and laity, at which he presided and during which he called on the three candidates to settle the matter of the election quietly.[19] The meeting proposed that the three candidates should appoint representatives to examine the lists of voters already canvassed and committed to each of them, after which the candidate with the least number of votes pledged should retire. The secretary of the meeting, Patrick Cullen, administrator of St. Nicholas, south, then wrote the three candidates, informing them of the results of the meeting. St. Lawrence and Blennerhassett agreed at once, but O'Flaherty, in a blistering reply on November 2, refused.[20] On election day, November 21, however, O'Flaherty was given a very real taste of the extent of the sway of the bishop and his clergy in the borough of Galway. In a formidable demonstration, the clerically endorsed candidates, St. Lawrence and Blennerhassett, received 826 and 804 votes, respectively, while O'Flaherty placed a poor third in the voting with only 432.[21]

More than six weeks later MacEvilly was still obviously in an elated mood when he wrote Kirby about his recent electoral victory in Galway. "The Elections," he explained on January 8, 1869, "were a

19. Ibid., November 6, 1868.
20. Ibid.
21. Walker, p. 109.

great success. Here in Galway it was a glorious triumph. It was the first Election I ever took an active part in, and indeed, I ardently hope it may be the last. It could not be called with truth a *political* contest. It was eminently *religious*. Our poor people came forward like men and backed myself & the clergy" (K). "We are to be subjected," he reported, "to the ordeal of a Petition from one of the defeated candidates, a nominal Catholic called Flaherty. He declares his whole object is to expose me & the clergy. This is all a feint. No doubt he and all his Fenian Followers, (He was one of the 1848 runaways,) would crucify the Clergy, but this is not his object. What it is will soon be seen. The clergy may set him at Defiance; never was so peaceable an Election conducted in Galway." "*Entre nous*," MacEvilly confided, going on to refer to his metropolitan, the archbishop of Tuam, "I have some reason to fear that a certain *Antistes* [high priest], who never forgives, is at the bottom of it, to see if he could annoy me. But let this pass. When I shall have the pleasure of seeing you, we will *talk* it over." "There was more violence," he finally assured Kirby, again referring to MacHale, "in *any one* Parish in the Co. Mayo, than could be found in the entire borough of Galway."

The real significance of both the Galway and the Dublin elections was to be found in what they revealed about the increased politicization of the Irish bishops as a body since the last general election in 1865. The basic lesson to be learned from these elections was that MacEvilly and Cullen did not simply commit themselves, as they had in 1865, to the principles of a constitutional program, but also chose to become personally involved in the election process in order to put that program into effect. It was this commitment to the means as well as the ends of constitutional politics by the great majority of the Irish bishops in 1868 that gave this general election its clerical intensity. Indeed, as MacEvilly inadvertently pointed out to Kirby, this election marked the return to the political arena of the greatest clerical gladiator of them all, the redoubtable archbishop of Tuam. For more than ten years, in fact, MacHale had been politically passive in what had been at one time his electoral strongholds, the counties of Galway and Mayo. In 1857, it will be recalled, George Henry Moore, a Mayo landlord and a Catholic and the favorite of MacHale and his clergy, had been returned in a very stiff three-cornered fight for one of the two county Mayo seats and then unseated on petition for alleged clerical intimidation during the election.[22] In the ensuing by-election Lord John Browne, the third son of the marquis of Sligo and a Whig in

22. Emmet Larkin, *The Making of the Roman Catholic Church in Ireland, 1850–1860* (Chapel Hill, N.C., 1980), p. 381.

politics, was returned unopposed for Moore's vacated seat. In the two general elections following, in 1859 and 1865, Browne, in company with a Conservative, was returned unopposed for county Mayo.[23]

In order to understand this sequence of events, and those that are to follow, it is first necessary to know something about the structure of politics in county Mayo. There were three political formations in Mayo of varying electoral strength. The first and strongest of these, with something less than half (about 47.5 percent) of the voting strength in the county, was composed of those Catholic and Protestant landlords who were Whigs in politics. The second political formation, which made up something more than a third (about 35.0 percent) of the electorate, was composed of those Catholic townsmen and tenant farmers who were more prosperous and independent, who were backed by MacHale and his clergy, and who looked upon themselves as Nationalists. The third group was made up of the Conservative landlords, who numbered something less than a fifth (about 17.5 percent) of the electorate. A combination, therefore, of any two political formations at an election could exclude the third. In 1857 the Nationalist party members in Mayo had become so angry at the political conduct of their Whig member, G. G. O. Higgins, who shared the representation with Moore, that they decided to effect an alliance with the Conservatives and put Higgins out. Moore and the Conservative candidate were duly returned, but as has been pointed out, Moore was unseated on petition. In the by-election that followed the Conservatives apparently decided to remain neutral, and the Nationalists of necessity had to allow the Whig candidate, Lord John Browne, a walkover. In 1859 and 1865 the Whigs took a lesson from the Nationalists and effected a coalition with the Conservatives, which resulted in the unopposed return of a Whig and a Conservative in both general elections.

In 1868, however, MacHale decided that ten years in the political wilderness was long enough. On August 6, therefore, he and his clergy, with representatives of the bishops and clergy of the dioceses of Achonry and Killala, met in Castlebar, where "they prepared resolutions for the public meeting" that was to follow immediately on their private meeting.[24] The first resolution presented to the public meeting was an interesting example of the political principles of MacHale and the Mayo clergy, as well as of what they thought ought to be the order of priority with regard to those principles in 1868:

23. Walker, p. 303.
24. *Freeman's Journal*, August 8, 1868.

That having met to confer together on the respective merits of the candidates for the representation of Mayo, in connection with which we deem most necessary for the prosperity of Ireland and her people, we hereby pledge ourselves to give our strenuous support to those candidates only who shall advocate the fullest measure of tenant right, unqualified freedom of Catholic denominational education, the disestablishment and disendowment of the Protestant Church, and above all, the Repeal of the Legislative Union, and who likewise shall not enter into coalition with any candidate not holding those principles or who shall decline to cooperate with the candidate who maintains them.

The second resolution presented to the meeting endorsed the candidacy of Moore and pledged those present to exert themselves to the utmost on his behalf in the upcoming election. Before the resolutions were put and seconded, however, MacHale made a long and impassioned speech in which he denounced the landlords of Mayo, Whig and Tory alike, for depriving their tenants of their legitimate rights by coercing them into voting against their consciences. Both resolutions were then put and seconded by clergymen, but to the obvious consternation of nearly all present, James Browne, the parish priest of Burriscarra and Ballintober, near Castlebar, in the diocese of Tuam, moved an amendment to the second resolution. Browne proposed to enlarge the resolution endorsing Moore to include a second candidate, Valentine O'Connor Blake, who, like Moore, was a Mayo landlord and a Catholic.

In the discussion that followed on Browne's amendment, both Browne and Blake (who was not present) were taken very severely to task by the clergy, and Browne's amendment was apparently lost for the want of a seconder. The clergy were very annoyed at Browne for breaking clerical ranks at the public meeting. He undoubtedly had had his say with regard to Blake's candidacy at the clerical meeting that had preceded the public meeting, and he was therefore bound to be silent at the public meeting if he could not in good conscience support the resolution framed by his clerical colleagues. In any case, whatever support Browne's amendment may have had at the clerical meeting, it was a tribute to the discipline of the Mayo clergy that not one priest supported Browne in the discussion following his amendment.

Browne, however, must have been as politically naive as he was mischievous, for he apparently missed MacHale's point at both meetings. MacHale was obviously determined to break up the landlord coalition by nominating Moore. What he really wanted was one of the

Mayo seats, and what he was threatening the Mayo landlord interest with was a revolt of their tenantry at the polling booths backed by him and his clergy. He made this clear in his long address at the public meeting by making pointed reference to the agitation for Catholic Emancipation, and he reminded his audience that it was those elections in 1826 in which the Catholic tenantry had first defied their landlords and voted for the Emancipation candidates that had finally turned the political tide in Ireland. He also reminded the Mayo landlords in his address that the greatest security for their own legitimate rights in their property and their status was to be found in the Catholic clergy. What MacHale was really saying, of course, was that the clergy also had a natural interest in the order and hierarchy of Irish society, and given their responsibilities in helping to sustain basic law and order in that society, they were entitled to a share of the power. In short, if the Mayo landlords did not soon want to face worse, they must surrender one of their seats. Father Browne's proposal to run both Moore and Blake was therefore basically subversive of MacHale's real purpose, because it would mean that the Nationalist party in Mayo was determined on having both seats. The Mayo landlords would then have no choice but to fight if they did not want to be immediately extinguished as a political force in the county.

The worst was not yet over for MacHale, however, because Browne was apparently not the only politically naive priest in Castlebar that day. After the discussion that followed on Browne's amendment was concluded, Peter Reynolds, the parish priest of Kilcolman, near Claremorris, and chancellor of the diocese of Tuam, raised the question whether it was prudent or practical to challenge the landlords to a contest unless there was a good prospect of success, for if the challenge failed, the price that would have to be paid by the tenantry— that is, evictions—would be very high. What Reynolds did not appear to realize was that the only way that MacHale's threat to raise a revolt among their tenantry would be taken seriously by the landlords was if they were convinced that the clergy were determined on a fight to the finish if they refused to surrender one of their seats. At this point the celebrated Patrick Lavelle, the parish priest of Partry, declared that though it was well known that he did not have much faith in parliamentary agitations, he was of the opinion that they must fight this election in order to free the tenantry from landlord tyranny. MacHale then intervened and magisterially and abruptly brought both the discussion and the meeting to an end. He realized, of course, that an extended discussion of Reynolds's question would only reveal the extent to which the Mayo clergy might be reluctant to proceed to a fight to the finish with the landlords, and this would only increase the chances for a contest; therefore, the sooner the meeting was brought to an end, the better.

His concluding remarks are worth quoting because they are as much a measure of the will and determination as they are a mark of the ability and astuteness of this very remarkable clerical politician:

> I thought it quite unnecessary to say a word after the resolutions that have been passed. They are perfectly intelligible and I cannot understand persons who come forward and say that nothing practical has been done. If there is any meaning in words, these resolutions should be intelligible to every one present. We have considered all the difficulties of a contested election, and the fact that some persons are thrown into the arms of the landlords. As far as I could express myself, and as far as Mr. Moore could express himself, and he did so eloquently, and as far as I could understand the responsive cheering of the auditory, the question at issue is, and must be until it is settled, whether these landlords will be allowed to take upon themselves contrary to law and consciences, to control the liberties of the people (hear, hear).

He concluded defiantly, "Whether we shall encounter obloquy or dissatisfaction, or indignation on the part of those gentlemen, this question must remain at issue until it is settled, and I say at this moment that so long as the tenants have a vote, and until they are again disenfranchised for their own benefit, so long as they are reported to be freemen, I shall not cease to encourage them to take a part at those elections until the landlords get tired of their tyranny and are ready to grant their freedom."[25]

In the next three months Moore, backed by the Mayo clergy, canvassed the constituency with great energy, because Blake, who was now being supported by the Whig landlords, gave every indication that he would contest the election. Shortly before nomination day, MacHale issued a pastoral letter to be read in all the chapels in his diocese after twelve o'clock mass on November 15, in which he again attacked the Mayo landlord coalition with great bitterness for tyrannizing over their tenantry in electoral matters.[26] In the end, though the Mayo landlords were undoubtedly very impressed with MacHale's determination to proceed to a contest, they were probably more im-

25. Ibid.
26. Ibid., November 16, 1868.

pressed with the inroads the Mayo clergy had made in canvassing the votes of their tenantry, for shortly before nomination day, Blake withdrew from the contest. In Castlebar, therefore, on nomination day, November 23, Lord Bingham, the Conservative candidate, and Moore were duly nominated and returned unopposed.[27] In proposing Moore to a vast throng of gentry, clergy, electors, and nonelectors, MacHale could not resist a final political crow. In a long and exultant speech, dwelling on the revolt of the tenantry, MacHale sounded the death knell for landlord political power in Mayo. It was, in fact, the last time that a candidate was ever returned for county Mayo on the landlord interest.

Though MacHale's political tour de force in the Mayo election was certainly as remarkable as it was typical of the man, the success of the bishops and clergy situated in county Cork was perhaps more representative of the political part that would be played by the clergy, high and low, in displacing the landlords as the essential makeweights in the election process over the next decade in Ireland. Cork was the largest county in Ireland, and with sixteen thousand electors, the largest constituency as well. It comprised the whole of three Irish dioceses, Cork, Cloyne, and Ross, and a part of a fourth, Kerry. The chief electoral problem facing the bishops and clergy of the county, therefore, was how to coordinate their political efforts effectively. Their inability to mobilize their political resources in recent years had resulted in the Conservatives' capturing one of the county seats, a feat that they had not been able to achieve since Catholic Emancipation. In any case, the bishops and clergy of county Cork in 1868 had obviously decided to remedy that anomaly. "I went to Cork last week," the bishop of Limerick, George Butler, informed his good friend William Monsell on August 16, "to meet Drs. Keane & O'Hea [bishops of Cloyne and Ross]. I was glad to find them both quite determined to admit no candidate for County or Borough except on a distinct pledge of opposing D'Israeli [and] supporting Gladstone at least until the Established Church is disestablished and disendowed."[28] "Drs. Keane & O'Hea were to have a meeting," Butler then reported, "with Drs. Delany & Moriarty [bishops of Cork and Kerry] so as to have perfect unanimity for Cork."

Shortly after the bishops met they issued the following circular letter to their clergy for their guidance in the approaching election:

> We are of opinion that no candidate aspiring to represent an Irish constituency in Parliament ought to be accepted unless on a

27. Ibid., November 26, 1868.
28. M, 8317 (2).

distinct pledge to support the policy enunciated by Mr. Gladstone with reference to the Established Church and to oppose any ministry which is not prepared to carry it into immediate effect.

We are also of opinion that candidates should make a distinct declaration of principles in conformity with those enunciated by the Church and people of Ireland on the all-important questions affecting land tenancy and public education.

While the latter questions must be kept prominently before the people without any relaxation of our efforts to carry them the disestablishment and disendowment of the Protestant Church must be insisted upon as of absolute and pressing necessity.

Should a number of candidates solicit the suffrages of the constituencies of Cork we recommend to our clergy to ascertain the views of the gentry and people, and to arrange, if necessary, for the holding of a county meeting to whose arbitrament the choice of candidates may be referred.

Our representatives should be men whose antecedents and position may be a guarantee for their fidelity to this pledge.[29]

The two sitting members for county Cork were Nicholas P. Leader, a Conservative-Protestant landlord of large estate in the county, and A. H. Smith-Barry, a very wealthy young Whig-Protestant landlord and a declared supporter of Gladstone. Because Smith-Barry was the sitting member and because he was willing to subscribe to the conditions laid down in the episcopal circular, his seat was not considered to be at stake in this election. There were, however, two Liberal aspirants soon in the field for Leader's seat. The first was Robert Boyle, a cousin of the earl of Cork and also a representative of the Whig-Protestant landlord interest in the county. The second candidate was T. McCarthy Downing, a Catholic solicitor and landlord from Skibbereen, who had recently achieved prominence in the affairs of the National Association by advocating that Tenant Right should have priority over all other questions. Both candidates were, of course, willing to subscribe to the pledge demanded by the bishops, but Downing had the added advantages of being the favorite of the tenant farmers and the close personal friend of the bishops of both Cloyne and Ross.

With two orthodox Liberal candidates in the field, the parish priests of county Cork convened those meetings of the gentry and people recommended by the bishops in their circular in case of such an eventuality. The representative clergy subsequently met in Bantry on Sep-

---

29. M, 8319, n.d., quoted in Thornley, p. 38.

tember 10 and adopted Downing as their candidate.[30] That same day, and only eighteen miles away, the bishops of Cork, Cloyne, and Ross met in Skibbereen and also approved the choice of Downing. Though the clerical meeting in Bantry was reported as having been numerously attended, the actual attendance apparently left something to be desired. It appears that a number of the clergy did not convene the local meetings recommended by the bishops because they did not agree with their parishioners about which of the Liberal candidates should be adopted. Most of these clergy apparently preferred Boyle, and out of deference to their parishioners and respect for the clerical consensus that would be arrived at in Bantry, they preferred to be passive and thus avoid political dissensions. In spite of the bishops' and clergy's endorsement of Downing, however, Boyle refused to withdraw and insisted on going to the poll. Downing was returned at the head of the poll with 8,011 votes, while Smith-Barry received 6,610 votes, and Boyle placed a poor third with only 3,717.[31] The victory was, in truth, a very real tribute to the organizing power and the discipline of the bishops and their clergy in county Cork. The abiding lesson of the election, however, was essentially the same as that in the Mayo contest. This was to be the last time that a candidate on the landlord interest was ever elected for the county. Indeed, the tenant-farmer interest, as represented by the election of Moore in Mayo and Downing in Cork, would soon become the dominant interest in Irish politics.

But, as with all mainstreams, the current of Irish politics in 1868 was complicated by its crosscurrents, its eddies, and its pools, and the election in Queen's county is perhaps the best example of how complex Irish politics really were even when the issues were relatively simple. The sitting members for the county were Gen. F. P. Dunne, a Conservative-Protestant landlord of very considerable estate in the county, and J. W. Fitzpatrick, a Whig-Protestant landlord and longtime political supporter of Lord John Russell. Fitzpatrick, an illegitimate son of the earl of Ossory, had had a very curious career in Irish politics. He had been first elected to Parliament for Queen's county in 1837 but had retired in 1841.[32] He was then returned for the county unopposed in 1847 and had the dubious distinctions of having voted for the Ecclesiastical Titles Act in 1851 and having defended his action in his election address in the general election of 1852. He prudently withdrew from that contest, but contested Queen's county

30. *Freeman's Journal*, September 11, 1868.
31. Walker, p. 108.
32. Ibid., p. 309.

again in 1857, when he was defeated. He ran again in 1865 and was returned with General Dunne in a three-cornered contest. Throughout his long and checkered political career, Fitzpatrick managed to retain the loyalty of a very significant section of the clergy in Queen's county. When it became evident that there would soon be a general election, one of the most influential of these clergy, Dr. John Magee, parish priest of Stradbally, wrote Fitzpatrick, gently explaining what would be required to gain the general support of the clergy in the county. "It seems to us," Magee pointed out on June 15, "as a just and natural compromise, that the Conservative party, who possess so much of the property of the county, should have a representative of their views; and in the selection of a Liberal candidate most of the clergy, if not all would (forgetful of some things in the past) place their confidence in you, provided your views on the land question and tenant right are as enlightened as those you entertain in regard to the Church."[33]

What both the clergy and Fitzpatrick were looking forward to, of course, was an uncontested election, with the sitting members, Conservative and Liberal, being returned unopposed. The clergy, however, had not reckoned on the Queen's county Independent Liberal Club, which had been formed more than two years before against the wishes of the local bishop, James Walshe, of Kildare and Leighlin.[34] The club, which was composed largely of professional men—barristers, solicitors, doctors, and ambitious local politicians—had been founded because of the resentment aroused by the clergy's success in reimposing Fitzpatrick on the constituency, after a forced retirement of some thirteen years, at the general election of 1865. The club members determined, therefore, to run their own candidate in 1868. They had some difficulty in finding a local candidate and were obliged to look outside the constituency. About the middle of August they finally settled on T. Mason Jones, a Protestant and a native of the county, who had lived elsewhere for most of his life and who had achieved considerable prominence recently in the radical English Reform Union as a lecturer on the evils of the established Church in Ireland.[35]

Shortly after the club had adopted Jones, the Queen's county clergy gave notice in a series of resolutions by public advertisement that Fitzpatrick was their candidate, and that they did not take kindly to carpetbaggers. After endorsing Fitzpatrick, the clergy resolved:

33. Thornley, pp. 40–41.
34. Ibid.
35. *Freeman's Journal*, August 13, 1868.

2. That in the event of a Candidate of position, intelligence, and personal worth—pledged to carry out the "Gladstone Policy" on Irish Questions—offering himself for the Representation of our County, we also pledge ourselves, in turn, to make use of every constitutional means to return him to Parliament instead of the gallant General [Dunne] who, throughout the session just closed, has uniformly disregarded the petitions and misrepresented the wishes of the vast majority of his Constituents.

3. That we cannot too strongly condemn the candidature of persons obtruding themselves upon the Electors without introduction or guarantee from any party or individual possessing the confidence of the people—in thus seeking to divide the Liberal Party they prove themselves the real enemies of the Popular Course, and facilitate the return of some supporter of Ascendancy and "No Surrender."

4. That in selecting a Candidate we give a decided preference to a gentleman residing or having property within the county. The reasons for such preference are too obvious to require further notice.[36]

The message of these resolutions, signed by the great majority of the clergy of Queen's county, was that Fitzpatrick's seat was not at stake in this election and that if an appropriate candidate, that is, one that met with their approval, now came forward, they would make every effort to elect him in place of the sitting Conservative member, General Dunne. Most important of all, of course, they were making it perfectly clear that whoever might do, T. Mason Jones would not. The Independent Club, however, does not appear to have been much intimidated by the clerical *pronunciamento*; it announced through its secretary, P. Cahill, that the only reason it was not entering another Liberal candidate besides Jones was that it was afraid the constituency could not secure the return of two Liberals.[37]

The Saturday after Jones had declared his candidacy, he was accused in the *Nation*, the influential nationalist weekly, by the proprietor and editor, A. M. Sullivan, of being a friend and supporter of Garibaldi.[38] The charges created a sensation and were carried into other Dublin and provincial newspapers. A meeting of the Independent Club was called for August 27, in Maryborough, to discuss the charges and to offer Jones the opportunity of rebutting them. At the meeting it was

---

36. Ibid., August 15, 1868.
37. Ibid., August 17, 1868, P. Cahill to the editor of the *Freeman's Journal*.
38. *Nation*, August 15, 1868.

decided that there would first be a public discussion open to all, and then the members of the club would meet to take the action it deemed necessary.[39] In answering to the charges Jones explained that he had been in Naples as a tourist shortly after Garibaldi had taken that city, and he had made the acquaintance of the Italian general out of a natural curiosity, but that step was a very far cry from being a friend of his. Jones admitted also that he had been at that time, and still was, an advocate of the cause of political freedom for the Italian people, but argued that it was hardly fair to hold him responsible for what Garibaldi and his followers had done since that time. After Jones had concluded his remarks, the secretary of the Independent Club reported that he had received a letter from Sullivan, but he was in a quandary about reading it because although Sullivan had said that he was at liberty to use it, he had also stipulated that the letter was not for publication. The chairman of the meeting resolved the difficulty by ruling that the secretary was bound to read the letter.

In his letter Sullivan explained that it was he who had written the paragraph in the *Nation* "unmasking" Jones and that he now wrote to set the members of the Independent Club right about Jones.[40] He had himself been in Liverpool in September 1861, Sullivan further explained, when Jones delivered his celebrated "Three Orations on Garibaldi" in the Philharmonic Hall, and he well remembered the furor they created "amongst the ultra anti-papal Englishmen of Liverpool." "Just at that time," he added, "Garibaldi was at the zenith of his career, the English people were going wild about him, and most opportunely for a grand sensation Mr. Jones appeared announcing himself as direct from Garibaldi's camp—nay, from Garibaldi's presence—and honoured by Garibaldi's friendship." He felt it keenly and bitterly, Sullivan admitted, "to see an Irishman go over to the English camp and pander to the applause and favour of the foes of Ireland and Catholicity. But I feel more keenly and more bitterly now to think that such a man, having cast his lot with those foes, should now try back upon us and seek at our hands a representative position." Sullivan then concluded by pointing out that if Jones were returned for Queen's county, it would be a reneging on all that Irishmen had done and sacrificed for the cause of Pio Nono in recent years.

Though both the secretary and the president, Richard Lalor, of the club attempted to rally support for Jones, the general sense of the meeting was that he should withdraw his candidacy. One of the more

39. *Freeman's Journal*, August 28, 1868.
40. Ibid. The letter was dated August 24, 1868.

influential of the local worthies, E. J. Maher, argued that the question was no longer whether the charges made against Jones were true, because the impression was now definitely abroad among the people that there was some truth in them. Maher then proceeded to put his finger on the heart of the matter when he pointed out that he did not think that one clergyman in the county had promised Jones his support. When Jones then remarked that he had not canvassed them yet, Maher replied, "I am afraid that I am only too true a prophet when I say that you will not have the support of the clergy, and if you don't have their support you won't be supported by the people (hear, hear)."[41] The regular meeting of the club was then convened, and after some further discussion it was agreed that both Jones and the club should be at liberty to ascertain the opinions of the electors regarding Jones before the next meeting. In testing the political water, Jones apparently learned that he had no chance, and on September 6 he prudently withdrew from the contest.[42]

The club then chose as its candidate Kenelm Digby, who, it may be recalled, had been recommended by John Blake Dillon to the bishop of Elphin as an appropriate candidate to contest county Sligo for the National Association interest in 1865.[43] Digby, who was a Catholic and owned some property in Queen's county, proved to be acceptable to the clergy as well, and they canvassed very assiduously on his behalf. The intensity of the clerical canvass is well illustrated by an exchange of letters between one of the more prominent Conservative landlords, Maj. H. D. Carden, and the parish priest of Maryborough, James I. Taylor. "It was with great surprise," Carden complained to Taylor on November 9, "that I heard today that you had sent round to my Roman Catholic tenants begging of them to attend at the chapel in Maryborough yesterday, and there obliged them to sign a paper pledging themselves to support the two Liberal candidates at the coming election. You must have been aware that these men had promised me that they would give one vote to General Dunne, and it is therefore with surprise that I hear that you, their pastor, should coerce them to break that promise which they had willingly made to me."[44] "It must be apparent to all," Carden added, "that there is little freedom of election in such conduct, and it must also be clear that the friendly feelings between landlords and tenants which should exist, and which would exist but for the inflammatory addresses and interference on

---

41. Ibid.
42. Ibid., September 7, 1868.
43. Ibid., September 28, 1868. See for the announcement of Digby's candidacy.
44. *Freeman's Journal*, November 16, 1862.

the part of the Roman Catholic priesthood, must cease, and these poor deluded people have to seek in other quarters the assistance and kindness which they naturally would expect from their landlords."

In his reply on November 12, Taylor proceeded to read Carden a sermon on the subject of lawful promises. "In your note of Monday last," Taylor pointed out, "you express your surprise at my having, as you say, caused your tenantry to sign a paper pledging themselves to vote for the two Liberal candidates at the ensuing election."[45] "If earnest advice and request be coercion," Taylor added,

I cheerfully admit the charge. I have persuaded them and the other Catholic tenants in this parish, as well as I was able, to do their duty at the election resolutely and fearlessly. Would it not be more suitable for you to reserve your surprise for cases where gentle men order their poor dependent Catholic tenants, to vote in the interest of an Establishment always hostile to them and their forefathers from the day it was first planted amid the ruins of our Catholic churches, and religious houses to this very hour? I have exhorted all Catholic voters as they would consider themselves bound in conscience not to vote for the Established Church, so they would feel it to be their conscientious duty not to vote for the members of Parliament who would go into the House of Commons to support it. Are you surprised at this? Is this coercion? And in cases where a terror-stricken tenant had promised his vote to his landlord, I have explained to him that a promise extorted under such fears as his was not binding; and, again, it has been my instruction to the tenant that if he made his promise (as not infrequently happens) in ignorance of the important religious question now at issue, and consequently of his own *duty* as a Catholic elector, he was not bound by such promise. Be not surprised at this, nor say that it is mere "Popish" doctrine. It is according to the teaching of moralists, Protestant as well as Catholic. Look at Paley, one of the first authorities on ethics in your own church. See his chapter on Promises, where he treats of promises that are not binding, and you will find it laid down that if a promise interfere in the event with *duty*, the duty must be discharged though at the expense of the promise and the peril of good name: *non meus est sermo* [not mine is the learned discourse].

"You talk," Taylor further noted, "of 'inflammatory addresses' from the Catholic clergy. Let me in turn express my surprise that you know

45. Ibid.

so little of all the Catholic clergy are doing for peace and order in this country. They are now labouring in the cause of religious equality, to abolish an institution which has done more to inflame and keep alive bad passions in Ireland than was ever effected by the harangues of all our agitators. You have the courage to speak of the kindness of land-lords, and of good feeling between them and their tenants. There are, I am happy to say, some kind landlords holding property in this parish, and I have borne testimony in public to their goodness; gladly would I persuade myself that you were one of the number." "If kindness con-sist," Taylor added ironically in conclusion, "in letting bad land at a high rent and exacting that rent rigourously from an impoverished tenantry, living on potatoes, and glad to have enough even of them, this county could supply a specimen of astonishing benevolence; and as for friendly feeling between landlord and tenant, if that is to be fostered by the amiable intervention of bailiffs, and notices, and driv-ers, I know tenants who might be the envy of their neighbours."

The clergy of Queen's county were apparently so successful in can-vassing the Catholic tenants of the Conservative landlords in the county that General Dunne finally decided to withdraw from the con-test, and on election day, November 23, Fitzpatrick and Digby were duly returned unopposed. This was really a very impressive political performance by the clergy. Not only had they imposed Fitzpatrick once again on the constituency, and forced Mason Jones to retire from the contest, but even more significantly they had persuaded the Catholic tenants of the powerful Conservative landlord interest to pledge their votes to Digby rather than to Dunne. This was, in fact, the first time since the Act of Union in 1800 that the Tory landlord interest had failed to return at least one of the two members of the county. The real lesson of the election in Queen's county, however, was what it had also been in the counties of Mayo and Cork: it sig-naled the end of landlord political power on the parliamentary level in those counties forever.

Though the Irish bishops and clergy certainly increased their political power and influence during the general election of 1868, that does not mean that the increase was either uniform or always determinant in its effect. The key to the effective exercise of clerical political power in the constituencies, of course, was that the clergy had to remain united. When they did not, they contributed in no small measure to that tendency toward factionalism that appeared endemic to Irish politics, especially in the smaller constituencies, where politics were always a good deal more personal. In 1868 the boroughs of Dungarvan and Dundalk provided apt illustrations of what could happen in a constituency when the clergy were not of one mind. The sitting member for the borough of Dungarvan, which was situated in county Waterford, was Charles R. Barry, a barrister by profession and a queen's counsel. He had been returned as a Liberal in 1865, defeating the Conservative candidate by 112 votes to 94. Barry, who before his election had served as the crown prosecutor in Dublin, was unlucky enough after his election to be assigned as chief government prosecutor in the trials of those Fenians who had been arrested in September 1865 and sentenced to long terms of penal servitude. When Barry offered himself again as a candidate for Dungarvan in 1868, there was therefore a considerable resentment against him in the constituency. This was all the more serious for Barry because the Liberal and Conservative electors in Dungarvan were evenly matched at about a hundred votes each, and the Nationalist electors, who were most resentful and numbered about fifty, held the balance.

The problem for those opposed to Barry was to find a candidate on whom both the Nationalist and the Conservative electors could agree. That problem was solved at the end of August in the person of Henry Matthews, an English Catholic barrister and queen's counsel, who at the request of a numerous body of electors announced his candidacy for the borough of Dungarvan. In his election address Matthews explained that though he was an Englishman, he was also a Catholic who was at one with his Irish co-religionists on all the great issues of the day—disestablishment, tenant compensation for improvements, and denominational education. He also supported the development of manufactures in Ireland to give sufficient employment and prevent emigration. "I desire to enter Parliament," Matthews explained in concluding his address, "devoted, not to party, but to the interest of our common country, and free to support measures proposed by either party which will tend to make Ireland prosperous and contented."[46] What Matthews was in effect saying in his address was that he would support all those issues that were dear to the hearts of the Liberal electors of Dungarvan and that as far as the Conservative electors were concerned, he was no Gladstonian. The Nationalists, of course, would vote for him to put Barry out.

At first, it does not appear that Matthews's candidacy was taken very seriously. On the first Sunday after Matthews announced that he

---

46. S.R.C., vol. 36, fol. 385, incorporating the *Cork Examiner*, August 31, 1868.

would seek election, Barry's chief clerical supporter, the parish priest of Dungarvan, Jeremiah Hally, who had long been prominent in the politics of the borough, denounced Matthews from his altar. "Our new English acquaintance," the somewhat bemused Dungarvan correspondent of the *Cork Examiner* reported on Monday, September 7, "attended first Mass yesterday, and had the pleasure of hearing himself . . . pointedly referred to by the Very Rev. Dr. Hally. The Doctor did not mention Mr. Mathews' [sic] name but he made it tolerably plain that the gentleman came over as the instrument of Disraeli, Stanley, and Co., to prevent the success of Gladstone in disendowing the Church and doing justice to the Irish people."[47] "The effect of the Doctor's speech," the Dungarvan correspondent further assured his readers, "was what might have been expected. Since his return matters have been looking peculiarly blue for the Mathew's party, and Mr. Mathews appears to be considerably nettled. He delivered a terrific tirade against the Doctor out of the windows of Buckley's Hotel last night."

If Matthews was a man who was easily nettled, he was obviously also a man who was not easily intimidated. When it then became obvious, moreover, that he not only had effected a coalition between the Nationalist and Conservative electors but also had secured the support of the influential prior of the Augustinians, James Anderson, in Dungarvan, the contest for the allegiance of the voters in the borough really began in earnest.[48] During the campaigning and canvassing that took place throughout the month of September, Hally continued with the aid of his curates to denounce Matthews's candidacy from the altar of his parish church on successive Sundays as well as to intimate that Father Anderson had been induced to support Matthews from pecuniary motives.[49] Toward the end of September, it was becoming obvious that Barry and his clerical supporters were being very hard pressed by the Nationalist-Conservative coalition. "Dr. Hally," George Commins, a curate in Waterford city, reported to Kirby on September 25, "is in the thick of a raging contest in Dungarvan, already there is preaching and speeching and of course fighting, and it will go

47. Quoted in the *Freeman's Journal*, September 10, 1868.
48. On Matthews's side were Lavelle; Jeremiah Vaughan, the parish priest of Doora in the diocese of Killaloe, who had been prominent in the affairs of the Brotherhood of St. Patrick in the early 1860s; and Thomas O'Shea, the parish priest of Comeris in the diocese of Ossory, who had been much involved with the Tenant Right League in the 1850s. Dominic O'Brien, bishop of Waterford, weighed in on Barry's side. Those opposed to Matthews could not appear on the hustings because Hally was the parish priest of Dungarvan and they needed his permission to appear in his parish. See Thornley, p. 60.
49. S.R.C., vol. 36, fols. 378–81, Matthews to Barnabò, January 1869.

hard with the Dr. to hold the boasted figurative trophy 'the key of the Borough' " (K). "However," Commins added more hopefully, "he has the influence and the weight of the town with him against a noisy faction."

The fact was, however, that the way those electors influenced by the "noisy faction" voted on election day would determine the outcome of the contest. In an effort, therefore, to bring some further pressure to bear on the Nationalist or Fenian supporters of Matthews, Hally enlisted the aid of the bishop of Waterford, Dominic O'Brien. Hally apparently wrote O'Brien complaining about Father Anderson's bringing an American Fenian, a Mr. Train, to lecture in Dungarvan about Fenianism.[50] O'Brien then wrote the provincial of the Augustinians in Ireland, Martin Crane, enclosing Hally's letter and requesting him to remove Anderson from Dungarvan.[51] When the provincial refused, O'Brien apparently decided to take action himself. Before he could do so, however, he received an interesting letter from Cullen. A member of Parliament, Cullen explained on November 8, had just called to see him and asked if he could do anything about preventing the return of Matthews, who was a Tory and a supporter of Protestant ascendancy, for Dungarvan.[52] Cullen suggested that O'Brien write a few lines to the electors telling them to vote against Protestant ascendancy and avoid rioting, drunkenness, and bribery. This step would have the double effect of curbing the violence in Dungarvan and electing a Liberal. With regard to Father Anderson, who was reported to be the cause of the disturbances in Dungarvan, Cullen advised O'Brien that his faculties should be withdrawn.

O'Brien obviously acted immediately on receiving Cullen's letter, for on November 9 he informed Anderson that he thereby withdrew from him "all *faculties* and *approbation* to hear confessions" in the diocese of Waterford and Lismore.[53] Several days later O'Brien also followed up on Cullen's suggestion about addressing a few lines to the electors of Dungarvan. On November 14, the Saturday before the election, he wrote Hally a remarkable letter, which was read at all the masses in the Dungarvan parish church on Sunday morning. "I am much surprised," O'Brien confessed, referring to Father Anderson, "that any Catholic, and much more a Catholic professing devotion to

---

50. Peadar MacSuibhne, *Paul Cullen and His Contemporaries*, vol. 4 (Naas, 1974), pp. 241–42, quoting Cullen to O'Brien, November 8, 1868.

51. K, O'Brien to Kirby, February 28, 1869.

52. MacSuibhne, 4:242. The M.P. who called was most likely The O'Donoghue, who had personally been very active in supporting Barry for reelection.

53. S.R.C., vol. 36, fol. 379.

St. Augustine, should vote for Matthews, who supports the no Popery Ministry of Disraeli. Such a Catholic I look upon as a favourer of heretics, and an advocate of No Popery doctrine and Protestant ascendancy. Such a Catholic does not love his religion, for he votes against it and does what he can to destroy it; for 'No Popery' mean[s] down with the Catholic Religion."[54] The Dungarvan correspondent of the *Cork Examiner* noted that after Hally had read this letter at first mass, "the matters therein referred to were discussed by the very rev. gentleman with his usual force and eloquence," and that the letter "was also read and commented [on] with great force by the other clergymen at each mass." "The letter and the remarks of the reverend gentlemen," the correspondent finally assured his readers, "have made a profound impression, and are regarded as deciding th[e] election against the Tory candidate."

Several days later Cullen wrote Kirby, alerting him about Father Anderson's conduct and especially about his Fenian propensities. "An Augustinian friar," he explained on November 18, two days before the election took place, "is opposing the Liberal candidate[,] Mr. Barry[,] a good Catholic and an eloquent defender of the Pope's authority. The Augustinian has formed an alliance between the Tories and the Fenians: these last will vote against Barry because he prosecuted their associates. The Tories go against him in order to get in an English Catholic, one of the Tablet clan determined to assist Disraeli in keeping up the Protestant Church in Ireland" (K). "I will send an account of this friar's doings to Rome," Cullen promised. "He is acting under the guidance of Father Lavelle, whose letter to him has been published. This same friar had a High Mass and a month's memory, and I am told a funeral oration for the poor Fenians who were hanged in Manchester." "Poor Father Hally," Cullen finally concluded, "is without prudence and unable to fight the friar properly." Indeed, all of the efforts of Father Hally and the bishop of Waterford proved to be of no avail, for when the poll was finally declared on November 21, Matthews received 155 votes to Barry's 105.[55]

After the election Anderson appealed his suspension to Rome, and Matthews in supporting him presented a long memorial to Cardinal Barnabò. In explaining the case to Barnabò in great detail, and enclosing the relative documents, Matthews pointed out that the conduct of both Father Hally and the bishop of Waterford in the recent election was reprehensible and that Father Anderson's deportment in the same

54. Ibid., fol. 386, incorporating the *Cork Examiner*, November 16, 1868.
55. Walker, p. 109.

affair had been a model of tact and prudence. Matthews further maintained that Anderson had been suspended because he exercised his legitimate rights as a citizen in promising him his vote in the recent election and that the suspension therefore was unjust. Matthews's memorial and documents were accompanied by a covering letter from Sir George Bowyer, former member for the borough of Dundalk, to Barnabò, dated January 16, 1869, which not only endorsed Matthews's views but also charged that the Irish bishops and priests had become fanatical about Gladstone and Bright and that Liberalism was now the religion of Ireland.[56] Bowyer's letter, however, and his later correspondence with Barnabò, must be taken with a rather large grain of salt: he had just been defeated in the borough of Dundalk, which he had represented for sixteen years, and he attributed his defeat to the refusal of the archbishop of Armagh, Michael Kieran, to support him.

Barnabò prudently turned over the whole correspondence to the archbishop of Westminster, Henry Edward Manning, who was then in Rome on English ecclesiastical business, for his opinion. "It is not possible to conceal," Manning explained to Barnabò on January 27, 1869, "that the Bishop in suspending the Augustinian has acted, at least, it seems to me, in an excessive way. It is true that I have not received his justification, but I hardly believe that it is possible to justify the suspension."[57] "In fairness," Manning added, "I believe it my duty to add that the letter of Mr. Bowyer seems to me egregiously irrational. It hardly contains, a sentence that is not exaggerated or *perverse*. He has lost his election because he has associated himself in Parliament with the party that always acts against the various interests, religious and political, of the Catholic people of Ireland. Cardinal Cullen has sustained him, I am certain, not because he approves of his politics, but because he esteems the loyal but odd character of Mr. Bowyer." Over the next several months, however, Bowyer took advantage of the opportunity occasioned by his letter covering Matthews's memorial to enlarge on his views to Barnabò about the dangers inherent in the Irish clergy's commitment to the Liberal alliance in general, and his own recent experience of that commitment in his defeat at Dundalk in particular.

Bowyer, who like Matthews was an English Catholic and a barrister, had long been prominent in English and Irish-Catholic affairs. He had been first elected to Parliament as a Liberal for Dundalk in the general election of 1852, and he had continued to be returned for that

56. S.R.C., vol. 36, fols. 383–84.
57. Ibid., fol. 387.

borough in three successive general elections, largely through the influence of the parish priest of Dundalk, Michael Kieran. By the time Kieran had been appointed archbishop of Armagh in 1866, he had become so attached to the town of Dundalk that he exchanged it for Drogheda as one of his two mensal parishes. He was, therefore, in effect, still the parish priest of Dundalk when Bowyer in 1868 decided to offer himself as a candidate for the borough once again. In the last several years, Kieran had become very uneasy about Bowyer's obvious Conservative propensities in Parliament, and particularly about his ambivalence regarding Gladstone's policy for Ireland. Therefore, when Cullen wrote Kieran on Bowyer's behalf in late August, the primate replied that he was sorry that it was not in his power to give effect to Cullen's wishes. "A large number of the liberal electors of Dundalk," he explained on August 25, "were opposed to Sir George from the beginning and many of them have been heard to say that they voted for him solely at my request. His conduct for the last three years has increased the number of those who are dissatisfied with him. Judging him by his public acts and by information which I have received from Myles O'Reilly and others, I cannot help thinking that he is more favourable to the Tory than to the liberal party and that he would rather see Mr. Disraeli than Mr. Gladstone in office" (C). "Not wishing to remain any longer," Kieran added, "under the imputation of using my clerical influence to force a member on Dundalk and believing as I firmly do that Sir George is anything but friendly to the liberal party, I signified to him a few months ago that I would not oppose him but that I would not support him at the next election." "He called on me yesterday," Kieran further reported, "to say that he did not expect my support but that he thought I was bound to say that I was not opposed to his Candidature. I have given him a letter to that effect which he is at liberty to read to the electors. He wished me to say in addition that I was satisfied with the explanation he gave me of his past conduct, but I have not done so, because I could not do it with truth." "I will support him privately," he finally assured Cullen, "as far as I can, but I feel that I could not join in any public demonstration in his favour without seriously compromising my character and position." Kieran's uneasiness about Bowyer's politics was obviously shared by a very large number of the electors of Dundalk, because when Bowyer began in the last week of August to canvass his supporters, it was reported that he met with a very cool reception and that his chances of retaining his seat were not very great.[58] By this time two

58. *Freeman's Journal*, August 27, 1868.

other candidates has also declared themselves. The first was Philip Callan, a local barrister and the popular candidate, and Charles Russell, also a barrister and queen's counsel, who had important and influential local connections. Both Callan and Russell, moreover, were strong supporters of Gladstone's Irish policy.

Given Bowyer's unpopularity and the emergence of Callan and Russell as serious candidates with considerable support in the town, Kieran decided to remain neutral in the contest. Several months after the election, on February 17, when Bowyer took the occasion of writing to Kieran to remonstrate with him for not giving his support in the recent contest, Kieran responded in a long and dignified letter explaining why he had acted as he did.[59] "I did not support you at the last election," he told Bowyer plainly on February 19, 1869, "1st because your absence from the House on one very important occasion as well as some of your speeches and acts convinced me that you are not friendly to Mr. Gladstone whom I believe to be the most sincere and zealous friend to Ireland that has ever appeared among English Statesmen and 2ndly because I wished to free myself from the imputation often cast in my face of using my clerical influence to force you on the electors of Dundalk. But neither did I oppose you at the last election. I feel perfectly confident that no single elector can be produced to say I asked him to vote against you or to vote for Callan or Russell."[60]

Kieran's decision to remain neutral had been immediately compromised by the action taken by two of his curates in allowing their signatures to be appended to a list of Callan's supporters, although Kieran wrote an open letter on September 8 protesting the action of his curates and publicly affirming his neutrality in the contest.[61] The rest of his letter, however, created more problems than it solved. "I have no desire," Kieran maintained,

> to dictate to the clergy of this diocese the opinions they should hold on political matters, nor control their choice of persons whom they consider best fitted to represent them in Parliament. But I have a very strong desire, indeed, that, when divisions prevail among their flocks, they would carefully abstain from all acts and words calculated to give offense to either party, and employ their best efforts to promote concord and harmony among the people entrusted to their care. It is a subject of great affliction to me to see the people of Dundalk so divided at a time when

59. S.R.C., vol. 36, fols. 419–21.
60. Ibid., fols. 413–14, copy.
61. *Freeman's Journal*, September 10, 1868.

union among Irishmen is so necessary to enable the Liberal party in England to carry the measures on which the future happiness of this country depends. If, owing to divisions among ourselves, a member is returned for Dundalk who will go to Parliament to vote for the continuance of the Protestant Church Establishment and thus endeavour to keep open the bitter source to which our principal calamities may be mainly traced, we will stand before our countrymen in a very unenviable position.

"I still, however," Kieran concluded, "entertain a confident hope that the Liberal electors of Dundalk will sink all personal feelings and predictions in one common desire to assist in obtaining the great object we all have at heart, by sending to Parliament as their representative, a man who will cordially support the great leader of the Liberal party."

Needless to say, this well-intentioned but badly conceived letter only made matters worse by making it clear that Kieran was not about to impose his example of neutrality authoritatively on the clergy of Dundalk. Because his letter was in the form of an exhortation rather than a command, he had, in effect, publicly given his clergy their political head. Indeed, his clergy apparently took him at his public word, especially those of his own household, who out of respect for their parish priest and archbishop might have been expected to follow his political example. Instead, all of the four curates in his mensal parish supported one or the other of the candidates during the election. That Kieran had expected something different, not to say better, especially from his curates, was made clear in the letter of explanation he wrote Bowyer several months after the election. "If some of my Curates opposed you," he explained to Bowyer on February 19, 1869, "they did so in opposition to my expressed desire."[62] He added somewhat inaccurately, "I wrote a public letter in which I advised my Curates to abstain from all interference in the last election, particularly as the Catholics were divided into three parties. I regret much that they did not take my advice." "Two of them," he further explained, "supported Callan, one of them supported you and the other supported Russell. If only one of them disregarded my advice I would have removed him from Dundalk. But I did not wish to make a victim of one when all were equally guilty and I felt it would be a very strong measure to remove them all." Besides his own curates, moreover, both the parish priest and the curate of the other parish situated in Dundalk were active on behalf of Russell in the contest.[63] By his ill-ad-

62. S.R.C., vol. 36, fol. 413.
63. Freeman's Journal, October 2, 1868.

vised open letter of September 8, therefore, Kieran had basically undermined his own best efforts to keep his clergy united under his control through a policy of neutrality.

What Kieran did not appear to realize, but what Bowyer certainly did, was that he had also compromised his policy of strict neutrality in his letter by exhorting the electors to vote only for a candidate who would support Gladstone and the Liberal party. Such advice, of course, precluded the return of Bowyer, whose views with regard to Gladstone and the Liberal alliance were common knowledge. Bowyer was apparently so furious at Kieran's treatment of him that when he remonstrated with the archbishop in his letter of February 17, he also accused him of supporting notorious Garibaldians and enemies of the pope's temporal power for parliamentary seats within his spiritual jurisdiction, while refusing to aid him, who had always been a true friend of the pope's temporal power. One of those whom Bowyer named as a Garibaldian was Benjamin Whitworth, a Protestant manufacturer, who had just been returned as a Liberal for the borough of Drogheda. "All I have done," Kieran protested to Bowyer on February 19, "in favour of Mr. Whitworth was to say in a letter to the P. Priest of Drogheda that if any of the electors of Dundalk asked my opinion about him, I would say that he would be a very desirable representative."

> In justification of having done this much in his favour, I am prepared to make . . . the following statements to any person or persons to whom I may feel bound to explain my conduct[:] 1st that Mr. Whitworth's father fought many a hard battle for the Catholics of Drogheda in very bad times[,] 2ndly that Mr. Whitworth himself rendered very valuable services to the inhabitants of that town[,] 3rdly that the late Primate [Joseph Dixon] one of the most ardent friends to the Holy See that ever was found in the Irish episcopacy supported Mr. Whitworth[,] and 4thly that all the clergymen of Drogheda secular and regular (17 in number) not only supported him but went so far in the direction that their strenuous exertions on his behalf were made one of the grounds on which the petition against his return was based.[64]

"I am moreover," Kieran finally assured Bowyer, "prepared to declare and make oath if necessary that I never read or heard from any person until I heard from you that Mr. Whitworth was the friend of Garibaldi."

64. S.R.C., vol. 36, fol. 414.

Bowyer was not to be appeased, however, and on February 26 he forwarded copies of his correspondence with Kieran to Cardinal Barnabò, with a bitter covering letter complaining about the archbishop's conduct toward him and his support of the enemies of the pope's temporal power. Barnabò, meanwhile, had written the bishop of Waterford to ask for an explanation of his suspension of the Augustinian, James Anderson. O'Brien replied on February 28 that he had suspended Anderson because he had been promoting Fenianism in the town of Dungarvan, and he did not feel that it was safe to allow Anderson to hear confessions and administer the sacrament of penance.[65] By attributing the cause of Anderson's suspension to his alleged Fenianism rather than his involvement in the election contest in Dungarvan, O'Brien astutely voided the whole grounds on which Matthews had based his complaint and created, in effect, an entirely new case. Meanwhile, Barnabò had apparently written Cullen to ask his opinion about the Anderson and Bowyer imbroglios. Cullen, who had promised Kirby as long ago as the previous November that he would write Rome about Anderson, had not been able to do so because in early December he was once again laid low by another of those attacks of sciatica and rheumatism to which he was periodically subject. In any case, he wrote Barnabò about Anderson on March 10, and though his letter does not appear to have survived, he undoubtedly told Barnabò what he had told Kirby the previous November.[66]

When Cullen received Barnabò's request for his opinion about the Bowyer affair, he took occasion on March 23 not only to report on it but also to expand on what he had already said about Anderson's alleged Fenian activities in the light of new information he had received since he last wrote.[67] As far as Bowyer was concerned, however, Cullen wasted very few words. After treating Barnabò to a very able short review of the facts of the case, Cullen pointed out that in the course of the whole dispute, the archbishop of Armagh refused to involve himself. "This was why Mr. Bowyer was angry," Cullen explained, "but it seems to me without reason; it being a question of three Catholics, the archbishop did not want to offend any of them, and then there was no reason to declare himself for Mr. Bowyer, he being very undecided about the questions that are more urgent to us than anything else." Cullen then turned to the case of Anderson. Since last writing, he explained to Barnabò, he had received some further information in regard to the conduct of that friar in Dungarvan:

65. Ibid., fols. 376–77.
66. Ibid., fol. 435. See also Cullen to O'Brien, March 11, 1869, quoted in Mac-Suibhne, 4:245, reporting that he had written Barnabò about Anderson.
67. S.R.C., vol. 36, fols. 435–36.

In that part of the county there is a house of the Christian Brothers, who there as elsewhere do much good. It happens, however, the superior general came to know that a brother named Grace kept company with Fenians, and it seems became imbued with their ideas, whence he considered it necessary to remove him to some other house. When the local superior announced this decision to Brother Grace, he asked permission to remain for one more day, and he then would leave. It ensued that the same brother had an interview in the garden of the house with Father Anderson for two hours, and then he presented himself to the local superior notifying him that he did not wish to leave for at least three weeks, and when he was reminded of his vow of obedience replied that the superiors could excommunicate or expel him from the congregation, but that he would not leave the house. After several days, however, he yielded and obeyed! Hardly had he departed, a warning was sent to the superior that he would answer with his life (*col suo sangue*) for what he had done, and the night after some rascals broke the windows of the Brothers' house and tried to throw some bottles of Greek fire, or some other explosive material, to which were attached short fuses, into the house. A bottle broke against the grating of the window, and exploded with a great noise—the fuses of the other two bottles fizzled out, and the superior who was within was able to remove them without any damage. If they had exploded, the house and the brothers would have been all sent to the other world.

"Letters that came from Dungarvan," Cullen further maintained, "put all this wickedness down to Father Anderson, and if it is not true, he is at least to be blamed for his having associated with men capable of such crimes. The account given here is very trustworthy because I have taken it from a letter of the superior of the Brothers in Dungarvan who saw all with his own eyes."

"I enclose," Cullen continued, "an extract from a newspaper that gives an account of a dinner given in honor of some Fenians freed from jail by the government.[68] Some of these gentlemen showed their gratitude by threatening new turbulence, declaring that the only remedy for Ireland was the sword and giving vent to their feelings by other such means."

68. Ibid., fol. 439, clipping from the *Dublin Evening Mail*, March 19, 1868. Both Anderson's and Lavelle's letters and the report of the meeting were appropriately marked.

Two priests were invited to the dinner, namely the celebrated Father Lavelle, and Father Anderson—both excused themselves, but manifested their approval of the honor given to the Fenians— Father Lavelle spoke with his usual energy, Father Anderson said that although absent in body, he was present in heart and in soul. "I am destined,["] said he, "like all those who love their country well and wisely, to suffer the greatest restraint that can be inflicted as a priest. The reflection however that I in a humble way am participating in the sacrifices made by our living martyrs (*namely the Fenians freed from jail*)[69] I am more than compensated for all that I have had to suffer." These are his own words which demonstrate how closely connected this sainted martyr is to the Fenians.

"It seems to me," Cullen finally added, "that the Father Provincial would deserve a good rebuke for having protected one of his religious so unworthy as Father Anderson." Cullen's endorsement of the actions taken by both Kieran and O'Brien in their respective quarrels was apparently decisive. Bowyer received little satisfaction from Barnabò or the Roman authorities, and he continued to lick his political wounds for some six years until he was returned for county Wexford in the general election of 1874 as a Home Ruler. Father Anderson was eventually transferred from Dungarvan to the Augustinian's house in Cork, where he continued to officiate for some years.

In spite of these examples of constituencies where the clergy were either divided or ambivalent about their political preferences, and some few other examples, such as the boroughs of Sligo and Youghal, where they were united but still unable to elect their candidates, the general election of 1868 was a very definite turning point as far as the level of clerical participation in Irish politics was concerned. Indeed, the point was particularly well illustrated in the report of the commissioners appointed after the election to inquire into alleged corrupt practices in the borough of Sligo.[70] Besides the usual charges of bribery, treating, and violence attributed to both candidates and electors, the commissioners also had some very hard things to say about the conduct of the bishop of Elphin, Laurence Gillooly, and a number of his clergy in regard to the charge of spiritual intimidation. "On the Sunday before the election," the commissioners reported,

the most rev. prelate addressed his flock in the Roman Catholic parish church, and in the course of his address stated, according

69. Cullen's addition.
70. *Freeman's Journal*, March 29, 1870.

to the evidence of Martin Boyle (p. 294), that if any of the Roman Catholic party voted for the Tory candidate [Major Knox] they would be considered rotten branches, and should be "lopped off." The bishop denied the accuracy of this account, and gave (answer 15,000) the following version of what took place: —"I referred to rotten branches, and I said most probably, although I cannot now remember the words I used, that it would be better that rotten branches should be cut off than they should be left hanging to the tree, injuring the vitality of it; and that it would be better that the member which was rotten should be cut off rather than it should infect the body. I then said I feared that some of those persons had cut themselves off by their misconduct, and by persevering in a course of conduct they knew to be criminal." And in answer to another question (15,004), he admitted that in a discourse before the election he had stated "that the Catholic voters who voted for Major Knox should make reparation before they could be reconciled to God."

"Whichever version of what occurred on this occasion be the correct one," the commissioners observed, "we cannot doubt that the bishop's words were understood by his hearers as a strong declaration of ecclesiastical censure against those Roman Catholics who should vote against the Catholic candidate—a censure which, as the bishop admitted (answer 15,057–8), implied a withholding of the rites of the church till a proper reparation should be made."

"We find that on that Saturday after the election," the commissioners continued,

the bishop, before commencing his sermon, directed that those who had voted for Major Knox should go to the porch. The bishop stated to us that he did not intend by this more than an advice, with a view to prevent a collision between parties; but he admitted that he had been understood to have meant prohibition on the persons alluded to going to any part of the church. Martin Boyle, sergeant of the permanent staff of the Sligo Militia, whose duty it was to attend Mass at the Roman Catholic parish church, was present there on this occasion. In consequence of what occurred, he (having voted for Major Knox) obtained from his commanding officer leave to hear Mass for the future at another Roman Catholic church (the Friary). We find that on the following Sunday he was ordered to leave the place he was occupying in the Friary church by the Rev. Thomas Hibbits, and this was in consequence of his having voted for Major Knox. We find that on the following Christmas morning two other persons—Laurence Burke and John M'Geurk—who had abstained from voting, were not allowed into the gallery of the Roman Catholic parish church, but were required by the Rev. J. Morris to hear Mass in the porch, which was considered under the circumstances, as a degradation.

"These rev. gentlemen were examined before us," the commissioners noted finally, "and stated that their reason for so acting was the feeling of indignation amongst the members of their congregation against those Roman Catholics who had not voted for Captain Flanagan [the Liberal candidate]."[71] The real moral of the Sligo borough election, of course, was not that the unseemly efforts of the bishop and clergy were unsuccessful, or even that Knox and his supporters, who spent more than £4000, were successful, but rather that Gillooly, who had hitherto been among the most politically circumspect of the Irish bishops, had been prepared to turn his altars into hustings before the general election and into jury boxes after.

In any case, in at least forty of the forty-five constituencies outside Ulster in which the bishops and their clergy were active, the candidates they endorsed were returned, and as has been pointed out, the great difference between the general election of 1868 and that of 1865 was that in 1868 the bishops and their clergy were not simply committed to the issues embodied in Gladstone's program of justice to Ireland but prepared to enter personally into the electioneering and practical politics necessary to the achievement of the desired ends. Indeed, the elections in Dungarvan and Dundalk were the exceptions that proved the rule of the clergy's very real power and influence in the constituencies, for when the clergy were united with the laity in the choice of candidates they were virtually unbeatable. Even in the few constituencies where they were defeated in 1868, as in Sligo and Youghal, the margins by which their candidates lost were extremely narrow.[72] In any case, the formula for electoral success in the constituencies had now emerged. The clergy had to remain united and as a body effect a consensus with the laity in finding a candidate acceptable to both. The point, of course, was that any attempt by the clergy to impose an unsuitable candidate, as had happened in Dungarvan and Dundalk, must result in a revolt of the laity in the long run, and any attempt by the laity to ignore the wishes of a united clergy must result, at the very best, in an extremely stiff contest, and at the very

71. Walker, p. 111. The Sligo tally was Knox, 241; Flanagan, 229.
72. Ibid. The figures for Youghal were Weguelin (Liberal), 127; McKenna (Liberal), 106. Ibid. The figures for Dundalk were Callan, 164; Russell, 143; Bowyer, 72.

worst, in a deep split in the community, utterly subversive of the concept of consensus.

The general election of 1868, however, not only resulted in the further politicization of the Irish bishops as a body in the interests of promoting the Irish-Liberal alliance but also provided Gladstone and the Liberal party with a formidable majority in the new House of Commons. Besides the eight seats they gained in Ireland, the Liberals also gained some twenty-five seats in Great Britain and were now able to muster an overall majority of nearly 130 for the immediate redeeming of Gladstone's pledge to solve the Irish problem by doing justice to Ireland. The buoyancy and optimism among the Irish as Gladstone took up the reins of power were extraordinary. What is most important to appreciate is that the great expectations were a function less of the Gladstonian promise to legislate to redress Irish grievances regarding the established Church, land law, and education than of the knowledge that these grievances were to be remedied according to Irish ideas. In a word, future Irish legislation was to be a function not merely of what the English thought was good for the Irish but rather of what the Irish thought was necessary for their well-being and happiness. What no one realized at the time, however, was that the Gladstonian pledge to do justice to Ireland according to Irish ideas was really an incipient form of Home Rule, and whether even Gladstone and his Liberal majority could fulfill the expectations excited was to be the dominant question in Irish politics in the next several years.

XII

Consolidation

December 1868–May 1870

The basic confidence in the Liberal alliance in Ireland, underlined by the general election of 1868, remained a fundamental feature of the first year and a half of Gladstone's new ministry, and no one was more forward in the support of that alliance than the Irish bishops and their clergy. There were, of course, some elements among the bishops and clergy, as there were among Gladstone's cabinet colleagues and party, who were suspicious of the alliance, but the sincere commitment of both Cullen and Gladstone to the alliance was enough to allay the doubts and fears of most of their colleagues and followers. Gladstone's Irish appointments, on assuming office on December 3, were certainly reassuring. The Earl Spencer, whose late uncle, Father Ignatius, a Passionist priest, had been a convert to Catholicism and a popular preacher in Ireland, was appointed lord lieutenant, and Chicester S. Fortescue, who was especially pleasing to Cullen, again became chief secretary of Ireland. The appointment that was greeted with the greatest enthusiasm in Ireland, however, was that of Thomas O'Hagan, who became lord chancellor of Ireland. He was the first Catholic ever to be appointed to that high office, and the enthusiasm both for the appointment and for what it represented was well reflected in a letter to Kirby from one of his former students in Rome. Timothy J. O'Mahony reported from Cork city on December 9, "Our Elections are over—we are very hopeful of the future. It is admitted on all hands that Gladstone means thorough reconciliation & justice to

Ireland. His appointment of Tom O'Hagan to the Chancellorship of Ireland is an earnest of his policy—a Catholic Lord Chancellor & a good & practical Catholic, is a *double* novelty. I am sure the Cardinal is greatly pleased" (K).

Shortly after assuming office, however, Gladstone was somewhat upset to learn that perhaps the Roman authorities were not as pleased as he had been led to believe about his proposed policy with regard to the established Church in Ireland. The new foreign secretary, the earl of Clarendon, read the dispatches of his predecessor, Lord Stanley, regarding Rome and apparently informed Gladstone that the situation was not entirely satisfactory. On November 24 Odo Russell, the British government's unofficial representative in Rome, had informed Stanley that "Cardinal Antonelli, who hitherto has avoided the subject of the Irish Church in conversation with me volunteered to ask me this morning what course our new Parliament was likely to follow in regard to that question."[1] "I was, of course," Russell explained, "unable to tell him, but the result of a very long conversation was that his Eminence distinctly said that the Church of Rome could never approve or sanction the principle of disendowment of any Church, — or the principle of separation of Church and State in any country, — nor could they ever allow their clergy to be salaried by an 'ACatholic' government—the only privilege they claimed was the liberty of education." "His Eminence," Russell noted in conclusion, "earnestly requested me to consider his observations as strictly private, and not as an official communication from the Pontifical Cardinal Secretary of State."

This was apparently one of the very few occasions on which Antonelli said too much, for Gladstone, after consulting the queen, wrote Russell on December 17, instructing him "to take an opportunity of pointing out to the Cardinal that it would be difficult for Her Majesty's Government to give the weight they might wish to give to any such communications, when they are precluded from quoting the authority which in any given case they might have allowed to influence any of their proceedings."[2] "I told Cardinal Antonelli this morning," Russell reported to Clarendon on December 22,

> that I should feel very much obliged to him if he could enable me to report to your Lordship, for the information of Her Majesty's Government, what were the opinions professed by the Papal Government on the subject of the Irish Church, as that question

1. F.O., 43/101.
2. Ibid.

was about to be discussed and settled by Parliament in February next. His Eminence replied that he would willingly do so, but he was not really prepared at the present moment to express a categorical opinion in the name of his government on the subject, but that in the future, the reports of the Irish and English Roman Catholic Bishops to the Propaganda, whose local knowledge naturally influenced the views of the Papal Government in such matters, would enable him to answer my question with more precision.

I asked his Eminence whether I was to understand from his answer that the opinions preached and published on the subject by Cardinal Cullen and Archbishop Manning were likely to be adopted by the Court of Rome?[3]

"Cardinal Antonelli replied," Russell noted in conclusion, "that the Court of Rome had the highest opinion of the judgment and capacity of Cardinal Cullen and Archbishop Manning and that as a general rule I might consider the opinions publicly expressed by them as those of the Papal Government, —nevertheless, and all things considered, he preferred to reserve the expression of his own opinion on the Irish Church for the present, as he was not really prepared to speak officially on a subject of such magnitude without more study and thought than he had yet been able to give it."

Some three weeks later, on January 12, 1869, Antonelli finally gave the assurance that Gladstone had been waiting for, by telling Russell that the British government might rest assured that Cullen and Manning's views on the established Church were the papal government's views.[4] Antonelli had obviously had very satisfactory conversations with Manning, who had arrived in Rome about the middle of December on English ecclesiastical business, and was now prepared to leave the whole matter in his and Cullen's hands. Manning had apparently convinced the cardinal secretary of state that the cry raised by some English Catholics (such as Bowyer) about the separation of Church and state and the confiscation of Church property was in the case of the Irish Church a false cry. As he explained to Barnabò on January 27, when writing him about Bowyer, all these cries "were nothing other than a superficial invention of certain Catholics who wished to justify their cooperation with the political party that systematically opposed the Catholic Church."[5] "They are those who sustained again last year

3. Ibid.
4. Ibid., 43/103B.
5. S.R.C., vol. 36, fol. 388.

the law against the Hierarchy," he charged, referring to the Ecclesiastical Titles Act. "Separation of the Church from the State is one thing, liberation of the State from a heresy is entirely another. And perhaps the separation of the State from every form of anti-Catholic and a-Catholic religion will be the absolute condition required to return the State to a true and normal relation with the Catholic Church."

Meanwhile, on January 12, the day when Antonelli was advising Russell in Rome that all was now in the hands of Cullen and Manning, the National Association convened a general meeting in Dublin to discuss the question of the established Church. Though none of the Irish bishops attended the meeting, letters were read from a number of them. Cullen's letter was a model of propriety. He advised that on the question of the established Church Irishmen should now repose their trust in Gladstone and Bright, and that was in effect what the meeting did. Several of the other bishops, notably those of Cloyne and Ross, were somewhat more insistent in their letters that the terms of the Liberal alliance must be fully lived up to, but really no one went further than that. The London *Times*, however, found that the tone of these letters was one of defiance and mistrust. Gladstone's foreign secretary, the earl of Clarendon, who disliked Cullen intensely and read more into the letters than was there, wrote Russell in Rome instructing him to ask Antonelli what he thought of Cullen's and his episcopal colleagues' letters to the National Association. "Cardinal Antonelli," Russell reported on February 5, "had neither seen nor heard of them but he had quite recently again discussed the Irish Church question with Dr. Manning and he could not sufficiently repeat how much impressed he had been by the Archbishop's knowledge, opinions, sentiments, views and arguments and how entirely he subscribed to them . . . and Lord Clarendon cannot do better than consult him as regards our views and wishes in Rome."[6]

Before this dispatch could have reached Clarendon, however, Cullen had already done what was needed to reassure Gladstone and his cabinet colleagues of his loyal support of the Liberal alliance. The occasion on which he chose to make this important political act of faith was February 8, at the traditional dinner of the lord mayor of Dublin, which he had also attended in 1867. He reported to Kirby on February 12,

> I went to the Lord Mayor's dinner last Monday. My health was proposed and I had to make a speech. I just referred to the chari-

6. F.O., 43/103B.

table works of Dublin, and said that we were rewarded for them by great peace. I contrasted our condition with that of North America and South America, Spain and Italy. I said that Italy was hurrying to destruction with the exception of one little spot where a venerable old man held the keys of Peter, maintaining peace and order and defending the rights of society and authority. I added that he was so little afraid of Mazzinian conspiracies and Garibaldian gladiators, that he was now about to hold a General Council of all the Bishops in Christendom in order to promote Christ's Kingdom on earth. Was not this a spectacle worthy of men, of angels, and of God himself[?] [K]

"I then returned to ourselves," he further explained, "and said that the peace we enjoyed permitted our legislators to engage in peaceful reforms and undertake to redress the evils brought on the country by former bad Government. Here we are so peaceable that a large army is not required whilst on the continent of Europe 6 millions of men are in arms, here we are free from the tyranny of conscription and oppressive taxes."

I then said that in such circumstances we were filled with hope, that we had great confidence in Mr. Gladstone and the English people, that our confidence was increased by the selection of Lord Spencer to be Lord Lt, whose name was dear to the poor people on account of his connection with Father Spencer, who had announced the glad tidings of salvation in every part, and who was dearly beloved by all the Irish. I then referred to the new Lord Chancellor and gave him and others as much Blarney as I could. The Lord Chancellor [correctly, Lieutenant] thanked me for all I said about his uncle and Lady Spencer was quite grateful.

"Yesterday," Cullen interestingly added, referring to an interview with the lord lieutenant, "I spent an hour with His Excellency. I gave him a history of all the proselytizing institutions of Dublin and showed how wicked they are." "I spoke to His Excellency also," he then concluded, "about the necessity of having Catholic schools and several other important matters. I think he and his Lady are very well disposed." Among the other "important matters" discussed was the established Church question, and in reporting their interview to his cabinet colleagues, Spencer expressed himself as delighted with Cullen's attitude.[7]

7. E. R. Norman, *The Catholic Church and Ireland in the Age of Rebellion, 1859–1873* (London, 1965), p. 360.

In the interim between Cullen's interview with Spencer on February 11 and Gladstone's introduction in the House on March 1 of his bill to disestablish the Irish Church, rumors began to spread that the Irish bishops in general, and Cullen in particular, had changed their minds about not accepting for their church any of the property that might be left over after the established Church was disendowed. These rumors were apparently the result of a memorial presented to Gladstone by the archbishop of Cashel, Patrick Leahy, requesting a provision in the disestablishment bill to allow for the purchase of historical sites, such as the "Rock of Cashel," which were owned but not used by the established Church as places of worship. Indeed, the rumors of Cullen's change of heart had by the middle of February spread apparently as far as Rome, for Kirby wrote Cullen explaining that some reassurance to the Roman authorities might be appropriate.

On February 28, therefore, Cullen complied in one of his long, carefully written set pieces in Italian to Kirby. "Here," he reported, "we are awaiting what is to be done with the Established Church. There will be a stiff fight, but it is believed that the heretical Church will succumb" (K). "I am sorry to hear" he added, after his short preface, "that someone has spread the rumor in Rome that I have abandoned the wise resolution adopted at a meeting of our Bishops in October, 1867, namely, not to accept any portion of the property of the Established Church, but to continue to live in the same way that has been practised with such advantage in the past, and in maintaining ourselves independent of the secular power. Whoever has spread the rumor that I have changed my views in this matter has been strangely deceived." He assured Kirby,

I continue to think as I thought when the Bishops adopted the well-known declaration, and I have neither said nor written anything to the contrary. I am convinced that if we demanded anything for the Catholic Church, the effect would be to offend the Liberals in England, who are now favorable to us because we do not demand anything, and to make them unite with those who support the party of the Protestant Church.

We shall be strong if we do not take anything, but if we agree to ask for a portion of the property of the Protestant Church we will be abandoned to all our enemies, and not obtain anything.

The way of proceeding will leave us as poor as we are, but we shall have at least the benefit of being free from the domination of heresy, and this will be to us a great advantage.

I fear that the bishop of Kerry is inclined to bargain with the authorities to obtain an endowment for his church, but I believe the other bishops are very hostile to his mode of proceeding, and condemn him. However about this matter I am not certain.

"In order that no one can say that I have lowered the flag," Cullen finally explained, "I have written a letter to Mr. O'Reilly that he will be able to read in Parliament, declaring that there has been no change in my sentiments, and that the Bishops continue to think as they thought when they published the resolutions against the Church."

Two days later, on March 1, Gladstone finally introduced his long-awaited bill to disestablish the Irish Church. The question of disestablishment was simple compared to the problems involved in dealing with the very considerable property and income of the Church. The Irish Church was worth about £16,000,000, and the real question was what was to be done with this enormous sum. Cullen and the Irish bishops, with the possible exception of Moriarty, thought that the established Church should be completely disendowed and thereby placed on an equal footing with all the other churches in Ireland as a voluntary association. Gladstone, however, had to contend with the Whig element in his cabinet and party, who viewed any such policy as mere confiscation. In the end a compromise was arrived at, and the Irish Church retained some £8,000,000, which was, in effect, the capitalized annual income of the bishops and clergy, who were to retain a life interest in that income. The remaining £8,000,000 was reserved to the state, which could use it for works of charity that could not be met by the ordinary charges on the poor law, but which was not to use it for the maintenance of any church or clergy, nor for the teaching of any religion. In other words, no other church was to be endowed out of the property of the established Church appropriated by the state. In keeping with the principle of disendowment all around, the annual incomes given by the state to the Catholic and Presbyterian Churches, in the form of the Maynooth grant and the Regium Donum respectively, were also abolished. As a form of compensation, however, the Maynooth grant and the Regium Donum, which amounted respectively to some £26,000 and £45,000 a year, were converted into capital sums calculated on the basis of fourteen years' purchase. The Catholics therefore received some £370,000 and the Presbyterians £650,000 as final settlements.

Though there was some grumbling among Catholics about the financial arrangements, the Irish bishops were generally pleased and loyally supported Gladstone's measures. The most full and explicit endorsement of the bill, surprisingly enough, came from Rome. "Cardinal Antonelli told me this morning," Russell reported to Clarendon on March 9, "that he had read Mr. Gladstone's speech of the 1st instant on the Irish Church with great interest, and that the plan proposed for solving that difficult question appeared to him both prudent and wise [*aussi prudent que sage*] because it gave full time for an equitable *rectification* of Church interests without bearing the character of a *confiscation* of Church property like the odious measures adopted in Italy two years ago."[8] Shortly after the first reading, Gladstone considerately forwarded Cullen a copy of his Irish Church bill. "Since it has appeared," Cullen reassured him on March 11, "I have seen several of my colleagues in the episcopacy and many persons of every class among Catholics, and they all agree in expecting that the new legislation will inaugurate an era of peace and prosperity for this country."[9] "Though all are well pleased," Cullen added, "with the bill as a whole, some few objections are made to it." "It is not for example," he then pointed out most interestingly, "considered desirable that twelve cathedrals should be maintained at the expense of the State for Protestant worship. Such an arrangement would be looked on as a symbol of religious inequality. If some of the cathedrals were handed over to Catholics they would assume the burthen of keeping them in repair, and others ought to do the same. Here in Dublin there are two cathedrals both built long before the reformation. Both are valuable monuments of art—but there are not sufficient congregations to fill them. If we had one of them, we would fill it and preserve it at our own expense."

"Nothing is so much descried in Ireland," Cullen further maintained, making an even more interesting suggestion, "as the introduction of small proprietors. If it were possible to sell the See lands to the farmers who are in actual possession [and] not to the gentlemen who hold large tracts of land from the church, and [who] sublet those lands to the smaller tenants, the industrial [i.e., industrious] classes would get a stake in the country, and would be more desirous to maintain peace and to preserve the rights of property." "Perhaps what I suggest," Cullen added, a little more diffidently, "is not practicable, and if so, it ought not to be allowed to interrupt the progress of legislation." In his reply two days later, on March 13, Gladstone dealt with Cullen's suggestion that, in effect, some of the property of the established Church be given to Catholics, which would have fundamentally undermined the principle of disendowment all around in his bill, in a gentle but firm manner.[10] "I will not take this occasion," he adroitly explained,

8. F.O., 43/103B.
9. Gl, 44419.
10. Ibid.

"of entering upon any lengthened statement of the views with which we have introduced into the Bill a provision not for *maintaining* but for contributing *towards* the maintenance of a limited number of great churches. All I need say is that this has been advisedly done as likely to contribute on the whole to the most easy and satisfactory settlement of the questions of Churches & Church Sites, used & unused, including in that matter the interest of other communions as well as of the Established Church." "I have explained this matter orally," he further assured Cullen, "to one or more of the Irish members." With regard to Cullen's second suggestion, that the land-purchase clauses in the bill should make certain that the property of the Church was sold directly to the occupying tenants, rather than to those middlemen who held their land on long leases from the Church and who in turn had subletted their leased land to occupying tenants, Gladstone apparently took Cullen at his word that his advice might be ignored if it was not practicable: he made no reference to it in his reply.

On March 16 the Irish Church bill received its second reading in the House of Commons, and after a week of debate, in which the supporters of the Church vainly tried to distinguish between disestablishment and disendowment (confiscation), the vote for the bill on March 23 was 368 for and 250 against.[11] "The majority for Mr. Gladstone," Cullen reported to Kirby on March 24, "was 118 over the Tories" (K). "I petitioned Mr. Gladstone privately to give us some of the old Cathedrals," Cullen confided, "and I hope he will do so—but no one knows that I have written on the matter. The Protestant ministers and Bishops and other *impiegati* [employees] will get about 8 millions compensation, the Presbyterians [correctly, Nonconformists] get £800,000 and Maynooth £360,000." "However Dr. Russell," Cullen added more sharply, naming the president of Maynooth, "and some others of the College went over to London and secured their own life interest. This will diminish very much the income of the College. It wd be as well if it were disendowed altogether." "There is a new bill," he noted finally, "to enable Catholic Bishops and priests to purchase sites for churches, glebes and glebe houses. This will be of gt value." After the vote on the second reading of the main bill, the House adjourned for Easter recess, and when it met again, it went into committee on April 15 to examine the bill clause by clause.

There was little doubt, given Gladstone's large majority and mandate, that the bill would have a safe, if long, passage through the

11. *Hansard Parliamentary Debates*, 3d ser., 194:2128.

House of Commons. What worried the supporters of the bill in Ireland was that the House of Lords might either reject it or amend it out of all recognition. The bill did not receive its third and final reading in the Commons until May 31, when it was then passed and duly sent to the Lords for their consideration.[12] Cullen was at this stage particularly apprehensive. "I fear," he confessed to Manning on June 8, "the Lords will reject the Irish Church Bill. If so, we shall have unpleasant work for some time longer in Ireland. If Mr. Gladstone resigns, and lets the Tories in again, it is much to be feared that we shall have serious disturbances."[13] "I hope," he added soberly, "nothing will induce him to take so ruinous a step." In the event, Cullen proved to be a false prophet. On June 14 the bill received its second reading in the Lords, and four days later, after the customary debate, it passed by a vote of 179 to 146.[14] The Lords, however, then went into committee and began to amend the bill with a vengeance. They abolished the preamble, which provided that no church or clergy or teaching of religion was to be endowed out of the surplus appropriated from the Irish Church, and then proceeded to restore to the Church some £7,000,000 of the £8,000,000 appropriated to the state by the Common's version. The bill as amended by the Lords also established the principle of concurrent endowment for the Catholics and Presbyterians by providing them with free glebes and houses for their clergy. The bill, so amended, passed its third reading in the Lords on July 12 and was then sent back to the Commons for consideration.

Cullen, needless to say, was furious. As soon as he learned what the Lords had done he wrote Manning a bristling letter. "The concurrent endowment of the Lords," Cullen complained on July 13, "appears to be only a device to get an argument to defend the renewed endowment of the Protestant church, and to silence us by throwing us some crumbs. The idea of the Lords appears to be to give £15,000,000 to the Protestants, that is £30 per head for each of the half million of Protestants in Ireland—to the Catholics they seem disposed to give £1,000,-000, or 5 shilling[s] per head for each of our four millions of Catholics—that is about 120 times more for each Protestant than for each Catholic."[15] "If the Lords," Cullen pointed out, "give 15 millions to the new Prot. church, to put things on a footing of equality, they ought to give us 120 millions." "I think the Irish Catholics," he added,

---

12. Ibid., 196:1078. The vote was 361 for and 247 against.

13. Shane Leslie, "Irish Pages from the Postbags of Manning, Cullen, and Gladstone," *Dublin Review* 165 (1919): 174–75.

14. *Hansard*, 197:304.

15. Gl, 44249, Cullen to Manning, July 13, 1869.

"ought not and will not submit to such terms. It is certainly very insulting to the Irish Catholics to be told that they are put on a footing of equality with Protestants whilst each Protestant gets as much as 120 Catholics." "If the concurrent endowment were adopted," he then warned Manning in conclusion, "it w^d be difficult for us to maintain the voluntary system whilst the endowment given us w^d be quite trifling and not sufficient to maintain one tenth of our clergy."

Manning forwarded Cullen's letter to Gladstone as soon as he received it, but Cullen also wrote Gladstone that same day to explain that the bill as amended made the principle of equality in Ireland a delusion. "Before this measure will be finally settled," Cullen warned Gladstone on July 14, "I now think it well to say that in my opinion that Bill will do no good in Ireland as it has been amended by the Lords. The Protestants are satisfied with it, the Catholics look on it as a measure for giving renewed strength to Protestantism and endowing the proposed new church in such a way as to render it richer than almost any other church in Christendom."[16] "The Fenians alone," he noted ironically, "will be gratified by the adoption of the amended bill, as it will give them an opportunity of proclaiming that Ireland can expect nothing good from British legislation." "I mention this matter," he then assured Gladstone, after going over much the same ground as in his letter to Manning, "not with the view of asking anything for the Catholic clergy, but merely to show that according to the amended bill the promised religious equality is a mere delusion." "To show how far we are from seeking any part of the property of the Establishment," Cullen finally concluded, invoking the authority of his colleagues, "I take the liberty of laying before you a copy of the resolutions of the Irish Catholic Bishops on this matter. The Bishops have not altered, nor are they at all likely to alter their views. Perhaps in the final arrangement of the question, it may not be useless to know how they feel."

Cullen had little cause to worry, however, because no one was more determined than Gladstone to maintain the principle of disendowment all around. He insisted, first of all, that the original preamble of the bill, which precluded any form of concurrent endowment, be restored in its integrity. He then refused to allow the additional £7,000,-000 assigned by the Lords to the Irish Church, and only after some very hard bargaining, and the intervention of the queen, did he agree to allow the original £8,000,000 to be increased by another £500,000. The bill then passed the Lords on July 20 and the Commons on the

16. Gl, 44421, Cullen to Gladstone, July 14, 1869.

twenty-third, and it finally became law on July 26, when it received the royal assent. On July 31 Cullen wrote Barnabò, briefly reporting the fall of the established Church.[17] Two weeks later, on August 14, he wrote Barnabò again more fully on the subject:

> The fall of the Protestant Church in Ireland has occasioned the greatest confusion among its adherents. Parliament has allowed them to form a new ecclesiastical body, which will be given the right of possession of the little property that will remain after having provided the life-interest pensions that are awarded to the clergy of the suppressed Church, as also to form a new code of doctrine and discipline. This new ecclesiastical body must be formed and approved by the Protestant bishops, ministers, and laity. These various parties begin already to wage a furious war among themselves; probably the affair will end in a true Babylon, in which case, I am convinced, that many Protestants to avoid the quarrels will take refuge in the Catholic Church.[18]

The day before he wrote Barnabò, Cullen had written Kirby about the demise of the established Church. "I intend," he explained on August 13, enclosing some £2,000 Peter's pence for the pope, "to have a Te Deum for the downfall of the old church of Elisabeth. The people who mix with Protestants think we ought to say nothing about the matter but I think it will do good to return thanks to God" (K). "The Protestants," Cullen reported, "have now to institute a new Church Body—they are tearing each other's eyes out already about the constitution and doctrines of the new Church, and I am persuaded they will make a sad mess of it. They can unite only on one subject i.e. the hatred of Catholicity." "Next week we shall have a Board of Maynooth to determine on what we are to do," he then informed Kirby, referring to the consequences of the recent legislation in regard to Maynooth. "I think all the Bishops will attend. I suppose we must reduce the no. of students, lessen the salaries of the Professors, and do away with the pocket money, £5,000 per annum that Sir. Rob. Peel granted to the students." A week later Cullen reported to Kirby on the result of the meeting. "We had a meeting of the bishops about Maynooth," he explained on August 20 (K). "The college will get £369,000[,] an enormous amount. For the past it had £27,000 per annum—the future income will be only £12,000 per annum. Still it will be one of the richest Colleges in the world—the professors have right to their full

17. S.R.C., vol. 36, fols. 662–63.
18. Ibid., fol. 564.

salaries i.e. £6,000 per annum—there will be only £6,000 remaining for the support of the students. With this sum 3 or 400 students can be supported—and that is quite enough." "We shall have the education and land questions on our hands immediately," he noted in conclusion. "I hope they may terminate well."

Indeed, the gratitude of Irish Catholics to Gladstone and the Liberal alliance on the passing of the Irish Church Act was exceeded perhaps only by their rising expectations. Cullen was certainly not alone among the bishops in his hopes for the future, and the attitude of the bishop of Cloyne, who was among the more politically advanced of the bishops, was probably typical of the body at this time. "The disestablishment of the Protestant Church," William Keane assured Kirby on September 6, "has wrought a great change in Ireland. It is only the first of other measures that will bring about in due time, confidence, union, peace, and happiness" (K). The commitment of the great body of the Irish bishops and clergy to Gladstone and the Liberal alliance in September 1869 was as deep and as real as it had ever been since the informal inception of that alliance some eighteen months before, in March 1868. The alliance was not, of course, without its critics in Ireland, even among the clergy, but their chief problem was that they were themselves deeply divided. Given the fundamental difference between constitutional Nationalists and revolutionary Fenians about means, those opposed to the Liberal alliance were not able to unite to counter its effects. During the general election, however, there had occurred a small event, no larger than the proverbial cloud, which would in the long run not only help to undermine the Liberal alliance as understood by Gladstone and the Irish bishops but also transform the whole structure of Irish politics.

On the evening of November 12, 1868, at the Mechanics Institute in Dublin, a meeting was held to inaugurate an Amnesty Committee, to petition the government for the release of the Fenian prisoners.[19] The chair was taken by Isaac Butt, a prominent barrister and politician who had achieved national prominence by his defense of the Fenian leaders arrested and convicted in 1865. Also present were A. M. Sullivan, editor of the *Nation*, who was an uncompromising constitutional Nationalist, and T. N. Underwood, who had served as president of the

19. *Freeman's Journal*, November 13, 1868. See also David Thornley, *Issac Butt and Home Rule* (London, 1964), pp. 53–55.

now-defunct Brotherhood of St. Patrick and who, if he was not a sworn Fenian, was certainly a trusted fellow traveler. There were apparently no Catholic clergy present, though a letter was read from John O'Hanlon, a Dublin curate, who some years before had officiated at the marriage of James Stephens. All the speakers were most moderate in attempting to enlist the support of all patriotic and merciful men, whatever their political persuasion. The committee then launched a petition movement, and at its usual weekly meeting on December 22, it was announced that some half dozen letters enclosing petitions had been received from Catholic clergymen.[20] It was also reported that the committee had received a somewhat amended version of its petition from the archbishop of Cashel, Patrick Leahy, signed by that prelate and by the clergy and laity of his district. The most interesting news of the evening, however, was the announcement that "a deputation of the committee had waited upon his Eminence Cardinal Cullen in reference to the petition. They were, however, unable to see his Eminence, who was ill, but they had seen Monsignor Moran, who brought them word that his Eminence would gladly sign the petition."[21]

Cullen, however, soon changed his mind about signing the petition. His second thoughts were apparently prompted by what he perceived to be a Fenian resurgence, and he came to view the Amnesty Committee as a part of the renewed Fenian effort. "Here," he reported to Kirby on January 3, 1869, "the Fenians are very busy again. I think they are swearing in new members. The Government knows everything they are doing and it lets them go on because it can crush them at any moment" (K). "The Fenian committee," Cullen then explained, "has sent round a petition in favour of the Fenian prisoners asking the Bishops to sign it. Dr. McHale, Dr. Keane and Dr. Conaty have signed it. Dr. Leahy of Thurles [correctly, Cashel] objected to the form of the petition. I think it is drawn up in a tone of defiance which can only do mischief, and I will not sign it. However I will get plenty of abuse for abstaining." The Amnesty Committee, however, pressed forward with its petition campaign, and on February 22, in the House of Commons, Gladstone announced that the government would release unconditionally forty-nine of the eighty-one Fenian prisoners.[22] The other thirty-two, soldiers convicted of Fenianism and responsible leaders of the conspiracy, would not be amnestied. The reaction in Ireland was one of considerable disappointment, and the Amnesty Committee in-

---

20. *Freeman's Journal*, December 23, 1868.
21. Ibid.
22. Patrick J. Corish, "Political Problems, 1860–1878," in *A History of Irish Catholicism*, gen. ed. Patrick J. Corish (Dublin, 1967), p. 37.

creased its efforts to influence public opinion by organizing receptions and dinners for the forty-nine Fenians who had been released. The committee also decided to hold a national church-door collection on St. Patrick's Day in tribute to "Ireland's martyrs."[23]

Cullen, however, would allow no such church-door collection in his diocese, and on March 12, in a letter to his clergy, he forbade it.[24] In writing Barnabò on March 23 about letters sent to the Cork reception committee for the Fenian prisoners by Fathers Lavelle and Anderson, Cullen also took occasion to explain what he had done about the collection:

> Here in Dublin we have had a little uneasiness with the Fenians. Some associates of that sect, or at least supporters, decided to make a collection in all the churches of Ireland in order to provide for forty or fifty Fenians who had been liberated. They fixed on St. Patrick's day in this diocese for the work. Some days before they intimated to me what they had resolved on, and demanded my cooperation—at the same time they wrote to all the priests instructing them to announce the collection at the masses, and to nominate collectors to receive the offerings. All was done without ever consulting me or the clergy. As soon as I learned of the project I wrote a letter to all the pastors of the various churches and prohibited the proposed collection. The Fenians are very angry, they covered the walls with tricolor handbills, ordering the collection, and they threatened to come to have it done. In any case when St. Patrick's day came, they had not the hardihood to appear at the churches and matters passed off quietly. The only thing that they were able to do was to give vent to their feelings in rudeness to me, and write letters full of insults and threats. Three or four bishops, those of Cloyne, Ross and Limerick allowed the collection, and it seems to me they have not acted prudently.[25]

"The Fenians," Cullen pointed out in conclusion, "did not thank them, but said that they had yielded for fear, and besides the fostering of Fenians now is displeasing to all those in England who for the first time seek to have a great act of justice done to Ireland in the abolition of the Established Church."

Cullen, however, was not just concerned about the possible effect

23. Ibid.
24. *Freeman's Journal*, March 13, 1869.
25. S.R.C., vol. 36, fol. 436.

on the Liberal alliance of this renewed Fenian effort through the Amnesty Committee. He was also concerned about the effect it was having on the Irish clergy, and that was why he reported to Rome the names of the bishops who had signed the petition and supported the collection. He was particularly worried about the influence of Father Lavelle, who was prominent in the affairs of the Amnesty Committee and who had recently become involved in a one-sided quarrel in the press with the bishop of Birmingham, W. B. Ullathorne. Ullathorne had condemned the activities of the Fenians in his diocese and had been taken to task for it by Lavelle, who maintained that the Fenians were not condemned by the Church because they were not against either the Church or the legitimate authority of the state. What the Fenians opposed in Ireland, he argued, was the illegitimate authority of the English state. Ullathorne prudently wrote Manning, who was then in Rome, asking him to bring the matter to the attention of Barnabò and Propaganda. "I will go over the Fenian question with C. Barnabò," Manning promised Ullathorne on February 17, "and will give him a full account of your letter and Pamphlet; and you shall have the result. We owe you thanks for speaking out. I wish both in Ireland and England we had all done so together some time ago. Many might have been saved. Still it is not too late" (Ma). "I feel sure," Manning then noted in conclusion, "that multitudes of good Catholics are misled by various causes into Fenianism: & that more will be unless we guide them."

Several days later Manning wrote Ullathorne again. "Card[l] B. desires me to say," he reported on February 20, "that the Prop[da] has in no way deviated from the answer of the H. Office respecting Secret Societies, including Fenianism: that any statement taken contrary is false: that you may act on the documents you refer to" (Ma). "F. Lavelle," Manning added, "was twice suspended by the H.F. Once he made a retraction in Prop[da]: but on his return went back to his old courses. The Abp of Tuam rehabilitated him: & now Propda will not touch him." The next day Manning added a postscript to this letter. "I omitted in my last letter," he explained on February 21, "to say that when F. Lavelle attacked me Card[l] Cullen repeatedly urged me not to reply. The same opinion is expressed here in your case" (Ma). Another letter from Lavelle was published in the Nationalist weekly the *Irishman*, on March 13, 1869, in which he again maintained that the Fenians were not condemned by the Church. In writing Barnabò on May 7, in reference to the trouble caused by the appointment of James Lynch as the coadjutor to the bishop of Kildare and Leighlin, Cullen took occasion to report Lavelle once again. "Here I shall only add,"

Cullen noted, "that the writings and the letters of Father Lavelle have done great harm among those members of the clergy who do not have respect for authority, and that in every diocese there are some few, especially among the younger, that belong to their class."[26] "The latest work of Father Lavelle," he added, "is a very long letter (or tract) against Monsignor Ullathorne, in which he defends the Fenians, and says that it is a laudable thing to resist the English government because it is not the legitimate government and does not have the right to demand obedience."

In the meantime, Cullen's worst fears about the Amnesty Committee were being realized. The collection for the prisoners was apparently a success, but owing to the government's refusal to make any further concessions, the initiative in the committee fell to the more radical element, who wanted to raise an agitation in the country by inaugurating a series of monster meetings. The moderates resisted the efforts of the radicals and Fenians in the committee, but the result, amid bitter recriminations and fisticuffs, was that the radicals and Fenians withdrew to form a new organization, the Amnesty Association. The new association was launched at a meeting on May 28; Issac Butt was elected its president, and Father Lavelle, A. M. Sullivan, and John Martin, the former Young Irelander and now Repealer, were among those who formed the executive committee. The new association soon eclipsed the old committee, carrying most of the popular element with it by its more active policy. Shortly before the Amnesty Committee split, however, Cullen was greatly heartened by a large Catholic-Nationalist demonstration on May 13, on the occasion of the translation of the remains of Daniel O'Connell from a temporary grave to a permanent one marked by a traditional Irish round tower in Glasnevin cemetery. Cullen, nine bishops, and some six hundred clergy, regular and secular, attended, as about fifty thousand people assisted at the pontifical high mass. "The police," Cullen reported to Kirby on May 16, "sent notice to some of the judges that there would be a great Fenian demonstration—but nothing of the kind took place. Not a Fenian emblem was displayed. The immense body of people assisted in profound silence at the Mass and procession, it was delightful to see the vast crowds kneeling on the grass and praying most fervently. The Mass was celebrated under a vast canopy at the foot of the round tower, and the platform for the altar and clergy was elevated that all the people could see the celebrant and assist at the Holy Sacrifice" (K). "I think the day's proceedings," he then informed Kirby in

26. S.R.C., vol. 35, fol. 1096. This letter has been misfiled; it should be in vol. 36.

conclusion, "have done a great deal to put down Fenianism. All the Fenians are the enemies of the pacific policy of O'Connell."

The Amnesty Association, which now represented a coalition of Fenians and the more radical constitutional Nationalists, proceeded from June until the following October to hold a series of some forty monster meetings all over Ireland. The agitation climaxed on Sunday, October 10, with a meeting at Cabra in Dublin, at which it was reported some two hundred thousand people attended. Gladstone, however, was not to be moved; on October 18 he announced that in the interests of public safety he could not release any more prisoners. At this point the leadership of the association prudently decided to suspend any further monster meetings.[27] The more extreme Fenian elements in the association, however, were so upset and frustrated by Gladstone's decision that they determined to break up every meeting that gave any countenance to him or his program. Their immediate target was those meetings being held by the new Tenant League, which had been recently organized to promote land reform and to encourage Gladstone in legislating for it. The great irony in the mounting Fenian violence against the league was that Isaac Butt had been elected president of the league, and as he was also president of the Amnesty Association, he was virtually obliged to preside over a civil war.

Cullen was appalled by the increasing violence. "I fear our Fenians," he reported to Kirby on November 2,

> are likely to do great mischief, and to prevent all useful legislation. At Limerick on yesterday a meeting in favour of tenant right was to be held, but the Fenians pulled down the platform, and disturbed the people. There was a meeting in Navan some time ago to obtain an amnesty for the Fenians. The railroad company refused a special train to bring people to the meeting but they gave a train to all who were going to a tenant right meeting ere yesterday. Now to show their spite some fellows supposed to be Fenians took up some of the rails of the railroad, and had this not been discovered in time very probably a couple of hundred passengers going to Navan would have been destroyed. [K]

"I think," Cullen maintained, "the Fenians have got too much encouragement. You know that F. Lavelle and the West [i.e., MacHale] always encouraged them. Dr. Butler gave them a collection in Limerick, Dr. Keane in Cloyne—in this way they have encreased [*sic*] in number and audacity." "The Government," he added, in obvious exasperation, "did

27. Thornley, p. 67.

wrong to let out a lot of them on the country and now it allows them to publish a whole lot of vile newspapers all against the Government itself, and also against the Catholic priests and Bishops. Rome has something also to answer for on account of the way in which they let F. Lavelle go on." "I dare say," he concluded grimly, "the winter coming on will be the witness of many scenes of outrage and bloodshed in Ireland."

Whatever the responsibilities of his fellow prelates, the government, or even Rome for the spread of Fenianism, it must be said that Cullen himself had not yielded an inch to the society, nor would he. Some ten days after Gladstone had refused to release any more prisoners, Cullen again denounced the Fenians in a pastoral letter to his clergy on the occasion of the Jubilee indulgence granted by the pope in connection with the approaching Vatican Council; he emphasized that because they were excommunicated the Fenians would not be able to partake of the benefits of the papal indulgence.[28] On November 24, less than a month later and three days before he set out for Rome for the council, Cullen addressed a letter to his clergy and laity in honor of the feast of the Immaculate Conception, in which he explained that he felt "compelled once more to raise my voice against the leaders, organisers, and adepts of the Fenian societies, and to deplore the evils their members are bringing, or likely to bring, upon themselves and upon our beloved country."[29] Besides his usual fulminations against the iniquities of Fenianism, Cullen went out of his way in this pastoral both to stress the dangers that the Fenians posed to the Liberal alliance and to emphasize his own allegiance to that alliance. In asking what Fenianism aimed at, Cullen replied that at present it appeared "to be altogether occupied in preventing the adoption of any good measures calculated to promote the welfare and peace of this country."

"Indeed," he then maintained, "the leaders of this body seem to have formed an unholy league with low Orangemen and interested land agents to prevent all useful legislation, and to drive, if possible, from power, the Statesmen who have rendered such signal services to Ireland during the last session of Parliament, hoping in this way to prevent the redress of great evils and grievances, and to keep the country in a state of chronic discontent, in order that they themselves may have grounds to justify their conspiracies and revolutionary movements, and may cast their nets more profitably in troubled waters." "It

28. Patrick Francis Moran, ed., *The Pastoral Letters and Other Writings of Cardinal Cullen* (Dublin, 1882), 3:264–65, October 27, 1869.
29. Ibid., p. 277.

is to be hoped," Cullen added, "that the wicked machinations of the few will not be allowed to blast the fair prospects of the whole country, and that the mischievous ingratitude of a reckless party will not prevent the great Statesmen now at the helm of the State from carrying out the wise and benevolent measures which they have in contemplation for the welfare of our afflicted country—measures which will soon make us forget past centuries of misrule and oppression." Cullen then took the incredible step of complimenting the government for its great forebearance in putting down the recent Fenian rising: "Considering that our people have escaped from such imminent dangers with very little bloodshed, and without any general suffering, we cannot but be grateful to the public authorities for the humanity they have displayed and the moderation with which they have acted when suppressing the movements of those by whom they were so foolishly and recklessly assailed."

What prompted Cullen to such an unusual exhibition of "West Britonism" was an open letter addressed to the Irish bishops a few days before by Father Lavelle, a letter that, in its sheer audacity, transcended all his previous efforts. The occasion for the letter, dated November 9, was Cullen's pastoral of October 27 maintaining that the Fenians were excommunicated. The letter, which appeared in the *Irishman* on November 20, the eve of the execution of the Manchester Martyrs should be allowed to speak for itself. "My Lords," Lavelle began, "Much as I have written within the last decade of years on the unhappy condition of our dear common country, viewed in its social, political, and religious aspects, I hardly ever sat down to address any body of my fellow-countrymen with a sense of deeper responsibility than now fills my breast. The ground of that very grave responsibility is the yet more grave diversity of public teaching on a matter of vital importance to tens of millions of our cherished fellow-countrymen at home and abroad—if, indeed if I can speak of 'home' at all in reference to Irishmen, whose 'home' is everywhere but 'at home.' . . ." Lavelle then proceeded to quote Cullen's late pastoral on the excommunication of the Fenians. "Now, my lords," he continued, "while I fully share with his Eminence all his horror and detestation of Continental 'secret societies,' which have for their object social and political anarchy, with a contempt and denial of religion and God, while I also, hold as really 'condemned' such associations as either expressly or equivalently have fallen under the censures of our Holy Church, I feel called upon to take issue direct with his Eminence on the fact that the society known throughout the globe as the *Fenian Brotherhood* has been, either by name or by implication, condemned." Lavelle went on:

He says it has, and, as a consequence, that not alone all its members, but even more, all its countenancers and votaries are "excommunicated," "Cut off like rotten branches from the mystic vine," and thereby accursed of God and His Church.

I maintain it has not; and, therefore, that none of these awful consequences flow from connexion with, or countenance of, that association.

Firstly, it has not been condemned. On the contrary, the very documents relied on for an express condemnation positively negative the fact.

There are two letters addressed by Cardinal Barnabo, Prefect of the Propaganda—the one on the 7th June, 1864, to the Archbishop of Dublin—the other on the 13th July, 1865, to the Archbishop[s] of Baltimore, Cincinnati, and New York, and other American prelates, on the very subject of the Fenian society. These two letters are identical, word for word, in their first paragraph, which I translate as follows: —

Many reports have been conveyed to the Holy See regarding a society which is called the Fenian Brothers, or the Fenians, and these have been submitted to the supreme congregation of the Universal Inquisition, that it might be decided what was to be thought about them. Now, our Most Holy Father, Pius P.P. IX., having heard the decision of the Most Eminent Inquisitors, ordered that the decree of 5th of August, 1846, should be notified to your Grace—which runs thus: —"The occult societies of which there is question in the pontifical constitutions, are all those which propose to themselves anything against the Church or government, whether they exact or do not exact an oath from their members to keep the secret. Furthermore, his Holiness wished it should be intimated to you that recourse should be had to the Holy See, and that with full and ample explanations of the facts and circumstances of the case, should any difficulty be found in the application of the foregoing decree."

The following is the translation of the additional clause in the letter to the American Bishops: —

But since it has been recently asserted in some journals, and especially in the *Connaught Patriot*, that a declaration has proceeded from the Holy See, according to which *the Fenians were not to be disquieted*, therefore, the Supreme

Congregation of the Holy Office decreed that you should be informed that the foregoing assertion was altogether false.

"Here, then," Lavelle maintained, "are the only grounds for the repeated assertions to the effect that the Fenians are expressly condemned. A word or two of critical examination will dissipate the assumption." He elaborated:

And, firstly, the only reference by name to the Fenians in the first letter, is the statement that reports concerning them had been transmitted to the Holy See. If the Holy See meant to condemn them, what was easier for it to say than this: —"The foregoing Pontifical constitutions apply to the Fenians?" But, instead of this plain, intelligible censure, what does it say? Why, that recourse should be actually had to itself on the very question—the one great question of "application:" and that, too, on its being furnished with full and ample information of all the facts, circumstances, and details of the case. Therefore, in that letter, so far from the Fenians being condemned, their case is expressly reserved for future consideration to the Holy See itself.

And since the date of this reservation up to the present day, the only other public utterance of the Holy See or the Holy Office (two very different things, as the case of Galileo proves) is the addendum to the American document. Now what is the meaning of that little clause? Why, simply a denial of an unfounded statement to the effect that the Holy See had actually taken the Fenians under its protection in forbidding any disquietude to be practised towards them. But how widely does this contradiction of a false report differ from positive condemnation? It leaves the Fenians just as they were, neither specially protected nor specially condemned, but subject to the application, should they be found on close scrutiny by the Holy See itself, deserving thereof, of the general constitutions of previous Popes.

"Let us now come to examine, secondly," Lavelle proposed, "how far these constitutions apply to the Fenian society—*i.e.*, how far the Fenians and their ends answer the description of the ends and characters condemned. As your lordships, and, indeed, most lay people in the country are fully aware, four predecessors, of happy memory, of his present Holiness—Clement XII., Benedict XIV., Pius VII., and Leo XII., issued constitutions entitled respectively, 'In Eminenti, Providas VI, Ecclesiam VI, and Quo graviora,' at once bewailing the evils which certain secret organisations were entailing on society in general, and on the Church in particular; and, accordingly, and most meritedly, visiting their members with the dreadful penalty of major excommunications." "But my lords," Lavelle pointed out, "the essential point is to ascertain what the end, aim and nature of these associations were; or were all political societies, no matter of what description, included in the terrible sentence? To suppose this latter would be simply ridiculous, absolutely derogatory to the justice at once and the dignity of the Holy See, as representing it as hurling its anathemas equally against the innocent and the guilty, equally against the friends and defenders, the enemies and the assailants of good government and the Church."

Given the absurdity of such an hypothesis, Lavelle further argued, the only recourse left was to examine the character of the organizations condemned in the constitutions issued by the various popes to determine whether they did indeed apply to the Fenians. Lavelle thereupon entered into a long review of the censures contained in the four papal constitutions against the Freemasons, Carbonari, and Universalitarians, and concluded:

> Thus, then, the Popes themselves qualify, with no small precision, the associations and men whom they meant to censure—associations which propose to themselves those things which we have above enumerated against the Church and the supreme civil powers, *i.e.*, "plots against Christ," "ambushes for extirpating the Church," "enemies of the Christian name," "who scoff at the most sacred mysteries of our religion and the most pure precepts of Christ, and assail all *legitimate* power," bound by "an impious oath to put to death any associate guilty of revealing their secret"—"who say, not alone in their hearts but aloud, 'There is no God;'" "indifferent to all religion," ["]giving every one license to form a religion of his own;" in one word, human monsters.

"My lords," Lavelle asked, "are the Fenians all or any of this?" "Nay," he answered, "has it not been established beyond cavil that they are the very reverse—men, as a rule, of stainless character, of a high sense of honour, of profound religious convictions, and of unaffected piety."

"Peter Crawley," Lavelle noted by way of example, referring to one of those few Fenians who had lost his life in the rising in March 1867, "of whom I make special communication on Sunday, and for whom I shall offer the Holy Sacrifice tomorrow, was found with his scapular and medal around his neck as he lay riddled with British bullets for not hating his country. Perhaps not within the walls of those abodes of

Christian sanctity and perfection may be found deeper piety than that practised by the Fenian convict, General Burke." "Ask the chaplains, my lords," he suggested, "of the several convict hells in which our dear countrymen are tortured, what manner of life they lead? Do they prove themselves 'enemies of the Christian name,' 'scoffers of religion,' 'conspirators against the Church,' 'Deniers of God'[?] Why, in these patriot souls, the sample virtues of Ireland are incarcerated; and yet they are made to herd in public estimation with off-scourings of mankind!!!" "No doubt, in an organisation embracing millions of men," Lavelle admitted, "there must of necessity be, even many if you will, in whose life there is much room for improvement; but we might as well make the vices of many Catholics an argument against our Holy Church as the irregularities of some individual Fenians, a proof of the 'wickedness and folly' (those are the stereotyped words) of Fenianism itself." "Again, I ask," Lavelle posed in conclusion, "are we to suppose all these true, warm-hearted men anathema if only they belong to that organisation which embraces millions of their fellow-countrymen equally warm and disinterested? Cardinal Cullen says yes. I say no. The best interests of religion—the vital interests of the faith among millions of Irishmen throughout the globe, demand that the truth should be unequivocally proclaimed—that this simple question should be plainly answered: —'Are Irishmen the banned of God's Church, and the accursed of God, for conspiring against a foreign, grinding, crushing, murderous, exhausting, depopulating government?' For so far, I have shown that they are not." "In my next," he finally promised the bishops boldly, "I shall try and give reasons why they ought not."

Two days after Lavelle's letter appeared, the political situation became even more intense. On November 22, at the nomination of candidates for a by-election in Tipperary occasioned by the death of Charles Moore, the local Fenians put forward Jeremiah O'Donovan Rossa, who had been sentenced to life imprisonment at hard labor in 1865 for his Fenian activities. The nomination of Rossa came as a complete surprise to the constituency. Indeed, in early October Issac Butt had been asked to stand for election by the Tenant League, and the archbishop of Cashel, Patrick Leahy, had indicated that he was willing to endorse him.[30] Butt, however, declined to run, and a county meeting of the electors then nominated Denis Caulfield Heron, a Catholic barrister of some prominence, who addressed the electors with a program of fixity of tenure, denominational education, and am-

---

30. L, Leahy to Thomas Ryan, October 10, 1869.

nesty, in that order. Heron was also endorsed by Butt, the local Tenant League party, the *Freeman's Journal*, and the clergy of county Tipperary. The contest, in effect, came down to a test of strength between the Fenian-amnesty party and the Liberal-land reform supporters of the Gladstonian program for Ireland, and there appeared to be little reason to doubt that Heron would win. The result, however, was a dreadful defeat for the supporters of the Liberal alliance, for Rossa received 1,131 votes to 1,028 for Heron.

By the time the results of the election were announced on November 27, most of the Irish bishops were on their way to Rome to attend the opening session, on December 8, of the first Vatican Council. Cullen had left Dublin on the day the election took place and did not, therefore, learn of the disaster until after he had reached Rome. There was, however, even worse news to come from Ireland as far as the supporters of the Liberal alliance among the Irish bishops were concerned. In the first week of December the dean of Limerick, Richard B. O'Brien, addressed a circular to all of the Irish clergy asking them to sign a declaration in support of amnesty for the Fenian prisoners.[31] Within a week some six hundred clergy had signed the declaration, and during the next several weeks about eight hundred more added their names.[32] Given that there were some three thousand priests serving in the Irish mission in 1869, this was a very significant demonstration of sympathy—especially when it is considered that the vicars-general of Dublin immediately warned their clergy, who numbered more than four hundred, that in the absence of the cardinal it would be imprudent of them to sign the declaration.[33] The warning was effective, for apparently only one prominent Dublin priest, James Redmond, the archdeacon of Glendalough, signed the declaration, and he was soon called to account for it by Cullen.[34]

When Cullen and the nineteen other Irish bishops who were in Rome attending the council learned of Dean O'Brien's circular, the great majority of them were very annoyed. Since their arrival in Rome, the bishops had been holding general meetings about once a week. At their meeting on January 12, 1870, as Cullen informed his secretary,

31. See the *Freeman's Journal*, December 16, 1869, for O'Brien's circular, the declaration, and the signatures of six hundred priests.
32. Ibid., December 24, 1869. See also Corish, p. 41.
33. *Freeman's Journal*, December 11, 1869.
34. C, Cullen to Conroy, December 31, 1869. All of the Cullen letters to Conroy quoted in this volume are from typescript copies in C. The originals are in the Ardagh Diocesan Archives in Longford. The typescripts have also been reprinted in Peadar MacSuibhne, *Paul Cullen and His Contemporaries*, vol. 4 (Naas, 1974), pp. 257–73; vol. 5 (1977), pp. 26–145.

George Conroy, that same day, all of the bishops except MacHale and John Derry, the bishop of Clonfert, had joined in condemning O'Brien's proceedings (C). The bishops, Cullen further assured Conroy, had lectured Butler "rather severely" about the conduct of his dean, and in writing Conroy again the next day, Cullen added that he was sure this step would keep O'Brien quiet for the future (C). "The Irish Bishops in Rome at a general Meeting," the bishops had formally resolved, "have expressed their decided disapprobation of Dean O'Brien's recently canvassing and seeking the signatures of the Priests of their respective Dioceses to a document emanating from him as they deem the proceeding an improper interference with the Priests of their respective dioceses, and have requested the Rt. Rev^d. D^r. Butler to make known this their disapprobation to Dean O'Brien" (C). What had upset the bishops, of course, was not simply that the dean had appealed over their heads to their clergy but that he had done so when most of them were in Rome and in no position to make their views on the subject known to their clergy. Even those bishops who had favored amnesty, such as Keane of Cloyne and O'Hea of Ross, joined in condemning the dean. The circular, moreover, given Gladstone's refusal to release any more prisoners, was essentially subversive of the Liberal alliance, to which Cullen and the great majority of the Irish bishops were now committed. Both their own authority and their declared public policy, therefore, demanded that they not allow the dean of Limerick's proceedings to pass unchallenged.

Another challenge, however, had incensed the bishops, and particularly Cullen, even more, and that was the public letter recently addressed to them by Father Lavelle. At their first general meeting in Rome on December 16, one of the bishops brought up the subject of Lavelle's letter, and it was agreed that it should be translated and brought under the notice of Propaganda.[35] When the bishops met again the following week, Lavelle's letter was the subject of a more extended discussion. "As in this letter," the bishops finally resolved on December 23, "the Rev. P. Lavelle asserts, contrary to the teaching of his Eminence Cardinal Cullen and the other Bishops of Ireland, that the Members of the Fenian Society do not incur the censures attached to Secret Societies by the Bulls and Constitutions of the Sovereign Pontiffs; and as he endeavours to sustain his opinion by certain theological arguments calculated to mislead the Public, the Prelates believe that Public Order and Ecclesiastical Discipline in Ireland require a speedy and definitive decision—whether Fenianism, as it exists in

---

35. C, Cullen to Conroy, December 16, 1879 [misdated, December 17, 1869].

Ireland comes under the Pontifical condemnations against Secret Societies" (C). The bishops also called on Propaganda to effect some "adequate reparation" from Lavelle for his interference with ecclesiastical authority and some effective measure to prevent a recurrence of it.

"With Dr. McHale and Dr. Derry dissenting," Cullen reported to Conroy on December 23, "all the other bishops have agreed to send a letter to Propaganda to call on the cardinals to give an explicit condemnation of Fenianism and to punish Lavelle" (C). "When the bishops had all spoken," Cullen explained, "I told them that I did not consider Lavelle's letter as addressed to me, but written against me; that it was an indictment directed to censure my teaching, that I would not take part in their proceedings but that I would bring Lavelle's letter before the Pope, my only judge. If his Holiness approved of it I would be satisfied and never write a line again on the subject of Fenianism." "Dr. McHale," Cullen added, "got a little frightened at this and said he would join the other bishops in their recourse to Propaganda. Dr. Leahy of Cashel, Dr. Gillooly, Dr. McCabe and Dr. Moriarty, all opposed to Fenianism[,] were deputed to bring Lavelle's letter to Propaganda and to call for justice." "Dr. McHale," Cullen assured Conroy, "heard more truth at the meeting than ever was told to him in Ireland. Some of the bishops told him that Fr. Lavelle was only an interpreter and that by promoting him to the best parish in his diocese he had shown that he sanctioned all the acts of that firebrand." "Dr. McHale was very patient," Cullen concluded; "I hope some good will be done."

When the episcopal delegation waited upon Cardinal Barnabò at Propaganda, however, he apparently told them what he had told Manning earlier in the year in reference to the Lavelle-Ullathorne affair—that the cardinals of Propaganda would not have anything more to do with Lavelle. As to Fenianism, he apparently advised them that their best course was to refer the matter directly to the Holy Office, especially because the pope was himself the head of that congregation. Cullen, meanwhile, had begun to draw up his own memorial to the pope in reference to Lavelle and Fenianism. When the bishops met again on December 30, they apparently decided to act on the cardinal prefect's advice. "We had a meeting of the Irish bishops today," Cullen reported to Conroy that same day, "and adopted a petition to have it expressly condemned by the Holy Office *et nominatim* [and by name]. Dr. McHale and Dr. Derry *non aderant* [not adhering]" (C). "All the other bishops signed the petition; perhaps the other two absentees may give their names." MacHale and Derry remained adamant in their refusal to sign the bishops' petition, but Cullen was certain, nevertheless, that Fenianism would be condemned by the Holy Office.[36]

In the meantime, Odo Russell, the British government's unofficial representative in Rome, had become so upset at the recent conduct of Lavelle and another Irish priest, John Ryan, parish priest of New Inn, near Cahir in the diocese of Cashel, that he decided on January 1, 1870, to recommend to Cardinal Antonelli that both priests be suspended.[37] In reporting this interview to Clarendon, the foreign secretary, Russell explained what had prompted him to take action. "As neither Cardinal Cullen nor Dr. MacHale," Russell complained on January 2,

> appear to notice the writings and sermons of Fathers Lavelle and Ryan in Ireland, and none of the Irish bishops appear to reprove them, I took it upon myself to talk over the subject of Ireland once more with the Cardinal Secretary of State and to remind his Eminence that the Pope was neglecting the interests of the Roman Church in not supporting his clergy against the Fenians.
>
> Cardinal Antonelli said that the Pope had repeatedly condemned Fenianism and had in the Bull of Censures "Latae Sententiae" published only the other day, renewed in article 4 the condemnation of secret societies to which the Fenians belonged.
>
> I said that no one in Ireland would read the Bull of Censures and that unless the Pope struck at the root of the evil by some visible and tangible measure Father Lavelle would go on writing in favour of Fenianism and Father Ryan would go on preaching in favour of agrarian outrages and the bishops would be open to suspicion so long as the Pope did not silence the enemies of his Church by some ex-cathedra utterance.[38]

"I need not weary your Lordship," Russell concluded, "with a repetition of all the well known arguments I employed, which ended in a strong recommendation to his Eminence to suspend the offending priests and shew the Fenians that the Pope's hand was *really* against them. Suffice it to say that I found Cardinal Antonelli well disposed and willing to call the Pope's attention to the necessity of immediate action."

When Russell had his customary New Year's audience with the

36. C, Cullen to Conroy, January 12, 1870.
37. F.O., 43/106, Russell to Clarendon, telegram, January 1, 1870.
38. F.O., 43/106.

Pope a short time later, he again raised the question of a formal condemnation of Fenianism. "After some unimportant observations," Russell reported to Clarendon on January 13, "His Holiness asked me whether I knew many bishops? There were he added, five or six very good English bishops and the Irish were all good."[39] "I said," Russell explained, "that I had endeavoured to know the Irish bishops with a view of ascertaining and consulting their wishes because Her Majesty's Government were about to introduce important reforms in Ireland which would require their cordial and powerful cooperation but unfortunately they were all in Rome when their presence was most needed at home to combat Fenianism, the enemy of Church and State." Russell went on:

> The Disestablishment of the Church was an enormous measure carried at a great cost as it alienated the Protestants but it was intended as a message of peace to Ireland and a hand cordially offered to the Roman Catholic subjects of Her Majesty. The bishops, I was happy to say, had received it in a Christian spirit and Her Majesty's Government were grateful for their support, but among the lower clergy, were many who sympathized with the Fenians, denounced their bishops, criticised their theology, condemned their pastorals, encouraged disobedience, crime and sedition, and undermined the spiritual authority of the Pope in Ireland. If His Holiness would consult the bishops, he would find that they needed his immediate interference and assistance to pacify Ireland and that they could do no more than they had done without his support, to reestablish their authority over the lower clergy, and enforce respect for law and religion among the people.

"The Pope said," Russell continued, "that he pitied the bishops, who in their pursuit of their calling were constantly exposed to a 'Bastonata' [beating] from the Fenians, who were the Garibaldians of England." Russell reported the rest of the conversation:

> I said that a message, a single word from His Holiness to the Irish clergy in support of episcopal authority—and stringent instructions to the bishops to suspend offending priests, would give the example of respect to authority, so much needed at present in Ireland, and the clergy could always reckon on the cordial cooperation of the civil authorities whenever they were

39. Ibid.

themselves willing to accept it. I then entered into a detailed account of the state of Ireland and the policy of Her Majesty's Government, and referred His Holiness to the Irish bishops for a confirmation of all I had said.

The Pope deigned to listen, and question with interest, and showed no signs of impatience or displeasure at my repeated and urgent appeals for some practical measures to strengthen the authority of the bishops who had admitted to me that they no longer had the power to do good where Fenianism prevailed in Ireland.

Finally after a very long conversation the Pope authorised me to tell your Lordship that although he had already condemned Fenianism, he would again consult the Irish bishops and take such measures as might be deemed expedient by them in accordance with the wishes I had expressed.

I ventured to suggest the necessity of immediate action, and His Holiness replied that as he expected to receive the Irish bishops that evening, I might consider his renewed condemnation of Fenianism as an accomplished fact.

"I can in conscience," Russell finally noted, "assure your Lordship that I said all in my power and even risked arousing Pontifical impatience to bring His Holiness to promise me that he would do something towards the pacification of Ireland."

Indeed, a week later, on January 20, Cullen received a letter from the pope's vicar-general, Cardinal Patrizzi, announcing the decree of the Holy Office condemning Fenianism by name. The decree, which was dated January 12, 1870, read:

Since it has been doubted by some whether the society of the Fenians is deemed to be included amongst the societies condemned by the Pontifical Constitutions, our Most Holy Lord Pius IX, by divine Providence, Pope, having first taken the suffrages of the Most Eminent Fathers the Cardinals Inquisitors General against heretical depravity in all Christendom and in order to prevent the hearts of the faithful, especially the simple, from being perverted with evident danger to the soul, adhering moreover to the decrees at other times issued in like cases by the Sacred Congregation of the Universal Inquisition, especially the decree of Wednesday, the 5th of July 1865, has decreed and declared that the American or Irish society called the Society of the Fenians, is included amongst the societies forbidden and condemned in the Constitutions of the Sovereign Pontiffs, and especially in the very recent one published by his present Holiness on the 4th of October, 1869, beginning with the words *Apostolicae Sedis*, in which under number 4 those persons are declared to incur the excommunication *latae sententiae* reserved to the Roman Pontiff: —"Who join the rest of the Freemasons, or the Carbonari, or other sects of the same kind, which plot openly or secretly against the Church or the lawful powers, and moreover those persons who show any favour whatsoever to the same sects, or those who do not denounce the secret ringleaders and chiefs thereof, so long as they shall not have denounced them." And this answer his Holiness has commended to be given to all bishops applying.[40]

In forwarding the decree to Conroy on January 20, Cullen instructed him to show it to his vicar-general, Edward McCabe, and to inform the clergy about the condemnation, but not to publish it until he should write again.

Russell did not learn about the decree until several days later, and then he immediately wrote Clarendon. "I have seen Archbishop Manning and Bishop Moriarty," he reported on January 23, "who tell me that the Pope has authorized the condemnation of the Fenians in Ireland."[41] "Archbishop Manning," Russell explained, "said that he had read the document and that he might call it a 'dynastic measure.' He hoped Her Majesty's Government would appreciate the importance of the Pope's support of the civil authority as it would undoubtedly expose his bishops to great hostility and persecution in Ireland. In authorizing me to communicate this information to your Lordship they expressed a hope that Her Majesty's Government would refrain from mentioning their knowledge of the existence of the document referred to, until its publication in Ireland, in order not to weaken in any way the authority of the bishops over their excitable flocks." "Neither of the two prelates," Russell then informed Clarendon, "seemed to know that I had spoken to the Pope on the 13th inst. as reported to your Lordship, and attributed the measure in question to Cardinal Cullen's influence, who had called a meeting of the Irish bishops to propose this measure to the Pope—so I thought it best not to mention my conversation with His Holiness on the subject to them."

On January 23, then, Russell was obviously under the impression that the decree condemning Fenianism had been secured mainly

---

40. *Irish Ecclesiastical Record* (February 1870), 6:240.
41. F.O., 43/106.

through his own recent efforts, and given that he did not know that the decree was dated January 12, this was a natural assumption for him to make. He simply concluded that the meeting of the bishops called by Cullen had taken place after his audience with the pope on January 13, and he naturally assumed a cause-and-effect relationship between the audience and the issuance of the decree. Though he was mistaken—the bishops had met on December 30—it is curious that the pope was not more candid with Russell at their audience on January 13. Because the pope was the prefect of the congregation of the Holy Office, and probably presided at the congregation that recommended the condemnation, and because the date of the issuing of the decree, January 12, must have been also the day he gave it his authoritative approval, he could not but have known at his audience with Russell that he had already condemned Fenianism *nominatim*. The only explanation would appear to be that though the pope had approved the decision to issue the decree on January 12, he had reserved the formal promulgation of it until after his scheduled audience with the Irish bishops on the evening of January 13 because he wanted to consult them again on a matter so vitally important to the Irish Church. In allowing Russell and the British government to assume that their influence had been crucial in persuading him to condemn Fenianism, the pope could not have been unaware that he was increasing the small store of British gratitude and goodwill toward his government at a very small cost to himself.

Whatever were the reasons for the pope's timing, the real question, as far as the Irish Church was concerned, was why the bishops as a body had finally decided to ask Rome for a definitive condemnation of Fenianism. For some eight years they had been ambivalent about taking any corporate action against the Brotherhood, and in late years that ambivalence appeared to have increased rather than decreased. Why, then, in less than a month after their arrival in Rome, did they petition the Holy Office for a formal condemnation? The answer to that question is very complicated, because the action they finally did take was more the result of the hardening or the crystallizing of a conviction than the working out of a simple cause-and-effect relationship. The bishops as a body, if MacHale and Derry be excepted, had long been of one mind about the dangerous nature of Fenianism. What they had not been of one mind about was the prudence of their taking corporate, and especially public, action against the Brotherhood, given the political temper of the Irish people. The key to their thinking was that as long as they could maintain a grip on their clergy, and their clergy a grip on the people, they could in time ride out the Fenian storm. Throughout the whole of the Fenian ordeal, however, the great symbolic threat to their hold on their clergy was Father Lavelle. Because that priest was believed to represent the views of Archbishop MacHale, the question naturally raised by both the clergy and the laity in other dioceses was, Why cannot our bishop be like the patriarch of the west? In the last analysis, MacHale's license in regard to Lavelle was subversive of his episcopal colleagues' authority over their own priests, at least as far as Fenianism was concerned.

The bishops as a body had been able to live with their situation as long as Lavelle remained essentially a symbol. With the launching of the amnesty movement, however, the ground swell among the people of sympathy for Fenians, if not for Fenianism, soon included the clergy, and even some of the bishops. The clearest sign, perhaps, of the difficulty in meeting this latest Fenian tactic was Cullen's own early ambivalence about amnesty. With the eclipse of the Amnesty Committee by the Amnesty Association, and particularly with the increasing violence of the more extreme Fenian elements in the association in October and November, after Gladstone's refusal to release any more prisoners, the bishops who had been initially sympathetic must have had serious second thoughts. When Lavelle issued his challenge to the bishops as a body on November 20, just when most of them either were about to leave or had already left for Rome, this was undoubtedly the drop that filled the cup to overflowing. Still, at their first meeting in Rome on December 16, they determined only on bringing Lavelle's letter under the notice of Propaganda, and it was not until December 23 that the bishops decided, with MacHale and Derry dissenting, to ask Propaganda not only to punish Lavelle but also to issue an explicit condemnation of Fenianism.

The bishops' newfound resolve to petition Propaganda for a formal condemnation was undoubtedly the result of their having learned soon after their arrival in Rome of the recent electoral disaster in county Tipperary and Dean O'Brien's amnesty declaration. On analysis, the bishops must have realized that the victory of Rossa over Heron in Tipperary was not only a triumph for Fenianism but also an indictment of the policy of supporting the Liberal alliance. After all, on two previous occasions in Tipperary in 1865, the Fenian-endorsed candidate, Peter Gill, polled more than 900 votes. The shock of this election, therefore, was less that Rossa had polled 1,131 votes than that Heron had polled only 1,028 votes in a constituency where he should have received between 2,500 and 3,000. Heron had lost, that is, because there was such a low poll, and there was such a low poll because the clergy of Tipperary had not thrown themselves into the contest with their customary vigor and enthusiasm. The bishops certainly understood that their recently acquired political power and influence at the national level under the terms of the Liberal alliance was dependent, in the last analysis, on their ability to mobilize their clergy in the constituencies. If their clergy would not be mobilized in the interests of the alliance, then the bishops' recently acquired political efficacy at the national level was threatened, and so were the expected land and educational reforms that were to be the fruit of that alliance.

What was perhaps even worse from the bishops' point of view was that the Tipperary clergy had obviously been as much intimidated by the violence of the Fenian mobs in this election as had the voters, and the Fenians were not simply jeopardizing the Liberal alliance on which the bishops had pinned their constitutional hopes but were also, through their violence and their tactics of radical confrontation, attempting to subvert the constitutional system itself by demoralizing and intimidating those who participated in it.[42] Previous to their involvement in the amnesty movement, the Fenians would have nothing to do with constitutional politics, maintaining that such politics were irrelevant to the immediate task at hand, the establishment of an Irish Republic by force of arms. Now, it appeared, the Fenians were prepared to use any means, including the subversion of the constitutional system, to achieve their ends. From the episcopal point of view, therefore, the Fenians had now gone too far. They would have to play the game of constitutional politics, and play it by the rules, or they would have to remain politically outside the pale, and a formal condemnation would make the issue perfectly clear. The bishops' resolve, moreover, could only have been strengthened by the arrival of the news of Dean O'Brien's amnesty declaration, and more especially the news of their clergy's reaction to it. When they learned that some six hundred of their clergy had signed the dean's declaration in the first week, they must have realized that such unauthorized symbolic gestures by the clergy had to be checked quickly and authoritatively if clerical discipline was not to be further eroded. Not only, therefore, would a Roman decree strengthen the hands of the bishops vis-à-vis their clergy on the subject of Fenianism, but it would effectively check any similar effusions in the future.

For all these reasons, then—the preservation of their political power and influence, the need to maintain their control over their clergy, the

---

42. James O'Shea, *Priest, Politics, and Society in Post-Famine Ireland: A Study of County Tipperary, 1851–1891* (Dublin, 1983), pp. 163–64.

obligations of the Liberal alliance, the realization of their legislative hopes and expectations, and their genuine commitment to the system of constitutional politics—the bishops finally decided to ask Rome to condemn Fenianism when they did. In the process of making up their minds, the bishops also made a very significant contribution to the consolidation of their own body. Their ordeal with Fenianism resulted, in fact, both in an increase in their corporate consciousness and in the better definition of their relationship as a body with Cullen. Part of the reason for both of these developments was that Rome provided the bishops with an atmosphere much more conducive to serious discussion and mature reflection than did Ireland. This was the first time since the Synod of Thurles in 1850 that the bishops had spent any considerable amount of time together as a body. Their general meetings in Dublin and Maynooth over the previous nineteen years had seldom lasted more than three or four days, and because of the considerable amount of work to be got through, they were always hurried and busy, with little opportunity for informal discussion or the exchange of ideas. In Rome, during the month of December, on the other hand, the bishops had at least three formal meetings over as many weeks (December 16, 23, and 30), as well as a considerable number of informal meetings. The main topic in nearly all of these meetings, formal and informal, was Fenianism, and there was, therefore, nothing hurried and rushed about the decision finally reached.

In Rome, moreover, the bishops not only had more control over their agenda but also had the added advantage of being able to deal with the authorities directly, without having to depend on Cullen as their intermediary. Indeed, it was the opportunity of the bishops as a body to consult with Barnabò that apparently allowed them to resolve the crisis that had arisen between Cullen and the body at their meeting on December 23. At that meeting, it will be recalled, after all the bishops had spoken, Cullen had maintained that he would have nothing to do with their petition to Propaganda on Fenianism. He would appeal instead directly to the pope. Because he had been the only Irish bishop, except for Moriarty, to condemn the Fenians *nominatim*, so that Lavelle's letter was an explicit censure of his formal teaching as a bishop, Cullen argued, quite rightly, that the pope was his only judge in such a matter. The bishops then deputed four of their number to bring the petition of their body before Propaganda, while Cullen began to prepare his own memorial to the pope. When the episcopal deputation consulted Barnabò, he apparently resolved the crisis by advising them to submit their petition to the Holy Office instead of Propaganda. The bishops would find in that congregation the proper tribunal for their petition, and Cullen would also be able to subscribe to their petition because the prefect of the Holy Office was the pope; thus the question of submitting Cullen's formal teaching as a bishop to a lesser authority would no longer signify. That is why MacHale and Derry did not attend the formal meeting on December 30, at which the bishops decided, with Cullen concurring, to submit their petition to the Holy Office. By attending, MacHale and Derry could not have avoided, if they had persisted in their views, an act of disrespect to the pope by refusing to agree to submit the matter to his pontifical authority. The petition submitted to the Holy Office and signed by eighteen of the twenty bishops then in Rome, therefore, was an authoritative, if not unanimous, act of the Irish bishops as a body.[43]

Once Fenianism had been finally and formally condemned by Rome, the real question for the Irish bishops was how that decision would be received in Ireland. If the reaction of the American bishops in Rome was a portent of the future, the Irish bishops had very good cause to be apprehensive. The Americans were very upset because the decision, which certainly concerned them as much as the Irish, had apparently been made without consulting them. "The American bishops (at least some of them)," Cullen informed Conroy on January 28, "are displeased with the Irish bishops for getting the Holy Office to act in this case" (C). "Dr. Spalding," he reported, naming the archbishop of Baltimore, "says we have done great mischief. I told him ... what was sport in America was death to us and to religion in Ireland. He admits that the Fenians even in America are very bad, but he thinks a condemnation will make them worse." "I told him," Cullen further explained, "about the infidelity and blasphemies of the *Irish Republic* [a Fenian weekly published in New York]; he never saw it or heard of it before. Dr. Woods of Philadelphia fully agrees with us. He says he condemned the Fenians publicly and always refused them absolution. Hence he had very little trouble with them. I will get some of those bishops to read the *Republic* and to see the sort of food that the Fenians are submitting to their flocks for the last four years."

Earlier in this letter, however, Cullen indicated that he was somewhat apprehensive about how the decree would be received in Ireland. "It was fortunate," he assured Conroy, "we got the rescript from the

43. L; see draft of petition in Latin, dated December 29, 1869, and signed by eighteen bishops.

Holy Office. It will keep priests from promoting the interests of the sect at least publicly. It will be hard to know what Lavelle *ejusque asseclae* [and his followers] may do privately." Several days later Cullen wrote Conroy again in the same vein. "I hope the rescript about Fenianism," he noted on February 2, "will silence Father Lavelle and company. I daresay if the priests were united and active, Fenianism would soon die out" (C). The Irish bishops, though prepared to do their duty, were no less apprehensive about the effects of the decree in Ireland than was Cullen. "The American bishops," Odo Russell informed Clarendon on February 20, "are angry at the Decree because they prefer the Fenian to the Britisher—but the Irish bishops generally with the exception of MacHale, are well disposed and ready to write vigorous pastorals as you will see, and the more so as their Vicars-General will have to bear the brunt of the condemnation in Ireland, while they are safe in Rome—for all expect and dread the vengeance of the Fenians."[44] Cullen and most of the Irish bishops apparently decided that the best way of promulgating the decree officially in Ireland was to have it published in the February issue of the *Irish Ecclesiastical Record* and then to proceed individually in their Lenten pastorals, to give to their flocks whatever explanations they thought necessary.

Because his council duties as a cardinal imposed a very heavy load of ceremony and work, Cullen was unable to finish his Lenten pastoral until the end of February. Finally, on February 28, he sent it to Conroy, instructing him to have five hundred copies printed immediately and distributed to all of the Dublin clergy, secular and regular. He also requested Conroy to have several copies of the printed pastoral sent to him as soon as possible and to see that the portions of the pastoral touching on Fenianism and the council were inserted in the newspapers. In touching in the pastoral upon the formal Roman condemnation of Fenianism, Cullen cleverly attempted to soften its impact by pointing out that the "Holy See has of late renewed its condemnation of this Society, and declared that the Fenians and their abettors, incur all the censures which have been fulminated against the followers of Mazzini, the Freemasons, and others who conspire secretly or publicly against the Church of God or against civil society."[45] Cullen then went on to denounce once again the wicked machinations of the Fenians, and most especially the wickedness of their press. When the pastoral was finally read in all the Dublin churches on Sunday, March 13, there were disturbances in both of Cullen's mensal parishes—in the procathedral in Marlborough Street

44. Norman, p. 132.
45. Moran, 3:285.

and at St. Andrews, Westland-Row—as some of the congregations left the church in protest.

By the middle of March 1870, in fact, Ireland was in a rare state of political ferment. First of all, the more extreme constitutional Nationalists and their Fenian allies began to contest by-elections wherever they could seriously embarrass a Liberal candidate. Secondly, there were a series of agrarian outrages and murders in Westmeath and Mayo that caused the government serious difficulties in Parliament because of its apparent inability to protect life and property in Ireland. Finally, the reception accorded Gladstone's long-awaited land bill in Ireland was very disappointing. The cumulative effect was to dampen the enthusiasm of the supporters of the Liberal alliance on both sides of the Irish Sea. The return of O'Donovan Rossa for Tipperary in November had so encouraged the more independent Nationalists that when another by-election occurred in county Longford a month later, they decided to enter another candidate. Their choice was John Martin, the former Young Irelander and late Repealer, who was then visiting the United States. The clergy and Liberal electors of Longford, meanwhile, had selected a younger son of Lord Greville, R. S. M. Greville-Nugent, as their candidate. The contest was a very violent and stormy one, and the clergy were very active in canvassing and electioneering for their candidate. They were also very successful in their efforts, for on election day, December 31, Greville-Nugent received 1,538 votes and Martin only 411.[46] The clergy, however, apparently overplayed their hand, for Greville-Nugent was eventually unseated on a petition, and a new election writ issued, because the clergy were adjudged guilty of corrupt practices in the form of "systematic treating with intoxicating drink."[47]

In the meantime, in Rome, Cullen was heartened by the news of the magnitude of the Longford victory as well as the unopposed return several days later, on January 4, of the Liberal candidate, Edward Dease, at a by-election in Queen's county.[48] He was also apprehensive, however, that a Fenian might be returned at the approaching by-election for the borough of Mallow, and he was undoubtedly much relieved when an orthodox Liberal won there on February 3 in a straight fight with a Conservative.[49] After a very short respite, two more by-elections took place in quick succession in Waterford and Tipperary at the end of February. In Waterford city, the sitting member, Sir Henry

46. Brian M. Walker, ed., *Parliamentary Election Results in Ireland, 1801–1922* (Dublin, 1978), p. 113.
47. Corish, p. 45. See also *Freeman's Journal*, March 30 and 31 and April 1, 1870.
48. C, Cullen to Conroy, January 7 and 12, 1870.
49. Walker, p. 113.

Winston Barron, had been unseated on petition by the candidate, Ralph Bernal Osborne, whom he had just defeated in a by-election. Barron was disqualified from contesting the seat again, and the local independent Nationalists seized on the opportunity and nominated another Young Irelander, P. J. Smyth, to oppose Osborne, who was running as a Liberal. In a very hard fought and close contest, Osborne defeated Smyth on February 25, 483 votes to 475.[50] In county Tipperary the contest proved to be even closer and fiercer. After Rossa had been elected the previous November, he had been disqualified from taking his seat because he was a convicted felon, and a new writ was accordingly issued. The Nationalists then proceeded to nominate Charles Kickham, who had also been tried and convicted as a Fenian in 1865 and who was serving a sentence of twenty years' penal servitude. He was opposed by Denis Caulfield Heron, the Catholic barrister who had run as a Liberal against Rossa. On election day, February 28, Heron won by only four votes, polling 1,668 to Kickham's 1,664.[51] Though Liberal candidates had won in Waterford and Tipperary, the contests were, in effect, moral victories for those opposed to the Liberal alliance.

Meanwhile, Conroy had been writing Cullen regularly to keep him informed about the situation in Ireland. By early March Cullen was obviously very uneasy about the recent developments. "I was sorry to hear," he explained to Conroy on March 6, "that the country was so disturbed in many places and that so much violence had been displayed in Tipperary and Waterford. It is hard to see how things will terminate" (C). What must have made Cullen even more apprehensive than the increasing political and agrarian violence in Ireland was the developing reaction both in Ireland and in Rome to the measure that had been expected to do most to allay that violence—Gladstone's land bill. The great difficulty facing Gladstone was that Irish views on what was a proper solution to the land question had radically changed since the days when the National Association had advocated compensation for improvements if a tenant was evicted from his holding. In late 1869 the recently formed Irish Tenant League had declared for fixity of tenure and a fair rent. In January Sir John Gray, M.P. for Kilkenny city and proprietor of the influential *Freeman's Journal*, in company with a number of other prominent politicians, had issued a requisition for a land conference to meet in Dublin in early February. The conference, which met on February 2 and 3, proved to be a very repre-

50. Ibid.
51. Ibid.

sentative one, and it was unequivocal in endorsing the principles advocated by the league and its president, Isaac Butt. "They were," Butt declared at the conference, "done with compensation for improvements—they were done with the sale of right of occupancy—they were done with everything that could leave a loop-hole for escape, and fixity of tenure, with fair rents was now the rallying-cry of Ireland."[52] Resolutions were passed at the conference demanding continual right of occupancy, subject only to eviction for nonpayment of rent or subletting without the consent of the landlord, and the valuation of rents by a local land tribunal.

In Rome, meanwhile, the Irish bishops were also very much concerned about the kind of land measure Gladstone was about to frame for Ireland. As Odo Russell reported to Clarendon on January 24, the Irish bishops wished Gladstone to know that "fixity of tenure" was the greatest blow Parliament could strike at Fenianism.[53] He also reported that he was now getting on better with the Irish bishops, and though Cullen was not very accessible, Manning was. Indeed, on February 5 Manning reported to Gladstone that he had just received a visit from three of the Irish bishops, who had come to represent the views of the body on the land question and who had asked him to convey those views in the strictest confidence.[54] They were concerned that some of the points they considered vital to a satisfactory solution to the land question might not find a place in the bill. They were particularly worried about capricious evictions, and they suggested local tribunals, which could decide if the landlord had good cause. They also suggested some form of arbitration machinery to guard against excessive rents. Finally they urged that the Ulster custom—compensation for improvements and "goodwill"—be included in the proposed land bill. On all these points, Manning assured Gladstone, the bishops were very decided and unanimous. "They urged also," Manning concluded, "that they have so openly staked their influence over their people in the confidence of a satisfactory Land Bill, that if in this they seemed to have failed, their power for good will be gone." The most interesting aspect of the recommendations of the Irish bishops was how much in concert they independently were with the resolutions of the recent land conference in Dublin.

In introducing his bill in the House of Commons on February 15, however, Gladstone virtually ignored the recommendations of both

52. Thornley, p. 75.
53. Norman, p. 395.
54. Gl, 44429.

the land conference and the bishops.[55] In his introductory remarks he specifically rejected the principle of "fixity of tenure" as "virtual expropriation." The effect of such a provision, he further argued, would be that the landlord would become "a pensioner and rentcharger on what is his own estate." The principle of fixity of tenure was obviously in Gladstone's mind subversive of the idea of private property. Instead, he proposed to protect the tenant from capricious eviction by making the Ulster custom law where it already prevailed and, where the custom did not exist, establishing a sliding scale of compensation for disturbance based on the rental of the holding. In this way he hoped to make the eviction process so costly that the landlord would be deterred from using it. The bill was vitiated by its legal complexity, however, and especially by a clause that specifically excluded tenants evicted for nonpayment of rent from receiving compensation for disturbances. A landlord desirous of evicting a tenant without compensating him for improvements, therefore, had merely to raise the rent to the necessary level, and because the great majority of Irish tenants were tenants at will and did not have leases, they were particularly vulnerable to such a procedure.

The general reaction in Ireland to the bill was mixed at first, but when the *Freeman's Journal* declared on February 20, after some initial hesitation, that the bill as it stood was hopeless, the tide began to turn against the measure in the country. Over the next several weeks the *Freeman* continued to argue with great effect that only fixity of tenure with a periodic valuation of rents could meet the needs of the Irish tenant farmers. In Rome, meanwhile, the initial and informal reaction of the Irish bishops to the bill was favorable. "Today," Manning informed Gladstone on February 24, "I have seen Cardinal Cullen & many of the Irish Bishops. They were unanimous, & they spoke also in the name of their absent colleagues, in commendation of the Land Bill."[56] "The Cardinal said," Manning further reassured Gladstone, "that he had written to Ireland to give it all support. The other Bishops spoke most warmly of it; which was not affected by one or two expressions of doubt whether in the scale for computing compensations the outgoing tenant is sufficiently protected. They also spoke most warmly & gratefully of you; and said that they prayed for you, as the truest friend & benefactor of Ireland." "The Archbishop of Tuam," Manning explained, "was not there but I inquired especially as to his opinion, & I was assured that he speaks very favourably of the Bill."

55. *Hansard*, 199:333–87.
56. Gl, 44429.

The following day, February 25, Cullen wrote William Monsell, M.P. for county Limerick and a staunch supporter of Gladstone and the Liberal alliance, asking him to inform Gladstone of both his and the Irish bishops' approval of the bill.[57] Manning had also obviously conveyed the good news to Odo Russell, for he reassuringly telegraphed Clarendon on February 27, "All Irish Bishops are very favourable to your Irish Land Bill."[58]

Cullen and Manning, however, had been more optimistic about the Irish bishops' approval of the land bill than was warranted. When they met formally on February 28 to consider it, they drew up a memorandum entitled "Amendments Required in the Proposed Land Bill of 1870," which included six major and four minor revisions that would render the bill unobjectionable from their point of view. The "Amendments" read:

1. Let the Act recognise & legalise, not for Ulster only but for all Ireland, the Right of all Agricultural Tenants to continue in occupation of their holdings and freely to improve them for their own profit, unless there be just cause shown in Land Court for their Eviction or for the prevention of certain improvements.

2. Let the Tenant if he considers his rent too high, be free to submit it for adjustment to the Land Court.

3. Let all Agricultural Tenants, on parting with their Holdings voluntarily or otherwise have the Right to dispose freely of their Goodwill & Improvements, the Landlord to have in each case a prior right to purchase, and the solvency of the incoming Tenant to be, on demand of Landlord, submitted to the Decision of the Land Court.

4. Let no lease for a Term less than 60 y^{rs}, and in case of Waste Lands 90 y^{rs} be deemed full Compensation for Goodwill; and in the Landlord as well as Public Interest, let no terminable Lease deprive the Tenant of his Improvements.

5. Let the Penal Clauses regarding the Subdivision of Holdings, be so modified as to allow Tenants, to subdivide, with permission of the L Court, in favor of their own Children.

6. As many Provisions of the Bill, purporting to favor the small agricultural Tenant may naturally lead to the maintenance & even extension of large Grass Farms, some means sh^{d} be provided in this & other Bills to Counteract such an evil ten-

57. Gl, 44425, Gladstone to Cullen, March 6, 1870. See also MacSuibhne, 5:73–74.
58. F.O., 43/106.

dency. The following are suggested: Let an Agricultural holding under this Act, mean only the Farm of which 1/5th at
least of the arable land will be kept under tillage—As the extension of Pasturage diminishes employment and thereby increases pauperism, let Grass Farms be subjected, thro' Union
Rating, to a heavy proportion of the Poor Rates—Let the Rent
of Grass Farms be recoverable only as a Common debt, by
Civil Bill, &c. &c.

The following Provisions, tho less important, are most desirable.

1. Let Landlords, who will not reclaim, be obliged to sell their
   Waste Lands.
2. Let the Church Lands be disposed of by Gov^mt *in a liberal
   spirit* in favor of the occupying Tenants.
3. Let no Agricultural Tenant be subject to more than one half of
   the County cess and let the Taxing & Fiscal Powers of Grand
   Juries be transferred to an Elected Body, duly representing the
   Tenant Class.
4. Let Loans be given liberally, especially to [the] Middle Class of
   Tenants; and let claims for Loans be settled by the local Land
   Court. The Board of Works sh^d be thoroughly reformed—so as
   to merit the Confidence of the Tenant Class.[59]

The Irish bishops then asked Manning to be their medium in breaking to Gladstone the news of their apparent change of heart; he did so
in a letter of March 1, enclosing the text of their memorandum.[60]
"The enclosed paper," Manning explained, obviously somewhat un-
comfortable, "was drawn up by the Irish Bishops, and brought to me
by two of them with a request that I would forward it to you. They
prefer for reasons of their own to communicate through a channel that
cannot be regarded as official: & they desire me to say that though
they feel strongly & unanimously on the subjects mentioned in their
note, they regard your measure as a great boon to Ireland, and the
beginning of a new & happier state. They say that as the measure now
stands they fear that it cannot be regarded as a settlement of the question: & that in the points they have noted both dissatisfaction & litigation may arise." "They fear in chief," he further reported, "that no
money checks will restrain evictions as the incoming tenant will re-
pay the Landlord: and that no sufficient security is provided against

59. Gl, 442–49.
60. Ibid.

exorbitant raising of the rent which is equivalent to eviction." "But I do not attempt," Manning noted in concluding his hapless assignment, "to enter into a matter of which I am only the channel. I cannot conclude without repeating the very strong expressions of the Irish Bishops towards yourself."

Cullen, who was obviously much more favorably disposed to the land bill than his episcopal colleagues, had also begun to trim on this issue. On February 28, it will be recalled, he had forwarded to Conroy his Lenten pastoral for distribution and reading in all the churches of Dublin. "After sending away the pastoral today," Cullen explained to Conroy later that same day, apparently shortly after the bishops had met, "it occurred to me that the few words about the land bill of Gladstone might be considered too laudatory. If so you can mitigate them by adding something to the effect 'that the difficulties of the measures are great and the defects of the bill may be gradually corrected'" (C). "It is well however," he added, "to give praise to Gladstone for his good intentions in the land question and more so than for the Church Act. Change and correct anything you like in the pastoral." By the time Conroy had received this cautionary note (probably on Monday, March 7), Irish public opinion had become so critical of the land bill that he decided not merely to mitigate Cullen's laudatory remarks but to eliminate them altogether. After referring briefly to the great benefit to Ireland of the Church Act of the previous year, Conroy revised the pastoral to read simply: "At present the great Statesmen who conferred so signal a benefit on this kingdom, and who still guide the helm of State, have manifested their resolve to remove other grievances and to heal other wounds of Ireland."[61]

The conduct of Cullen and the Irish bishops in regard to the land bill is certainly on the face of it both curious and perplexing. The great difficulty is that there are no firsthand accounts of the two formal meetings of the bishops during February in regard to the bill, and the evidence that does exist about their views, formal and informal, has been refracted through the medium of Manning's correspondence with Gladstone. In effect, Manning reported three stages in the opinions of the bishops, and it is difficult not to lay the charge of inconsistency against the bishops. At their first meeting in early February, it will be recalled, they took a very high line in declaring for greater security of tenure, fair rent, and the legalizing of the Ulster custom for all Ireland. When Manning then met many of the bishops on February 24, shortly after the text of the bill had arrived in Rome, he reported to Gladstone

61. Moran, 3:285–86.

that the Irish bishops, both those present and those absent, unanimously approved of the bill, and that their approval was not affected by one or two misgivings about whether the outgoing tenant was properly protected. When the bishops met formally four days later, on February 28, and drew up their proposed "Amendments," they reverted, in effect, to the very high line they had advised Gladstone to take earlier in the month.

The obvious question is, of course, Why did the bishops apparently change their minds between February 24 and February 28? In the first place, when the bishops spoke to Manning on February 24, they had not had very much time to examine the text of the bill, as it had only just arrived in Rome, and they were undoubtedly very much impressed initially with Gladstone's introduction of the bill in the House of Commons, which was a most persuasive rhetorical performance. In his introduction Gladstone had attempted to meet the bishops' greatest concern, insecurity of tenure, not with a measure for fixity of tenure, which he considered to be subversive of the rights of property, but with an elaborate machinery for compensation for disturbances, which he argued would make capricious evictions more difficult by making them uneconomic for the landlord. In the second place, many of the bishops did not apparently realize when initially considering the bill that all of Gladstone's elaborate safeguards against capricious evictions were undermined by the clause that allowed the landlord to evict for nonpayment of rent, which rent an unscrupulous landlord could raise to an intolerable level to effect his purpose. In the third place, and most important of all, when all the various criticisms of the bill began to arrive in Rome from Ireland, especially the condemnation of the bill on February 20 by the *Freeman's Journal*, the bishops' initial optimism and unanimity about the bill gradually evaporated.

The problem of the bishops at their February 28 meeting, given the great dissatisfaction most of them felt by then with the land bill, was how to break the news to Gladstone without jeopardizing the Liberal alliance, while at the same time retaining their credibility with their people. The most embarrassed bishop at the meeting was undoubtedly Cullen, who not only had assured Manning that he approved of the bill but also had written to Ireland in support of it, and who now found himself in a small minority in the body. In order to solve their dilemma, the bishops decided to forward their proposed "Amendments" unofficially and privately to Gladstone through Manning, while at the same time allowing each individual bishop, if he so chose, to write the members of Parliament within his spiritual jurisdiction to explain his views on the bill. In this way, those bishops who, like Cullen, were more hopeful could still support the bill privately, while those who were more doubtful, or even negative, could also discharge their conscientious duty by informing their representatives of their views. Indeed, about a week after the bishops had met, their dissatisfaction with the land bill was given full vent in a letter from Thomas Furlong, the bishop of Ferns, to M. P. D'Arcy, the member for county Wexford. "Most of the Irish bishops now assembled in Rome," Furlong reported on March 7, "have conferred together on Mr. Gladstone's Land Bill and being fully impressed with the belief that its provisions are totally inadequate to the attainment of the objects contemplated by it, deem it advisable to intimate their views on the subject to the members of Parliament from their respective districts merely as suggestions, but not with the intention of interfering with any course of action with regard to the Bill which they may deem more prudent and more effective."[62]

Furlong then proceeded to outline, in effect, the "Amendments" proposed by the bishops in their memorandum to Gladstone. "These are some of the improvements," he explained, "the Bishops would wish to see introduced into Mr. Gladstone's Land Bill." "Of course," he added revealingly, "the difficulty of recasting the Bill in that form is such as to render the task well nigh hopeless, yet the Bishops deemed it desirable to intimate to the Irish Members their own sentiments, that they might carry them out as far as it might be found practicable, if according with their own views." Furlong concluded, most imprudently, "As I am at the present moment very busily engaged, I regret that it is not in my power to communicate directly with all the members of Co. Wexford, but I take the liberty of asking you to present it to each of them for perusal and to bespeak their kind consideration in regarding it as addressed to himself." It would be very interesting to know whether Furlong marked the original of this letter "private."

The depth of the bishops' dissatisfaction with the land bill as it stood was given even greater emphasis several days later in a letter from Laurence Gillooly, the bishop of Elphin, to John George MacCarthy, the member for the borough of Mallow in county Cork. In thanking MacCarthy on March 11 for sending him a copy of his recent book on the Irish land question, Gillooly noted that the "remedies it proposes for the present vicious and impolitic system of land tenure in Ireland are just, practical, and moderate."[63] "I regret deeply, in common with my Irish friends here," he added, discreetly alluding to his

62. *Irish Times*, March 28, 1870.
63. *Freeman's Journal*, March 25, 1870.

episcopal colleagues, "and, I may add, with all who are sincerely interested in the peace and prosperity of our dear country, that such remedies have not been made the basis of the new Land Bill." He went on:

> The draft bill introduced into Parliament by Mr. Gladstone, though containing many provisions intended to improve the position of the tenant farmer, leaves almost untouched the source of all the tenant's grievances, his absolute dependence as regards the occupation and rent of his holding on the will of the landlord. Now, so long as this unjust degrading dependence continues established by law, the law will be neither respected nor cordially obeyed; its enforcement will be an intolerable unceasing violence; contentment, peace, prosperity, the union of classes, will be a sheer impossibility. The new land law, to be a message of peace and justice, and to become the basis of public order and prosperity, must be such as to make the tenant class feel that their natural right to occupy, improve, and enjoy the soil of their country is legally recognised and secured, that they are no longer slaves or aliens on the land of their birth, and that a new era of just and enlightened statesmanship, in which the sole object of every law for Ireland shall be the general good of the Irish people, without distinction of class or creed, has been opened at the call and with the sanction of the whole empire. It is, I am fully convinced, the interest of landlords, quite as much as of tenants, that a land bill, with provisions such as I allude to, and such as you have so ably advocated in your book, should be adopted by Parliament. No half measure will save either the landlord interest or public order, and if the landlord class be not blind or insensible to their social duty as well as to their private interest, they will unite with the representatives of the tenants of Ireland in demanding the amendment of Mr. Gladstone's bill so as to make it a just and final settlement, not for Ulster only, but for all Ireland, of the relations between landlord and tenant.

"A bill," Gillooly concluded, "just in principle, simple in machinery, adapted alike to the political and social wants of the country, and harmonising with the spirit of our people, is what was expected from Gladstone and Bright. Let us hope that the present bill will come out of committee in a form that will realise those expectations, and enable us to forget *our disappointment.*"

Gladstone, meanwhile, had been growing more and more upset about the deteriorating agrarian and political situations in Ireland, and especially about the reception of his land bill both in Ireland and among a considerable number of influential Irish members of Parliament, led by Sir John Gray. On Sunday, March 6, therefore, the day before the bill was to receive its second reading in the House of Commons, and apparently before he received Manning's letter of March 1 enclosing the Irish bishops' memorandum, Gladstone wrote Cullen a long letter, in his best circumlocutionary style, complaining about the reception of his bill in Ireland and predicting the ruin of the Liberal alliance if the Irish bishops did not publicly, and soon, throw their weight into the political balance in Ireland. After explaining that he had been pleased to learn from Monsell and a number of other sources that Cullen and the Irish bishops took a favorable view of the bill, Gladstone assured Cullen that public opinion in Britain was also favorable to it. "The only serious danger," he warned, "is in Ireland itself. A perverse and vengeful spirit seems to meet every pacific and just indication on the part of Parliament by a multiplication of outrages, and an extension of terrorism, which create on this side of the channel not apprehension but disgust."[64] "The action of this vengeful spirit," he explained,

is at present twofold. Having for its object perpetual war between England and Ireland, it works in the disguise of agrarian crime, and likewise under the mask of demands for changes in the Land Bill, which it knows to be impossible.

It seeks to triumph by the double means of convincing Great Britain that reasonable legislation will not be accepted and of alarming it into the destruction or suspension of constitutional freedom.

The language which I now hold to your Eminence, the government have as yet studiously avoided in public. But the crisis is a solemn one, and it is becoming more solemn every day. By the Bill we offer to the cultivators of the soil in Ireland legal shelter, legal privilege and immunity, such as has never been dreamed of for his brother cultivators in England and Scotland. And this under the circumstances is right. But if the demands now talked of for alteration in the Bill shall be passed, they will require for the profit of the half million who now occupy land in Ireland, a social revolution throughout the three countries.

"To say," Gladstone warned again, "that we will be no parties to such a change is saying little. The existence of this or that government, with reference to so profound a question, is no more than dust

64. Gl, 44425, quoted in MacSuibhne, 5:73–74.

in the balance. But let us rise for a moment to the higher considerations, national and moral, which the case involves."

> Ireland has been strong in her controversy with Great Britain,
> because she has had justice on her side, and at her back the de-
> liberate judgement of the civilised and Christian world. I need
> not say what she would have been, but for those indestructible
> and invincible elements of power. We are reduced, so to speak,
> to deprive her of them, by doing justice. I am afraid the day may
> be at hand, unless salutary influences intervene, when a portion
> of the Irish people actively, and a large portion passively, may
> be deluded into a continuance of the contest, without the aid
> of these old and indispensable allies, nay when justice and man-
> kind have changed sides in the controversy, conformably to the
> change in the balance of right and wrong.

"I assure you," he maintained in conclusion, "that we are not very
distant from the point when the unanimous people of this island will
be driven to abandon in despair the work of conciliation, and will
fearlessly challenge the verdict of all nations as to the good faith and
sincerity of efforts, the failure of which may usher in a period resem-
bling the years gone by in the exercise of force, though differing from
them as to the right and the necessity which put it into use."

What Gladstone was really telling Cullen, of course, was that
though he appreciated the Irish bishops' private endorsement of his
land bill, and, in effect, of the Liberal alliance, the political situation
in Ireland had now so deteriorated that unless there was some interference by the "salutary influences" still operative there, the Liberal alliance would soon be in great danger in England. By "salutary influences," Gladstone meant the Irish bishops, and what he wanted was a
public endorsement of his bill by them as it went into the critical
amendment stage in the House of Commons. His reaction when he
received their proposed amendments to his bill through Manning may
be easily imagined. The bishops had, in effect, recommended those
measures that Gladstone had assured Cullen were "impossible" because they would require a "social revolution" in Britain and Ireland,
to which his government could not be a party. Gladstone must have
immediately realized that he could expect no more than a muted endorsement of his land bill by the bishops, and that he was also virtually on his own as far as the restoration of law and order in Ireland was
concerned. On March 17, therefore, shortly after the land bill was
approved on its second reading by a vote of 431 to 11 and then committed to the amendment stage, Gladstone introduced a peace preser-

vation bill for Ireland. As far as Irish coercion bills went in the nineteenth century, this was not a stringent one, though it did contain some strong and unusual measures for the control of the press. The bill became law on April 4, meeting opposition from only some dozen Irish members in its passage. Cullen and most of the Irish bishops were enthusiastic about the new Peace Preservation Act because they viewed the government's action as complementary to their own recent condemnation of Fenianism. Cullen had long been critical of what he regarded as the government's culpability with regard to the Fenian and seditious press in Ireland. In late months, however, his concern had become almost an obsession. In asking Conroy, on December 30, for example, to give the lord chancellor, Thomas O'Hagan, his best respects and to wish him many happy new years, Cullen also took occasion to read O'Hagan a small homily on the license of the press in Ireland. "Tell him," Cullen instructed Conroy, "that as long as the government authorises a set of worthless writers to publish the worst doctrines and opinions, and to glorify treason every day, they have no right to ask either priests or people to be correct in their language or their views. All classes will speak and think in accordance with what they read every day coming from the pens of self-constituted public instructors" (C). "If poison is to be sold freely to everyone," Cullen added, drawing his moral, "we cannot wonder if some be injured by it."

When Cullen received Gladstone's long letter of March 6 complaining about the deteriorating situation in Ireland, and attributing it to the political perverseness of those who were trying to prevent justice being done to Ireland by wrecking his land bill, he took occasion to read the prime minister, not a simple homily as in the case of the lord chancellor, but a complete sermon on the consequences of allowing too much civil and personal freedom in Ireland. After assuring Gladstone on March 12, in a letter marked "Private," that he and "several other Prelates" in Rome not only approved of his land bill but thought that any defects in it might be easily remedied, Cullen explained that he thought the fault lay less with those who opposed his bill than with the system they lived under.[65] "But without entering into the merits of the question," Cullen pointed out,

> I beg to assure you that I sincerely regret that your attempt to benefit Ireland has met with so determined an opposition. However in my opinion the blame is not to be thrown on the people

65. Ibid.

CONSOLIDATION

but to be attributed to external causes which perhaps the government might remove. The first cause is the presence in Ireland of a great number of adventurers from America, who have plenty of money at their disposal and who seem to have nothing in view but to disturb the minds of poor simple people, and to prepare them for resistance to authority. I cannot understand why Parliament should not adopt means to drive that dangerous class of adventurers from the country. When the Habeas Corpus Act was suspended some years ago, many if not all of them left the country or found it necessary to be quiet. The second cause is the publication of several Fenian and seditious papers in Dublin. Very probably some of these papers are supported by American money. Anyhow, they are widely circulated at a very low price, and they preach up treason and sedition from one end of the year to the other. The poison is brought home to our unsuspecting people, and it would be strange if the evils produced were not widely spread. I must add that I believe the papers of a most revolutionary character printed in America are also circulated in Ireland. One of them called the *Irish Republic* is regularly sent to my house in Dublin by some unknown agency, and I must say that it is as hostile to religion as it is to the English government. The evils produced by this low sort of revolutionary literature on our people not well instructed and not accustomed to such dangerous reading are very great, and I cannot see why the Parliament or government in the interest of peace and morality would not take measures to save her majesty's subjects from them. Such publications may not do much harm in England, but as they pretend to promote patriotism in Ireland and to supply a panacea for all the evils of the country, the mischief they cause on our side of the channel is incalculable. Indeed in my opinion nothing good can be effected for Ireland until something shall have been done to prevent the ravages of an infidel and revolutionary press, subsidised and maintained to a great extent by foreign gold.

"I must now beg pardon," Cullen finally assured Gladstone again, "for troubling you with these observations, and I shall conclude by saying that whether your land bill will become law or not, Ireland is bound to be eternally grateful to you for the glorious efforts you have made to remove the effects of past grievances and to put her on a footing of equality with other parts of the empire."

Gladstone probably received this letter of March 12 on March 17, the day he introduced his peace preservation bill in the House of Commons, and though he must have been reassured by Cullen's recommending a much more severe coercion measure than any he contemplated, he could not have been pleased by anything else in the letter. What Cullen was telling him was that though he approved of his land bill, and esteemed him personally for all that he had done and intended to do for Ireland, Gladstone could expect little more than the passive goodwill of the bishops as a body toward his land bill. By marking his letter "Private," moreover, and pointing out that "several other Irish Prelates" agreed with him, Cullen was politely informing Gladstone that he was speaking for himself and only a few of his colleagues, not for the episcopal body. Cullen and a number of his colleagues had undoubtedly been willing to go much further than the bishops as a body in endorsing Gladstone's bill, but he and they were now obviously constrained, as Manning had explained to Gladstone on March 1, by the fact that the bishops as a body were "strongly and unanimously" in favor of their proposed amendments to the bill. What is obvious from Manning's and Cullen's letters to Gladstone is that the bishops had seized the initiative with regard to the land bill, and in spite of their equivocation about it, they retained that initiative throughout. Even more significant perhaps is that in the whole affair of the land bill, Cullen hewed to the line laid down by the body and loyally deferred to a policy that certainly did not have his wholehearted approval. In successfully containing Cullen, therefore—in policy on the land bill, in procedure in the condemnation of Fenianism, and in episcopal appointments (by blocking his choice for Armagh)—the Irish bishops took their final step in Rome in effecting the institutionalization of their body.

In the meantime, the news received in Rome from Ireland continued to be alarming. "Yours of the 11th," Cullen reported to Conroy on March 16, "reached me yesterday. I am much obliged for all the news, though a great deal of it about the state of the country is very bad. There is, however, some hope that things may improve, as I hear that Mr. Gladstone is about to restrain the newspapers, but it may be that he will prevent the publication of treason, allowing the attacks on religion to go on" (C). "Let us hear," he then added, "all about the Fenians. What has become of the pastoral? I have not got any copy or seen anything about it in the papers." Several days later Cullen received another letter from Conroy, dated Sunday, March 13, in which he reported the Fenian protest in the procathedral when his Lenten pastoral was read. "I have just got yours of the 13th," Cullen noted hurriedly at the end of a letter on March 19. "No account of the pastoral. I mean no copy. It is clear that the *Freeman* does not wish to publish such things. The Fenians appear to be very wicked. I fear for S. Patrick's Day. The rising up in the church was bad enough. It would be well to catch someone" (C).

On March 18 Conroy wrote Cullen again about that disturbance in the procathedral, informing him also that there had been another Fenian disturbance in the second of his mensal parishes, St. Andrew's, Westland-Row, when the pastoral was read. "As yet," Cullen replied on March 22, "I have not got a copy of the late pastoral, nor has any of it been given in the papers we receive except a short extract. Send us some few copies. The bishops wish to see what it is about" (C). "It would be worth a great deal," Cullen then added, "if it could be proved that three students from Trinity C. were engaged in disturbing the peace at Marlboro Street. Every effort ought to be made to verify the fact." He directed Conroy to the administrators of his mensal parishes: "Recommend the matter to Canon Murphy, and the search after the delinquents in Westland Road to Father Doyle." "The accounts we get from Meath," he then explained, referring to the recent election in county Longford, where a petition charging the Ardagh clergy with illegal treating of the electors with intoxicating liquors had been entered, "are not very cheering. One of the bishops of a diocese bordering on Meath received a letter here from one of his priests, in which the priests stated that he had been at an office in Meath, and that 10 or 12 priests, whom he met there, were all friends and supporters of Martin, and A. M. Sullivan, and spoke most violently against Dr. McCabe and the priests of Ardagh." "I fear those last mentioned clergymen," Cullen concluded sadly, "will fare badly at the approaching trial."

The news from Ireland in the next few weeks did not improve, and Cullen became more and more concerned.[66] On Wednesday, April 6, he had an audience with the pope in which he apparently explained how worried he was about the worsening situation in Ireland, for the pope gave him leave to return home for Easter. Cullen left Rome the following day, Thursday, April 7, accompanied by his cousin and secretary, Patrick Moran, and arrived in Dublin via Civitavecchia, Marseilles, Paris, and London on Monday evening, April 11.[67] On arriving in Dublin neither Cullen nor Moran was reassured by the state of the country. Indeed, if anything, the situation had actually worsened in

66. C, Cullen to Conroy, March 26 and April 1, 1870.
67. K, Cullen to Kirby, April 9, 1870. See also MacSuibhne, 5:98, quoting Cullen to Margaret Cullen, April 15, 1870.

the last several weeks. The Liberal alliance had been much shaken by the publication in the press of the letters written by the bishops of Ferns and Elphin earlier in the month, in criticism of Gladstone's land bill. The bishop of Elphin's letter had been published in the *Freeman's Journal* on March 25, and the depth of the consternation of Gladstone's colleagues may be gauged from the fact that his foreign secretary denounced Gillooly's letter as "infamous."[68] When Furlong's letter was then published in the *Irish Times* on March 28, the Liberals felt that injury had been added to insult. In Rome, for example, Odo Russell, who had of late been getting on better with the Irish bishops, was outraged. "The Irish Bishops," he explained to Clarendon on April 10, "are a hopeless set of humbugs, talking one way, writing another and acting a third, ignorant, cunning and deceitful like Neopolitans."[69] "To me," he maintained, "their language is most satisfactory, full of praise and gratitude to H.M. Govt., but they do not act as they speak, and since Bishop Furlong has published his extraordinary letter not one of them, or even of the English Bishops, will in conversation with me blame, criticize, or venture to disagree with a brother Bishop's published opinions!" "They all express themselves delighted," Russell further reported, "with the stringency of the peace preservation law for Ireland and more particularly with the suppression of the pestilent newspapers and with the Law to be extended to Liverpool, Glasgow &c. &c. where they fear the Fenians will now publish their papers and send them to Ireland." "But who," Russell concluded skeptically, "can tell whether they are sincere?"

To add to the difficulties, the case of the Longford election petition was heard during the first week in April, and on April 7 J. D. Fitzgerald, justice of the Queen's Bench and a Catholic, laid before Parliament the case charging the Ardagh clergy with corrupt practices in securing the return of R. S. M. Greville-Nugent over John Martin.[70] Moran reported to Kirby from Dublin on April 13, "He returns the names of ten Priests as having been guilty of corrupt practices i.e. illegal treating with the electors. The whole election has done a terrible amount of injury to our poor country, and the promoters of Fenianism exult & gloat over the humiliation of the Clergy" (K). "The Liberal party here," Moran then explained, "is terribly annoyed with Dr. Furlong's letter, and with the imprudence of the person who published it." "In Dublin everything is very quiet," he then added, "but I am

68. E. D. Steele, *Irish Land and British Politics* (Cambridge, 1974), p. 314.
69. Noel Blakiston, ed., *The Roman Question* (London, 1962), pp. 418–19.
70. *Freeman's Journal*, April 8, 1870.

told that during the past few months terrible injury was done by the wicked newspapers. Their attacks against the Cardinal and Clergy, as if we were bought by the Government, have told on the poor people to some extent." "With the blessing of God," Moran concluded, "they will soon be disabused of such an error and all will be as tranquil & religious as before."

Two days later, on Good Friday, Cullen was equally gloomy in replying to a letter he had just received from Laurence Gillooly, the bishop of Elphin, who was still in Rome. "I send you the *Irishman*," Cullen reported on April 15.[71] "Read the articles marked; they show that we are surrounded by dangers." "The churches here," he then added, "are crowded today, and they were quite full yesterday, so Fenianism is not able to root out the faith altogether. The outrages continue. No newspaper has been punished as yet. The *Nation* has become quite loyal." "The decision of the judge in Longford was very unfortunate," Cullen noted; "Dr. McCabe [bishop of Ardagh] would do well to caution the priests against taking money for distribution, or using violent language." "The land question," he then finally reported, "is in *statu quo*. It is thought by some that the opposition given to the land bill by the Irish liberals will drive Mr. Gladstone from power, and that we shall be put into the hands of Orangemen for eight or ten years to come."

However, when Cullen wrote Kirby several days later, on Easter Monday, April 18, he had been greatly heartened by the devotions in Dublin during Holy Week (K). "We had immense crowds," he reported, "in attendance on every morning and evening and the people assisted with the greatest devotion. Yesterday there was an immense multitude[,] from 6 to 8000[,] at Communion. At the last Mass I preached and gave the Pope's blessing to the congregation. The crowd was so great that many were obliged to remain out in the street. Before I gave the benediction, I explained the doctrine of scripture and tradition regarding the Pope's Infallibility, & all appeared to take great interest in the matter." "So you see," he assured Kirby, "Fenianism has not rooted out the faith as yet. Indeed the Fenians do not appear to have been able to do much mischief. The priests have all opposed them, and in this way they have not got on in Dublin. Yesterday all the parish churches were crowded with communicants. The Fenians are now very quiet as they are afraid of the Coercion Bill." "It is said," Cullen added, in a more gloomy vein, "Gladstone will not be able to pass the Land Bill, and that he will have to resign. The Orangemen, Fenians and several ecclesiastics joined Gladstone's enemies and the

71. MacSuibhne, 5:253.

result now anticipated is that we shall get no Land Bill, and the Irish Orangemen will get power into their hands for perhaps ten years to come. These said Orangemen, though now leagued with the Fenians, will when they get into office give such annoyance to the good poor people as may drive the country to violence or rebellion."

In writing Kirby a week later from Dublin, Moran was in a still more hopeful mood. "The news here," he assured Kirby on April 25, " 's all very good. The people in Easter time never frequented the chu rches in such crowds, and never were there such numbers going to the s. raments as during Holy Week. What is also curious, the offerings of the faithful for the Clergy were never so large at Marlborough Street so the canker of Fenianism has not got very far. The few who are infected with it are very active and violent and unscrupulous and hence they appar strong whilst they are nothing" (K). "The death of G. H. Moore," he further reported, "has been a death blow to the party that would seek to weaken us by divisions. He had made an appointment to meet Father Lavelle at Moore Hall on Monday at 3 o'clock. Father Lavelle called but Mr. Moore wished him to return next morning. He did so but I fear that Mr. Moore had got the attack of apoplexy before he arrived, and thus instead of arranging the program for the coming months, Father Lavelle had to administer the last sacraments to him." "Dr. Forde will be amused to hear," Moran then added, indicating that Cullen had also been active in the interests of Gladstone's land bill, "that Canon Redmond has written a letter withdrawing his furious denunciations against Mr. Gladstone's bill. It will appear in the *Freeman's Journal* tomorrow morning. Sir John Gray has also changed his opinion in regard to the tactics hitherto pursued by the national party and so I hope everything will get on more smoothly now for the future."

Before leaving Dublin to return to Rome, Cullen decided to consolidate the gains made with the faithful during Holy Week by issuing a pastoral, "On the Month of May," in honor of the Virgin Mary.[72] He took occasion in this pastoral, which was dated April 26 and was to be read in all Dublin churches on the following Sunday, May 1, to warn against the great evil of "Masonic, Fenian, Ribbon, and other secret societies in this country." After denouncing the Masons, Cullen then turned to the Fenians. "As to Fenianism," he explained,

> I have spoken so often of it that I have nothing new to say. All I shall now add is, that the experience of the last few years shows

72. Moran, 3:290–304.

that the leaders of this organization, or many of them, have been men without principle or religion, and that, to carry out their own reckless projects they have driven their unsuspecting followers into the most foolish undertakings, and exposed them to the greatest dangers. By their mad enterprises at Tallaght and elsewhere they have brought disgrace upon this country, and made us a laughing-stock to the nations of the earth. Indeed, all their undertakings, conceived, in a spirit of folly, have failed. They have displayed neither wisdom nor courage; so far from rendering services to their country, and promoting its prosperity and its liberties, they have obstructed every useful improvement; they have turned the minds of their followers to foolish pursuits; and they have brought on the country, and on its peaceful inhabitants, the evils of coercive and exceptional legislation.

"Of course," Cullen pointed out, "there was not a shadow of hope for the success of this party; but had it prevailed, or had the masses of the people joined in its undertakings, we should have had nothing but confusion, anarchy, and despotism, and our poor country would have been overwhelmed with unheard-of calamities."

Cullen then went on to denounce the agrarian murders and outrages lately so frequent, and most particularly the wickedness of the poisonous and seditious press, reminding his flock of the O'Connellite adage that he who commits a crime is a traitor to his country. Cullen admitted that the Irish had much to complain of, and it could not be otherwise after centuries of misrule and persecution, but he urged that time and patience were now necessary to remedy the effects of so many persecutions and so much misrule. At this point Cullen then entered the most unequivocal endorsement of the Liberal alliance that he had ever made, or was ever to make again:

The Statesmen now in power, encouraged by the good dispositions and growing liberality of the English people, have determined to obliterate the memory of past wrongs, to bind up the wounds of the country and to put us on a footing of equality with all other classes of Her Majesty's subjects. By a great measure, carried last year, they commenced the good work of conciliation, and this year they are determined to go on in the same direction, settling the relations between landlord and tenant, and providing protection for the existence and welfare of the great masses of our poor people. This is a great undertaking, but it is surrounded by innumerable difficulties in itself, and it is opposed by the interests and passions of many. Let us pray during this month that

God may direct our legislators to adopt everything good in the proposed measure, to correct what is wrong in it, and to adapt it to the wants and claims of a long-afflicted country. The distinguished Statesmen who have displayed so much love for the public good and the welfare of Ireland, by undertaking a work of such magnitude and difficulty, may be defeated by their opponents, but in any case they deserve our warmest thanks, and the lasting gratitude of the country.

"In the meantime it appears to be our duty," Cullen further maintained, "not only to avoid all uncalled-for opposition to a measure admittedly containing the seeds of much good, but rather to assist, as far as possible in passing it, with any necessary amendments." "In my humble opinion," he warned his flock finally, "it would be a foolish and fatal policy to do anything to weaken the hands of those who are anxious for our welfare, or to assist in driving them from power in order to hand over the reins of government to patrons, perhaps, and abettors of Orange lodges, always the curse and bane of Ireland, to men who, if in power, would think of nothing but the interests of a faction, and the most efficacious means of upholding old abuses."

Though this was Cullen's best effort ever on behalf of the Liberal alliance, it should be noted that his endorsement, in several important respects, was a qualified one. First of all, he did not mention either Gladstone or his colleagues by name, referring to them only and obliquely as "Statesmen." The point Cullen was making, of course, was that there was nothing formal or official in his endorsement. Secondly, he was extremely cautious in dealing with the land bill and was careful not to enter into any detail in wishing the "legislators" well in their efforts to transform it into law. Finally, in pointing out that it was, in his "humble opinion," a foolish and fatal policy to drive their friends from power in order that their hereditary enemies should enjoy it, Cullen was making it perfectly clear that he was speaking only for himself and not for the bishops as a body. Indeed, the real significance of this pastoral was the same as that of his "Private" letter to Gladstone nearly two months before. Cullen once again had hewed loyally to the line laid down by the bishops on the land bill at their meetings in Rome, and in thus publicly deferring in his pastoral to his episcopal colleagues, while at the same time trying to do justice to the Liberal alliance, he gave yet another good example of how he had learned as a cardinal to negotiate the strait and narrow as far as the bishops as a body were concerned.

Epilogue

Fundamental to the consolidation of the modern Irish Church in the 1860s was the successful response by the Irish bishops to all the various challenges—political, educational, and constitutional—posed to their unity as a body. In meeting these challenges, the Irish bishops finally institutionalized that corporate wholeness they had focused with such effect in the making of the modern Irish Church in the late 1850s. All that is made, however, whether in church or in state, is not always successfully consolidated. Indeed, most consolidations are only partially successful, in that the great ends promised in their making are seldom fully realized. The degree of success of any consolidation, therefore, is perhaps best measured by the achievement of those ends for which the institution was originally made. By this measurement, it may be safely affirmed that the modern Irish Church realized to a very remarkable degree in the 1860s those ends for which it had been made in the late 1850s.

Chief among those ends was the reaffirmation of the role of the bishops as a body in the governing of the Church. In the 1850s the authority of the body had been fundamentally threatened by the on-going struggle for power in the Church between Archbishops Cullen and MacHale. Though that struggle had been resolved by the victory of Cullen, the real achievement of the bishops was in their ability then to contain the very considerable power and influence Cullen had acquired in winning his victory over MacHale. In this achievement the constitution of the Irish Church was effectively made, in that the distribution of power in the governing of the Church was regularized among Cullen as the leader, the bishops as a body, and Rome as the ultimate authority.

The task of the 1860s, therefore, was the consolidation of the constitutional distribution of power. Central to that consideration was the way in which the bishops would be appointed. In other words, the real question was whether the procedures governing the appointment of Irish bishops would be observed. In fact, the constitutional modus vivendi arrived at in the making of the Irish Church in the late 1850s was duly observed. Indeed, in the established procedure—the senior clergy of a diocese commending three names, or a *terna*; the bishops of the province then reporting on those names; and the cardinals of Propaganda finally making their recommendation to the pope for his authoritative approval—the report of the bishops came to be the most important factor in the 1860s. This was made patently clear in the period before Cullen became a cardinal, and though it became somewhat blurred after his appointment in 1866 because of some very special and unusual circumstances, the procedure was dramatically vindicated by the appointment of Daniel McGettigan as archbishop of Armagh in early 1870, in spite of Cullen's strenuous efforts on behalf of his secretary and protégé, George Conroy. This due observance of procedure, with an increasing weight being given to the voice of the bishops in that procedure during the 1860s, caused the integrity of the bishops as a body to be given a greater guarantee and also made their corporate will determinant in both the governing of and the making of policy for the Irish Church.

Second in importance only to this reaffirmation of the determinant role of the bishops as a body in fulfilling the promise of the making, or consolidation, of the modern Irish Church was the success of the bishops in achieving virtual unanimity during the 1860s on the education question on all its levels. That achievement was fundamental to their being able to adopt the aggressive line toward the British state that resulted in their acquiring by 1870 effective control over a de facto denominational system of primary education outside Ulster. The beginning of the end of state control over the primary system, of course, had been initiated when Edward Cardwell, the chief secretary for Ireland, agreed in 1860 to give the Catholics parity among the commissioners who governed the Board of National Education, a step that, because the Protestants were divided, allowed the Catholics the working majority they needed to modify the rules of the system, by degrees and over time, to suit the views and interests of the bishops. The success of the bishops in emptying the model schools of Catholic teacher trainees and students by 1865 was yet another proof of both their ability and their determination to prevent the state from encroaching on what they had come to regard as their special purview. The various concessions made by the Liberal government immediately before its demise in June 1866, especially in regard to the model schools and the obnoxious Stopford rule, were only another sign of the cumulative effectiveness of the bishops' persistent and uncompromising policy. As one scholar has perceptively noted in summing up this cumulative effect of the efforts of the bishops:

> The Catholic prelates' aggressiveness was reinforced, rather than extinguished by their being rewarded with a concession almost every time they attacked the commissioners of national education. Since their complaints regularly produced results, the prelates passed another set of resolutions on education at their October 1867 meeting. . . . Once more the prelates' noise-making brought results. In 1868 a parliamentary circular was sent to each of the Irish bishops asking their opinion upon the national system and asking what modification they desired. In the same year the government appointed a royal commission to investigate the national school system and to make recommendations for reform. With the appointment of this commission it appeared that the prelates had won.[1]

By 1870 the bishops had indeed won, and it was this new aggressiveness on all levels of Irish education that became their hallmark during the 1860s. The mettle they had shown in their approach to the primary level was also evidenced at the secondary and university levels. The achievement at the secondary or intermediate level has gone largely unnoticed, however, because there has been no systematic study of Catholic secondary education in the nineteenth century. What is clear is that though the secondary system was not all that could be desired in either quality or quantity, it was at least adequate to Catholic needs, and the facilities—diocesan colleges and Christian Brothers schools for boys and convent schools staffed by nuns for girls—were considerably augmented during the 1860s. Though the bishops were undoubtedly hard pressed financially to support a burgeoning secondary system, they did manage to keep it economically viable until the state finally gave them some monetary relief in the

---

1. Donald H. Akenson, *The Irish Education Experiment* (London, 1970), pp. 309–10.

Intermediate Education Act of 1878, without interfering with either their control or the denominational character of the system.

The same determined and aggressive line was maintained by the bishops with even greater fierceness, although with considerably less success, in regard to university education. The real irony in this situation, of course, was that in the negotiations with both Whig and Tory governments for a charter and endowment for the Catholic University between 1865 and 1868, Cullen, who had been the main architect of episcopal education policy in the 1850s and early 1860s, came to find that he had become a moderating influence in the body and that his colleagues had actually become more Roman than the Romans on this question. The basic lesson to be learned, as Archbishop Manning found out both to his cost and to his annoyance, was that the determinant voice on the education question, though it might be modified by Cullen's astuteness and influence, was really that of the bishops as a body.

In regard to both the constitutional and educational questions, therefore, the ends for which the modern Irish Church had been made in the late 1850s were realized to a remarkable degree during the 1860s. On the other hand, the success of the bishops in dealing with the challenge posed by the political question during the 1860s, while no less real or remarkable, was a good deal more clouded because of the very complex nature of the issue. Though the complexity of the question was partly the result of its acquiring a revolutionary dimension during the 1860s, in the last analysis the real difficulty involved lay ultimately with the constitutional rather than the revolutionary side of the question. The great political achievement of the bishops as a body in the making of the Irish Church in the late 1850s had been their success in being able finally to curb the conduct of their priests in political matters. Not only was this episcopal control made evident on the constitutional side of politics during the 1860s, but it was made even more clear in regard to the revolutionary politics of Fenianism. Though a good many of the clergy undoubtedly sympathized with the Fenian end of an independent Irish Republic, and a lesser number even with the physical force advocated by the Brotherhood as the effective means to that end, there was not one priest in a body of some three thousand, if Father Lavelle be excepted, who was prepared to endorse those ends and/or means publicly under his own name.

Indeed, Lavelle was the exception that proved the rule of episcopal control, for if he had not had the approval and protection of his diocesan, Archbishop MacHale, he could never have survived his public endorsements of the Brotherhood. The reason why the bishops had been able to let the Fenian fever run its course during the 1860s was that they had been able to maintain a firm grip on their clergy. However, when Lavelle finally challenged them publicly and directly in November 1869 about whether Fenianism had really been condemned, and when several weeks later Dean O'Brien of Limerick proceeded to threaten their authority over their priests by issuing his circular to the Irish clergy, asking them to endorse his call for the amnesty of the Fenian prisoners still in jail, the bishops decided to settle the Fenian question once and for all by securing a Roman condemnation of the Brotherhood. By firmly reestablishing their control over their clergy on this issue, the bishops fulfilled in large part the promise to curb the political propensities of their clergy that had accompanied the making of the Irish Church more than ten years before.

The challenge of controlling their clergy on Fenianism, however, was a relatively simple one compared to that which the bishops faced in dealing with the constitutional side of politics. As long as the task was essentially *negative*, that is, to prevent their priests from indulging in unbecoming political behavior, whether on the revolutionary or the constitutional side, the bishops were able to maintain over the long run an effective control. When they decided to take up a more *positive* role in constitutional politics, with the founding of the National Association in late 1864, the problem became not so much how they would prevent their clergy from going too far on the hustings as rather whether they could successfully enlist them in the new departure. As soon became evident from their experience in the association, the bishops did not have much success in involving their clergy, and the movement never acquired any real vitality at the grass roots. Constitutional politics, therefore, especially after the death of John Blake Dillon in the summer of 1866, soon lapsed into the sad condition they had been in before the founding of the association, and they did not begin to revive until Gladstone promised to do justice to Ireland in December 1867 by adopting, in effect, the original program of the association. In the ensuing general election in 1868, the bishops succeeded in enlisting their clergy in what can only be described as a religious crusade in the constituencies on behalf of Gladstone and the Liberal party. The result was a sweeping electoral victory in Ireland for Gladstone and his program. The real lesson of the election, however, was less the number of Gladstonian Liberals returned than the fact that the bishops not only had succeeded in mobilizing their clergy for political action in the constituencies but had in doing so again become, as a body, a force to be reckoned with in constitutional politics.

All this had been done, moreover, with the bishops' still maintaining a firm grip on their clergy. Indeed, if there were to be complaints about clerical conduct on the hustings in 1868, or in the future, they would be made about bishops in political conjunction with their clergy rather than about the clergy alone.

The politicization of the bishops as a body in the general election of 1868 resulted in a new set of political givens, which in turn involved a novel set of challenges for the body that were a good deal more complex than those signified in their successful efforts to keep a grip on the political conduct of their clergy. In subscribing so enthusiastically to the Gladstonian Irish-Liberal alliance, the Irish bishops had seriously compromised both the emerging Irish political system and their place in it. The alliance was in fact utterly subversive of the consensual elements of leader, party, and bishops that made up the indigenous Irish political system, because it in effect made Gladstone the leader, reduced the party to the mere tail of the Liberal party, and endowed the bishops with considerable power without any corresponding responsibility. The reason why the bishops took up the alliance with such determination, of course, was not simply that Gladstone had promised to remedy the outstanding Irish grievances about the established Church, Tenant Right, and educational reform; it was rather that he promised to give the Irish satisfaction on those matters according to their own ideas about what was necessary, and not merely to legislate according to what the English thought might be good for them. In other words, the Irish were to receive an incipient form of Home Rule by being treated equally in the greater political partnership known as the United Kingdom, and their warrant for that equality was the assurance that their voice would be the determinant one as far as their basic interests in the partnership were concerned.

In such a scenario the bishops, as the only body functioning at the national level, would become the real power brokers in Irish politics, because the individual members of Parliament would be at each bishop's particular political mercy in the constituencies; further, there would be no real need for a distinct Irish political identity embodied in a leader or a party because the Irish representatives, one and all, would be subsumed in the politics of the dominant British system. This was why those constitutional Nationalists on the extreme left of the Irish political spectrum reacted so violently and did everything in their power to embarrass Gladstone and the bishops by launching an amnesty movement for the Fenian prisoners and, failing that, endorsing Fenian prisoners as candidates at successive by-elections. The constitutional Nationalists instinctively realized that the alliance was both destructive of any hope of national self-government and subversive of the building of the necessary constitutional means to that desired end. In retrospect, it is easier to understand that, given the exigencies of British politics, Gladstone had little chance of fulfilling his promise to govern and legislate for Ireland according to Irish ideas, and that the Irish bishops as a body made a serious political mistake in so unreservedly committing themselves to his cause.

Still, it is perhaps unfair, and even unhistorical, to ask for a political prescience in the bishops that was not much demonstrated generally in the Irish political spectrum. Besides being drawn by the hope of a final political solution to the Irish question, the bishops had, in their recent frustrations, some very good reasons for taking up the Irish-Liberal alliance when they did, and for sustaining it as long as they did. The failure of the National Association, the death of John Blake Dillon, the success of the Fenians in making mischief, if not revolution, and the humiliating experience of being thrown over by the Conservatives on the University question all cumulatively made the bishops anxious for some tangible political achievement of consequence. Once they were committed to the alliance, the political difficulties inherent in the situation were masked for them for a time by Gladstone's great success in disestablishing the Irish Church. The bishops were slow to understand that Gladstone's ability to mobilize the British Nonconformists for disestablishment could not be easily translated into success on questions concerning property rights and denominational education. When the bishops finally realized how deeply they were committed to the alliance during their discussions in Rome on the land question, and how precarious their position had become in regard to Irish public opinion because of that commitment, they not only began to equivocate on the land bill but began to trim on the alliance.

Indeed, the beginning of the end of the bishops' commitment to the Irish-Liberal alliance may be dated from Gladstone's inability to respond to their proposed amendments to his land bill in late February 1870. The end, of course, did not come until three years later, when the bishops as a body called on their parliamentary representatives to vote against Gladstone's proposed University bill, and succeeded in defeating it. The reason why the end was so long in coming was that the bishops were reluctant to break with Gladstone until they learned what kind of an education measure he would introduce. For his part, Gladstone continued to drag his feet for three years on the measure because he was only too well aware that his ministry was likely to be wrecked by his inability to satisfy either the Nonconformists in his own party who were opposed to denominational education or the Catholics who were in favor of it. When the moment of truth finally came in late February of 1873, however, the temper of the bishops had not been much improved by the long delay. A considerable part of their very negative reaction to Gladstone's bill, in fact, may be attributed not to its failure to meet their expectations but to their deep annoyance about the awkward position in which their continued tacit support of the alliance had placed them; while they had been thus engaged, the recently emerged Home Rule movement had posed a developing and increasingly successful challenge to their political power and influence in the constituencies. This, however, is to anticipate the sequel to the present volume. Suffice it to say here that the bishops' realization in the late winter and early spring of 1870 that the Irish-Liberal alliance was becoming a distinct political liability, and their consequent coolness in distancing themselves from it, allowed them in the long run to preserve their very considerable effectiveness in the emerging Irish political system.

During the 1860s, then, the ends for which the modern Irish Church had been made in the 1850s had been largely fulfilled, and the Church may be said to have been successfully consolidated. The greatest achievement was undoubtedly in the crystallization of the constitution of the Irish Church; and the institutionalization of the bishops as a body was the feat sine qua non. Without the achieving of the necessary unity in the episcopal body, the considerable accomplishments in education, politics, and pastoral reform would not have been possible. The unanimity achieved in each of these areas, moreover, contributed cumulatively to the strengthening and hardening of the corporate will of the body. On the education issue, the bishops had firmly established their authority by 1870, and it was obvious that no one, be he British or Irish, could have their unequivocal political support without accommodating them absolutely on that issue. In politics, the basis of their power and influence was their ability to maintain control over their clergy, and although individual bishops had lost or might again temporarily lose control of their clergy because of personal or political differences, these were the rare exceptions that in the long run proved the rule of episcopal control. In pastoral reform, the great majority of the bishops had provided for the devotionalization of their laity by 1870, and not only had the Irish people as a people been virtually transformed into pious and practical Catholics, but that unique and recent creation known as Irish Catholicism was rapidly becoming, through mass emigration, part of the religious land-scape of the English-speaking world. In the last analysis, what allowed the bishops to respond successfully to all of the various challenges during the 1860s was that they were finally institutionalized as a body, and the modern Irish Church was, in effect, consolidated.

Bibliographical Note

The sources of this study were mainly archival, and the printed materials used were few in number. I have not listed the books, articles, and newspapers in a formal bibliography, because the reader will easily find what is pertinent in the footnotes. A number of works that have been liberally used in the writing of this volume, however, deserve especial mention. They are Patrick J. Corish's "Cardinal Cullen and the National Association of Ireland," *Reportorium Novum* 3, no. 1 (1962): 13–61, and "Political Problems, 1860–1878," in *A History of Irish Catholicism*, gen. ed. Patrick J. Corish (Dublin, 1967), 5: 1–59; E. R. Norman's *The Catholic Church and Ireland in the Age of Rebellion, 1859–1873* (London, 1965); volumes 3, 4, and 5 of Peadar Mac-Suibhne's *Paul Cullen and His Contemporaries* (Naas, 1965, 1974, 1977); and Sean Cannon's "Irish Episcopal Meetings, 1788–1882: A Juridico-Historical Study," *Annuarium Historiae Conciliorum: Internationale Zeitschrift für Konziliengeschictsforschung*, vol. 13 (1981), pp. 270–422. Monsignor Corish's essays and Norman's book are really basic works, which no scholar or student of the period can fail to profit by. The late Father MacSuibhne's volumes contain a considerable number of Cullen letters, and though some lack location designations, some are not quoted in full, and some are unfortunately paraphrased, they are, taken all together, very valuable. Father Cannon's illuminating study of Irish episcopal meetings is one of the most original pieces of work to appear on the modern Irish Church in recent years. The exhaustiveness of the research and the fine handling of the conceptual framework make this book a significant contribution not only to knowledge but to interdisciplinary studies as well. The archival materials consulted are to be found mainly in Dublin, London, and Rome.

In Dublin the main bodies of material consulted were:

1. The papers of Paul Cullen. Dublin Diocesan Archives.

2. The papers of John Blake Dillon. Trinity College Library.

3. The papers of Laurence Gillooly. C. M. Elphin Diocesan Archives, Sligo. They have been microfilmed and are on deposit in the National Library of Ireland.

4. The papers of Patrick Leahy. Cashel Diocesan Archives, Thurles. These are also available on microfilm in the National Library of Ireland.

5. The papers of William Monsell, first Baron Emly. National Library of Ireland.

6. The papers of George Henry Moore. National Library of Ireland.

7. The papers of Bartholomew Woodlock. Dublin Diocesan Archives.

In London the main bodies of material consulted were:

1. Foreign Office Papers for Italy and Rome. Public Record Office, Chancery Lane.

2. The papers of William Ewart Gladstone. British Library.

3. The papers of Henry Edward Manning. Westminster Diocesan Archives.

4. The papers of Earl Russell. Public Record Office.

In Rome the main bodies of material consulted were:

1. The papers of Tobias Kirby. Archives of the Irish College.

2. The papers of Bernard Smith, O.S.B. Archives of St. Paul's Basilica outside the Walls.

3. The Irish correspondence in the Archive of the Sacred Congregation for the Evangelization of the People, formerly the Society for the Propagation of the Faith. Piazza d'Espagna.

Index